PEREGRINE BOOKS

SOCIAL ORIGINS OF
DICTATORSHIP AND DEMOCRACY

Dr Barrington Moore Jr was born in Washington,
D.C., on 12 May 1913. He was educated at Williams
College, where he took a degree in Greek and
Latin, and at Yale University where he gained a
Ph.D. in Sociology. He is now lecturer in Sociology
and Senior Research Fellow at the Russian Re-
search Center at Harvard University. His books
include *Soviet Politics – The Dilemma of Power, Terror and
Progress – USSR, Political Power and Social Theory, A
Critique of Pure Tolerance* (co-author with Robert P.
Wolff and Herbert Marcuse). Among his most
recent essays in periodicals are 'Thoughts on Vio-
lence and Social Change', 'Urban Riots: Violence
and Social Change', and 'Revolution in America?'
He was awarded the Woodrow Wilson Foundation
Award (1967), and the MacIver Award (1968) for his
book *Social Origins of Dictatorship and Democracy*.

SOCIAL ORIGINS OF DICTATORSHIP AND DEMOCRACY

*Lord and Peasant in the
Making of the Modern World*

BARRINGTON MOORE, JR

PENGUIN BOOKS

Penguin Books Ltd, Harmondsworth, Middlesex, England
Penguin Books Australia Ltd, Ringwood, Victoria, Australia

—

First published in the U.S.A. 1966
Published in Great Britain by Allen Lane The Penguin Press 1967
Published in Peregrine Books 1969

—

—

Made and printed in Great Britain by
Hazell Watson & Viney Ltd
Aylesbury, Bucks
Set in Monotype Spectrum

—

*This volume was prepared under a grant from
the Carnegie Corporation of New York. That Corporation
is not, however, the author, owner, publisher, or proprietor of this
publication and is not to be understood as approving
by virtue of its grant any of the statements
made or views expressed therein.*

—

To E. C. M.

Contents

PART THREE

THEORETICAL IMPLICATIONS AND PROJECTIONS

Preface and Acknowledgments

THIS BOOK ENDEAVORS TO EXPLAIN the varied political roles played by the landed upper classes and the peasantry in the transformation from agrarian societies (defined simply as states where a large majority of the population lives off the land) to modern industrial ones. Somewhat more specifically, it is an attempt to discover the range of historical conditions under which either or both of these rural groups have become important forces behind the emergence of Western parliamentary versions of democracy, and dictatorships of the right and the left, that is, fascist and communist regimes.

Since no problem ever comes to the student of human society out of a blue and empty sky, it is worthwhile to indicate very briefly the considerations behind this one. For some time before beginning this work in earnest more than ten years ago, I had become skeptical of the thesis that industrialism was the main cause of twentieth-century totalitarian regimes, because of the very obvious fact that Russia and China were overwhelmingly agrarian countries when the communists established themselves. For a long time before that I had been convinced that adequate theoretical comprehension of political systems had to come to terms with Asian institutions and history. Hence it seemed at least a promising strategy to investigate what political currents were set up among the classes who lived off the countryside and to devote as much attention to Asian as to Western societies.

The book presents first (in Part I) a discussion of the democratic and capitalist route to the modern age as this transformation worked itself out in England, France, and the United States. My original intention had been to complete this section with similar chapters on Germany and Russia in order to show how the social origins of fascism and communism in Europe differed from those of parliamentary democracy. With some misgivings I decided to discard these two chapters, partly because the book was already quite long, partly because first-rate accounts became available during the course of writing to which it was impossible for me to add anything by way of interpreting the social history of these two countries. At the same time I have still drawn freely on German and Russian materials for the purpose of comparative illustration and in the theoretical discussion of Part III. The bibliography lists the sources that have formed the basis of my conception of German and Russian social history. Abandoning explicit accounts of Germany and Russia has at least the compensating advantage of permitting more extended discussion (in Part II) of the Asiatic versions of fascism, communism, and parliamentary democracy, in Japan, China, and India, where agrarian problems remain acute. Since the history and social structure of these countries is often quite unknown to educated Western readers, critics may show some indulgence to an author who writes more about what he knows less.

Against such a selection of cases it is possible to object that the range is too wide for effective coverage by one person and too narrow to yield sound generalizations. About the possibility that the undertaking was too big it would be inappropriate for the author to say more than that there have been many times when he would have agreed heartily. Critics of the second type might point out that none of the smaller states — Switzerland, Scandinavia, or the Low Countries on the democratic side, the smaller areas of communist victory or control on the other, such as Cuba, the satellites of Eastern Europe, North Vietnam, North Korea — receive any consideration. How is it possible to generalize about the growth of Western democracy or of communism while excluding them? Does not the exclusion of the smaller Western democratic states produce a certain antipeasant bias throughout the whole book? To this objection there is, I think, an impersonal answer. This study concentrates on certain important stages in a prolonged social process which has worked itself out in several countries. As part of this process new social arrangements have grown up by violence and in other ways which have made certain countries political leaders at different points in time during the first half of the twentieth century. The focus of interest is on innovation that has led to political power, not on the spread and reception of institutions that have been hammered out elsewhere, except where they have led to significant power in world politics. The fact that the smaller countries depend economically and politically on big and powerful ones means that the decisive causes of their politics lie outside their own boundaries. It also means that their political problems are not really comparable to those of larger countries. Therefore a general statement about the historical preconditions of democracy or authoritarianism covering small countries as well as large would very likely be so broad as to be abstractly platitudinous.

From this standpoint the analysis of the transformation of agrarian society in specific countries produces results at least as rewarding as larger generalizations. It is important, for example, to know how the solution of agrarian problems contributed to the establishment of parliamentary democracy in England and the failure as yet to solve very different ones constitutes a threat to democracy in India. Furthermore, for any given country one is bound to find lines of causation that do not fit easily into more general theories. Conversely too strong a devotion to theory always carries the danger that one may overemphasize facts that fit a theory beyond their importance in the history of individual countries. For these reasons the interpretation of the transformation in several countries takes up the largest part of the book.

In the effort to understand the history of a specific country a comparative perspective can lead to asking very useful and sometimes new questions. There are further advantages. Comparisons can serve as a rough negative check on accepted historical explanations. And a comparative approach may lead to new historical generalizations. In practice these features constitute a single intellectual process and make such a study more than a disparate collection of interesting cases. For example, after noticing that Indian peasants have suffered in a material way just about as much as Chinese peasants during the nineteenth and twentieth centuries without generating a massive revolutionary movement, one begins to wonder about traditional explanations of what took place in both societies and becomes alert to factors affecting peasant outbreaks in other countries, in the hope of discerning general causes. Or after learning about the disastrous consequences for democracy of a coalition between agrarian and industrial élites in nineteenth- and early twentieth-century Germany, the much discussed marriage of iron and rye — one wonders why a similar marriage between iron and cotton did not prevent the coming of the Civil War in the United States; and so one has taken a step toward specifying configurations favorable and unfavorable to the establishment of modern Western democracy. That comparative analysis is no substitute for detailed investigation of specific cases is obvious.

Generalizations that are sound resemble a large-scale map of an extended terrain, such as an airplane pilot might use in crossing a continent. Such maps are essential for certain purposes just as more detailed maps are necessary for others. No one seeking a preliminary orientation to the terrain wants to know the location of every house and footpath. Still, if one explores on foot — and at present the comparative historian does exactly that a great deal of the time — the details are what one learns first. Their meaning and relationship emerges only gradually. There can be long periods when the investigator feels lost in an underbrush of facts inhabited by specialists engaged in savage disputes about whether the underbrush is a pine forest or a tropical jungle. He is unlikely to emerge from such encounters without scratches and bruises. And if he draws a map of the area he has visited, one of the natives may well accuse him of omitting his own house and clearing, a sad event if the researcher has actually found much sustenance and refreshment there. The outcry is likely to be all the sharper if at the end of the journey the explorer tries to set down in very brief form for those who may come later the most striking things that he has seen. That is exactly what I shall try to do now, to sketch in very broad strokes the main findings in order to give the reader a preliminary map of the terrain we shall explore together.

In the range of cases examined here one may discern three

main historical routes from the preindustrial to the modern world. The first of these leads through what I think deserve to be called bourgeois revolutions. Aside from the fact that this term is a red flag to many scholars because of its Marxist connotations, it has other ambiguities and disadvantages. Nevertheless, for reasons that will appear in due course I think it is a necessary designation for certain violent changes that took place in English, French, and American societies on the way to becoming modern industrial democracies and that historians connect with the Puritan Revolution (or the English Civil War as it is often called as well), the French Revolution, and the American Civil War. A key feature in such revolutions is the development of a group in society with an independent economic base, which attacks obstacles to a democratic version of capitalism that have been inherited from the past. Though a great deal of the impetus has come from trading and manufacturing classes in the cities, that is very far from the whole story. The allies this bourgeois impetus has found, the enemies it has encountered, vary sharply from case to case. The landed upper classes, our main concern at the start, were either an important part of this capitalist and democratic tide, as in England, or if they opposed it, they were swept aside in the convulsions of revolution or civil war. The same thing may be said about the peasants. Either the main thrust of their political efforts coincided with that toward capitalism and political democracy, or else it was negligible. And it was negligible either because capitalist advance destroyed peasant society or because this advance began in a new country, such as the United States, without a real peasantry.

The first and earlier route through the great revolutions and civil wars led to the combination of capitalism and Western democracy. The second route has also been capitalist, but culminated during the twentieth century in fascism. Germany and Japan are the obvious cases, though only the latter receives detailed treatment in this study for reasons given above. I shall call this the capitalist and reactionary form. It amounts to a form of revolution from above. In these countries the bourgeois impulse was much weaker. If it took a revolutionary form at all, the revolution was defeated. Afterward sections of a relatively weak commercial and industrial class relied on dissident elements in the older and still dominant ruling classes, mainly recruited from the land, to put through the political and economic changes required for a modern industrial society, under the auspices of a semi-parliamentary regime. Industrial development may proceed rapidly under such auspices. But the outcome, after a brief and unstable period of democracy, has been fascism. The third route is of course communism, as exemplified in Russia and in China. The great agrarian bureaucracies of these countries served to inhibit the commercial and later industrial impulses even more than in the preceding instances. The results were twofold. In the first place these urban classes were too weak to constitute even a junior partner in the form of modernization taken by Germany and Japan, though there were attempts in this direction. And in the absence of more than the most feeble steps toward modernization a huge peasantry remained. This stratum, subject to new strains and stresses as the modern world encroached upon it, provided the main destructive revolutionary force that overthrew the old order and propelled these countries into the modern era under communist leadership that made the peasants its primary victims.

Finally, in India we may perceive still a fourth general pattern that accounts for the weak impulse toward modernization. In that country so far there has been neither a capitalist revolution from above or below, nor a peasant one leading to communism. Likewise the impulse toward modernization has been very weak. On the other hand, at least some of the historical prerequisites of Western democracy did put in an appearance. A parliamentary regime has existed for some time that is considerably more than mere façade. Because the impulse toward modernization has been weakest in India, this case stands somewhat apart from any theoretical scheme that it seems possible to construct for the others. At the same time it serves as a salutary check upon such generalizations. It is especially useful in trying to understand peasant revolutions, since the degree of rural misery in India where there has been no peasant revolution is about the same as in China where rebellion and revolution have been decisive in both premodern and recent times.

To sum up as concisely as possible, we seek to understand the role of the landed upper classes and the peasants in the bourgeois revolutions leading to capitalist democracy, the abortive bourgeois revolutions leading to fascism, and the peasant revolutions leading to communism. The ways in which the landed upper classes and the peasants reacted to the challenge of commercial agriculture were decisive factors in determining the political outcome. The applicability of these political labels, the elements that these movements do and do not share in different countries and at different times, will I hope become clear in the course of subsequent discussion. One point, on the other hand, is worth noticing right away. Though in each case one configuration emerges as the dominant one, it is possible to discern subordinate ones that become the dominant features in another country. Thus in England, during the latter part of the French Revolution and until after the end of the Napoleonic wars, there existed some of the elements of a reactionary configuration recognizable as a dominant feature in Germany: a coalition between the older landed élites and the rising commercial and industrial ones, directed against the lower classes in town and countryside (but able at times to attract significant lower-class support on some issues). Indeed this reactionary combination of elements turns up in some form in each society studied, including the United States. To illustrate further, royal absolutism in France shows some of the same effects on commercial life as do the great bureaucratic monarchies of tsarist Russia and Imperial China. This type of observation encourages somewhat greater confidence in the possibility that empirically based categories may transcend particular cases.

Nevertheless there remains a strong tension between the demands of doing justice to the explanation of a particular case and the search for generalizations, mainly because it is impossible to know just how important a particular problem may be until one has finished examining all of them. This tension is responsible for a certain lack of symmetry and elegance in the presentation, which I deplore but have been unable to eliminate after several rewritings. Again the parallel with the explorer of unknown lands may not be amiss: he is not called upon to build a smooth and direct highway for the next band of travellers. Should he be their guide, he is thought to acquit himself adequately if he avoids the time-consuming back-tracks and errors of his first exploration, courteously refrains from leading his companions through the worst of the underbrush, and points out the more dangerous pitfalls as he guides them warily past. If he makes a clumsy misstep and stumbles into a trap, there may even be some in the party who not only enjoy a laugh at his expense, but may also be willing to give him a hand to set him forth on his way once more. It is for such a band of companions in the search for truth that I have written this book.

*   *   *

Harvard's Russian Research Center gave me the precious boon of time. Because they displayed sympathetic curiosity without the least trace of impatience, I am especially grateful to several officers of the Center during whose tenure the book was written: Professors William L. Langer, Merle Fainsod, Abram Bergson as directors, Marshall D. Shulman, as associate director. Amid numerous distractions Miss Rose DiBenedetto typed and retyped countless pages of manuscript with endless good humor.

Throughout the whole undertaking my very good friend Professor Herbert Marcuse fortified me with his unique blend of warm encouragement and penetrating criticism. He may have helped me most when he believed me least. Another good friend, the late Professor Otto Kirchheimer, read through the entire manuscript and brought to the surface some implicit theses that I have tried to make explicit. At all stages the help that Elizabeth Carol Moore gave was so fundamental and so varied that only an author and a husband can appreciate it. We both drew often and successfully on the intelligence and quiet resourcefulness of staff members of Widener Library, especially of Mr. Foster M. Palmer and Miss Y. T. Feng.

Several colleagues with special factual knowledge, by their comments on individual chapters, have saved me from some foolish mistakes and made valuable suggestions. Their generosity in telling me they had found food for thought and further questioning in their own specialities has been a treasured reward. No matter what disclaimer I might set down, to list their names here would identify them in some degree with my views and confer upon this book an unwarranted hint of scholarly consensus. Hence their thanks have been private. From those not named here, as well as those who are, I have learned that the notion of a community of scholars is more than pure rhetoric.

BARRINGTON MOORE, JR.

PART ONE
Revolutionary Origins
of Capitalist Democracy

CHAPTER ONE

England and the Contributions of Violence to Gradualism

1. Aristocratic Impulses behind the Transition to Capitalism in the Countryside

As ONE BEGINS THE STORY of the transition from the preindustrial to the modern world by examining the history of the first country to make the leap, one question comes to mind almost automatically. Why did the process of industrialization in England culminate in the establishment of a relatively free society? That contemporary England has been such for a long time, perhaps even considerably more liberal than the United States in the crucial areas of freedom of speech and the tolerance of organized political opposition, seems plain enough. The aristocratic component in this toleration by the dominant classes is equally apparent. To suggest all the important reasons why this situation came about is a larger task than ours need be, even if it is necessary to keep in mind possible causes other than those pursued here in order to maintain a proper perspective. The focus in this chapter will be on the particular and very significant part that the classes in the countryside played in the transformation to industrialism.

If the emphasis on the fate of nobles and peasants — and the numerous gradations in between that were a distinctive feature of English society — comes from the general plan of this book and the questions with which it started, another axis of inquiry emerges from examining the evidence. It is not necessary to read English history for very long, or to be more skeptical than the degree prescribed in standard texts on scientific method, in order to realize that there is an element of myth in common notions about the peculiar British capacity to settle their political and economic differences through peaceable, fair, and democratic processes. Such notions are a partial truth rather than a myth. Simple debunking will not clear up matters. The conventions of historical writing which begin the story of English industrialization at some point after 1750 help to perpetuate this partial truth by highlighting peaceful domestic history, very peaceful in contrast to France, during the eighteen and nineteenth centuries and by leaving in the shadow the era of the Puritan Revolution or Civil War.[1] Merely to notice this fact is to confront the question of what has been the connection between violence and peaceful reform: first of all in modern democracy and more generally in the whole transformation from societies based on agriculture to those based on modern industrial technologies.

The social struggles that erupted in the English Civil War of the seventeenth century have their origins in a complicated process of change that began several centuries earlier. Just when it began is impossible to say, just as it is impossible to prove that it had to take the form of a civil war. Still the character of the process itself is reasonably clear. A modern and secular society was slowly pushing its way up through the vigorous and much tangled overgrowth of the feudal and ecclesiastical order.[2] More specifically, from the fourteenth century onward there are several signs pointing toward the increasing importance of commerce in both the countryside and the towns, the dismounting of feudalism and its replacement by

[1] Schweinitz, *Industrialization*, 6, remarks: "The political reforms which, starting with the Reform Bill of 1832, brought full democracy to Great Britain took place in the nineteenth and early twentieth centuries. But these measures were successful largely because of the *gradual evolution of constitutional and parliamentary institutions in the centuries prior to 1832.*" (Emphasis added) Elsewhere (pp. 10–11) the author argues rather cautiously that it is impossible to repeat the capitalist and democratic solutions to the problems of modernization, a thesis with which I agree.

[2] Feudalism means something different to the social, economic, legal, and constitutional historians, and the different aspects changed at different rates. See the helpful discussion in Cam, "Decline and Fall," 216.

England's relatively weak version of royal absolutism, both carried on within the framework of an increasingly bitter religious struggle that was partly reflection and partly cause of the anxieties and bitterness that necessarily accompany the decline of one kind of civilization and the rise of a new one.

Though the wool trade had long been known in England, by the late Middle Ages that country had become the largest and most important source of fine wool.[3] The reverberations of the wool trade were felt not only in the towns but in the countryside as well, possibly even more there, and certainly in politics. Since English markets for wool were on the continent, particularly in Italy and the Low Countries, it is to the growth of trading towns there that one would have to turn in order to find the beginnings of the strong commercial impulse that was eventually to rule English society. To analyze these would take us too far afield; it is only necessary to accept this decisive influence as a raw datum for our purposes. Other important factors were at work too. The Black Death in 1348 – 1349 cut a deep swathe in England's population and reduced the supply of labor. In Lollardy not long afterward there appeared the first ominous rumblings of religious revolt, to be followed in 1381 by a serious peasant rebellion. Later there will be occasion to examine these stirrings among the lower classes and their meaning.

For the present we shall concentrate mainly upon the upper classes. During the latter part of the fourteenth century and much of the fifteenth, important changes in their position were working themselves out. The land and tenurial relations based on it had largely ceased to be the cement binding together lord and man. Though other aspects of feudalism remained powerful, the king had for a long time been attempting with varied success to turn these arrangements to his own purposes, working within them to strengthen his own power. Cut off from its roots in the soil, feudalism had become parasitic, deriving its strength from the maneuvers of powerful magnates and the countermoves of the monarch.[4]

The Wars of the Roses (1455 – 1485) were for the landed aristocracy a social rather than a natural catastrophe, a bloodletting

[3] Power, *Wool Trade*, 16.
[4] Cam, "Decline and Fall," 218, 225, 232.

that severely weakened them and enabled the Tudor dynasty which emerged from the struggle to resume with greater success the process of consolidating royal power. Under Henry VIII, political and religious considerations may have had the consequence of giving another push toward commercial agriculture. A Marxist historian has suggested that Henry VIII's confiscation of the monasteries in 1536 and 1539 may have helped to promote new and commercially minded landowners at the expense of the older aristocracy and its centrifugal traditions.[5] It seems more likely, however, that the main significance of Henry VIII's rule was to damage one of the pillars of the old order, the church, and to set an example on this score that his successors were to regret. Deeper stirrings were already at work that needed no prompting from the crown, which more and more set its face against them as a menace to good order.

Combined with the continuing stimulus of the wool trade, the Tudor peace generated a powerful stimulus to the growth of a commercial and even capitalist outlook in the countryside. Along with other works, R.H. Tawney's unsurpassed study of the economic life of England before the Civil War shows how these forces ripped apart the feudal framework long before the war:

> In the turbulent days of the fifteenth century land had still a military and social significance apart from its economic value; lords had ridden out at the head of their retainers to convince a bad neighbour with bows and bills; and a numerous tenantry had been more important than a high pecuniary return from the soil. The Tudor discipline, with its stern prohibition of livery and maintenance, its administrative jurisdictions and tireless bureaucracy, had put down private warfare with a heavy hand, and, by drawing the teeth of feudalism, had made the command of money more important than the command of men. . . . [This change . . .] marks the transition from the mediæval conception of land as the basis of political functions and obligations to the modern view of it as an income-yielding investment. Landholding tends, in short, to become commercialised.[6]

---

[5] Hill, *Puritanism*, 34 – 35.

[6] Tawney, *Agrarian Problem*, 188 – 189. So also Hexter, *Reappraisals*, 144 – 145, where the same fact is presented as part of a criticism of Tawney's

Royal peace and wool had to combine in a specific way to set up one of the significant forces propelling England toward both capitalism and a revolution that would make capitalism eventually democratic. In other states, notably Russia and China, strong rulers made their writ to run over far-flung territories. Indeed in England the fact that the rulers' success was very limited contributed heavily to the eventual triumph of parliamentary democracy. Nor is there any necessary connection between the wool trade as such and democracy. In Spain during the same period, the effect of sheep growing was if anything the reverse, since the migratory herds and their owners became one of the instruments used by the centralizing monarch in opposition to local and particularist tendencies and thus contributed to the growth of a stultifying royal absolutism.[7] The key to the English situation is that commercial life in both town and countryside during the sixteenth and seventeenth centuries grew up mainly though not entirely in opposition to the crown, for reasons that will appear in due course.

---

overemphasis on economic factors. A brief modern review of the ground Tawney covers is Thirsk, *Tudor Enclosures*. Emphasizing the variety of geographical and social conditions behind enclosures, the author comes to the same general conclusions (see 19 – 21). Tawney too was careful to draw such distinctions. The main difference is that Thirsk holds natural increase in population to be one of the more significant factors (9). Kerridge, "Depopulation," 212 – 228, gives good grounds for distrusting statistics on enclosures. His main point is that many of those accused of enclosing were later acquitted and that the statistics are exaggerated. Given the preponderant political influence, even under the Tudors, of those who were doing the enclosing, this fact is not surprising. Though the actual figures are not to be taken seriously, there is no doubt that the problem was serious in important parts of England. Neither Tawney nor Kerridge is cited in the brief review of the literature given at the end of Thirsk, *Tudor Enclosures*.

A half century after Tawney, modern investigators still stress the connection between the wool trade and agrarian changes. By the midsixteenth century, however, the impulse to switch from grain to wool was weakening, land becoming scarcer, labor more abundant, while grain prices rose sharply. Though the character of the wool trade changed, the movement of wool prices was steeply upward, with occasional sharp fluctuations, from 1450 to 1650. See Bowden, *Wool Trade*, xviii, 6, and table on 219 – 220.

[7] Thus concludes Klein, *The Mesta*, 351 – 357.

Under the pressure of circumstances, the medieval notion of judging economic actions according to their contribution to the health of the social organism began to collapse. Men ceased to see the agrarian problem as a question of finding the best method of supporting people on the land and began to perceive it as the best way of investing capital in the land. They began to treat land more and more as something that could be bought and sold, used and abused, in a word like modern capitalist private property. Under feudalism too there had been, of course, private property in land. But in all parts of the world where feudalism grew up, the ownership of land was always burdened and hedged with a great variety of obligations to other persons. The way in which these obligations disappeared, and who was to win or lose by the change, became crucial political issues in every country that knew feudalism. In England the issues came to the surface early. There, long before Adam Smith, scattered groups of Englishmen living in the countryside began to accept self-interest and economic freedom as the natural basis of human society.[8] In view of the widespread notion that economic individualism arose chiefly among the bourgeoisie, it is

[8] Lipson, *Economic History*, II, lxvii - lxviii. Hexter, *Reappraisals*, 94 - 95, vulgarizes and misrepresents Tawney's analysis of this trend by asserting that Tawney tries to squeeze the Puritan Revolution into a predetermined doctrinaire conception of an inevitable bourgeois revolution by weaving the "legend that the arrival of the townsmen in the country broke the old patriarchal rural economy and replaced it with a hard ruthless bourgeois commercialism." This is simply untrue. Tawney's whole analysis stresses the more or less spontaneous adaptation of the landed upper classes to a new situation created by the increasing importance of commerce, whose main focus of development he sees in the towns. (See *Agrarian Problem*, 408.) That is a very different matter from the simple migration of townsmen with new ideas to the countryside. In support of his strictures Hexter cites, with a flourishing *passim, Agrarian Problem*, 177 - 200, and Tawney's essay "Rise of the Gentry." For Tawney's real point, see "Rise of the Gentry," 184 - 186. On the very first page of Hexter's first citation (*Agrarian Problem*, 177) Tawney has written one of the best eloquent warnings against doctrinaire determinist history that has ever come to my attention. There may be isolated sentences in these long passages that mention the purchase of estates by townsmen and their farming on commercial lines; that is not the main thrust of Tawney's argument.

worthwhile noticing that the enclosing landlords prior to the Civil War already provided at least as important a breeding ground for these subversive doctrines.

One of the most striking signs of the changed outlook was a boom in the land market that began around 1580 and lasted for about half a century. Annual rentals climbed to a third of what estates had sold for a few decades earlier.[9] Such a boom would be most unlikely without far-reaching structural changes in the conduct of agriculture itself and may be interpreted as a consequence of these changes.

The most important of these were the enclosures. The word itself has a variety of meanings describing quite different things, all of which were happening at the time and whose relative importance is not absolutely clear. During the sixteenth century the most significant were "encroachments made by lords of manors or their farmers upon the land over which the manorial population had common rights or which lay in the open arable fields."[10] Propelled by the prospect of profits to be made either in selling wool or by leasing their lands to those who did and thereby increasing their rents, the lords of the manors found a variety of legal and semilegal methods to deprive the peasants of their rights of cultivation in the open fields and also their rights to use the common for pasture of their cattle, the collection of wood for fuel, and the like. While the actual area affected by such enclosures appears to have been small — less than one-twentieth of the total area in the counties most heavily subject to enclosure — yet this fact, if it is indeed a fact, does not mean that the situation in those sections was not serious. One might as well argue, as Tawney points out, that urban overcrowding is of no importance in England because the total area of the country divided by the population yields a quotient of about an acre and a half for every human being. "The drifting away of one tenant from

[9] See Hexter, *Reappraisals*, 133.

[10] Tawney, *Agrarian Problem*, 150. In English usage "farmer" usually means tenant-farmer or one who rents and cultivates a holding, with or without hired labor, depending on the amount of capital he has. More rarely does "farmer" refer to an owner. See *The Shorter Oxford English Dictionary, s.v.* "farmer."

each of fifty manors, and the eviction of fifty tenants from one manor, yield precisely the same statistical results" — and very different social ones. Finally, the political and social turmoil of the time must have had a real basis. "Governments do not go out of their way to offend powerful classes out of mere lightheartedness, nor do large bodies of men revolt because they have mistaken a ploughed field for a sheep pasture."[11]

Clearly a substantial amount of land formerly subject to customary rules prescribing the methods of cultivation was becoming land to be used at the discretion of the individual. Simultaneously the commercialization of agriculture meant a change from the feudal seigneur who was at worst a lawless tyrant and at best a despotic parent to an overlord who was closer to an acute man of business exploiting the material resources of the estate with an eye to profit and efficiency.[12] The habits were not entirely new in the sixteenth century. Nor were they as extensive as they were to become following the Civil War and during the eigtheenth and early nineteenth centuries. Nor were they confined to the landed upper classes. They were widespread in the upper ranks of the peasantry as well.

These were the yeomen, a class whose boundaries shaded off into the smaller gentry at the top and the less prosperous peasants at the bottom.[13] Though by no means all of them were freeholders or enjoyed modern rights of private property in land, they were rapidly thrusting forward in this direction and sloughing off the remaining feudal obligations.[14] Economically they were a "group of ambitious, aggressive, small capitalists, aware that they had not enough surplus to take great risks, mindful that the gain is often as much in the saving as in the spending, but determined to take advantage of every opportunity, whatever its origin, for increasing their profits."[15] Their estates may have run from twenty-five to two hundred acres in arable areas and up to as much as five or six

11 Tawney, *Agrarian Problem*, 264 – 265, 224.
12 Tawney, *Agrarian Problem*, 217, 191 – 193.
13 Campbell, *English Yeoman*, 23 – 27.
14 Campbell, *English Yeoman*, chap IV.
15 Campbell, *English Yeoman*, 104.

hundred in grazing territories. Though the big sheep farmers could, of course, operate at lower unit costs and market their wool more profitably, sheep farming was widely engaged in by yeomen and even less prosperous peasants.[16] Growing marketable grain was also a major source of income for the yeomanry. Those close to London or to the growing towns, as well as those who had access to transportation by water, must have had enormous advantages over the others.[17]

The yeomen were the chief force behind peasant enclosures. Directed toward land for tillage, these enclosures were quite different from those of the lordly sheep farmers. They were mainly a form of nibbling away at wastes, commons, and very frequently at the fields of neighbors, including landlords who did not keep a sharp lookout to defend their rights. At other times peasant enclosures were mutual agreements to consolidate plots and abandon the system of strips in the open field. Within the limits of their situation, the yeomen too were eager to break away from traditional agricultural routines and try new techniques in the hope of profit.[18]

From the comparative standpoint, sixteenth-century yeomen look rather like the *kulaks* of the late nineteenth-century and even of postrevolutionary Russia, though living in an environment much more favorable to individual enterprise than their Russian counterparts. Yeomen are generally the heroes of English history, *kulaks* the villains of Russian history for both conservatives and socialists, a contrast in attitudes that reveals much about the different societies and their respective paths into the modern world.

Those who promoted the wave of agrarian capitalism, the chief victors in the struggle against the old order, came from the yeomanry and even more from the landed upper classes. The main victims of progress were as usual the ordinary peasants. This happened not because the English peasants were peculiarly stubborn and conservative or clung to precapitalist and preindividualist habits out of

[16] Campbell, *English Yeoman*, 102, 197–203; Bowden, *Wool Trade*, xv, 2.

[17] Campbell, *English Yeoman*, 179, 184, 192.

[18] Campbell, *English Yeoman*, 87–91, 170, 173. See also Tawney, *Agrarian Problem*, 161–166.

sheer ignorance and stupidity, much as this seemed to be the case to contemporaries. Persistence of old habits no doubt played a part; but in this instance, as in many others to be encountered in the course of this study, it is necessary to ask why the old habits persisted. The reason is fairly easy to perceive. The medieval system of agriculture in England, as in many other parts of the world, was one where each peasant's holdings took the form of a series of narrow strips scattered helter-skelter amid those of his fellows in unfenced or open fields. Since cattle grazed on these fields after harvesting, the harvest had to come in about the same time for all concerned, and the operations of the agricultural cycle had to be more or less coordinated. Within these arrangements, there was some leeway for individual variation,[19] but mainly there was strong need for cooperative organization that could easily harden into custom as the easiest way to settle matters. To rearrange the use of the strips each season, though this did happen, would obviously be quite an undertaking. The peasants' interest in the common as a source of extra pasture and fuel is obvious. More generally, since the English peasants had won for themselves a relatively envious position under the protection of the custom of the manor, it is no wonder that they looked to the protection of custom and tradition as the dike that might defend them against the invading capitalist flood from which they were scarcely in a position to profit.[20]

Despite some help, now and then, from the monarchy, the dike began to crumble. In the language of the day, sheep ate men. The· peasants were driven off the land; ploughed strips and commons alike were turned into pastures. A single shepherd could manage flocks grazing over land that once had fed many humans.[21] To measure these changes accurately is probably impossible, though there is no doubt that they were substantial. Yet, as Tawney himself is careful to point out, the waters that broke through in the sixteenth century were but a trickle compared to the rush that came after the Civil War had destroyed the dike.

[19] Cf Campbell, *English Yeoman*, 176–178, citing research by G.E. Fussell on early farming methods.

[20] Tawney, *Agrarian Problem*, 126, 128, 130–132.

[21] Tawney, *Agrarian Problem*, 232, 237, 240–241, 257.

Thus in England the chief carriers of what was eventually to be a modern and secular society were at this time fundamentally men of commerce in both the countryside and the towns. In sharp contrast with what happened in France, these men pushed forward mainly on their own instead of under the umbrella of paternalist royal patronage. At times of course some were happy to cooperate with the crown, since there were rich pickings to be had. But, especially as the Civil War approached, the wealthier townsmen turned against royal monopolies, if not as fetters on production, at least as barriers to their own ambitions.[22] The crown under Elizabeth and the first two Stuarts made some effort to mitigate the effects of these trends on both the peasants and the poorer classes in the towns. Large numbers of the peasants, cast adrift, were becoming a menace to good order, to the point where intermittent revolts occurred.[23] One careful historian calls royal policy one of spasmodic benevolence. During the Eleven Years' Tyranny, when Charles I ruled through Strafford and Laud without a Parliament, the attempt to apply benevolence may have been more vigorous. Such royal courts as the Star Chamber and the Court of Requests gave the peasant what protection he did obtain against eviction through enclosures.[24]

[22] For the contrast with France, see Nef, *Industry and Government*. For the attack on chartered companies see also Lipson, *Economic History*, II, lviii – lix.

[23] Peasant revolts have apparently received scant attention. Tawney perhaps exaggerates their connection with enclosures. The best material I could find was in Semenov, *Ogorazhivaniya*, especially 349, 277, 284, 287 – 291, 300 – 304, 307, 309, 321, 324, 327. The burden of this material, limited to the sixteenth century, is the following. There were three main upheavals in which peasants took part: 1) The Pilgrimage of Grace, 1536 – 1537, mainly a feudal and antiroyal movement in which peasants rose with their lords; 2) Devonshire and Cornwall in 1549, an economically backward area; and 3) in the area of Norfolk in the same year where there is evidence of a connection with enclosures. Trevor-Roper, "Gentry," 40, refers to the revolt of the Midland peasants in 1607 as "the last purely peasant rebellion in England," where the terms Levellers and Diggers appear. This one too was clearly directed against enclosures.

[24] Lipson, *Economic History*, II, lxv, 404 – 405; James, *Social Problems*, 79, 241 – 243.

At the same time the crown was not above lining its own pockets by fines in the attempt to enforce these policies. A vigorous enforcement was in any case beyond its reach. Unlike the French monarchy, the English crown had not been able to build up an effective administrative and legal machinery of its own that could force its will upon the countryside. Those who kept order in the countryside were generally members of the gentry, the very ones against whom the crown's protective policies were directed. Thus the chief consequence of the crown's policy was to antagonize those who upheld the right to do what one liked — and thought socially beneficial — with one's own property. Royal policy tended to weld commercially minded elements in town and countryside, united by many other bonds as well, into a coherent opposition to the crown.[25] In the agrarian sector, Stuart agrarian policy was definitely a failure and helped to precipitate the Civil War, a conflict "between individual rights and royal authority, conceived of as resting in the last resort, on a religious sanction."[26] By this point it should be reasonably clear whose individual rights were at stake and that they were certainly not those of the mass of the peasantry, still the overwhelming bulk of England's population.

2. Agrarian Aspects of the Civil War

In the light of this general background there would seem to be little reason to question the thesis that commercially minded elements among the landed upper classes, and to a lesser extent among the yeomen, were among the main forces opposing the King and royal attempts to preserve the old order, and therefore an important cause, though not the only one, that produced the Civil War. The growth of commerce in the towns during the sixteenth and seventeenth centuries had created in the English countryside a market for agricultural products, thereby setting in motion a process leading toward commercial and capitalist agriculture in the countryside itself. The intrusion of commercial influences created more and more extensively a new situation to which different groups

[25] For an excellent analysis see Manning, "Nobles," in Aston, ed, Crisis in Europe, 247 – 269, esp 252, 263.

[26] James, Social Policy, 80.

within each of the agrarian classes, no one of which was sharply marked off from the others or from those in the towns, adapted in different ways and with varying degrees of success. Titled aristocrats with expensive habits of display and court connections were by and large less likely to make the shift, though some did adapt.[27] The main rural body whose more enterprising members adapted successfully was that large and somewhat diffuse body below the peerage and above the yeomanry, in other words, the gentry. But their success was not entirely due to agricultural activities alone. The gentry who looked ahead had all sorts of personal and business connections with the upper ranks of the townsmen or bourgeoisie in the accepted narrower sense of the term.[28] From the gentry as a class, then, came the main representatives of a decisive historical trend modifying the structure of English rural society. In terms of the contrast between types of economy, social structure, and corresponding outlooks to be found among the gentry and landed aristocracy there was "a struggle between economies of different types, which corresponded more closely with regional peculiarities than with social divisions. There are plenty of gentry who stagnate or go down-hill. It would be easy to find noble landowners who move with the times, and make the most of their properties."[29] The gentry who "stagnated" were apparently those who were relatively unenterprising in improving their economic situation on the land and lacked profitable urban connections of a

[27] Tawney, "Rise of the Gentry," 181. On this point see the very thorough study, which appeared while this book was in press, Stone, *Crisis of the Aristocracy*, chap IV, esp 163. The author concludes that the peers' share in the rapidly growing wealth of England had declined sharply and that this change in their relative financial position, not their absolute one, was what mattered.

[28] Tawney, "Rise of the Gentry," 176, 187 – 188.

[29] Tawney, "Rise of the Gentry," 186. Tawney's achievement is in recognizing and drawing attention to the structural changes in English society, though the statistical underpinning of his argument is probably its weakest part. He may have exaggerated the number of titled nobles who were making heavy weather of the new situation and the number of gentry who were profiting from it. For a criticism of Tawney's statistical procedures, see Cooper, "Counting of Manors," 377 – 389, and the Appendix on interpretations of statistical data.

commercial or official nature. These "growlers and grumblers" may have supplied a portion of the radical element behind Cromwell and the Puritan Revolution, though this impetus had its main origins further down the social scale.[30] Thus, under the impact of commerce and some industry, English society was breaking apart from the top downward in a way that allowed pockets of radical discontent produced by the same forces to burst temporarily in the limelight. As we shall see in due course, a similar sequence of developments is roughly characteristic of the other major modern revolutions as well, the French, the Russian, and the Chinese. In this process, as the old order breaks up, sections of society that had been losing out due to long-run economic trends come to the surface and do much of the violent "dirty work" of destroying the *ancien régime*, thus clearing the road for a new set of institutions.

In England the main dirty work of this type was the symbolic act of beheading Charles I. The chief demand for justice against the king came from the army. Here popular influences were quite strong. They stemmed from strata below the gentry, very likely urban journeymen and peasants.[31] By the time of the execution, Cromwell and his officers had already succeeded in curbing them. The execution itself had to be rammed through Parliament practically at the point of a musket. Even then a substantial number (49) refused to judge the king; 59 signed the death warrant. There are indications of a preponderance of poorer gentry among the regicides and of wealthier gentry among those who refused to judge the king. But the two groups overlap considerably; mechanical sociological analysis will not accurately sift the political sentiments of the day.[32] Conceivably constitutional monarchy could

[30] See Trevor-Roper, "Gentry," 8, 16, 24, 26, 31, 34, 38, 40, 42, 51. While his case is not watertight, Trevor-Roper has presented a good deal of evidence pointing to substantial influence by "mere gentry" in Cromwell's armies. For modifications of Trevor-Roper's position see Yule, *Independents*, 48 – 50, 52, 56, 61, 65, 79, 81, and esp 80, where Yule agrees that the lesser gentry made up the Army officer Independents. Incisive criticism of Trevor-Roper's thesis appears in Zagorin, "Social Interpretation," 381, 383, 385, 387.

[31] Firth, *Cromwell's Army*, 346 – 360.

[32] See Yule, *Independents*, 129 for table.

have come about in another way. But Charles I's fate was a grisly reminder for the future. No subsequent English king tried to take royal absolutism seriously again. Cromwell's attempt to establish dictatorship seems merely a desperate and unsuccessful attempt to patch things together afterward and is not really comparable to the semidictatorial phase in the French Revolution, where there was still much destruction of the *ancien régime.* Nor did the peasants and urban plebs, those who did the dirty work of the other revolutions, come to the surface during the English Civil War, except in certain very important brief symbolic acts.

There were many ties that held modernizers and traditionalists together in the same social strata, including common fears of the lower orders, the "meaner sort." Such bonds help to explain why class alignments were far from clear in this revolution. Charles I did his best to court the gentry. There is evidence that he succeeded on a very wide scale.[33] Despite Stuart opposition to enclosures, the support of many wealthy gentry for the royal cause is scarcely surprising. One would scarcely expect men of substance to have an easy conscience about kicking over two of the main props, king and church, that supported the social order. Eventually they were to welcome them back in a changed form more suited to their requirements. The same ambiguous attitude toward those aspects of the old order that supported property rights came to the surface in the three great revolutions elsewhere that succeeded the Puritan Revolution, as well as in the American Civil War. On the other hand, the policy of the leaders of the rebellion was clear and straightforward. They opposed interference with the landlord's property rights on the part of the king and on the part of radicals from the lower orders. In July 1641, the Long Parliament abolished the Star Chamber, the main royal weapon against enclosing landlords, as well as the general symbol of arbitrary royal power. Radical threats from within the army, from the Levellers and the Diggers, Cromwell and his associates fended off with firmness and skill.[34]

Other factors too account for the fact that the Puritan Revo-

[33] Zagorin, "Social Interpretation," 390, collects the relevant evidence. See also Hardacre, *Royalists,* 5 – 6.

[34] See James, *Social Policy,* 117 – 128.

S.D.D. – 2

lution did not develop at any point into a clear-cut struggle between the upper and lower strata. The struggle involved a combination of economic, religious, and constitutional issues. There is not enough evidence yet to show conclusively the extent to which these issues coincided: the social basis of Puritanism awaits analysis. But the indications are that opinion crystallized on these issues at different times. Hence as the dramatic events of the Revolution unfolded and men were confronted by events they could not control and whose implications they could not foresee — in short, as the process of revolutionary polarization advanced and receded, many high and low felt themselves in terrible predicaments and could reach a decision only with the greatest difficulty. Personal loyalties might pull in a direction opposite to principles that the individual only half-realized and vice versa.

In economics the Civil War did not produce any massive transfer of landed property from one group or class to another. (On this score Tawney is almost certainly mistaken.) The effects on land ownership were probably even less than they were in the French Revolution, where modern research has sustained de Tocqueville's contention that the growth of a class of property-owning peasants preceded the Revolution and was not the consequence of the sale of *émigré* properties. In England the Parliamentary side was chronically short of money and financed the war partly by taking over the operation of Royalist estates and partly through outright confiscation. In the meantime Royalist agents managed to repurchase estates, thereby making their contribution to the finances of their enemies. Many more estates were recovered afterward. One study of these transactions in southeastern England, which the author holds to have wider applications, shows that more than three-quarters of the properties sold under the Commonwealth can be traced back to their owners by the Restoration. Just short of a quarter were recovered before 1660. Purchasers of crown and church lands do not seem to have been able to retain their holdings after the Restoration, though the author provides no statistics on this point.[35]

It will not do, however, to cite this evidence in support of the thesis that the Puritan Revolution was no revolution at all. Its revo-

[35] Thirsk, "Restoration Land Settlement," 323, 326–327.

lutionary consequences were deep and lasting in the area of law and social relationships. With the abolition of the Star Chamber, the peasants lost their chief protection against the advance of enclosures. Some attempts were made under Cromwell, especially in the later phase of the rule of the major generals, to check their effects. But this was the last effort of its kind.[36] Though there may be room for doubt about the social characteristics of those gentry who supported the revolution, it is clear who won the victory. "With the Restoration the encloser carried all before him," though the full effects were not to be felt for some time.[37] Through breaking the power of the king, the Civil War swept away the main barrier to the enclosing landlord and simultaneously prepared England for rule by a "committee of landlords," a reasonably accurate if unflattering designation of Parliament in the eighteenth century.

The critics of those who label the Civil War a bourgeois revolution are correct in their contention that the conflict did not result in the taking of political power by the bourgeoisie. The upper classes in the countryside remained in firm control of the apparatus of politics, as we shall see in due course, not only during the eighteenth century but even after the Reform Bill of 1832. But seen against the realities of social life the point is a trivial one. Capitalist influences had penetrated and transformed much of the countryside long before the Civil War. The connection between the enclosing landlord and the bourgeoisie was close and intimate to the point where it is often difficult to decide where the one begins and the other leaves off in the ramified family circles of the day. The outcome of the struggle was an enormous if still incomplete victory for an alliance between parliamentary democracy and capitalism. As one modern historian puts the point, "The aristocratic order survived, but in a new shape, for money more than birth was now its basis. And Parliament itself became the instrument of landed capitalists, Whig and Tory both, and their connections and allies, whose interests the state now unswervingly pursued."[38]

[36] James, *Social Policy*, 118, 120, 122, 124.
[37] James, *Social Policy*, 343.
[38] Zagorin, "English Revolution," 681.

To perceive the magnitude of the Civil War's accomplishments it is necessary to step back from the details and glance forward and backward. The proclaimed principle of capitalist society is that the unrestricted use of private property for personal enrichment necessarily produces through the mechanism of the market steadily increasing wealth and welfare for society as a whole. In England this spirit eventually triumphed by "legal" and "peaceful" methods, which, however, may have caused more real violence and suffering than the Civil War itself, during the eighteenth and early nineteenth centuries on the land as much as in the towns. While the original impulse toward capitalism may have come from the towns far back in the Middle Ages, it proceeded on the land as strongly as in the cities, receiving a perpetual draft from the towns that caused the flames devouring the old order to spread through the countryside. Both the capitalist principle and that of parliamentary democracy are directly antithetical to the ones they superseded and in large measure overcame during the Civil War: divinely supported authority in politics, and production for use rather than for individual profit in economics. Without the triumph of these principles in the seventeenth century it is hard to imagine how English society could have modernized peacefully — to the extent that it actually was peaceful — during the eighteenth and nineteenth centuries.

3. Enclosures and the Destruction of the Peasantry

Revolutionary violence may contribute as much as peaceful reform to the establishment of a relatively free society and indeed was in England the prelude to a more peaceful transformation. But not all historically significant violence takes the form of revolution. A great deal may occur within the framework of legality, even a legality that is well along the road to Western constitutional democracy. Such were the enclosures that followed the Civil War and continued through the early Victorian era.

A half century ago many scholars saw the enclosures of the eighteenth century as the main device by which a nearly omnipotent landed aristocracy destroyed the independent peasantry of

England.[39] Subsequent scholarship has slowly and patiently chipped away at this thesis. Few professional historians, except perhaps some Marxists, would accept it today. Unquestionably the older interpretation is wrong in details and dubious in some points crucial to the central argument. Yet the earlier writers grasped firmly one point that often disappears in modern discussions: the enclosures were the final blow that destroyed the whole structure of English peasant society embodied in the traditional village.

As we have just seen, peasant society had come under attack well before the outbreak of the Civil War. The war itself eliminated the king as the last protection of the peasantry against the encroachments of the landed upper classes. Though the Tudor and Stuart bureaucracy had not been very effective, on occasion it had at least endeavored to stem the tide. After the Restoration and the Glorious Revolution of 1688, the last rumblings of the earthquake, England settled down in the eighteenth century to government by Parliament. While the king was by no means a mere figurehead, he did not attempt to interfere with the advance of enclosures. Parliament was more than a committee of landlords; urban commercial interests had at least some indirect representation through the system of rotten boroughs.[40] Local government, with which the peasants came directly in contact, was even more firmly in the hands of the gentry and titled aristocracy than it had been before. As the eighteenth century advanced, the transaction of public business in the parishes, some 15,000 of which formed the cells of the English body politic, came to be conducted more and more behind closed doors, losing whatever vestiges of a popular and democratic character that it may have had during the Middle Ages.[41]

Furthermore it was Parliament that ultimately controlled the process of enclosure. Formally the procedures by which a landlord put through an enclosure by act of Parliament were public and democratic. Actually the big property owners dominated the

[39] See, for example, the classic monograph by the Hammonds, *Village Labourer*. Cf Johnson, *Disappearance*.

[40] Namier, *England*, 4, 22, 25.

[41] Hammond and Hammond, *Village Labourer*, 16 – 17; Johnson, *Disappearance*, 132.

proceedings from start to finish. Thus the consent of "three-fourths to four-fifths" was required on the spot before Parliament would approve a proposal to enclose. But consent of what? The answer turns out to be property, not people. Suffrages were not counted, but weighed. One large proprietor could swamp an entire community of smaller proprietors and cottagers.[42]

The political and economic supremacy of the larger landlords during the eighteenth century was partly the result of trends that long antedate the Civil War, chiefly the authority of local notables and the absence of a strong bureaucratic apparatus to check this authority, even under the Tudors and the Stuarts. The outcome of the Civil War itself, in sharp contrast to that of the French Revolution, was to strengthen greatly the position of the landed upper classes. There has already been occasion to notice some evidence indicating relatively little change in the distribution of landed property during the Puritan Revolution.[43] With only two exceptions, all the great families that were in Northamptonshire and Bedfordshire in 1640 were still there a century later.[44]

Adapting early to the world of commerce and even taking the

[42] Hammond and Hammond, *Village Labourer*, 49–50. A subsequent study attacked the Hammonds for overdoing the element of corruption and bias in Parliament's handling of enclosures. See Tate, "Members of Parliament," 74, 75. The author studied every occasion of which he could find record in which members of Parliament gathered to consider petitions for enclosure in one area, the county of Nottinghamshire. He found that in 71 percent of the 365 occasions examined, "There seems no reason to suppose that injustice was done on account of the private self-interest of the members concerned, *except insofar as injustice must necessarily occur to some extent when, in a class society, members of one class legislate concerning the livelihoods and properties of those occupying a very different position in the social order*." (Emphasis added.) When the author remarks further on, "Probably a parliament of landlords was almost as biased in considering the case for the preservation of a landed peasantry as would be a parliament of coal owners deliberating as to the necessity for the continued existence of coal-owners," the reader may conclude that he has destroyed his own case.

[43] See the studies of Thirsk cited above.

[44] Habakkuk, "English Landownership," 4.

lead in the march into the new era, the landed aristocracy of England was not swept away by the convulsions that accompanied the change. Although the interlocking between the bourgeoisie and the landed aristocracy was less in the eighteenth century than under Elizabeth and the early Stuarts, the connection between the two remained very close.[45] As Sir Lewis Namier has observed, the English ruling classes in the eighteenth century were not "agrarians" like their contemporaries in Germany, while the civilization they created was neither urban nor rural. They lived neither in fortified castles nor in manor houses, nor in town palaces (as in Italy), but in mansions planted on their estates.[46]

There is widespread agreement among historians that the period from about 1688 to the end of the Napoleonic Wars was the golden age of the great landed estate. In important parts of the country, the estates spread out over the land, sometimes at the expense of the smaller gentry, and more significantly at the expense of the peasants. No one has yet arisen to deny the general importance of the enclosures or that innumerable peasants lost their rights on the common lands of the villages as the great landlords absorbed these lands. This was an age of improvement in agricultural techniques, such as the increased use of fertilizer, new crops, and crop rotation. New methods could not be applied at all in fields subject to the rules of common cultivation; their expense made them harder for the farmer of small and even middling means. Undoubtedly a large part of the increase in the size of farms came from the higher profits and lower costs of the larger unit.[47]

Contemporaries were enthusiastically, perhaps too enthusiastically, aware of these advantages. Like his counterpart in the towns, and indeed like all modern revolutionaries, the rural capitalist justified the misery he caused by appealing to the benefits he created for society at the same time that he made immense personal gains. Without these ideas of benefit to society and the substantial ele-

[45] Habakkuk, "English Landownership," 17.

[46] Namier, *England*, 16, see also 13; also Goodwin, ed, *European Nobility*, chap I on England by Habakkuk.

[47] Mingay, "Size of Farms," 480.

ments of truth they contained, it would be impossible to understand the ruthlessness of the enclosure movement.[48]

I have spoken here as if the rural capitalist were one person. Actually he was two: the big landowner and the large tenant farmer. The large landlord was an aristocrat who did no work with his hands and often left the actual details of management to a bailiff, though he generally kept a sharp eye on this figure. Walpole read reports from his steward before he looked at state papers. The large landholder's contribution to the development of capitalist farming at this stage was mainly legal and political; it was usually he who arranged the enclosures. Lacking serfs to work the land, he generally let it out to large tenant farmers. Many of these used hired labor. Quite early in the eighteenth century landowners were "clear as to what was a good estate. It was one tenanted by large farmers holding 200 acres or more, paying their rents regularly and keeping the holdings in repair. The three most important methods of improvement in this period were all devices to this end — consolidation of holdings, enclosure, and the replacing of leases for lives by leases for a term of years—and in practice they were related to each other in a great variety of ways."[49] The big tenant farmers made the economic contribution. Though the landlords shouldered the heavy tax burden — the tenants were in a strong enough position to force this issue — they seldom provided working capital for their tenants.[50] Nor were they expected to. But the big tenants, along with the wealthy freeholders, and not the celebrated handful of "spirited landlords," were the real pioneers of agricultural development, in the judgment of a recent historian.[51]

[48] For all their sympathy with the victims, the Hammonds grasped this point firmly, saying that it was "maddening to have to set your pace by the slow bucolic temperament of small farmers, nursed in a simple and old-fashioned routine, who looked with suspicion on any proposal that was strange to them." See *Village Labourer*, 36.

[49] Habakkuk, "English Landownership," 15. Cf Namier, *England*, 15.

[50] Habakkuk, "English Landownership," 14.

[51] See Mingay, "Size of Farms," 479, 472, drawing on the evidence of Arthur Young's *Tours*. Elsewhere Mingay cites considerable evidence showing that the very large landholders were not economically progressive, adding to their property, when they did, mainly by advantageous marriages

The span of time when these changes were most rapidly and thoroughly taking place is not absolutely clear. It seems most likely, however, that the enclosure movement had gathered considerable force by about 1760. It may have surged forward at its greatest speed during the Napoleonic Wars, to die out after 1832, by which time it had helped to change the English countryside beyond recognition. Rising food prices and probably also difficulties in obtaining labor appear to have been the main factors both tempting and compelling landlords to enlarge their holdings and rationalize their cultivation.[52]

Thus over substantial parts of England, as the large estate became larger and was operated more and more on commercial principles, it finally destroyed the medieval peasant community. It is rather likely, though not absolutely certain, that the wave of parliamentary enclosures during the eighteenth and early nineteenth centuries merely gave legal sanction to a process of eroding peasant property that had been going on for some time.[53] We know from

---

and getting their hands into public funds. The impulse toward improved methods of cultivation came from "publicists, country gentlemen, owner-occupiers, and large tenant farmers." See Mingay, *Landed Society*, chap III and 166, 171. Enclosure, he agrees (179), was the landowner's principal contribution to economic progress.

[52] See Ashton, *Economic History*, 40, and the table of wheat prices for 1704–1800 on 239; Deane and Cole, *British Economic Growth*, 94, for a table showing the annual number of parliamentary enclosure bills 1719–1835 (not in itself more than a very rough indication about the number of peasants and the amount of land affected); Gonner, *Common Land*, 197; Levy, *Large and Small Holdings*, 10, 14, 16, 18, 19. For a different point of view see Johnson, *Disappearance*, 87, 136. Note also the remark in Chambers, "Enclosure and Labour Supply," 325, note 3. An older view that placed the disappearance of the small landowner prior to 1760 was based partly on the study of land tax records (as in Johnson cited above). But see objections to reliance on such data by Mingay, "Land Tax Assessments," 381–388.

[53] See Mingay, *Landed Society*, 99, 180–181, 184, 186. If this conclusion is correct, the main fault of the Hammonds would have been overemphasis on parliamentary enclosures as such. In contrast to my views, Mingay minimizes the hardship and extent of enclosures. See his *Landed Society*, 96–99, 179–186, 268–269.

the experience of other countries that the intrusion of commerce into a peasant community generally sets in motion a tendency toward the concentration of land in fewer hands. This tendency had been noticeable in England at least as early as the sixteenth century. In the heart of an area heavily hit by enclosure, seventy percent of the land in one village had been withdrawn from the peasant economy before the village was enclosed by act of Parliament. By 1765 only three families in ten occupied land in this area of advancing industry. The rest were laborers, knitters, small tradesmen. Seventy small peasants out of less than a hundred owned less than a fifth of all the land, while a dozen select families at the top owned three-fifths.[54] A similar situation probably prevailed over much of the area that was heavily subject to enclosure after the middle of the eighteenth century. If, in order to discover the area affected, one looks at a map of England shaded according to the total areas of counties in which the enclosure of common fields took place, one will notice that rather more than half the country had been subject to such enclosure. Perhaps half of this area in turn, mainly in the Midlands but with a broad tongue extending northwards, experienced the heaviest impact, running from just under a third to a half and more of these areas.[55]

As is usually the case in such social upheavals, the fate of those who lost out by the change is very difficult to discern. Those who had property rights to defend in the course of enclosure proceedings tended by and large to make better weather of the storm than those who did not. Even at that many small owners had heavy costs to bear connected with enclosure proceedings, as well as capital charges for hedging and ditching, that made their situation precarious.[56] The ones whose property rights were tenuous to nonexistent fail to appear in the historical record because they lacked

[54] Hoskins, *Midland Peasant*, 217, 219, 226 – 227.

[55] See map on enclosures of common fields in the 18th – 19th centuries, facing p. 20 in Clapham, *Economic History*, I. The map is based on Gonner, *Common Land*, which appeared in 1912 and made use of earlier studies whose statistics may well be open to criticism.

[56] Gonner, *Common Land*, 201 – 202, 367 – 369; Hoskins, *Midland Peasant*, 260.

property rights to defend. "These landless or semi-landless workers, together with the small tenants who disappeared through consolidation, represent the real victims of enclosure, and unless they
are kept constantly in mind, they may also become the victims of
statistical method."[57] Within these bottom layers, before enclosure,
there had been some variety of economic and legal position. Most
poor families — tenant cottagers, for example — had a small dwell-
ing and the right to cultivate a few strips of land as well as to keep
perhaps a cow, a few geese, or a pig or so. Men and beasts had
generally scratched out an existence in which the rights of common
played a large part. For cottagers and certainly for the landless
laborers who had only customary but not legal usage of the common, the loss of this right or privilege meant disaster. "The appro-
priation to their own exclusive use of practically the whole of the
common waste by the legal owners meant that the curtain which
separated the growing army of labourers from utter proletarianiza-
tion was torn down. It was, no doubt, a thin and squalid curtain
. . . but it was real, and to deprive them of it without providing a
substitute implied the exclusion of the labourers from the benefits
which their intensified labour alone made possible."[58] The little men
at the bottom of the rural heap were thus swept aside, either to
swell the new army of rural laborers, needed for some time to put
in enclosure hedges, ditches, roads or to carry out new agricultural
practices not yet possible to execute by labor-saving machinery or
to join the wretched workers in the disease-ridden towns. Modern
scholars tend to believe that the dispossessed cottagers and landless
laborers generally stayed on the soil, while the remaining "unab-
sorbed surplus" laborers and cottagers became industrial workers.[59]
But generally only the young, the unmarried, or the village craftsmen were willing to leave home — and only such individuals were
wanted by the new industrial employers. Mature men with families
were not as trainable nor could they as easily tear themselves com-

---

[57] Chambers, "Enclosure and Labour Supply," 326 – 327. See also
Hoskins, *Midland Peasant*, 268.

[58] Chambers, "Enclosure and Labour Supply," 336.

[59] See, for example, Chambers, "Enclosure and Labour Supply," 332 –
333, 336.

pletely out of the fabric of rural life. Remaining on the soil, they had recourse to their "last right" — the right of poor relief.[60] In one village in Leicestershire, "as in thousands of other parishes in the Midlands and the South," the enclosures of common fields, together with the loss of commons and the requirements of a money economy, had resulted in a steady rise of poor rates in order to support by 1832 "nearly one half the families in the village in regular receipt of poor relief and many more receiving intermittent relief." In the previous century these families had been self-supporting small farmers or not too badly off cottagers, able to obtain the necessaries of life in an open-field economy.[61] Where the open-field system worked at all well in terms of supplying enough of what was needed, it had been the basis of a rough degree of economic equality in the village. It had also served to bolster up the network of social relationships based on the division of labor that, in effect, *was* the society of the village. When, in the past, village society had been strong, the peasants had fought vigorously with some success to defend their rights. In the eighteenth century, with the final blow of enclosures and commercial influences, these small farmers generally failed to resist or to fight back.[62] Thus it seems quite clear that when the common fields disappeared and a new economic system began to win out in the countryside, the old peasant community finally gave way and disintegrated.[63]

Looking back over the enclosure movement as a whole and taking account of the results of modern research, it still seems plain enough that, together with the rise of industry, the enclosures greatly strengthened the larger landlords and broke the back of the English peasantry, eliminating them as a factor from British political life. From the standpoint of the issues discussed here, that is,

[60] Thompson, *Making of the Working Class*, 222 – 223.

[61] Hoskins, *Midland Peasant*, 269 – 270.

[62] Ashton, *Economic History*, 36, asserts that ". . . if large numbers had been evicted they would hardly have gone quietly. But there are no records of agrarian risings or even local battles of any consequence at this time. The process was one of attrition." For the last agrarian revolt, in 1830, see Hammond and Hammond, *Village Labourer*, chaps XI, XII.

[63] See Hoskins, *Midland Peasant*, 249 – 250, 254 – 255.

after all, the decisive point. Furthermore, for the "surplus" peasant it made little difference whether the pull from the towns or factories was more important than the push out of his rural world. In either case he was caught in the end between alternatives that meant degradation and suffering, compared with the traditional life of the village community. That the violence and coercion which produced these results took place over a long space of time, that it took place mainly within a framework of law and order and helped ultimately to establish democracy on a firmer footing, must not blind us to the fact that it was massive violence exercised by the upper classes against the lower.

4. *Aristocratic Rule for Triumphant Capitalism*

The nineteenth century itself was the age of peaceful transformation when parliamentary democracy established itself firmly and broadened down from precedent to precedent. Before examining what part agrarian changes played in this process, it is well to pause briefly and consider in what ways the violence of the seventeenth and eighteenth centuries — the first open and revolutionary, the second more concealed and legal but nonetheless violent for that — prepared the way for peaceful transition in the nineteenth. To break the connection between the two is to falsify history. To assert that the connection was somehow necessary and inevitable is to justify the present by the past with an argument that is impossible to prove. All that the social historian can do is point to a contingent connection among changes in the structure of society.

Perhaps the most important legacy of a violent past was the strengthening of Parliament at the expense of the king. The fact that Parliament existed meant that there was a flexible institution which constituted both an arena into which new social elements could be drawn as their demands arose and an institutional mechanism for settling peacefully conflicts of interest among these groups. If Parliament emerged from the Civil War mainly as an instrument of a commercially minded, landed upper class, it was not just that and, as experience was to show, it could become a great deal more. The fact that this class had developed an economic base which had brought it into violent opposition to the crown before the Civil

War had a great deal to do with the strengthening of Parliament, a point that will stand out more clearly when we can see the course of English developments against other cases where this did not happen. The strong commercial tone in the life of the landed upper classes, both gentry and titled nobility, also meant that there was no very solid phalanx of aristocratic opposition to the advance of industry itself. Despite a good many expressions of contrary sentiment from their own members, it is fair to say that the most influential sector of the landed upper classes acted as a political advance guard for commercial and industrial capitalism. This they continued to do in new ways during the nineteenth century.

The other main consequence was the destruction of the peasantry. Brutal and heartless though the conclusion appears, there are strong grounds for holding that this contribution to peaceful democratic change may have been just as important as the strengthening of Parliament. It meant that modernization could proceed in England without the huge reservoir of conservative and reactionary forces that existed at certain points in Germany and Japan, not to mention India. And it also of course meant that the possibility of peasant revolutions in the Russian and Chinese manner were taken off the historical agenda.

At the end of the eighteenth century and the beginning of the nineteenth there was certainly nothing inevitable about the victory of parliamentary democracy. Indeed it is unlikely that more than a very few people had any but the haziest notions as to what the words could mean or what kind of a society might lie over the horizon. During the eighteenth century commerce had made considerable progress. There were now beginning to appear signs of conflict between the landed interests and those connected with commerce. Influential elements in the latter sought to promote an aggressive foreign policy in pursuit of raw materials and markets, while many gentry hung back for fear of higher taxes in an age when the land tax was the main source of revenue. In the meantime radical voices about the need to overhaul England's antiquated social structure, especially her corrupt Parliament, began to make themselves heard. The cliché that eighteenth-century politics was a battle of cliques without issues is simply false. There were the same issues between new and old forms of society and civilization as in the seventeenth century, transposed to a new era, though it is perhaps too much to claim that after the loss of the American colonies England was on the verge of revolutionary action.[64]

The outbreak of the French Revolution put an end to all hope of reform. More specifically, as soon as the Revolution passed beyond its liberal phase, when Louis XVI's flight to Varennes and recapture "tore the veil of illusions" from liberal prospects and the Revolution began to enter a radical phase, those in England who sympathized with it found their position more and more awkward. Pitt the Younger stopped all talk of reform. England began to enter a phase of repression that lasted until after the Napoleonic Wars. Its fundamental feature was that the upper classes, in both the town and the countryside, closed ranks around patriotic and conservative slogans against the menace of radicalism and tyranny in France and against the remotest threat to their privileges.[65] If the menace of revolution and military dictatorship had not ended at the Battle of Waterloo, it is highly unlikely that England would have resumed in the nineteenth century those slow and halting steps toward political and social reform that she had given up at the end of the eighteenth. Acceptable regimes in Europe, the absence of a threat from that quarter, was one of the prerequisites for peaceful democratic evolution in England.

To understand why the reactionary phase was relatively brief and why the movement toward a freer society commenced anew during the nineteenth century, it is necessary to look beyond the

---

[64] Plumb, *England*, 132. This excellent survey brings out very clearly the conflict between landed and commercial interests. See also Mingay, *Landed Society*, 260 – 262, 265, for conflicts of interest between large proprietors and the small gentry, farmers, and urban middle class, whose dissatisfaction, he asserts, mounted to a peak during the American war.

[65] Much of what took place resembles American reactions to communist expansion after 1945. There is the same ambiguity about the character of the revolutionary enemy, the same exploitation of this ambiguity by the dominant elements in society, the same disillusionment and dismay among its original supporters as the revolution abroad deceived their hopes. In a later chapter and in connection with other types of reactionary movements, I shall try to discuss this phase more fully.

landed classes. They had reached the zenith of their combined economic and political power before the turn of the century; the subsequent story is one of defense and concessions rendered easier by the fact that the process of erosion was slow, and their economic base remained firm. Commonplace mechanical metaphors are misleading here. Though the capitalist elements in the towns "rose"; the landed upper classes did not "fall" — at least not for a very long time. By the end of the Napoleonic Wars, the more modern capitalists in the towns had already achieved considerable strength on the basis of their economic achievements, which, as modern historians now stress, had a long history behind them. Under the leadership of the landed classes, much of the road had been smoothed for them. The English capitalists in the nineteenth century did not have to rely on a Prussia and its Junkers to achieve national unity, tear down the internal barriers to trade, establish a uniform legal system, modern currency, and other prerequisites of industrialization. The political order had been rationalized and a modern state created long before. With a minimum of help from that state they could, as the first fully capitalist bourgeoisie, convert a large part of the entire globe into their trading area. Temporarily dammed up during the Napoleonic Wars, English industrial capitalism could spread out, mainly through peaceful means, to draw on foreign resources and make England the workshop of the world during the nineteenth century. Other capitalist tasks, such as the further disciplining of the labor force, English industrial leaders could carry out on their own with a minimum of help from the state or the landed aristocracy. They had to do so because the repressive apparatus of the English state was relatively weak, a consequence of the Civil War, the previous evolution of the monarchy, and of reliance on the navy rather than on the army. In turn the absence of a strong monarchy resting on an army and a bureaucracy, as in Prussia, made easier the development of parliamentary democracy.

In the meantime the landed gentry and those above it in the social scale retained a firm hold on the levers of political power. They filled the Cabinet, monopolized the representation of the rural areas, and sat in Parliament as representatives of the towns as well. At the local level, their influence remained very strong. As one recent historian has pointed out, the old governing class was still in firm control in the middle of the nineteenth century. "The political system was still to a remarkable extent the plaything of the nobility and gentry, and in particular of the hereditary owners of the great estates." The nucleus of this system contained perhaps no more than 1200 persons.[66]

On the other hand, they worked these levers within the context of strong challenges from other classes. To concentrate on the strength of their position in the formal and even the informal apparatus of politics would give a misleading impression of the power of the gentry and the nobility.[67] Even if the Reform Bill of 1832, which gave the industrial capitalists the vote, disappointed the hopes of its more ardent advocates and belied the fears of its more ardent opponents, its passage mean that the bourgeoisie had shown its teeth.[68] The same can be said about the striking down of the Corn Laws in 1846. The landed upper classes suffered no disaster, but they learned the limits of their power.

In the face of Chartist agitation too, during the decade 1838 – 1848, no very strong diehard policy of reaction emerged. It is true

[66] Clark, *Victorian England*, 209 – 210, 214, 222.

[67] Thompson, *Landed Society*, 273 – 280, recognizes this fact and provides detailed evidence on the character of this relationship after 1830. Though this very good study was published too late for me to take full advantage of its findings, it renders superfluous anything more than the sketch of nineteenth-century developments given here.

[68] The leadership behind the passage of the Bill were Whig landed aristocrats with characteristic family and clique connections among the "money interest" in the City of London and a good share of the manufacturing interest in the industrial provinces. Secure and aristocratic, they were prepared to accept reform to avoid worse dangers, i.e., a revolutionary outbreak such as happened in France in 1830. Nor were they averse to the use of force if necessary. Lord Melbourne in the Home Office, who epitomized the leadership, put down the revolt of the village laborers (1830) ruthlessly: 9 laborers were hanged, 457 transported, nearly as many imprisoned for varying terms. He refused to consider positive measures to relieve distress. Thus the Whig leaders made plain their intention to keep England safe for property. See Briggs, *Age of Improvement*, chap V, for an analysis of the forces behind and opposing the Reform, esp 237, 239, 249 – 250; also the very readable and instructive biography by Lord Cecil, *Melbourne*.

that the Conservative government, under proddings from Queen Victoria and the Duke of Wellington, used troops, opened private correspondence in search of information, and prosecuted some of the leaders for conspiracy, though the jury responded leniently. The Conservative government also used the occasion to mount an attack on the radical press of the day. The Whigs, who were in power at the beginning and the end of this period, were much more lenient. Lord John Russell, the Home Secretary, forbade interference with the Great Chartist meetings held in the autumn of 1838. Except for comparatively brief periods, the government paid very little attention to the Chartists. Russell's private papers contain only an occasional reference to the movement. The only bloodshed occurred when twenty-two Chartists were shot dead in a riot, an episode that took place, ironically, some days after the Whig attorney general had boasted of suppressing the movement "without one drop of blood being spilled."[69]

Since the Chartist movement displayed strong overtones of violence, it constituted a severe test of liberal principles. The comparatively mild treatment that it received at the hands of the ruling classes may be traced to three factors. There was then a strong current of opinion in favor of doing something to alleviate mass distress, as well as marked reluctance to use force. This current of opinion is in turn traceable to England's historical experience, at least as far back as the Puritan Revolution. Russell was a doctrinaire Whig devoted to the ideal of liberty and anxious to avoid encroaching on the free discussion of political issues.[70] Secondly, England in any case lacked a strong repressive apparatus. Thirdly, a combination of legislation to improve the situation of the poor and a favorable turn in the economic situation may have taken the steam out of the movement before it could become a really serious threat.

The situation during the first half of the nineteenth century and even considerably later contrasts very sharply with that found in Germany where at that time (and also later) a much weaker bourgeoisie leaned on the landed aristocracy to protect them against popular discontent and to carry through political and economic

[69] Mather, "Government and Chartists," 375 – 376, 383, 393 – 398.
[70] Mather, "Government and Chartists," 374.

measures necessary for modernization. In England the landed interest to some extent engaged in a popularity contest with the bourgeoisie for mass support. After 1840 the landowning class found in the support of factory laws a convenient way of answering manufacturers' attacks on the Corn Laws, though it should be noted that there were enlightened supporters of shorter hours among the manufacturers themselves.[71]

Thus the theme of diehard opposition to the march of democracy is a rare and minor current among the landed aristocracy of England in the nineteenth century.[72] One cannot find in English history the counterpart to those German conservatives whose parliamentary representatives rose in demonstrative applause to the ringing challenge of Herr von Oldenburg auf Januschau: "The King of Prussia and the German Emperor must always be in a position to say to any lieutenant: 'Take ten men and shoot the Reichstag!' "[73]

One of the reasons why such a scene seems incongruous in England of the nineteenth century is that, unlike the Junkers, the gentry and nobility of England had no great need to rely on political levers to prop up a tottering economic position. Even the abolition of the Corn Laws failed to have the dire effects predicted by some. If anything, the condition of agriculture may have been better after 1850 than before. Prices continued to rise. Estate management took on more and more the attributes of running a capitalist business enterprise as the operators tried to take advantage of the great improvements in agricultural techniques developed in previous decades. Naturally there was considerable variety on this score. At the upper reaches it was fairly common practice to turn over a great deal of responsibility to an agent. In this fashion the owner gained leisure for sport, culture, and politics, while the task of the agent took on many of the qualities of a profession. Still the great landlord made the main decisions or took responsibility for them, leav-

[71] Woodward, *Age of Reform*, 142.
[72] What there was of it may be found in Turberville, *House of Lords*, esp chaps XI – XIII.
[73] Schorske, *German Social Democracy*, 168.

ing routine to the agents. Among the gentry the choice was more between careful management on their own or turning the matter over to lawyers in the town, who were often ignorant of rural ways and who became rich, so some gentry thought, through the poverty of the owner.[74] Sharing in the general Victorian advance and having continued to acquire bourgeois and capitalist traits, the landed upper classes had much less reason than their continental counterpart to oppose the advance of either capitalism or democracy.

In the nineteenth century, as in earlier periods, the lines between wealthy nobility, gentry, and the upper reaches of business and the professions were blurred and wavering.[75] In numerous individual cases it is very difficult to decide whether a person belongs in one category or another. This difficulty, the despair of anyone undertaking a statistical analysis of English class structure, constitutes in itself one of the most important facts about this structure.[76]

Quantitatively the osmosis between business and the landed aristocracy may not have been very different in nineteenth-century England and Germany. There is even some statistical evidence to suggest that it was, surprisingly enough, larger in Prussia. One investigator claims to have found that the Prussian House of Representatives included among its members in a long series of years prior to 1918 an average of slightly more than 78 percent drawn from the ranks of commoners (*Bürgertum*) and the new nobility. In diplomacy and administration, on the other hand, the real keys to power in Germany, the proportions of commoners were respectively 38 and 43 percent. For England a study of Parliament for the years 1841 – 1847 uncovers only 40 percent of the members with business connections, the remaining 60 percent having no ties with

[74] Clark, *Victorian England*, 216 – 217; Thompson, *Landed Society*, chap VI, brings out the variety of practices.

[75] During the late eighteenth century there were signs of sharp antagonism between the older squirearchy, clinging to its monopoly of local political power, and the new industrialists. Later these were often peacefully absorbed. On the other hand, the man who owned a small business has remained outside the circle of gentlemen up to the present day.

[76] See the interesting appendix on the business interests of the gentry, a study of those who sat in Parliament between 1841 and 1847, by Aydelotte, in Clark, *Victorian England*, 290 – 305.

the world of business at all.[77] There are thorny technical problems in the use of such evidence; for example, are the statistical piles for each country really comparable? Is it appropriate to set alongside one another the 40 percent of the English Parliament with business connections and the 78 percent of the Prussian House of Representatives drawn from the *Bürgertum?* I am skeptical about doing so, but believe that, even if the technical problems could be solved, we would not have made worthwhile progress.

By itself a quantitative measure of social mobility tells us little about social anatomy and its workings. In nineteenth-century Prussia the members of the bourgeoisie who became connected with the aristocracy generally absorbed the latter's habits and outlook. Rather the opposite relationship held in England. Thus if we did have a technically perfect measure of mobility that gave an identical numerical reading for the amount of fusion in England and Prussia, we would make a disastrous mistake in saying that the two countries were alike on this score. Statistics are misleading traps for the unwary reader when they abstract from the essence of the situation the whole structural context in which social osmosis takes place. As statistics are fashionable now, it is worthwhile stressing this point. Men who hold power do not necessarily exercise it simply in the interests of the class from which they arise, especially in changing situations.

There was some tendency toward the adoption of aristocratic traits by the commercial and industrial élite in England. All accounts of England prior to 1914, and to some extent even beyond that date, give the strong impression that rolling green acres and a country house were indispensable to political and social eminence. But from about the 1870s onward, landed estates became more and more symbols of status rather than the foundations of political power.

Partly because the end of the American Civil War and the rise of the steamship started to make American grain available in Eu-

[77] For Germany, see von Preradovich, *Führungsschichten,* 164; for England, Aydelotte in Clark, *Victorian England,* 301. Unfortunately Aydelotte does not present separate figures for the House of Commons, which might alter the impression considerably.

rope, an agricultural depression set in at this time, which seriously commenced to erode the economic base of the landed upper strata.[78] Roughly the same thing happened in Germany, and once again it is instructive to view England against the German background. There the Junkers were able to use the state in the effort to preserve their position and also to form a united agricultural front with the peasant proprietors in the rest of Germany. At no point did Germany go through an experience comparable to the abolition of the Corn Laws. Instead, leading sectors of industry entered the marriage of iron and rye (fully consummated in the tariff of 1902), gaining as their part of the bargain a program of naval construction. The whole coalition of Junker, peasant, and industrial interests around a program of imperialism and reaction had disastrous results for German democracy. In England of the late nineteenth century, this combination failed to put in an appearance. Imperialist policies in England already had a long history behind them. They were an alternative, perhaps even an adjunct to free-trade policies, rather than an altogether new social phenomenon arising out of advanced capitalism.[79] In regard to agricultural problems, the Conservative governments of 1874 – 1879 took only small palliative measures; the Liberals from 1880 onward either let matters take their course or actively attacked agrarian interests.[80] By and large agriculture was allowed to shift for itself, that is, to commit decorous suicide with the help of a few rhetorical tears. This could scarcely have been allowed to happen except for the fact that by this time the English upper strata had largely ceased to be agrarian. The economic base had shifted to industry and trade. Disraeli and his successors showed that, with some reforms, a popular basis for conservatism could be maintained and sustained within a democratic context. There were still struggles to come, as in Lloyd George's attack on titled landowners in his budget of 1909 and the constitutional crisis that grew out of it. But by this time, despite the furor, the agrarian problem

---

[78] Thompson, *Landed Society*, 308 – 318, discusses the varied impact of the depression on different sections of the landed interest.

[79] See the brilliant article by Gallagher and Robinson, "Imperialism of Free Trade," 1 – 15.

[80] Clark, *Victorian England*, 247 – 249.

and the question of the power of the landed aristocracy had receded into the background to give way to new questions, centering on ways to incorporate the industrial worker into the democratic consensus.

As one looks back over the nineteenth century, what factors stand out as responsible for England's progress toward democracy? Those inherited from a violent past have already been mentioned: a relatively strong and independent Parliament, a commercial and industrial interest with its own economic base, no serious peasant problem. Other factors are specific to the nineteenth century itself. Governing in the context of rapidly growing industrial capitalism, the landed upper classes absorbed new elements into their ranks at the same time that they competed with them for popular support — or at the very least avoided serious defeat by well-timed concessions. This policy was necessary in the absence of any strong apparatus of repression. It was possible because the economic position of the governing classes eroded slowly and in a way that allowed them to shift from one economic base to another with only a minimum of difficulty. Finally, policies that were necessary as well as possible became facts because influential leaders saw and handled problems accurately enough and in time. There is no need to deny the historical significance of moderate and intelligent statesmen. But it is necessary to perceive the situation within which they worked, one created in large measure by men who were also intelligent but scarcely moderate.

CHAPTER TWO

Evolution and Revolution in France

1. Contrasts with England and their Origins

AMONG THE DECISIVE FACTORS in the development of democracy in England were the independence of the landed gentry and nobility from the crown, their adoption of commercial agriculture partly in response to the growth of a trading and manufacturing class with its own strong economic base, and the disappearance of the peasant problem. French society entered the modern world by a very different path. Instead of thrusting its way through to a high degree of independence, the French nobility, or more specifically its leading sector, became a decorative appanage of the king. Though this trend was reversed in the latter part of the eighteenth century, the ultimate consequence was the destruction of the aristocracy. Instead of a landed upper class turning to commercial agriculture in the English manner, we find in France of the Bourbon monarchy mainly a nobility living from what it can extract through obligations resting upon the peasants. In the place of the destruction of peasant property we perceive its gradual consolidation both before and after the Revolution. Commerce and manufacturing in France lag behind that in England. All the main structural variables and historical trends in French society of the *ancien régime* differed sharply from those in England from the sixteenth through the eighteenth centuries. How and why there was any similarity at all in the final political outcome during the nineteenth and twentieth centuries constitutes, along with some of the important differences, the central puzzle that I shall try to unravel in this chapter. Since without the Revolution it is most improbable that there would have been any similarity at all, this great event will be the central concern of the discussion.

In comparison with their counterpart in England during the eighteenth century, the French nobility lived very largely from dues collected in kind or in cash from their peasants. The origins of this difference reach sufficiently far back into the mists of early French history to make it unwise for an amateur to try peering very far into them, especially since the great French historian Marc Bloch threw up his hands rather than suggest an explanation. Suffice it to say that, by the late fourteenth century and during the fifteenth, many of the basic features had already begun to appear: a seigneur who devoted relatively little attention to the cultivation of his own demesne, which was rather small in size. The demesne seems to have shrunk as the overlord granted out sections of it in small parcels to the peasants in return for a portion of the crop. Where possible the seigneur preferred to let out his land *en bloc* and in many cases on terms showing that he hoped to regain it at some future date. But this was not always possible. The nobleman was often far away at war, while hands to work the land were hard to come by. The best solution, at least for many, appears to have been to throw the burden of cultivation as much as possible on those tenants who would manage large units or, more often, directly on the peasant.[1] Somewhat earlier the French nobility had begun to acquire a more precise juridical status through rules strictly defined in law.[2]

These two traits of a more definite legal status, even if a far from crystal clear one, and dependence on peasant dues were to distinguish the French nobility from the English gentry for the remainder of its history. At quite an early date the peasant had managed to escape from personal servitude, mainly by capitalizing on the demand for labor in the countryside that increased as the growing

[1] Duby, *Economie rurale*, II, 572 – 599; Bloch, *Histoire rurale*, I, 95 – 105. Duby's account, written about thirty years after that by Bloch, is generally similar (though more detailed), except that it puts the main trends a century and a half later.

[2] Bloch, "Passé de la noblesse," 366.

towns presented the possibility of another way of making a living. By the time of the Revolution, peasants possessed close to *de facto* property rights.[3]

Underlying this continuity were also important elements of change. The system of large landholdings worked by serfs began, as we have just seen, to undergo modification at least as early as the latter part of the fourteenth century. At the end of the Middle Ages and during the early modern period, perhaps especially during the sixteenth century when an increase in the supply of gold and silver seems to have driven up prices, there are indications of something approaching a crisis in seigneurial incomes. Large sections of the old fighting nobility, the *noblesse d'épée,* lost out heavily. The disappearance of their economic underpinnings may have made it easier for the kings and their talented ministers to extend the royal authority, a process that culminated in the long reign of Louis XIV (1643 – 1715). Naturally the nobility did not accept their fate passively. Faced with catastrophe, many attempted to backwater, to cease being *rentiers* and to reconstitute the demesne.[4] But by and large they lacked the economic basis, such as the wool trade, that made such a policy possible in England.

Members of the bourgeoisie who had made money in the towns and begun to acquire land from distressed nobles had somewhat greater success. The process began in the fifteenth century and continued on through the eighteenth. Through this influx of urban wealth there was some reconstitution of estates. In parts of France it brought about a situation that had some resemblances to England, as the new owners lived on and managed their estates with an eye to profit. But the resemblance is superficial. In seventeenth-century France, as well as later, the profit came not from selling produce on the market but still from collecting rents from peasants. As Bloch observed, the fortune to be gained from a big estate came from collecting a series of small dues, some of them in kind, from a series of

[3] Bloch, *Histoire rurale,* I, 120 – 121; Sée, *Histoire économique,* I, 125, 129, on the emancipation of the serfs; Lefebvre, *Études,* 251.

[4] In addition to Duby, *Economie rurale,* see Sée, *Histoire économique,* I, 93; and mainly Bloch, *Histoire rurale,* I, 107, 111 – 112, 134 – 135, 150 – 153.

small units. Though the task might be turned over to an intermedi-
ary, the best prospect of success came from careful, detailed, and
rather pettifogging administration.[5]

The situation was an ideal one for lawyers, and in more than
one respect. The spreading tentacles of the royal bureaucracy
needed lawyers in its struggle against the older nobility. And the
rich bourgeois who acquired land moved into higher social circles
either through being granted nobility or through purchase of a bureaucratic position (*office* or *charge*).[6] Though the *noblesse de robe*
was often troublesome to the king — only Louis XIV was able in
time to treat them with deliberate contempt — they furnished one
of the main instruments of absolutism in its struggle with localist
tendencies and with the older fighting nobility. As there were often
good pickings in the royal bureaucracy, especially in the eighteenth
century as royal control slackened, its attractions may have served
to diminish any tendency to operate an estate along English lines.

In any case the "return" of the big estate was a relatively
limited affair. They were not nearly as common in France as in
England or Eastern Germany. Large sections of the country were
in the hands of the peasants. Thus the system as a whole was one
where large and small units coexisted.[7] France did not undergo an
extensive enclosure movement. By and large, the large proprietor
was interested in preserving peasant tenures because they provided
the basis of his own existence.[8] Only in the latter part of the eighteenth century did the situation begin to change.

The decline of the *noblesse d'épée* was part of the same process
by which the king consolidated and extended his authority. In the
course of the sixteenth century and afterward, the king deprived
the nobles of many of their judicial functions, raised soldiers and
taxes on their lands, intervened generally in their affairs, and forced
them to submit to his Parlements.[9] By the time of Louis XIV, the
nobility seemed reduced to a role of magnificent indolence at Ver-

---

[5] Bloch, *Histoire rurale*, I, 142 – 143, 145, 149 – 150; II, 169 – 170.
[6] Göhring, *Feudalität*, 69 – 70.
[7] Bloch, *Histoire rurale*, I, 154.
[8] Sée, *Histoire économique*, I, 395.
[9] Sée, *Histoire économique*, I, 83; Sagnac, *Société française*, I, 209 – 210.

sailles or else of peaceful vegetation in the provinces. However, this impression is somewhat deceptive. To be sure the Sun King had rendered them largely harmless. But he had to pay certain costs that were only partly advantageous to the crown. He could get good positions for many in the church, which had enormous revenues, at that time much larger than those of the state. In return for the church's assistance in taking care of a sector of the nobility, the king protected the church against heresy.[10] One consequence was the revocation of the Edict of Nantes. A second form of the cost to the crown was war. Though Louis drove the nobility away from the center of government, he gave over to them the army as well as the church.[11] Perpetual war was the perpetual topic of conversation among the nobility at court and helped to create an atmosphere of loyalty to the king.[12]

The system of compulsory conpicuous consumption at Versailles ruined many nobles. In the provinces too Colbert's inquiry, conducted through the intendants, revealed widespread poverty.[13] Hence it is tempting to make a connection between royal absolutism and a failure of commercial agriculture to take hold, both factors mutually reenforcing one another over a long period of time. Until quite recently the historians' accounts of a brilliant and parasitic aristocracy in Paris and of the rural nobleman proudly molding away in the countryside amidst a generally stagnant agriculture pointed toward some such explanation of the background of the Revolution and the disappearance of the aristocracy through revolutionary violence. Research published since 1960, the work of an American scholar Robert Forster, has sharply modified this familiar image. By enabling us to locate more precisely the structural differences between modernization in the English and French countrysides, he has made a most valuable contribution to an understanding of the background and consequences of the Revolution. Since the

[10] Sagnac, *Société française*, I, 32, 35.

[11] Sagnac, *Société française*, I, 56.

[12] Cf Lavisse, ed, *Histoire de France*, VII, pt 1, 383. This volume, written by Lavisse himself, remains despite its age one of the most illuminating accounts of French society under Louis XIV.

[13] Lavisse, *Histoire*, VII, pt 1, 377.

role of commercial agriculture is crucial to the general argument of the present book, it will be wise to pause and examine the situation closely.

2. *The Noble Response to Commercial Agriculture*

For the latter part of the seventeenth century and the opening decade of the eighteenth, there is little reason to doubt the thesis that the impulse toward commercial agriculture was weak in comparison to that in England, not only among the nobility but in France generally. As it was in England too, the key agricultural problem was to get grain to the classes that ate bread but did not grow wheat. The grain trade presented a picture of stagnation broken by some impulse toward production for the market in the neighborhood of the big cities. There the wealthier peasants rather than the landed aristocracy appear to have been the main beneficiaries. Market areas generally did not extend beyond the vicinity of a few big cities and certain export depots on the frontiers. Only Paris drew on a substantial hinterland. Most of the territory drew its supplies from nearby areas.[14]

The general conception of the grain problem was one of controlling a limited supply from a limited area. The pull of a few big cities was felt mainly in times of scarcity, and then as a disruptive factor.[15] In the latter part of the seventeenth century and the early part of the eighteenth, merchants and their agents in some localities, mainly near Paris, adopted the practice of scouring the countryside to buy up any surplus they could find. This practice aroused much resentment as a disturbance of local sources of supply and grew up in opposition to both prevailing custom and legislation.[16] Though rich estate owners might receive grain in the form of feudal dues to dispose of it through commission merchants in the towns, it was quite the common practice to buy grain from the wealthier peasants, a clear indication they competed successfully with the noble-

[14] Usher, *Grain Trade,* in which the frontispiece maps show the situation as of 1660 – 1710.

[15] Usher, *Grain Trade,* 5, 11, 17.

[16] Usher, *Grain Trade,* 20, 21, 25 – 26, 42 – 43, 101, 105 – 106.

man for a limited market.[17] If there were enterprising landlords in France of the late seventeenth and early eighteenth centuries, laying field to field in the English manner, they have escaped the notice of historians. Possibly there were a few. But it is highly unlikely that they were of any importance at all. When commercial attractions became more important during the eighteenth century, French noblemen responded in an entirely different way.

To consider only the grain trade runs the risk of giving a very misleading impression. Wine was a commercial product and a very important one. Indeed wine was to French agriculture, perhaps even to eighteenth-century French society as a whole, what wool was to English agriculture and society in the sixteenth and seventeenth centuries. One statistically inclined scholar has calculated that in an ordinary year during the latter part of the *ancien régime* France produced enough wine, some thirty million *hectolitres*, to provide cargo for the entire British merchant fleet of the day.[18] It was just as impossible for one man to drink all the wine he could produce in a year as to wear all the wool he could raise. Hence to grow grapes or to raise sheep meant to be propelled into the market, to become dependent on the acts of kings and chancellors and to try to influence them, to find businesslike methods and account books more congenial than the *beau geste*, the sword, *largesse*, and other aristocratic ways. But the similarities stop there and short of what really matters.

The economic and political consequences of the wine trade and sheep raising are quite different. In what seems to have been a burst of Gallic enthusiasm, coupled with an American statistical mania, the distinguished French economic historian C.E. Labrousse has endeavored to demonstrate with mountainous statistics that a long depression in the wine trade was a decisive factor in accounting for the generally backward state of the French economy and the outbreak of the Revolution. The result is to me more overwhelming than convincing. The link with industrial backwardness

[17] Usher, *Grain Trade*, 7, 8, 16, 87, 88, 91 – 93.

[18] Labrousse, *Crise de l'économie*, I, 208. As far as I know, only two parts out of a promised six ever appeared. Thus evidence for some of Labrousse's generalizations is not at hand.

is not demonstrated. His two massive studies, only a small part of the whole undertaking as originally planned, limit themselves almost entirely to agricultural matters. While it is pleasant to contemplate wine drinking as at least a potential cure for economic backwardness, some facts adduced by Labrousse himself indicate that, for eighteenth-century France, the prospect was unrealistic. Nine-tenths of the wine, he estimated, was consumed in France itself. Wine growing took place all over France: out of the thirty-two *généralités* or fiscal divisions of the *ancien régime*, only three in the north and northwest were not wine producing areas.[19] Bad transportation, vine culture spread over the country, most of the wine drunk in France — all these facts point to the conclusion that most of the wine was *vin ordinaire*, probably a good deal more wretched than now, and not a luxury product from which it was possible to make a fortune and put a shoulder to the economy.

Wines that yielded a good commercial profit seem to have been produced in the same limited areas of France as now. The advantages of proximity to water transport must have given the port of Bordeaux a huge advantage during the eighteenth century. Wine provided the economic basis for a very prosperous and very commercially minded provincial nobility in and around Bordeaux during the eighteenth century. Grapes were transmuted into gold and gold into many attractive forms of culture, varying all the way from dancing girls to Montesquieu's *Esprit de lois*. (This distinguished philosopher was at times what moderns would call a lobbyist for the wine industry.)[20] By themselves, profits from wine stop there, as they seem to have done in Bordeaux. Viniculture cannot form the basis of a textile industry as can sheep raising. Nor can it provide for feeding the city population as does wheat growing. In any case the impulse for change comes from the cities, not the countryside. What happens in the countryside becomes important mainly through the social changes that may or may not overspread what is still the overwhelming majority of the population during the early stages of industrial growth.

[19] Labrousse, *Crise de l'économie*, 586, 207.
[20] Forster, "Noble Wine Producers," 19, 25, 33.

Wine growing in France did not produce the kind of changes among the peasantry, such as massive enclosures, that were the consequence of commercial agriculture in England. Viniculture, particularly in the days before artificial fertilizers, was what economists call a labor-intensive variety of agriculture, requiring large amounts of fairly skilled peasant labor and relatively small amounts of capital either in the form of land or equipment. The English situation by and large was the other way around. Now French rural society in the eighteenth century was such as to be able to take care of the problems of labor-intensive agriculture quite satisfactorily — from the point of view of the aristocracy if not that of the peasantry. Since there is surprisingly little difference between the social arrangements in an advanced wine-producing area and in grain-growing areas where commercial influences had penetrated and become strong, we may skip the details here. The essential distinction is fairly simple: the French aristocrat kept the peasant on the land and used feudal levers to extract more produce. Then the nobleman sold the produce on the market. In the case of wine, his legal privileges were especially useful, since through them he could do a great deal to prevent peasants from bringing wine into Bordeaux where it could compete with that from a noble chateau. Lacking the privilege of bringing wine into the city, as well as the resources to postpone sale until the most favorable moment, the smaller producers found it necessary to sell their wine to the noble landlord.[21]

In eighteenth-century Bordeaux, good-sized fortunes based on wine were to be found only among the *noblesse de robe*, the judicial nobility whose origins were mainly bourgeois, though, in many eighteenth-century *robe* families in France as a whole, the bourgeois origin might be a matter that belonged to the remote past. The old military nobility, the *noblesse d'épée*, was neither rich nor illustrious. And they seem to have constituted the overwhelming mass of the four hundred-odd noble families in the Bordeaux area. Only a few cut good figures in Bordeaux society. Most lived in or near sleepy townships, often in chateaux screened by poplar trees or hidden away in the villages. Wheat domains of about a hundred

[21] Forster, "Noble Wine Producers," 26.

acres and royal pensions of a few hundred *livres* provided the basis of a life that was neither austere nor affluent, but provincial in the extreme. Parish seigneurs, many of them retired army officers, had an income of no more than 3000 *livres* a year, near indigence by the standards of a well-to-do nobleman with vineyards to support his affluence.[22] At least in this area the contrast between the old military nobility and the newer *noblesse de robe* was striking. And there must have been many nobles throughout France who resembled these parish seigneurs. Very likely unenterprising nobles were a majority — I suspect an overwhelming majority — though there is no evidence yet that would clinch the point. As one notices such a contrast certain questions spring to mind almost automatically for a present-day sociologist. Were there some sort of legal and cultural barriers that prevented the *noblesse d'épée* from making a success of commerce? How important were such barriers in explaining the economic and political characteristics of the French nobility or the fact that a great revolution overwhelmed them?

Cumulative evidence leads me to offer a very firm negative to the question and to argue that it is the wrong question to ask if one wishes to understand the connection between economic changes and political ones. Both Marx and Weber have led their followers, particularly those who try to be most literally scientific, thoroughly astray on certain of these issues, invaluable as their contribution certainly is on other scores. But let us see the evidence first.

Cultural and legal obstacles there certainly were in the form of aristocratic prejudice against commerce and the rule of derogation, i.e., that any nobleman who engaged in a demeaning occupation lost his noble status. Legislation about derogation applied mainly to urban commerce and industry. It tried to draw a line between large scale activities such as wholesaling and international trade, which the monarchy actively encouraged, sometimes over the objections of the Third Estate, and petty ones, such as operating a retail shop, which were prohibited. In agriculture there was a definite rule renewed in 1661 against a gentleman's working more than a small amount of his own land, four *charrues*, or four times the area that

[22] Forster, "Noble Wine Producers," 19–21.

could be worked with a single plough.[23] The main force that maintained these laws and the public opinion that supported them was
the monarchy. Nevertheless, even under Louis XIV, its policy in
this area was ambivalent and confused. The monarchy wanted a
prosperous nobility as a decorative adjunct to the crown and as help
in keeping the people in their proper place, and expressed concern
on frequent occasions when it came across evidence of poverty
among the nobility. But the crown did not want the nobility to
establish an independent economic base that could enable it to challenge royal power.

The prejudice against trying to make money out of farming
was probably very influential among the highest nobility and those
subject even less directly to the mores of court life. A life of strenu-
ous indolence and intrigue at Versailles would certainly be vastly
more exciting than superintending cows and peasants and would
soon teach a man to be embarrassed at the smell of manure on his
boots. On the other hand, a good many aristocrats evaded the rules
by making their fortunes in the West Indies, often working with an
axe in their hand at the head of their own bands of negroes. Then
they would come back to Versailles or Paris to take part in court
life. In other words, successful commercial farming for the high
aristocrat involved a temporary escape from French society.[24] In
the first quarter of the eighteenth century, the general prejudice
against mean occupations seems to have been quite strong: Carré
cites some material from contemporary letters including the case of
a duke who opened up a store selling spices, by which he aroused
the jealousy of the spice corporation. When the matter became
public, street youngsters ran after the duke crying, "Il a chié au
lit."[25] Later in the century a strong current of opinion ran in the
opposite direction, favorable to commercial activities for the aristocracy. England and everything English, including their agricultural practices, became very fashionable in high circles and had for
a brief time some influence on policy. There was a vigorous war of
pamphlets about the propriety of commerce for the nobility. In the

[23] Lavisse, *Histoire*, VII pt 1, 378; Carré, *Noblesse*, 135 – 138.
[24] Carré, *Noblesse*, 140, 149, 152.
[25] *Noblesse*, 137 – 138.

course of time there came to be widespread evasion of the rules against it. Many aristocrats were involved in commercial enterprises, hiding their presence behind fronts and dummies.[26]

All these facts indicate that the cultural and legal barriers were becoming much less important during the eighteenth century. For the provincial nobleman, in whom we are mainly interested here, they were largely a dead letter. As a contemporary pamphlet pointed out, when the country nobleman had his wheat, wine, cattle, or wool sold, no one accused him of derogation.[27] Where they had the opportunity, or perhaps one should say the temptation to do so, the nobility of the sword showed no reluctance to make money out of commerce. Near Toulouse, an area where there were fine profits to be had from wheat farming, the habits and mores of the older nobility became thoroughly businesslike and indistinguishable from the quasi-bourgeois nobility of the robe.[28] Speaking of the provincial nobility generally Forster has put forth the following thesis:

> Far from an idle, dull, and impoverished *hobereau*, the provincial noble was as likely to be an active, shrewd, and prosperous landlord. These adjectives are meant to suggest more than a swollen pocketbook. They imply an attitude toward the family fortune characterized by thrift, discipline, and strict management usually implied by the term "bourgeois."[29]

From such evidence it is perfectly clear that legislation and prejudice as such were not significantly hindering the spread of a commercial outlook and commercial behavior among the French landed aristocracy. That is not the place to look for any explanation of the supposed backwardness of French agriculture in relation to that of England.

Was it so backward then? How representative was the kind of nobleman just sketched by Forster? The answer to such a set of questions can at present be no more than highly tentative. If it were possible to construct some index of the degree of commercial penetration in agriculture and plot the differences on a map of late

[26] *Noblesse*, 141 – 142, 145 – 146.
[27] *Noblesse*, 142.
[28] Forster, *Nobility of Toulouse*, 26 – 27.
[29] Forster, "The Provincial Noble," 683.

eighteenth-century France, one would certainly find substantial patches where something that could be called the spirit of agrarian capitalism was very strong. The execution of such a task would be very laborious and from the standpoint of the questions raised here far from rewarding. Statistics alone will not solve our problem because it is mainly a qualitative one.

Much more is at issue here too than the emergence of a new psychological attitude and its possible causes. Those who follow Weber, especially those who speak in terms of some abstract drive for achievement, neglect the importance of the social and political context in which such changes manifest themselves. The problem is not merely whether French rural nobles tried to run their estates efficiently and sell their produce on the market. Nor is it simply how many nobles developed such an outlook. The key question is whether or not in so doing they altered the structure of rural society in a way similar to what took place in those parts of England where the enclosure movement was strongest. The answer to this question is simple and decisive. They did not. Those nobles who represented the leading edge of commercial advance in the French countryside tried to extract more from the peasants.

Fortunately Forster has presented us with a detailed study of the nobility in a part of France, the diocese of Toulouse, where the commercial impulse was strong and where grain growing for the market was a noble occupation par excellence. His account makes it possible to put one's finger rather precisely on the similarities and differences between the improving gentry in England and their no less businesslike counterpart in France.

In southern France, and perhaps more widely in other parts of France than is realized, the incentive to grow grain for the market was quite strong. Population in the kingdom and locally was rising rapidly. So were grain prices in this area. Local political pressures had produced great improvement in transportation, making it possible to sell grain at a considerable distance from Toulouse and in quantities that were substantial by eighteenth-century standards. On all these counts the situation was basically similar to that in England. The nobles of Toulouse, those of the sword as well as those of the robe as we have already noticed, made just as successful an adaptation to circumstances they had helped to create as did the hearty squires of England.[30] Perhaps a larger share of Toulousan income came in the form of *rentes*. Since a large part of these were *rentes* on the Estates of Languedoc, and since the area was primarily agricultural with a weak and backward bourgeoisie, most of the money that flowed into their pockets was still based on wheat.[31]

The way in which the Toulousan nobility took up farming for the market was, on the other hand, entirely different from that of the English gentry. Except for the introduction of maize during the sixteenth century as a forage crop for animals, which increased greatly the amount of wheat that could be marketed, there were no important technical innovations. Agriculture continued to be carried on in fundamentally the same technical and social framework as had existed during the Middle Ages. Possibly geographical factors, differences in soil and climate, prevented change,[32] though I suspect that political and social factors were more important. In broad outline what took place can be expressed very simply: the nobles used the prevailing social and political framework to squeeze more grain out of the peasants and sell it. Unless the nobles had been able to do this and overcome the peasants' reluctance to part with his grain, the townsfolk would have had nothing to eat.[33]

In a way that resembles what took place more than a century later in parts of China and Japan, the peasants were left in occupation of the soil but under a series of obligations enabling the nobles, who became in effect commercial landlords, to take a large share of the crop. Here lies the principal difference from the English situation. The Toulousan nobles, unlike those in many other parts of France, owned almost half of the land and derived the overwhelming portion of their strictly agricultural revenues from the demesne. But the demesne itself was broken into a series of small

[30] Forster, *Nobility of Toulouse*, 47 – 48, 68 – 71. Unless otherwise indicated, comparisons with England are mine.

[31] Forster, *Nobility of Toulouse*, 118 – 119, 115, 22 – 24.

[32] Forster, *Nobility of Toulouse*, 41 – 42, 44, 62.

[33] Cf Forster, *Nobility of Toulouse*, 66.

plots.[34] On these small plots the peasants continued to live. Some known as *maître valets* received a cottage, oxen, a few primitive tools, and an annual wage in grain and coin. The entire grain harvest went into the lord's storage bin. To the undiscriminating observer the *maître valet* with his cottage may have looked like a peasant as he worked his small farm with the help of his family. Possibly he even felt like a peasant: Forster tells us that he had a certain prestige because often his family had worked the lord's farm for generations. In strict economic terms nevertheless he was a wage laborer.[35] Other peasants worked the land for the lord as sharecroppers. In theory lord and tenant divided the harvest between them equally; in practice the contract became weighted more and more in favor of the lord, partly because the lord managed through the manipulation of seignorial rights to capture the lion's share of the livestock, the principal farm capital of the area. Rising population, too, favored the lord by increasing the competition for holdings.[36]

In practice, too, the difference between *maître valet* and sharecropper was slight. The basic unit of production was the *métairie*, a farm of thirty-five to seventy acres, worked by a single peasant family either as a wage laborer or sharecropper. In the case of the wealthier nobles, the unit of property might be larger and contain several *métairies*. The overwhelming majority of noble estates were administered in this way. Leasing land to a large farmer for money rents, the English practice, existed in the area but was rare.[37]

This system of keeping the peasants on the land as a labor force was buttressed by legal and political institutions inherited from feudalism, but these rights were of minor importance as a source of income in the diocese of Toulouse. Nevertheless the right of seigneurial justice, for example, provided a convenient way of forcing delinquent tenants to pay arrears and was part of the whole series of political sanctions that enabled the nobility to extract its eco-

---

[34] Forster, *Nobility of Toulouse*, 35, 38 – 39, 40 – 41.
[35] Forster, *Nobility of Toulouse*, 32 – 33, 55 – 56.
[36] Forster, *Nobility of Toulouse*, 56 – 58, 77 – 87.
[37] Forster, *Nobility of Toulouse*, 32 – 34, 40 – 44, 58.

nomic surplus.[38] Before long the peasants were to find allies that would enable them to storm these political ramparts and cripple the nobility.

In contrast to England, commercial influences as they penetrated into the French countryside did not undermine and destroy the feudal framework. If anything, they infused new life into old arrangements, though in a way that ultimately had disastrous consequences for the nobility. That is the lesson one can derive from Forster's detailed studies, as well as from older standard sources and more general descriptions if one looks at them with the insights that come from more detailed descriptions. If we try to visualize the situation in France as a whole toward the end of the *ancien régime,* what we are likely to see is a series of peasants on the one side working the land, and the nobleman collecting a share of what they produced either directly in the form of produce or indirectly in the form of cash. Quite possibly the older standard descriptions underemphasize the extent to which the nobleman was making what economists would call a managerial contribution to the total output. But he was caught in an awkward situation. Whatever political and social contribution he may have made under feudalism in the form of providing political order and security had been taken over by royal officials, though he was able to retain certain rights of local justice and exploit these for economic purposes. Nor was he yet a full-blown capitalist farmer. Essentially what the landed proprietor possessed were certain property rights, whose essence were claims, enforceable through the repressive apparatus of the state, to a specific share of the economic surplus. Though in formal and legal terms the burden of property rights rested on the land, and land was what the nobleman's carefully preserved title deeds (*terriers*) described, land was useful to the nobleman only insofar as the peasants on it produced an income for him. Thus he might collect his income in sharecropping arrangements, which covered somewhere between two-thirds and three-quarters of France. Sharecroppers were often identical with small peasant *propriétaires* who, if fortunate, were able to lease small bits of land on a sharecropping basis

[38] Forster, *Nobility of Toulouse,* 29, 34 – 35.

in order to add to the insufficient yield of their own tiny plots.[39] Usually the land was let out to peasants whose holdings were seldom more than ten to fifteen hectares.[40] In some areas nobles scraped together an income from the peasantry through their right to collect a series of feudal dues, without owning any substantial estate.[41]

The main forces that created the economic relationships just described were capitalist influences radiating out from the towns and the monarchy's long efforts to hold the nobility in check. As in England, relationships with commercial and industrial elements and with the king were decisive influences in determining the characteristics of the nobility. Again as in England, the response to the new world of commerce and industry included a very substantial fusion between the landed upper classes and the bourgeoisie. But if these abstract variables, king, nobility, and bourgeoisie, were the same in both countries, their qualitative character and relationship to each other were very different. In England the fusion between countryside and town was in the main directed against the crown, not only before the Civil War but for much of the subsequent period. In France the fusion took place through the crown with very different political and social consequences.

3. Class Relationships under Royal Absolutism

A glance at commerce, manufacturing, and town life at the apogee of French royal absolutism in the seventeenth century is sufficient to make one wonder where the strength could come from to generate a bourgeois and capitalist revolution in the eighteenth, and whether those who thus characterize the French Revolution may have fallen victim to a doctrinal mirage, a point best discussed later. Under the seventeenth-century monarchy, the French bourgeoisie was not the spearhead of modernization taking the countryside along with it toward the still invisible world of industrial

[39] See Lefebvre, *Etudes*, 164, 210–211; Sée, *Histoire économique*, I, 175; Bois, *Paysans de l'Ouest*, 432–433, where Bois emphasizes his agreement with other scholars that to the peasant it was total yield rather than the type of right to work the land that was most important.

[40] Sée, *Histoire économique*, I, 178.

[41] Göhring, *Feudalität*, 68.

capitalism that their English counterpart had already become. Instead, it was heavily dependent on royal favor, subject to royal regulation, and oriented toward the production of arms and luxuries for a restricted clientele.[42] Except for the much greater degree of control and higher level of technology, especially in the military arts, the situation resembles late Tokugawa Japan or even India of Akbar's day somewhat more than it does England of the same period. Politically too municipal life was subject to royal controls that had been increasing intermittently since the reestablishment of peace and order under Henri IV. Though there was a brief municipal revival during the *Fronde* at Bordeaux, Marseille, Lyon, and Paris, Louis XIV decided not to tolerate any more opposition from his *bonnes villes*. In the older portions of France royal controls developed rapidly in his reign. Through the cities the king held the provinces, though there was much local variation, with the king sometimes allowing municipal elections to continue but appointing the mayor directly or indirectly.[43]

From the foregoing it is evident that, under Louis XIV, the impulse toward establishing the bases of a modern society, i.e., a unified state and even some of the habits of precision and obedience, came much more from the royal bureaucracy than from the bourgeoisie. That, however, was scarcely the deliberate intention of the crown. At the time its real function in the French polity was to maintain order, supervise the economy, and squeeze out of French society whatever resources it could to sustain the royal policy of war and magnificence. Of the two, war was far more expensive than magnificence, though exact measurements are impossible. That the royal bureaucracy of Louis XIV's day was far less effective in performing these tasks than the administrative apparatus of a twentieth-century state goes without saying.

The French royal administration faced the same difficulty that plagued other agrarian bureaucracies such as those of Tsarist Russia, Mogul India, and Imperial China. In preindustrial societies it was practically impossible to generate and extract enough of an economic surplus to pay the members of the bureaucracy a salary

[42] Nef, *Industry and Government*, 88.
[43] Sagnac, *Société française*, I, 46, 63.

that would ensure their real dependence on the crown. Other methods of payment are possible, such as the grant of revenues from specified lands or the Chinese device of allowing corruption to make up the difference between an income appropriate to official status and what the monarch can afford to pay in salaries. Indirect compensations such as these, however, run the risks of diminishing control from the center and encouraging exploitation that may arouse popular discontent. The French monarchy tried to solve this problem by selling positions in the bureaucracy. Though the practice was not unique to France, the extent to which French kings resorted to it and the way in which the practice not only permeated the entire royal bureaucracy but also influenced the character of French society as a whole distinguish France quite sharply from other countries. French society of the seventeenth and eighteenth centuries presents us with an illuminating mixture of competing traits that scholars sometimes regard as characteristically Western and characteristically Oriental: feudalism, bourgeoisie, and bureaucracy. The sale of offices epitomizes this mixture of commercial and precommercial institutions and was also an attempt to reconcile them.

For a long time the sale of offices made good political sense. Inasmuch as it gave the bourgeoisie access to the royal administration, it made allies among this class.[44] Probably under French conditions it was an indispensable device in creating the king's power and hence in pushing aside the older nobility and overcoming the barriers of feudalism to create the foundations of a modern state. And from the king's point of view it was both an important source of revenue and a cheap method of administration, though neither of these features was advantageous to French society as a whole.[45]

There were at the same time inherent disadvantages that became increasingly important with the passage of time. The sale of an office meant in effect that the position became a form of private property that passed from father to son. Hence the king tended to lose control over his subordinates. The famous Paulette of 1604 in

[44] Cf Göhring, *Ämterkäuflichkeit,* 291.
[45] Exact figures are unobtainable. But see the estimates of Göhring, *Ämterkäuflichkeit,* 232, 260, for the late seventeenth century.

the reign of Henri IV granted full property rights to the holders of offices in return for the payment of a tax and thereby sealed the transition from bureaucratic office to property. To counter this situation, the kings resorted characteristically to the creation of new officials, the intendants, to watch over the activities of others.[46] Even these offices became in time indirectly subject to purchase.[47]

At first the status of nobility acquired by purchase of an office was limited to the person of the purchaser. Then it became hereditary. Under Louis XIV the rule disappeared that three generations in the same office were necessary to confer hereditary nobility. Since high offices tended to remain in the same family anyway, the change was mainly symbolic.[48] The bourgeois drive toward property found considerable satisfaction through the royal bureaucracy, while any drive toward political independence was blunted by converting the bourgeois into an aristocrat. Later this aspect was to limit very severely the power of the monarchy to adapt itself and French society to ever more pressing problems.

At the height of absolutism the contradictions and paradoxes of the system were already visible. Without resort to the sale of offices, "the manna that never fails," Louis XIV would probably have had to seek the consent of the nation through the Estates General to raise money.[49] Hence the sale of offices was at the root of the king's independence of the aristocracy, of any effective control by a parliament. It was the key prop of royal absolutism.

At the same time the practice undermined the king's independence. It is at the root of the paradox that the most powerful king in Europe against whom no domestic resistance was possible or even imaginable still appears to historians so badly obeyed that he had to regard disobedience as perfectly normal.[50]

[46] Göhring, *Ämterkäuflichkeit*, 290.

[47] Göhring, *Ämterkäuflichkeit*, 301.

[48] Göhring, *Ämterkäuflichkeit*, 293 – 294.

[49] Lavisse, *Histoire*, VII, pt 1, 369.

[50] Lavisse, *Histoire*, VII, pt 1, 367; Sagnac, *Société française*, I, 61, points out that Louis XIV had only about thirty-odd officials who acted in his name and were responsible to him. There were at this time, according to Göhring, *Ämterkäuflichkeit*, 262, some 46,000 officials in a population of perhaps 17 million.

If, in the earlier stages of the monarchy's growth, the sale of offices had helped to rally the bourgeoisie to the monarch's onslaught on feudalism, continued resort to this device increasingly revealed that it also imparted feudal characteristics to the bourgeoisie. In 1665 Colbert supported his proposal to abolish the sale of offices with the argument that the amount of money tied up in the traffic in offices would thus be returned to real commerce which would be useful to the state. He suggested that this amount might be as much as the value of all the lands in the kingdom.[51] No doubt Colbert's claim was exaggerated. But his thesis is undoubtedly correct that the system diverted energy and resources from commerce and industry. Furthermore, by giving bourgeois commoners a title of nobility and then making it impossible to supervise their activities closely, the sale of offices helped to build up a sense of corporate identity, immunity from outside influences, and *esprit de corps*. Holders of office sealed themselves off from royal influence and became stubborn defenders of local interests and vested privileges.

The process is most clearly visible in the *parlements*, judicial organs that had acquired, as judicial organs have been known to do even in twentieth-century America, considerable administrative power. During the Middle Ages they had provided one of the king's main weapons against the nobility. At the time of the *Fronde* and subsequently, they posed as the one bulwark of freedom against absolute despotism. By the eighteenth century they had become the main bastion of reaction and privilege, "the unyielding barrier against which the reforming spirit of the century broke itself in vain."[52] Other corporate bodies joined the *parlements* in this struggle with the king. According to Martin Göhring's now classic study of the problems, they gave the monarchy the final push that toppled it over.[53]

One episode in this struggle, the attempt of Louis XV and his chancellor Maupeou to abolish the sale of offices and the venality of justice, deserves retelling here for the light it casts on our problem.

[51] Lavisse, *Histoire*, VII, pt 1, 361 – 362.
[52] Cobban, *"Parlements of France,"* 72.
[53] Gohring, *Ämterkäuflichkeit*, 306.

The incident took place in 1771, shortly before the death of Louis XV and at once stirred up a hornet's nest of opposition. Led by the nobility, the opposition expressed itself in terms of the natural rights of man, freedom of the individual and political liberty, even the social contract. Voltaire saw through the sham and supported Maupeou. In any case he detested *parlements* as the persecutors not only of Calas but also of literary men such as himself.[54]

It would be a mistake to dismiss the appearance of revolutionary slogans in the service of a reactionary cause as no more than an instance of selfish privilege seeking to justify itself by any convenient argument. For one thing, no less a mind than Montesquieu's defended the sale of offices as part of his famous theory of intervening powers. As Göhring points out, the conceptions of the inviolability of property and freedom of the individual received a powerful impulse from this concrete historical situation.[55] This was neither the first nor the last occasion when a stubborn aristocracy clinging to reactionary privileges helped to set in motion revolutionary ideas. Still it would be difficult to find a sharper illustration of the interpenetration of bureaucratic, feudal, and capitalist features characterizing French society in the late eighteenth century than the appearance of such ideas in this context.

When Louis XV died, it seemed as though Maupeou's reform might succeed.[56] Louis XVI ascended the throne in 1774. One of the first acts of his reign was to undo the work of Maupeou and restore the *status quo*. This is one of the more striking facts that have led a number of historians, including even the socialist Jaurès, to take the view that a strong king might have been able to prevent the Revolution and lead France along the road to modernization by peaceful means.[57] Impossible though it is to answer such a question, reflection on it forces one to ask other questions that bring the decisive issues into the open. Exactly what alternatives were actually open to the monarchy, let us say, at the death of Louis XIV in

[54] Lavisse, *Histoire*, VIII, pt 2, 397–401. This volume is by H. Carré.

[55] *Ämterkäuflichkeit*, 309–310.

[56] Lavisse, *Histoire*, VIII, pt 2, 402.

[57] Jaurès, *Histoire socialiste*, VI, 37. See also Mathiez, *Révolution française*, I, 18, 21, who expresses a similar view but with greater doubts.

1715? What lines of political development had the course of previous history already closed off?

It was unlikely that French society could generate a parliament of landlords with bourgeois overtones from the cities in the English fashion. The growth of the French monarchy had largely deprived the landed upper classes of political responsibility and diverted much of the bourgeois impulse to its own purposes. But this was not necessarily the only possibility. To perceive the alternatives open to the crown is more difficult. Clearly if the king were going to pursue any active policy at all he would have had to reforge an effective instrument of rule, a renovated bureaucracy. That would have meant the abolition of the sale of offices and venal justice and a reform of the tax system to distribute the burden more evenly and to collect the revenue more efficiently. It would also have been necessary to reduce, at least for a time, the expensive policy of war and magnificence. The very large remaining internal barriers to trade would have had to go and the legal system to be considerably modernized to allow room for the growth of commerce and industry that began to show some signs of independent vitality toward the end of the eighteenth century. Distinguished statesmen from Colbert to Turgot put forward large parts of this program. As an explanation for the monarchy's failure, we can quickly rule out any argument to the effect that in the intellectual climate of the time nobody in a position of influence could see the problem. They saw it very clearly. That there would have been strong resistance from vested interests is blatantly obvious. Still it would be difficult to argue that such obstacles were insurmountable. Would they have been any more severe than those faced by an Henri IV in forging French unity?

For the present it is enough to indicate the direction in which such considerations lead. Conceivably France might have followed the conservative path of modernization in the manner of Germany or Japan. Then, on the other hand, and for reasons that can be brought out only gradually in the course of the whole book, it is likely that the obstacles to democracy would have been even greater. In any case, the monarchy did not pursue a consistent policy and did not survive. Agrarian problems played a very important part in bringing about this result.

4. *The Aristocratic Offensive and the Collapse of Absolutism*

During the last half of the eighteenth century the French countryside witnessed the seigneurial reaction and experienced a brief and limited enclosure movement. To call the former a feudal reaction is misleading. What was happening, as we have seen earlier in this chapter, was a penetration of commercial and capitalist practices into agriculture by feudal methods. Such things had been going on for a very long time but became more widespread in the latter part of the eighteenth century. One form this penetration took was the restoration of feudal rights and dues where they had been allowed to fall into neglect. Some economic historians see its origins in the lord's steadily increasing need for cash.[58] Much of the pressure may have come from the recently ennobled who took a more commercial and less patriarchal attitude toward their estates, tightening up on administration, exploiting old feudal rights, and reviving new ones wherever possible.[59] The economic feature of the revival seems to have been the lords' efforts to get a larger share of the peasants' crops in order to sell them. To get control of the peasants' land was secondary to getting the crops. Feudal dues paid in kind brought in the best return among agricultural incomes, partly because feudal dues were levied as a direct proportion of the crop.[60]

To stress the purely economic aspects would nevertheless be to miss the main point. As pointed out repeatedly in these pages, feudal arrangements combined with those of royal absolutism constituted the political mechanisms through which the French landed aristocracy extracted an economic surplus from the peasants. Without these political mechanisms the economic system in the country-

[58] Sée, *Histoire économique*, I, 189.

[59] Göhring, *Feudalität*, 72 – 73.

[60] Labrousse, *Mouvement des prix*, 378, 381 – 382, 420 – 421. As I think Labrousse is probably right about the general trend but am skeptical as to whether his statistics measure it accurately, I have not tried to summarize his measurements. Forster's institutional findings support Labrousse's conclusion.

side could not work. This was the concrete meaning of privilege. It was also the essential feature that distinguished the French aristocracy from the English landed upper classes who developed entirely different methods of extracting the surplus. It is also at this point that any simplified version of Marxism, any notion that the economic substructure somehow automatically determines the political superstructure, can lead one astray. The political mechanism was decisive, and the peasants at the time of the Revolution revealed sound political instinct when they sought to smash these gears and levers, an instinct they did not always display, as we shall see shortly. By helping to smash these levers beyond repair they helped to destroy the *ancien régime*. The significance of the seigneurial reaction, I would urge, lies in whatever impulse it gave to these political changes.

The enclosure movement was a more open form of capitalist transformation in agriculture. It began to gain force during the latter part of the eighteenth century, though it never became as widespread as in England, except perhaps in Normandy where textile industries, especially in the neighborhood of Caux, grew up in both town and countryside.[61] The French enclosure movement thus was partly a response to commerce, as in England. But in France, while it lasted, it was much more a matter of government policy and of intellectual discussions in the salons than in England where it was an indigenous movement among the gentry. The physiocrats managed for a time to get the ear of important royal officials, and the policy was pushed for a brief time.[62] As the government encountered resistance, it drew back. The main impulse died down by 1771. Timidity was the dominant note of the *ancien régime* down to its end.[63] The physiocratic attack lasted longer. For a long time they did not dare attack feudalism. But in 1776 under Turgot's ministry his friend and secretary Boncerf proposed, at least for the next generation, the financial redemption of feudal dues.[64]

[61] Bloch, *Histoire rurale*, I, 210, 212.

[62] Bloch, *"Individualisme agraire,"* 350, 354 – 356, 360. Göhring, *Feudalität*, 76, 80.

[63] Bloch, *Histoire rurale*, I, 226; Bloch, *"Individualisme agraire,"* 381.

[64] Göhring, *Feudalität*, 92.

Hence capitalism was seeping into the French countryside by every possible cranny, in the form of feudalism through the seignorial reaction, in the form of an attack on feudalism, and under the banner of "progress" and "reason" through the officially sponsored enclosure movement. More rapid penetration had to await the measures of the Revolution, and even much later action. Certain rights of common pasture, for instance, were not abolished until 1889.[65]

Though limited capitalist penetration failed during the eighteenth century to revolutionize agriculture or eliminate the peasantry, it came in such a way as to increase very sharply peasant hostility to the *ancien régime*. Peasants resented the increase in feudal dues and revival of old ones by clever lawyers. Even more important, the government's flirtation with enclosures turned the peasants against the monarchy. Many *cahiers* of the communes in 1789 energetically demanded the restoration of the old order and the withdrawal of enclosure edicts.[66] The consequence was to encourage the unity of the Third Estate, to throw many peasants and a section of the town dwellers into more vehement opposition to the old order. These trends go a long way toward explaining why the most prosperous peasantry in Europe could become a major force for revolution.

Through the *parlements* the higher echelons of the *noblesse de robe* supported and intensified the seigneurial reaction. Formerly, as we have seen, the royal bureaucracy had served to attract commercial wealth to the royal cause. However, it had also had the consequence of turning a small but influential section of the bourgeoisie into vehement defenders of privileges conceived of as private property attached to the individual. Here again capitalist ways of thinking and acting were seeping through the pores of the old order. During the eighteenth century these trends continued and intensified. As early as 1715 there were signs that the newer judicial nobility had won acceptance, that the bars were steadily coming down, and that in effect France would soon see a single nobility defending a single set of privileges against royal and popular en-

---

[65] Bloch, "Individualisme agraire," 549 – 550.
[66] Göhring, *Feudalität*, 82 – 84, 96; Lefebvre, *Etudes*, 255 – 257.

croachment. By 1730 the fusion was very visible.[67] Since the older nobility lacked any institutional base that could effectively challenge the king and since the newer group possessed this base in the system of sovereign courts, the older stratum found it necessary to concede social acceptance for the sake of political advantages. As the style of life of the two sections steadily became more similar, the difficulties steadily diminished.[68] Under Louis XVI, the king's judicial apparatus continued to work as a major recruiting center that brought wealthy commoners into that part of the establishment which was the focal point of opposition to reform. Of 943 *parlementaires* recruited during the period 1774 – 1789 and still in office in 1790, no less than 394 or 42 percent were former *roturiers* who became noble by virtue of their new position.[69]

As its share of the bargain in the rough working coalition we have been discussing, the older nobility managed to reserve certain key positions for itself. Toward the end of the *ancien régime* it managed to raise more and more barriers to the power of money. High offices and the army constituted preserves where the power of money found its frontier.[70] By the 1780s the aristocratic coalition as a whole had "ruined Maupeou and Turgot, reconquered every bishopric in the realm, imposed the rule of four quarterings of nobility for high army appointments, and forced the monarchy into a cowed, ultimately fatal solicitude for privileged interests."[71]

This absorption of many bourgeois into the nobility casts much doubt on one familiar explanation of the Revolution: that a major cause was the closed character of the French aristocracy, closed, that is, in comparison with the fluid boundaries and easy access that prevailed at the same time in England. The evidence just discussed indicates that this contrast was mainly a legal formality.

[67] Ford, *Robe and Sword,* 199 – 201.

[68] Ford, *Robe and Sword,* 250 – 251 and chap XI.

[69] Ford, *Robe and Sword,* 145 – 146, discussing a paper by Jean Egret from whom the figures are taken.

[70] Göhring, *Feudalität,* 74. The question would bear further detailed investigation. Göhring includes the magistrates in this category too. But Egret's evidence cited by Ford in the previous footnote raises doubts on this score.

[71] Ford, *Robe and Sword,* vii.

In actual practice, access to aristocratic status may not have presented more difficult hurdles in late eighteenth-century France than in England of the same period. Statistics are lacking. Here once again, however, we encounter a question where quantitative measurements fail to penetrate to the important qualitative differences. As pointed out above, the whole situation surrounding upward mobility and fusion was a different one in the two countries. In England the fusion took place in large measure outside the monarchy's range of influence and against the king. Enclosing landlords did not want the king meddling in the affairs of their peasants. Wealthy townsmen did not want the crown to make profitable business opportunities its private preserve for selected favorites. Important segments of these classes in England neither needed nor wanted political weapons borrowed from the arsenal of a dead feudalism or royal absolutism. In France, on the other hand, the monarchy turned commoners into landed aristocrats needing feudal protection. Hence it made them into stubborn defenders of privilege and vigorous opponents of its own intermittent efforts at reform. It did so in such a way as to make enemies among the sections of the bourgeoisie that were not identified with the old order.

These bourgeois in the meantime were growing stronger. So far they have not received the attention of historians and sociologists to the same degree as have the nobility and the peasants.[72] Nevertheless a few moderately well established points important for the present analysis do stand out. Basically the century was one of great economic progress for commerce and industry. Foreign commerce especially increased, even more rapidly in fact than in England.[73] About the latter years of the regime there is a difference of opinion. C. E. Labrousse, who has made a detailed study of prices, sees the period from about 1778 onward as one of wide-

[72] An exception is Barber, *Bourgeoisie in Eighteenth Century France*, but the economic foundations are slighted.

[73] Labrousse, *Crise de l'économie*, xxvii, xxviii, xlviii. On p. xxxviii the author calls attention to the fact that foreign trade in the last third of the eighteenth century was based on the reexport of colonial products, mainly sugar and coffee, and hence cannot be taken to indicate any improvement in domestic production. See also Sée, *Histoire économique*, II, xiv – xv; more details in his *Evolution commerciale*, 245 – 249.

spread depression affecting industry as well as agriculture.[74] In an older work, Henri Sée describes the last two decades of the old order as one in which there was a spurt in big industry, even though France remained backward in relation to England at the outbreak of the Revolution, since she started from a position far behind her rival across the Channel.[75] Government regulation of industry remained very important during the eighteenth century although the stream of edicts suggests that the regulations were not very effective. In the second half of the century government control diminished.[76] Thus commerce and to a lesser extent industry were expanding the social basis for demands that the old fetters on trade and production be thrown aside.

Turgot served as a spokesman for these forces. He took office, a firm believer in enlightened despotism and in liberty of production and exchange in both industry and agriculture. A glance at his attempted reforms and the opposition they aroused helps us to gauge the strength of the forces behind a classical version of capitalism, that is, one based on private property and free competition without support from precapitalist institutions. His program, only parts of which went into effect, included a reform of the tax system, free trade in grain (introduced by the edict of 13 September 1774), the suppression of the *corvée*, suppression of the guilds, and the free choice of occupation by the workers.[77] Turgot's policies antagonized the small consumers of food, greatly upset by the rise in prices that followed free trade in grains. Riots flared up all over the country; some rioters even invaded the courtyard of Versailles demanding that the bakers be forced to reduce their bread prices in a way that foreshadows the problems of the Revolution at the height of the Terror. Though Louis XVI held firm on this occasion, the incident scarcely strengthened Turgot's credit at court.[78] Evidently there was still a strong popular demand for a controlled

[74] *Crise de l'économie*, xxxii, xxxvi.

[75] *Evolution commerciale*, 303 – 305.

[76] Sée, *Histoire économique*, I, 348, 351. Labrousse, *Crise*, l.

[77] Lavisse, *Histoire*, IX, pt 1, 28, 43, 45.

[78] Lavisse, *Histoire*, IX, pt 1, 32. See Mathiez, *Vie chère* for later developments.

economy of a very old-fashioned variety, i.e., one where the emphasis was not on increasing production but where a benevolent authority would ensure a "fair" distribution of necessities to the poor. This sentiment, based on the lower strata of the peasants and the urban plebs, the famous *sans-culottes*, was to be the main source of radical measures in the Revolution itself. In addition, Turgot's proposal aroused the opposition of those financiers who profited from the corrupt features of the bureaucracy and that of manufacturers who were indignant that he refused to protect French industry, particularly cotton and ironworking, against foreign competition or to prohibit the exportation of raw materials needed by industry.[79]

The coalition of interests against Turgot is one more indication that the forces seeking to break the lingering fetters of feudalism and establish anything resembling private property and free competition were far from being the dominant ones in French society on the eve of the Revolution, even if they were growing stronger during much of the eighteenth century. To speak of the Revolution as bourgeois and capitalist in this simple sense is plainly mistaken. As it came to France, capitalism often wore a feudal mask, especially in the countryside. The demand for property rights within the prevailing system was very strong, as the sale of offices and the seigneurial reaction demonstrates. Capitalism, as Jaurès, the great socialist historian of the Revolution perceived without drawing the necessary conclusions, permeated the *ancien régime*, twisting it in such a way as to antagonize important segments of the privileged classes as well as the peasants, turning them too against the monarchy. Partly for this reason the radical thrust behind the Revolution, based on the *sans-culottes* and sections of the peasantry, was explicitly and strongly anticapitalist. The rich peasants, as we shall see, set the limits to which radical anticapitalism could go. Ultimately the forces behind a private property free of ancient fetters won important triumphs in the city and the countryside. To achieve this victory the capitalists frequently required the help of their bitterest enemies.

[79] Lavisse, *Histoire*, IX, pt 1, 40.

5. The Peasants' Relationship to Radicalism during the Revolution

Up to this point the discussion has tried to illuminate the sources of both rigidity and demands for change that gradually accumulated among the dominant classes. In analyzing the Revolution itself the facts compel a change of focus with concentration on the lower classes. French society broke apart from the top downward as the monarchy, for institutional and personal reasons, became increasingly unable to control the divisive forces discussed in the preceding sections. The collapse increased latent discontents among the lower classes and allowed them to come to the surface. There is evidence that these had been simmering for some time. Peasant uprisings in which the little people of the towns also took part strew the record of the seventeenth century. They occurred in different parts of France in 1639, 1662, 1664, 1670, 1674, and 1675.[80] By itself, however, popular resentment could not make a revolution. Whether it increased just before the Revolution is not absolutely clear; very likely it did. Nevertheless, only when popular grievances could coalesce even briefly with those of more powerful groups would they help to bring the monarchy crashing down amid fire, blood, and smoke.

The causes of earlier outbreaks, the nature of the peasants' world, the problems of those who constituted the great bulk of the French population appear but dimly in studies of the great days of royal absolutism.[81] As the Revolution approaches, more details appear until at least some of the main outlines of peasant society become reasonably distinct. In the absence of the kind of commercial revolution that took place in England or of a manorial reaction such as that which happened in Prussia and also in Russia for quite different reasons, many French peasants had become in effect small property owners. Though it is impossible to give precise numbers of these *coqs de paroisse* — their counterpart will be called *kulaks* at a later

[80] Sée, *Histoire économique*, I, 214–215; Sagnac, *Société française*, I, 139–143. Abundant material in Porchnev, *Soulèvements populaires*.

[81] See, e.g., Goubert, *Beauvais*, which concentrates mainly on statistical information for a single area and is not very helpful on the working of institutions.

stage in Russia — they were certainly a substantial and very influential minority. The large majority of the peasants trailed off beneath them by imperceptible gradations, through those who had tiny *lopins de terre*, down to those who had none at all and lived as agricultural laborers. One gets the impression — but it is no more than an impression — that the number of the land-short and the landless had been slowly and steadily growing for at least two centuries. Lefebvre asserts that by 1789 the large majority of rural proprietors did not have enough land to live on and had to work for others or find some auxiliary trade. Again general figures are not to be had. But in many parts of the country families without any land at all may have run from twenty to as high as seventy percent of the peasant population.[82]

One may discern two major demands among the poorer peasants. First, and perhaps above all, they wanted a plot of land if they had none, a slightly larger plot if they had any at all. Secondly, they were anxious to preserve those specific customs of the village community that served their own interests. The poor peasants had no generalized attachment to the village community. When they caught a glimpse of the opportunity to get a plot of land out of dividing up the common lands of the village during the Revolution, they were loud in their cries to do so. It was mainly the rich peasants who prevented the breaking up of the commons, partly because the rich peasants were often the only ones to use the commons for pasture for the stock with which they worked their farms.[83] On the other hand, certain collectivist practices were important to poor peasants. The most valuable was the right of *vaine pâture*. On cultivated territory this right was part of the ancient open-field system that prevailed through much of France in the absence of a powerful movement toward enclosures. The cultivated fields lay in strips, surrounding the cluster of dwellings that was the village. All this land had to go through each stage of the agricultural cycle at the same moment, a practice known in France as *assolement forcé*, in

[82] Lefebvre, *Etudes*, 209–212.
[83] Cobban, *Social Interpretation*, 112–117 corrects the widespread view that poor peasants generally opposed division of the common lands.

German-speaking lands as *Flurzwang*. After the harvest had been gathered in, the rights of the proprietor, as Bloch vividly remarks, went to sleep, and cattle wandered freely over unfenced fields. In meadows used for hay growing, which by this time might be the property of a seigneur, of the village as a whole, or of a well-to-do peasant, a similar arrangement prevailed in many areas: after the hay had been gathered, the meadows would be thrown open for the cattle to graze and eat the second growth (*regain*). To the poorer peasants the right of *vaine pâture* was important because they were liable to be prevented from making much use of communal lands. Even if they often lacked horses and ploughs, they were likely to possess a cow or sheep and a few goats that they used for meat or to raise a bit of cash. Gleaning rights, when hordes of poor peasants might swarm over the fields for a specified number of days under the anxious eyes of the owners of the fields, and rights to collect fuel and pasture animals in the woods, were also significant to them.[84]

The political consequence was a split within the peasantry and a very marked disintegration of the peasant community. Like those in many other parts of the world, the poorer peasants in France were the main victims as the forces of modernization pried apart the ancient village society that had governed the division of labor and had provided them a modest but recognized place within their small world for as long as anyone could remember. Though French villages, of which there were many different types, by and large suffered later and less and for different reasons than their English counterparts, still this society was under very visible attack as the

[84] For a lucid general description of collective practices and resistance to attacks on them see Bloch, "Individualisme agraire," esp 330 – 332, 523 – 527. In the latter passage Bloch notes that the attitude of the poor toward dividing up the land in village commons varied according to local circumstances, while moves to withdraw common rights through limited enclosures generally hurt them. See also Lefebvre, *Paysans du Nord*, 72 – 114 on collective rights and 424 – 430 on their revival during the Revolution. Lefebvre's actual evidence points in the same general direction: that the poor often wanted to divide up village commons but clung to other common rights.

eighteenth century drew toward its close.[85] The situation of the rural poor drove many toward violent egalitarian theories. For them modernization meant mainly that the prosperous peasants were blocking them from dividing up the land (including that which became available through confiscation during the Revolution) and starving them out by restrictions on gleaning and pasture rights as part of the drive toward modern forms of private property in land. At the height of the Revolution, radicalism in the cities and the countryside could join hands, a fact that helps to explain the depth and violence of the French Revolution in comparison with its English precursor. There was not just a single peasant revolution going its own way, sometimes joining, sometimes opposing the revolution in the cities and the capital. There were at least two peasant revolutions, that of the peasant aristocracy and that of the larger and more diffuse majority, each following its own course and also from time to time fusing or opposing revolutionary waves in the cities.

Turning now to the upper ranks of the peasantry, it seems at least moderately clear that their discontents came from their half-way position: they possessed the land without really owning it.[86] As is well known, the legal and social position of the French peasantry, at any rate at its upper levels, was subject to fewer repressive restraints than in any other large country on the continent. Most of them were personally free. To the extent that we can glimpse their demands through the refractions of the *cahiers*, we can see that they wanted mainly to eliminate the arbitrary aspects of the feudal system that had been increasing in the last years of the old order. In sharp contrast with the bourgeoisie, they did not attack the social position and special privileges of the nobility. Instead, they often expressly acknowledged them,[87] a fact which suggests that they could not understand any general connection between the privileges of the nobility and their own problems. Evi-

[85] It is possible to follow many details of the process in a single area in an excellent account by Saint Jacob, *Paysans de la Bourgogne,* esp 435 – 573.

[86] Göhring, *Feudalität,* 57 – 58, 60.

[87] Göhring, *Feudalität,* 115 – 116.

dently in 1789 it would still take serious shocks to turn the peasants into an active revolutionary force. These shocks were not long in coming.

One impulse came from the actions of the nobility and the vacillations of the king preceding and following the meeting of the Estates General. Certainly the peasants neither understood nor cared much about such questions as voting by order or voting by head, which agitated the rest of France. Nor were they very likely to be deeply concerned about the rickety character of Bourbon finances and the prospect of bankruptcy. The distribution of the tax burden among the various orders could not have been much more exciting; the peasant was interested in *his* share of the tax in *his* village, which varied from place to place in too bewildering a fashion for all but specialists to understand.[88] On the other hand, all these questions very definitely agitated a large portion of educated townsfolk. The nobility was trying to take over the state through the mechanism of the Estates General, a natural continuation of what they had been trying to do during the so-called feudal reaction. Their reluctance to compromise on these issues made for the moment what was no more than a legal label for all that was neither noble nor clergy — the *Tiers Etat* — into something resembling a single political mind.

Many of the wealthier and especially the liberal nobles who played conspicuous parts in this early phase of the Revolution were quite willing to make substantial concessions. On agrarian questions they were even willing to sacrifice some of the more oppressive feudal rights without indemnity. The reactionary pressure that temporarily fused the *Tiers Etat* very likely came in large part from the crowd of rural petty seigneurs who lived off their dues and had neither willingness nor capacity nor opportunity to manage their affairs as commoners even if they were indemnified for the loss of feudal rights.[89]

Other impulses were more fortuitous. In 1786 the French gov-

[88] Standard observations about the oppressive character of taxation under the old order may be an exaggeration. Goubert, *Beauvais*, 152, stresses the fundamental fairness of the system in the area he studied.

[89] Lefebvre, *Etudes*, 258.

ernment had reduced sharply its duties on English manufactures, which threw many people out of work. It affected the peasants in some areas by reducing or eliminating outside employment. A decree of 1787 removed restrictions on the grain trade, including those requiring the cultivators to bring their grain to the local market. The harvest in the autumn of 1788 was disastrously short. The winter that followed was unusually harsh, while spring brought severe storms and floods.[90] Natural disasters combined with political uncertainties and anxieties by the summer of 1789 to set off a series of panics and peasant uprisings in many parts of France.

The radical potential of the peasantry began to show. Though the troubles lumped under the *Grande Peur* took different forms in different parts of France, opposition to feudalism came to the surface everywhere. Even where the peasants did not rise, they refused their feudal obligations.[91] All sorts of rumors flew thick and fast; fears of an aristocratic plot, not by any means altogether unfounded, made it easy for the peasants to get the support of the poorer classes in the towns. As the authority of the central government deteriorated, France seemed to be breaking up into a network of little towns and communities. The disintegration of public order made solid and substantial citizens among the bourgeoisie welcome the liberal nobles into their ranks. The poorer classes, on the other hand, distrusted them and tried to push them out. Thus in the areas where the panic prevailed, middling property owners in town and countryside formed themselves into local defense groups to protect themselves against brigands and bandits, supposedly let loose on the country by a scheming aristocracy.[92]

On the other hand, where there were real agrarian revolts and *jacqueries*, there was no *Grande Peur*.[93] In these areas, the peasant on the march *was* the brigand. There was no need to imagine brigands, and no possibility of imagining that he was the tool of the aristocrat. Full-scale peasant violence frightened the bourgeoisie, particularly those for whom feudal rights were as sacred a form of

[90] Lefebvre, *Grande Peur*, 13 – 14; Göhring, *Feudalität*, 129.

[91] Lefebvre, *Grande Peur*, 119.

[92] Lefebvre, *Grande Peur*, 30, 31, 103 – 105, 109, 157 – 158.

[93] Lefebvre, *Grande Peur*, 165 – 167, 246.

property as any other, and threw them into the arms of the nobility. After the storming of the Bastille the bourgeoisie in some areas, especially Alsace where uprisings were particularly violent, co-operated wholeheartedly with the privileged classes in suppressing them.[94]

The Revolution had already let loose social forces anxious and willing to put an end to it. Counterrevolution had leadership of a sort in Paris and influence with the king. Momentarily, success seemed possible. On July 11, 1789, Necker was hastily discharged and banished from France. The nobility had shown signs that it was unwilling to accept the victory of the *Tiers Etat*, which had split off from the Estates General, taking the clergy and forty-seven nobles with them to form the Constituent Assembly, formally established on July 7, 1789. Troops were gathering around Paris. The countryside was agitated for the reasons we have seen. Famine threatened. There were suspicions that the king planned a coup. The Constituent Assembly expected the worst. At this moment a popular uprising saved the moderate revolution from capitulation and propelled it forward. The population of Paris had no intention of saving the Assembly; they did so "by ricochet" and in the form of a defensive reaction. Panics were continuous in those days, the first expressions of the *Grande Peur*. Seeing Paris surrounded by royal troops and "brigands," fearing they would be bombarded and delivered over to pillage, masses of citizens erected barricades and sought out arms, taking 32,000 rifles at the Invalides. The morning of the fourteenth they went to find more arms at the Bastille and ended by storming the famous symbol of arbitrary authority.[95]

In the capture of the Bastille and the brief wave of popular vengeance that followed it, there already appeared, as Lefebvre points out, certain major traits of the radical component in the French Revolution: the fear of counterrevolutionary plots, the defensive uprising among the masses, mainly poor artisans and journeymen, and the will to punish and destroy their enemies.[96]

These characteristics reappeared in each of the main popular

[94] Lefebvre, *Grande Peur*, 56, 139.
[95] Lefebvre, *Révolution française*, 125 – 126, 134 – 135.
[96] *Révolution française*, 133.

surges of the Revolution. It is well known that the Revolution began with an offensive by the nobility and became more radical as it
proceeded. More radical sections of the bourgeoisie came to power
and followed more radical policies until shortly before the fall of
Robespierre on 9 Thermidor or July 27, 1794. Each time that the
conservative forces, who were of course less conservative and a different group on succeeding occasions, tried to halt the Revolution,
a radical offensive from below propelled them forward. Three great
popular upheavals, three famous *journées*, marked this series of leftward lurches. The first was the storming of the Bastille on July 14,
1789. The second was the storming of the Tuileries on August 10,
1792, which led to the execution of Louis XVI. The third uprising,
that of May 31, 1793, took place in similar but more serious circumstances and was part of the chain of events leading to the reign of
terror and Robespierre's brief supremacy. The main impulse behind
each surge came from the Parisian *sans-culottes*. Each surge succeeded as long as it could draw on active support from the countryside. When this support dried up, when the demands of the *sans-
culottes* came to conflict with those of property-owning peasants,
the impulse behind the radical revolution petered out, and its urban
remnants were easily repressed.

It is fair, therefore, to hold that the peasantry was the arbiter of
the Revolution, though not its chief propelling force. And even if it
was not the main propelling force, it was a very important one,
largely responsible for what in retrospect seems the most important
and lasting achievement of the Revolution, the dismantling of feudalism.

To resume the narrative, the taking of the Bastille was significant in a symbolic sense rather than as a concrete political or military victory. The mortal blow given to feudalism a few weeks later
on the famous night of August 4, 1789, turned out to be more important and, as just indicated, was directly traceable to peasant disturbances. The Constituent Assembly was in a ticklish position. Its
members were mainly men of law and order who had been saved
by a popular uprising. Substantial property owners in general had
no desire to see peasants on the rampage. But if they turned to the
king and what was left of the royal apparatus to restore order, they

would play into the hands of the intransigeant elements in the aristocracy and forfeit the gains of the Revolution. In this situation a minority managed to maneuver the Assembly into passing the decrees.

Though the text of the declaration begins with the assertion that the Assembly entirely destroyed feudalism, this was an exaggeration. The abolition of those feudal dues that rested on the land was subject to redemption payments, which would have meant their survival for quite some time. Other remnants, including honorific prerogatives, survived too. Only later in more radical phases of the Revolution did subsequent legislation finish most of the work of dismounting the remains of the feudal structure, in this way of course continuing, as de Tocqueville emphasized, the work of royal absolutism. Nevertheless the Assembly voted equality before the law, the abolition of feudal obligations that rested on persons (without indemnification), equality of punishments, the admission of all to public services, the abolition of the sale of offices, and suppression of the tithe (without indemnity). These were enough to justify the results of this famous occasion as the "death certificate of the *Ancien Régime*."[97]

Let it be emphasized that this was no sudden act of spontaneous generosity. The Assembly acted with a pistol at its head, in the form of popular disorders.[98] To take occasions such as this, when the upper classes showed a willingness to make concessions, out of

[97] Lefebvre, *Révolution française*, 140–141. It is worth noticing that the revolutionary leaders proceeded rather more cautiously in dismounting traditional practices among the peasants. The Constituent Assembly did not try to abolish *assolement forcé*, the obligation on each member of a village to plough, sow, and harvest at the same time as the rest, until June 5, 1791. Then it did so indirectly by a decree that allowed the proprietor a free choice of crops. Neither the Constituent Assembly nor the Convention suppressed *vaine pâture obligatoire*, the corresponding right to turn cattle loose on the cultivated fields as soon as the harvest had been gathered. See Bloch, "Individualisme agraire," 544–545.

[98] See Lefebvre, *Grande Peur*, 246–247 and his *Révolution française*, 113, 119. About the August 4th concessions Marat wrote, "It is by the light from the flames of their burning chateaux that they magnanimously renounce the privilege of holding in chains men who have already forcibly recovered their freedom." Translation in Postgate, ed, *Revolution*, 27.

their context in order to argue that revolutionary radicalism was therefore unnecessary would be to falsify the situation completely.

The second radical phase was also provoked by an attempt at reaction. The same pattern repeated itself but with greater intensity. The king's attempted flight, frustrated at Varennes (June 20 – 25, 1791), destroyed whatever possibility there might have been that the Revolution would come to rest in a constitutional monarchy and rule by the upper classes as in England. War broke out in the spring of 1792. The leaders of the Gironde, in which commercial and shipping interests were heavily represented, sought war to spread the revolutionary gospel as well as for more material reasons. Lafayette intended to use the war for exactly the opposite reason, to restore order. The danger of a military coup was real.[99] From November of 1791 onward there was a series of popular uprisings in many parts of the countryside, protesting ·against the export of grain in a time of acute scarcity. In itself the notion that grain was being sent out of the country – when it cost more in France than abroad – was certainly absurd. The riots, though suppressed without great difficulty, reveal the state of excitement and disorder. The city poor, too, were hard hit by increasing inflation.[100] Military reverses added to the highly charged atmosphere. The coup that cleared the air, the storming of the Tuileries and the famous slaughter of the Swiss Guards, August 10, 1792, was again the work of the Paris crowd, mainly poor artisans, journeymen, etc.[101] Though Paris was the center, the popular and radical movement received active support from the provinces. This was the occasion of Rouget de Lisle's song of war and revolt, sung by the Jacobin battalions on their march from Marseilles to come to the aid of their comrades in Paris. The overturn of August 10 was not at all a Parisian one like that of July 14th, but a national uprising.[102]

In national politics the consequence was the virtual abdication

[99] Lefebvre, *Révolution française*, 225, 227 – 228, 243.

[100] Mathiez, *Vie chère*, 59 – 71; esp 67; Lefebvre, *Révolution française*, 241.

[101] Rudé, *Crowd*, provides detailed information on the composition of the Paris crowd for the great *journées* of the Revolution.

[102] Lefebvre, *Révolution française*, 246.

of the Legislative Assembly, which had replaced the Constituent Assembly in October 1791; the trial of Louis XVI, which did not take place until the end of 1792; and, more immediately, popular vengeance in the September 1792 massacres. These massacres appear to have started about as spontaneously as mass actions ever do. A waiting crowd seized and summarily executed a batch of prisoners under escort. Then the massacres spread to the jails. Between 1100 and 1400 lost their lives, the great majority common thieves, prostitutes, forgers, and vagrants. Only about a quarter were priests, nobles, or "politicals" of any sort.[103] Similar scenes took place in other French cities and towns. The massacres are significant mainly as revealing the blindness and irrationality of popular vengeance. The Terror, of which they were a prelude and which appeared in the next phase, was more organized and less capricious in its results.

As a consequence of the uprisings during 1791 – 92 the peasants had won important gains by the summer of 1792. On the 25th of August feudal dues disappeared, without indemnity unless the original title survived. By another act on the 28th, villages received back their common lands where the lord had usurped them. Still another decree sought to make it easier for the rural proletariat to acquire land by arranging for the sale of confiscated *émigré* properties in small units. In Paris itself the Commune enrolled the unemployed for work on fortifications.[104] By these measures the government made a move toward meeting some of the demands of the submerged majority of tiny property holders and the propertyless in the countryside, in an effort to attach them to the interests of the Revolution. But it was only a halfhearted move. The revolutionary government in Paris backed and filled on the crucial question of dividing up communal and *émigré* lands among the small peasants. The effect was to sharpen the split between rich and poor. The aroused richer peasants proclaimed that to give property to the landless was the same as the *loi agraire:* it meant communism of property.[105]

[103] Rudé, *Crowd,* 109 – 110.

[104] Lefebvre, *Révolution française,* 254.

[105] Cobban, *Social Interpretation,* 115. See also Bourgin, ed, *Partage des biens communeaux,* xvii for further details on the legislation. The speech

In the meantime the government's uncertainty promoted the circulation of radical notions among the peasantry. The enemies of peasant radicalism lumped such ideas together under the general scarcecrow label of *loi agraire*. Equality of property was probably the notion that had the widest appeal among the poorer peasants. But there were other ideas that transcended the conceptions of private property within whose framework the revolutionary leaders remained even during the next and most radical phase. These were a mixture of Christian and collectivist ideas. Just how much of an echo they found among the peasants it is difficult to say, not only due to the absence of records, but also because of rigid suppression. Carnot, who hated the radicals, undoubtedly exaggerated when he wrote on October 7, 1792, from Bordeaux that the idea of the *loi agraire* had spread terror everywhere.[106] Obviously peasant radicalism was frightening the authorities. In a fiery speech to the Convention·Barère demanded action to make plain to the countryside that the slightest attacks on property would not be tolerated. The next day, March 18, 1793, the Convention set the death penalty for preaching the *loi agraire*.[107] Enough of the content of these notions nevertheless survived to show that they were relevant to the needs of the poor peasants and met some of their needs. Hence it becomes important to examine this underground radical stream with some care.

The first radical attack arose in connection with the riots over the alleged exports of grain mentioned a few moments ago as part of the background of the August 10, 1792 uprising. In the course of

---

by the Chairman of the Committee of Agriculture (337–373) is a revealing attempt to combine characteristic capitalist notions about progress in agriculture, via private property and the abolition of common lands *à l'anglaise*, with an effort to meet the demands of the poor. "Cependant, Messieurs, si le droit de propriété est sacré, la cause du pauvre l'est aussi," he observes at one point (360). Leafing through a number of the petitions printed in Bourgin has convinced me that Cobban's interpretation of the peasants' demands is correct and that prevailing ones about the opposition of the poor to dividing up the commons are mistaken.

[106] Quoted by Guérin, *Lutte de classes*, I, 350.

[107] A long quotation from Barère's speech may be found in Soreau, "Révolution française et le proletariat rural," 121–122.

one of these disturbances the peasants of the neighboring communes murdered a rich tanner of Étampes in Beauce. The case sent a ripple throughout France; his funeral was made a national fete. However, a Jacobin *curé* from the neighborhood, Pierre Dolivier, had the courage to oppose this wave of sentiment. In May 1792 he presented to the Legislative Assembly a petition attacking the murdered victim as a rich and greedy figure, suggesting that he was a speculator in grain and that he roundly deserved his fate. At this point Dolivier went on not only to ask for price controls on behalf of the poor and hungry but also to attack the right of property itself: "La nation seule est véritablement propriétaire de son terrain."[108] Mathiez correctly points out the archaic element in Dolivier's thinking. Louis XIV had claimed to be the master of the property of his subjects. Now the nation had succeeded to the king. On the other hand, there is also a note in Dolivier and his successors that strikes the present-day reader as very modern: the state has the obligation to see to it that the less fortunate majority of its citizens do not starve, and this obligation overrides the selfish rights and interests of property.

In defending the violent action of outraged peasants and in attacking property, Dolivier shocked the assembly. But Robespierre spoke up for the *curé* in a way that both foreshadows and contrasts with his later behavior during the Terror. He attacked the entire class of avid bourgeoisie who had seen in the Revolution nothing but a means to succeed the nobility and the clergy and who defended wealth with the same harshness as the privileged classes had defended birth.[109] Thus the ideas of the extreme radicals were not altogether uncongenial to those of the small property holders epitomized by Robespierre.

After the storming of the Tuileries, similar notions cropped up in other parts of France along with sporadic but unsuccessful efforts to put them into practice. Another *curé* told his parishioners, "Les biens vont être communs, il n'y aura qu'une cave, qu'un grenier où chacun prendra tout ce que lui sera nécessaire." He advised his

[108] Quoted by Mathiez, *Vie chère*, 73.
[109] For the story of Dolivier see Mathiez, *Vie chère*, 66, on the murder and 72–76, on Dolivier himself.

flock to set up common stores upon which they could draw as they needed and hence do away with money. In this connection we must remember that inflation had already sent prices soaring and that a sector of the peasantry consumed more food than it produced on its own property. The landless were of course completely without means to produce their own food. Elsewhere an inhabitant of Lyons, this time a city man, worked out and published a detailed system for nationalizing basic necessities. The state was to buy up the harvest at fixed prices; then, guaranteeing peasants against the fluctuations of the market, store it in *greniers d' abondance;* and, in addition, distribute bread at a fixed price. The notion resembles the "ever-normal granary" of more recent times, though the latter was a response to excess production instead of to shortage.

Another pamphlet was much more religious, calling down the wrath of Jehovah on the proud rich and invoking in his name "la loi des Francs . . . AGRAIRE!" Like English radicals at the time of the Puritan Revolution, this pamphlet writer looked back to a mythical past and tried to prove that the Gauls and Germans redistributed their land every year.[110]

Certain themes, it is easy to see, run through all these radical agrarian protests. They seek either the abolition of private property altogether or its very strict limitation along egalitarian lines. Secondly, they propose measures to get around the workings of the market, such as storage depots and free distribution of products on a local scale or the more elaborate *greniers d'abondance.* Townsmen were perhaps more inclined to advocate the prominent display of the guillotine as a way of prying the necessities of life out of greedy and reluctant hands.[111] Here lay the seeds of later divisions. For the moment it is enough to notice that agrarian radicalism was quite obviously a response not only to the disturbed conditions of the time, but also to the intrusion of capitalism into the countryside.

[110] Mathiez, *Vie chère,* 90 – 94. The author's citations from Caesar and Tacitus show that he could scarcely have been a peasant himself. On the other hand it seems obvious that *prevailing* equalitarian practices among the peasantry (such as *vaine pâture*) and the attacks on these must have provided the impetus to search for legitimation in historical precedents.

[111] Mathiez, *Vie chère,* 91 – 92.

The whole thrust of these ideas is against those who got rich by working the market. What people needed was, it seemed, just too expensive and too hard to come by. Poor peasants and even those not so poor could agree with the *sans-culottes* in the towns on these simple opinions. As long as the interests of these groups converged, the radical revolution could keep a fire under the revolution on behalf of private property and the rights of man. Also the bourgeois revolution needed the help of the radical revolution, as we have already seen in connection with the events of July 14 and August 4, 1789. Up to a point the two revolutions — actually a fusing of several smaller ones into two major and easily distinguishable currents — could work together and reenforce each other. But the two were fundamentally incompatible due to incompatible attitudes toward property: the incompatibility of those who have property and those who don't.[112] When the radical stream split and the property holders had no more use for their help, the Revolution would lurch to a halt. The final convergence and separation of the radicals and men of property is the process we have to analyze in the third phase.

The final radical thrust, like its predecessors, began with a popular uprising in Paris at the end of May 1793. Again it was a punitive response to real danger. In March, General Dumouriez had turned traitor after his defeat by the Austrians. With them he concluded an armistice in order to march on Paris, set Louis XVII on the throne, and reestablish the Constitution of 1791.[113] Royalist revolt was under way in the Vendée. Marseilles had been the victim of anti-*sans-culottes* and Lyon of anti-Jacobin uprisings and had escaped from the control of the revolutionaries.[114] The May upris-

---

[112] To call the urban *sans-culottes* a proletariat or even a protoproletariat at this point in French history, as does Guérin in *Lutte de classes*, seems to me quite misleading. The whole radical push came mainly from a series of strata being crowded off the historical stage, a phenomenon characteristic of modern revolutions, as I hope to show in due course. It is fashionable to criticize Guérin for his misconception without trying to replace it by a more tenable interpretation. I find such criticism small spirited and would like to record publicly my debt to Guérin. Without his book and of course Mathiez's *Vie chère* I could not have written these pages.

[113] Lefebvre, *Révolution française*, 334.

[114] Lefebvre, *Révolution française*, 340.

ing itself was a well engineered affair, "the best organized *journée* of the Revolution," which enabled the more radical faction of the bourgeoisie led by Robespierre to get the upper hand over the Gironde.[115]

In the meantime the radicalism of the Parisian poor had begun to find articulate expression at about the same time as the scattered pockets of agrarian radicalism came to light in the countryside. The Gironde's policies of attempting to let food prices find their natural level through the operation of supply and demand in the midst of war and revolution brought together small artisans, journeymen, workers, and the miscellaneous floating population of Paris — in a word the *sans-culottes* — in common misery. The inflation made matters worse; it was in effect a way of shifting the cost of the war onto the backs of the poor.[116] By January 1793, even the Gironde leaders found it necessary to confess that the price of wheat would not go down of its own accord.[117]

Such then was the situation in which Jacques Roux and the *enragés* began to attract attention in Paris. Their ideas were if anything simpler than those of the agrarian radicals discussed a moment ago and amounted to two propositions: 1) Freedom of commerce played into the hands of the speculators and caused intense suffering to the poor. 2) Force should be used to put an end to speculation. There was also a significant backward-looking note. At one point, in June of 1793, Jacques Roux contrasted before the bar of the Convention itself the ease of existence under the *ancien régime* with the miseries that plagued the people under a revolution supposedly carried out on their behalf. He went on to express open regret for the days when paternalist regulations prevented the poor from having to pay three times their value for elementary necessities. Beyond these notions Roux's program, if it can be called that, did not go. But to say even this was to attack the right of property

[115] Lefebvre, *Révolution française*, 340–342.
[116] As Mathiez, *Vie chère*, 613, pointed out, on account of the inflation of the *assignat* the little people bore the cost of the Revolution as much as did priests and *émigrés*.
[117] Mathiez, *Vie chère*, 113.

and the legitimacy of the whole Revolution, and certainly took courage.[118]

Thus both the rural and the urban radicals shared a common hostility at this point to the rich who were profiting from the Revolution and to the unfettered workings of the market. Further evidence that urban and rural radicalism were seeking compatible objectives comes from a significant detail reported by Mathiez about the uprising of May 31, 1793. Some months before, delegates from the *fédérés* of eighty-three *départements* had come to Paris. Though the Gironde leaders hoped to use this group in its struggle against the Paris Commune and the Montagne, the delegates fell under the influence of the *enragés*.[119] That provincials whom the Gironde hoped to use were susceptible to such ideas indicates the general strength of anticapitalist radicalism at this juncture.

Probably for this reason the Montagne, shortly after the uprising of May 31, 1793, found it advisable to make important concessions to the peasantry. On June 3 it decreed the sale of *émigré* property in small units, payable in ten years; on the 10th, the voluntary division of village common lands among individual inhabitants—whether this ever went into effect is unknown — and, on July 17th, the abolition without indemnity of all that remained of seigneurial rights.[120] To sum up the meaning of the uprising and the events surrounding it, the bourgeois revolution had been pushed sharply to the left under radical pressure and forced to shed the moderates (dramatized in the arrest of thirty-one Girondist deputies on June 2), while the urban radicals and the peasants were still marching together even if in ragged formation.

The popular upsurge helped to make possible the heroic and desperate period of the Revolution, the reign of terror and the so-called dictatorship of the Committee of Public Safety, the creation of a new army, the driving of those allied against France back

[118] Mathiez, *Vie chère*, 212, 218, with extensive quotations from Roux. For a much more detailed analysis of the social composition and aspirations of the *sans-culottes*, see Soboul, *Sans-culottes*, esp pt II.

[119] Mathiez, *Vie chère*, 120 - 121.

[120] Lefebvre, *Révolution française*, 344; Cobban, *Social Interpretation*, 117.

across the Rhine, the defeat of the counterrevolution in the Vendée. Actually, of course, the dictatorship of the Committee of Public Safety was a ramshackle and primitive affair by twentieth-century standards. The technical means of communication and transportation precluded centralized control of the economy. No nationwide measure to ration the consumption of the population was attempted.[121] This failure to ration food was one of the main reasons why the urban *sans-culottes* failed in the end to stand by Robespierre. On the agrarian side, the key problems were to get grain to the armies first, secondly to Paris and the big cities, and finally to ensure its movement from areas where there was a surplus to areas in short supply. The last aspect was a continuation under new and revolutionary conditions of a difficulty that had long plagued the old order. To solve this series of problems the revolutionary government resorted to requisitioning and price controls. In many cases requisitioning merely involved transfers to a nearby *département* or to an army active in the vicinity.[122] Conflicts of jurisdiction continually plagued the complicated administrative system. Quite often the representatives of the Committee of Public Safety took the side of local interests in opposition to those of Paris and the Revolution.[123] Yet despite strong resistance and confusion the system did work: it got food to the cities and to the armies, saved the Revolution, and prevented famine. Patriotic and Revolutionary necessity overcame the theoretical scruples of the leaders who were enthusiastic partisans of economic liberalism.[124]

Despite such convictions, the pressure of the emergency led to a few scattered experiments that pointed in a socialist direction and that are significant as antecedents of twentieth-century collective farms. There was some talk of turning big estates confiscated from the *émigrés* into national farms or some variety of communal undertaking in order to feed the cities.[125] As part of the *levée en masse*

[121] Lefebvre, *Paysans du Nord*, 647. For an excellent general account of the Committee's program of controls see Mathiez, *Vie chère*, pt III, chap III.

[122] Mathiez, *Vie chère*, 479.

[123] Mathiez, *Vie chère*, 464 – 470, 477.

[124] Mathiez, *Vie chère*, 483 – 484.

[125] Mathiez, *Vie chère*, 436; see also 423 – 425.

or national conscription, decreed on August 23, 1793, the government attempted to have the holders of confiscated estates turn over the produce to national storage depots, *greniers d'abondance*, putting into effect, though probably not consciously and deliberately, one of the key notions of agrarian radicalism. However, the attempt was a failure.[126]

The wealthier peasants, those who produced a substantial surplus above their own needs, were the ones who felt the impact of the Committee of Public Safety's controls most keenly and who were the main source of resistance. Though anticlerical legislation had made some peasants uneasy as early as 1790 (when the Civil Constitution of the Clergy was instituted), it was the emergency measures of 1793 – 1794, regarding food supplies, that turned large numbers of them against the Revolution. As producers, the peasants evaded the system of price controls. To do so was relatively easy; there were really rather few risks despite efforts to prevent clandestine sales. The old regime's compulsion on the peasant to bring his produce to the market no longer existed.[127] In response to evasions and its own imperious needs, the government tightened the screws. Requisition began by allowing peasants to retain enough for their families and for seed, an elastic regulation that peasants stretched when they could. The Convention soon suppressed the *réserve familiale* on the 25th Brumaire (November 15, 1793).[128] In the villages the government's efforts to find grain and to compel its sale through legal channels and at legal prices, supported by the threat of the guillotine and perhaps overt measures against the priest, hardly looked like temporary war measures. The radical phase of the Revolution

[126] Mathiez, *Vie chère*, 462, 464.

[127] Lefebvre, *Paysans du Nord*, 648, 671. Though Lefebvre's information comes only from the North, it is highly likely that these circumstances prevailed very widely.

[128] Mathiez, *Vie chère*, 471. Here and elsewhere the date in parentheses, giving the one which in the Gregorian calendar corresponds to that in the Revolutionary calendar, represents my calculation from the convenient table provided in Soboul, *Sans-culottes*, 1159 – 1160. Historians of the Revolution have the vexing habit of giving dates without mentioning the year, and, when they do so only according to the Revolutionary calendar, the prospect of a slip is considerable.

was in many places an outright attack on the substantial peasants, even if it was brief and spotty.[129] Perhaps worst of all, townsmen and "outsiders" — often much more ruthless than the administrators and tax collectors of the monarchy — were its main agents in the countryside, sometimes aided by a revolutionary army. At the height of the "popular terror," that is, between the adoption of the *maximum général* of September 15, 1793, and the execution of Hébert and other *sans-culotte* leaders, March 24, 1794, the government allowed the formation of revolutionary "armies" whose purpose was more to collect grain than to fight the enemy.[130]

The obvious and decisive fact of the radical phase is this: the urban *sans-culottes* had been able to push the Jacobin leaders into policies that saved the Revolution but at the cost of turning the peasants against it. The radical phase might have gone further if the government in Paris had been able to count on the mass of the poorer peasants against the wealthier ones. But the government's limited capacity and willingness to enforce price controls helped to prevent this split from materializing. Rising prices worked hardship on the small-plot owners who had little to sell and on agricultural workers who had to buy at least part of their food. These suffered the most from the violation of the maximum. For a time their situation remained tolerable, according to Lefebvre's detailed and thorough studies of the North, because the price of bread rose less rapidly than wages. By the end of 1793 these groups were in worse straits, Lefebvre holds, than the town dwellers.[131] To the extent that these conditions prevailed elsewhere in the countryside, they alienated radical support from the Revolution and dried up the sources of rural radicalism.

In measures they proposed in March 1794, just before the execution of the *sans-culotte* leaders, Robespierre and Saint-Just showed

[129] Lefebvre, *Paysans du Nord*, 846 – 847.

[130] Guérin, *Lutte de classes*, I, 166 – 168, 189 – 191. According to Cobb, *Armées révolutionnaires*, II, 403, resistance was strongest in the areas rich in grain. In others the armies were often welcomed as bringing justice against speculators, rich merchants, and farmers. However, Cobb's main information concerns popular reactions in small towns rather than among the peasants themselves.

[131] Lefebvre, *Paysans du Nord*, 673, 678, 651 – 652, 702.

signs of being aware of the fact that they needed to prop up their government by concessions to the poor peasants. Whether or not the proposals they made at this time, known as the Ventôse decrees,[132] were more than a political maneuver is a question still under discussion. What the episode does demonstrate is that Robespierre and Saint-Just knew very little about the peasants' problems and that their proposals fell far short of meeting demands of the peasants expressed in petitions whose general content the revolutionary leaders must have known.[133] Even if they hàd wanted to do more, Robespierre and Saint-Just had precious little room within which to maneuver. Lands confiscated from the *émigrés* would not have provided enough to meet the needs of the poor. To divide up what land was available and grant it on easy terms to the mass of small and landless peasants would have reduced the value of the *assignat* even further.[134] It would have been very difficult, perhaps impossible, to meet the expressed desires of the poorer peasants without putting a spike into the wheels of the bourgeois and capitalist revolution. As it was, even these mild proposals encountered strong opposition in the Convention and the Committee of Public Safety itself and hence came to nothing.

Thus during the radical phase the needs and aspirations of the urban *sans-culottes* finally came into direct and open conflict with all sections of the countryside. The main symptom was the deterioration of exchanges between the city and the countryside, especially the provisioning of the city, a problem that was to have great influence on the course and consequences of the Russian Revolution as well. During the winter of 1793 – 1794 the economic situation of the Parisian *sans-culottes* deteriorated sharply, as the peasants, resenting the forays of *sans-culotte* organizations into the countryside, brought in less and less.[135] A government inquiry at the time of Hébert's trial brought out the fact that the peasants were no longer bringing food into Paris because individuals went out into

---

[132] See Lefebvre, *Questions agraires,* 1 – 3, 43 – 45.

[133] Lefebvre, *Questions agraires,* 57, 129.

[134] Lefebvre, *Questions agraires,* 55. See also his *Paysans du Nord,* 915.

[135] Lefebvre, *Révolution française,* 373 – 374; Soboul, *Sans-culottes,* 1029.

the countryside to buy produce at more than the fixed price. Obviously this escape was open only to those Parisians who had some money. The peasants, on the other hand, complained that there was no use going to Paris since they could not get what they needed there.[136] Nor was this situation confined to Paris. Elsewhere in France the city closed itself off from strangers while village merchants found they could not procure what they needed.[137]

Marxist historians explain the failure of the radical revolution and Robespierre's dramatic fall by the assertion that a bourgeois revolution could not meet the demands of the Parisian *sans-culottes*.[138] Though partially enlightening, this explanation seems to me metaphysical and one-sided. It is true that the *sans-culottes* did not rise to Robespierre's defense and that Robespierre himself did not really seek their help during the crisis, though others did try to rouse them. *Sans-culotte* disgust was clearly enough the immediate cause of Robespierre's downfall. His mass support had evaporated. But why did this mass support evaporate? At this point to speak of a conflict between a bourgeois revolution and a more radical one confuses the issue. Robespierre and the Committee of Public Safety had shown themselves quite willing to go well beyond the limits of a revolution on behalf of private property. The trouble was that this policy, though it worked well enough to ensure military victory, brought the countryside into direct conflict with the urban poor and did so in such a way as to aggravate, rather than alleviate, the misery of the city dweller.

Actually the revolutionary *élan* of the *sans-culottes* did not dissipate itself with Robespierre's execution. After Thermidor and the dismounting of the remaining economic controls, the material situation of the Parisian poor, if anything, deteriorated still further. They responded with riots in the spring of 1795, perhaps even more violent than the great revolutionary days of July 14, 1789, August 10, 1792, and May 31, 1793. The mob invaded the hall of the Convention, killed one of its members and hoisted his head on

[136] Mathiez, *Vie chère*, 557.

[137] Lefebvre, *Paysans du Nord*, 652, 672.

[138] Guérin, *Lutte de classes*, II, chap XIV; Soboul, *Sans-culottes*, 1025 – 1035 is more concrete and penetrating.

the tip of a pike.[139] But this popular revolutionary fervor produced no results. The countryside refused to budge on behalf of Paris. Nor did the revolutionary government have any reason to make concessions to radicalism. The king was out of the way, the nobility too it seemed, and revolutionary armies were victorious on the frontiers. Hence the forces of order and property could and did use the army (which here moved against popular insurrection for the first time) to put down the last powerful surge of the *sans-culottes*.[140] The repression that followed inaugurated the White Terror. No matter how radical the city was, it could do nothing without the help of the peasants. The radical revolution was over.

6. *Peasants against the Revolution: The Vendée*

Before examining the general consequences of the radical impulse in the Revolution, it will be useful to pause briefly for an analysis of violent peasant resistance in the famous counterrevolution of the Vendée. Simmering beneath the surface for some little time, it flared into open warfare in March 1793 and lasted off and on until 1796. Weakened imitations occurred again in subsequent political crises, Napoleon's downfall in 1815 and in an ill-conceived Legitimist uprising in 1832. The counterrevolution in the Vendée is a particularly piquant topic today because it is the only major peasant uprising directed against what is loosely called the Left. The rebels fought under the cries of "Long Live the King and Our Good Priests! We want our King, our priests, and the old regime!"[141] It may be significant that in these spontaneous moments they omitted to ask for the return of the nobles, though the peasants accepted noble leaders. In looking a little more closely we see that the paradox of an apparently conservative peasant revolution dissolves. The main thrust of the counterrevolution was anticapitalist, against the merchants and manufacturers in nearby towns and those scattered through the heart of the Vendée itself. In its violent rejection of intruding capitalism, the counterrevolution of the Ven-

[139] Guérin, *Lutte de classes*, II, 330–331.

[140] Guérin, *Lutte de classes*, II, 331–338. Lefebvre, *Révolution française*, 426–428.

[141] Tilly, *Vendée*, 317.

dée resembles the great peasant upheavals that were the main popular force breaking apart the old regimes of Russia and China before
the communist victories of the twentieth century.

Naturally there were features specific to France and to an age
before Marxist anticapitalist movements had arisen. As we have
just seen, anticapitalism was a strong force in the French countryside. What factors permitted and encouraged it to break out here in
the form of an actual counterrevolution?

In order to find the answer to this question two scholars have
studied intensively the ways in which French society in the Vendée
differed from that in the adjacent areas that adhered to the main
current of the Revolution.[142] Their researches have established very
convincingly that differences existed. The counterrevolutionary
area was one where commercial agriculture had not penetrated.
Peasants lived not in villages surrounded by open fields laid out in
characteristic strips but on isolated individual farms or in scattered
hamlets, farming plots of land enclosed by hedges. Agricultural
techniques were stagnant. Absentee nobles owned more than half
of the land. In the adjacent "Patriot" and revolutionary areas, commercial influences were strong but prevailed alongside the ancient
system of cluster villages and open fields. The nobles were less influential but more numerous.

With the information that is now available it would be possible to proceed to draw a reasonably complete portrait of society
in the Vendée and the way it differed from surrounding areas loyal
to the Revolution. But do these differences in social structure provide an answer to our question? On this score I have serious doubts.
They would if the literature demonstrated that there was some kind
of conflict inherent in their relationship to each other. For example,
if there were evidence to indicate that the more commercial area
needed constantly increasing amounts of land and therefore encroached on the Vendée, it would be easy to believe that sooner or

[142] Tilly, *Vendée*, and Bois, *Paysans de l'Ouest*. Tilly's book concentrates on differences between counterrevolutionary and Patriot areas in
southern Anjou; that by Bois on corresponding differences in the *département* of the Sarthe. Both represent a convergence of historical and sociological approaches.

later there would have been a very severe struggle. But those who have studied the problem do not really attempt to make this type of argument. What the literature does show is the existence of differences and the fact of conflict. The link between these two, the connection between specific forms of society and the political fact of a counterrevolutionary outburst, is obscure, at least to me.[143] In the next chapter we shall encounter a similar problem on a larger scale when we try to grasp the connection between plantation slavery and industrial capitalism in the American Civil War. By themselves social and economic differences never explain conflict.

In the case of the Vendée, general reflection readily suggests two possible connections between social trends in the area and the counterrevolutionary upsurge. It is natural to suspect that the burden of the nobility upon the peasantry might have been substantially lighter in this part of France. Similarly one might suspect that the growth of trade and manufacturing, either in the Vendée itself or in neighboring areas that might have somehow encroached on it, could have gradually taken place in this context in a way that rendered the townsmen peculiarly oppressive and offensive to the underlying population. Neither hypothesis finds much support in the evidence. Indeed the evidence runs mostly the other way.

Since all the sources stress the isolation of the Vendée, its remoteness and inaccessibility to the main forces that were modernizing France, the monarchy and commercial currents, the general conception of commercial permeation and consequent social discontent rapidly seems unpromising. There was, to be sure, a textile industry scattered through towns in the heart of the Vendée and engaged in making fine linens for markets outside the area. In the years before 1789 there was a severe depression in textiles that hit

[143] Bois, *Paysans de l'Ouest* (in Book III) tries much more explicitly than Tilly to connect social differences with political behavior. Nevertheless just what precise political consequences arose from the "personnalité sociale de la paysannerie" remains puzzling. Here and elsewhere I have no intention of playing the cheap trick of just poking logical holes in the results of hardworking investigators. The real use of other people's research (as opposed to merely summarizing and reproducing it) sooner or later amounts to asking questions that go beyond their explicit answers. Their hard work is what makes it possible to perceive these questions.

the weavers hard. There are clues suggesting that some weavers therefore became vehemently antibourgeois. However, the evidence about the weavers is ambiguous and contradictory.[144] Furthermore their connection with the peasants, the mass of the population, was almost nonexistent. Unlike other parts of France, the peasants of the Vendée did not take up artisan occupations to supplement their earnings. A man was either a peasant or a weaver. By and large the commercial economy, such as it was, existed alongside the rural one without having much of any contact with it. To speak of a bourgeois exploitation of the countryside for this area would stretch the evidence beyond all recognition. At most there was a certain amount of acquisition of land by prosperous bourgeois families in the towns. In some parts of the Vendée the acquisition was indeed considerable.[145] On the other hand, this process went on in many parts of France without generating a counterrevolution. All in all, the relationship between the townsmen and the peasants prior to the outbreak of the Revolution yields very little that accounts for the bloody events of 1793. Those that come afterward are another story.

The weight of the seigneurial regime on the peasants is more difficult to assess. In this part of France the nobles owned a great deal of the land — in the heartland of the counterrevolution, the lion's share, around sixty percent.[146] Most of the nobles were absentees. Modern research has demolished the notion that loyalty to the aristocrats who lived in their midst, sharing their rustic life, moved the peasants to raise the flag of counterrevolution.[147] The income of the nobility came from leasing out their land to the peasants. Many nobles hired full-time intermediaries who were bourgeois. (It is hardly likely that this situation could have been the cause of an especially virulent hostility to the bourgeoisie because it existed in many other parts of France.) Whether rents increased in the latter years of the *ancien régime* is unclear. Though the ab-

[144] See Tilly, *Vendée*, 136–137, 219–224; Bois, *Paysans de l'Ouest*, 620–621.

[145] Tilly, *Vendée*, 54, 55, 71, 81, 144; Bois, *Paysans de l'Ouest*, 628–629.

[146] Tilly, *Vendée*, 74–75.

[147] Tilly, *Vendée*, 77, 119–120.

sentee nobles are said to have been mainly interested in a fixed income, it is difficult to see why they should have been less exposed to the temptations of conspicuous consumption than other absentees. There are also some signs of a seigneurial reaction and a general tightening up toward the end.[148]

One piece of evidence might indicate that the burden was lighter: there are in the *cahiers* of 1789 rather fewer complaints about strictly "feudal" questions from the counterrevolutionary areas than from neighboring ones. On the other hand, as Tilly is careful to point out, this fact merely means that groups critical of noble privilege carried little weight in the public deliberations that led up to the drafting of the *cahiers*. In other words, critical voices might have been unwilling to speak up under the long shadow of the lord and his agents. Furthermore there *was* a substantial body of criticism, and, on other closely related aspects of the *ancien régime*, the *cahiers* fail to reveal any very distinctive lack of local grievances. Nearly all the standard complaints turned up.[149]

So far there is very little to suggest that agrarian relationships were any easier on the peasants in the counterrevolutionary areas, at least in the matter of the strictly economic burden. As we have noted above, one major alleged difference often stressed by older authors — the supposed residence of the nobility among the peasants and the sharing of a common cultural outlook — has turned out to be a myth. There was nevertheless one aspect of agrarian relationships that was sufficiently distinctive in the counterrevolutionary area to make it a worthwhile candidate for bearing a substantial part of the explanatory load.

In contrast to the adjacent Patriot countryside, where the peasants lived in good-sized villages and farmed open fields laid out in strips, the core of the counterrevolutionary territory was a land of enclosures. When and why enclosure took place does not appear in the literature I have examined, though it is clear that the system of separate farms had been part of the established order for as long as anyone could remember by the time the Revolution broke out. Peasants rented farms from the nobility, in size generally of twenty

[148] Tilly, *Vendée*, 122 – 123, 125; 131.
[149] Tilly, *Vendée*, 177 – 183.

to forty hectares, rather large by French standards, though there
were smaller units too. Rye for subsistence was generally the main
crop. The leases ran for periods of five, seven, or nine years. Despite the fact that they were renters, not owners, the larger farmers, those who could be expected to set the political tone in the
countryside, were able to renew quite easily. Often they held the
same land in their family for generations.[150]

The political meaning of this fact, I would suggest, is that the
leading peasants in the areas that were to become counterrevolutionary already had some of the major benefits of private property
in land. They were not subject to the collective decisions of the
village about the times of ploughing, sowing, and harvesting and of
turning the cattle into the fields after the harvest had been gathered
up. These decisions the occupying farmer could make for himself.
And, if a good tenant, he could pass the land to the next generation.
The stubborn individualism and independence of the Vendée peasant is probably not just a literary stereotype, since it had strong
roots in the social order of the countryside, with its near-private
property and widely scattered homes. In many instances a man
would not see his neighbors for long stretches of time.[151] If a revolutionary wave on behalf of unfettered private property came upon
these peasants from the outside in such a way as to mean no more
rents for the nobles, it is not unreasonable to suggest that they
would have welcomed it. But what else could they expect from
such a revolution? Beneath them, it is worth noticing, there was no
land-hungry near-proletariat of agricultural laborers to help propel
the revolution leftward once it arrived.[152] On the other hand, what
might be expected to happen if the Revolution failed to abolish
rents and took more taxes out of the peasants than had been the
case under the old order? What if the Revolution promoted a substantial bourgeois land grab? Finally, what if the Revolution came
as a wholesale attack on peasant society?

These are the things that *did* happen.

Rents were a "bourgeois" form of property and continued to

[150] Tilly, *Vendée*, 67–68, 114–115, 121, 125.
[151] Cf Bois, *Paysans de l'Ouest*, 610–617.
[152] Tilly, *Vendée*, 79.

be exacted up to the counterrevolution, and perhaps later. When the value of the *assignat* fell, the landlords took their rents in kind and may thereby have increased them. The dismounting of more strictly "feudal" obligations does not seem to have helped the peasants. When the tithe was abolished, landlords simply upped their rents by the corresponding amount.[153] The revolutionary government exacted much more in taxes than the *ancien régime* had. In theory landlords were to absorb this burden; there are indications that in practice they put it onto the tenants.[154] Revolutionary tax policy, however, probably was not decisive, since roughly the same thing occurred in other parts of France. What mattered most in the specific conditions of the Vendée was the attack on the clergy because it was part of a general offensive: economic, political, and social at once.

One phase of the offensive was the forced reorganization of local government in the Vendée during 1790. The main effect was to install a new elected official, the mayor, as spokesman for the local community, the commune. In many instances the inhabitants responded in a revealing fashion by electing the *curé* as mayor. The *curé* was the "natural" leader in the Vendée because he stood at the center of the relatively few networks of cooperation that existed in this society of isolated farmhouses and scattered hamlets. Religious affairs provided the more important occasions when the peasants came together in the Vendée, a situation in sharp contrast with that prevailing in the ordinary village where peasants rubbed elbows daily. Almost every formal organization a countryman could belong to — school, brotherhood, vestry, charity, and of course the church itself — was religious. What money the seigneur gave for good works, the *curé* administered. He was essentially, even into the early revolutionary period, the master of the commune's internal affairs.[155] To invoke the special religious sentiments of the peasants in the Vendée to explain the fact that they followed their *curés* into the counterrevolution is to look at the situation the

---

[153] Bois, *Paysans de l'Ouest*, 628, 633; Tilly, *Vendée*, 201.
[154] Bois, *Paysans de l'Ouest*, 632–633.
[155] Tilly, *Vendée*, 103–110, 155; Bois, *Paysans de l'Ouest*, 614–615.

wrong way around. Very likely these sentiments were stronger here. But if they were, what could have kept them alive other than the fact that the *curé* played a special role in this distinctive rural society, that he did things a good many countrymen wanted done for rather obvious reasons? An attack on the *curé* was an attack on the linchpin of rural society.

The main revolutionary offensive came in the form of the seizure of church properties and the demand that priests should swear their loyalty to the new government of France in the Civil Constitution of the Clergy. In this part of France the effects began to be felt in 1790, that is, simultaneously with the attack on the communes. The sale of church properties led to a very substantial land grab by the bourgeoisie. Wealthier peasants made a try for some properties and lost out. A number of the buyers were not outsiders but local merchants, notaries, and officials, those responsible for translating the general reforms of the Revolution into changes in their rural communities.[156] Important as the land grab was, there is no reason to believe that it was decisive. The *curé* in the heart of the Vendée, though a man of substance, generally lived from tithes alone.[157] Hence it is unlikely that much visible or accessible land disappeared from under the eyes of the peasants.

The key measure was the demand that the *curé* take an oath of loyalty to the revolutionary government and the effort to replace him by an outsider if he refused. The oath was administered in 1791 in this area. Practically all the clergy refused in what were to be the main centers of the counterrevolution, while in adjacent Patriot areas the refusal was less than half.[158] New priests who had taken the oath and were sent in from the outside soon found themselves at best isolated in the midst of a hostile population, at worst in serious physical danger. Meanwhile the population flocked to clandestine masses, some in closed and abandoned churches, but more and more often in barns and open fields, any place where a local Patriot

[156] Tilly, *Vendée*, 232, also 206, 211 – 212; and Bois, *Paysans de l'Ouest*, 650. In the area studied by Bois the bourgeois *outsiders* were the victors in the struggle for these properties.

[157] Tilly, *Vendée*, 105.

[158] Maps in Tilly, *Vendée*, 238, 240.

could not find them. Clandestine services meant enthusiastic ones.[159] Here was the break with prevailing legality. At one stroke, the society that had been the world that was taken for granted passed over intact to the world that was counterrevolution. The attempt to enforce conscription in 1793 did no more than toss the sparks into a situation already explosive. We have reached the end of our tale.

In revolutions, as well as counterrevolutions and civil wars, there comes a crucial point when people suddenly realize that they have irrevocably broken with the world they have known and accepted all their lives. For different classes and individuals this momentary flash of a new and frightening truth will come at successive points in the collapse of the prevailing system. There are also unique moments and decisions — the storming of a palace, the beheading of a king, and in reverse the overthrow of a revolutionary dictator — after which there is no return. Through these acts a new crime becomes the basis öf a new legality. Huge sections of the population become part of a new social order.

These features the counterrevolution in the Vendée shared with other violent social upheavals, even if often on the minute scale of the parish or the commune. What seems rather more unique is the simple transformation of the prevailing social organization in the countryside from being the legal and accepted order to being the basis of rebellion. I detect no sign in the literature of the breakdown of the older society into masses of wandering individuals, of revolutionary crowds, and the corresponding forging of new revolutionary organizations and new forms of solidarity, processes that the communists in a later age were to learn by trial and error to turn to their purposes. Nevertheless in many of its features the counterrevolution of the Vendée foreshadows what was to happen as capitalism impinged on premodern peasant societies. An account of the actual fighting we may forego, since what happened beforehand contains the main lessons for our purposes. Suffice it to say that the repression of the counterrevolution was the bloodiest domestic act in the French revolutionary drama. Let us turn instead to a general assessment of revolutionary terror,

[159] Tilly, *Vendée,* 252–257.

in which vengeance taken by peasants and upon peasants claimed a huge and tragic toll.

7. Social Consequences of Revolutionary Terror

The experience of the Terror and the French Revolution in general gave a strong impulse to that very influential current of Western political thought which recoils from political violence in any form. Today many educated people are still likely to think of the Terror as a daemonic outburst of mob violence indiscriminate in its choice of victims, later as the expression of blind hatred and extremism, indeed of a special utopian mentality that lies at the roots of twentieth-century totalitarianism. I shall try to show that this interpretation is a distorted caricature.

Like any caricature, this conception contains some truthful elements without which the resulting image would bear no recognizable relation to reality. As the victims of the September massacres show — mainly poor people who happened to be in jail when the mob burst in — popular resentments could erupt in sudden acts of indiscriminate vengeance. Nevertheless a dispassionate analysis cannot just draw back in horror at this point; it is necessary to perceive the causes. They are clear enough in the aggravating circumstances of the moment and the history of degradation and oppression to which the mass of people at the very bottom of the social order were subject. To express outrage at the September massacres and forget the horrors behind them is to indulge in a partisan trick. In that sense there is no mystery here. In another there is. As we shall see most clearly later, when we come to consider India, severe suffering does not always and necessarily generate revolutionary outbursts, and certainly not a revolutionary situation. That problem must wait. For the moment we may take it that popular desperation and anger were comprehensible reactions to cirmumstances.

For the Terror to become an effective instrument of policy, that is, for it to produce significant political results, the popular impulse had to be brought under some degree of rational and centralized control. This impulse came mainly from the *sans-culottes*. From the very beginning there was more than sheer resentment in the call for the guillotine. It was a protest against the workings of the market that were producing untold misery and a primitive way of forcing rich speculators to disgorge hoarded goods. Though the situation and requirements of the poor peasants paralleled that of the urban poor for a time, the peasants were not at all a significant force behind the organized Terror of 1793 – 1794. Peasant violence did play a decisive part in the French Revolution, especially as a force behind the dismantling of feudal practices, but mainly in the earlier phases.

As matters turned out, the popular and bureaucratic impulses were partially fused and partially contradictory. Essentially what happened was that Robespierre and the Montagne took over a large part of the program of the *sans-culottes,* including the Terror on a massive scale, tried to use it for their own purposes, and in time turned the weapon back against popular forces.[160] By and large the consequences were rational. Detailed researches show that the Terror was mainly used against counterrevolutionary forces and was most severe where the counterrevolution was strongest.[161] Certainly there were exceptions and injustices. But the Terror was not in its major features a case of shedding blood for the insane pleasure of doing so.

Within France counterrevolutionary forces had two distinct geographical bases, the Vendée, and the commercial and port cities of Lyon, Marseilles, Toulon, and Bordeaux. The contrast between these two foci of counterrevolution sheds a revealing light on the

[160] Guérin, *Lutte de classes* tells the story in circumstantial detail.

[161] Greer, *Incidence of the Terror.* The two maps of France used as a frontispiece tell this part of the story with striking clarity. One shows the areas of counterrevolution and invasions, grading the *départements* from areas without dangerous disturbances through those of civil war entailing major military operations. The other map shows the incidence of executions, grading the *départments* from those with less than ten to those with more than one hundred. With the understandable exception of Paris, the connection is extremely close. This connection between counterrevolution and the incidence of executions constitutes in my view strong evidence against Greer's central thesis that the split in French society was perpendicular and that the Terror was not an instrument of class warfare, a matter discussed more fully in the *Appendix.*

social character of the Revolution itself. The Vendée was the part of France where commercial and modern influences had penetrated least; the southern cities, the area where they had penetrated furthest. In the Vendée, as might be expected, the Terror claimed the largest number of victims. The situation in the south was almost exactly the opposite, especially in Lyon where the silk industry had proceeded to the point of crippling the artisans and producing an incipient modern proletariat. Throughout much of southern France the wealthier commercial element in the towns showed a strong inclination to join hands with the nobility and the clergy, who hoped to use the Gironde and the federalist movement as an entering wedge for the restoration of the monarchy. As the Revolution became more radical, a seesaw struggle developed in several of the cities. Lyon, Marseilles, Toulon, and Bordeaux fell under the control of the wealthier element in alliance with the privileged orders and turned against the Revolution. Recapture by the Revolution took different forms, depending on local circumstances and personalities. It proceeded peacefully in Bordeaux; in Lyon there was severe fighting and later one of the more bloody repressions of the terror.[162] The executions in the Vendée and the port cities were, however, only a relatively small aspect of the red terror as a whole. Less than 17,000 victims died in executions carried out by the revolutionary authorities. How many died in prison or otherwise, and were also real victims of the Revolution we do not know. Greer estimates that 35,000 to 40,000 persons in all may have lost their lives as a direct result of revolutionary repression, a figure that Lefebvre regards as quite a reasonable guess, though it is little more than that.[163] That this blood bath had its tragic and unjust aspects no serious thinker will deny. Yet in assessing it, one has to keep in mind the repressive aspects of the social order to which it was a response. The prevailing order of society always grinds out its tragic toll of unnecessary death year after year. It would be enlight-

[162] See Greer, *Incidence of the Terror*, 7, 101–103, 30, 36, 120. Greer draws on a series of valuable local monographs on the economy and social structure.

[163] Greer, *Incidence of the Terror*, 26–27, 37; Lefebvre, *Révolution française*, 404–405.

ening to calculate the death rate of the *ancien régime* from such factors as preventable starvation and injustice if that were at all possible. Offhand it seems very unlikely that this would be very much below the proportion of .0016 which Greer's figure of 40,000 yields when set against an estimated population of around twenty-four million, the lowest one that Greer cites.[164] I think it would be vastly higher. The figures themselves are open to dispute. The conclusion to which they point is less so: to dwell on the horrors of revolutionary violence while forgetting that of "normal" times is merely partisan hypocrisy.

Still the reader who feels that there is something inhuman in this balancing of grim statistics is by no means altogether mistaken. Even if they were perfect they would not answer some of the most important and difficult questions. Was the terror and bloodshed of the Revolution necessary? What if anything did it accomplish? We may close with a few comments on these points.

The radical revolution was an integral part of the revolution on behalf of private property and the rights of man since it was in very substantial measure a negative response to the bourgeois revolution. The anticapitalist elements in the *sans-culottes'* revolution and the protests of the poorer peasants were a reaction to the hardships arising out of the steady spread of capitalist features into the economy during the latter phase of the *ancien régime* and the Revolution itself. To regard the radicals as an extremist band, an excrescence on the liberal and bourgeois revolution, is to fly in the face of this evidence. The one was impossible without the other. It is also quite clear that the bourgeois revolution would not have gone as far as it did without pressure from the radicals. There were several occasions, as we have seen, when the conservatives of the moment tried to stop the Revolution.

That they failed is the real tragedy, the democratic opponent of violence might be quick to point out. Had they succeeded, to continue the argument for moderation, had the French Revolution ended in the kind of compromise achieved by the English revolutionary impulse by 1689, democracy could have gradually established itself in roughly the same way as in England, sparing France

[164] Greer, *Incidence of the Terror*, 109.

unnecessary bloodshed and subsequent upheavals. Even if ultimately unprovable, the thesis deserves a serious answer. The main argument against it has already been given in considerable detail: the underlying social structure of France was fundamentally different and hence ruled out the kind of peaceful transformation — which, we have seen, was actually quite far from peaceful — that England experienced in the eighteenth and nineteenth centuries.

In a word, it is very difficult to deny that if France were to enter the modern world through the democratic door she had to pass through the fires of the Revolution, including its violent and radical aspects. The connection seems to me, at any rate, about as close as any historical research can ever establish, certain as it is to be debated as long as there are historians of different persuasions. To anyone who accepts such a conclusion it is legitimate to put the second question: what visible contribution to democratic institutions did all this bloodshed and violence make?

One cannot make nearly as strong a case for the contribution of violence to democratic gradualism in the case of the French Revolution as in that of the Puritan Revolution. The Napoleonic Wars by themselves rule out such an interpretation. To mention just one other point, students of twentieth-century France point to the gashes left by the Revolution as a major cause of the instability of French political institutions. Nevertheless certain changes in French society wrought through the Revolution were ultimately favorable to the development of parliamentary democracy.

The Revolution mortally wounded the whole interlocking complex of aristocratic privilege: monarchy, landed aristocracy, and seigneurial rights, a complex that constituted the essence of the *ancien régime*. It did so in the name of private property and equality before the law. To deny that the predominant thrust and chief consequences of the Revolution were bourgeois and capitalist is to engage in a trivial quibble. What is questionable in the view that it was a bourgeois revolution is any argument to the effect that a relatively solid group of commercial and industrial interests had achieved enough economic power in the last quarter of the eighteenth century to throw off feudal shackles mainly by its own efforts in order to initiate a period of industrial expansion. Put this way, the thesis greatly overemphasizes the independent influence of such interests. That the ultimate outcome of all the forces at work was a victory for an economic system of private property and a political system based upon equality before the law, the essential features in Western parliamentary democracies, and that the Revolution was a crucial feature in this general development, are truths undeniable even if they are familiar.

During the Restoration, it is quite true, a Bourbon king reigned for another decade and a half, from 1815 to 1830, and the old landed aristocracy regained temporarily a great deal of what it had lost. Some scholars estimate that it recovered about half the landed property lost in the Revolution. Certainly it was the dominant, indeed the only, political group in France. That indeed was its undoing. The failure to share power with the *haute bourgeoisie*, or to make this class its ally instead of its enemy, was an important cause of the Revolution of 1830. At this point the old aristocracy disappeared from the political arena as a coherent and effective political group, even if it retained considerable social prestige for a long time afterward.[165]

From the standpoint of the questions raised in this book, the destruction of the political power of the landed aristocracy constitutes the most significant process at work in the course of French modernization. Ultimately it is largely though not completely traceable to the response of the French nobility to the problems of agriculture in an increasingly commercial society. Royal absolutism was able to tame and control an aristocracy that had difficulty in establishing an independent economic base. The Revolution finished the work of the Bourbons, as de Tocqueville recognized long ago. The consequence was the destruction of one of the indispensable social bases of right-wing authoritarian regimes that show a strong tendency to culminate in fascism under the impact of advanced industry. In this very broad perspective the French Revolution appears as a partial substitute or historical alternative to the development of commercial agriculture free of preindustrial traits. Where the impulse behind the bourgeois revolution has been weak or abortive, the consequences have been in other major countries either fascism

[165] See Lhomme, *Grande bourgeoisie,* 17 – 27.

or communism. By destroying one of the major causes of such an outcome, the survival of a landed aristocracy into modern times, and doing so in the late eighteenth century, the French Revolution made a major contribution to the development of parliamentary democracy in France.

Thus, on the score of the landed aristocracy, the contribution of the Revolution seems to have been favorable and even decisive. But the very same processes that were destroying the landed aristocracy were also creating small-peasant property. In this respect the consequences were much more ambiguous. Lefebvre reminds us that the sale of lands confiscated from the church and the *émigrés* was *not* the source of peasant property, which reaches much further back in French history. Actually the bourgeoisie were by and large the main ones to profit by the sales, though there were locally important increases in peasant property.[166] Simultaneously the peasant aristocracy was a major beneficiary of the Revolution. However, the experience of requisitioning, the attempt to place ceilings on the prices of grain, and the encouragement given to small holders and agricultural workers during the radical phase of the Revolution, turned the upper stratum of the peasants decisively against the Republic. This legacy was a baneful one for a long time.[167]

About peasant society during the nineteenth and even the twentieth centuries there is less solid information than for the eighteenth century.[168] Still the following generalizations command considerable support. First, the influential peasants cared next to nothing about democracy as such. They wanted effective guarantees for property and social position in their own villages. Concretely these demands meant guarantees against any serious challenge to property acquired through the *vente des biens nationaux* from aristocratic sources or any radical notions that hinted at a redistribution

[166] Lefebvre, *Etudes*, 232, 237, 239, 242.

[167] Lefebvre, *Paysans du Nord*, 911 – 912, 915 – 916.

[168] The generalizations that follow are based mainly on Lefebvre's writings and on Augé-Laribé, *Politique agricole;* Hunter, *Peasantry and Crisis in France;* and two illuminating articles by Wright, "Agrarian Syndicalism in Postwar France" and "Catholics and Peasantry in France." For recent reflections on this topic see Wright, *Rural Revolution in France.*

of property. In the second place, the continued advance of capitalist industry tended to undermine small peasant property, which was
at a disadvantage in producing for the market. Peasant spokesmen
often complained that the terms of trade were against them. For
this combination of reasons peasant property has ambiguous consequences: it appears as a threat to big property — in both its capitalist
and precapitalist aristocratic forms — and as an outer rampart pro-
tecting such property. In the twentieth century the ambiguity appears most sharply where peasants support the French Communist
Party.

Actually such a paradox is more apparent than real. As a precapitalist group, peasants frequently display strong anticapitalist
tendencies. In the course of the inquiry I shall try to indicate the
conditions under which such tendencies take reactionary or revolutionary forms.

8. Recapitulation

The central message that I have been able to discern in the
origins, course, and consequences of the Revolution is that the
violent destruction of the *ancien régime* was a crucial step *for
France* on the long road toward democracy. It is necessary to un-
derscore the point that the step was crucial for France, where the
obstacles democracy faced were different from those in England.
French society did not and probably could not generate a parliament of landlords with bourgeois overtones, in the English manner.
Previous trends in France had made the upper classes into an enemy
of liberal democracy, not part of democracy's entering wedge.
Hence, if democracy were to triumph in France, certain institutions
would have to be gotten out of the way. To assert that such was
the connection, implies no claim that French history was inevitably
bound to culminate in liberal democracy or that the Revolution was
in any sense inevitable. Instead there are grounds for holding that
the whole process could have worked itself out very differently and
that, for this very reason, the Revolution was all the more decisive.

Under the conditions of royal absolutism the French landed
upper classes adapted to the gradual intrusion of capitalism by put-

ting greater pressure on the peasants, meanwhile leaving them in a situation approaching *de facto* ownership. Up until about the middle of the eighteenth century the modernization of French society took place through the crown. As part of this process there grew up a fusion between nobility and bourgeoisie quite different from that in England. This fusion took place through the monarchy rather than in opposition to it and resulted, to speak in what may be here a useful if inaccurate shorthand, in the "feudalization" of a considerable section of the bourgeoisie, rather than the other way around. The eventual result was to limit very severely the crown's freedom of action, its ability to decide what sectors in society were to bear what burdens. This limitation, accentuated by Louis XVI's defects of character, I would suggest, was the main factor that brought on the Revolution, rather than any extraordinarily severe conflict of interests along class or group lines. Without the Revolution, this fusion of nobility and bourgeoisie might have continued and carried France forward into a form of conservative modernization from above, similar in its main outlines to what took place in Germany and Japan.

But the Revolution did prevent all that. It was not a bourgeois revolution in the restricted sense of the seizure of political power by a bourgeoisie that already had won the commanding heights of economic power. There was a group of this variety within the ranks of the bourgeoisie, but the previous history of royal absolutism had prevented its growing strong enough to accomplish much on its own. Instead, parts of the bourgeoisie rose toward power on the backs of radical movements within the urban plebs, released by the collapse of order and the monarchy. These radical forces also prevented the Revolution from turning backward or halting at a point suitable to such sections of the bourgeoisie. Meanwhile the peasants, mainly the upper layer at this point, had taken advantage of the situation to force the dismounting of the seigneurial system, the main achievement of the Revolution. For a time rural and urban radicalism, which shared a contradictory mixture of small-property and backward-looking collectivist aims, could work together, as they did up to and through the most radical phases of the Revolution. But the need to get food to the poorer townsmen and the

Revolutionary armies ran up against the interests of the more well-to-do peasants. Increasing resistance from the peasants deprived the Parisian *sans-culottes* of food, thereby removed Robespierre's popular support, and brought the radical revolution to a halt. The *sans-culottes* made the bourgeois Revolution; the peasants determined just how far it could go. The incompleteness of the Revolution on the other hand, an incompleteness quite largely traceable to the structure of French society in the late eighteenth century, meant that it would be a long time before a full-blown capitalist democracy could establish itself in French society.

CHAPTER THREE

The American Civil War:
The Last Capitalist Revolution

1. Plantation and Factory: An Inevitable Conflict?

THE MAIN DIFFERENCES between the American route to modern capitalist democracy and those followed by England and France stem from America's later start. The United States did not face the problem of dismounting a complex and well-established agrarian society of either the feudal or the bureaucratic forms. From the very beginning commercial agriculture was important, as in the Virginian tobacco plantations, and rapidly became dominant as the country was settled. The political struggles between a precommercial landed aristocracy and a monarch were not part of American history. Nor has American society ever had a massive class of peasants comparable to those in Europe and Asia.[1] For these reasons one may argue that American history contains no revolution comparable to the Puritan and French Revolutions nor, of course, the Russian and Chinese twentieth-century revolutions. Still there have been two great armed upheavals in our history, the American Revo-

---

[1] Like many such terms it is impossible to define the word peasantry with absolute precision because distinctions are blurred at the edges in social reality itself. A previous history of subordination to a landed upper class recognized and enforced in the laws, which, however, need not always prohibit movement out of this class, sharp cultural distinctions, and a considerable degree of *de facto* possession of the land, constitute the main distinguishing features of a peasantry. Hence Negro sharecroppers in the present-day South could be legitimately regarded as a class of peasants in American society.

lution and the Civil War, the latter one of the bloodiest conflicts in modern history up to that time. Quite obviously, both have been significant elements in the way the United States became the world's leading industrial capitalist democracy by the middle of the twentieth century. The Civil War is commonly taken to mark a violent dividing point between the agrarian and industrial epochs in American history. Hence in this chapter I shall discuss its causes and consequences from the standpoint of whether or not it was a violent breakthrough against an older social structure, leading to the establishment of political democracy, and on this score comparable to the Puritan and French Revolutions. More generally I hope to show where it belongs in the genetic sequence of major historical upheavals that we can begin arbitrarily with the sixteenth-century peasant wars in Germany, that continues through the Puritan, French, and Russian Revolutions, to culminate in the Chinese Revolution and the struggles of our own time.

The conclusion, reached after much uncertainty, amounts to the statement that the American Civil War was the last revolutionary offensive on the part of what one may legitimately call urban or bourgeois capitalist democracy. Plantation slavery in the South, it is well to add right away, was not an economic fetter upon industrial capitalism. If anything, the reverse may have been true; it helped to promote American industrial growth in the early stages. But slavery was an obstacle to a political and social democracy. There are ambiguities in this interpretation. Those that stem from the character of the evidence are best discussed as the analysis proceeds. Others lie deeper and, as I shall try to show at the end of the chapter, would not disappear no matter what evidence came to light.

Aside from questions of space and time at the reader's disposal as well as the author's, there are objective reasons for passing over the American Revolution with but a few brief comments. Since it did not result in any fundamental changes in the structure of society, there are grounds for asking whether it deserves to be called a revolution at all. At bottom it was a fight between commercial interests in England and America, though certainly more elevated issues played a part as well. The claim that America has had an anticolonial revolution may be good propaganda, but it is bad history and bad sociology. The distinguishing characteristic of twentieth-century anticolonial revolutions is the effort to establish a new form of society with substantial socialist elements. Throwing off the foreign yoke is a means to achieve this end. What radical currents there were in the American Revolution were for the most part unable to break through to the surface. Its main effect was to promote unification of the colonies into a single political unit and the separation of this unit from England.

The American Revolution can be trotted out from time to time as a good example of the American (or sometimes Anglo-Saxon) genius for compromise and conciliation. For this, the Civil War will not do; it cuts a bloody gash across the whole record. Why did it happen? Why did our vaunted capacity for settling our differences fail us at this point? Like the problem of human evil and the fall of Rome for Saint Augustine, the question has long possessed a deep fascination for American historians. An anxious if understandable concern seems to underlie much of the discussion. For some time, it often took the form of whether or not the war was avoidable. The present generation of historians has begun to show impatience with this way of putting the problem. To many the question seems merely a semantic one, since if either side had been willing to submit without fighting there would have been no war.[2] To call it a semantic problem dodges the real issue: why was there an unwillingness to submit on either side or both?

It may be helpful to put the question in less psychological terms. Was there in some objective sense a mortal conflict between the societies of the North and the South? The full meaning of this question will emerge more clearly from trying to answer it on the

[2] Donald in the preface to Randall and Donald, *Civil War*, vi. Fully documented and with an excellent bibliography, this general survey provides a most helpful guide to the present state of historical opinion. An enlightening general survey of past discussions may be found in Beale, "Causes of the Civil War" (1946). Stampp, *Causes of the Civil War* (1959), provides an illuminating collection of contemporary and modern historical writings about the reasons for the war. In his editorial preface (p. vi) Stampp repeats Beale's observation, made more than a dozen years before, that the debate remains inconclusive while modern historians often merely repeat partisan themes set out at the time.

basis of specific facts than through theoretical discussion at this point. Essentially we are asking whether the institutional requirements for operating a plantation economy based on slavery clashed seriously at any point with the corresponding requirements for operating a capitalist industrial system. I assume that, in principle at any rate, it is possible to discover what these requirements really were in the same objective sense that a biologist can discover for any living organism the conditions necessary for reproduction and survival, such as specific kinds of nourishment, amounts of moisture, and the like. It should also be clear that the requirements or structural imperatives for plantation slavery and early industrial capitalism extend far beyond economic arrangements as such and certainly into the area of political institutions. Slave societies do not have the same political forms as those based on free labor. But, to return to our central question, is that any reason why they have to fight?

One might start with a general notion to the effect that there is an inherent conflict between slavery and the capitalist system of formally free wage labor. Though this turns out to be a crucial part of the story, it will not do as a general proposition from which the Civil War can be derived as an instance. As will appear shortly, cotton produced by slave labor played a decisive role in the growth not only of American capitalism but of English capitalism too. Capitalists had no objection to obtaining goods produced by slavery as long as a profit could be made by working them up and reselling them. From a strictly economic standpoint, wage labor and plantation slavery contain as much of a potential for trading and complementary political relationships as for conflict. We can answer our question with a provisional negative: there is no abstract general reason why the North and South had to fight. Special historical circumstances, in other words, had to be present in order to prevent agreement between an agrarian society based on unfree labor and a rising industrial capitalism.

For clues as to what these circumstances might have been, it is helpful to glance at a case where there was an agreement between these two types of subsocieties within a larger political unit. If we know what makes an agreement possible, we also know something about circumstances that might make it impossible. Once again the German record is helpful and suggestive. Nineteenth-century German history demonstrates quite clearly that advanced industry can get along very well with a form of agriculture that has a highly repressive system of labor. To be sure, the German Junker was not quite a slave owner. And Germany was not the United States. But where precisely did the decisive differences lie? The Junkers managed to draw the independent peasants under their wing and to form an alliance with sections of big industry that were happy to receive their assistance in order to keep the industrial workers in their place with a combination of repression and paternalism. The consequence in the long run was fatal to democracy in Germany.

German experience suggests that, if the conflict between North and South had been compromised, the compromise would have been at the expense of subsequent democratic development in the United States, a possibility that, so far as I am aware, no revisionist historian .has explored. It also tells us where we might look with profit. Why did Northern capitalists have no need of Southern "Junkers" in order to establish and strengthen industrial capitalism in the United States? Were political and economic links missing in the United States that existed in Germany? Were there other and different groups in American society, such as independent farmers, in the place of peasants? Where and how were the main groups aligned in the American situation? It is time now to examine the American scene more closely.

2. *Three Forms of American Capitalist Growth*

By 1860 the United States had developed three quite different forms of society in different parts of the country: the cotton-growing South; the West, a land of free farmers; and the rapidly industrializing Northeast.

The lines of cleavage and cooperation had by no means always run in these directions. To be sure, from the days of Hamilton and Jefferson there had been a tug-of-war between agrarians and urban commercial and financial interests. The expansion of the country westward made it seem for a moment, under President Jackson in the 1830s, that the principles of agrarian democracy, in practice an absolute minimum of central authority and a tendency to favor debtors over creditors, had won a permanent victory over those of Alexander Hamilton. Even in Jackson's own time, however, agrarian democracy had severe difficulties. Two closely related developments were to destroy it: the further growth of industrial capitalism in the Northeast and the establishment of an export market for Southern cotton.

Though the importance of cotton for the South is familiar, its significance for capitalist development as a whole is less well known. Between 1815 and 1860 the cotton trade exercised a decisive influence upon the rate of growth in the American economy. Up until about 1830 it was the most important cause of the growth of manufacturing in this country.[3] While the domestic aspect remained significant, cotton exports became an outstanding feature at about this time.[4] By 1849, sixty-four percent of the cotton crop went abroad, mainly to England.[5] From 1840 to the time of the Civil War, Great Britain drew from the Southern states four-fifths of all her cotton imports.[6] Hence it is clear that the plantation operated by slavery was no anachronistic excrescence on industrial capitalism. It was an integral part of this system and one of its prime motors in the world at large.

In Southern society, the plantation and slave owners were a very small minority. By 1850 there may have been less than 350,-000 slave owners in a total white population of about six million in the slaveholding areas.[7] With their families, the slaveholders numbered perhaps a quarter of the white population at the most. Even within this group, only a small minority owned most of the slaves: a computation for 1860 asserts that only seven percent of the whites owned nearly three-quarters of the black slaves.[8] The best land

[3] North, *Economic Growth*, 67, 167, 189.

[4] North, *Economic Growth*, 194.

[5] Gates, *Farmer's Age*, 152.

[6] Randall and Donald, *Civil War*, 36.

[7] Randall and Donald, *Civil War*, 67.

[8] Cited by Hacker, *Triumph of American Capitalism*, 288. Randall and Donald's figures are close to these.

tended to gravitate into their hands as well as the substance of political control.[9]

This plantation-owning élite shaded off gradually into farmers who worked the land with a few slaves, through large numbers of small property owners without slaves, on down to the poor whites of the back country, whose agriculture was confined to a little lackadaisical digging in forlorn cornpatches. The poor whites were outside of the market economy; many of the smaller farmers were no more than on its periphery.[10] The more well-to-do farmers aspired to owning a few more Negroes and becoming plantation owners on a larger scale. The influence of this middling group may have declined after the Jacksonian era, though there is a whole school of Southern historians that tries to romanticize the yeomen and "plain folk" of the old South as the basis of a democratic social order.[11] That, I believe to be utter rubbish. In all ages and countries, reactionaries, liberals, and radicals have painted their own portraits of small rural folk to suit their own theories. The element of important truth behind this particular notion is that the smaller farmers in the South by and large accepted the political leadership of the big planters. Writers tinged with Marxism claim that this unity within the white caste ran counter to the real economic interests of the smaller farmers and came about only because fear of the Negro solidified the whites. This is possible but dubious. Small property owners in many situations follow the lead of big ones when there is no obvious alternative and when there is some chance of becoming a big property holder.

Since plantation slavery was the dominant fact of Southern life, it becomes necessary to examine the workings of the system to discover if it generated serious frictions with the North. One consideration we can dispose of rapidly. Slavery was almost certainly not on the point of dying out for internal reasons. The thesis is scarcely tenable that the war was "unnecessary" in the sense that its

[9] Gates, *Farmer's Age*, 151, 152.

[10] North, *Economic Growth*, 130.

[11] Owsley, *Plain Folk*, 138 – 142. This study impresses me as folklorish sociology that misses nearly all the relevant political and economic issues.

results would have come about sooner or later anyway by peaceful means and that therefore there was no real conflict. If slavery were to disappear from American society, armed force would be necessary to make it disappear.

On this question the best evidence actually comes from the North, where peaceful emancipation during the Civil War faced nearly insuperable difficulties. Union states that had slavery dragged their feet and expressed all sorts of apprehension when Lincoln tried to introduce a moderate scheme of emancipation with compensation for the former owners. Lincoln had to drop the plan.[12] The Emancipation Proclamation (January 1, 1863), as is well known, excluded slave states in the Union and those areas of the South within Union lines; that is, it emancipated slaves, in the words of a contemporary English observer (Earl Russell, ancestor of Bertrand Russell) only "where the United States authorities cannot exercise any jurisdiction."[13] If peaceful emancipation faced these difficulties in the North, those in the South scarcely require comment.

These considerations point strongly toward the conclusion that slavery was economically profitable. The author of a recent monograph argues cogently that slavery persisted in the South primarily because it was economically profitable. Southern claims that they were losing money on the operation he dismisses as part of the rationalizations through which Southern spokesmen tried to find a higher moral ground for slavery, an early version of the white man's civilizing burden. Ashamed to justify slavery on crude economic grounds, which would have made them resemble money-grubbing Yankees, Southerners preferred to claim that slavery was the natural form of human society, beneficial both to the slave and the master.[14] More recently still, two economists dissatisfied with the evidence upon which previous studies rested, mainly fragmentary and incomplete accounting records from early plantation activities, have tried to find the answer by examining more general

---

[12] Randall and Donald, *Civil War*, 374, 375.
[13] Randall and Donald, *Civil War*, 380 – 381.
[14] Stampp, *Peculiar Institution*, esp chap IX.

statistical information. In order to find out whether slavery was more or less profitable than other enterprises, they have collected statistics about average slave prices, interest rates on prime commercial paper, costs of maintaining slaves, yields per prime field hand, cotton marketing costs, cotton prices, and other relevant facts. Though I am moderately skeptical about the reliability and representative value of the original statistics, their conclusions are in line with other considerations and about as close to reality as we are likely to get in this fashion. They, too, conclude that plantation slavery paid, moreover that it was an efficient system which developed in those regions best suited to the production of cotton and other specialized staples. Meanwhile, less productive areas in the South continued to produce slaves and export the increase to the main regions producing staple crops.[15]

To know that plantation slavery as a whole was a money-making proposition is important but insufficient. There were differences of time and place among the plantation owners that had significant political consequences. By the time the war broke out, plantation slavery had become a feature of the lower South. It had disappeared from the tobacco plantation before 1850 mainly because there were no great advantages to large-scale operations. In Maryland, Kentucky, and Missouri even the term "plantation" had become almost obsolete before the Civil War.[16] Around 1850 really fat pickings were to be had, chiefly in virgin areas; at first such places as Alabama and Mississippi provided such opportunities; after 1840, Texas. Even in virgin lands, the best way to make money was to sell out and move on before the soil gave out.[17]

To the extent that plantation slavery migrated from the South toward the West, it did create a serious political problem. Large parts of the West were still unsettled or sparsely settled. Though cotton growing had obvious limitations of climate and soil, no one could be certain just what the limitations were. If slavery spread,

[15] Conrad and Meyer, "Economics of Slavery," 95–130; see esp 97 for the general thesis.

[16] Nevins, *Ordeal*, I, 423.

[17] Gates, *Farmer's Age*, 143; Gray, *Agriculture in Southern United States*, II, chaps XXXVII, XXXVIII for more detail.

the balance between slave and free states might be upset — something that mattered of course only if the difference between a society with slavery and one without mattered. By 1820 the problem was already acute, though a settlement was reached in the Missouri Compromise, balancing the entry of Missouri as a slave state by that of Maine as a free state. From then on the problem erupted intermittently. Solemn and statesmanlike political bargains hopefully settled the question for good, only to become unstuck after a short while. The issue of slavery in the territories, as partly settled areas that had not yet become states were called, played a major part in bringing on the war. The inherent uncertainty of the situation very likely magnified economic conflicts out of all proportion.

The migratory tendency of the plantation economy was important in other ways as well. As cotton planting declined in the old South, there was some inclination to adapt to the situation by breeding slaves. The extent to which this took place is difficult to determine. But there are at least moderately clear indications that it was not enough to meet the demand. The costs of slaves rose rather steadily from the early 1840s until the outbreak of the war. The price of cotton also tended to rise, but with much more marked fluctuations. After the financial panic of 1857, the price of cotton fell off, while the price of slaves continued to climb steeply.[18] Slaves could not be legally imported, and the blockade seems to have been moderately effective. Together with Southern talk about reopening the slave trade, talk that became fairly vigorous just before the final outbreak of hostilities, such evidence points in the direction of a serious labor shortage facing the plantation system. How serious? That is much harder to tell. Since capitalists are nearly always concerned about the prospect that labor may be short, it will be wise to treat Southern laments on this count with a touch of skepticism. It

[18] See table in Phillips, *Life and Labor*, 177, and the discussion of alleged overcapitalization of the labor force in Conrad and Meyer, "Economics of Slavery," 115 – 118. Even if the plantation owner was not caught in a net of his own making — Phillips's thesis that Conrad and Meyer combat — it seems clear enough, and not denied by these two authors, that many planters did face increasing labor costs. See further, Nevins, *Ordeal*, I, 480, for some contemporary views.

is very doubtful that the plantation system was about to expire from Northern economic strangulation.

So far the argument that the requirements of the plantation economy were a source of economic conflict with the industrial North does not turn out to be very persuasive. After all, was not the plantation owner just another capitalist? Nevins observes correctly: "A great plantation was as difficult to operate as a complicated modern factory, which in important respects it resembled. Hit-or-miss methods could not be tolerated; endless planning and anxious care were demanded."[19] Might it not therefore have been perfectly possible for the plantation owner to get along with his equally calculating capitalist brethren in the North? In my estimation it would have been quite possible had strictly rational economic calculations been the only issue. But, *pace* Max Weber, the rational and calculating outlook, the viewing of the world in terms of accounts and balances, can exist in a wide variety of societies, some of which may fight one another over other issues.[20] As we have already noticed in examining the French nobility, this type of outlook is not by itself enough to generate an industrial revolution. Certainly it did not in the South, where urban growth, outside of a few major entrepôts such as New Orleans and Charleston, remained far behind that in the rest of the country. The South had a capitalist civilization, then, but hardly a bourgeois one. Certainly it was not based on town life. And, instead of challenging the notion of status based on birth, as did the European bourgeoisie when they challenged the right of aristocracies to rule, Southern planters took over the defense of hereditary privilege. Here was a real difference and a real issue.

The notion that all men were created equal contradicted the facts of daily experience for most Southerners, facts that they had themselves created for good and sufficient reasons. Under the pressure of Northern criticism and in the face of worldwide trends

[19] *Ordeal*, I, 438.

[20] Nevin's description of the plantation is strikingly similar to the rational methods of calculation that prevailed, even without the use of writing, on the medieval English manor. See the vivid description in Bennett, *Life on the English Manor*, 186–192, esp 191.

away from slavery, Southerners generated a whole series of doctrinal defenses for the system. Bourgeois conceptions of freedom,
those of the American and the French Revolutions, became dangerously subversive doctrines to the South, because they struck at the
key nerve of the Southern system, property in slaves. To grasp how
a Southern planter must have felt, a twentieth-century Northerner
has to make an effort. He would do well to ask how a solid American businessman of the 1960s might feel if the Soviet Union existed
where Canada does on the map and were obviously growing
stronger day by day. Let him further imagine that the communist
giant spouted self-righteousness at the seams (while the government denied that these statements reflected true policy) and continually sent insults and agents across the border. Southern bitterness and anxiety were not just the expressions of a fire-eating
minority. In his appeal for compromise among the sections Henry
Clay, the most famous of Southern moderates, made this revealing
and much quoted statement: "You Northerners are looking on in
safety and security while the conflagration I have described is raging in the slave States. . . . In the one scale, then, we behold sentiment, sentiment, sentiment alone; in the other, property, the social
fabric, life, and all that makes life desirable and happy."[21]

As industrial capitalism took more and more hold in the North,
articulate Southerners looked about themselves to discover and emphasize whatever aristocratic and preindustrial traits they could find
in their own society: courtesy, grace, cultivation, the broad outlook versus the alleged money-grubbing outlook of the North.
Shortly before the Civil War, the notion took hold that the South
produced in cotton the main source of American wealth upon
which the North levied tribute. As Nevins points out, these ideas
parallel physiocratic doctrines to the effect that the profits of manufacture and trade come out of the land.[22] Such notions crop up
everywhere as industrialization takes hold, even to some extent
without industrialization. The spread of commercial agriculture in
a precommercial society generates various forms of romantic nostal-

[21] Quoted after the version in Nevins, *Ordeal*, I, 267.
[22] Nevins, *Emergence of Lincoln*, I, 218.

gia, such as Athenian admiration of Sparta or that of late Republican Rome for the supposed virtues of early days.

Southern rationalizations contained a substantial portion of truth. Otherwise they would have been too hard to believe. There were differences between Northern and Southern civilizations of the type suggested. And Northerners did make profits, big ones too, in marketing cotton. There was no doubt a much larger proportion of sheer fake in the Southern rationalizations. The supposed aristocratic and precommercial or anticommercial virtues of the plantation aristocracy rested on the strictly commercial profits of slavery. To try to draw the line between what was true and what was fake is extremely difficult, probably impossible. For our purposes it is not necessary. Indeed to do so may darken counsel by obliterating important relationships. It is impossible to speak of purely economic factors as the main causes behind the war, just as it is impossible to speak of the war as mainly a consequence of moral differences over slavery. The moral issues arose from economic differences. Slavery was the moral issue that aroused much of the passion on both sides. Without the direct conflict of ideals over slavery, the events leading up to the war and the war itself are totally incomprehensible. At the same time, it is as plain as the light of the sun that economic factors created a slave economy in the South just as economic factors created different social structures with contrasting ideals in other parts of the country.

To argue thus is not to hold that the mere fact of difference somehow inevitably caused the war. A great many people in the South and the North either did not care about slavery or acted as if they did not care. Nevins goes so far as to assert that the election of 1859 showed that at least three-quarters of the nation still opposed radical proslavery and antislavery ideas at what was almost the last moment.[23] Even if his estimate exaggerates the strength of neutral sentiment, one of the most sobering and thought-provoking aspects of the Civil War is the failure of this mass of indifferent opinion to prevent it. It is also this substantial body of opinion that has led intelligent historians such as Beard to doubt the importance

[23] *Emergence of Lincoln,* II, 68.

of slavery as an issue. That I hold to be an error, and a very serious one. Nevertheless the failure and collapse of moderation constitute a key part of the story, one on which those with Southern sympathies have shed valuable light. For a situation to arise in which war was likely to occur, changes had to take place in other parts of the country besides the South.

The main impetus behind the growth of Northern capitalism itself through the 1830s came, as we have seen, from cotton. During the next decade the pace of industrial growth accelerated to the point where the Northeast became a manufacturing region. This expansion ended the dependence of the American economy on a single agricultural staple. The Northeast and the West, which had in the past supplied the South with much of its food and continued to do so, became less dependent on the South and more on each other. Cotton remained important to the Northern economy, but ceased to dominate it.[24] Measured by the value of its product, cotton still ranked second among Northern manufactures in 1860. On the other hand, the North by this time produced a wide variety of manufactured goods, generally, to be sure, in small factories. A high proportion of the output was to meet the needs of an agricultural community: flour milling, lumber, boots and shoes, men's clothing, iron, leather, woolen goods, liquor, and machinery.[25] As we shall see in a moment, Northern manufacturing output came to be exchanged very heavily with the rapidly growing Western areas of the country.

Though the diminution of Northern dependence on Southern cotton and the development of some economic antagonisms were the dominant trends, there are others that deserve our attention. It will not do to overemphasize the divisive tendencies. In its relation to the plantation economy, the Northeast provided the services of financing, transportation, insurance, and marketing.[26] The bulk of the cotton exported left from Northern ports, of which New York was the most important. Thus — and this was a source of friction — Southern incomes were spent very largely in the North to purchase

[24] North, *Economic Growth*, 204 – 206.
• [25] North, *Economic Growth*, 159 – 160.
[26] North, *Economic Growth*, 68.

services for the marketing of cotton, to buy what was needed on the plantation that could not be produced on the spot, and, no small item, for holidays from the heat by rich planters. Furthermore both the North and the West still sold manufactured goods and food to the South. The 1850s were the heyday of the Mississippi steamboat trade.[27] Most important of all, the relative efficiency of New England cotton textile mills in relation to foreign competition improved between 1820 and the outbreak of the war. From 1830 onward, they enabled the United States to enter the export market.[28] Had this push been stronger, Northern and Southern interests might have come closer, and conceivably the war might not have taken place. In any event Northern business interests were very far from bellicose advocates of a war of liberation or even war for the sake of the Union. An adequate study of the political attitudes and activities of Northern industrialists remains to be written.[29] It seems wide of the mark, however, to entertain any notion to the effect that Northern industrialists were itching to work the levers of the federal government on behalf of their purely economic interests.

What Northern capitalism needed from any government was the protection and legitimation of private property. It took some very special circumstances, however, to make the owners of Southern plantations and slaves appear as a threat to this institution. What Northern capitalists also wanted was a moderate amount of government assistance in the process of accumulating capital and operating a market economy: more specifically, some tariff protection, aid in setting up a transportation network (not all of which need be strictly ethical — though many of the big railway scandals came later), sound money, and a central banking system. Above all, the

[27] North, *Economic Growth;* 103.

[28] North, *Economic Growth,* 161.

[29] As in the case of the French bourgeoisie prior to the bourgeois revolution, I have not found a good monograph that deals with the decisive political and economic questions. Foner, *Business and Slavery,* is very helpful as far as it goes but cannot be depended on for a general analysis because it concentrates on New York business interests closely connected with the South. The author is a well-known Marxist but in this study seems quite undogmatic. Industrial interests in Pennsylvania and Massachusetts need to be considered, but no adequate studies exist here either.

ablest Northern leaders wanted to be able to do business without bothering about state and regional frontiers. They were proud of being citizens of a large country, as of course others were too, and in the final crisis of secession reacted against the prospect of a balkanized America.[30]

The economic issue that aroused the most excitement was the tariff. Since American industry made remarkable progress under relatively low tariffs after 1846, the Northern demand for a higher tariff and Southern opposition to it look at first like a false issue, one that people quarrel about when they are really mad about something else. If Northern industry was booming, what earthly need did it have for political protection? The whole thesis that the South was trying to exercise some sort of veto on Northern industrial progress begins to look very dubious as soon as one asks this question. A closer look at the time sequence dispels much of the mystery, though it will be necessary to discuss the point again after other relevant facts have appeared. There was a very rapid industrial growth after 1850. But trouble became acute in certain areas, iron and textiles, during the middle of the last decade before the war. By the end of 1854 stocks of iron were accumulating in every market of the world, and the majority of American mills had shut down. In textiles Lancashire had learned to produce low-priced goods more cheaply than New England mills; between 1846 and 1856 imports of printed dyed cotton leaped from 13 million yards to 114 million, those of plain calico from 10 million to 90 million. In 1857 came a serious financial crash. A tariff passed in that year, reflecting Southern pressures, gave no relief and actually reduced duties in these two areas.[31] Partly *because* they followed a period of prosperity and rapid growth, it seems, these events aroused sullen indignation in Northern industrial circles.

[30] On sentiment about the Union see Nevins, *Ordeal*, II, 242, and on contemporary editorial opinion Stampp, *Causes of Civil War*, 49–54. The selection from the Buffalo *Courier*, April 27, 1861, (pp. 52–53) is interesting for its protofascist language.

[31] Nevins, *Emergence of Lincoln*, I, 225–226. In his final assessment of the causes of the war, Nevins deprecates the role of the tariff and economic factors generally. See *Emergence of Lincoln*, II, 465–466. More on this later, but at least on the tariff his argument seems to me contradictory.

Northern capitalists also needed a reasonably abundant force of laborers, to work at wages they could afford to pay. Here was a serious sticking point. Free land to the west tended to draw off laborers, or at least many people thought so. And a major thrust behind the Jacksonian system had been a working coalition of planters, "mechanics" or workers, and free farmers on the one hand against finance and industry in the Northeast. Where then was the labor to come from? And how was Northern capital to break out of its economic and political encirclement? Northern political and economic leaders found a solution that enabled them to detach the Western farmers from the South and attach them to their own cause. Significant alterations in the economy and social structure of the West made these changes possible. It will be necessary to examine them more closely in a moment. But we may perceive their significance at once: by making use of these trends, the Northern capitalists freed themselves from any need to rely on Southern "Junkers" in order to keep labor in its place. Perhaps more than any other factor, these trends set the stage for armed conflict and aligned the combatants in such a way as to make possible a partial victory for human freedom.

Between the end of the Napoleonic Wars and the outbreak of the Civil War what is now known as the Midwest, but was then simply the West, grew from the land of pioneers to that of commercial farming. Indeed many of those who lived through the rugged age of the pioneer seem to have left it rapidly behind for others to praise. Marketable surpluses of food with which to buy a few necessities and still fewer amenities appeared quite early. Up until the 1830s the bulk of this surplus made its way South to feed the more specialized economy of that area, a trend that was to continue but lose its significance when the Eastern market became more important.[32] Thrown heavily still on their own resources, the small independent farmers in the first third of the nineteenth century were keen to wrest control over the public lands from politicians in Washington who either speculated in land on a large scale or were otherwise indifferent to the claims and needs of the West.

[32] North, *Economic Growth*, 143, 67 – 68, 102.

They sought local autonomy sometimes at the expense of slim ties that connected them to the Union.[33] They were sympathetic to Andrew Jackson's attacks on the Eastern citadels of wealth and formed one wing of the superficially plebeian coalition that then ruled the country.

The growth of manufacturing in the East and the consequent rise in an effective demand for Western grain and meat changed this situation. Waves of expansion into the West in 1816 – 1818, 1832 – 1836, 1846 – 1847, and 1850 – 1856 reflect the increasing profitability of wheat, corn, and their derivatives.[34] From the 1830s onward, there was a gradual redirection of Western produce toward the Eastern seaboard. The "transportation revolution," the rise of canals and railroads, solved the problem of cross-mountain haulage, making possible a new outlet for Western farm products. The West's trade with the South did not decline absolutely, but actually increased. It was the proportions that shifted and helped to draw the West closer to the North.[35]

The demand for farm products gradually transformed the social structure and psychological attitudes of the West in such a way as to make a new alignment possible. The outlook of the early individualist and small-scale capitalist, characteristic of the Northeast, spread to the dominant upper stratum of the Western farmers. Under the technological conditions of the day, the family farm was an efficient social mechanism for the production of wheat, corn, hogs, and other marketable products.[36] "As quick transportation carried farm produce to eastern markets and brought ready cash in return," says Beard in one of the many passages that capture the essence of a basic social change in a few rolling sentences, "as railways, increasing population, and good roads lifted land values, brick and frame houses began to supplant log cabins; with deep political significance did prosperity tend to stifle the passion for 'easy money' and allay the ancient hatred for banks. At last beyond the mountains the chants of successful farmers were heard above the laments of poor

---

[33] Beard and Beard, *American Civilization*, I, 535 – 536.
[34] North, *Economic Growth*, 136, and chart on 137.
[35] North, *Economic Growth*, 103, 140 – 141.
[36] North, *Economic Growth*, 154.

whites. . . ."[37] A further consequence was the spread and deepening of antislavery sentiment, probably traceable to the rooting of the family farm as a successful commercial venture in Western soil.[38] There are puzzles here, since the family farm run without slaves was very common in the South as well, though it seems to have been less of a commercial affair and more of a subsistence undertaking. In any case it is clear that growing up outside the shadow of the plantation, and depending mainly on family members for labor, the Western system of farming generated considerable fear of competition from slavery.[39]

Before the middle of the nineteenth century, Southern planters who had once welcomed Western farmers as allies against the plutocracy of the North came to see the spread of independent farming as a threat to slavery and their own system. Earlier proposals to divide up Western lands on easy terms for the small farmer had antagonized Eastern seaboard areas that feared emigration and loss of labor, including even some in the South, such as North Carolina. Initiatives in support of free land had come from the Southwest. With the establishment of commercial farming in Western areas, these alignments altered. Many Southerners dug in their heels against "radical" notions of giving land away to farmers that would "abolitionize" the area.[40] Plantation interests in the Senate killed the Homestead Bill of 1852. Eight years later President Buchanan vetoed a similar measure, to the delight of nearly all Southern congressmen who had been unable to prevent its passage.[41]

The response in the North to the changes in Western agrarian society was more complex. Northern mill owners were not auto-

[37] Beard and Beard, *American Civilization,* I, 638. Nevins, *Ordeal,* II, chaps V, VI, tells essentially the same story.

[38] A map of the distribution of Abolition Societies in 1847 (Nevins, *Ordeal,* I, 141) shows them to be nearly as thick in Ohio, Indiana, Illinois as in Massachusetts.

[39] See Nevins, *Ordeal,* II, 123. As support for Seward was strong in rural New York (Nevins, *Ordeal,* I, 347), there is reason to suspect that the same sentiment was strong among Eastern farmers.

[40] Zahler, *Eastern Workingmen,* 178–179, 188, esp note 1, p. 179.

[41] Beard and Beard, *American Civilization,* I, 691–692; more details on the attitudes in Congress in Zahler, *Eastern Workingmen,* chap IX.

matically ready to give away land to anyone who asked for it, since doing so might merely diminish the number of willing hands likely to appear at the factory gates. Southern hostility to the West gave the North an opportunity for alliance with the farmer but one that Northerners were slow to grasp. The coalition did not become a political force until very late in the day, in the Republican platform of 1860 that helped to carry Lincoln to the White House, even though a majority of the country's voters opposed him. The rapproachement appears to have been the work of politicians and journalists rather than businessmen. The proposal to open up Western lands for the smaller settlers provided a way that a party attached to the interests of those with property and education could use to attract a mass following, especially among urban workers.[42]

The essence of the bargain was simple and direct: business was to support the farmers' demand for land, popular also in industrial working-class circles, in return for support for a higher tariff. "Vote yourself a farm — vote yourself a tariff" became Republican rallying cries in 1860.[43] In this fashion there came to be constituted a "marriage of iron and rye" — to glance once more at the German combination of industry and Junkers — but with Western family farmers, not landed aristocrats, and hence with diametrically opposite political consequences. On into the Civil War itself, there were objections to the wedding and calls for a divorce. In 1861 C.J. Vallandigham, an advocate of the small farmers, could still argue that "the planting South was the natural ally of the Democracy of the North and especially of the West," because the people of the South were an agricultural people.[44]

But these were voices from the past. What made the realignment possible, in addition to the changes in the character of Western rural society, were the specific circumstances of industrial growth in the Northeast. The existence of free land gave a unique twist to

[42] Zahler, *Eastern Workingmen*, 178.

[43] Beard and Beard, *American Civilization*, I, 692. For further information on the background of this rapprochement, which represented a significant reversal of earlier notions prevalent in the East, see Zahler, *Eastern Workingmen*, 185; Nevins, *Emergence of Lincoln*, I, 445.

[44] Beard and Beard, *American Civilization*, I, 677.

the relations between capitalists and workmen in the beginning stages of American capitalism, stages which in Europe were marked by the growth of violent radical movements. Here energies that in Europe would have gone into building trade unions and framing revolutionary programs went into schemes providing a free farm for every workman whether he wanted it or not. Such proposals sounded subversive to some contemporaries.[45] The actual effect of the Westward trek, nevertheless, was to strengthen the forces of early competitive and individualist capitalism by spreading the interest in property. Beard is too colorful when he speaks of the Republicans' flinging the national domain to the hungry proletariat "as a free gift more significant than bread and circuses," after which the socialist movement sank into the background.[46] There was hardly time for all that to happen. The Civil War itself, as he remarks a few sentences later, cut short the drift to radicalism. And just how much help Western land may have been to the Eastern workingman before the Civil War remains a very open question. Already speculators were getting their hands on big chunks of it. Nor is it likely that the really poor in Eastern cities could leave the mine shaft and the factory bench to buy a small farm, equip it even with simple tools, and run it profitably, even if they benefited from the prospect that others might be able to do so.

Despite all these qualifications, there is a vital remnant of truth in the famous Turner thesis about the importance of the frontier for American democracy. It lies in the realignment of social classes and geographical sections that the open West produced at least temporarily. The link between Northern industry and the free farmers ruled out for the time being the classic reactionary solution to the problems of growing industrialism. Such an alignment would have been one of Northern industrialists and Southern planters against slaves, smaller farmers, and industrial workers. This is no abstract phantasy. Quite a few forces pushed in this direction before the Civil War, and it has been a prominent feature in the American political landscape ever since the end of Reconstruction. In the circumstance of midnineteenth-century American society,

[45] Beard and Beard, *American Civilization*, I, 648 – 649.
[46] Beard and Beard, *American Civilization*, I, 751.

any peaceful solution, any victory of moderation, good sense, and democratic process, would have had to be a reactionary solution.[47] It would have had to be at the expense of the Negro, as it was to be eventually anyway, unless one is ready to take seriously the notion that more than a hundred years ago both Northerners and Southerners were ready to abandon slavery and incorporate the Negro into American society. The link between Northern industry and Western farmers, long in preparation if sudden in its arrival, for the time being did much to eliminate the prospect of a straightforward reactionary solution of the country's economic and political problems on behalf of the dominant economic strata. For the very same reason, it brought the country to the edge of Civil War.

3. *Toward an Explanation of the Causes of the War*

The alignment of the main social groupings in American society in 1860 goes a long way toward explaining the character of the war, or the issues that could and could not come to the surface — more bluntly what the war could be about. It tells us what was likely *if* there was to be a fight; by itself the alignment does not account very well for *why* there actually was a fight. Now that some of the relevant facts are before us it is possible to discuss with greater profit the question of whether or not there was an inherent mortal conflict between North and South.

Let us take up the economic requirements of the two systems one by one in order of 1) capital requirements, 2) requirements for labor, and 3) those connected with marketing the final product.

Though the point is open to some dispute, it is possible to detect definite expansionist pressures in the plantation economy. Fresh virgin lands were necessary for the best profits. Thus there was some pressure on the side of capital requirements. There are corresponding indications that the labor supply was tight. More slaves

---

[47] Drawing on Latin-American experience, Elkins, *Slavery*, 194–197, presents a "catalogue of preliminaries" that might have helped to eliminate slavery without bloodshed: to bring the slaves under Christianity, safeguard the sanctity of the slave family, allow the slave use of free time to accumulate his purchase price. These measures still seem to me highly reactionary, a form of tokenism within the framework of slavery.

would have been very helpful. Finally, to make the whole system work, cotton, and to a lesser extent other staples, had to fetch a good price in the international market.

Northern industry required a certain amount of assistance from the government in what might be called overhead costs of capital construction and the creation of a favorable institutional environment: a transportation system, a tariff, and a sufficiently tight currency so that debtors and small men generally did not have undue advantages. (Some inflation, on the other hand, that would keep prices moving up would probably be rather welcome, then as now.) On the side of labor, industry needed formally free wage laborers, though it is not easy to prove that free labor is necessarily superior to slavery in a factory system, except for the fact that someone has to have money in order to buy what industry produces. But perhaps that is a sufficient consideration. Finally, of course, growing industry did need an expanding market, provided still in those days quite largely by the agricultural sector. The West furnished much of this market and may be regarded as part of the North for the sake of this crude model.

It is difficult to perceive any really serious structural or "mortal" conflict in this analysis of the basic economic requirements, even though I have deliberately tried to bias the model in that direction. Here it is indispensable to remember, as revisionist historians of the Civil War correctly point out, that any large state is full of conflicts of interest. Tugging and hauling and quarreling and grabbing, along with much injustice and repression, have been the ordinary lot of human societies throughout recorded history. To put a searchlight on these facts just before a violent upheaval like the Civil War and call them the decisive causes of the war is patently misleading. To repeat, it would be necessary to show that compromise was impossible in the nature of the situation. From the analysis so far this does not seem to be the case. The most one can say along this line is that an increase in the area of slavery would have hurt the free farmers of the West badly. Although the areas where each kind of farming would pay were determined by climate and geography, no one could be sure where they were without trying. Still this factor alone does not seem sufficient to account for the war. Northern industry would have been as happy with a plantation market in the West as with any other, if such considerations were all that mattered, and the conflict could very likely have been ironed out. The other points of potential and actual conflict seem less serious. Northern requirements in the area of capital construction, the demand for internal improvements, a tariff, etc, cannot be regarded as threatening a crushing burden for the Southern economy. To be sure quite a number of marginal planters would have suffered, a factor of some importance. But if Southern society was run by the more successful planters, or if this influence was no more than very important, the smaller fry could have been sacrificed for the sake of a deal. In the question of slave labor versus free there was no real economic conflict because the areas were geographically distinct. Every account that I have come upon indicates that Northern labor was either lukewarm or hostile to the antislavery issue.

In addition to the conflict between free farmers in the West and the plantation system, about the strongest case one can make in strictly economic terms is that for the South secession was not an altogether unreasonable proposal mainly because the South did not need much that the North really had to offer. In the short run the North could not buy much more cotton than it did already. The most that the North could have offered would have been to reopen the slave trade. There was talk about taking over Cuba for slavery, and even some desultory action. As quite recent events have shown, under other circumstances such a move might be an extremely popular one in all parts of the country. At that time it seems to have been both impractical and impolitic.

To sum up, the strictly economic issues were very probably negotiable. Why, then, did the war happen? What was it about? The apparent inadequacy of a strictly economic explanation — I shall argue in a moment that the fundamental causes were still economic ones — has led historians to search for others. Three main answers are distinguishable in the literature. One is that the Civil War was fundamentally a moral conflict over slavery. Since large and influential sections of the public in both the North and the South refused to take a radical position either for or against slavery, this explanation runs into difficulties, in effect the ones that Beard and others tried to circumvent in their search for economic causes. The second answer tries to get around both sets of difficulties by the proposition that *all* the issues were really negotiable and that the blunderings of politicians brought on a war that the mass of the population in the North and in the South did not want. The third answer amounts to an attempt to push this line of thought somewhat further by analyzing how the political machinery for achieving consensus in American society broke down and allowed the war to erupt. In this effort, however, historians tend to be driven back toward an explanation in terms of moral causes.[48]

Each of the explanations, including that stressing economic factors, can marshal a substantial body of facts in its support. Each has hit at a portion of the truth. To stop at this observation is to be satisfied with intellectual chaos. The task is to relate these portions of the truth to each other, to perceive the whole in order to understand the relationship and significance of partial truths. That such a search is endless, that the discovered relations are themselves only partial truths, does not mean that the search ought to be abandoned.

To return to the economic factors, it is misleading, if at times necessary, to take them separately from others with the traditional labels political, moral, social, etc. Similarly, it is a necessity for the sake of comprehensible exposition to break the issues down one by one in some other series — such as slavery as such, slavery in the territories, tariff, currency, railroads and other internal improvements, the alleged Southern tribute to the North. At the same time, the

[48] Nevins stresses moral causes at the same time that he reports most people were unconcerned about them, a paradox that, as far as I can see, he does not directly confront. See *Emergence of Lincoln*, II, 462–471, for his general explanation; on the widespread desire for peace, ibid, 63, 68. But Nevins does give much factual material helpful in trying to resolve the paradox. For a succinct statement of the thesis that the politicians were responsible, see the extract from Randall's *Lincoln the Liberal Statesman*, reprinted in Stampp, *Causes of the Civil War*, 83–87. Nichols, *Disruption of American Democracy*, and Craven, *Growth of Southern Nationalism*, present versions of the third thesis. No one author, it should be noted, presents a pure version or a lawyer's brief for a specific explanation. It is a matter of emphasis, but very strong emphasis.

breakdown into separate categories partially falsifies what it describes because individual people were living through all these things at once, and persons who were apathetic about one issue could become excited about another. As the connection among issues became apparent, the concern spread among articulate people. Even if each individual issue had been negotiable, a debatable point, collectively and as a unit they were almost impossible to negotiate. And they were a unit, and so perceived by more than a few contemporaries, because they were manifestations of whole societies.

Let us begin the analysis afresh with this viewpoint in mind. Primarily for economic and geographical reasons, American social structure developed in different directions during the nineteenth century. An agrarian society based on plantation slavery grew up in the South. Industrial capitalism established itself in the Northeast and formed links with a society based on farming with family labor in the West. With theWest, the North created a society and culture whose values increasingly conflicted with those of the South. The focal point of the difference was slavery. Thus we may agree with Nevins that moral issues were decisive. But these issues are incomprehensible without the economic structures that created and supported them. Only if abolitionist sentiment had flourished in the South, would there be grounds for regarding moral sentiments as an independent factor in their own right.

The fundamental issue became more and more whether the machinery of the federal government should be used to support one society or the other. That was the meaning behind such apparently unexciting matters as the tariff and what put passion behind the Southern claim that it was paying tribute to the North. The question of power at the center was also what made the issue of slavery in the territories a crucial one. Political leaders knew that the admission of a slave state or a free one would tip the balance one way or another. The fact that uncertainty was an inherent part of the situation due to unsettled and partly settled lands to the West greatly magnified the difficulties of reaching a compromise. It was more and more necessary for political leaders on both sides to be alert to any move or measure that might increase the advantages of the other. In this larger context, the thesis of an attempted Southern veto on Northern progress makes good sense as an important cause of the war.

This perspective also does justice, I hope, to the revisionist thesis that it was primarily a politician's war, perhaps even an agitator's war, if the terms are not taken to be merely abusive epithets. In a complex society with an advanced division of labor, and especially in a parliamentary democracy, it is the special and necessary task of politicians, journalists, and only to a somewhat lesser extent clergymen to be alive and sensitive to events that influence the distribution of power in society. They are also the ones who provide the arguments, good and bad alike, both for changing the structure of society and for maintaining things as they are. Since it is their job to be alert to potential changes, while others keep on with the all-absorbing task of making a living, it is characteristic of a democratic system that politicians should often be clamorous and intensify division. The modern democratic politician's role is an especially paradoxical one, at least superficially. He does what he does so that most people do not have to worry about politics. For that same reason he often feels it necessary to arouse public opinion to dangers real and unreal.

From this standpoint too, the failure of modern opinion to halt the drift to war becomes comprehensible. Men of substance in both North and South furnished the core of moderate opinion. They were the ones who in ordinary times are leaders in their own community — "opinion makers," a modern student of public opinion would be likely to call them. As beneficiaries of the prevailing order, and mainly interested in making money, they wanted to suppress the issue of slavery rather than seek structural reforms, a very difficult task in any case. The Clay-Webster Compromise of 1850 was a victory for this group. It provided for stricter laws in the North about the return of fugitive slaves and for the admission of several new states to the union: California as a free state, New Mexico and Utah at some future date with or without slavery as their constitutions might provide at the time of admission.[49] Any

---

[49] On social groupings that supported the Compromise in the South, see Nevins, *Ordeal*, I, 315, 357, 366, 375. On 357 he remarks, "the . . . largest element was a body of moderates . . . who believed both in South-

attempt to drag the slavery issue out into the open and seek a new solution made large numbers of these groups cease being moderates. That is what happened when Senator Stephen A. Douglas put an end to the Compromise of 1850 only four years later by reopening the question of slavery in the territories. Through proposing in the Kansas-Nebraska Act that the settlers decide the issue for themselves one way or the other, he converted, at least for the time being, wide sections of Northern opinion from moderation to views close to abolitionism. In the South, his support was not much more than lukewarm.[50]

By and large the moderates had the usual virtues that many people hold are necessary to make democracy work: willingness to compromise and see the opponent's viewpoint, a pragmatic outlook. They were the opposite of doctrinaires. What all this really amounted to was a refusal to look facts in the face. Trying mainly

---

ern Rights and the Union, but hoped they could be reconciled." In other words, they wanted to have their cake and eat it too. On general reactions and those in the North, see Nevins, *Ordeal*, I, 346, 293 – 294, 348; more detail on selected Northern business reaction in Foner, *Business and Slavery*, chaps 2 – 4. Excitement about fugitive slaves in both the North and the South seems to have been greatest in states where the problem was least likely to occur. But it was Clay and Webster who provided the evidence for this thesis. See Nevins, *Ordeal*, I, 384.

[50] On reactions to Douglas's proposal in the North and the South see Nevins, *Ordeal*, II, 121, 126 – 127, 133 – 135, 152 – 154, 156 – 157. A sympathetic treatment of Douglas may be found in Craven, *Coming of the Civil War*, esp 325 – 331, 392 –393. On the Kansas-Nebraska affair Craven makes a plausible case for the thesis that dishonest Northern politicians stirred up slavery as a false issue. On the Lincoln-Douglas debates he argues that Lincoln's own high-sounding moral ambiguities had the effect of making Douglas appear thoroughly indifferent to moral issues. This treatment is diametrically opposite to that in Nevins. Commenting on Douglas's action in reopening the issue of slavery by the Kansas-Nebraska bill, Nevins remarks (*Ordeal*, II, 108), "When indignation welled up like the ocean lashed by a hurricane, he [Douglas] was amazed. The fact that the irresistible tidal forces in history are moral forces always escapes a man of dim moral perceptions." This is commencement oratory, not history. Successful political leaders have to be morally ambiguous in their efforts to cope with conflicting moral forces. Subsequent historians make the politicians that win into moral heroes. Generally Nevins does not succumb to such nonsense.

to push the slavery issue aside, the moderates were unable to influence or control the series of events generated by the underlying situation.[51] Crises such as the struggles over "bleeding Kansas," the financial panic of 1857, John Brown's melodramatic attempt to put himself at the head of a slave insurrection, and many others eroded the moderate position, leaving its members increasingly disorganized and confused. The practicality that tries to solve issues by patiently ignoring them, an attitude often complacently regarded as the core of Anglo-Saxon moderation, revealed itself as totally inadequate. An attitude, a frame of mind, without a realistic analysis and program is not enough to make democracy work even if a majority share this outlook. Consensus by itself means little; it depends what the consensus is about.

Finally, as one tries to perceive American society as a whole

[51] During the winter of 1858–1859 plans were afoot in the South to create a new party, characterized by Nevins, *Emergence of Lincoln*, II, 59, as "a conservative, national, Union-exalting party which should thrust aside the slavery issue, denounce all secessionists, push a broad program of internal improvements, and on constructive grounds overthrow the Democrats." It drew on men of substance, political leaders, journalists, tried to appeal to small farmers versus big slaveholders, but made hardly any dent. During the last phase, when secessionists were in charge of events, the main opposition seems to have come from those who had direct trade connections with the North, i.e., merchants and professional men in some Southern ports, and the smaller farmers. See Nevins, *Emergence of Lincoln*, II, 322, 323, 324, 326. New York business circles blew hot and cold. After being vigorous defenders of the Compromise of 1850, they turned nearly abolitionist over Douglas's Kansas-Nebraska action, reversing themselves again shortly afterward. As Foner remarks (*Business and Slavery*, 138), "Ever since 1850, the great majority of New York merchants had operated under the illusion that the sectional struggle would right itself in time if 'politicians and fanatics' would only leave the controversial incidents alone." This desire to dodge the issues seems to be the one constant theme in their outlook. Excitement was bad for business. On October 10, 1857, the *Herald* predicted (Foner, *Business and Slavery*, 140–141): "The nigger question must give way to the superior issues of a safe currency, sound credits, and solid and permanent basis of security upon which all the varied commercial and business interests of the country may repose." On this platform, at least, moderates North and South could agree. In time it became the one upon which the Civil War and its aftermath were liquidated.

in order to grásp the causes and meaning of the war, it is useful to recall that searching for the sources of dissension necessarily obscures a major part of the problem. In any political unity that exists for a long time, there must bé causes to produce the unity. There have to be reasons why men seek accommodation for their inevitable differences. It is difficult to find a case in history where two different regions have developed economic systems based on diametrically opposite principles and yet remained under a central government that retained real authority in both areas. I cannot think of any.[52] In such a situation there would have to be very strong cohesive forces to counteract the divisive tendencies. Cohesive forces appear to have been weak in the midnineteenth century in the United States, though there is always the risk of exaggerating their weakness because the Civil War did happen.

Trade is an obvious factor that can generate links among various sections of a country. The fact that Southern cotton went mainly to England is almost certainly a very important one. It meant that the link with the North was so much the weaker. English partiality to the Southern cause during the war itself is well known. But it will not do to put too much weight on the direction of trade as an aspect of disunity. As pointed out earlier, Northern mills were beginning to use more cotton. When the Western market fell off sharply after the crash of 1857, New York merchants relied for a time more heavily on their Southern connections.[53] In a word, the situation in trade was changing; had the war been averted, historians who look first for economic causes would have had no difficulty in finding an explanation.

Though the fact that cotton still linked the South with England more than with the North was significant, two other aspects of the situation may have been more important. One has already been mentioned: the absence of any strong radical working-class threat to industrial capitalist property in the North. Secondly, the United States had no powerful foreign enemies. In this respect, the

[52] The British Commonwealth may be the most obvious candidate. Its breakup into independent units in the last fifty years supports the above generalization.

[53] Foner, *Business and Slavery*, 143.

situation was entirely different from that facing Germany and Japan, who both experienced their own versions of political modernization crises somewhat later, 1871 in Germany, 1868 in Japan. For this combination of reasons, there was not much force behind the characteristic conservative compromise of agrarian and industrial élites. There was little to make the owners of Northern mills and Southern slaves rally under the banner of the sacredness of property.

To sum up with desperate brevity, the ultimate causes of the war are to be found in the growth of different economic systems leading to different (but still capitalist) civilizations with incompatible stands on slavery. The connection between Northern capitalism and Western farming helped to make unnecessary for a time the characteristic reactionary coalition between urban and landed élites and hence the one compromise that could have avoided the war. (It was also the compromise that eventually liquidated the war.) Two further factors made compromise extremely difficult. The future of the West appeared uncertain in such a way as to make the distribution of power at the center uncertain, thus intensifying and magnifying all causes of distrust and contention. Secondly, as just noted, the main forces of cohesion in American society, though growing stronger, were still very weak.

4. *The Revolutionary Impulse and its Failure*

About the Civil War itself, it is unnecessary to say more than a few words, especially since the most important political event, the Emancipation Proclamation, has already been mentioned. The war reflected the fact that the dominant classes in American society had split cleanly in two, much more cleanly than did the ruling strata in England at the time of the Puritan Revolution or those in France at the time of the French Revolution. In those two great convulsions, divisions within the dominant classes enabled radical tendencies to boil up from the lower strata, much more so in the case of the French Revolution than in England. In the American Civil War there was no really comparable radical upsurge.

At least in major outline the reasons are easy to see: American cities were not teeming with depressed artisans and potential *sans-culottes*. Even if only indirectly, the existence of Western ·lands reduced the explosive potential. In the second place, the materials for a peasant conflagration were lacking. Instead of peasants at the bottom of the heap, the South had mainly black slaves. Either they could not or they would not revolt. For our purpose it does not matter which. Though there were sporadic slave outbreaks, they had no political consequences. No revolutionary impulse came from that quarter.[54]

What there was in the way of a revolutionary impulse, that is, an attempt to alter by force the established order of society, came out of Northern capitalism. In the group known as the Radical Republicans, abolitionist ideals fused with manufacturing interests to ignite a brief revolutionary flash that sputtered and went out in a mire of corruption. Though the Radicals were a thorn in Lincoln's side during the war, he was able to fight the war to a successful military conclusion mainly on the basis of preserving the Union, that is, without any serious offensive against Southern property rights. For a brief time, about three years after the end of the fighting, 1865 – 1868, the Radical Republicans held power in the victorious North and mounted an offensive against the plantation system and the remnants of slavery.

Leading members of this group perceived the war as a revolutionary struggle between a progressive capitalism and a reactionary agrarian society based on slavery. To the extent that the conflict between the North and the South really had such a character, a conflict some of whose most important struggles came after the actual fighting stopped, this was due to the Radical Republicans. From the perspective of a hundred years later, they appear as the last revolutionary flicker that is strictly bourgeois and strictly capitalist, the last successors to medieval townsmen beginning the revolt against their feudal overlords. Revolutionary movements since the Civil War have been either anticapitalist, or fascist and counterrevolutionary if in support of capitalism.

From abolitionist ideologues and Free Soil radicals, a small

[54] The well-known Marxist scholar Aptheker collects these instances in his *American Negro Slave Revolts,* chap XV.

band of Republican politicians took over the conception of slavery as an anachronistic "remnant of a dying world of 'baron and serf — noble and slave.'" The Civil War itself they perceived as an opportunity to root out and destroy this oppressive anachronism in order to rebuild the South in the image of the democratic and progressive North, based on "free speech, free toil, schoolhouses, and ballot boxes." Though his public statements were somewhat milder, the leader of the Radical Republicans in the House of Representatives, Thaddeus Stevens, wrote privately to his law partner during the year that what the country needed was someone in power (i.e., *not* Lincoln) "with sufficient grasp of mind, and sufficient moral courage, to treat this as a radical revolution, and remodel our institutions. . . . It would involve the desolation of the South as well as emancipation, and a repeopling of half the Continent. . . ." What put steam behind this movement and lifted it out of the realm of noisy talk was the fact that it coincided with the interests of crucial segments of Northern society.[55] One was the infant iron and steel industry of Pennsylvania. Another was a set of railroad interests. Stevens acted as a Congressional go-between for both of these interests, from each of whom he received cash favors in accord with prevailing political morals.[56] The Radical Republicans also received substantial support from Northern labor. Even though Northern workers were very cool to abolitionist propaganda, fearing Negro competition and regarding New England abolitionists as hypocritical representatives of the mill owners, they were enthusiastic about Radical conceptions of tariff protection and going slow on the contraction of inflated Northern currency.[57] Financial and commercial interests, on the other hand, were unenthusiastic about the Radicals. After the war, principled Radicals turned against the "plutocracy of the North."[58]

Thus the Radical offensive did not represent a united capital-

[55] See the excellent study by Shortreed, "The Antislavery Radicals," 65 – 87, esp 68 – 69, 77, from which the remarks in quotations are taken.

[56] Current, *Old Thad Stevens*, 226 – 227, 312, 315 – 316.

[57] See Rayback, "American Workingman and Antislavery Crusade," 152 – 163.

[58] Sharkey, *Money, Class and Party*, 281 – 282, 287 – 289.

ist offensive on the plantation system. It was a combination of workers, industrialists, and some railroad interests at the time of its greatest power. Still it would not be amiss to label it entrepreneurial and even progressive capitalism; it attracted the main creative (and philistine) forces that Veblen later liked in American society and repelled those that he disliked: snobbish financiers who made their money by selling instead of doing. In Thaddeus Stevens and his associates, this combination had skilled political leadership and sufficient minor intellectual talent to provide a general strategy. Radicals had an explanation of where society was heading and how they could take advantage of this fact. For them the Civil War was at least potentially a revolution. Military victory and Lincoln's assassination, which they welcomed with scarcely disguised joy, gave them a brief opportunity to try to make it a real one.

Thaddeus Stevens again provided the analysis as well as the day-to-day political leadership. Essentially his strategy amounted to capturing the machinery of the federal government for the benefit of the groups for which he was spokesman. To do so it was necessary to change Southern society lest the old type of plantation leadership return to Congress and frustrate the move. Out of this necessity came what little revolutionary impulse there was to the whole struggle. Stevens had enough sociological insight to see what the problem was and to cast about for a possible remedy, as well as enough nerve to make a try.

In his speeches of 1865 Stevens presented to the general public and to Congress a surprisingly coherent analysis and program of action. The South had to be treated as a conquered people, not as a series of states that had somehow left the Union and were now to be welcomed back. "The foundation of their institutions both political, municipal, and social *must* be broken up and *relaid*, or all our blood and treasure have been spent in vain. This can only be done by treating and holding them as a conquered people."[59] They should not be allowed to return, he asserted, "until the Constitution shall have been so amended as to make it what its framers in-

[59] Speech of September 6, 1865, in Lancaster, Pennsylvania, as given in Current, *Old Thad Stevens*, 215.

tended; and so as to secure perpetual ascendency to the party of the Union," that is, the Republicans.[60]

If the Southern states were not "reconstructed" — the revealing euphemism for revolution from above has passed from contemporary usage into all subsequent histories — they might easily overwhelm the North, Stevens calculated carefully and openly, and thus enable the South to win the peace after losing the war.[61]

Out of these considerations, came the program to rebuild Southern society from top to bottom. Stevens wanted to break the power of the plantation owners by confiscating estates over two hundred acres, "even though it drive (the Southern) nobility into exile." In this way, he argued, citing statistics, the federal government would obtain enough land to give each Negro household some forty acres.[62] "Forty acres and a mule" became in time the catchword slogan to discredit the supposedly utopian hopes of the newly freed Negroes. But the Radical Republicans were no utopians, not even Stevens. The demand for sweeping land reform reflected realistic awareness that nothing else would break the power of the planters. These had already set about to recover the substance of their old power by other means, something they were able to do because the Negroes were economically helpless. All this, at least a few Radicals saw quite clearly. And there are indications that dividing up the old plantations to give the Negroes small farms was feasible. In 1864 and 1865, Northern military authorities made two experiments along these lines in order to take care of the troublesome problem of thousands of destitute Negroes. They turned over confiscated and abandoned lands to more than 40,000 Negroes who are said to have been successful in working the land as small farmers until President Johnson returned the estates to their former white owners.[63] Still the experience of slavery was scarcely one to prepare Negroes to manage their own affairs as small rural capitalists. Stevens was aware of this and felt that the Negroes would need supervision by his friends in Congress for a long time to come. At

[60] *Reconstruction, Speech, December 18, 1865,* p. 5.
[61] *Reconstruction, Speech, December 18, 1865,* p. 5.
[62] Speech of September 6, 1865, in Current, *Old Thad Stevens,* 215.
[63] Stampp, *Reconstruction,* 123, 125 – 126.

the same time he saw that, without minimal economic security and minimal political rights, including the right to vote, they could do little for themselves or for Northern interests.[64]

In a nutshell, the Radical version of reconstruction came down to using the North's military power to destroy the plantation aristocracy and create a facsimile of capitalist democracy by ensuring property and voting rights for the Negroes. In the light of Southern conditions at the time, it was indeed revolutionary. A century later, the movement for civil rights for the Negroes seeks no more than this, indeed not quite all that, since the economic emphasis remains muted. If being ahead of the times is revolutionary, Stevens was that. Even sympathetic Northerners professed shock. Horace Greeley, editor of the *New York Tribune*, long sympathetic to the abolitionist cause, wrote in response to Stevens's speech of September 6, 1865, ". . . we protest against any warfare on Southern property . . . because the wealthier class of Southerners, being more enlightened and humane than the ignorant and vulgar, are less inimicable to the blacks."[65] Greeley's misgivings give a hint of what was to come when men of substance North and South were to bury their differences and, by another famous compromise, leave the Negroes to make what they could of their freedom.

It is not surprising therefore that defeat came soon to the Radicals, or more precisely to what was radical in their program, as soon as it encountered Northern property interests. The Radicals were unable to force confiscation into the reconstruction acts of 1867 against the wishes of more moderate Republicans. In the House, Stevens's "40 acres" measure received only 37 votes.[66] Influential

[64] "Without the right of suffrage in the late slave States, (I do not speak of the free States,) I believe the slaves had far better been left in bondage." — *Reconstruction, Speech, December 8, 1865*, pp. 6, 8.

[65] Quoted from the issue of September 12, 1865, by Current, *Old Thad Stevens*, 216 – 217. Greeley also criticized Stevens for failing to include a suffrage plank in this speech, which he did in the later one, mainly it seems in response to pressure from Senator Charles Sumner of Massachusetts. I have not tried to present differences of opinion within Radical ranks, but have concentrated on Stevens as its most revolutionary figure, as well as its most influential day-to-day strategist when the movement was at its height.

[66] Current, *Old Thad Stevens*, 233.

Northern sentiment was in no mood to tolerate an outright attack on property, not even Rebel property and not even in the name of capitalist democracy. The *Nation* warned that "A division of rich men's lands amongst the landless . . . would give a shock to our whole social and political system from which it would hardly recover without the loss of liberty." The failure of land reform was a decisive defeat and removed the heart of the Radical program. Without land reform the rest of the program could be no more than palliatives or irritants, depending on one's viewpoint. To say that this failure cleared the way for the eventual supremacy of Southern white landholders and other propertied interests may nevertheless be an exaggeration.[67] The Radicals had never even really managed to bar the way. Their failure at this moment revealed the limits American society imposed upon the revolutionary impulse.

In the absence of confiscation and redistribution of land, the plantation system recovered by means of a new system of labor. At first there were attempts with wage labor. These failed, at least partly because Negroes were inclined to draw their wages in slack months and abscond when the cotton had to be picked. Hence there was a widespread turn toward sharecropping which gave the planters superior control of their labor force. The change was significant. As we shall see in due course, sharecropping in many parts of Asia has constituted one way of extracting a surplus from the peasant through economic rather than political methods, though the latter are often necessary to buttress the former. Hence it is instructive to see fundamentally similar forms appear in America without the prior existence of a peasantry.

The country merchant gave a local twist to the American situation, though similar devices occurred also in China and elsewhere. The country merchant was often the large planter. By making advances of groceries to tenant and sharecropper, charging much higher rates for them than ordinary retail prices, he kept control of the work force. Tenants and sharecroppers could trade at no other store, since they had credit at no other and were usually short of

[67] See the excellent account in Stampp, *Reconstruction*, 128–130; the quotation from the *Nation* occurs on 130.

cash.[68] In this fashion economic bonds replaced those of slavery for many Negroes. How much real improvement, if any, the change meant is very difficult to say. But it would be a mistake to hold that plantation owners prospered greatly under the new system. The main effect appears to have been to make the South even more of a one-crop economy than before, as banker pressed planter, and planter pressed cropper to grow crops that could be quickly turned to cash.[69]

Political recovery proceeded along with economic recovery, reenforcing each other rather than in any simple relationship of cause and effect. There is no need to recount here the political twistings and turnings of the successors to the antebellum ruling groups in the South as they sought for political leverage, though it is worth noticing that "scalawags" — white collaborationists they might be called today — included numerous planters, merchants, and even industrial leaders.[70] A good deal of violence, perhaps deprecated by the better elements, though skepticism is in order here, helped to put the Negroes "in their place" and reestablish overall white supremacy.[71] Meanwhile industrialists and railroad men were becoming increasingly influential in Southern affairs.[72] In a word, moderate men of substance were returning to power, authority, and influence in the South, as they were in the North as well. The stage was being set for an alliance of these across the former battle lines. It was consummated formally in 1876 when the disputed Hayes-Tilden election was settled by allowing the Republican Hayes to take office in return for removing the remnants of the Northern occupational regime. Under attack from radical agrarians in the West and radical labor in the East, the party of wealth, property, and privilege in the North was ready to abandon the last pretense of upholding the rights of the propertyless and oppressed

[68] See Shannon, *American Farmers' Movements*, 53 for a succinct description.

[69] Randall and Donald, *Civil War*, 549 – 551.

[70] Randall and Donald, *Civil War*, 627 – 629, sketches these maneuvers.

[71] Randall and Donald, *Civil War*, 680 – 685.

[72] Woodward, *Reunion and Reaction*, 42 – 43. Chapter II provides a first-rate analysis of the whole process of moderate recovery.

Negro laboring class.[73] When Southern "Junkers" were no longer slaveholders and had acquired a larger tincture of urban business and when Northern capitalists faced radical rumblings, the classic conservative coalition was possible. So came Thermidor to liquidate the "Second American Revolution."

5. The Meaning of the War

Was it a revolution? Certainly not in the sense of a popular uprising against oppressors. To assess the meaning of the Civil War, to place it in a history that is still being made, is just as difficult as to account for its cause and course. One sense of revolution is a violent destruction of political institutions that permits a society to take a new course. After the Civil War, industrial capitalism advanced by leaps and bounds. Clearly that was what Charles Beard had in mind when he coined the famous phrase, "the Second American Revolution." But was the burst of industrial capitalist growth a consequence of the Civil War? And how about the contribution to human freedom that all but the most conservative associate with the word revolution? The history of the Fourteenth Amendment, prohibiting the states from depriving any person of life, liberty, or property, epitomizes the ambiguity on this score. As every educated person knows, the Fourteenth Amendment has done precious little to protect Negroes and a tremendous amount to protect corporations. Beard's thesis that such was the original intent of those who drafted the amendment has been rejected by some.[74] That in itself is trivial. About the consequence, there is no doubt. Ultimately the way one assesses the Civil War depends on the assessment of freedom in modern American society and the connection between the institutions of advanced industrial capitalism and the Civil War. Another whole book would scarcely serve to argue these issues. I shall do no more than try to sketch a few of the more important considerations.

Certain very important political changes did accompany and

[73] Woodward, *Reunion and Reaction*, 36 – 37.
[74] Randall and Donald, *Civil War*, 583; see also 783 – 784 for a review of the literature.

follow the Northern victory. They may be summed up in the remark that the federal government became a series of ramparts
around property, mainly big property, and an agency to execute
the biblical pronouncement, "To him that hath shall be given."
First among the ramparts was the preservation of the Union itself,
which meant, as the West filled up after the war, one of the largest
domestic markets of the world. It was also a market protected
by the highest tariff to date in the nation's history.[75] Property received protection from state governments with unsound inclinations through the Fourteenth Amendment. Likewise the currency
was put on a sound footing through the national banking system
and the resumption of specie payments. Whether such measures
hurt the Western farmers as much as was once supposed is dubious;
there are indications that they were doing quite well during the war
and for some time afterward.[76] At any rate they received some
compensation through the opening of the public domain in the
West (Homestead Act of 1862), though it is on this score that the
federal government became an agency of the bibilical statement
just quoted. Railroads received huge grants, and disposal of public
domains also formed the basis of great fortunes in timber and min-
ing. Finally, as a compensation to industry that might lose laborers
in this fashion the federal government continued to hold open the
doors to immigration (Immigration Acts of 1864). As Beard puts
it, "All that two generations of Federalists and Whigs had tried to
get was won within four short years, and more besides."[77] "Four
short years" is a rhetorical exaggeration; some of these measures

[75] The Morrill Tariff of 1861 was the beginning of a sharp upward
climb in tariffs. It raised average tariff rates from 20 percent of value to 47
percent, more than double the rates prevailing in 1860. Designed
at first to raise revenues for the wartime Union treasury, it established pro-
tectionism deeply in American economic policies. The acts of 1883, 1890,
1894, and 1897 granted even more protection. See Davis and others, *American Economic History*, 322 – 323.

[76] Sharkey, *Money, Class, and Party*, 284 – 285, 303.

[77] Beard and Beard, *American Civilization*, II, 105; see pages 105 – 115
for a survey of the measures summarized here; also Hacker, *Triumph of
American Capitalism*, 385 – 397, for a similar and in some ways more concise
analysis.

were also part of Reconstruction (1865 – 1876), and the resumption of specie payment did not take place until 1879. But that is a small matter, since Reconstruction was definitely a part of the whole struggle. If one looks back and compares what happened with the planter program of 1860: federal enforcement of slavery, no high protective tariffs, no subsidies nor expensive tax-creating internal improvements, no national banking and currency system,[78] the case for a victory of industrial capitalism over the fetters of the plantation economy, a victory that required blood and iron to occur at all, becomes very persuasive indeed.

Reflection may make much of this conviction evaporate. It is worth noticing that Beard's own position is quite ambiguous. After recounting the victories of Northern capitalism just summarized above he remarks, "The main economic results of the Second American Revolution thus far noted would have been attained had there been no armed conflict. . . ."[79] But Beard's views are not in question except insofar as the provocative writings of a first-rate historian shed light on the issues. Three related arguments may be brought to bear against the thesis that the Civil War was a revolutionary victory for industrial capitalist democracy and necessary to this victory. First, one might hold that there is no real connection between the Civil War and the subsequent victory of industrial capitalism; to argue in favor of this connection is to fall victim to the fallacy of *post hoc, ergo propter hoc*. Second, one might hold that these changes were coming about of their own accord through the ordinary processes of economic growth and needed no Civil War to bring them about.[80] Finally, one could argue on the basis of evidence discussed at some length earlier in this chapter that the economies of North and South were not really in serious competi-

[78] Beard and Beard, *American Civilization*, II, 29.

[79] Beard and Beard, *American Civilization*, II, 115.

[80] Cochran, "Did the Civil War Retard Industrialization?" 148 – 160 seems to me a version of this and the preceding argument. I do not find it persuasive because it merely shows on the basis of statistics that the Civil War temporarily interrupted industrial growth. It touches only briefly and tangentially on the problem of institutional changes, which I hold to be the center of the question.

tion with one another: at best they were complementary; at worst, they failed to link up with each other due to fortuitous circumstances, such as the fact that the South sold much of its cotton to England.

All such arguments would receive an effective answer only if it were possible to demonstrate that Southern society, dominated by the plantation, constituted a formidable obstacle to the establishment of industrial capitalist democracy. The evidence indicates very clearly that plantation slavery was an obstacle to democracy, at least any conception of democracy that includes the goals of human equality, even the limited form of equality of·opportunity, and human freedom. It does not establish at all clearly that plantation slavery was an obstacle to industrial capitalism as such. And comparative perspective show clearly that industrial capitalism can establish itself in societies that do not profess these democratic goals or, to be a little more cautious, where these goals are no more than a secondary current. Germany and Japan prior to 1945 are the main illustrations for this thesis.

Once again the inquiry leads back toward political questions and incompatibilities between two different kinds of civilizations: in the South and in the North and West. Labor-repressive agricultural systems, and plantation slavery in particular, are political obstacles to a *particular kind* of capitalism, at a specific historical stage: competitive democratic capitalism we must call it for lack of a more precise term. Slavery was a threat and an obstacle to a society that was indeed the heir of the Puritan, American, and French Revolutions. Southern society was based firmly on hereditary status as the basis of human worth. With the West, the North, though in the process of change, was still committed to notions of equal opportunity. In both, the ideals were reflections of economic arrangements that gave them much of their appeal and force. Within the same political unit it was, I think, inherently impossible to establish political and social institutions that would satisfy both. If the geographical separation had been much greater, if the South had been a colony for example, the problem would in all probability have been relatively simple to solve at that time — at the expense of the Negro.

That the Northern victory, even with all its ambiguous consequences, was a political victory for freedom compared with what a Southern victory would have been seems obvious enough to require no extended discussion. One need only consider what would have happened had the Southern plantation system been able to establish itself in the West by the middle of the nineteenth century and surrounded the Northeast. Then the United States would have been in the position of some modernizing countries today, with a latifundia economy, a dominant antidemocratic aristocracy, and a weak and dependent commercial and industrial class, unable and unwilling to push forward toward political democracy. In rough outline, such was the Russian situation, though with less of a commercial emphasis in its agriculture in the second half of the nineteenth century. A radical explosion of some kind or a prolonged period of semireactionary dictatorship would have been far more probable than a firmly rooted political democracy with all its shortcomings and deficiencies.

Striking down slavery was a decisive step, an act at least as important as the striking down of absolute monarchy in the English Civil War and the French Revolution, an essential preliminary for further advances. Like these violent upheavals, the main achievements in our Civil War were political in the broad sense of the term. Later generations in America were to attempt to put economic content into the political framework, to raise the level of the people toward some conception of human dignity by putting in their hands the material means to determine their own fate. Subsequent revolutions in Russia and China have had the same purpose even if the means have in large measure so far swallowed up and distorted the ends. It is in this context, I believe, that the American Civil War has to be placed for its proper assessment.

That the federal government was out of the business of enforcing slavery was no small matter. It is easy to imagine the difficulties that organized labor would have faced, for example, in its effort to achieve legal and political acceptance in later years, had not this barrier been swept away. To the extent that subsequent movements toward extending the boundaries and meanings of freedom have faced obstacles since the end of the Civil War, they have done so in large measure because of the incomplete character of the victory won in 1865 and subsequent tendencies toward a conservative coalition between propertied interests in the North and the South. This incompleteness was built into the structure of industrial capitalism. Much of the old repression returned to the South in new and more purely economic guises, while new forms appeared there and in the rest of the United States as industrial capitalism grew and spread. If the federal government no longer concerned itself with enforcing the fugitive slave laws, it either acquiesced or served as an instrument for new forms of oppression.

As far as the Negro is concerned, only in quite recent times has the federal government begun to move in the opposite direction. As these lines are being written, the United States finds itself in the midst of a bitter struggle over the Negroes' civil rights, a struggle likely to ebb and flow for years to come. It involves a great deal more than the Negroes. Due to the peculiarities of American history, the central core of America's lowest class are people with dark skins. As the one major segment of American society with active discontents, the Negroes are at present almost the only potential recruiting ground for efforts to change the character of the world's most powerful capitalist democracy. Whether this potential will amount to anything, whether it will splinter and evaporate or coalesce with other discontents to achieve significant results, is quite another story.

At bottom, the struggle of the Negroes and their white allies concerns contemporary capitalist democracy's capacity to live up to its noble professions, something no society has ever done. Here we approach the ultimate ambiguity in the assessment and interpretation of the Civil War. It recurs throughout history. There is more than coincidence in the fact that two famous political leaders of free societies chose to express their ideals in speeches for their fallen dead given more than two thousand years apart. To the critical historian both Pericles and Lincoln become ambiguous figures as he sets what they did and what happened alongside what they said and in all likelihood hoped for. The fight for what they expressed is not over and may not end until mankind ceases to inhabit the earth. As one peers ever deeper to resolve the ambiguities of history, the seeker eventually finds them in himself and his fellow men as well as in the supposedly dead facts of history. We are inevitably in the midst of the ebb and flow of these events and play a part, no matter how small and insignificant as individuals, in what the past will come to mean for the future.

PART TWO

*Three Routes to the
Modern World in Asia*

Problems in Comparing European and Asian Political Processes

THERE WAS A TIME in the still recent past when many intelligent thinkers believed there was only one main highway to the world of modern industrial society, a highway leading to capitalism and political democracy. The experience of the last fifty years has exploded this notion, although strong traces of a unilinear conception remain, not only in Marxist theory, but also in some Western writings on economic development. Western democracy is only one outcome, and one that arose out of specific historical circumstances. The revolutions and civil wars discussed in the three preceding chapters were an important part of the process leading to liberal democracy. As we have just seen, there were sharp divergences within the same general line of development that led to capitalist democracy in England, France, and the United States. But there are differences far greater than those which exist within the democratic family. German history reveals one type of development culminating in fascism, Russian history a third. The possibility of an eventual convergence among all three forms is not one to be dismissed offhand; certainly there are some ways in which all industrial societies resemble one another and differ from agrarian societies. Nevertheless, if we take the seventh decade of the twentieth century as our point of observation, while continuing to realize that like all historical vantage points it is arbitrarily imposed, the partial truth emerges that nondemocratic and even antidemocratic modernization works.

For reasons that will become clearer in subsequent chapters, this claim may be less true of forms of modernization culminating in fascism than in communism. That remains to be seen and is not the issue here. What is beyond all doubt is that by very different means both Germany and Russia managed to become powerful industrial states. Under Prussian leadership Germany was able to carry out in the nineteenth century an industrial revolution from above. What impulse there was toward a bourgeois revolution — and what was revolutionary was not bourgeois — petered out in 1848. Even the defeat of 1918 left essential features of the preindustrial social system intact. The eventual if not inevitable result was fascism. In Russia the impulse toward modernization prior to 1914 was very much less effective. There, as every one knows, a revolution whose main destructive force came from the peasants destroyed the old ruling classes, still mainly agrarian as late as 1917, to make way for the communist version of an industrial revolution from above.

All these familiar facts serve to press home the point that such words as democracy, fascism, and communism (and also dictatorship, totalitarianism, feudalism, bureaucracy) arose in the context of European history. Can they be applied to Asian political institutions without being wrenched beyond all recognition? At this moment it is not necessary to take a position on the general question of whether or not it is possible to transfer historical terms from one context and country to another beyond remarking that, without some degree of transferability, historical discussion breaks down into a meaningless description of unrelated episodes. On a strictly philosophical plane these questions are sterile and insoluble, leading only to tiresome word games as a substitute for the effort to see what really happened. Objective criteria, it seems to me, do exist for distinguishing between superficial and meaningful historical resemblances, and it may be helpful to say just a few words about them.

Superficial and accidental resemblances are those unconnected with other significant facts or that lead to a misapprehension of the real situation. For example, a writer who stressed similarities in the political styles of General de Gaulle and Louis XIV — let us say their punctilious enforcement of the etiquette of deference — would be setting out misleading trivialities if he were doing this as more than a joke. The different social bases of their power, the differences between seventeenth and twentieth-century French society, are far more significant than these superficial resemblances.[1] On the other hand, if we find that in both Germany and Japan prior to 1945 there was a whole series of causally related institutional practices whose structure and origins are similar, we are justified in calling this complex unit by the name fascism in both cases. The same is true of democracy and communism. The nature of the connections has to be established by empirical investigation. It is quite likely that in themselves the essential features that go to make up communism, fascism, or parliamentary democracy will fall short of providing an adequate explanation of the principal political characteristics of China, Japan, and India. Specific chains of historical causation that do not fit into any recognizable family of sequences may have to bear a substantial share of the explanatory burden. This has been the case in the study of Western societies; there is no reason to expect it to be otherwise as we turn to Asia.

[1] If it were possible to demonstrate that the resemblances between de Gaulle and Louis XIV were indeed symptoms and consequences of a deeper and more significant connection, they would cease to be superficial. One cannot in advance rule out the possibility of such discoveries. Slips of the tongue seemed trivial until Freud uncovered their connection with serious human concerns. Once again it is necessary to stress that such questions can be settled only through studying the facts.

CHAPTER FOUR

The Decay of Imperial China
and the Origins of the Communist Variant

1. The Upper Classes and the Imperial System

A LONG, LONG TIME AGO there was a school of philosophers in China whose tenets called for a "rectification of names." They apparently believed that the beginning of political and social wisdom was to call things by their right names. Those who study China today are busy on a similar task; the names that they bandy about are words such as "gentry," "feudalism," and "bureaucracy." The issue beneath this terminological debate is the decisive one with which our inquiry must begin: how were the upper classes connected with the land in this society where the overwhelming majority were tillers of the soil? Did their power and authority rest ultimately on control of landed property or was it an outcome of their near monopoly of bureaucratic posts? If it was a combination of the two, what was the nature of this combination? Since the debate carries a heavy freight of contemporary political implications, it will be well to bring these out into the open first, in the hope of clearing the way toward an accurate grasp of the way Imperial Chinese society actually worked.

Some Western scholars stress the bureaucratic character of the Chinese Empire and de-emphasize the link between the Imperial service and landed property. Such an interpretation serves the dual purpose of suggesting grounds for criticizing the Marxist derivation of political power from economic power and for criticizing modern communist states as a throwback to an alleged form of Oriental despotism.[1] Marxists, and especially the Chinese Communists, on the other hand, treat the Imperial era and even the Kuomintang period as a form of feudalism, meaning a society in which most of the land is owned by landlords whose main income derives from rent.[2] By de-emphasizing its bureaucratic character, Marxists conceal uncomfortable resemblances to their own practices. Feudalism is, if anything, an even less apt characterization than bureaucracy. There was no system of vassalage in Imperial China and only very limited grants of land in return for military services. Nevertheless the Marxist stress on landlordism is thoroughly justified, as we shall see. In sum it seems to me that Western scholars are struggling desperately to deny the connection between landholding and political office, while Marxists try equally desperately to establish such a connection.

What, then *was* the connection? What were the decisive characteristics of Chinese society during the last great dynasty, the Manchus (1644 – 1911)? How did these structural features impart a direction to the subsequent development of China that culminated in the middle of the twentieth century in the Communist victory? What characteristics of the Chinese landed upper class help to account for the absence of any strong push toward parliamentary democracy as the Imperial system broke down?

A few simple points stand out upon which there is widespread agreement and that enable us to take preliminary bearings. First of all, long before our story begins, the Chinese polity had eliminated the problem of a turbulent aristocracy tied to the land. The stages

[1] Wittfogel's *Oriental Despotism* is the best known version of this thesis.

[2] I have not seen Chinese Communist historical treatments myself. For a survey see Feuerwerker, "China's History in Marxian Dress," 323 – 353. Russian sources on the problems raised here I have found disappointing. For the Manchu period a diligent search failed to uncover any work, except for a few recent articles cited below, that deserved serious consideration; for the period 1911 – 1949, examined less closely, the Russian studies do not give any indication of being less cut off from what was taking place in the countryside (in Chinese Soviet as well as Nationalist territory) than were Westerners. Nor do their biases seem to have been any less stultifying than ours.

by which this enormous transformation took place do not concern us, except to mention that the famous system of examinations, which helped the emperor to recruit a bureaucracy with which to fight the aristocracy, played a part in it. The examination system was in working order during the T'ang dynasty which ended in 907 A.D. By the succeeding Sung dynasty, not much was left of the ancient aristocracy.[3] Whether this aristocracy was feudal, whether the earlier stage of Chinese society prior to its first unification under the Ch'in during the third century B.C. deserves the appellation feudal, are questions that we may happily leave aside.[4]

On the other hand, it is necessary to pay close attention to the problem of whether or not a landed aristocracy continued to exist under a façade of administrative centralization during the Manchu era, or the Ch'ing dynasty, as it is generally known among sinologists. Every one would agree to the existence of a class of wealthy landed proprietors, though problems would arise in just where to draw the line between wealthy and merely well-to-do. There is similar widespread agreement on the existence of a class of officials and scholars, and again problems of drawing the line within this group, though the line between those who did and did not have a tincture of academic culture was a sharp one. There is also agreement on the point that the two groups overlapped and were not absolutely identical. There were at least moderately rich landlords who did not hold any form of academic degree, and there were degree holders who owned no landed property. The exact degree of overlap is uncertain.[5]

To stop short at this agreement, however, is to obscure the essentials. Even if we had information about the exact proportion of individuals who belonged to both groups, who were both landlords and officials or scholars, we would not know very much. No

[3] There is a convenient and concise history of the examination system in Franke, *Reform and Abolition of Examination System*. I have drawn these items of information from p. 7.

[4] For a discussion generally opposed to Wittfogel's theses, see Eberhard, *Conquerors and Rulers*.

[5] In addition to the sources mentioned in the next footnote, see Chang, *Income*, 125, 142, 146.

physiologist would be content with knowing what percentage of the human body was bone and what percentage was muscle. He wants to know how bone and muscle work together in the course of the body's activities. The same kind of knowledge is necessary to understand the connection between landed property, degree holding, and political office in China.

The mechanism that linked all of these was the family, or more precisely the patrilineal lineage. In the agriculturally more productive areas, especially the South, the lineage was more extended and is known as the clan. The family as a social mechanism worked in the following manner. Fortunes acquired through the Imperial service were invested in land, a practice that continued well into modern times. A man accumulated this property for the sake of the lineage. In turn any family with aristocratic pretensions had to substantiate them by having a degree holder or prospective degree holder whom it supported in the quite justifiable hope that he would get an official position and use it to advance the family's material fortunes. Through the Imperial post, the scholar recouped or extended the family fortune and maintained the status of the lineage, thus closing the circle. The clan worked in the same way, though as a larger group it included a substantial proportion of straightforward peasants. While official rank was in theory open to the meanest peasant with talent and ambition, the absence of any widespread system of popular education usually required that the student have the support of a wealthy family for the long years of arduous study. Sometimes a wealthy family whose children lacked academic promise would provide for a bright boy from a poor background. Hence the link between office and wealth through the lineage was one of the most important features of Chinese society. For these reasons it is justifiable to refer to this upper class of scholar-officials and landlords as the gentry.[6] There are also other

[6] See Balázs, "Aspects significatifs," 81, 84 – 85. This analytical essay is indispensable for the problems raised here. Some material on the clan is in Liu, *Clan Rules*, 110, 129, 140. See also Chang, *Chinese Gentry*, 186, and his *Income*, 42.

In the West there is considerable discussion of the term "gentry" for the Chinese upper class. Though those who would reject it because of its West-

significant aspects of the connection that will appear if we look closely at each in turn.

Without assuming that the landlord's role was either more or less important than the official's, we may begin with him. The first question that arises is how he managed to get the peasants to work for him in the absence of feudal compulsions. Though details are lacking and the subject to date one that scholars have yet to examine, the general answer is fairly clear: by tenancy arrangements that do not differ in any essential way from those under modern capitalism. With some regional variations, the tenancy was in essence a form of sharecropping supplemented by hired labor, at least by the beginning of the nineteenth century.[7] The landlord, who

---

ern and particularly English connotations have some persuasive grounds, it seems pedantic to boggle at this word after it has passed into widespread usage to designate the landed upper class in Russia as well as in China. See Ho, *Ladder of Success*, 40, for arguments against its use for China.

For a definition of the gentry that seeks to distinguish degree-holding from landownership see Chang, *Gentry*. Freedman's review in *Pacific Affairs*, XXIX, 78 – 80, points out the difficulties of limiting the definition to degree holders. Ho, *Ladder of Success*, 38 – 41, differs from Chang on decisive points, such as the social status of those who purchased degrees and holders of elementary degrees. As he has little information on the economic status, the book makes very little contribution to problems raised here. His discussion of wealth as an aspect of social mobility limits itself to the secondary problem of mercantile wealth, saying almost nothing about landed wealth.

On this and other questions I am happy to acknowledge a special debt to Owen Lattimore, who gave me detailed written comments on an earlier version of this chapter. A few of these that struck me as very penetrating after I had read several additional sources have been incorporated almost *verbatim* in my text. Since the evidence elsewhere seems to me to point in a different direction, the usual exculpating phrase that he bears no responsibility for views expressed here accurately reflects the real situation.

[7] I have been unable to uncover any monographic treatment. A brief historical and geographical treatment may be found in Ho, *Population*, 217 – 226. Note also Chang, *Income*, 127; Hsiao, *Rural China*, 384, 385, 389. Hsiao has combed through an enormous mass of material, much of it from local gazetteers, excerpted it, and arranged it in some sort of order with a minimum of comment and a maximum of direct quotation. The effect is roughly similar to a clipping file from newspapers and travellers' remarks on the

was undoubtedly a more prominent figure in some areas than in others, furnished the land, and the peasants furnished the labor. The crop was divided between the two. Since the landlord hardly produced land in the same way that a peasant produced labor, we already have one good clue to the services provided by the Imperial bureaucracy: it guaranteed his control over the land.[8] A rich peasant who did not have any pretensions to academic culture himself, but who might have hopes for his son, would work in the fields like any other. But the scholar did not work with his hands. Though the scholar-landlords lived in the countryside, unlike their English and German counterparts (even *some* of their Russian and French ones), they seemed to have played no part whatever in the actual work of cultivation, not even a supervisory one.[9] Their social position presents the sharpest of all contrasts to the Japanese overlord, as we shall see in due course. Many of the differences between the political fates of China and Japan, in modern times as well as earlier, may be traced to this distinction.

Though there are frequent references to the buying and selling of rice on a fairly large scale, it is a safe inference that sharecrop-

---

shady side of American politics. As long as one remembers that such materials overemphasize the slightly shady aspect of society — fundamental defects seldom find direct mention except in the occasional remarks of an acute traveller — such a book is extremely useful, more useful than the attempts to collect dubious statistics that often conceal the actual workings of the system. Indeed one could make a case that a book like Hsiao's provides better material for the sociologist than many a brilliant monograph which filters the facts through a thesis, no matter how honest and intelligent the author. Still, it would be dreadful to have to read many like this one.

[8] A Soviet scholar, Khokhlov, "Agrarnye otnosheniya," 110, claims that about 1812, eighty percent of the cultivated land was taken up by the upper classes while the peasants held the remaining twenty percent. Though the figures are dubious, there seems no reason to doubt that the lion's share was in the possession of the former group.

[9] Conceivably this impression might rest on the absence of information. But the clan genealogy cited by Chang, *Income*, 127, above takes it for granted that management is to be avoided. The attitude toward manual labor renders it highly unlikely that the scholar could ever show a peasant how to do a piece of work. As indicated below, the "economic" contribution of the rich landlord was to wangle favors from the government.

ping constituted the predominant pattern, with the landlord receiving his share in grain (rice in the South, wheat and other grains in the North) rather than in money. Even the Emperor was a superlandlord who collected grain from his subjects.[10] If the Imperial system relied to such a great extent on collections in kind, we may be sure that it prevailed quite widely elsewhere. Since a wealthy landlord would not be able to eat all the rice collected in rents, he might well sell part of the surplus. But this was a secondary affair and certainly not the way to make a killing.

Under this arrangement the landlords had a definite interest in what is loosely called overpopulation. An excess of peasants bid up the rents for the landlord. If one hungry peasant was willing to bid half the crop in order to have land to cultivate, a still hungrier one would be willing to bid a trifle more. Such competition, of course, was not all there was to the relationship. Both custom and the landlord's own interest in the quality of his tenants prevented him from tightening the screw as far as possible. Still the landlord's interest in having numerous peasants as at least potential tenants was a decisive element in the situation.

Two features deserve special attention. Population pressure would serve the landlord's interests only so long as there was a strong government to keep order, guarantee his property rights, and ensure the collection of his rents. This was the task of the Imperial bureaucracy. Hence the overpopulation was not a simple arithmetic ratio between land and men, but in China, as in Japan and India, it had specific economic and political causes. Secondly, the institutional causes long antedate the Western impact. Imperial concern lest the rising tide of population might break through the dikes

[10] In the flourishing days of the Manchu dynasty, government junks brought it through the Grand Canal, an engineering feat comparable to the pyramids. The Imperial court, a large number of scholar-officials, and some of the Imperial military forces, depended heavily on the annual voyage of the junks for their food supply. Hinton, *Grain Tribute System,* esp 5, 97. The system presents a revealing contrast with the supply of grain to the city of Paris under the corresponding phase of royal absolutism. The Parisian system was quite unorganized, outside of the law and effective administrative control, and depended almost entirely on the stimulus of a money economy to private avarice.

thrown up by Chinese society and sweep away the entire system began to display itself as early as before the end of the second quarter of the eighteenth century.[11] Thus the pressure of population on the land is not, as some Marxists have claimed, merely the consequence of the Western impact, or the prevention of industrialization, the destruction of native handicrafts, and the consequent "damming up" the people on the land. All these things happened — and greatly intensified a situation that already existed. Still the parasitic landlord, whom we shall encounter in different forms and at different stages of development in Japan and India, originated in China, too, prior to the Western impact.

As already indicated, the landlord depended on the Imperial bureaucracy to guarantee his property rights and to enforce the collection of rents in kind or in cash.[12] The bureaucracy served his purposes in several other important ways. The landlord had a strong interest in proper irrigation in order to enable his tenants to grow good crops. Hence local landlord families were constantly pressuring the government to construct water-control systems, something they could do effectively only if some member had an academic degree and the official contacts that such a degree made possible.[13] This type of wire-pulling appears to be the main economic contribution of the landlord, taking the place of direct supervision in the course of the agricultural cycle. Larger projects on a provincial scale were the work of provincial landlord cliques. Imperial projects were the work of still more powerful cliques with a national vision. As Owen Lattimore has remarked, behind each Imperial project was a powerful minister, and behind each minister a powerful body of landlords. These facts, it seems to me, bring the notions of water control and Oriental bureaucracy into correct perspective.[14] Secondly, the bureaucracy, rather than land itself, offered

[11] Ho, *Population*, 266–268; some illuminating texts are translated in Lee, *Economic History*, 416, 417, 419, 420.

[12] Detailed information in Hsiao, *Rural China*, 386–395.

[13] Hsiao, *Rural China*, 284–287, 292. See also Ch'ü, *Local Government*, chap X.

[14] See Lattimore, "Industrial Impact on China," 106–107. Chang, *Income*, 49, writing from a viewpoint very different from Lattimore's, also stresses the local origin of irrigation works.

the biggest material prizes.[15] In the absence of primogeniture, a wealthy family might find itself reduced to penury in a few generations through equal division at inheritance. The main way to prevent this misfortune was to send someone with academic aptitudes into the bureaucracy. Making his fortune in this way, through formally illegal but socially accepted corruption, this member could add to the family fortunes. The practice of buying land as an investment and retiring to it after a career in office was quite common. Thus the bureaucracy constituted an alternative way of squeezing an economic surplus out of the peasants and city dwellers as well, about whom we shall have more to say shortly. By and large, bureaucracy seems to have been a more powerful and effective instrument than landholding, though the one could not exist without the other. Landed wealth came out of the bureaucracy and depended on the bureaucracy for its existence. On this score, the critics of a simplified Marxist view have a strong point. Finally, for the landlord, Confucian doctrines and the system of examinations gave legitimacy, at least in his own eyes, to his superior social status and freedom from manual labor as long as some member of the

---

[15] This is the burden of Chang, *Income*. The fact that the best pickings were to be had in the bureaucracy does not contradict the view that landownership constituted the main economic basis of the gentry, since these pickings, as Chang himself shows, went to a small group. Indeed the same generalization would apply to Tudor and Stuart England. On p. 147 Chang asserts that only a small portion of the gentry in the nineteenth century received their main income from the land. What his data show are that a small *proportion of the income of the gentry as a whole* came from landed rent, quite a different matter. I find no figures indicating how many of the gentry were not landowners. Probably there were a substantial number among the bottom rung, the *sheng-yüan*, whom Ho does not consider as real gentry. Chang concludes that income from rent may have been somewhere between 34 and 29 percent of the total received by the gentry as a whole (table 41, p. 329), which is still a sizeable chunk. And as Chang is careful to point out, the statistics are far from trustworthy.

In any case this is a technical and somewhat secondary point. Landed property certainly needed the bureaucracy to buttress its rights and often arose out of a career in the bureaucracy. As far as I am aware, there is no disagreement on this major point.

family, or an adopted bright youngster, could manage to acquire a degree.

In addition to the public works, mainly the irrigation projects already mentioned, the chief task of the Imperial bureaucracy in actual practice was keeping the peace and collecting taxes that became transmuted into books, painting, poetry, concubines, and similar paraphernalia that in other civilizations also make life rather bearable for the upper classes. The problem of keeping the peace was in China mainly a domestic one before the Western intrusion, which began in earnest during the middle of the nineteenth century when internal decay had already made one of its periodic reappearances.[16] On the whole, the foreign threat was limited to periodic conquests by barbarians. When these had conquered enough territory and established themselves as a new dynasty, they adapted themselves to the prevailing social pattern. During the Imperial era, Chinese rulers did not face the problem of continuous military competition on more or less equal terms with other rulers. Hence the standing army did not absorb a large proportion of the society's resources nor impose a bias on the development of the state as it did in France and even more in Prussia. Nor was the problem of keeping the peace one of checking powerful barons at home, though there were some similarities in a time of decay. Rather, it was one of not squeezing the peasants so hard that they would run off and become bandits or feed an insurrection led by dissatisfied elements in the upper class.

The absence of any effective mechanism to prevent such a squeeze may have been one of the fundamental structural weak-

[16] To discuss the dynastic cycle is beyond the writer's competence. Modern sinologists are prone to deny that Chinese history has been fundamentally unchanged for two thousand years, asserting that this is an illusion due to our ignorance. Nevertheless to a nonspecialist it seems quite obvious that, in comparison with Europe, Chinese civilization did remain largely static. What changes are there in China comparable to the Western sequence of city state, world empire, feudalism, royal absolutism, and modern industrial society? Take architecture: is there in China any variety over time comparable to the Parthenon, the cathedral at Chartres, Versailles, the skyscraper?

nesses of the system. It was in the interests of the dynasty to collect taxes fairly and efficiently. But it had few means to ensure that this was done, and very limited personnel. On the other hand, the individual official had a strong incentive to line his pockets as best he could, merely refraining from such flagrant corruption and extortion as to cause a scandal and hence damage his career. This point deserves closer examination.

In any preindustrial society, the attempt to establish a large-scale bureaucracy soon runs into the difficulty that it is very hard to extract enough resources from the population to pay salaries and thereby make officials dependent on their superiors. The way in which the rulers try to get around this difficulty has a tremendous impact on the whole social structure. The French solution was the sale of offices, the Russian one, suitable to Russia's huge expanse of territory, was the granting of estates with serfs in return for service in tsarist officialdom. The Chinese solution was to permit more or less open corruption. Max Weber cites an estimate that the extra-legal income of an official amounted to about four times his regular salary; a modern investigator comes up with the much higher figure of some sixteen to nineteen times the regular salary.[17] The exact amount will probably remain an historical secret; we may be content with the assurance that it was large.

Naturally this practice substantially reduced the effectiveness of control from the center, which varied a great deal at different historical periods. The officer at the lowest rung in the ladder, administering a *hsien*, ordinarily comprising one walled city and the surrounding countryside, was theoretically in charge of at least 20,000 people and often many more.[18] As a temporary sojourner in the area, the usual term being about three years, he could not possibly get to know local conditions. If anything were to be done, it would have to be with the consent and support of local notables, that is, substantial landholding scholars, who were after all "his kind of people." Direct contact with the peasants seems to have been al-

<hr />

[17] Weber, "Konfuzianismus und Taoismus," I, 344; Chang, *Income*, 30, 42.

[18] Ch'ü, *Local government*, 2.

most nonexistent. Runners from the magistrate's office (*yamen*), a low class of people debarred from taking the examinations and improving their lot, did the legwork of collecting taxes, taking *their* share en route.[19] It seems fair to say that the system was highly exploitative in the strictly objective sense of taking more out of the society in resources than it put back in the form of services rendered. On the other hand, because it had to be exploitative in order to work at all, it also had to leave the underlying population very much to its own devices. There was simply no possibility of reordering the daily life of the people in the way modern totalitarian regimes do, or even as formally democratic ones to a lesser extent do in the course of prolonged national emergency. There were futile attempts to control the life of the people, as will be discussed shortly. But deliberate cruelty on a massive scale, as compared with neglect and selfishness, was beyond the range of the system.[20]

Before discussing more specific problems connected with the final agony of this system, it will be well to notice one further structural feature, partly because of its comparative interest in relation to Japan. The examination system tended to breed an oversupply of prospective bureaucrats, particularly·in its later years.[21] At the bottom of the official system of ranking was a large number of degree candidates (*sheng-yüan*), a transitional group between those qualified to hold office and the commoners. Whether they should be counted as regular members of the gentry or not is a matter of dispute among specialists. Their difficult position at the bottom of the ladder of privilege recalls that of the lower ranks of the *samurai* in Japan during the nineteenth century. Both contributed nuclei of opposition to the prevailing system. While in Japan a significant minority in this group provided much of the impetus toward mod-

[19] Ch'ü, *Local government*, chap IV, and p. 137.

[20] The point cannot be pressed too far. When threatened, individually or collectively, the Chinese were as capable of terror as anyone else. Frying alive in oil was one of the punishments I have noticed. See also DeGroot, *Sectarianism and Religious Persecutions,* an instructive reaction to early Western idealization of China.

[21] Ho, *Ladder of Success,* 220 – 221.

ernization, in China this energy mainly dissipated itself in fruitless revolt and insurrection within the prevailing framework.[22] Doubtless the cramping effect of the examination system was partly responsible for the difference. Still, the reasons run much deeper. They have to do with the way in which Chinese society choked off modernization until it was too late for piecemeal adoption. To some of the more recent aspects of this huge problem we may now turn.

2. The Gentry and the World of Commerce

Imperial Chinese society never created an urban trading and manufacturing class comparable to that which grew out of the later stages of feudalism in Western Europe, though at times there were some starts in this direction. Imperial success in uniting the country may be advanced as one of the more obvious reasons for the difference. In Europe the conflict between Pope and Emperor, between kings and nobles, helped the merchants in the cities to break through the crust of the traditional agrarian society because they constituted a valuable source of power in this many-sided competition. It is noteworthy that in Europe the breakthrough occurred first in Italy where the feudal system was generally weaker.[23] The Chinese examination system also deflected ambitious individuals away from commerce. This aspect is noticeable in one of the later abortive spurts toward commercial expansion during the fifteen century. A French historian goes so far as to speak of a "grande bourgeoisie financière" competing with the gentry for first place at this time, but adds significantly that this new bourgeoisie directed its children toward the examinations.[24] Another historian makes the interesting suggestion that the diffusion of printing may have increased the absorptive capacities of the mandarinate. Printing made it possible for some of the smaller merchants to acquire sufficient literary culture to obtain an official post. Though the expense of taking the examinations remained an important barrier, access to official posts

[22] Hsiao, Rural China, 448, 450, 473, 479; Ho, Ladder of Success, 35 – 36.

[23] See Pirenne, Histoire économique, 365 – 372 for a perceptive survey of the political factors at the end of the thirteenth century.

[24] Maspéro and Escarra, Institutions de la Chine, 131.

became somewhat easier. He presents some striking evidence of the attractiveness of the Imperial service. A number of these merchants castrated themselves in order to become eunuchs and enjoy a position close to the throne. Those who castrated themselves enjoyed a special advantage, since they already had the education ordinary eunuchs (the main competitors of the scholar-officials at court) were forbidden to seek.[25]

Probing a little deeper, one may readily perceive that money-making activities represented a dangerous threat to the scholar-officials because it constituted an alternative ladder of prestige and an alternative ground of legitimacy for high social status. No amount of Confucian talk and no amount of sumptuary legislation could be expected to conceal forever the simple fact that someone who made lots of money could buy the good things of life, including even a substantial measure of deference. If the situation were allowed to get out of hand, all the painfully acquired classical culture would become useless and obsolete. Behind this conflict of cultures and value systems, and at its very root, were powerful material interests. Tradition as such was a feeble barrier to commerce; those who wanted to could find justification for it in the Confucian classics.[26] At any rate the gentry were perspicacious enough, in the short run, to see to it that the situation did not get out of hand. They taxed commerce to absorb the profits for themselves. Or they turned it into a state monopoly and kept the most lucrative positions for themselves. The salt trade was the most important monopoly. The attitude of the officials was mainly exploitative. Commerce, like the land, was something to be milked for the benefit of a cultivated upper class. Once again we see that the Imperial bureaucracy served as an instrument for pumping resources out of the population and into the hands of the rulers, who remained careful in the meantime to control any developments that might threaten their privileges.

With the decay of the Imperial apparatus, noticeable before the end of the eighteenth century, its capacity to absorb and control commercial elements inevitably declined. Even if the Imperial

[25] Eberhard, *Chinas Geschichte*, 280 – 282.
[26] Chang, *Income*, 154 – 155.

system had been in full vigor, it could scarcely have resisted the new forces undermining it. For behind these forces came the military and diplomatic thrust of the West, blunted only as the greed of one power checked the cupidity of its rivals. By the second half of the nineteenth century, the traditional rule of the scholar-official had disintegrated in the coastal cities. There a new hybrid society had already emerged in which power and social position no longer rested securely in the hands of those with a classical education.[27] After the conclusion of the Opium War in 1842, the *compradores* spread through all the treaty ports of China. These men served in a variety of capacities as intermediaries between decaying Chinese officialdom and the foreign merchants. Their position was ambiguous. By shady methods they could accumulate great fortunes to live a life of cultivated ease. On the other hand, many Chinese condemned them as servants of the foreign devils who were destroying the foundations of Chinese society.[28] From this point onward, much of China's social and diplomatic history becomes a record of Chinese attempts to keep this hybrid society in check and of contrary efforts by stronger powers to use it as an entering wedge for their commercial and political interests.

When Chinese industry began on its own in a modest way in the 1860s, it did so under the long shadow of provincial gentry, who hoped at this time to turn modern technology to their own separatist purposes. Military problems were in the forefront, and the early plants were exclusively military affairs, such as arsenals, navy yards, and the like. Superficially the situation recalls the mercantilist era in Western social history because of the rulers' interest in forms of industry that would enhance their power. The differences are far more important. In Europe the governments were strong and getting stronger. In China the Manchu dynasty was weak. A mercantilist policy in the manner of a Colbert was impossible because the commercial and industrial element was foreign and largely outside Imperial control. The main Chinese push

[27] On the whole process, see Lattimore, "Industrial Impact."
[28] Wright, *Last Stand of Chinese Conservatism*, 84, 146–147; Levy, and Shih, *Chinese Business Class*, 24.

toward industrialization came from provincial foci of power, with very little from the Imperial government.[29] Hence it was more of a disruptive than a unifying factor. Commercial and industrial elements on the make can be expected to turn for protection to whatever political groups have real power. If it is the king, well and good; his power will wax. If it is a local official, the opposite will be true. Marxists make too much of the way Western imperialists stifled industrial development in China. (Nationalists in India also use this convenient scapegoat.) None of this could have happened without prior stifling by purely domestic forces.

Not until 1910 did the Chinese business class begin to show some definite signs of emerging from official influence and domination.[30] A recent study even gives the impression that the Chinese merchant was well on the way toward emancipation from dependence on the foreigner by the end of the nineteenth century.[31] Still, the decisive areas remained in foreign hands for much longer. The whole indigenous commercial and industrial impulse remained .puny. By the end of the Imperial regime, there were said to be some 20,000 "factories" in China. Of these, only 363 employed mechanical power. The rest used only human or animal power.[32]

Thus China, like Russia, entered the modern era with a numerically small and politically dependent middle class. This stratum did not develop an independent ideology of its own as it did in Western Europe. Nevertheless it played an important part in undermining the mandarin state and creating new political groupings in the attempt to replace it. The growth of this class along the coast combined with the breakup of the Empire into regional satrapies in a way that foreshadowed the combination of "bourgeois" and militarist roles in the hey-day of the warlords (roughly 1911 to 1927) and on into the Kuomintang era. An early example (1870 – 1895) of this general development is Li Hung-chang, who for twenty-

[29] Feuerwerker, *China's Early Industrialization*, I, 12 – 13; Levy and Shih, *Chinese Business Class*, 27, 29.

[30] Levy and Shih, *Chinese Business Class*, 50.

[31] Allen and Donnithorne, *Western Enterprise*, 37, 49.

[32] Feuerwerker, *China's Early Industrialization*, 5.

S.D.D. – 7

five years "moved toward single-handed control over foreign affairs, domination of the maritime customs revenue, monopoly of
armaments production, and complete control of the military forces
in the northern half of the empire."[33] Furthermore a substantial
amalgamation gradually took place between sections of the gentry
(and later their successors turned landlords pure and simple) and
urban leaders in trade, finance, and industry.[34] This amalgam provided the chief social underpinning of the Kuomintang, an attempt
to revive the essence of the Imperial system, that is, political support
of landlordism with a combination of gangsterism indigenous to
China and a veneer of pseudo-Confucianism that displays interesting resemblances to Western fascism, to be discussed in more detail
later. This combination arose in very large measure out of the gentry's failure to make the transition from preindustrial to commercial forms of farming. The reasons for this failure will now occupy
our attention.

3. *The Failure to Adopt Commercial Agriculture*

A cultural and psychological explanation, to the effect that the
methodical pursuit of profit even in agriculture was incompatible
with the Confucian ideal of stylized leisure, rapidly runs into difficulties. Western scholarship, it seems to me, has overemphasized
the significance of the condescending attitude of the Chinese upper
stratum toward the Western barbarians. As mentioned in the preceding section, where the Chinese gentry had the opportunity to
take up the technical civilization of the West and even some of its
social habits, there were a number who did not hesitate to do so.
Writing about the early stage of the Western impact, one careful
scholar noticed that "a conspicuous phase of the period before 1894
was the initiation of industrial and mechanical enterprises by prominent members of the official class, that group ordinarily thought of
in the West as composed of arch conservatives."[35] A more recent
student has commented that, among serious Chinese thinkers of the
1890s, the study of Western technology was considered almost a

[33] Cf Feuerwerker, *China's Early Industrialization*, 13.
[34] Levy and Shih, *Chinese Business Class*, 50; Lang, *Chinese Family*, 97.
[35] Cameron, *Reform Movement*, 11.

panacea for China's economic backwardness.[36] If there was some cultural barrier to technical improvement, it does not seem that it could have been an insuperable one. Since the Chinese upper class did display considerable interest in technology for military and industrial purposes, one might expect *a fortiori* that they would display an even greater interest in regard to agriculture because it was so central to their whole way of life. (We may be practically certain that such an explanation would have been presented if technically advanced commercial agriculture had taken hold.) Instead, with a few random exceptions, confined to programmatic statements, they displayed no such interest.[37]

A more convincing explanation may be constructed from an examination of the material and political conditions that existed in China at the time that the modern world made its impact. Although cities existed in China, there was no rapidly growing urban population with at least moderately diffused and increasing prosperity that could act as a stimulus to rationalized production for the market. To judge from the situation at a later date, the proximity of a town or city mainly served to stimulate peasant truck gardening, the cultivation of fruit and vegetables that could be taken into the market by hand. Imperial policy in the early and vigorous days of the dynasty may have opposed the formation of large landed estates. In the second half of the nineteenth century, such big estates did dominate parts of the Empire.[38] Although the point would bear further investigation, it seems that a big estate was often simply an agglomeration of small properties, that is, composed of more peasants who therefore gave the proprietor a larger aggregate rent.

Here we approach the nub of the matter. The Chinese landlord-tenant relationship was a political device for squeezing an economic surplus out of the peasant and turning it into the amenities of civilization. (What the peasant did and did not get out of the relationship is an important aspect that we may neglect for the

[36] Feuerwerker, *China's Early Industrialization*, 37.

[37] Feuerwerker, *China's Early Industrialization*, 34.

[38] Jamieson et al, "Tenure of Land in China," 100, mentions huge holdings in Kiangsu. Khokhlov, "Agrarnye otnosheniya," 110, asserts that in the beginning of the nineteenth century they existed nearly everywhere.

moment.) In the absence of a big urban market, there was little reason to change it, perhaps even less possibility of doing so. Ambitious and energetic individuals under the Empire got themselves a bureaucratic post in order to add to the family acres.

Chinese agriculture did not, of course, remain entirely static during the latter part of the nineteenth century and the first decades of the twentieth. As urban life increased, it had far-reaching effects on the agrarian sector, some of which have already come to our attention, while others will do so subsequently. Here we need to notice only one salient point. Under the conditions of a simple technology and abundant labor, there was no need for a Chinese landowner to rationalize production on his farm to produce for the urban market. If his farm were in the neighborhood of a city, it was much simpler and easier for him to sit back and rent his land to peasant tenants, letting the competition for land drive up his income with very little effort on his part. Similarly, the more prosperous town dwellers could easily find a profitable investment in land. Economically this process meant the growth of absentee landlordism near the cities. Sociologically it contributed to the partial fusion of sections of the former gentry and the wealthier elements in the cities. But this situation could be stable only as long as political methods could be found to keep the peasants at work and collect rents from them. In the not-so-long run, this problem was to prove insoluble.

Thus it does not appear that any innate lack of adaptability prevented the Chinese gentry from making a successful transition to the modern world. More important was the lack of incentive and the presence in this historical situation of other and readier alternatives. For much of the time there was not enough of a market to make the effort worthwhile. When and where the market did appear, it turned the gentry into *rentiers* with political connections rather than into agrarian entrepreneurs. Only a minority made this step. But this minority formed the leading edge of a powerful historical trend. Given the conditions that they faced, it is very difficult to see what else they could have done. Like the decline of any ruling class, the fate of the Chinese gentry, far from the most unattractive ruling class in history, has its share of tragedy.

4. Collapse of the Imperial System and the Rise of the Warlords

In all the major countries of Europe the struggle between the nobility and the crown was for a very long time one of the decisive. elements of politics. Everywhere, even in Russia, one may perceive at some point the development of estates, what German historians call *Stände*, status groups with a substantial degree of corporate identity and publicly recognized immunities that they defended jealously against other groups and especially against the crown. The onset of modernization affected this struggle in a variety of ways depending on the time and situation in which it began. In England it was favorable to the development of parliamentary democracy; on the continent, it was much less so or even generally unfavorable, though there was usually at some point an aristocratic liberal opposition.

During the period under discussion, the Chinese landed upper classes did not develop any significant principled opposition to the Imperial system. There were no doubt some who took up Western parliamentary notions as an intellectual plaything, but there was no political movement of opposition with substantial roots in Chinese conditions. Some circumstances favoring such a development were present. The Chinese official class — here I speak of degree holders whether landlords or not — had a strong sense of corporate identity, as well as privileges and immunities recognized by the Emperor and to a considerable extent by wide sections of the public.[39] In Europe under feudalism aristocrats created privileges, immunities, and a sense of corporate identity, institutions that some historians regard as a major part of the impulse that culminated in parliamentary democracy. In China any such impulse faced much greater obstacles. Landed property in Chinese society would not easily serve as a basis for political power separate from the political mechanism that made it pay. The Imperial system was not only a way of making property pay, it was a way of getting property too.

[39] Good brief summary in Ch'ü, *Local Government*, 173–175. Ho, *Ladder of Success*, 99, asserts that members of the same examination class called one another brothers and that this fictive kinship relationship often passed on to the next generation.

The fact that circumstances generally precluded the emergence of a liberal aristocratic opposition decreased the flexibility of China's response to a totally novel historical challenge and helps to explain one new feature that we encounter in the Chinese case, the nearly complete disintegration of the central government. A regime, many of whose key features had lasted for centuries, simply fell apart in less than a hundred years under the impact of Western blows.

There was to be sure a brief period in the Russian response to somewhat similar stresses when the central government in effect disappeared. But in Russia, from the perspective of fundamental social trends, this period of collapse was scarcely more than an episode. In China, on the other hand, the final period of near anarchy lasted much longer. As a minimum, one might date it from the proclamation of the Republic in 1911 to the formal victory of the Kuomintang in 1927. The latter initiated a weak reactionary phase, to be discussed in more detail below, that also differs from the Russian experience since it followed rather than antedated the collapse. In this section I shall try to point out some of the reasons for the disintegration and draw attention to the ways in which the upper strata managed to save themselves as the old building broke into pieces over their heads.

A serious dilemma faced the Manchu government during the last half century of its rule. On the one hand, it needed greater revenue to put down internal rebellion and face foreign enemies. On the other hand, it could not obtain this revenue without destroying the whole system of gentry privileges. To raise adequate revenue would have required the encouragement of commerce and industry. The fact that foreigners managed the customs made such a policy even more difficult. Raising the government's revenues would also have made necessary the introduction of an efficient system of taxation and putting an end to the officials' habit of pocketing the lion's share of what the government took from its subjects. Thus the government would have had to eliminate a major source of the gentry's income and encourage the growth of a social class that inevitably would have competed more and more successfully with the gentry. As long as the government itself rested on the gentry, such a course was most unlikely.[40] A shrewd and powerful ruler such as Bismarck can afford to alienate substantial segments of his support in the course of pursuing policies that he hopes will bring greater benefits and more powerful underpinning for the regime. To win such a gamble assures the statesman a prominent place in history textbooks, the "judgment of history" to which all politicians appeal. No ruler can simply dispense with his main body of support and ask it to commit political suicide.

To say that successful reform in nineteenth-century China was unlikely under the circumstances does not imply that the government failed to make any efforts. Neither the government nor the gentry let themselves drift down the tide of history. There were attempts at reform, whose failure serves to bring out the formidable obstacles the rulers faced.

The most energetic effort, described by Mary C. Wright in an illuminating monograph, lasted a dozen years from 1862 to 1874 and is known as the T'ung-chih Restoration. The distinguished officials who led the movement met the problems of internal rebellion and foreign aggression with a resolute backward-looking policy. One of their main policies consisted in efforts to strengthen the position of the gentry. They scrupulously respected its legal and economic privileges, restored the *status quo ante* in land titles where revolution had upset them, and used tax relief primarily for the relief of landlords. Trade and commerce they treated as "parasitic excrescences" on an ordered agrarian society.[41] By no means altogether oblivious of the economic and social problems of their society, they spoke mainly in ethical terms of finding the "right" man with the "right" character to do the "right" thing, "right" of course being defined in Confucian terms. Such an upsurge of traditional rhetoric often occurs when a ruling class finds itself in a tight corner. Though the T'ung-chih Restoration succeeded for the moment, this very success may have hastened the ultimate end by temporarily strengthening those forces most opposed to a funda-

[40] See Wright, *Last Stand*, 184 – 190; Cameron, *Reform Movement*, 163; Morse, *Trade and Administration* in which chap IV is well worth reading.

[41] Wright, *Last Stand*, 129, 167.

mental readjustment of Chinese society. In this way, Restoration statesmen may have contributed to the violent overthrow of the class and social institutions they sought to restore.

The flurry of reforms under the Dowager Empress in the opening years of the twentieth century were of a different character and bring out another aspect of the problem. Her attempts to modernize the educational system and to abolish the examination system we can only mention. There followed in 1906 the throne's proclamation of adherence to the principle of constitutional government, though the principle was not to be put into effect until the country was ready. Along with this, she proposed and made some energetic attempts to carry out a reform of the bureaucracy. When her plans ran into stubborn opposition, she dismissed four of her six ministers in the Grand Council, showing she meant business.[42] Though this spurt of reforming energy came to nothing, though it stands in almost ludicrous contrast with the earlier behavior of this irascible archreactionary and skilled intriguer, to dismiss it with a smile as a meaningless gesture would be to misinterpret a revealing episode. The pattern of her actions strongly suggests that her real goal was the establishment of a strong centralized bureaucratic government over which she would be able to exercise direct personal control, roughly along the lines of a Germany or a Japan.[43]

The main point for our purpose is that the social basis for such a regime was lacking in China — even more lacking than in Russia. The central feature of such regimes, as shown also by the experience of Italy and Spain, is a coalition between sections of the old agrarian ruling classes that have considerable political power and a shaky economic position with an emerging commercial and industrial élite with some economic power but political and social disadvantages. In China at this time, native urban commercial groups were not strong enough to provide a useful partner for such an alliance. A quarter of a century was to elapse before such an at-

[42] Cameron, *Reform*, 103, 105. See also Bland and Backhouse, *China*, 431–432.

[43] For further evidence on this point, see her decree of January 21, 1901, quoted by Bland and Backhouse, *China*, 419–424, esp 423.

tempt at reaction could be carried out under new auspices, those of the Kuomintang, with at least some prospect of success.

The ground had been prepared during the latter third of the nineteenth century when important changes in the character and position of the gentry were taking place. The Confucian scholarly ideal, and with it the traditional system of status in China as a whole, had been crumbling away as the material basis of the scholar-official's role and its significance in Chinese society steadily diminished. We have already had occasion to notice the government's awkward predicament — caught between the need for additional revenue and fear of damaging the gentry's position. The expedients to which it resorted contributed to the ultimate collapse of the regime.

In its search for revenue, after the Taiping Rebellion (1850 – 1866) had devastated huge areas of China, the government opened somewhat wider the back door to service in the state, allowing more persons to purchase rank instead of obtaining it through the regular route of examinations.[44] Though new and wealthy recruits did not swamp the hierarchy, the prestige of the examination was almost certainly reduced and a major prop of the old regime severely damaged. The formal abolition of the examination system, after attempts to modernize it that did no more than antagonize traditional scholars fearful that their skills were becoming obsolete, took place by proclamation in 1905. As there was nothing to put in its place, the system tottered along for a few years under its own momentum.

As the possibility of exercising the traditional role of the scholar declined and the power of the central government weakened, the gentry took control of local affairs more and more into their own hands, foreshadowing the long period of chaos and internecine warfare that did not really come to an end until the Communist victory in 1949. In many parts of the country, the gentry simply collected their own taxes and forbade others to pay them to the central government.[45] By establishing the famous *likin*, a tax

[44] Chang, *Chinese Gentry*, 111, 141; for a different assessment of the character of the "irregulars," see Ho, *Ladder of Success*, 38 – 41.

[45] Chang, *Chinese Gentry*, 46, 66, 70.

collected from shopkeepers and travelling merchants, the Imperial government intensified disruptive trends. The tax was an emergency measure to raise funds needed as a result of the Taiping Rebellion that it could not collect through traditional methods. It is scarcely surprising that several Restoration leaders favored the *likin* in preference to a heavier tax on land.[46] Control of the tax fell out of the hands of the Imperial government, while the tax itself remained to help provide an economic base for new regional authorities, prototypes of the warlord era.[47]

The end of the Manchu dynasty in 1911 and the proclamation of the Republic in 1912 merely gave oblique constitutional recognition to the fact that real power had passed into the hands of the local satraps where it would remain for at least another decade and a half. During this period, important sections of what had been the gentry clung to power either by turning into warlords or by allying themselves with individual militarists. The whole social and cultural apparatus that had given them legitimacy was smashed beyond hope of repair. Their successors were to be landlords pure and simple, gangsters, or a combination of the two, a tendency that lay just below the surface in Imperial times.

There was a symbiotic relationship between the landlord and the warlord gangster. It appears most clearly in the workings of the system of requisitions, taxes in labor and kind, which continued to be the chief way to compel the peasantry to support the élites in the countryside. Merchants too played their part, foreshadowing the coalition between commercial groups and landlords that underlay the Kuomintang.

Theoretically, military requisitions were based on the land tax. The system was highly flexible, mainly to the disadvantage of the peasant, who lost much of what protection he once had from Imperial officials and the code of limited "legitimate" exploitation, a deterioration that had already been taking place for some time. An original assessment of two *catties* of flour might become two and a half, three *catties* of hay might turn into six, four carts into sixteen, and so on. Grain dealers in collusion with requisition collectors and

46 Wright, *Last Stand*, 168 – 169.
47 Beal, *Origin of Likin*, 41 – 44; cf Chang, *Chinese Gentry*, 69.

often acting as agents of landlords could make a profit by paying the sum when due and then raising the prices of grain, sharing the difference between the fixed and the market price. Sometimes collections would be made continuous even though troops had moved away. Larger landholders, often militarists themselves, generally made their tenants pay the requisitions for them.[48] Though I suspect that the sources from which this information has been gleaned may exaggerate peasant distress, there can be no doubt about the existence of appalling man-made suffering.

Leaving the position of the peasantry aside for discussion at an appropriate point, we may notice certain more general features of the warlord era. The system of requisitions represented a continuation of the gentry's relation to politics under the mandarinate, whereby political power begat and supported economic power to generate political power once more. With the disappearance of the central government, the landed upper class lost one of the main mechanisms that had helped to keep Chinese society in its ancient mold, if by no means unmarred by serious cracks and rifts. In earlier ages, according to some authorities, the society had recovered as the gentry and the peasants worked out a new *modus vivendi* and a new and vigorous dynasty came to power. In the twentieth century new forces were at work, and the successors to the old ruling class would turn without success to new allies. That is the tale of the Kuomintang, to whose fate we may now turn.

5. The Kuomintang Interlude and its Meaning

By the 1920s, commercial and industrial interests had become a significant factor in Chinese political and social life, though their continuing dependence upon both the foreigner and their subordination to agrarian interests forced them to play a very different role from their Western European counterpart. In the meantime, as will appear in more detail shortly, a numerically small but politically significant sector of the landlords near the port cities had begun to amalgamate with this class and turn into *rentiers*. The

[48] *Agrarian China,* 101 – 109. The article from which this is taken appeared in 1931. Despite a primitive Marxist bias in many of these studies this is a useful source of information on a little-known period.

urban workers too had made their appearance on the historical stage in a stormy and violent fashion.

It was in this situation that the Kuomintang became active. The story of its rise to power has been told too often to bear detailed repetition here.[49] Though still somewhat clouded in controversy, the essential points for our purpose appear to be the following ones.

With important native Communist and Soviet assistance, the Kuomintang by late 1927 had won control of a substantial part of China, working out from its base in the south. Up to this moment, its success had been mainly due to its ability to harness and ride the tides of discontent among the peasants and the workers. Thus the Kuomintang's social program distinguished it from the warlords and gave it an advantage over them. For a time, hopes ran high that the Kuomintang's military force might overcome the warlords and unify China on the basis of a revolutionary program.

Such was not to be the case, though formal unification did occur. The Kuomintang's partial success brought to the surface latent conflicts among the disparate elements that a program of nationalist unification had temporarily brought together. The landed upper classes, who provided officers for the military force, became increasingly nervous lest the peasants might get out of hand. Ironically enough the Chinese Communists, under some prodding from Moscow, supported the successors to the gentry at this juncture on the ground that the national revolution took precedence over the social one.[50] The role of the urban merchants and financiers is less clear.[51] But they could scarcely have been any happier than the gentry about the prospect of a Kuomintang victory with a left-wing program.

[49] Holcombe, *Chinese Revolution*, is a pioneering study. Isaacs, *Tragedy of the Revolution*, seems to me the best general account. Schwartz, *Chinese Communism*, and Brandt, *Stalin's Failure*, throw additional light on Russian and Chinese Communist actions during this period.

[50] Brandt, *Stalin's Failure*, 106 – 107, 125.

[51] A journalist asserts that Chiang obtained the promise of heavy financial support from leading bankers and merchants in Shanghai who agreed to raise the money on the understanding that the new government was to be definitely anti-Communist. See Berkov, *Strong Man of China*, 64.

In these circumstances, Chiang Kai-shek, who had firm control over an important section of the military forces, managed to disassociate himself from the revolution, amid a welter of intrigue and by a series of military coups. Toward the end of this disengagement Chiang turned upon the workers in the classic pattern of the agrarian-bourgeois alliance. On April 12, 1927, his agents, together with others on the spot, including French, British, and Japanese police and military forces, carried out a mass slaughter of workers, intellectuals, and others accused of sympathizing with the Communists.[52] Chiang and his military machine were not, however, a mere passive instrument of this alliance. He also turned on the capitalist elements themselves, subjecting them to confiscation and compulsory loans, amid threats of prison and execution.[53]

Chiang's victory inaugurated a new phase in Chinese politics. Both in word and deed, the Kuomintang gave priority to national unification as something that had to precede political and agrarian reform. In reality this meant the search for a solution to the agrarian problem through military force, that is, the suppression of banditry and communism. It is too much to assert that this prospect was hopeless from the start. Modernization did take place under reactionary auspices and with a substantial dose of repression in Japan as well as in Germany, the latter a country that also faced the task of national unification. Nevertheless the problems facing China were vastly more difficult.

To specify the agrarian aspects in any detail soon runs into gaps in the data, especially the almost complete absence of dependable statistics, lacunae far wider in the case of China than the other countries studied for this book. Nevertheless the main outlines of the problem are quite clear. The first point that deserves to be made is a negative one. Except perhaps in some areas, China, after the First World War, was not a country where a class of aristocratic owners of huge *latifundia* exploited a mass of poor peasants and landless laborers. To emphasize this fact, however, would seriously distort the image of what was actually taking place. Under the

[52] Isaacs, *Tragedy of the Revolution*, chap 11. The role of foreign forces is described on p. 180.
[53] Isaacs, *Tragedy of the Revolution*, 181.

impact of advancing commerce and industry, China was steadily moving toward a system of absentee ownership with increasing differences in wealth. This change was most marked in the coastal areas, especially near large cities. In many parts of the interior, too, tenancy problems were acute, though there they seem rather the legacy of former practices than the consequences of new forces.[54] That Chinese agriculture involved tremendous amounts of human labor and very little in the way of expensive implements or live-stock — a few rich families in the wheat-growing North did have horses — is a fact so well known as scarcely to bear repeating. As usual, Tawney puts the point in its political and social context, in rolling classical prose. The distinctive note of Chinese agriculture, he observes, was "economy of space, economy of materials, econ-omy of implements, economy of fodder, economy of fuel, econ-omy of waste products, economy of everything except of forests, which have been plundered, with prodigal recklessness, to the ruin of the soil, and of the labor of human beings, whom social habits have made abundant and abundance cheap."[55]

In the absence of a tradition of privileged feudal estates, the relationship between landlord and tenant contained strong elements of a business contract. But it was still a preindustrial business con-tract heavily flavored by local custom. Thus the statistical category of tenancy covered a wide variety of situations. Some landlords who had overburdened themselves with debt in buying land might be worse off than many tenants. On the other hand, those who rented land might be either well-to-do persons with spare cash and implements, or else poor peasants with little or no land, whose least misfortune might put them under conditions approaching slavery.[56] Considerations such as these show the difficulty of connecting the specific terms landlord and peasant to any general notion of social classes. Still one must not fall victim to the opposite illusion: that

[54] Tawney, Land and Labour, is by far the best account. Buck, Land Utilization, does contain some useful statistical information gathered under Buck's direction.

[55] Tawney, Land and Labour, 48.

[56] Tawney, Land and Labour, 63, 65; China-U.S. Agricultural Mission, Report, 53; Agrarian China, 59.

one cannot speak of social classes because the statistical data fail to bring them out clearly. The extent to which there was an explosive class struggle in the countryside is a more complicated problem to which we shall come in due course.

A few statistical estimates are worth bringing to the reader's attention. By the end of the first quarter of the twentieth century, land in China had become almost entirely private property. The State held only about seven percent. Almost all of the remaining ninety-three percent was in the hands of individuals. Of this about three-quarters was owned by the farmer himself, and about one-fourth rented.[57] At first glance, such figures would seem to indicate that tenancy was not a serious problem. A breakdown by regions tells a different story. In the wheat-growing regions of the North, ownership accounted for about seven-eighths of the land, according to the most dependable estimate.[58] Such tenancy as there was often took the form of share renting, generally preferred by tenants in areas where there was great risk from flood or drought.[59] In the light of subsequent Communist entrenchment in many parts of the North, I am suspicious of these statistics but unable to do more than state the existence of the problem. According to one source, land-lordism was clearly rampant and deep rooted in the social structure of an area in northeastern China later under Communist control.[60] In the South, particularly in the rice-growing areas, the landlord was a much more important figure. Over several provinces, the area of rented land came to forty percent and more, though in the rice region as a whole three-fifths of the land was still owned.[61] Near

[57] Buck, *Land Utilization*, 9. Compare China-U.S. Agricultural Mission, *Report*, 17.

[58] Buck, *Land Utilization*, 194.

[59] China-U.S. Agricultural Mission, *Report*, 55.

[60] Crook and Crook, *Revolution in a Chinese Village*, 3, 12, 13, 27 – 28. This study, conducted by a Canadian and an Englishman under Communist auspices in 1948 has the advantage of being less inhibited about the seamy side of Kuomintang rule. Though the authors maintain standards of scientific objectivity and the book is in no sense a Communist tract, I sense that they have accepted somewhat uncritically the Communist version of the recent past in the village.

[61] Buck, *Land Utilization*, 194, map on 195.

the big cities, occupying ownership was rare indeed. Here the absentee landlord, collecting rents chiefly in cash, had become the characteristic figure by the late 1920s if not earlier.[62] Thus the map tells a familiar historical story, that of a society in which commercial influences were eating away at the peasant proprietorship and concentrating wealth in the hands of a new social formation, a fusion between parts of the old ruling class and new elements rising in the cities.

As this fusion formed the main social basis of the Kuomintang, its agrarian policy was one of trying to maintain or restore the *status quo*. In addition, the presence of the Communist rival with *de facto* independence tended to polarize the situation and make Kuomintang policy more reactionary and oppressive. An American scholar sympathetic to the Kuomintang offers this general characterization: "The Communists act as the inheritors to temporarily fanatical peasant rebellions: the National Government and the Kuomintang to ascendant mandarinates."[63] Certainly not the whole story, the appraisal is nevertheless an accurate one. Elsewhere the same scholar writes on the basis of direct observation:

> Since [the Kuomintang] . . . does not promote rural class warfare, pre-existing class relationships continue. The Party and the Government have sought, not always efficiently or faithfully to the *n*th degree to carry out the programs of land reform. . . . The Kuomintang has tolerated widespread sharecropping, land destitution, usury, and rural despotism — because it found these in existence, and was preoccupied with building a national government, a modern army, adequate finance, and with eradicating some of the worst evils, such as opium, bandits, and Communists. . . .[64]

In this passage the author accepts at face value the Kuomintang statements about the reasons for their policy. Nevertheless the passage is important testimony from a witness friendly to the Kuomintang to the effect that their policy was one of maintaining

---

[62] Tawney, *Land and Labour*, 37 – 38; China-U.S. Agricultural Mission, *Report*, 55.

[63] Linebarger, *China of Chiang*, 233.

[64] Linebarger, *China of Chiang,* 147 – 148.

the *status quo* in the countryside, in itself a form of class warfare.

The Kuomintang's inability to carry out a serious overhauling of agrarian relations does not mean that there was no improvement at all. From time to time, the Kuomintang issued decrees and pronouncements aimed at improving the condition of the peasantry.[65] In some areas, such as Szechuan, there was probably real improvement, as the rule of the Kuomintang replaced the exactions of the warlord.[66] In a number of areas, according to an American official report, landlords received an average of one-third of the gross farm receipts, or slightly less than the 37.5 percent set at one time as a ceiling by the Communists and by the Kuomintang in its legislation.[67] Liberal elements were able to promote efforts at gradual reform, such as the rural reconstruction movement, that were tolerated as long as they remained "politically innocuous." The purpose of the reconstruction movement was "to improve the entire community without revolutionizing its class structure."[68] Similar was the "living social laboratory" of Ting Hsien, a northern district of 400,000 people where for the first time intellectuals went deliberately to the people.[69]

The point that emerges most clearly from both friendly and hostile testimony is that the Kuomintang's reforms were window dressing inasmuch as they stopped short of altering the élites' control of local life. In areas untouched by attempted reform, there was no question about their retention of power. Even as friendly a source as Linebarger observes that "Many *hsien* are under local machines which permit wealthy conservatives to evade tax payments, steal government funds, and repress genuine farmer organ-

---

[65] Some of these are summarized in Lamb, *Agrarian Movement,* 45 – 46, 78 – 79.

[66] Linebarger, *China of Chiang,* 222.

[67] China-U.S. Agricultural Mission, *Report,* 56. The date of the Kuomintang legislation is not given.

[68] Linebarger, *China of Chiang,* 220 – 221. The characterization is Linebarger's.

[69] Linebarger, *China of Chiang;* 218 – 219. See also the report on this community by Gamble, *Ting Hsien.* It may be significant that the social structure of this community is scarcely visible behind the mass of statistical data in this study.

ization."[70] Over wide areas of China, the end of the Imperial regime did not produce fundamental changes in the political and economic role of the landed upper classes. They continued to behave in the same fashion in the loosely unified satrapies of the Kuomintang as they had under the warlords and under the Manchus. Sources critical of the Kuomintang bring this point out even more clearly. Discussing a revision of land legislation issued by the Kuomintang in 1937, whose purpose was the encouragement of peasant farms, one Chinese writer observes that political power in the village remained in the hands of the former gentry. "It cannot therefore be expected that these gentlemen will carry out with any degree of faithfulness the rental policies of a new law which would tend to loosen the economic strong stranglehold they have on the peasantry."[71] Similarly a study of local government showed that elective procedures had not been put into effect at the *hsien* (or county) level in most provinces, due not only to the continuing turbulence of the times, but also to sabotage of the procedures by both local and higher officials of the government.[72] Often landlords, according to another source, threatened to accuse tenants who insisted on rent reduction of being Communists, for which they could be arrested.[73]

The situation, of course, almost certainly was not as bad everywhere as these scattered criticisms might suggest. That they could be published at all in the early to midthirties is in itself a significant fact, especially when one recalls Chiang's bloody repression a few years before. Anthropological studies of several Chinese communities during this period indicate that patriarchal attitudes and institutions continued in many places to hold the grosser forms of exploitation in check. As part of the same picture, however, they document the continuity of ex-gentry rule at the local level. Thus they reenforce the conclusion that the Kuomintang agrarian policy amounted to an effort to retain the old order.

There were important regional variations in the extent to

[70] *China of Chiang*, 220.

.[71] *Agrarian China*, 155, quoting an article published in 1937.

[72] See Shen, "Local Government," 190 – 191, 193, for an instructive episode.

[73] *Agrarian China*, 147. The original article appeared in 1932.

which older institutions survived into the Kuomintang period. As already noted, these regional differences reflect successive stages of historical development. In some remote interior villages, by accepting what would seem to Westerners an abysmally low standard of living, a few leading families could still take on some of the traits of a leisure class, such as freedom from physical labor and adherence to a philosophy of contentment, aided in some instances by opium smoking, though they fell far short of the ideal of the classically educated gentry.[74] At the opposite end of the scale would be a village near a big city where traces of the former gentry had practically disappeared but where absentee landlords from the city had come to own two-thirds of the subsoil, leaving "ownership" of the surface soil to the cultivator.[75] In another village, however, not far from Nanking, studied just prior to the Communist takeover, the survival of the former ruling class and some of the same methods of maintaining its position appear much more clearly. There the status of a "gentleman" was one that only affluent landlords held. There too, however, the landlords' power reached only as far as the local garrison could extend its protection, a significant sign of the times. Areas on the edge of the county, removed from the police power of the town "defied the landlords and paid no rent."[76] These facts tell us a great deal about the real relation between military force, the bourgeoisie, and the wealthy landlords or neo-gentry during the latter part of the Kuomintang period.[77]

Still more evidence on the survival of the former landed upper classes and their continuing political importance comes from the strategic policies of the Kuomintang prior to and during the war with Japan. It is well known that commercial and industrial inter-

[74] For an example see Fei and Chang, *Earthbound China*, 19, 81 – 84, 92.

[75] See the pioneering study carried out by Fei during the 1930s, *Peasant Life*, 9 – 10, 185, 191. On the significance of· dual ownership of the soil Fei agrees with Tawney, *Land and Labour*, 36 – 38.

[76] Fried, *Fabric of Chinese Society*, 7, 17, 101, 196.

·[77] For further information on the survival of the former ruling class in new circumstances see M. C. Yang, *Chinese Village*, 1, 183 – 186. In another village, near Canton, according to C. K. Yang, *Village in Transition*, 19, there was one unemployed teacher of traditional learning. Large landlords lived in the city and took no part in agricultural work.

ests failed to register significant advances under the Kuomintang. At first glance, this fact might seem attributable to the Japanese blockade and occupation. But this can scarcely be the whole story since the blockade began only in 1937. A significant factor appears to have been the continuing agrarian opposition to China's transformation into an industrial power. A military historian without the remotest Marxist sympathies notes that, before the war began, China preferred to import whatever equipment seemed indispensable rather than to build up a native industrial base.[78] Tactics on the battlefield likewise reflected China's social structure, though Liu does not draw this fairly obvious conclusion. In the absence of superior weapons, China simply used masses of peasant manpower, urging her soldiers to be brave in the defense of the country. This "death-stand" attitude resulted in enormous casualties. The battles of 1940 alone are said to have cost the Chinese 28 percent of their forces. The same source estimates that an average of 23 percent of all the able-bodied men drafted in the 8 years of war were casualties.[79] One might object that any preindustrial state caught in the same situation would have suffered approximately the same experience. This objection, I think, misses the main point: China remained preindustrial largely because the successors to the gentry retained the substance of political control.

Let us now change our focus and look at the Kuomintang regime from the standpoint of comparative institutional history. As we step back from the details (though we would like to have many more accurate ones than we do), the two decades of Kuomintang rule take on some of the essential characteristics of the reactionary phase of the European response to industrialism, including important totalitarian features. The main social basis of the Kuomintang, as we have already seen, was a coalition, or perhaps better, a form of antagonistic cooperation between the successors to the gentry and urban commercial, financial, and industrial interests. The Kuomintang, through its control of the means of violence, served as the link that held the coalition together. At the same time its control of violence enabled it to blackmail the urban capitalist

[78] Liu, *Military History*, 155.
[79] *Military History*, 145.

sector and to operate the machinery of government both directly and indirectly. In both these respects the Kuomintang resembled Hitler's NSDAP.

There are, however, important differences in both the social bases and the historical circumstances that distinguish the Kuomintang from its European counterparts. These differences help to account for the relatively feeble character of the Chinese reactionary phase. An obvious one is the absence of a strong industrial base in China. Correspondingly, the capitalist element was very much weaker. It is a safe guess that the Japanese occupation of the coastal cities reduced the influence of this group even further. Finally, the Japanese invasion, though it provided a direct target for nationalist sentiment, effectively prevented China's reactionary phase from becoming one of foreign expansion, such as took place under German, Italian, and Japanese fascism. For these reasons, the Chinese reactionary and protofascist phase resembles that of Franco's Spain, where an agrarian élite also managed to stay on top but could not execute an aggressive foreign policy, more than it does corresponding phases in Germany or Italy.

It is in the area of doctrines, where realistic considerations are somewhat less pressing, that one may observe the most striking resemblances between the Chinese reactionary period and its European counterparts. During its revolutionary phase prior to attaining power, the Kuomintang had identified itself with the Taiping Rebellion. After obtaining power and with Chiang Kai-shek's emergence as the real leader, the Party did an about-face, identifying itself with the Imperial system and its apparent success during the Restoration of 1862 – 1874,[80] a switch that recalls the early behavior of Italian fascism. After victory, the doctrine became a curious amalgam of Confucian elements and scraps taken from Western liberal thinking. The latter, as is well known, had entered through the influence of Sun Yat-sen, who remained as the most revered ancestor of the movement. The analogies to European fascism arise mainly from the pattern and shadings of emphasis that Chiang Kai-

[80] Wright, *Last Stand*, 300. For a penetrating analysis of the strictly Chinese aspects of Kuomintang doctrine see 301 – 312.

shek, or those who wrote his doctrinal pronouncements, placed upon these disparate elements.

The main diagnosis of China's problems was couched in semi-Confucian moral and philosophical platitudes to the effect that matters went wrong after the 1911 revolution because the Chinese people did not think correctly. Chiang asserted in 1943 that the Chinese in general had failed to understand the true wisdom of Sun Yat-sen's deep philosophical statement that "to understand is difficult; to act is easy" and still thought that "to understand is easy; to act is difficult." The only concrete element in the diagnosis is the harm that foreign domination and the unequal treaties wrought in China, with a few comments on the weakness and corruption of the Manchu dynasty.[81] There is practically no discussion of the social and economic factors that had brought China to her current plight. To bring these out in the open in any candid fashion would have run the serious risk of alienating upper class support. Thus in its lack of any realistic analysis and in some of the reasons for this absence, Kuomintang doctrine recalls European fascism.

The same is true of Kuomintang proposals for future action. There are occasional remarks scattered through Chiang's semi-official book about the importance of the People's Livelihood, a term that served in part as a euphemism for the agrarian question. But, as we have already noted, very little was actually done, or even proposed, in order to solve the question. There was also a ten-year plan for industrialization, again mainly a matter of putting marks on paper. Instead the stress was on moral and psychological reform from above, but without social content. Both the diagnosis and the plan of action are summed up in these sentences by Chiang Kai-shek:

> From what has been said we know that the key to the success of national reconstruction is to be found in a change of our social life, and the change of our social life in turn depends upon those who have vision, will power, moral conviction and a sense of responsibility, and who, through their wisdom and efforts, lead the people in a town, a district, a province or throughout the country, to a new way until they grow accustomed to it unawares. As I have

[81] Chiang Kai-shek, *China's Destiny*, chaps I and II.

also pointed out, national and social reconstruction could be easily
accomplished, provided the youth throughout the nation resolve
to perform what others dare not perform, to endure what others
cannot endure. . . .[82]

Here the Confucian theory of a benevolent élite has, under the
pressure of circumstances, taken on a martial and "heroic" character. The combination is already familiar to the West in fascism.

The resemblance becomes still stronger as we see the organizational form that this heroic élitism is supposed to take, namely the
Kuomintang itself. There is an important difference nevertheless.
The Kuomintang was closer to the concept of the nation in arms.
Everybody was supposed to be equally excited by the force of its
ideals and the moral example of its leaders. Though the idea of an
all-embracing party went back to Sun Yat-sen, it had a certain
tactical advantage. Chiang was carefully keeping the door open for
the Communists in the hope that they might merge with his organization.[83] Actually of course the Kuomintang, like European
totalitarian parties of both right and left, remained a very small
minority in the population at large.[84]

The avowed purpose of this moral and psychological reform
and its ostensible organizational embodiment was of course military
power. In turn, military power was to achieve national defense and
national unification. Over and over again, Chiang put military unification first as the prerequisite for any other reform. Chiang's main
justification for this point of view has a definite totalitarian ring.
He cites Sun Yat-sen's judgment that Rousseau and the French
Revolution could not serve as models for China because the Europeans at that time did not have liberty while the Chinese at present
had too much. The Chinese, according to a favorite metaphor of
both Chiang and Sun, resembled a heap of loose sand, ready victims
of foreign imperialism. "In order to resist foreign oppression,"
Chiang continues in direct quotation from Sun, "we must free ourselves from the idea of 'individual liberty' and unite ourselves into

[82] *China's Destiny*, 212.
[83] *China's Destiny*, 212–216, 219–221, 233.
[84] Linebarger, *China of Chiang*, 141–142, in the absence of official data
estimates the membership at around two million.

a strong cohesive body, like a solid mass formed by the mixing of cement with sand." Chiang amplifies with the following comment:

> In other words, if the Chunghua nation [i.e., China] is to be consolidated into a strong unit for national defense, as solid as a rock, it goes without saying that individuals cannot enjoy excessive liberty as if they are loose sand. To put it more concretely, we may say that China must develop herself into strong national defense unit if she is to win final victory in this war, and in the postwar period, together with the other independent and free nations of the world, to safeguard permanent world peace and work for the liberation of mankind. Hence . . . excessive personal liberty . . . cannot be allowed to exist either during wartime or in the postwar period.[85]

Three features stand out in this brief review of Kuomintang doctrine as formulated by Chiang Kai-shek. The first is the almost complete absence of any social and economic program to cope with China's problems, and indeed a very marked ritual avoidance of the realities of these problems. The talk about "political tutelage" and preparation for democracy was mainly rhetoric. Actual policy was to disturb existing social relationships as little as possible. Such a policy did not exclude blackmail and forced contributions from any sector of the population that provided a convenient target. Gangsters do the same thing in American cities, without any real attempt to upset the existing social order, upon which they actually depend. The second feature, one may call the concealment of the lack of specific political and social objectives through somewhat grotesque efforts to revive traditional ideals in a situation that had for a long time increasingly undermined the social basis of these ideals. Since Professor Mary C. Wright has argued this point cogently and with abundant concrete evidence in *The Last Stand of Chinese Conservatism*, we need only remind ourselves here that this distorted patriotic idealization of the past is one of the main stigmata of Western fascism. The third and last feature is the Kuomintang's effort to resolve its problems through military force, again a major characteristic of European fascism.

[85] *China's Destiny*, 208.

To stress these three traits is not to say that the Kuomintang was identical with European fascism or earlier reactionary movements. Identity never occurs in history and is not the issue here. Our point is that these similarities constitute a related whole that is significant not only for understanding China but for the dynamics of totalitarian movements in general. In other words, we do not have here a loose collection of accidental resemblances in which certain minor Chinese traits happen to recall major European ones. As a single complex unit, they dominated for a time the political, social, and intellectual climate of both Europe and China.

The Kuomintang's effort to push China along the reactionary road to the modern state did end in complete failure. So had a similar and more promising attempt failed in Russia. In both countries this failure was the immediate cause and forerunner of Communist victories. In Russia Communists have succeeded in creating a first-class industrial power; in China the issue is still somewhat in doubt. Again in both cases, peasant insurrection and rebellion made a decisive contribution toward pushing these countries toward the communist path of modernization instead of the reactionary or the democratic variants of capitalism. In China this contribution was even more important than in Russia. Clearly it is high time to examine more carefully the peasants' part in these huge transformations.

6. Rebellion, Revolution, and the Peasants

The frequency of peasant rebellions in China is well known. Fitzgerald lists six major ones in China's long history prior to 1900.[86] There were many other local and abortive ones. Here I shall try to indicate some of the main reasons why premodern Chinese society was prone to peasant rebellions, limiting the discussion mainly to the latter phase of the Manchu dynasty, though it is probable that several of the factors to be discussed operated during earlier dynasties as well, a point that lies outside the scope of this work and indeed the author's competence. We may nevertheless take judicial notice of the fact that these were rebellions, not revolu-

[86] *Revolution in China,* 13.

tions; that is, they did not alter the basic structure of the society. Secondly, I shall endeavor to show how this original structural weakness facilitated a real revolution under the impact of new strains created by the impact of commerce and industry during the nineteenth and twentieth centuries. The whole story constitutes a most instructive contrast with India where peasant rebellions in the premodern period were relatively rare and completely ineffective and where modernization impoverished the peasants at least as much as in China and over as long a period of time. The contrast with Japan is also illuminating even if less striking. There the rulers were able to keep in check impulses toward peasant rebellion generated in the course of modernization partly because Japanese peasant society was organized on principles differing from those in China. Their success in turn enabled Japan to follow a reactionary pattern of modernization that, like Germany's, culminated in fascism.

Before discussing the peasantry in China, it is well to recall that the political structure of China during the nineteenth century displayed certain serious weaknesses that have only a very indirect connection with the peasantry and may be more properly regarded as due to the character and organization of the ruling stratum of landlords and officials. I have already suggested certain reasons why this segment of Chinese society generally failed to adapt to the modern world of commerce and industry. There are also reasonably clear indications of a defect in the political mechanism of traditional China. In their local habitat and as landlords, the gentry needed an Imperial system strong enough to enforce their authority over the peasants. At the same time, actions that were necessary to make the Imperial system strong ran counter to the short-run interests of the local gentry. They were very reluctant to pay their share of the taxes and generally wanted local affairs run in their own way.[87] About this situation there was not much the district magistrate could do. As corruption mounted and the usefulness of the central government became less obvious, so did centrifugal pulls increase, creating a vicious circle.

From the standpoint of our immediate problem, the most important structural defects were a series of weaknesses in the links

[87] Hsiao, *Rural China*, 125 – 127.

binding the peasantry to the upper classes and to the prevailing regime. As indicated above, members of the gentry do not appear to have played any role in the agricultural cycle, not even a supervisory one, that would give them a legitimate status as leaders of the peasant community. Indeed one of the main distinctions between a landed gentleman in China and a mere rich landlord seems to have been that the gentleman avoided any taint of manual labor and devoted himself to scholarship and the arts. The gentry did bargain with the government in order to improve irrigation. Though the results were certainly visible to the peasants, and we may be sure that the gentry did their best to impress on the peasants what they had done for them, by its very nature this could not be a continuous or frequently repeated activity. In any one area it is possible to get only so many irrigation ditches. Furthermore as the resources available to the central government and even a good many local ones declined, it became harder to keep old projects in working order and impossible to get new ones.

The gentry's well-known control of astronomic lore, necessary for determining the time at which to perform the various tasks of the agricultural cycle, comes to mind as one casts about for possible economic contributions that would have legitimated their status. Though the point would bear further examination — in general we need more and firmer information about the relation between the peasants and the gentry — there are several reasons for doubting that this monopoly was important at all in the nineteenth century.[88] Furthermore, peasants, generally out of their own practical experience, always develop a rich lore about every aspect of the agricultural cycle: the best time and location for planting each type of crop, for harvesting it, and so forth. Indeed, this lore is so firmly imbedded by experience and the risks of deviation from it are so great for most peasants, that modern governments have a great deal of difficulty in persuading peasants to vary their routines. Hence it

[88] Or perhaps at any time. See Eberhard, *Conquerors and Rulers*, 22 – 23. Hsiao's *Rural China*, tremendously valuable partly because it collects indiscriminately all kinds of information that might have any bearing at all on problems of social control in the countryside, does not mention this feature at all.

seems rather likely that the astronomers adapted whatever knowledge they had to what the peasants already did, rather than the other way around, and that they did not do anything in modern times that struck the peasant as indispensable.

What then did the government do for the peasant? Modern Western sociologists are perhaps too prone to dismiss as impossible the answer that it did practically nothing, which I suspect is the correct one. They reason that any institution which lasts a long time cannot be altogether harmful to those who live under it (which seems to me to fly in the face of huge masses of both historical and contemporary experience) and therefore undertake a rather desperate search for some "function" that the institution in question must perform. This is not the place to argue about methods or the way in which conscious and unconscious assumptions determine the questions raised in any scientific inquiry. Nevertheless it seems more realistic to assume that large masses of people, and especially peasants, simply accept the social system under which they live without concern about any balance of benefits and pains, certainly without the least thought of whether a better one might be possible, unless and until something happens to threaten and destroy their daily routine. Hence it is quite possible for them to accept a society of whose working they are no more than victims.

One might object that the Imperial bureaucracy, when it was working well, as it did in the seventeenth and eighteenth centuries, maintained law and order, enforcing an objective standard of justice well in advance of that prevailing in most parts of contemporary Europe. That is true enough. But the administration of justice and the enforcement of law and order had very little effect on the peasants. In theory, to be sure, criminal cases, homicide, robbery, theft, adultery, and kidnapping could be reported to the district magistrate at any time. One magistrate went so far as to permit the people to beat the gong in his *yamen* as a way of signalling their request for a hearing. The "busy season for farmers" was set aside as a time when no civil cases would be heard.[89] Such facts do make it look as though the magistrate played an important role in the life of the people. Looking further, one quickly sees how unlikely this

[89] Ch'ü, *Local Government*, 118–119.

would be. He was responsible for the administration of justice, even its pettier forms, over many thousands of persons. His *yamen* was located in the walled town that served as the seat of a district. Normally he had no direct contact with peasants at all.[90] What contact there was took place through the government runners, the dregs of the population in league with the criminal elements, and was largely exploitative. It seems likely that from time to time a case of homicide among the peasantry would come to the magistrate's attention. Otherwise contact was evidently minimal. The peasants in the family and the clan had their own arrangements for keeping order and administering justice according to their own lights. They had no need for the Imperial apparatus except to keep marauders and bandits away from their crops. But banditry on a large enough scale to be a serious menace to the peasants was in itself very largely the consequence of exploitative officialdom. During the nineteenth century the Imperial bureaucracy became less and less able to keep even a minimum of order over wide areas of China as its own policies helped to generate peasant outbreaks.

To sum up the discussion so far, the evidence points strongly toward the conclusion that the government and the upper classes performed no function that the peasants regarded as essential for their way of life. Hence the link between rulers and ruled was weak and largely artificial, liable to snap under any severe strain.

There were three ways in which the Imperial regime tried to compensate for the artificial character of this link. One was the system of granaries, local and Imperial storage depots for grain that could be distributed to the population in times of shortage. The rulers recognized very clearly the connection between hunger and peasant rebellion, though hunger was not the only cause of rebellion, as we shall see clearly enough in due course. However, the system of public granaries broke down and was largely abandoned in the nineteenth century, when it was most needed. Probably the main reason was the absence of any short-run profit for the gentry and prosperous landlords in selling grain to the government or in turning it over free. Also periods of shortage were times when those

[90] Ch'ü, *Local Government*, 116, 151.

who had grain could make a killing.[91] A second arrangement was the famous *pao-chia* system of mutual surveillance, which resembles and long antedates modern totalitarian procedures. Ten households were grouped into a *pao*, with a chief responsible for reporting the conduct of its members. A number of these *paos* (the number varied at different times) were put into a similar group with similar responsibilities, and so on upward in an ascending hierarchy. It was an attempt to extend the government's power of observation and supervision below the district magistrate. Modern students of China judge the *pao* system to have been quite ineffective.[92] Mutual surveillance became tangled up with the collection of taxes, which would scarcely endear it to the peasantry. Any such arrangement depends for its effectiveness on a substantial scattering of ordinary individuals who have both a sufficient stake in the system to make it possible to force them to play the unenviable role of talebearers and enough respect among the population so that they will learn what is going on. These conditions, one may infer, were not widely met in Manchu China. The third arrangement also recalls modern totalitarian practices, the *hsiang-yüeh* system of periodically lecturing the population on Confucian ethics. Apparently the practice began in the seventeenth century. Several emperors took it quite seriously. There is abundant evidence that the population did not and even regarded the lectures as unctuous nonsense. Though it lasted as late as 1865, the lecture system degenerated into empty formalism, taken seriously neither by the officials who had to give them nor by the people who had to listen to them.[93]

The whole combination of welfare policies, police surveillance, and popular indoctrination constitutes a revealing precursor of modern totalitarian practices. To my mind, they demonstrate conclusively that the key features of the totalitarian complex existed in the premodern world. But, in agrarian societies before modern technology made totalitarian instruments vastly more effective and cre-

[91] Hsiao, *Rural China*, chap V, gives details of the operation of the system.

[92] Ch'ü, *Local Government*, 151 – 152; Hsiao, *Rural China*, 26 – 30, 43 – 49, 55.

[93] Hsiao, *Rural China*, chap VI.

ated new forms of receptiveness to its appeals, the totalitarian complex was little more than an ineffectual embryo.

A fourth link between the peasants and the upper class was the clan, which seems to have been rather more effective in tieing the peasants to the prevailing order. The clan, as the reader may recall, was a group of people claiming descent from a common ancestor. Though clan affairs were run by its gentry members, the clan included a large number of peasants. It had rules of conduct that were repeated orally at the colorful ceremonies when all members gathered and visibly reasserted their membership in a collective unit. Through the clan a certain number of Confucian notions, such as respect for elders and ancestors, filtered down to the peasantry. At least such notions did as were compatible with the structure of peasant society. Respect for age was certainly one of these because of the value of cumulative experience in a world of very slow social change. Here we may observe one of the stronger forces creating peasant conservatism. The ritual land, held in collective ownership, provided the clan with its essential economic base. The land might be rented out to poorer members at less than the going market price. In some cases this land provided the means by which apt but indigent members of the clan could obtain a classical education and go forth to the world of officialdom, thereby to enrich the collective resources of the clan. Villages in which the clans were strong, especially those where the inhabitants constituted a single clan, are reported to have been much more cohesive and solidary units than others. Though clans existed in the North they were much stronger in the agriculturally richer South and were generally a phenomenon of greater agricultural wealth.[94] Thus clans did not exist everywhere. On the other hand, the clan was no more than an enlarged version of the patrilineal and patrilocal lineage with strong patriarchal features which was widespread among the upper classes. Therefore it seems safe to assume that in the other parts of China where clans were not prominent there were numerous smaller lineages that included both gentry and peasant households and that also served the same purpose: to bind rulers and ruled.

By and large then, the clan and patrilineal lineage emerge as

[94] See Hsiao, *Rural China,* 326 – 329 and Liu, *Clan Rules.*

the only important link between the upper and lower strata in Chinese society. As such their importance should not be underestimated, though, as will appear in due course, the clan was double edged: it could also serve as the key mechanism holding rebellious groups together. The general weakness of the link between rulers and ruled, in comparison with other societies, except Russia which was equally subject to peasant insurrection, seems reasonably well established at least for the Manchu era and, I would suggest, accounts in considerable measure for the fact that peasant rebellion was endemic in Chinese society. Were there, however, also structural aspects of the peasant community as such, that might explain this noticeable characteristic of Chinese politics?

On this point there is very little direct information concerning the Manchu period as such. However a number of anthropologists have made good field studies of modern Chinese villages, including studies of some villages in the interior, remote from modern influences. From these we can draw inferences about the earlier period, after omitting any facts that are clearly due to recent influences.

The Chinese village, the basic cell of rural society in China as elsewhere, evidently lacked cohesiveness in comparison with those of India, Japan, and even many parts of Europe. There were far fewer occasions on which numerous members of the village cooperated in a common task in a way that creates the habits and sentiments of solidarity.[95] It was closer to a residential agglomeration of numerous peasant households than to a live and functioning community, though less atomized than, for example, the modern South Italian village where life seems to have been a pacific struggle of all against all.[96] Still there is more than political rhetoric behind the frequent statements of Sun Yat-sen and Chiang Kai-shek that Chinese society was like a heap of sand.

In the village the primary unit of economic production (and consumption as well) was the household, a man with his wife and

[95] For a general analysis of this connection see Homans, *The Human Group*.

[96] See Banfield, *Moral Basis of a Backward Society*.

children.[97] The distinguished anthropologist Fei has claimed that using the hoe in cultivating rice fields has made most of the work very individualistic. "Group work yields no more than the sum total of individual efforts. It also does not increase efficiency very much."[98] Though less detailed information is available about the wheat-growing North, basically the same system of intensive human labor on a series of small scattered plots and the same type of village society prevailed there as well.[99] Hence it is rather unlikely that the technology alone accounts for the relatively weak development of cooperative practices.

Some cooperation did exist, and the brief comments on it in the sources suggest an explanation of why there was not more. Rice culture, to be most efficient, requires large amounts of labor at the time when the young seedlings are transplanted and again at harvest time. In due course we shall see the very effective organization that the Japanese village reached to meet this problem and the very inefficient one that prevails still in large parts of India. The Chinese met this need in several ways. They might exchange labor among themselves, staggering the dates of planting so that crops would not reach the same stage of maturity simultaneously and hence allow time to help out one's kin. Exchanges of labor within kinship groupings were considered most desirable.[100] If the kin could not supply enough labor at crucial points in the agricultural cycle, extra hands were hired. Surplus labor came from three sources. One was from local peasants who had too little land to support their families.[101] The existence of this group made it possible for those with

[97] See Lang, *Chinese Family*, 17, 155, 138 – 141; for the family in areas subject to commercial influences see Fei, *Peasant Life*, chap III and pp. 169 – 171; Yang, *Village in Transition*, 32, 37, 91 – 92.

[98] Fei, *Peasant Life*, 170, 172, and 162 – 163, for a vivid picture of rice transplanting, with the rhythmic cooperation of the family as a work group.

[99] Gamble, *Ting Hsien*, is heavily statistical; rather more illuminating is Crook and Crook, *Revolution in a Chinese Village*, esp 1 – 5.

[100] Fei and Chang, *Earthbound China*, 36, 144, 64 – 65; Yang, *Village in Transition*, 265.

[101] See Fei and Chang, *Earthbound China*, 299, where the authors estimate that the proportion of farmers who could not support their own

enough land to compel the others to work for them within the framework of the prevailing social and political system. A second source of labor came from those without any land and a third from men who could not eke out a living from insufficient land in a poorer, distant area. As late as the mid-1930s, many migrant workers were of different ethnic origin ("wandering souls," "boat people"), drifters who would accept very low pay, keeping local wage rates down. At times a few landless Chinese from another district might settle in the village but, without clan membership and access to a plot of land, they lived alone, outside the stream of village life.[102]

As long as labor was abundant and surplus because of the situation just described, it is not surprising that economic cooperation among any set of individuals in the Chinese village lacked permanence or the institutional basis that still exists in India under the caste system and in Japan in a different form. In premodern China, arrangements for the exchange or hiring of extra labor were fluid, temporary, and unhurried affairs. This was true in the north as well as in the rice-growing south.[103] Even among close kin, exchanges of labor were discussed and arranged anew each year, and, at peak periods of work, landowners could afford to wait until the last moment to hire extra workers at lowest wages.

The only frequently recurring activity that demanded cooperation was the management of the water supply. This was more a question of sharing a scarce resource than of working together on a common task and often resulted in fights within the village or among several villages.[104] In sharp contrast again with Japan and also premodern Europe, the main decisions in the agricultural cycle were made by the individual household. There is no trace of any-

---

families from the land, in the four villages studied, amounted to around seventy percent. See also ibid, 60–63, for the sources of extra labor in one backward village.

[102] Fei and Chang, *Earthbound China*, 58–62; Yang, *Village in Transition*, 11, 51–52, 101, 149.

[103] See Crook and Crook, *Revolution in a Chinese Village*, 63; Gamble, *Ting Hsien*, 221–222.

[104] Hsiao, *Rural China*, 419.

thing remotely resembling *Flurzwang:* the practice under which the European village community decided when all its member fields should become pasture for the winter — common land available to all — and when the separate strips should return to private responsibility for ploughing and seeding. Chinese property too was held in strips scattered throughout the territory of the village. But the rarity of animals and the intense pressure on the land ruled out this European practice, even in the northern wheat-growing areas.

Since historians of Russia and Japan have stressed the importance of collective responsibility for taxes in producing the solidary villages characteristic of these countries, it is worthwhile drawing attention to the fact that the Imperial system in China also imposed collective responsibility.[105] So far as evidence from a later time indicates, the Chinese system did not produce similar results. Evidently taxation practices are insufficient by themselves to create cohesive village communities, though they are undoubtedly an important factor. For its own purposes, as we have seen, the Empire tried to create solidarity through the *pao-chia.* The generally admitted failure of the *pao-chia* in China, and the greater success in Japan of a similar arrangement based on the Chinese model, considerably strengthen the thesis that cohesiveness was weak in the traditional Chinese villages of Imperial times. Quite possibly the impression of casual individualism and minimal organized cooperation may be somewhat exaggerated, due to the need to rely on anthropologists' accounts from fairly recent times. Still it is highly unlikely that the basic structural patterns of village life were fundamentally different in Imperial times from those recently observed. The system of sharecropping and the devotion of the upper class to stylized leisure, with its need for a labor force that it did not have to supervise directly, all point toward arrangements roughly similar to those just sketched here. Thus the political needs of the upper classes combined with agricultural practices to generate a combination of peasant individualism and surplus labor, leading to a relatively atomistic peasant society.

By these observations I do not mean to imply that the Chinese village at any time was a miniature war of each against all. There

[105] Hsiao, *Rural China,* 60, 84 – 86, 96, and esp 100.

was at least a limited sense of community. The village usually had a temple and numerous festivals in which all bona fide villagers could participate to some degree. Also in the local oligarchy of notables the village had a generally effective means of settling disputes among inhabitants and preventing explosions from the aggressions that arise in any group of people living in close proximity. One indication of this sense of community is the fact that many villages rigidly excluded. outsiders from membership. The reason was simple: there was not enough land to go around.

In this fact we encounter another basic principle of Chinese society: the possession of land was absolutely necessary if one were to be a full-fledged member of the village. We have already noticed how land provided the basis for the activities of the clan. The same is true on a smaller scale of the family. Since the family was the chief unit of economic production, occupation on the soil was uniquely conducive to strong and stable kinship ties.[106] The whole Confucian ethic of filial respect was impossible without property and was very much weaker among the poor peasants. Indeed, family life itself was often impossible for them. In contrast with the situation that prevailed for a long time in Western society, the poorer peasants in China had fewer children and of course fewer of them survived to maturity.[107] Many could not marry at all. Modern Chinese villages had a number of "bare sticks," bachelors too poor to marry. "They were objects of pity and ridicule in the eyes of the villagers, whose life centered on the family."[108] And, of course, it was the poor who sold their children, mainly girls but occasionally also boys, because it was impossible to bring them up.

In a word, no property: no family, no religion. That is a bit too extreme. There was a place, if only a small and precarious one, for the landless agricultural laborer in the Chinese village, though the situation that prevailed more widely was for land-short peasants to eke out their resources by working for their wealthier neighbors.

[106] Yang, *Village in Transition*, 80, 91–92.

[107] Yang, *Village in Transition*, 17–19. See also Crook and Crook, *Revolution in a Chinese Village*, 7–11, for a generally similar situation in a North China village.

[108] Yang, *Village in Transition*, 51.

Nevertheless the older conception among scholars of the patriarchal ethic uniting Chinese society through millions of peasant families is largely nonsense. This patriarchal image was an aristocratic costly ideal beyond the reach of most peasants. To the extent that it existed among the peasants, it did little more than provide a rationale for the petty despotism within the peasant family, made necessary by a brutally cramped existence. The Chinese peasant family had built into it a highly explosive potential to which the Communists in due course were to set the spark.[109]

To sum up, the cohesiveness of Chinese peasant society appears to have been considerably less than that of other peasant societies and to have depended very heavily on the existence of a sufficiency of landed property. In India, to anticipate again, the caste system provided a niche for landless laborers and tied them into the division of labor within the village, while its sanctions depended for their operation less directly on the existence of property. The political significance of such differences presents puzzling problems of assessment, especially as one recalls the fact that in Russia peasant revolts were endemic to tsarist society, although the peasants had developed strong solidary institutions. Evidently there are forms of solidarity that promote peasant insurrection and those that oppose it, a larger question best postponed for later discussion.

In China the structure of peasant society, together with the weakness of the links that bound the peasantry and the upper classes, helps to explain why China was especially subject to peasant insurrection as well as some of the obstacles and limitations to these insurrections. It indicates the lines of fracture in Chinese society that would become increasingly evident during the nineteenth century and on into the twentieth as poverty pressed harder and harder on many sections of the country. Then the bonds would snap. Peasants would break with their homes, wander off, and become bandits. Later they would become recruits for warlord armies. Chinese society was such as to make possible the creation of huge masses of human debris, tinder easily ignited by an insurrectionary spark. On

[109] On rather intense dissatisfaction among the young and the women under the traditional family system, in town and country, see Yang, *Chinese Family*, 192 – 193, 201.

the other hand, rebellion requires more than the destruction of prevailing social bonds; it also requires the forging of new forms of solidarity and loyalty. This was difficult in China since the peasants were not used to cooperating with each other beyond the limits of the family or clan. The task is even more difficult in the case of a revolution that attempts to introduce a new kind of society. Had not certain fortuitous circumstances intervened, fortuitous in the sense that they did not derive from anything taking place in China itself, the Communists might never have solved the problem. An examination of the concrete forms that violence took, in late Imperial times and subsequently, will help to give greater meaning to these necessarily general observations.

Even in "normal" times the inadequacy of the Imperial system for maintaining peace and security in the countryside left the inhabitants easy victims to what for lack of a better word we can call simply gangsterism, the use of violence to prey on the population indiscriminately without the slightest interest in altering the political system, not even in substituting a new set of rulers for an old one. It is necessary to beware of romanticizing the robber as a friend of the poor, just as much as of accepting the official image. Characteristically the local inhabitants would bargain with the bandits in order to be left in peace. Quite often local gentry leaders were on cordial terms with bandits. Professional and hereditary bandits existed.[110] As such, there is nothing remarkable here. Gangsterism is likely to crop up wherever the forces of law and order are weak. European feudalism was mainly gangsterism that had become society itself and acquired respectability through the notions of chivalry. As the rise of feudalism out of the decay of the Roman administrative system shows, this form of self-help which victimizes others is in principle opposed to the workings of a sound bureaucratic system. A bureaucracy to survive must obtain a monopoly on the making of victims and do it according to a rational principle, which was supplied in China by Confucianism. As the Imperial system decayed into warlord satrapies, feebly and temporarily united under the Kuomintang, the entire system took on more and more gangster attributes and became increasingly unpopular.

[110] Hsiao, *Rural China*, 430, 456, 462, 465.

In Manchu times the line between merely predatory banditry and organized rebellion was in any event a thin one. Still it is not enough for a rebellion to be able to draw off a steady stream of individuals from peasant villages, relatively easy as that was under the conditions of China's rural social structure. That might be indispensable as a beginning. By itself it could do no more than supply a steady recruitment for banditry. If a rebellion is to amount to a serious threat, it must acquire a territorial base independent of the government, and the territory must be continually extended. The acquisition of a territorial base in turn involves getting whole villages to change their allegiance. In China that meant getting the local notables, including resident gentry, to cooperate as well as offering better conditions to the peasants.

Unfortunately there is no good monograph on the great Taiping Rebellion of the 1850s written by a scholar sensitive to problems of social structure. There is, however, an instructive study of the Nien Rebellion (1853 – 1868) which temporarily cooperated with the Taiping rebels. This account allows us to perceive some of the causes and limitations of traditional rebellion in the nineteenth century. A few comments on this case will therefore be useful.

Like other rebellions of the nineteenth century, that of the Nien was the consequence of Imperial decay and served to intensify and accelerate the process. Maladministration and hunger, sometimes intensified by great natural disasters in the form of floods that sent many peasants wandering from their homes, were among the immediate causes of such outbreaks. To some extent the floods were not merely natural disasters: they had a political and social origin in the widespread neglect of dikes and systems of river control.[111] Since the Imperial government was unable to protect the local communities against marauders, these took local defense into their own hands, taxed the people, and took over the administration. In the Nien region, the rebels set up earth walls around the villages. Secret societies played an important part in this connection, using the pretext of assisting the villagers' defense when villages quarreled

[111] On this point see also Hinton, *Grain Tribute*, 16–23, for the shift in the course of the Yellow River.

among themselves. In the meantime the local gentry gained control of regional military forces. The central government found it necessary to use one local military force against another that was in open rebellion, by this compromise eventually weakening its power and authority still further. These two factors, the secret societies and the existence of military units under the gentry, took rebellion out of the category of mere banditry.[112]

The Nien extended their base by taking villages surrounded by earth walls, that is, already largely detached from the central government's authority. They persuaded local notables to cooperate, leaving them in power as long as they were willing to do so, which seems to have been the usual case. If officials who were loyal to the government remained in an area, they were publicly humiliated. The clan, it is worth noticing, formed the basis of the rebel organization. Only wealthy and influential families commanded enough support and clientele to make their adherence worthwhile. This was not all, however; clan loyalties formed the basis of passionate allegiance to their rebel leaders on the part of the peasantry.[113] Though the rebels worked mainly through the prevailing social organization, they had a rudimentary economic and social program. Relief of starving people, they recognized, was the key to gaining their loyalty. They emphasized the production of wheat and barley in their homeland. Struggles over harvests became an important item in campaigns along the margins of their territory.[114] Possibly under the influence of the Taipings they put into effect a crude version of land reform, dividing crops equally and limiting the authority of the larger landowners.[115]

Here we encounter some of the limitations of rebellion under the traditional system, which the Communists were to overcome, though not without difficulty. Gentry participation and leadership limited the possibility of any real change. Furthermore, the Nien system was itself essentially predatory, gaining food supplies by

[112] Chiang, *Nien Rebellion,* v – vii, 17, 32. The introduction by Renville Lund is particularly useful.
[113] Chiang, *Nien Rebellion,* 38 – 42, 48, 113.
[114] Chiang, *Nien Rebellion,* 41.
[115] Chiang, *Nien Rebellion,* 37.

raids on other areas, which it therefore antagonized.[116] This was self-defeating. Hence it is easy to understand why not all local groups identified themselves with the rebels. Some sought "neutral self-defense"; others even fought on the Imperial side.[117] Somewhat similar factors appear to have been at work in the case of the Taiping. At first the inhabitants in many areas regarded them as better than their Imperial rulers. Later, as the rebels proved unable to bring about real improvement, and perhaps as their exactions became harsher in the struggle against the government, they lost much popular support.[118]

For a long time the Imperial forces adopted a purely military policy against the Nien, endeavoring fruitlessly to destroy the earth walls. Eventually the great Imperial minister, Tseng Kuo-fan, who seems a Bismarck *manqué* in Chinese circumstances, achieved victory by taking over rebel tactics. He too worked with and through local leaders and offered concrete benefits to the peasants: support for cultivation and peace at a time when they had become tired of turmoil. Toward the end, money and the prospect of food in the government military forces induced many to surrender.[119] The rebellion, which had begun in the winter of 1852–1853, finally ended in 1868. One of the more striking features, from the point of view of our problems, is that both rebels and Imperial authorities could manipulate the local social structure with about the same degree of ease or difficulty. "Organizational weapons," it appears, were not decisive. Much more basic were the grievances of the peasantry. Shifts in their loyalty, manipulated and accelerated to be sure by both sides, determined both the outbreak and the end of the rebellion.

Thus the framework of traditional Chinese society both encouraged rebellion and put severe limitations on what it could accomplish. It might overthrow a dynasty, in which case, as a Chinese source remarks, later historians would whitewash the whole affair.[120]

[116] Chiang, *Nien Rebellion*, vii, xii, xiii.
[117] Chiang, *Nien Rebellion*, 90.
[118] Hsiao, *Rural China*, 183, 200–201, 483–484.
[119] Chiang, *Nien Rebellion*, 101–107, 116–117.
[120] See Hsiao, *Rural China*, 484.

Or it might turn into a worse form of oppression and gradually peter out as the Imperial forces regained a semblance of control. Only when the impact of the modern world had eaten away the superstructure in ways indicated earlier, did a real revolutionary attempt become possible. Let us now try to understand what the coming of the modern world did to the peasant, the base of this structure.

During the nineteenth century there appeared scattered but unmistakable signs of a decline in the peasant's economic situation: abandonment of tillage, deterioration of irrigation systems, increasing agricultural unemployment. Though signs of the peasant's plight were to be found in practically every part of the empire, perhaps more in the northern provinces than elsewhere, the regional diversity of China produces exceptions to any generalization. Some provinces continued to enjoy prosperity and abundance, while others suffered famine and near famine conditions.[121] Peasant handicrafts, an important supplement to the peasants' meager resources and a way of using surplus labor power during the slack times of the agricultural cycle, suffered severe blows at the hands of cheap Western textiles. Standard accounts until quite recent times have emphasized and possibly overemphasized this fact. It is conceivable that the peasants in time found other employment: anthropological accounts of modern villages frequently stress the importance of artisan occupations as a small but vital addition to the subsistence of the peasants.[122] In any event, the impact was undoubtedly severe for a time in many areas. The spread of opium, encouraged at first by the West and at a later date by the Japanese, spread further demoralization as well as reluctance to seek improvement.

In the meantime near the coastal cities and along large rivers, the local village market gave way to the large urban market, while the effects of a market economy penetrated more and more deeply into the rural areas. As an institution, the market and a money economy had long existed in China. These changes did not bring about something totally new. In the 1930s the lion's share of the produce still

[121] Hsiao, *Rural China*, 396 – 407, esp 397.

[122] Crook and Crook, *Revolution in a Chinese Village*, 4; Fei and Chang, *Earthbound China*, 173 – 177.

went no further than the local market town or at most the district (*hsien*) city.[123] Still the increasing importance of the market was sufficient to produce many of the same social and political dislocations that occurred during an earlier phase of European history. As the market evolved toward a more efficient and centrally organized institution, the peasant was left behind and his bargaining position deteriorated. Without reserves and operating close to the margin of subsistence, the peasant often had to sell immediately after the harvest when prices were falling. As might be expected in China, where transportation and storage facilities were poor, seasonal variations in prices were violent. The peasant's plight favored the dealer and speculator, generally in league with the landlord. Dealers had larger reserves, wider sources of information, and better opportunities for combination than the peasant. Sometimes they were strongly organized in a guild that fixed prices and forbade overbidding among its members. In the light of the circumstances, it is no wonder that the dealer generally got the better of the peasant.[124]

As the peasants fell into debt, they had to borrow, often at very high rates. When they could not repay, they had to transfer title to the land to a landlord, remaining on the soil to work it more or less indefinitely. All these processes had their heaviest impact in the coastal provinces. There too sprang up the peasants' rebellion of 1927, the greatest since the days of the long-haired Taipings, according to its historian, Harold Isaacs.[125]

In the light of the connection between property and social cohesion, perhaps the most important aspect of the changes under discussion was the growth of a mass of marginal peasants at the bottom of the social hierarchy in the village. Local modern studies indicate that they amounted to about half or more of the inhabitants.[126] How much of an increase, if any, this may represent

[123] Buck, *Land Utilization*, 349.

[124] Tawney, *Land and Labour*, 56 – 57.

[125] *Tragedy of the Chinese Revolution*, 221; further data on the connection with social changes in coastal areas in Tawney, *Land and Labour*, 74; Lang, *Chinese Family*, 64, 178.

[126] See Yang, *Village in Transition*, 61 – 62, 41, 44 – 45; Fei and Chang, *Earthbound China*, 299, 300.

over the nineteenth century, we have no way of knowing as yet. That they represented potentially explosive material is, on the other hand, reasonably clear.[127] They were marginal, not only in the physical sense of living close to the edge of starvation, but also in the sociological sense that the reduction of property meant that the ties connecting them to the prevailing order had worn thinner and thinner. Indeed their connections with the village were probably less than one might conclude on the basis of anthropological accounts, since these studies had to be carried out in areas where law and order and stability still prevailed. Wide areas of the country were in the throes of active revolution or else under bandit control. Thus the mass basis of the revolution that began in 1927 and culminated in the Communist victory of 1949 was a land-short peasantry. Neither in China nor in Russia was there a huge agricultural proletariat working on modern capitalist *latifundia*, the source of much rural upheaval in Spain, Cuba, and possibly elsewhere. It was different too from the situation in France in 1789, where there were many landless peasants, but where the revolution in the countryside came from the upper stratum of the peasantry, who put the brakes on the revolution when it showed signs of passing beyond the confirmation of property rights and the elimination of feudal vestiges.

Massive poverty and exploitation in and by themselves are not enough to provide a revolutionary situation. There must also be felt injustice built into the social structure, that is, either new demands on the victims or some reason for the victims to feel that old demands are no longer justifiable. The decay of the upper classes in China provided this indispensable ingredient. The gentry had lost their *raison d'être* and turned into landlord-usurers pure and simple. The end of the examination system spelled the end of their legitimacy and the Confucian system that had supported it. How much of this the peasants had ever actually accepted is somewhat doubtful. As Max Weber has pointed out, the religion of the masses was mainly a combination of Taoism and magic, more suited to their own needs. Still some Confucian ideas did permeate through

[127] For Imperial fears on this score see Hsiao, *Rural China*, 395-396, 687-688 (note 84).

the clan. In any case the self-respect had largely evaporated that had given the old ruling classes assurance in the presence of the peasants. All kinds of shady élites, racketeers, gangsters, and the like arose to fill the vacuum left by the collapse of the former ruling stratum. In the absence of a strong central power, private violence became rampant and essential in order for the landlords to continue their squeeze on the peasantry. Many landlords moved to the city where they enjoyed greater protection. Those remaining in the countryside turned their residences into fortresses and collected their debts and rents at the point of a gun.[128] Naturally not all land-lords were like this. Quite possibly only a small minority behaved this way, although to judge from anthropological accounts, those who did were likely to be the most powerful and influential figures in the area. Patriarchal relationships continued to exist alongside naked and brutal exploitation. This was widespread enough to help turn many parts of China into a potentially explosive situation that would give the Communists their chance. It is worth noticing that no comparable deterioration of the upper classes has so far taken place in India.

To say that a revolutionary situation existed does not mean that the conflagration was about to ignite of its own accord. The conservative half-truth that "outside agitators" make riots and revolutions — a half-truth that becomes a lie because it ignores the conditions that make agitators effective — finds strong support from Chinese data. In numerous accounts of village life, I have come upon no indication that the peasants were about to organize effec-tively or do anything about their problems of their own accord. The notion that peasant villages were in open revolt before the Communists appeared on the scene does not correspond with a large body of evidence from anthropological field studies.[129] Those

[128] Yang, *Village in Transition*, chap VII; Crook and Crook, *Revolution in a Chinese Village*, chap II.

[129] Conducted under Kuomintang auspices and in peaceful areas, the studies by anthropologists, except that by the Crooks, contain a built-in bias, intensified by methodological preconceptions too abstruse to discuss here. Even if discounted for these reasons, their evidence remains very sig-nificant and is confirmed by other data such as the failure of the Commu-nists to gain an extensive foothold prior to the Japanese occupation.

who found the situation intolerable very likely left their home villages, in many instances to join bandits, warlord armies, and in time the constantly swelling Communist forces. Within the old framework of the village, there was little spontaneous attempt to do anything. Just as in Manchu times, the peasants needed outside leadership before they would turn actively against the existing social structure. As far as the village itself is concerned, the situation almost certainly could have gone on deteriorating until most of the inhabitants simply died in the next famine. That is exactly what happened many times over.

These observations do not in the least imply that the Chinese peasants were innately stupid or lacked initiative and courage. The behavior of the revolutionary armies, even after due subtraction for propaganda and revolutionary heroics, demonstrates quite the contrary. The meaning is merely that, up to the last moment in many areas, the tentacles of the old order wrapped themselves around the individual with sufficient power to prevent him from acting as an isolated unit or, quite often, even thinking about such action. The lack of cohesiveness of the Chinese village, discussed earlier in another connection, may have helped the Communists by enabling a steady stream of recruits to slip away to Communist areas. It also probably made their task of breaking down and altering the old village structure easier. More precise information is necessary for any firm appraisal. Rickety as it was, the old order would not disappear through spontaneous action in the village as such. That, of course, has been the case in all the major modern revolutions.

Even the entry of the Chinese Communist Party upon this scene of widespread distress and decay was not sufficient in and by itself to produce a fundamental change. The Party was founded in 1921. Thirteen years later, the Communists had to abandon their main territorial foothold in Kiangsi and embark on the famous Long March to remote Yenan. Their fortunes, in the judgment of some historians, were then at their lowest ebb. About all they had demonstrated was a tough capacity to survive: Chiang's five major military offensives between 1930 and 1933 had failed to root them out. But they had not been able to extend their territorial base or to gain significant influence outside of the areas they immediately controlled.

To some extent the Communists' failure up to this point is explicable in terms of their mistaken strategy. Not until 1926 did they begin to display any serious interest in using the peasants as the base for a revolutionary movement.[130] After the break with Chiang Kai-shek in 1927, the Party still tried to win power through proletarian risings in the cities with disastrous and bloody consequences. Though the abandonment of this piece of Marxist orthodoxy and the adoption of Mao's strategy of reliance on the peasantry were indispensable, more was necessary to bring success.[131] For one thing it was necessary to adopt a milder attitude toward the well-to-do peasants, a policy not adopted until 1942, though there were adumbrations much earlier.[132] Important though all these changes were, it is unlikely that by themselves they would have enabled the Chinese Communists to win a revolutionary victory. The decisive ingredient was the Japanese conquest and the occupation policies of a foreign conqueror.

In reaction to the Japanese occupation, Kuomintang officials and landlords moved out of the countryside and into the towns, leaving the peasants to their own devices. Secondly, the Japanese army's intermittent mopping up and extermination campaigns welded the peasants into a solidary mass. Thus the Japanese performed two essential revolutionary tasks for the Communists, the elimination of the old élites and the forging of solidarity among the oppressed.[133] Negative evidence strongly supports this superficially paradoxical conclusion. Where the Japanese or their puppet regime gave the peasants some security, guerilla organizations made no headway. Indeed, the Communists were unable to establish guerilla

[130] Ch'en, *Mao*, 107–108.

[131] Schwartz, *Chinese Communism* deserves credit for being the first to trace out the history of this shift in strategy and for stressing (see p. 190) the importance of favorable external circumstances.

[132] For some key turning points see Ch'en, *Mao*, 162; Brandt et al, *Documentary History*, 39–40, 224–226, 275–285. It is well to remember that, especially in those chaotic times, what was decreed and what was done on the spot were far from the same.

[133] Johnson, *Peasant Nationalism*, esp 70, 110, 48–60, 116–117.

bases in regions that had no direct experience of the Japanese army.[134]

Important as the Japanese contribution was, it is necessary to perceive it in proper perspective. To see in this cooperation between fighting enemies some sort of devilish conspiracy between the Japanese and the Communists is of course silly. Circumstances favored the Communists, who pressed their advantage against *both* the Japanese and the Kuomintang, which showed strong collaborationist tendencies and of course had no desire to see the war culminate in a social revolution.[135] The war intensified a revolutionary situation and brought it to a head. From the standpoint of Chinese society and politics, the war was an accident. From the standpoint of the interplay of political and economic forces in the world as a whole, it was scarcely an accident. Just as in the case of the Bolshevik victory in Russia, which some historians see as an accidental outcome of the First World War, the inevitable analytical necessity of isolating certain manageable areas of history can lead to partial truths that are misleading and even false unless and until one subsequently puts them back into their proper context.

We may close with a few comments on the way in which the Communists used the lines of cleavage in the village in order to destroy the remnants of the old order. Fortunately we possess two good studies of different villages in the North and the South during the period of the Communist takeover which show successive stages and problems in this process.

The northern village was in the Shansi-Hopeh-Shantung-Honan Border Region where the Communists were able to gain a foothold and combine their social struggle with nationalist resistance to the Japanese. Since the wealthier elements in the area, including remnants of Kuomintang power, identified themselves with the Japanese in order to preserve their property, the Communists gained an important advantage in being able to combine their social program, at that time a very moderate one, with resistance to foreign oppression. Bit by bit they were able to set up in the village their own political organization beneath the existing one. This they

---

[134] Johnson, *Peasant Nationalism*, 66 – 67, 146.
[135] Johnson, *Peasant Nationalism*, 120.

combined with a program giving benefits to the numerous poor peasants and putting the burden on the richer ones. The program at first eliminated the levies that had formerly lined Kuomintang pockets and distributed the new burdens of organizing the rear roughly according to ability to pay. The new slogan was "Those with wealth contribute wealth; those with labour contribute labour." A decisive crisis arose at the point when the Japanese threatened to impose a tax on the village. By raising the question of whether the tax·should be paid on the Japanese flat rate or on the Communist system that put the burden on the rich, the Communists first split the village wide open into rich and poor. Meanwhile the Communists had been urging peasants to hide their grain in caves and prepare to evacuate the area. Since the rich had not done this, they now found themselves exposed to the prospect that the Japanese would come and take all of their grain. Hence they went along with the Communist proposal. The importance of the episode lies in showing how the Communists, like earlier revolutionaries, were able to compel whole villages and areas to go over to their side and accept their administration as well as how the Japanese helped to forge a new solidarity for the Communists. But the Communists went much further. Though they used the old and tainted leadership at times, they created new organizations among the poor peasants and even among the women, the most oppressed group in Chinese society. Above all, in their program of local economic self-sufficiency, as shown in the establishment of a cooperative, and in many other ways, they presented the peasants with concrete alternatives to submission and starvation. Land reform on any substantial scale was something that could wait. When it came, it was combined with vengeance on collaborators and former oppressors. Reading this account makes it easy to understand the revolutionary *élan* behind both resistance to the Japanese and the Communist sweep to victory over the Kuomintang.[136]

Some years later the Communist revolution came to Nanching, a little village near Canton, not in the form of aid in resisting the Japanese, but from above. A shattering blast, set off by retreating

[136] Crook and Crook, *Revolution in a Chinese Village*, chaps I – V, esp 31 –37.

Nationalist soldiers blowing up the steel bridge across the Pearl River, shook the village windows and announced the fall of the old government. In a few days well-armed detachments of Communist soldiers appeared who posted notices announcing the annulment of the previous political rule and commanding former government personnel to remain in their old posts until their duties and documents were transferred to new personnel. After ten months, during which very little happened, the land-reform cadres appeared, three men and one woman in their late teens or early twenties, disguising urban bourgeois backgrounds "under dirty gray uniforms and conscious attempts to imitate the peasants' mode of life."[137]

Once started, the process proceeded rapidly of destroying the old order and taking preliminary steps toward the creation of a new one, all by government direction. Essentially it amounted to taking land away from the wealthy and giving it to the poor. "The general strategy was to unite the poor peasants, agricultural laborers, and middle peasants and to neutralize the stand of the rich peasants so as to isolate the landlords."[138] The effect was rather different. Though the Communists used categories that corresponded reasonably well with the social realities of the village, the main consequence was general uncertainty, even among the poor peasants, who were the chief immediate beneficiaries but who seem to have been as uncertain as the others about how long all this was to last. Formerly there had been suppressed hatred between the two extremes: a rich, exploitative, and cruel landlord and his tenants. Under the new system the entire village was methodically partitioned into compartments, each set against the other.[139]

One aspect deserves special mention because of the light it sheds backward on the workings of the pre-Communist era, as well as on Communist tactics. Land was redistributed not to the family as a whole, but to each member on an equal-share basis, regardless of age and sex. Thus the Communists broke the village apart at its

[137] Yang, *Village in Transition*, 167, 134. This is a richer and fuller monograph than the Crooks' study. It is also quite objective and perhaps the best of the monographs on village life.

[138] Yang, *Village in Transition*, 133.

[139] Yang, *Village in Transition*, 145.

base, obliterating the connection between landed property and kinship. By destroying the economic basis for kinship bonds, or at least greatly weakening them, the Communists released powerful antagonisms across class lines as well as those of age and sex. Not until they had done this, did the struggle of peasants against landlords, tenants against rent collectors, victims against local bullies become open and bitter. The last to bring charges were the young against the old. Even here bitterness came to the surface.[140]

The Communist regime forged a new link between the village and the national government. It became evident to every peasant that his daily life depended on a national political power. Through this new link the Communists pumped out of the village, C.K. Yang estimates, even more than the landlord rentier and the Kuomintang had taken before. At the same time the new and larger burden was much more equally distributed than had previously been the case.[141] All these changes were temporary and transitional. To destroy the old order, to forge new links with the government, to extract more resources from the peasants could only be preliminary to solving the basic problem of increasing economic output all around in a world of competing armed giants. That part of the story falls outside the scope of this book. In China, even more than in Russia, the peasants provided the dynamite that finally exploded the old order. Once again they furnished the main driving force behind the victory of a party dedicated to achieving through relentless terror a supposedly inevitable phase of history in which the peasantry would cease to exist.

[140] Yang, *Village in Transition*, 178 – 179.
[141] *Village in Transition*, 174 – 175, 158 – 159.

CHAPTER FIVE

Asian Fascism: Japan

1. Revolution from Above: The Response of the Ruling Classes to Old and New Threats

DURING THE SEVENTEENTH CENTURY in Japan, China, and Russia, new governments came to power that in each country put an end to a prolonged period of internal disorder and fighting. In Russia and China the establishment of peace and order was the beginning, to the extent that we can ever speak of beginnings in history, of a long process that culminated in peasant revolutions. The agrarian bureaucracies in these two countries inhibited the growth of a class of independent merchants and manufacturers. Oversimplifying somewhat, we can say that, in the absence of a bourgeois revolution, there came a peasant revolution that in turn opened the road for totalitarian modernization. Japanese development, on the other hand, followed quite a different course, closer to that of Germany. Though mercantile influences undermined the agrarian order, there was here too, as in Germany, nothing that deserves the name of a successful bourgeois revolution. And the Japanese managed to contain and deflect peasant discontents in such a way as to prevent a peasant revolution. By the end of the third decade in the twentieth century the outcome showed a very strong resemblance to European fascism.

What explains the difference between the course of modernization in Japan and that in both Russia and China? At once feudalism leaps to mind as a possible explanation. Feudalism was a weak memory in both Russia and China if indeed it can be said to have existed at all, a matter of dispute among scholars. The Japanese version of feudalism, on the other hand, remained vigorous well into the nineteenth century. Since Japan is also the only Asiatic country that had become a substantial industrial power by the third decade of the twentieth century, the hypothesis that feudalism provides the key becomes very attractive through the wide range of history that it would help to render more orderly and intelligible.[1] Insofar as feudalism in Japan helped to make it possible for one section of the old ruling classes to detach itself from the prevailing order and carry out a revolution from above to make the social changes necessary for industrial advance, it does constitute an important part of the explanation. Nevertheless it is necessary to see why this was possible and precisely how the whole process of modernization was related to feudalism as it existed in Japan.

Both in explaining and assessing this transformation it is essential to remind ourselves of the limitations of our present historical perspective. A hundred years from now, or perhaps in much less time, the partial nature of Japan's social and industrial revolution, especially the very limited "revolution" of the Imperial Restoration in 1868, may seem to be the essence of Japan's tragedy. It is worth recalling here that modern historians are far from sanguine about Bismarck's success in combining old and new in Germany. On the

[1] For a recent discussion of the similarities and differences between European and Japanese feudalism see Hall, "Feudalism in Japan," 15–51. The notion that there is a connection between Japanese feudalism and its subsequent adoption of Western practices is fairly common among Orientalists, though I have not found any detailed examination of the nature of the connection. At the end of his instructive essay, "Japanese Feudalism," in Coulburn, ed, *Feudalism in History,* 46–48, Edwin O. Reischauer lists several characteristics of Japanese feudalism that he suggests may have eased the Japanese transition to modern social institutions. One of these, strong national consciousness, seems to me the exact opposite of feudalism. Another, the independent development of capitalist enterprise within feudalism, also refers to the growth of antifeudal institutions rather than a legacy of feudalism. But the Japanese case does support the thesis that capitalism can establish itself more easily within a feudal system than within an agrarian bureaucracy. Reischauer's list summarizes the legacy of Japanese historical experience *as a whole,* not that of Japanese feudalism.

other hand, contemporary Chinese society, despite severe difficulties and setbacks, shows signs of moving ahead. By learning from Soviet mistakes, China could conceivably surpass Russia. Naturally it is impossible to anticipate future perspectives. But at least we can avoid the parochialism of taking our own for granted. It is foolish to treat the Japanese response to the challenge of the modern world as a success and the Chinese one as a failure.

With these cautions in mind let us try to discover what characteristics in premodern Japanese society played a significant part in the course of modernization. Both vertical and horizontal fissures appeared as the old order eroded, and both were perhaps equally important. Furthermore, there were significant differences between Western and Japanese feudalism. To say this is to remain dreadfully abstract; it is necessary to plunge into the actual workings of the society over a specific period of time in order to see what these observations actually mean.

Through his victory in the battle of Sekigahara in the year 1600 Tokugawa Ieyasu, one of the most famous rulers in Japanese history, put an end to the period of warring barons and inaugurated an era of internal peace. In its formal political aspects this regime, known to historians as the Tokugawa Shogunate, lasted until the Restoration of the Emperor in 1868.[2] The leading political idea of the Shogunate was a static one, the maintenance of peace and order. Society was sharply divided into rulers and ruled. The latter were chiefly peasants, whom the ruling warrior classes regarded mainly as an instrument to work the land and produce taxes for their benefit.[3] In return, when the system was working well, the peasants received the benefits of at least a modicum of economic security and political justice. As much as possible, through a variety of devices ranging from severe sumptuary edicts to the sealing-off of Japan from nearly all contacts with the outside world between 1639 and the advent of Commodore Perry in 1854, the rulers attempted to repress any influences that might undermine the prevailing or-

[2] Excellent general description in Sansom, *Short Cultural History*, chap XXI. See also his *Western World and Japan*, chap IX. Sources on more specific points will be given below.

[3] Asakawa, "Notes on Village Government, I," 260, 278.

der. The merchants in the towns, to whom we shall come in due course, became in time one of the main sources of disruption and worry to the rulers.

Within the ruling groups there were important grades and distinctions. The Emperor was a shadowy and secluded figure, able only in the end to convert prestige into real power — for others. The *Shōgun* held the reins of authority in a system that resembled the absolutism of the *Roi Soleil* much more than the decentralized feudal institutions of earlier European history. Together with various branches of the Tokugawa family and his immediate vassals, the *Shōgun* possessed between one-fourth and one-fifth of the agricultural land of the country, deriving the major part of his resources from this source.[4] To manage his domain lands, he appointed about forty intendents with regular salaries.[5] Thus, as also in Western Europe at the same time, there was a strong bureaucratic infusion in Japanese feudalism.

Certain points in the Tokugawa system of authority are worth noticing. First, it represented an attempt to impose a degree of central bureaucratic authority on top of a fragmented feudal polity where it was important to play off the great fiefs against each other. Secondly, this fragmentation was never wholly overcome. When the Tokugawa polity ran into increasing difficulty in the middle of the nineteenth century, some of the most important vertical cleavages were the same as those plastered over by the system established in 1600.

Directly beneath the *Shōgun* in rank came the small body of great lords or *daimyō*.[6] There were 194 of them in 1614 and only 266 immediately before the Restoration of 1868. At the latter date the largest fief was registered as producing 1,022,700 *koku* of rice. The average was about 70,000 *koku*.[7]

[4] Allen, *Short Economic History*, 10.

[5] Asakawa, "Notes on Village Government, I," 261.

[6] They were classified into three groups according to their relationship to the Tokugawa house. See the discussion in Craig, *Chōshū*, 17 – 21.

[7] Asakawa, "Notes on Village Government, II," 160. One *koku* equals slightly less than 5.2 American bushels. The fact that a fief was registered at 70,000 *koku* did not mean that its overlord received that much as an annual income but merely that the land was theoretically capable of pro-

Beneath the *daimyō* was the main body of *samurai*, or warriors, among whom there were wide variations in power and wealth.[8] Together with their families they are estimated to have numbered around 2,000,000 persons or about one-sixteenth of the total population on the eve of the Restoration.[9] Formally, they were military retainers of the *daimyō* and received from them an annual stipend in rice. The Tokugawa Shogunate, by making them recipients of stipends, cut them off from independent bases of power in the countryside and eliminated at one stroke one of the chief sources of political instability of the preceding era.[10] At the same time, through the imposition of peace, the Shogunate deprived the *samurai* of any real function in Japanese society and contributed to the creation of a group — the impoverished *samurai* — that played a key role in its eventual overthrow.

The days had long since come to an end when the soldier in time of peace had farmed his own land. As early as 1587 Hideyoshi, the great general who helped to found the Tokugawa regime, had proclaimed that all farmers were to hand in their weapons. The measure was intended not only to eliminate the danger of an armed peasantry but to emphasize the clarity and stability of class distinctions.[11] Subsequently the right to wear a sword became the chief distinction between a *samurai* and a wealthy peasant.[12]

When away from the *Shōgun*'s court the *daimyō*, or overlord, lived surrounded by his *samurai*, or retainers, in a castle town. Few peasant villages were more than twenty miles away from such a town.[13] The castle towns were the local centers through which the warrior class extracted from the peasantry, in the form of taxes, the

---

ducing that much rice. On this point see Ramming, "Wirtschaftliche Lage der Samurai," 4. For further details, particularly on geographical distribution of high and low tax rates and the political implications thereof, see Beasley, "Feudal Revenue," 255 – 271.

[8] For more details on these divisions, see Ramming, "Wirtschaftliche Lage der Samurai," 4 – 5.

[9] Allen, *Short Economic History*, 11.

[10] Smith, *Agrarian Origins*, 1.

[11] Sansom, *Short Cultural History*, 430.

[12] Smith, *Agrarian Origins*, 179.

[13] Smith, *Agrarian Origins*, 68.

economic surplus that supported it. Essentially the tax-collecting administration consisted of two sets of officials: those who manned the central bureaus in the castle or nearby town and the district magistrates scattered about the fief itself.[14] In peaceful times at any rate the system worked with remarkably little use of force.

Within the fiefs, the great feudatories exercised power according to their own lights. However, they could not erect new castles, coin money, construct warships, or arrange marriages without the *Shōgun*'s sanction. The continuity of the fiefs as distinct units appears from the fact that, of the sixteen great Outside Houses that existed in the year 1664, all of them continued to rule their own fiefs down to the formal abolition of feudalism in 1871. In the beginning, to be sure, the *Shōgun* intervened quite freely in the local affairs of the fiefs, confiscating and transferring territories on a wide scale. After the middle of the seventeenth century, when the system had shaken down and the *Shōgun*'s position seemed secure, the policy of succeeding *Shōgun* became more cautious, and interventions in the internal affairs of a fief much rarer.[15] Such, then, in brief outline, was the regime established by the Tokugawa Shogunate. As we have seen, it was a relatively centralized and tightly controlled form of feudalism, so much so that one older writer refers to it as a police state,[16] a designation that no doubt seemed much more appropriate in 1900 than it would after Hitler and Stalin. Though this designation now seems inappropriate, the Tokugawa system was not one out of which was likely to grow the theory and practice of free society as known in modern Western civilization. Earlier Japanese feudalism, too, lacked features that in the West made important contributions to this growth. In the feudal bond uniting lord and vassal, the element of contract was very weak in Japan; the elements of loyalty and duty to superiors, on the other hand, received heavy emphasis.[17] Western discussions of the contrast make the Japanese feudal bond seem more primitive,

[14] Smith, *Agrarian Origins*, 202.
[15] Murdoch, *History of Japan*, III, 20–22.
[16] Fukuda, *Gesellschaftliche und Wirtschaftliche Entwickelung*, chap IV.
[17] Sansom, *History of Japan*, I, 359–360, 368.

less objective and rational than its European counterpart. It rested more on unwritten custom and ceremonial observance; it had the character of a fictive kinship relationship, something very widely used in Japanese society, and relied less than in Europe on written or oral contract to specify individual duties or privileges.[18] Indigenous trends in this direction received further reenforcement from the importation of Confucian philosophy which attained almost the position of an established religion.

By the time Commodore Perry's ships appeared in 1854, the Tokugawa system had suffered substantial decay. The decline of the old order, together with attempts to preserve the privileges of the agrarian élite, had already given rise to some of the social forces that eventually culminated in the regime that dropped its fateful bombs on Pearl Harbor in 1941.

The factors that produced this decay and rebirth were many and complicated. Their exact nature and relative importance will probably long remain a matter of dispute among specialists. Yet for our purposes it may not be too misleading to suggest that essentially they dissolve into two: peace and luxury. Peace permitted a commercial way of life to emerge not only in the towns but also in the countryside. Even though kept under close supervision, commercial influences eroded much of the feudal edifice. Just as the Tokugawa system may strike the comparative historian as a species somewhere between the centralized agrarian bureaucracy of China and the much looser feudalism of medieval Europe, so does the capacity of eighteenth- and nineteenth-century Japanese society to contain the divisive and destructive effects of commerce fall somewhere between these two extremes.

To a considerable extent peace and luxury radiated out from the center of the Tokugawa polity. Just as Louis XIV compelled his nobles to reside at Versailles, so did the *Shōgun* require the *daimyō* to spend specified periods of time in the capital Edo.[19] Up to a point the effects were similar in both cases. By encouraging

18 Hall, "Feudalism in Japan," 33 – 34.
19 The residence requirement remained in full effect until 1862, when its abandonment foreshadowed the end of Tokugawa power. See Murdoch, *History of Japan*, III, 723.

various forms of luxurious display the *Shōgun* weakened the position of his nobles and simultaneously gave a fillip to the trading classes in the towns. The expenses of the *daimyō* increased as they had to maintain a residence both at home and in Edo. For their establishment in the capital and the costs of travel for themselves and a large retinue they had to pay in specie, which they had no right to coin. These expenses put a heavy demand on the finances of many fiefs. To pay for them, *daimyō* generally had to ship their excess rice and other local products to the market, using the services of the merchant.[20] Often the feudal aristocrat became dependent on the merchant for credit, while the merchant, on the other hand, depended on the *daimyō* for political protection.

The *samurai*'s economic position, dependent on the *daimyō*, apparently deteriorated under the Tokugawa, especially after the middle of their reign. The evidence, however, is not conclusive. One of the ways in which the *daimyō* endeavored to meet their own expenses was by cutting the stipends of their *samurai*.[21] Cutting the stipend became possible only in Tokugawa times. Secured by the peace and authority of the *Shōgun*, the *daimyō* no longer needed to rely so heavily on their vassals and could afford to impose this sacrifice.

Whatever the actual economic situation of the *samurai*, there can be no doubt that their status in Japanese society was deteriorating. A good income in rice was for a *samurai* merely the material base for the life of a warrior. Under the enforced peace of the Tokugawa, the warrior had no obviously important social function to perform. In the meantime, other forms of prestige, based on the wealth of the merchants, were beginning to compete with the martial virtues. The old ethic was being undermined, though as yet no new one had taken its place. Signs of these changes began to appear as early as the beginning of the eighteenth century.

The loss of their function as warriors, together with the inroads of commerce, placed a severe strain on the loyalty of many *samurai*, setting them adrift in both a psychological and a literal sense. While we may treat as literary exaggeration the statement

[20] Sheldon, *Merchant Class*, 18.
[21] Some data in Ramming, "Wirtschaftliche Lage der Samurai," 34–35.

of an early nineteenth-century writer that "the *samurai* hate their lords as their worst enemies" on account of the practice of cutting stipends, we may be certain that the cuts were widely resented.[22] To make matters even more difficult, the warriors were prohibited from engaging in any form of commerce. Though many evaded the prohibition in order to make ends meet, whatever wealth they gained in this way could scarcely have contributed to their feeling of security as *samurai*.[23]

As a result, many warriors simply cut their ties and became *rōnin*, wandering masterless men, often ready for any violent enterprise, a group that contributed to the turbulence of the latter part of the Tokugawa period. *Chōshū*, the fief that played the key part in the Imperial Restoration of 1868, was a great refuge for the *rōnin*.[24] The notion of getting rid of the "barbarian" Westerners had a strong appeal for these men. Many opposed the opening of new ports, because the "expulsion of the barbarians would then be hopeless. . . . We should have to fold the left lappet over the right, to take to writing across the page, and to have to use their stinking calendar."[25] Thus the lower ranks of the *samurai* constituted a free-floating source of violence, a "lumpenaristocracy," available for a variety of reactionary purposes but certainly no revolution of the English and French type. In some of the crucial military struggles surrounding the Imperial Restoration they were ranged about equally on both sides.[26] Without the foreign threat and great political skill at the top, this potentially explosive force, a result of the way in which *pax Tokugawa* had profoundly altered the position of the warrior class, might have burst Japanese society at the seams and brought about a return to feudal anarchy.

The merchants (*chōnin*) were the immediate if not the ultimate source of these corrosive influences on the old order. Their role in Japanese society shows many similarities to that of the Jews

[22] Ramming, "Wirtschaftliche Lage der Samurai," 7.

[23] See Sheldon, *Merchant Class*, 32; Ramming, "Wirtschaftliche Lage der Samurai," 10.

[24] Murdoch, *History of Japan*, III, 737.

[25] Quoted in Murdoch, *History of Japan*, III, 720.

[26] Craig, "The Restoration Movement," 187–197, esp 190–191.

in late medieval Europe, particularly in Spain. In very general terms we may characterize the relationship between the warrior aristocracy and the merchants as one of symbiotic antagonism. The *daimyō* or *samurai* depended on the merchant to turn rice and other agricultural products produced by the peasants into cash and to supply them with many of the essentials and most of the amenities for their aristocratic style of life. The merchant, on the other hand, depended on the warrior aristocrat for political tolerance and protection in order to engage in trade, a degrading and generally parasitic way of life according to the warrior's code of ethics. Without by any means throwing off the feudal restrictions, or even attempting to do so, the merchants substantially improved their position in this relationship until by the end of the period they had become the dominant partner.

One consequence was that the rigid barriers between classes, upon which the Tokugawa system depended for much of its stability, showed serious signs of breaking down. Warriors became merchants and vice versa. Whether or not this trend increased throughout the period we do not know, though it would seem likely, on general grounds, that it did.[27] In the early nineteenth century, out of one group of 250 merchant families, 48, or almost one in five, had *samurai* ancestors. Impoverished *samurai* at times set aside the eldest son and adopted a rich merchant's son as heir. Though the *Shōgun* Yoshimune in the early eighteenth century forbade the sale of *samurai* status, the prohibition soon became a dead letter.[28]

Not until after the beginning of the eighteenth century did the feudal rulers realize that the merchants were in any sense a threat to their power. By then it was too late, even though the economic advance of the merchants had largely spent its force.[29] Indeed, recent writings give the impression that the feudal rulers might have been able to contain this threat and maintain some form of equilibrium, even if one rather different from early Tokugawa

[27] Sheldon, *Merchant Class*, 6, mentions that merchants of *samurai* descent were numerous and successful in the first years of the Tokugawa.
[28] Honjo, *Social and Economic History*, 204–205.
[29] Sheldon, *Merchant Class*, 165.

days, for quite some time if Western battleships had not made their ominous appearance on the Japanese scene.[30] At any rate the feudal aristocracy had a number of weapons they could and did use against the merchants: outright confiscation, forced loans (that became increasingly frequent toward the end of the Tokugawa regime), and refusal to pay debts. The effect of these measures, and especially confiscation, was in the latter part of the era simply to make the merchants more reluctant to grant loans.[31] Since the aristocracy was heavily though not universally dependent on these loans, it proved impossible to crush the merchants.

The stranglehold that many merchants obtained from time to time on sections of the nobility produced understandable resentment among the latter and other articulate segments of Japanese society. In a way that recalls European physiocratic notions of the same date and anti-Semitism at a later one, some Japanese thinkers argued that nobles and peasants were the only useful members of society. "Merchants, on the other hand, carry on an insignificant occupation . . . [and] it should be no concern of government if they ruin themselves."[32] As already indicated, the *Shōgun*'s government from time to time tried to put these or similar ideas into practice. In this clash between a decaying military aristocracy and an emerging commercial interest, we may notice the beginnings of that anticapitalist outlook which was to be so prominent in the Japanese variant of fascism.

Though the conflict between the feudal aristocracy and the merchants constitutes a very significant aspect of the background to later developments, it would be seriously misleading to stress this aspect alone. Unlike Western Europe, Japan did not develop self-governing towns with charters that expressed in concrete terms their political and legal independence of the surrounding feudal authority. To be sure, there were some promising starts in this direction in the beginning phases of the Tokugawa regime. But, as the regime consolidated itself in a form of centralized feudalism, it

[30] Suggestive in this connection is the interchange between Dore and Sheldon in *Journal of Asian Studies*, XVIII, 507 – 508, and XIX, 238 – 239.

[31] Sheldon, *Merchant Class*, 119, 122 – 123.

[32] Quoted by Sheldon, *Merchant Class*, 105.

cut short such tendencies. This "refeudalization," as it is sometimes called, imposed strict limitations on the merchants, carefully enclosing them in the feudal order, where, so the rulers hoped, they could do no harm.[33] The closing of the country, through the edicts of 1633 – 1641, had the effect of limiting the initiative of the merchants, partly through removing the stimulus of foreign contacts and competition.[34] As we have already noticed, the main thrust of mercantile development had spent much of its force by about a hundred years after imposition of the *pax Tokugawa*. After that, there was some tendency to settle down and enjoy the fruits of enterprise, as well as to cling to tried and proven methods of business.

For our purpose there is no need to discuss in any further detail the mechanism of political controls over the merchants that the Tokugawa rulers devised. It is enough to note that they were rather effective, particularly in the early period, and that, as a result, the merchants' rise to economic power was "almost an underground movement."[35] These political controls made the Japanese merchant a dependent figure in the society, even if there were occasions when his wrath could make a *daimyō* tremble.

There were, of course, significant variations. The merchants of Ōsaka were less dependent than those of the capital, Edo.[36] And, in the latter part of the period, the provincial merchants showed themselves less dependent on feudal relationships for their materials and markets than did the older urban monopolists.[37]

It is also true that in some of the arts and in the lighter pleasures of life the merchants developed some distinctive social traits and tastes that recall the pre-Puritan aspects of mercantile culture in the West. But this merchant culture, that reached the height of its flowering by the beginning of the eighteenth century, was no real threat in itself to the Tokugawa system.[38] Essentially this tol-

---

[33] Sheldon, *Merchant Class*, 8, 25, 37.
[34] Sheldon, *Merchant Class*, 20 – 24.
[35] Sheldon, *Merchant Class*, 32 – 36.
[36] Sheldon, *Merchant Class*, 88, 92, 108.
[37] Sheldon, *Merchant Class*, 163.
[38] Sheldon, *Merchant Class*, 99.

erated licentiousness, mainly restricted to a particular quarter of the capital, served as a safety valve. If anything, it helped to preserve rather than destroy the *ancien régime*.[39]

For all these reasons Japanese merchants of the Tokugawa period were suffused with the feudal ethic. They completely failed to develop any intellectual standpoint with which to oppose the traditional outlook. E. Herbert Norman searched through many varieties of Japanese writings "to discover whether any writer had ventured to express a sustained and penetrating criticism of the most oppressive aspects of Japanese feudalism, its social rigidity, its intellectual obscurantism, its scholastic sterility, its debasement of human values, and its parochial outlook on the outside world."[40] Though he was able to find in chronicles and literary writings a number of scattered expressions of disgust with the cruelties of feudal oppression, he was unable to find a single influential thinker who made a frontal attack on the system as a whole.[41] The failure of the Japanese merchant class to develop a critical intellectual standpoint comparable to that produced in the West cannot, in my opinion, be explained through psychological factors or some peculiar efficacy of the Japanese value system.[42] Such explanations are logically the same as the famous explanation of the effects of opium as being due to its "dormitive" properties. They beg the fundamental question: *why* did this particular outlook prevail when and where it did? The answer to this question is historical: the conditions under which the Japanese merchant class grew up from the seventeenth century onwards. The isolation of the country, the symbiotic relationship between the warrior and the merchant, and the long political dominance of the warrior would seem to constitute

[39] Norman, "Andō Shōeki," 75.

[40] "Andō Shōeki," 2.

[41] Norman finally chose to interpret in considerable detail an early eighteenth-century physician, Andō Shōeki, admittedly an isolated thinker without influence in his lifetime or later. Andō Shōeki's main work was never published and, though critical of feudalism, gives off an air of utopian agrarian primitivism rather than of a "bourgeois" critique of contemporary Japan. See "Andō Shōeki," chap I and 100 – 110, 224 – 226, 242 – 243.

[42] For such an interpretation, see Bellah, *Tokugawa Religion*.

the essential elements in any explanation of the merchants' limited horizon.

A large portion of the wealth that flowed into merchant coffers was originally pumped out of the peasants by the warrior aristocracy. Subsequently we shall have to discuss in some detail the factors that prevented the Japanese peasants from becoming a revolutionary force on the scale of their Russian and Chinese counterparts. Here the discussion will be confined to the peasant question as the dominant classes perceived it and as it impinged on their interests.

With their taxes, then, the peasant mass supported the rest of the population, as is largely the case in any agrarian state. Articulate circles within the warrior aristocracy seized upon this fact to claim that the peasant was the foundation of a healthy society — meaning, of course, by "healthy" one in which the *samurai* were dominant. This is the characteristic rhetoric of an agrarian aristocracy threatened by commercial interests. Admiration for the peasantry was an oblique criticism of the merchant. The much quoted cynical rhymed couplet, "Peasants are like sesame seeds; the more you press, the more comes out," comes closer to describing the *samurai*'s real relationship to the peasantry.[43] As Sir George Sansom remarks dryly, the Tokugawa had a high regard for agriculture, but very little for agriculturists.

In the early 1860s the peasant question became intertwined with the problem of creating a modern army. The solution to this question affected not only Japan's independence as a sovereign state but the very character of the society. In essence the government had to decide whether or not to arm the peasant in order to defend Japan against the foreign enemy. In 1863 it sounded out its higher administrative officials about the wisdom of this step. Revealing excerpts from the replies reflect two main concerns: that the *daimyō* in the fiefs might turn this force against the Tokugawa government and that the peasants themselves might be a source of danger to the established order.[44] Both fears turned out to be justified.

[43] Ramming, "Wirtschaftliche Lage der Samurai," 28.
[44] Norman, *Soldier and Peasant,* 73.

The hold of the authorities over the peasants was weaker in areas directly controlled by the *Shōgun* than in some of the outlying fiefs, especially in Chōshū. The strictly Tokugawa areas included the major cities of Edo and Ōsaka, out of which commercial influences radiated. The leaders of Chōshū, on the other hand, by an ingenious system of budgets and taxation, managed to keep their financial independence and avoid falling into the hands of Ōsaka moneylenders and merchants. Partly for this reason, the peasant base and traditional feudal ties remained relatively strong in Chōshū.[45] Though there had been moderately severe peasant outbreaks much earlier in Chōshū (in the years 1831 – 1836), it was only when foreign warships shelled Chōshū forts in 1864 that important circles in the fief became convinced of the necessity of reform on Western lines and argued that even the peasants ought to be armed. With the formation of these units in Chōshū the pro-Emperor forces gained an important power base.[46]

In other parts of Japan, the peasants contributed an antifeudal and even faintly revolutionary component to the Restoration movement. The later years of the Tokugawa era were characterized by numerous outbreaks of peasant violence with substantial antifeudal overtones. Even if they apparently lacked very clear political objectives, they were a threat to the rulers. A detailed monograph on these uprisings reports a total of around a thousand such affairs during the whole of the period, the majority of which displayed a direct relationship between the peasants and the governing class that controlled them. A chart of their frequency shows a sharp increase in the later years of the epoch, that is, from 1772 to 1867.[47] Imperial armies at times received help from peasant uprisings in the military clashes that accompanied the Restoration. In Echigo province, for example, 60,000 armed peasants blocked the commander of the Tokugawa forces in that region. Again, in other areas, the commanders of the Imperial forces exploited antifeudal sentiments by methods recalling contemporary political warfare. In one instance, the

"Pacifier and Commander-in-Chief of the Tosando" posted pla-
cards in prominent places and distributed manifestoes addressed
to the peasants and traders in these villages, inviting them to appear before the local headquarters of the Imperial army and bring
charges of tyranny and cruelty against the former Tokugawa administrators. They specifically appealed to the most impoverished,
orphans, widows, and those who had been persecuted by the feudal
authorities. All complaints were promised a careful and sympathetic hearing, and it was further stated that justice would be
meted out to guilty officials.[48]

The mildly revolutionary strand was of course not the only
peasant contribution. Peasants fought on both sides of the Restoration struggle for a variety of motives. As we shall see later, there
was also a strong reactionary component, not only among peasants
but among other supporters of the Emperor, harking back to a pure
and mythical feudal past. The interweaving of these strands is what
gives the Meiji Restoration its protean and, so far as the immediate
event is concerned, somewhat inconclusive character.

The reader will have certainly recognized by this point that
the Restoration was by no means pure class struggle and certainly
not a bourgeois revolution, as some Japanese writers, though not to
my knowledge any Western ones, have maintained. In some of its
decisive aspects it was an old-fashioned, feudal struggle between the
central authority and the fiefs.[49] And the fiefs that led the struggle
against the *Shōgun*, not only Chōshū, but also Satsuma — the "Prussia of Japan" about which we know rather less — were ones where
the traditional agrarian society and feudal loyalties remained relatively much stronger.[50]

In marked contrast to some of the larger fiefs, Tokugawa

[48] Norman, *Soldier and Peasant*, 38 – 39.

[49] A French scholar, writing on the fiefs during the last phase of the
Tokugawa, claimed that the *Shōgun*'s authority received strict obedience
only near the garrisons; the further one travelled from Edo, the more the
spirit of independence and particularism appeared. See Courant, "Clans
japonais," 43.

[50] On the traditional agrarian system see Norman, *Soldier and Peasant*,
58 – 65. Satsuma was the land of the *gōshi*, a country squire halfway between
peasant and *samurai*, and a survivor from pre-Tokugawa days.

finances became increasingly shaky toward the end of the period and, in the judgment of several historians, contributed to the final downfall of the Shogunate. But, as is usually the case with an *ancien régime*, the financial difficulties were no more than symptoms of deeper causes. The foreign danger daily increased the Shogunate's need for revenues — and for an army that seemed to be a threat to the Tokugawa if not to the Chōshū leaders. The merchant could not be pressed too hard without killing the goose. The only other source was the peasant, who had shown increasing restiveness under existing burdens.

Though these cleavages and issues formed the background to the Restoration, in the events that led up to it, from about 1860 onwards, they remained very much in the background. The ever-present threat of foreign armed intervention helped to make the Restoration a symbolic act that many groups could support for a wide variety of contradictory reasons. In itself the Restoration was not particularly decisive, and the implications for the future of Japanese society were not clear for some years. The struggles that accompanied it had very little of the character of programmatic conflicts among clearly defined interest groups. For these reasons, the account of these years seems to a Westerner no more than a confusing web of intrigues, intricate and purposeless. They appear this way, I would suggest, precisely because the main actors within the ruling class were generally agreed on what they wanted: the ousting of the foreigner and a minimum of disturbance to the *status quo*. Down to the very last, according to one standard account,[51] the Emperor wanted to act through the Shogunate in opposition to "extremist" and "disorderly" elements — in a word, against anything that smacked of revolutionary change.

Therefore the question became in effect: who should bell the cat? Much of the rivalry centered about who might get the credit for this daring act — if it could be carried out. In this struggle the Shogunate had the tremendous disadvantage of political responsibility. Whenever the Shogunate failed to keep a promise that it could not possibly keep, such as to expel the barbarian by a certain date, its incapacity was obvious. The *Shōgun*'s opponents, on the

[51] See Murdoch, *History of Japan*, III, 733.

other hand, naturally gravitated toward a figure that was "above politics." As much as any other factor, the disadvantages of political responsibility in an impossible situation contributed to the *Shōgun's* conclusive defeat.[52]

At this point it may be helpful to assess in more general terms the causes of the Restoration. The fundamental one, I believe, was the partial erosion of the feudal edifice through the rise of commerce, which was in turn due to the establishment of peace and order. Together with the foreign intrusion, this erosion created problems toward whose solution the Restoration was one important step. The politically reactionary aspects of the solution are to a great extent explicable in terms of the groups that the Imperial movement attracted. One was a section of the nobility at the Imperial court. Another consisted of a few disaffected leaders of fiefs where feudal institutions appear to have been particularly strong. *Samurai,* disaffected from their particular lord but by no means from feudal society as such, also made an important contribution. Among the commercial elements, the conservative old-line merchants were hostile to the idea of opening the country, as it would increase competition for them. Generally the merchants did not play an active part in the struggle itself, although Mitsui interests were on both sides of the fence.[53] Only among the peasants, and there far from universally, can one find signs of opposition to feudal institutions. In doctrinal terms, the Restoration took place under the banner of traditional symbolism, mainly Confucian. As we have seen, the old order faced no direct intellectual challenge, least of all one that stemmed from commercial interests.

In the light of the groups that supported the Restoration, what is surprising is not that the new government did so little but that it did so much. As we shall see shortly, the Meiji government (1868 – 1912) as the new regime is known, took many important steps toward remaking Japan in the image of modern industrial society. What prompted this largely feudal revolution to carry out a program with many undoubtedly progressive features? The reasons

[52] For an account of the principal events, see Craig, *Chōshū,* chap IX, and Murdoch, *History of Japan,* III, chaps XVIII – XIX.

[53] Sheldon, *Merchant Class,* 162, 172.

are not hard to find and have been emphasized by many historians of Japan. There was some shift in the character of the ruling class, though that is probably a subordinate factor. Since the lines of cleavage in Japanese society were vertical as well as horizontal, they enabled a section of the agrarian ruling class to detach itself from the Tokugawa system and put through a revolution from above. The foreign threat was decisive in this connection. Under its unifying force, the new government acted in such a way as to preserve the privileges of a small segment of the élite, open up opportunities for others, and ensure national survival.

From 1868 onward, the new rulers of Japan, drawn in substantial measure from the pool of *samurai* that had been losing out under the old regime, faced two major problems. One was to achieve a modern centralized state. The other was to create a modern industrial economy. Both were necessary if Japan was to survive as an independent state. Together these problems amounted to the dismantling of a feudal society and the erection of a modern one in its place.

Such at least is the way the problem appears to the social historian with the advantages and disadvantages of hindsight. It is scarcely the way the problem appeared to contemporaries. Many had joined the movement to "Restore the Emperor — Expel the Barbarian" in the hope of creating a new and better version of feudalism. Our formulation is too abstract and too concrete. Too abstract in that, by and large, the people behind the Restoration and the early years of the Meiji did not wish to see just *any* kind of modern state, but one that would preserve as much as possible of the advantages the ruling class had enjoyed under the *ancien régime*, cutting away just enough (which in practice turned out to be a great deal) to preserve the state, since they would otherwise lose everything. Too concrete in that it gives the impression of a specific unified program of modernization. The leaders of early Meiji Japan were no doctrinaire social theorists, catapulted like the Russian Marxists into the arena of political responsibility. Nevertheless, if these qualifications are kept in mind, this notion of the task before the Meiji leaders will help to sort out important facts of the period, their consequences, and their relationship to each other.

A most important first step toward the creation of an effective central government occurred in March of 1869, when the great Western fiefs of Chōshū, Satsuma, Hizen, and Tosa "voluntarily" offered their territories to the throne, declaring at the same time, "There must be one central governing body and one universal authority, which must be preserved intact." This must have been a very ticklish moment. Clearly the Restoration might have been no more than a redistribution of power within the feudal system.

Why then did these leading fiefs take this step? Magnanimity and farsightedness may have played a part, as some historians claim, though I am very skeptical about their importance. Much more significant may have been the fact that the *daimyō* were allowed to retain half their revenues after the extensive negotiations that preceded this step, even though this was not the final solution.[54] A still more important consideration was the fear on the part of these fiefs that, if they did not take this joint step, some one group of provincial leaders might step into the Tokugawa's shoes. Satsuma itself at the time nourished exactly such ambitions.[55] Rivalry, in other words, among the contenders for power strengthened the hand of a central authority that as yet was quite weak.

For the moment, the government was not prepared to put its new powers to the test and left the former feudal rulers in charge as Imperial legates with the title of governor. Only two years later, however, in August 1871, it took the final step of announcing in a brief decree that feudal domains were to become units of local administration (prefectures) under the central government. Shortly afterwards, in a move that recalled the methods of the Tokugawa, it ordered all the former *daimyō* to leave their estates and settle with their families in the capital. Indeed the similarity is more than fortuitous.[56] The Tokugawa in their victory of 1600 had laid the

[54] Sansom, *Western World and Japan*, 323–324, 327–328.

[55] Sansom, *Western World and Japan*, 324, where the author adds an illuminating general comment to the effect that the famous Charter Oath of 1868, Japan's first "constitutional" document providing for assemblies and open discussions, was "not a concession to rising democratic sentiment but a safeguard against the ascendancy of a single feudal group."

[56] Sansom, *Western World and Japan*, 326.

foundations of a modern centralized state. The Meiji completed the process.

At the same time that it was establishing itself politically, the government passed a whole series of measures whose effect would not become fully visible until later. Their general purport was to strike off the feudal shackles on the free movement of persons and goods and thus encourage development along capitalist lines. In 1869 the government declared equality before the law for social classes, abolished local barriers to trade and communication, permitted freedom of cropping, and allowed individuals to acquire property rights in land.[57] Though land had begun to emerge from feudal fetters under the Tokugawa, now it could take on the character of a commodity to be bought and sold like any other, with important consequences for the rest of society that we shall discuss in due course.

If these transformations were to be carried out at all peacefully, and from above instead of through a popular revolution, it was necessary to provide substantial compensation at least to key elements in the old order. In 1869 the government had granted to the *daimyō* one-half of their revenues upon the surrender of their fiefs. Such generosity could not continue. The government's freedom to maneuver was narrow. In 1871 the attempt to revise treaties in a way that would permit raising additional revenue did not succeed. In 1876 the government found it necessary to impose a compulsory reduction in the revenues of the *daimyō* and the stipends of the *samurai*. Although all but the least important *daimyō* received quite favorable treatment, the smaller feudal chieftains and the majority of the *samurai* suffered a severe cut.[58] In effect, then, the new government rewarded a few of its key supporters handsomely. On the other hand, the Meiji found it necessary to repudiate the discontented *samurai*, an important source of the energy that had overthrown the old order.

[57] Allen, *Short Economic History*, 27. According to Norman, *Japan's Emergence*, 137, the legal ban on the sale of land was not removed until 1872.

[58] Sansom, *Western World and Japan*, 327–328. For more information on the economic aspects of the problem, see Allen, *Short Economic History*, 34–37. The point will be discussed further below.

The reduction in *samurai* stipends was simply the culmination of a long trend. Actually the Meiji merely finished off the process of destroying the *samurai* that, as we have seen, was well under way during the Tokugawa period. Modernization in Japan did not involve the revolutionary liquidation of any section of the ruling class. Instead, there was a prolonged process of euthanasia lasting through three centuries. The social status of the *samurai* all but vanished with the proclamation of equality before the law, though they were allowed the empty distinction of being known as *shizoku*, or former *samurai*, a designation that carried with it no rights or exemptions. As warriors, they had already lost most of their function under the *pax Tokugawa*. The introduction of conscriptions in 1873 eliminated practically all of the distinctions that remained to them on that score. Finally, the opening up of property rights in land, as Sansom remarks, struck at the heart of feudal pride and privilege, since feudal society rested on the working of the land by the peasant and its ownership by the lord.[59]

All this was scarcely what the *samurai* had bargained for in supporting the Restoration. Very many of those who took part in the overthrow of the Tokugawa probably did so with the intention of altering the feudal system in their favor rather than destroying it.[60] Hence it is scarcely surprising that feudal forces revolted and attacked the new regime after the import of its policies had become clear. The Satsuma Rebellion of 1877 was the last bloody convulsion of the old order. As part of this final spasm, indeed actually as the direct offspring of expiring feudalism, there appeared Japan's first organized "liberal" movement. The auspices could scarcely have been less auspicious.[61]

[59] *Western World and Japan*, 330.

[60] Scalapino, *Democracy*, 36.

[61] For details on the background of "liberal" origins see Ike, *Beginnings of Political Democracy*, 55–58, 61, 65; Scalapino, *Democracy*, 44–49, and 57–58 for the related origins of the *Jiyūtō* (Liberal Party) which I shall discuss in the concluding section. Some useful facts too are in Norman, *Japan's Emergence*, 85–86, 174–175, and Sansom, *Western World and Japan*, 333. For many Japanese, Western liberalism was on a par with Western firearms, part of the Western magic with which Japan too could hope to become powerful and defeat the barbarians. Democracy was mainly

After quelling the Satsuma Rebellion, the Meiji government was firmly in the saddle. In the space of nine years it had managed to dismantle the feudal apparatus and replace it with much of the basic framework of modern society. This was indeed a revolution from above and accomplished with a relatively small amount of violence in comparison with the leftist revolutions of France in the eighteenth century or of Russia and China in the twentieth. On any account, it was a remarkable performance for a government that had to tread warily among the rivalries of great fiefs, lacking until after 1873 an army of its own and necessarily, as Sansom comments, much more anxious to preserve its own life than to examine its political and social anatomy.

Several factors contributed to Meiji success. The new rulers had used their opportunities wisely in terms of self-interest. As we have seen, they made large material concessions to the *daimyō* and took the risk of antagonizing the *samurai* later. As far as the reduction of *samurai* stipends goes, it is difficult to see what else their resources at this point would have allowed them to do. And they refrained from becoming prematurely involved in a foreign war. At a deeper level of historical causation, the Tokugawa regime had by its policies already undermined the dominance of the warrior and prepared the way for a centralized state without at the same time generating any overwhelming revolutionary potential. The Meiji regime was thus a continuation of previous trends and, as the rest of our account will show, left much of the original structure standing. Finally, the Imperial institution, as many historians of Japan have emphasized, provided a rallying point for fundamentally conservative forces and a framework of legitimate continuity within which to make a number of necessary adjustments.

Before carrying the analysis further, we may pause to reconsider the suggestion with which this chapter opened, to the effect that feudalism constitutes the key to the differing fates in modern times of Japan, Russia, and China. By this point it is perhaps apparent that differences in internal social structure constitute only one

---

a technique with which to achieve what we would now call totalitarian consensus. There are interesting parallels here to some American notions about counterinsurgency and communism.

major variable, albeit an extremely important one. There were also differences in timing and in the external circumstances under which premodern institutions broke down and adapted themselves to the modern era.

For Japan, the advent of the West was a relatively sudden affair. The superiority of Western arms and technology became evident to many Japanese leaders very rapidly. The question of national survival and the need to take appropriate steps to defend it pushed their way to the forefront with dramatic speed. China, to which we may limit these preliminary comparative remarks for the sake of simplicity, seemed superior to the West at first. For a long time its rulers could treat the representatives of Western civilization with polite curiosity and disdain. In the course of time, partly for this reason, Westerners were able to gain a substantial territorial foothold in China. Only gradually did the inadequacy of the Imperial system become evident. At crucial points the West chose to support the Manchu dynasty against internal enemies, as in the Taiping Rebellion, a factor that further slowed any awakening of the rulers to the dangers that threatened them. When important circles had become fully alive to the dangers, let us say by the time of the Boxer Rebellion, the process of dynastic decay had gone too far to be arrested.

In order to cope effectively with the foreign and domestic problems that faced it in the latter part of the nineteenth century, the Chinese bureaucracy would have had to encourage commerce and widen the tax base. But such a policy would have undermined the hegemony of the scholar-official and the whole static agrarian order on which this hegemony was based. Instead, therefore, officials and prominent families appropriated local resources as the central apparatus broke down. The regional warlords of the early twentieth century replaced the Imperial bureaucracy of earlier times.

It is conceivable that one of these warlords might have subdued the others and reunited China to inaugurate a politically reactionary phase with some degree of industrial modernization. Chiang Kai-shek once seemed close to succeeding. If that had happened, historians might now be stressing the similarities between China and

Japan rather than the differences. There would have been the important parallel of one segment of the society detaching itself from the rest to take over the government and to launch a conservative version of modernization.

But was such a possibility ever really "in the cards," as a losing gambler might phrase it? No flat answer is possible. Yet important factors were against it. In addition to the differences between Chinese bureaucracy and Japanese feudalism, there was, to repeat, the factor of timing. When Chiang sought to impose unity on China, he had to face an aggressive expanding Japan. There was also, to return to domestic differences, the contrast in character and outlook between the mandarin and the *samurai*, two figures that represent the precipitate of sharply different historical experiences. The pacific ideal of the gentleman-scholar-official turned out to be less and less adequate in the face of the modern world. The fate of the warrior ideal in Japan was substantially different. The ruling classes were looking for ways to recoup their fortunes. If they could shed certain anachronistic notions of feudal honor, they could make good use of modern technology in warlike ways that were not unfamiliar. As the Satsuma Rebellion shows, it was not easy to shed feudal romanticism. But it could be done and was done. On the other hand, what earthly use was modern technology to the classically trained Chinese scholar-official? It did not teach him how to deal with people in a way to keep them peaceful. At best it might provide a source of bribery, which corrupted the system, or serve as a toy and diversion. From the official's standpoint it was not particularly desirable for the peasants, as it might make them lazy and insubordinate.

Thus the feudal military tradition in Japan provided at first a congenial basis for a reactionary version of industrialization, though in the long run it may turn out to have been fatal. In China's premodern society and culture there was little or no basis out of which a militarist patriotism of the Japanese type could grow. In comparison with Japan, the reactionary nationalism of Chiang Kai-shek seems thin and watery. Only when China began to make over her own institutions in the communist image did a strong sense of mission appear.

Furthermore, despite the centralization of the Tokugawa government, the feudal units in Japan still retained their separate identities as going concerns. The Japanese fiefs were independent cells that probably could have survived reasonably well if they had been separated from the Tokugawa body politic. What their leaders derived from the *pax Tokugawa* was the peaceful enjoyment of aristocratic privilege. When the system as a whole was suddenly threatened, it was not too difficult for a few of the feudatories to detach themselves and execute a *coup d'état*. Thus the Imperial Restoration had some of the characteristics of a successful *Fronde*. But a better parallel, and one noticed nearly fifty years ago by Thorstein Veblen in his *Imperial Germany and the Industrial Revolution*, would be Prussia. Though there are very important differences to be discussed in due course, the essential similarity rests in the capacity of a segment of the landed aristocracy to promote industrialization against the will of its more backward members in order to catch up with other countries, as well as the disastrous culmination of the whole policy in the middle of the twentieth century. The survival of feudal traditions with a strong element of bureaucratic hierarchy is common to both Germany and Japan. It distinguishes them from England, France, and the United States where feudalism was overcome or absent and where modernization took place both early and under democratic auspices — fundamentally and with all due qualifications those of a bourgeois revolution. In this respect, Germany and Japan differ also from both Russia and China, which were agrarian bureaucracies rather than feudal polities.

Hence not feudalism itself, certainly not feudalism as a disembodied general category, holds the key to the way in which Japanese society entered the modern era. To feudalism one must add the distinct factor of timing. Secondly, it was Japan's particular variety of feudalism with substantial bureaucratic elements that made possible the leap. The special character of the Japanese feudal bond, with its much greater emphasis on status and military loyalty than on a freely chosen contractual relationship, meant that one source of the impetus behind the Western variety of free institutions was absent. Again, the bureaucratic element in the Japanese

polity produced its characteristic result of a tame and timid bourgeoisie unable to challenge the old order. The reasons for the absence of a serious intellectual challenge. lie deeper in Japanese
history but are part of the same phenomenon. The intellectual and
social challenges that made the Western bourgeois revolutions were
feeble to nonexistent. Finally, and perhaps most important of all,
throughout the transition and on into the era of industrial society,
the dominant classes were able to contain and deflect disruptive
forces arising out of the peasants. Not only was there no bourgeois
revolution, there was also no peasant revolution. To understand
how and why it was possible to tame the peasantry will be our next
task.

2. The Absence of a Peasant Revolution

Three interrelated reasons may account for the absence of a
peasant revolution during the transition from an agrarian to an industrial society in Japan. In the first place, the Tokugawa system
of taxation appears to have been such as to leave an increasing surplus among those peasants who were energetic enough to add to
their output. In this fashion it helped to stimulate production,
which began to rise in the later Tokugawa era and continued to do
so under the Meiji government. Secondly, in sharp contrast with
China, Japanese rural society was one with a close link between
the peasant community and the feudal overlord, also his historical
successor the landlord. Simultaneously, and again in contrast with
China (though the relevant information for China is sketchy) the
Japanese peasant community provided a strong system of social
control that incorporated those with actual and potential grievances into the *status quo*. This was the case because of a specific
division of labor, combined with the system of property, land
tenure, and inheritance that prevailed in late Tokugawa times. In
the third place, this set of institutions proved adaptable to commercial agriculture with the help of repressive mechanisms taken over
from the old order together with new ones appropriate to a modern
society. The key element in the transition was the rise of a new
landlord. class, recruited in substantial measure from the peasants,
which used the state and traditional mechanisms of the rural com-

munity to squeeze rice out of the peasants and sell it in the market. The shift from older feudal arrangements to tenancy furthermore had some advantages for the peasants at the bottom of the social ladder. All in all, it proved possible to take over the old order from the past and incorporate a peasant economy into an industrial society — at the price of fascism.

The transition was not easy. At times it was touch and go whether the dominant classes would be able to carry it off. Violent opposition from the peasants there was in good measure. For a variety of reasons, the present generation of Western historians tends to minimize the importance of peasant discontent. Therefore it will be wise to review the evidence before examining social trends and relationships in the countryside in any detail. Doing so right away may help to prevent illusions of inevitability. A bourgeois revolution does seem to me to have been out of the question. There is much less reason to believe that a peasant one was impossible.

The later years of the Tokugawa period were, as we saw, characterized by numerous outbreaks of peasant violence. Though it is naturally impossible to determine the objective circumstances that produced many of the uprisings, far less the motives of the participants, there is considerable evidence to show that the inroads of commercial influences played an important part. Merchants were a significant target in many instances. For example, in 1783 – 1787, after a series of crop failures, the peasants in the western provinces rose against the merchants, who had become landowners by appropriating land in exchange for money and goods borrowed by the peasants. In part also, the peasants rose against village officials who, as representatives of the ruling class, collected taxes, spied on the farmers, and added taxes for their own profit.[62] Again, in 1823, in one of the Tokugawa domains 100,000 farmers revolted because of the corruption of the local administrative officer who was allied with the rice merchants. In a similar large upheaval, the immediate cause of the outbreak appears to have been that local officials had prayed for a bad harvest and tried to enrage the dragon

[62] Borton, *Peasant Uprisings*, 18 – 19.

god, all in order to raise prices.[63]. Already by the middle of the Tokugawa period or mideighteenth century, we begin to hear about tenancy disputes,[64] a form of conflict that was to become much more important after the Restoration.

Outright violence was not the only weapon to which the peasants resorted. Some, like their Russian counterparts, "voted with their feet" before they ever heard of the ballot, though the opportunities to move away were very limited in Japan as compared with Russia. In some areas the practice developed of one or more villages' leaving their habitations *en masse* — a significant indication of the solidarity of the Japanese village. They crossed into the neighboring fief or province and petitioned the lord that they might be allowed to remain in his domain. According to Borton, there are records of 106 such desertions, the majority of them in Shikoku.[65]

Borton's evidence shows quite clearly that the intrusion of commercial relationships into the feudal organization of the countryside was creating increasingly severe problems for the ruling group. There were three main strands to the peasant violence: opposition to the feudal overlord, to the merchant, and to emerging landlordism. To the extent that these institutions were becoming interlocked, the peasant movement was definitely dangerous. One reason that the Meiji government was able to weather the storm may have been that this interlocking was relatively quite weak in the main territorial base of the Imperial movement, the great fief of Chōshū.

For a time, immediately after the Restoration, the danger continued to mount. The peasants had been promised that all state land (except that of the temples) would be divided up for their benefit. But they soon discovered that the promise was an empty one and that their tax burden to boot would not be lessened. It seemed obvious that they had nothing to gain from the new regime. Agrarian revolts reached a crescendo of violence in 1873, the year of the

[63] Borton, *Peasant Uprisings*, 27 – 28.
[64] Borton, *Peasant Uprisings*, 31, 32.
[65] *Peasant Uprisings*, 31.

new land tax,[66] to be discussed further in the context of the land-lords' problems. In the first decade of the Meiji government there were over 200 peasant uprisings, more by far than in any decade under the Tokugawa. "Never in modern times," says T.C. Smith, not one to exaggerate peasant violence, "has Japan been so close to social revolution."[67]

The dominant theme in the peasant movement of these ten years was "stubborn antagonism to rent, usury, and exorbitant taxa-tion," the usual reaction of the peasant to the intrusion of capitalist relationships in the countryside.[68] This reactionary response was very prominent in Japan. Many *samurai* were quick to exploit their knowledge of peasant psychology and even to set themselves at the head of peasant risings against the government. This was possible because, as we shall see, the *samurai* were the main victims of the Restoration. Where *samurai* leadership occurred, it helped to pre-vent the peasant movement from becoming an effective revolution-ary force.

The tax reduction of 1877 marked the end of the first and most serious wave of peasant revolt.[69] The second outbreak in 1884 – 1885 was a more local affair, confined to mountainous re-gions north of Tokyo, especially noted for the production of raw silk and the textile industry. There peasant households, working under the putting-out system, derived a large part of their income from these sources. After the dissolution of the *Jiyūtō*, Japan's early "liberal" movement, certain radical local affiliates, disap-pointed by their leaders' defection and goaded by continuing eco-nomic difficulties, turned to open revolt.[70] In one prefecture, Chichibu, the outbreak was severe enough to resemble a miniature civil war and required fairly extensive efforts by the army and the military police to put it down, after it had attracted wide popular

---

[66] Norman, *Japan's Emergence*, 71 – 72.

[67] *Political Change*, 30.

[68] Cf Norman, *Japan's Emergence*, 75.

[69] Norman, *Japan's Emergence*, 72, 75.

[70] Ike, *Beginnings of Political Democracy*, 164. See chap XIV for an account of the outbreak as a whole.

attention. One of the related and simultaneous outbreaks, of which there were several, produced straightforward revolutionary slogans and public statements with concrete objectives, such as tax reduction and revision of the conscription law. Yet significantly even this group called itself a patriotic society (*Aikoku Seirisha*, Patriotic Truth Society). Everywhere, however, the government succeeded in suppressing the revolts. Their main consequence was to intensify the split between the more prosperous elements in the countryside, mainly the new landlords, and the poorer sections of the peasantry.

Shortly afterward, in 1889, the government proclaimed the new constitution, which kept the right to vote securely in the hands of men of substance. Out of a population of about 50 millions, only some 460,000 obtained electoral rights.[71] Rural radicalism was not to be a serious problem again until the tenancy disputes following the First World War.

The peasant revolts described above document the existence of more than scattered resistance to the transition from the premodern agrarian system to a new one. They reflect many of the usual difficulties of the changeover to capitalism and commercial farming in the countryside. Why were they not more serious? For an answer to that question it is necessary to examine rural society more closely and the changes it underwent.

As in any agrarian society, the Japanese peasants generated most of the economic surplus that supported the upper classes, while the methods of extracting this surplus formed the core of nearly all political and social problems. Professor Asakawa, a distinguished historian of the older generation, has observed that the first problem of village administration under the Tokugawa was the collection of taxes. "Few provisions of the laws of the village had no bearing, direct or indirect, upon the subject of taxation; few phases of the entire structure of the feudal rule and of national welfare were not deeply influenced by the solution of this fundamental problem."[72] The feudal system of taxation accounts very largely for the tightly knit character of the Japanese village that has impressed a wide variety of historians and modern observers.

[71] Ike, *Beginnings of Political Democracy*, 188.
[72] "Notes on Village Government, I," 269.

Simultaneously, Japanese feudal structure tied the peasants closely to their rulers.

The main tax was the land tax, levied not upon the peasant as an individual person, but on the officially determined productive capacity of each holding. From the official standpoint the peasant was an instrument to make the holding yield what it should.[73] Until quite recently, authorities on Japan believed that by and large the feudal lord of Tokugawa times, pressed for greater expenses in the *Shōgun*'s capital and elsewhere, used the machinery of village administration to extract a larger and larger surplus out of the peasantry.[74] Detailed investigation of the incidence of taxation in several widely scattered villages have made this conclusion a most unlikely one. What appears to have happened is that the amount taken by the taxation remained static or nearly so, while the productivity of peasant agriculture markedly increased. The consequence was to leave a larger amount in the hands of the peasant.[75]

The taxation system penalized farmers who failed to improve the output of their lands and benefited those who increased their productivity. Though the details of its operation are obscure, it is easy to see that a taxation system that took a fixed amount of produce from each farm year after year would have this effect. We do not know exactly how the Japanese villagers allocated the tax, levied on the village as a whole in proportion to the lord's assessment of the yield on individual fields. But there is rather strong evidence that the tax system encouraged improved output.[76] There is, moreover, no indication of periodic redistribution of property and its burdens, such as we find in the Russian village. Without any deliberate intent then, it seems that Tokugawa taxation and agrarian policy, as worked out both by the ruling class and the peasants themselves, was a "wager on the strong."

Furthermore, the structure of Japanese society was such as to impose certain barriers to the growth of a revolutionary potential

[73] Asakawa, "Notes on Village Government, I," 277.
[74] Cf Norman, *Japan's Emergence*, 21.
[75] Smith, "Land Tax," 3 – 19, esp 5 – 6, 8, 10.
[76] Smith, "Land Tax," 4, 10 – 11.

among the peasants. Some of these, too, may be found in the operation of the Tokugawa system of tax collection. The separation of the warrior from the land by the early Tokugawa rulers meant that the peasant's financial obligations to the government took on the appearance of public taxes to the government rather than personal dues to the lord. There were no banalities, and the earlier personal *corvée* was gradually being incorporated into the *corvée* for the public.[77] Very likely this appearance of public obligations helped to ease the peasant's transfer of loyalty from the feudal overlord to the modern state, when the time came to do so in the Meiji Reform.

Alongside these bureaucratic traits that set it off as an impersonal "government" over and above the peasants, the Tokugawa government retained even more important feudal and paternalistic features that enabled the ruling warriors to send down their tentacles into peasant society.

To put teeth into their system of tax collection and paternalistic supervision of village life, the Tokugawa rulers revived the ancient Chinese system of village administration known as the *pao*. In China this device of dividing up village households into small groups who assumed responsibility for the conduct of their members seems never to have been very successful. In Japan it had been known ever since the great seventh-century borrowing from China but was no more than a lingering survival when the early Tokugawa seized it and forced it on the entire rural and urban population of their realm. Asakawa asserts that every inhabitant of the village, no matter what his tenure or status, was ordered to belong to one of these five-man groups and that this order was well carried out. Ordinarily the five-man group consisted of five landholding house fathers living near one another, together with their family members, dependents, and tenants.[78] From about the middle of the seventeenth century, the custom spread of having the five-man group pledge under oath to fulfill the orders of the lord, repeating the orders as nearly as was practicable in the form they were given.[79]

[77] Asakawa, "Notes on Village Government, I," 277.
[78] Asakawa, "Notes on Village Government, I," 267.
[79] Asakawa, "Notes on Village Government, I," 268.

The five-man group was supplemented by the device of public proclamations or the posting of notice boards in the villages exhorting the peasants to good behavior. Occasionally in modern writings one comes across statements to the effect that the Japanese peasant was so submissive to authority that these public notices were almost sufficient by themselves to keep peace and order. As I am trying to demonstrate, there were other and stronger reasons for this orderliness, an orderliness that in any case knew periods of serious turbulence. Nevertheless it is worthwhile to glance at the text of one of these messages, as it may modify this impression of "natural" orderliness. Though there is a reference to Buddha in this one from the middle of the seventeenth century, the tone is quite Confucian:

> Be filial to thy parents. The first principle of filial piety is to keep thyself healthy. It is especially pleasing to parents if thou refrain from drinking and quarreling, and love thy younger brother and obey thy elder brother. If thou hold to the above principle, blessings of goods and Buddha will be upon thee, and thou mayst walk in the right path and thy land shall bring forth good harvests. On the other hand, if thou become indulgent and lazy, thou wilt become poor and broken, and finally resort to stealing. Then the law shall overtake thee and bind thee with rope and put thee in a cage, and perhaps hang thee. If such a thing happens, how heartbroken thy parents must be! Moreover, thy wife and children and brothers must all suffer punishment because of thy crime.

The advice continues with some remarks on the material rewards for good behavior and draws to a close with this revealing admonition:

> Indeed, the farmer has the securest kind of life if only he pays his tax regularly. Keep, therefore, the above precept always in thy mind. . . .[80]

Through the five-man group and other devices, the entire village was made to take an active interest in the behavior of every household. Marriage, adoption, succession, and inheritance were subject to effective control. Peasants were expected to watch over

[80] Quoted in Takizawa, *Penetration of Money Economy*, 118.

and correct one another's conduct, settling disputes as far as possible by mutual conciliation. The peasants were strictly forbidden to own firearms, carry swords, study the Confucian classics, or take up novel religious practices.[81]

Another channel of official control was through the village headman. In most villages the office of headman descended from father to son along with the family headship or rotated among the leading families.[82] The appointment of the headman by the lord or his officer was also widespread.[83] Only in villages affected by commercial influences, where the traditional structure had begun to disintegrate, does it appear that the headman was elected.[84]

The lord did all in his power to exalt and support the dignity and power of the headman, the chief of the little oligarchy that was the Japanese village in Tokugawa times. Essentially the headman's power rested on a careful manipulation of leading opinion in the village. Rather than isolate himself from this opinion, in a crisis the headman sided with the village against the lord even though the consequence was almost certain death. But such circumstances were exceptional. Generally the headman was the individual who reconciled the lord's interests with those of the leading villagers into some consensus or notion of the common welfare.[85]

The Japanese village displayed a fierce demand for unanimity that recalls the Russian *sbornost'*. Personal affairs were given a public character lest they lead to deviant opinion or behavior. Since anything secret was automatically suspicious, a man with private business to conduct with someone in another village might be obliged to conduct it through his headman. Gossip, ostracism, and more serious sanctions, such as assembling at a man's gate and beating pots and pans in unison, or even banishment (which meant cutting a peasant off from human society so that he must soon starve or run afoul of the law), all helped to create a conformity that was probably far more severe than any lamented by modern

---

[81] Asakawa, "Notes on Village Government, I," 275.
[82] Smith, *Agrarian Origins*, 58.
[83] Asakawa, "Notes on Village Government, II," 167.
[84] Smith, *Agrarian Origins*, 58.
[85] Smith, *Agrarian Origins*, 59–60.

Western intellectuals. Only after he had learned the sense of the community by careful consultation with other leading figures, did the headman express his own opinion on any important issue. Villagers would go to great lengths to avoid any open conflict of opinion. Smith mentions one village where, as recently as the period after World War II, the village assembly met privately on the day before its public meeting in order that decisions might be unanimous. Similarly a headman in Tokugawa times would bring together the parties to a boundary dispute to reach a compromise. Only after the compromise had been reached and the matter settled, would he issue an "order."[86]

The system of taxation, along with the political and social controls that supported it, was the main external source of solidarity in the Japanese village. There were equally important internal sources: primarily the system of economic cooperation and, closely intertwined with this, the structure of kinship obligations and inheritance rules.

Though there are no indications of any system of collective cultivation, the land belonged to the village, which reserved to its own members the exclusive right of bringing it under the plough.[87] Common lands provided peasant families with fuel, fodder, compost, and building materials. Unlike common lands in Europe, they were not a potential reserve mainly for the poorer peasants but were subject to the effective control of the wealthier households.[88] Likewise the allocation of water for rice growing was a crucial matter for the whole village. Important though they were, the problems of irrigation probably would have been insufficient by themselves to create the kind of solidarity for which the Japanese village was noted. We have seen that village irrigation in China did not create any remarkable solidarity. Even in Tokugawa times, Japanese rice culture required a large and well-organized labor force for the spring planting. Rice was not sown directly in the fields but started from special beds from which the seedlings were transplanted later. This task had to be carried out within a very

[86] Smith, *Agrarian Origins*, 60 – 64.
[87] Smith, *Agrarian Origins*, 36.
[88] Smith, *Agrarian Origins*, 24, 42, 182 – 183.

short period of time in order to avoid damaging the seedlings. Enormous amounts of water were necessary to work the soil to the consistency of thick paste suitable to receive the seedlings. As few fields could be given the necessary amount of water simultaneously, it was necessary to flood and plant fields one after another, reducing the time available for transplanting in any one field to a few hours. To accomplish the transplanting in the available time required a labor force far larger than the individual family could muster.[89]

The Japanese peasants met the problem of an adequate labor force, which was most acute in rice growing but by no means confined to this crop, through their system of kinship and inheritance, stretching it with semi-kinship or even pseudo-kinship devices where necessary. In most seventeenth-century villages one or two or more holdings were very much larger than the rest. Part of the labor to work these holdings was supplied by expanding the family beyond the limits usual on small holdings, through keeping in the family the younger generation after marriage and also through retaining members of collateral lines of descent. Where the family was insufficient, as frequently happened, the possessors of the larger holding usually resorted to two devices. To some people, known as *nago* and by a variety of local names, they gave small holdings with separate dwellings in return for labor services. The other device was to use hereditary servants (*genin*, also *fudai*), persons who together with their children passed down in a family from generation to generation.[90]

Both the small holders and the hereditary servants were assimilated in large measure to the pattern of the large holding worked by branches of the original family stem. Their economic relations were similar in kind, if not in degree. Smith, our main authority for this information, warns us against regarding the small holders as a distinct class. They were distinct only in a formal, legal

[89] This summary was taken almost verbatim from Smith, *Agrarian Origins*, 50 – 51. Many of the purely technical problems remain the same in present-day Japan. See Beardsley et al, *Village Japan*, chap 7.

[90] Smith, *Agrarian Origins*, 8 – 11.

sense. Economically and socially their position was close to that of branch family members.[91]

Thus the Japanese village of premodern times was not a cluster of autonomous farming units. Instead, it was a cluster of mutually dependent ones, some large, some small. The large holding provided a pool of capital in the form of tools, animals, seed, fodder, and fertilizer, etc., on which the smaller ones could draw from time to time. In return the small ones provided labor.[92] The separation of capital from labor as far as ownership was concerned, and their recombination in the production process, show some similarities to the world of capitalist industry. A study of about one hundred seventeenth-century village registers from all parts of Japan reveals that in most villages from forty to eighty percent of the holders of arable land were without homesteads.[93] On the other hand, the paternalistic and quasi-kinship relationships between the possessors of the large holdings and the suppliers of labor helped to prevent the emergence of class conflict in the village. It would be difficult to claim that the possessors of large holdings held anything like a monopoly of power, though the system doubtless had its exploitative aspects — significantly the small holders usually could not grow rice on the poor soil allotted to them.[94] In hard times the large owners had to help their less fortunate dependents. Furthermore, the power to refuse help at the crisis of rice harvesting must have been an important sanction in the hands of those who provided the labor, even though such a refusal would have required the strongest justifications to be acceptable to village opinion.[95]

A few remarks on property and inheritance will help to complete this sketch of the village in premodern times. As we have seen, the small holders, very many of whom lacked homesteads, farmed mere slips of land incapable of supporting a family without the exchange of labor for other resources.[96] Turning to the larger holders,

[91] Smith, *Agrarian Origins*, 46, 49.
[92] Smith, *Agrarian Origins*, 50.
[93] Smith, *Agrarian Origins*, 42.
[94] Smith, *Agrarian Origins*, 25 – 26.
[95] Smith, *Agrarian Origins*, 51.
[96] Smith, *Agrarian Origins*, 48.

we learn that while property could be divided among heirs, the office of head of the family could not. The inheritance system was unequal, with the sanction of public opinion against undue generosity to the branch families. The rationale of unequal division was to relieve the main family of the obligation to support "excess" members. By keeping most of the land and settling the "excess" members on small plots, the main family could assure itself a satisfactorily large holding and an adequate labor supply.[97]

The political implications of late Tokugawa peasant society seem fairly obvious. Clearly one cannot explain the absence of full-scale peasant revolution in these fairly turbulent times as a consequence of rough equality in holdings. Rather, it was the series of bonds that connected those without property to those who possessed it that helped to maintain stability. The premodern Japanese village community gives every sign of having been a very powerful mechanism for incorporating and controlling individuals with real and potential grievances. Furthermore, the formal and informal channels of control between the overlord and the peasantry seem to have been quite effective. The lord could make his will known and the peasants indicate just how far they were willing to obey through clearly recognized procedures. One gets the strong impression that Tokugawa society, when it was working well, consisted of a series of descending and spreading chains of influential leaders and their coteries of close followers, linked all the way from the top to the bottom by patriarchal and personal ties, enabling those in superior position to know just how far they could push those beneath them. Perhaps there was something specifically feudal in this arrangement, though it is also characteristic of any stable hierarchy.

The key to the social structure of the premodern Japanese village was the exchange of labor for capital and vice versa, without the impersonal mechanism of the market, and through the more personal one of kinship. The coming of the market changed these arrangements, though they have left their imprint on later Japanese peasant society down to the present day. Our next task therefore is to trace the effects of the market or, more generally, the rise of commercial agriculture and especially the political consequences of

[97] Smith, *Agrarian Origins*, 37 – 40, 42 – 45.

this transformation, which began to be felt even in Tokugawa times.

The latter half of the Tokugawa period was one of very substantial improvements in agricultural techniques. After 1700 genuinely scientific treatises on agriculture began to appear, a curious parallel to simultaneous developments in England. After a few ritual bows to the Confucian doctrine of harmony with nature, these treatises at once settled down to the eminently practical business of improving on the ways of nature. There is clear evidence that the knowledge set forth in these treaties filtered down to the peasants. The main motives to which they appealed were self-interest, but of the family, not the individual. Nor was there any appeal to notions of the welfare of society or the state.[98]

To recount the technical improvements in any detail would take us too far from our main theme of political change. It is sufficient to mention improvements in irrigation that increased the use of paddy and added to the rice crop, the use of commercial fertilizers to replace the use of grass taken from the mountainside and trampled into the fields, and the invention of a new threshing device, said to thresh rice some ten times faster than the older method.[99] What is most important for our purposes is that these changes, in sharp contrast to the more striking mechanical revolution that swept over American agriculture in the last hundred years, increased rather than decreased the aggregate amount of labor required for Japanese agriculture. Although technical improvements, such as commercial fertilizer and the improved threshing device, lightened the work load at peak times of sowing and harvesting, the overall work load did not decline because the Japanese turned to various forms of double cropping. Peak work loads for the new crops were as far as possible timed to coincide with slack periods for the old. Thus the general result was to spread more work out more evenly during the year.[100]

Partly as a result of increased agricultural production, the exchange of goods through the market spread more and more into rural areas. So did the use of money, though money as such had

[98] Smith, *Agrarian Origins*, 87 – 88, 92.
[99] Smith, *Agrarian Origins*, 97 – 102.
[100] Smith, *Agrarian Origins*, 101 – 102, 142 – 143.

been known for a long time: a Korean ambassador of the fifteenth century reported that beggars and prostitutes would accept nothing else. By the time of the late Tokugawa, established markets held at ten-day intervals were to be found even in remote and backward areas.[101] Though there is evidence of a high degree of peasant self-sufficiency that lasted well into the Meiji period,[102] it is clear that Japan, unlike China, was beginning as early as the eighteenth century to make very substantial steps quite on her own toward becoming a modern nation. A large part of the difference may be attributed to the *pax Tokugawa* that contrasted with the disorder in China under the Manchu dynasty, already in decline at this time.

Meanwhile the advance of the economy had widespread effects in changing the traditional system of large holdings with their satellites and replacing them with family farms and landlord-tenant groupings. The fundamental cause was an increasing shortage of rural labor. The growth of rural trade and industry meant that the possessors of large holdings had to give more land to their dependent small holders in order to hold them against the pull of the towns. Too, the small holders (*nago*) were finding more and more opportunities to make money in handicrafts. Wage labor began to replace the older forms. As a legal category, and more slowly as an economic and social reality, the dependent small holder disappeared from the countryside. By the late nineteenth century only vestiges of this class remained. The general trend was to elevate the dependent small holders to the status of separate families, a few as proprietors but most as tenant farmers.[103]

A parallel process led to similar results in the case of the hereditary servants, the other main source of labor for the large holder, outside of the family. Here too the impact of the market released the rural laborer from traditional and familistic relationships, though his gain in independence was slight if any. The wage "contract" was often complicated by debt that could still keep the former servant in subjection for an extended period of time. Yet the

[101] Smith, *Agrarian Origins*, 72 – 73.
[102] Smith, *Agrarian Origins*, 72.
[103] Smith, *Agrarian Origins*, 33, 34, 83, 133, 134, 137.

fundamental advantage of scarcity was on the side of the laborer. By the time of the late Tokugawa, wage labor had become quite common. Scarcity drove up its price and freed it from traditional restraints. Thus slow improvements in the economic status of the former small holder and of the hereditary servant helped to hasten the rise of tenant farming.[104]

By the middle of the eighteenth century the shift to tenant farming had become a powerful trend.[105] Large landholders a half century earlier had already recognized that the high cost of labor in its changing forms had made it impossible to operate large holdings successfully. Not only did labor costs continue to rise during the next century but, by the midnineteenth century, many wage workers who found that they could nearly support a family by their earnings alone did not work well for landowners, often disappearing without warning when needed most. These conditions favored the family-size unit, farmed by tenants who had in former days been dependent small holders.[106] With big units reduced to manageable small ones worked by tenant farmers, the large landholders could retain and in some cases increase their profits from the land. Now the tenants had to bear the increasingly expensive burden of fertilizers and other costs of cultivation, which they could do in two ways: by keeping down their standard of living and by increasing their earnings in artisan occupations as trade and industry began to grow.[107]

The end result was, therefore, not the disappearance of large holdings but a change in their method of exploitation, from a system based on the family and its extensions to a system based on tenancy. The unit of cultivation became smaller; the unit of property if anything became larger. Far from liquidating their larger holdings, Smith points out, their possessors greatly expanded them after discovering the solution to their problem in tenant cultivation.[108] Paternalistic relations were being replaced by the explosive

[104] Smith, *Agrarian Origins*, 108 – 118, 120, 123.
[105] Smith, *Agrarian Origins*, 5, 132.
[106] Smith, *Agrarian Origins*, 127, 131 – 132, 124.
[107] Smith, *Agrarian Origins*, 127 – 131.
[108] *Agrarian Origins*, 126, 131, 141.

ones of landlord and tenant, as a landlord class emerged out of the peasantry — it would seem rather more than out of the aristocracy — as a result of the advent of commercial farming. The new problems that this relationship created were, as we already know, to plague Japan for a long time.

As might be anticipated on the basis of the experience of other countries, the new commercial relationships produced some tendency toward the concentration of land in fewer hands and the breakup of older familistic relationships within the peasant community.[109] The significant point about Japan, however, is that these tendencies did not go very far. After the rise of tenant farming as a solution to the problems of commercial agriculture, property relationships underwent very little change for nearly a century. Despite a few incipient signs of an expropriation of the peasantry, no such expropriation took place. Nor did the peasants rise to expropriate the dominant classes in Japanese society. By the midnineteenth century, the intrusion of commercial relationships in agriculture nevertheless had created a dangerous situation for the old order and left a legacy of serious problems for the Meiji.

Japan's first steps toward an industrial society in the early years of Meiji were the familiar ones of extracting more resources from the underlying population. As in Soviet Russia, it was mainly the Japanese peasant who paid for what Marxists call primary capitalist accumulation, the gathering of sufficient capital to make the leap from an agrarian to an industrial society. But, largely due to the different auspices under which the Meiji carried out industrialization, the Japanese experience was almost exactly the opposite of the Soviet one.

The new government needed a regular and dependable source of revenues. The Land Tax, adopted in 1873, was the device chosen, perhaps the only economically and politically feasible one under the circumstances. The peasants provided most of the revenue for the government.[110] Since the government undertook most of the

[109] Smith, *Agrarian Origins*, 145 – 146, 149, 157 – 163.

[110] According to Smith, *Political Change*, 25, about 78 percent of the ordinary revenue of the government between 1868 – 1880 came from the land tax. See also ibid, 73 – 82.

first steps in industrialization — to turn them over to private owners within a few years — the peasant did pay for the beginning stages of industrial growth. On the other hand, in the judgment of modern authorities, the Meiji land tax constituted no increase over the Tokugawa levy. The new government merely redirected it into new channels, thereby achieving modernization without reducing rural living standards.[111] It was possible to do this because agricultural productivity continued to rise, as it had done under the Tokugawa.[112] This increase was to continue through most of the period of Japanese history discussed in this book. Crop yields are estimated to have doubled between 1880 and 1940.[113] One should beware of leaping to optimistic conclusions about the possibility of a nonrevolutionary path to industrialism on the basis of these facts. Japan paid a price for the failure to modernize her agrarian structure — and other countries did too, as Japanese armies marched through China and Japanese bombs fell on American ships.

On the peasants, the immediate economic effect was to intensify certain trends already apparent under the Tokugawa. The peasant had to raise cash to pay the land tax and thereby became more dependent on the vicissitudes of the market and on the village usurer, who was often the leading landholder of the village. A good many peasants fell into debt and lost their farms. How many is a matter of dispute among specialists. Although the new regime had granted property rights to the peasants, in the actual settlement the little man often lost out because he had nothing but memory and oral tradition to rely upon, while the "law" — in the person of the village headman as well as officials — generally sided with the large holder.[114] All these factors helped to strengthen the position

[111] Smith, *Agrarian Origins*, 211.

[112] For some data see Morris, "Problem of the Peasant Agriculturist," 361 – 362.

[113] Dore, *Land Reform*, 19.

[114] Whether the peasants also suffered from the ruin of Japanese domestic handicrafts is more open to doubt. The present view of several Western scholars is that while there may have been severe dislocations, new exports of rural products, notably tea, silk, and rice, more than made up for these losses. Compare Smith, *Political Change*, 26 – 31 with Morris, "Problem of the Peasant Agriculturist," 366.

of the landlord at the expense of the tenant or small holder. They also constituted a continuation of the traditional pattern of reliance on the strong and sober, which may be one reason why peasant resistance to these measures failed.[115]

Meiji legislation and the operation of economic factors did not lead to a wholesale expropriation of the peasantry, despite some tendencies in that direction. The main results were, if anything, the opposite: the strengthening and legitimation of the landlord, and the legitimation of the peasant's possession of his plot, whether as tenant or proprietor. There was no huge exodus to the cities, no very significant consolidation or extension of the unit of land cultivated.[116]

The policy of the Meiji government was conservative in the sense that it had no thought of abdicating power to any other class. At the same time, modern authorities often observe, it was revolutionary in the sense that it broke down feudal distinctions and sought to incorporate the peasants into a conservative body politic. One very important step in this direction was the adoption of military conscription (1872 – 1873).[117] Another was the establishment of a system of universal and compulsory education, announced in the Imperial Rescript of 1890. By 1894, 61.7 percent of all eli-

[115] See Norman, *Japan's Emergence*, 138 – 144, and the criticism of Norman in Morris, "Problem of the Peasant Agriculturist," 357 – 370. Though Norman's picture of peasant distress as a result of increased exposure to the market is probably overdrawn, I am skeptical of the statistics advanced by Morris to show that there was little or no distress. His computations rest on the questionable assumptions: 1) that increasing productivity continued to be divided as it had been earlier (p. 362) and 2) that a money economy was by this time fully effective in the countryside – an assumption contradicted by contemporary observers (see pp. 360, 364). As noted below, Norman ultimately recognizes that there was no widespread expropriation of the peasants.

[116] Norman, *Japan's Emergence*, 149, 153.

[117] On this whole question see Norman, *Soldier and Peasant*. This is a most enlightening monograph, though, as Sansom points out in the introduction (p. xi), to call the peasant uprisings of late Tokugawa and early Meiji a "growing anti-feudal and democratic revolution" that was checked by the introduction of conscription is to credit the uprisings with political objectives not warranted by the evidence.

gible children were attending primary school; soon after the turn of the century all of them were. In addition to elementary skills in reading and writing, Japanese children received heavy doses of patriotic indoctrination.[118] Thus the revolutionary features were part of the government's policy of taking over from the West those features of its civilization that seemed necessary to intelligent Japanese for the purpose of creating a powerful national state. The contradiction between the revolutionary and the conservative features is more apparent than real. Naturally there were many sharp discussions among the Japanese leaders about exactly what was necessary for this purpose. A small minority may even have found themselves attracted to Western ways for their own sake. Nevertheless it is misleading to make too much of these discussions and divisions. If Japan were to become an independent modern nation, she would need a population that could read and write at least well enough to handle modern machinery, and an army to fight enemies abroad and keep order at home. Such a policy is scarcely revolutionary.

In sum then, Meiji policy amounted to using the peasant as a source of capitalist accumulation. In turn this required opening the peasant economy even wider to commercial influences and offsetting some of the strains incurred thereby through efforts to incorporate the peasants into a cohesive body politic. Dismounting feudalism from above was not so much an aim or a policy in its own right as a means to other ends.

Reviewing the process as a whole, we may discern more clearly and concretely some of the reasons why it took place without a revolutionary upheaval. The continuing rise in agricultural productivity was vital in making the whole transition bearable. In itself, of course, the rise requires an effort at explanation, best deferred to the next section. One consequence, however, was that there was no great hunger in the towns to produce plebeian allies for peasant radicalism — as there was at the height of the French Revolution. Nor was there in the town any substantial bourgeois antifeudal impulse with which more moderate peasant demands could join in overthrowing the old order. The advent of the market actually gave landed property to the poorer ranks of the peasants,

[118] Scalapino, *Democracy*, 295 – 298.

if usually only as tenants. Still, physical possession of a larger plot of land than before may have acted as a stabilizing factor.

The stake of the new landlords in emerging capitalism, to be discussed shortly, is fairly obvious. In large measure this group grew out of the class of wealthy peasants that had become increasingly prominent toward the close of the Tokugawa and, in the view of some historians, made an important contribution to the Restoration movement. By becoming landlords, a section of the peasant élite may have been drawn off and rendered politically safe. In addition, a substantial number of them acquired commercial interests and therefore were not averse to important changes in the old order. But in general the wealthy peasant proprietors had no desire to upset the oligarchial system of the Japanese village whose chief beneficiaries they were. As soon as the poorer peasants and tenants began to put forth radical demands under the Meiji, the wealthy peasants turned against them.[119] Thus Japanese rural society at this historical juncture contained important safeguards against any severe outbreak of anticapitalism and opposition to new social trends.

If there were checks against anticapitalist "excesses" at this stage, there also remained certain important safeguards against antifeudal ones. The penetration of the Japanese village by feudal influences through the five-man system of mutual surveillance and through the village headman were very significant here. These brakes on antifeudal influences could have led to a dangerous accumulation of resentment, and evidently did in some areas where feudal influences combined with incipient commercial ones to give the peasants the worst of both worlds, a repressive combination lacking in the main base of the Imperial movement (Chōshū).

The conflict between a feudal system that still had considerable vitality and the commercial influences steadily undermining it gave the Meiji government room to maneuver. When *samurai* on occasion put themselves at the head of a peasant insurrection, they were of course a danger. But on balance, the Meiji, by using their peasant conscript army, were able to direct antifeudal sentiments to

[119] For a penetrating analysis of the role of the rich peasants before and after the Restoration see Smith, "Landlords and Rural Capitalists."

their own advantage, as shown by the suppression of the Satsuma Rebellion, the greatest threat to the new government. Though at times the situation was precarious, the government, by threading its way through divisions among both its enemies and its allies, managed to survive and establish itself.

While it is doubtful that the foreign threat entered seriously into the consciousness of many peasants, it did play a significant part in the course of events and contributed to the conservative outcome. The revolutionary forces in Japanese society were not nearly strong enough to sweep away the obstacles to modernization by themselves. But they could and did provide a limited basis of support for such measures when the leaders sought them in order to preserve their own power through the creation of a strong state.

3. *The Meiji Settlement: The New Landlords and Capitalism*

Among the ruling classes, too, the Meiji era (1868 – 1912) was one where feudal and capitalist features were put to work alongside one another in the effort to create a powerful modern state. We shall concentrate on the political meaning of the fact that the commercial landlord replaced the feudal overlord, a process that had already begun under the Tokugawa. It is necessary to perceive the change against a more general background of the rulers' adaptation to the modern world and the extent to which new and different social formations replaced the older dominant groups. On this score it is necessary to distinguish sharply between the nature of the higher aristocracy or *daimyō* and the ordinary *samurai*.

All authorities agree that the Meiji government's "settlement of accounts" with the *daimyō* in 1876 was generous to a fault. The measure, as we have seen, both assured the new government the allegiance of the *daimyō* and deprived the latter of their original economic base. At the same time, it enabled some of the greatest lords to become members of the dominant financial oligarchy. Funds obtained in this way played an important part in promoting capitalist industry.[120] By 1880 slightly more than 44 percent of the stock in the national banks belonged to the new peers, mostly for-

[120] Norman, *Japan's Emergence*, 96; Reischauer, *Japan*, 68.

mer *daimyō* and members of the Imperial court (*kuge*).[121] Those
who made the transition to commerce, industry, and banking were
few in number but very important. Now they were able to push
the former merchant class aside, whereas in Tokugawa times they
had been forced to work with and through them.[122]

A few others turned to agriculture. With their capitalized pensions, they were able to buy large tracts of government land in
Hokkaidō at very cheap prices and become landlords on a huge
scale.[123] But these were only a handful. The upshot of trends under
the Tokugawa and the Meiji settling of accounts was to bring
Japan into the modern world without a numerous group of powerful landed aristocrats. Strictly speaking, Japan, after about 1880,
had no class of big Junkers (though plenty of small ones), no
equivalent of Burke's great oaks to shade her rice paddies. Almost
by a stroke of the pen their counterpart, in any case few in number,
were jerked forward a century to become the brethren of England's coal and beer barons. The coterie around the throne in the
late nineteenth century was to consist of former lords metamor-
phosed into capitalists by the commutation of feudal privileges, and
a few old merchant families together with princely new ones risen
from the ranks. Meanwhile a new and numerous landed upper class
was arising in the countryside, about which it will be necessary to
speak in a moment. Significantly, they referred to themselves as the
"middle class" of the new Japanese society.[124]

Of the old upper classes the *daimyō* by 1872 were only a very
small group, 268 all told. The number of *samurai*, however, was
quite large, somewhat short of two million persons, or between five
and six percent of the population in 1870.[125] Their fate was less fortunate, and, for a substantial proportion, no doubt disastrous. The

121 Norman, *Japan's Emergence*, 100.
122 Scalapino, *Democracy*, 93.
123 Norman, *Japan's Emergence*, 99.
124 Smith, "Landlords' Sons in the Business Elite," 98.
125 Norman, *Japan's Emergence*, 81, with reference to Japanese sources.
Taeuber, *Population of Japan*, 28, reports that the "registration compilation
of 1886 indicates that 5 percent of the total population were nobles, *samurai*, or members of the families of these groups," but gives no absolute
figure.

Meiji regime swept away *samurai* social, economic, and political privileges. Since we find the *samurai* in 1880 holding just under a third of the stock in the national banks,[126] the assertion that their claims against the government were liquidated with little more than token compensation may be too sweeping.[127] Their aggregate income from the bonds they received in 1876 has been estimated at about one-third the value of their rice stipends at the end of the Tokugawa period.[128]

Much as individuals in the highest circles might toy with the ideas of Herbert Spencer, the government could not afford to sit with folded hands and let the *samurai* shift for themselves or starve to death. At least they could not make this their publicly announced policy. Nor could they afford to put them on a permanent dole. A good part of the impetus behind the industrialization program, Smith suggests, came from the necessity of doing something for the *samurai*.[129] The government also took a number of more specific measures, such as encouraging agricultural reclamation by *samurai* and offering loans to set them up in business. According to a scholar who has examined these policies in some detail, they failed to provide a real solution.[130]

Though the evidence is not as firm as one could wish, it appears that the mass of the *samurai* did not find a satisfactory haven in the business world. To be sure, a small number became wealthy and powerful in business and politics. Many made their way as best they could into almost any crevice they could find in the social structure, becoming, among other things, police constables, army officers, teachers, lawyers, publicists, even jinricksha pullers and common thieves.[131] One clue to their fate comes from the writings of a contemporary political theorist (Ueki Emori): he opposed property qualifications for voting and eligibility to office because such

---

[126] Norman, *Japan's Emergence*, 100.

[127] Cf Smith, *Political Change*, 31.

[128] See Smith, *Political Change*, 32.

[129] *Political Change*, 33 – 34.

[130] Harootunian, "Economic Rehabilitation of the Samurai," 435, 443 – 444.

[131] Norman, *Japan's Emergence*, 75 (note 70); Scalapino, *Democracy*, 95 (note 3).

TABLE I

LAND TAX PAYMENTS IN JAPAN 1887*

	Total no. of persons	Persons paying 10-yen land tax	Proportions paying tax
Ex-samurai	1,954,669	35,926	0.018
Commoners	37,105,091	846,370	0.023

* Source: Computed from La Mazelière, *Japon*, V, 135 – 136. In terms of the figures alone it would be possible of course that the low percentage of ex-*samurai* paying the land tax of 10 yen was due to the fact that so many paid *more* than 10 yen. In terms of the rest of our information, this is most unlikely.

requirements would disqualify most of the *samurai*, in his opinion the class best suited for political life.[132]

On the land, the *samurai* fared scarcely any better than in business. Most of those who took their bonds and tried to make their way as farmers found that they were no match for peasants.[133] Though there were a number of experiments in large-scale farming during the nineteenth century conducted by enthusiastic former *samurai* newly returned from the West, most of these were failures.[134] Further indications of their fate come from some figures on the land tax in 1887 (Table 1), which also present the total number of ex-*samurai* (*shizoku*) and commoners (*heimin*) nearly two decades after the Restoration. Evidently the number of persons claiming the status of ex-*samurai* had not dropped appreciably, as there were somewhat short of two millions at the earlier date.

The failure of the bulk of the *samurai* in agriculture and industry is not quite the whole story. Under the Tokugawa the *daimyō* were not the only holders of land. The higher reaches of the *samurai* also held fiefs.[135] How many of these there were and how

[132] Ike, *Beginnings of Political Democracy*, 131, 134.

[133] Smith, *Political Change*, 32.

[134] Dore, *Land Reform*, 18. See also Harootunian, "Economic Rehabilitation of the Samurai," 435 – 439.

[135] La Mazelière, *Japon*, V, 108 – 109, lists several sections of the warrior nobility in addition to *daimyō* who held land. Craig, "Restoration Movement," 190, states that one *samurai* "had a fief of 16,000 *koku*, larger than that of many *daimyō*."

much land they held at the end of the Tokugawa period are facts I have not been able to determine. Probably neither their number nor the amount of land they held was very large. We do not hear of their expropriation at the time of the Restoration settlement. Presumably, therefore, this small group lived on into the Meiji era to constitute one sector of the new agrarian élite. The Imperial domains constituted another link with the past.

With these qualifications, we may conclude that Japan entered the modern age without a system of large estates handed down from feudal times. The substantial inequalities that are visible at a later date arose from other causes. Japan's modern landlord class seems to have emerged in large measure out of the peasantry as a result of changes that had begun to take place in the peasant economy during the Tokugawa era. The Tokugawa regime had already taken a crucial step toward the modern world by separating a large section of the ruling class from direct ties with the land, a separation that has taken place sooner or later in every industrialized country. In these important respects Japanese society embarked on the modern era with fewer remnants of the agrarian age than did England or Germany.

The early Meiji reforms removed the last of the feudal barriers to the development of commercial relations in agriculture. The productivity of agriculture, which had been improving during the latter part of the Tokugawa period, continued to rise. Between 1880 and 1914 the countryside managed to supply all but a small part of the increased demand for rice that arose from the increase in population. Food and drink imports as a whole formed a smaller proportion of total imports just before 1914 than in the early 1880s. This success was only partly due to an increase in the area cultivated. Most of it was due to an improvement in methods and to more intensive cultivation.[136] However, the atomized character of Japanese agriculture, like that of China a form of small peasant holdings, long prevented any widespread use of machinery, a possibility that appeared on the horizon only after World War II.

[136] Allen, *Short Economic History*, 57 – 58, 88. Further illuminating statistical measures and discussion in Ohkawa and Rosovsky, "Role of Agriculture," 43 – 67.

At the same time, commercial influences increased, as Japanese agriculture more and more entered the world market. In the early eighties Japan's main exports were raw silk, tea, and rice, of which raw silk was by far the most important.[137] The reform of the tax system in 1873 further encouraged the spread of commercial influences. To meet the new tax, the landholder had to convert his rice into money.[138]

Now that the barriers to the sale of land were removed, there were numerous transfers and some indications of a tendency toward concentration of landed property in fewer hands. Still Japan, unlike England, did not undergo on any widespread scale the process of expropriating its peasants, driving them to the cities, and creating large capitalist estates. Instead, in the conditions of Japanese society, opening the floodgates of commercialization intensified prior trends toward the creation of a system of landlords (mainly small ones by Western standards), tenants, and independent proprietors.

Between the Meiji Restoration and the end of the First World War, Japanese agriculture made what we can legitimately regard as a successful adaptation to the requirements of a modern industrial society, successful at any rate in strictly economic terms. After the war, certain inherent shortcomings became more obvious. For the moment we may leave these aside, though it is essential to remember they formed part of the price of earlier success. The feat was a rather remarkable one because it took place without any revolution, peaceful or violent, in agrarian social relationships. Since India has been attempting to execute the same feat for more than a decade and a half, so far with very indifferent results, it behooves us to look carefully for a few moments at what may be the reasons for the Japanese achievement. A few figures will help to give a rough notion of its magnitude. Around 1955 India's productivity, measured in bushels of rice per hectare, was about the same as that of Japan's in 1868 – 1878, more than 60 but less than 70,

---

[137] Allen, *Short Economic History*, 87. See pp. 306 – 308 below for effects on peasants of the decline in sericulture.

[138] Norman, *Japan's Emergence*, 161.

probably much closer to the lower figure. By 1902 Japan's productivity rose to a little more than 74 bushels per hectare, by 1917 to nearly 90 bushels, or by as much as a half in generally steady increases over a half century.[139]

One more piece of statistical information reveals a great deal about how the Japanese managed this early version of an economic miracle. The landlord took in the form of rent in kind and sold a large part of what the peasant grew, between 58 and 68 percent of the yield during the years 1878 – 1917 if we may trust the statistics.[140] The landlord wanted or needed cash. The way he was getting it is obvious: he used various forms of legal and social devices to take rice away from the peasants and sell it in the market.

Just what part the landlord played in getting the peasants to work harder and more efficiently is not clear in some of its details. According to R.P. Dore, Japan's new landlords, many of whom had come from peasant stock, persuaded their tenants to adopt technical improvements that greatly increased output.[141] Despite my respect for Professor Dore, I doubt very much that the landlord often played this active a role. As Professor Dore points out elsewhere, the peasants were doing a great deal of improving for their own good and sufficient reasons. Too, the landlord may have returned some of his profits to the tenants in order to encourage them to adopt improved techniques. The size of the share returned in this fashion may well be beyond accurate measurement; here the accounts become vague and general in a manner to suggest that it was quite small. Nevertheless it may have been just large enough to make the crucial difference. Without it, we read, tenants were unresponsive to instructions about how to add to their output.[142]

Even though the improvement would not have come about without the economic incentives, they are insufficient by themselves to explain it. Notions about how to improve output could

[139] Ohkawa and Rosovsky, "Role of Agriculture," 45 (Table 1), 65.
[140] Ohkawa and Rosovsky, "Role of Agriculture," Table 6, p. 52.
[141] "Agricultural Improvement," 69 – 91.
[142] Ohkawa and Rosovsky, "Role of Agriculture," 52 (note 15); Dore, "Agricultural Improvement," 81 – 82.

conceivably penetrate down to the peasants in the rice paddies because of the specific structure of the peasant community. As we have seen, it was a tightly knit society and at the same time highly permeable to influences from the immediate overlord in a way very different from both Indian and Chinese peasant communities. There were well-worn institutional grooves through which demands for innovation from above could reach the peasants and arouse a response as long as these demands were not very far-reaching. The last point deserves stress. As Dore observes, ". . . It is certain that a great part of the increase is attributable to increased use of commercial fertilizer, not, that is to say, to innovation, but to farmers doing more of what most of them were doing already."[143]

Once the system of land tenure had shaken down, certain of its major features remained remarkably stable up until (and probably even during) the Second World War. Thus, in 1903, 44.5 percent of the arable land was worked by tenant cultivators, while in 1938 the corresponding figure was 46.5 percent, with no significant fluctuations in the meantime.[144] Nor do the size of holdings and the distribution of landed property reveal any marked changes. It appears that in 1910 about 73 percent of owners with holdings of one *chō* or less owned only about 23 percent of the land, while less than one percent owned nearly a fifth of the land. By 1938 the concentration had increased somewhat: about 74 percent of the owners of one *chō* or less owned one-quarter of the land; and about one percent owned a trifle more than a quarter of the land.[145]

Certainly the advent of capitalism neither revolutionized nor disintegrated Japanese agriculture. Rather, the evidence shows an initial shock of some severity followed by prolonged equilibrium. The landlord was the key to the new system. What sort of a person was he in the broader social and political sense? Actually, the term "landlord" covers too wide a ground to be satisfactory, though

[143] "Agricultural Improvement," 89. See also pp. 77 – 78 on the use of the traditional social structure.

[144] Takekoshi, "Land Tenure," 118; Nasu, *Aspects of Japanese Agriculture*, 11 (Table 15).

[145] See Nasu, *Aspects of Japanese Agriculture*, 11 (Tables 13 and 14). The totals in these tables do not add up correctly in several of the rows, so one cannot rely on them except for rough approximations.

the character of the evidence compels its use.[146] It can include anyone from a man scarcely distinguishable from a peasant to one of the four giants with more than 1000 *chō* (about 2450 acres) of land. A trustworthy authority tells us that a holding of about 5 *chō* would be necessary for the social position suggested by the word "landlord" in English. There were about 28,000 who rented out more than 5 *chō*, just prior to the American land reform. Of these there were some 3000 really large landowners who owned more than 50 *chō*.[147]

When the nonspecialist attempts to grasp the political meaning of the landlord as the key figure in the rural landscape under the new regime, he is likely to be very confused at first. The evidence on which I have been drawing up to now suggests a figure analogous to the enterprising landlord of late eighteenth-century England, vigorous and out for the main chance economically. There is also a somewhat older tradition in the literature that stresses the parasitic aspect of the adaptation to capitalism.[148] Though it is possible to reconcile the two interpretations in a way I shall suggest shortly, it will be well to review the argument for a parasitic adaptation first.

The essence of the argument is simple and draws attention to important aspects of the landlord's situation. Under the political and economic circumstances created by the Meiji Restoration, many Japanese landlords did not have to become rural capitalists experimenting with new techniques. In the course of time the pressure of population on the land drove up rents. In Japan, as in China, there are clear indications that the rise in population antedates the Western impact. Indirect evidence suggests an increase that may be near to forty percent during the seventeenth century, that is, after the establishment of peace and order by the Tokugawa Shogunate.[149] The benefits of peace and order do not spread themselves equally among all sections of society. Both in preindustrial and in

[146] For a brief review of the problem criticizing the radical tradition that has until recently dominated most Japanese and Western writing, see Dore, "Meiji Landlord," 343 – 355.

[147] Dore, *Land Reform*, 29.

[148] Cf Nasu, *Aspects of Japanese Agriculture,* 130 – 131; Norman, *Japan's Emergence,* 150 – 151.

[149] Taeuber, *Population of Japan,* 20.

modern times, Japan's "surplus" population was "surplus" to a specific historical situation from which the dominant classes drew enormous benefits. In the course of time industrialists too profited from the way in which the huge reserve of manpower in the countryside pressed down on urban wages.

In other words, political factors played a part in creating the new landlord and the "surplus" population that sustained him. Since the process was a gradual one, it is scarcely surprising that historians of varying persuasions should debate the dates at which the parasitism becomes visible. By 1915, in any case, the parasitic landlord dominated the rural landscape as the observant English traveler Scott saw it.[150] Here I shall only mention what appear to be some early forms of the more important political landmarks.

The land tax revision of 1873 established the property rights of the landlord, often in opposition to the peasant.[151] By itself the security of property was a necessary condition for the emergence of the parasitic *rentier*, certainly not a sufficient one. The change in the land law of 1884, according to some interpretations, was crucial, since it pegged the land tax in a period of secular inflation. One of the landlord's main costs was to remain constant, while his revenues were to rise with the increasing demand for food and the general advance of the economy. A further symptom of the change may be seen in the activities of the landlord in the Liberal Party in the first Diet session of 1890. At this time the landlords wanted to slash the land tax and, in order to achieve this end, were willing to sacrifice agricultural subsidies, which would have done more for agriculture but less for landlords.[152]

Whether the new *rentier* managed to squeeze a greater surplus out of the peasantry than his feudal forebears did is open to doubt. The surplus he did extract is impressive testimony to the effective way in which the new regime served the landlord's interest. When a modern scholar sets out to correct early erroneous impressions about the hardships that early capitalism imposed on the Japanese

---

[150] *Foundations of Japan*, 261. The author visited many parts of rural Japan during World War I.

[151] Norman, *Japan's Emergence*, 138 – 139.

[152] Dore, "Meiji Landlord," 352, 351.

cultivators, the significance shows up when he estimates that the landlord took from three-fifths to two-thirds of the physical product of the land between 1873 and 1885.[153]

Scattered information about the situation in later times indicates that the institutional changes which did occur were not fundamental. By about 1937, Japanese landlords were selling 85 percent of their crops, which they acquired mainly through payment in kind from their tenants. Measured in terms of money, the rents for rice fields rose by more than 50 percent in the years following the First World War.[154] Under the system prevailing between the World Wars, the tenant turned over half his crop to the landlord. All that the tenant got in return was the use of the land, since he furnished all the capital.[155] From 1929 onward, there were attempts to enact a tenancy law. Some very minor improvements were made. But the landlords were able to block any real reforms.[156] Though we shall have to discuss the political implications of the agrarian situation more fully at another point, we may notice briefly here the kind of reasoning the Japanese landlords developed to protect their interests. Essentially, as might be expected, it was an appeal to nationalist traditions in order to deny the realities of conflicting economic interests, one of the main ingredients in fascism. The following statement issued by the Japanese Landowners' Association in 1926 reveals how Imperial and *samurai* tinsel served specific economic interests, as well as how easily it might turn into fascist demagoguery.

Remembering the splendid tradition of our nation, with sovereign and subjects forming one whole, and reflecting on the glorious history of our national development in the past, let us emphasize the harmonious relations between capital and labor, and especially cultivate peace between landowners and tenant farmers and thus contribute to the development of our agricultural villages. What sort of devils are they who furiously strike fire bells when there are no fires and incite to a class struggle, provoking animosity against

[153] Morris, "Problem of the Peasant Agriculturist," 359 (Table II).
[154] Ladejinsky, "Farm Tenancy," 431, 435.
[155] Ladejinsky, "Farm Tenancy," 435.
[156] Ladejinsky, "Farm Tenancy," 443–444.

landowners by exciting tenant farmers? If these malicious designs go unrestricted, what will become of our national existence? . . . We are determined, therefore, to cooperate with those who hold the same ideas, to arouse public opinion, and to establish a more suitable national policy.[157]

The evidence just reviewed establishes quite clearly that there was a repressive component in the adaptation of the rural upper classes to the rise of commerce and industry. That, I would urge, is the key, rather than parasitism *tout court*. From this standpoint the problem of the evidence concerning energy, ambition, economic drive, disappears.[158] Talk about a psychological drive for achievement tells us nothing unless we know how the drive manifests itself. Japanese society in the late nineteenth century may well have generated its own version of the enterprising landlord who so impressed foreign visitors to eighteenth-century England. In Japan, on the other hand, his relationship to the state was almost the reverse of that in England. The British squire used the state to drive off peasant proprietors and keep a few tenants. The Japanese squire did not drive them off the land; instead he used the state, along with more informal levers inherited from earlier times, to squeeze rents out of the peasants and sell the produce on the open market. Hence he was, sociologically speaking, much closer to the commercializing nobleman of eighteenth-century Toulouse than to the corresponding English gentleman.

Still the comparison with French developments seems too generous. In the eighteenth century these changes were still part of a forward movement, intellectually and socially. In Japan the advent of the modern world brought with it an increase in agricultural production, but mainly through the creation of a class of small property owners who extracted rice from the peasantry through a mixture of capitalist and feudal mechanisms. The peasants subsisted

---

[157] Quoted by Ladejinsky, "Farm Tenancy," 441 – 442.

[158] Note in this connection Smith, "Landlords' Sons in the Business Elite," 102 – 105, where the author argues that the landlord class contributed more than its share of business leaders because it had the means to educate its children, a belief in the virtues of hard work, and a desire to push them up the social ladder.

in large numbers very close to the margin of physical survival, though they were not pushed over the edge from time to time in widespread famines as happened in China and India. In return what did this new landlord class contribute to Japanese society? As far as I am able to judge the record, it offered neither the artistic culture nor the security of earlier rulers in the countryside, indeed scarcely more than pious protofascist sentiments. A class that talks a great deal about its contributions to society is often well along the road to becoming a menace to civilization.

A landed upper class which is not itself part of the vanguard of economic advance and which therefore relies on a substantial dose of repression to maintain its social position is liable in modern times to face the unpleasant task of coming to terms with the agents of capitalist progress in the towns. Where the bourgeois impulse is a weak one, as in Japan, capitalist leaders may welcome the contribution of the conservative countryside to order and stability. In practice what this really means is that capitalist elements are not strong enough to introduce new forms of repression on their own. When the Meiji Restoration opened the way to a new world, the commercial classes of the towns were by and large too much caught up in the older corporate system and too narrow in their outlook to be able to take advantage of new opportunities. A few, however, did see important opportunities in the struggles of the time and through this foresight later became the most important and powerful commercial combines in Japan, the well-known *zaibatsu*.

During the early Meiji, the main impulse to economic growth came formally at least from the government, now in the hands of a new wing of the agrarian nobility, and from a scattering of able and energetic *samurai* who had suffered disadvantages under the Tokugawa. Business continued to be in a dependent position. Economically it leaned on the government, which encouraged business partly to give Japan a sufficient modern base to resist foreign pressure (with an eye toward future conquests) and also to provide an occupation for a turbulent peasantry.[159] Thus from the

---

[159] Smith, *Political Change*, 31, emphasizes the latter point. The slogan "Rich Country — Strong Army" indicates clearly enough the character and auspices of economic reform, whose nationalist aspects are stressed in

beginning of the modern period we find agrarian and commercial interests combined in order to keep the populace in its place at home and enable Japan to seek martial glory abroad.

Even during the later decades of Meiji the business class was still socially and politically inferior to the élite that ruled Japan, whose cultural roots were in an agrarian past even if its economic roots reached into the world of modern industry. The social stigma on business continued. Toward public officials, businessmen continued to express themselves deferentially and apologetically. Avoiding public politics, businessmen engaged in effective private politics. Corruption was often the mechanism that reconciled the needs of business and politics. Still fighting the battle against aristocratic anticommercial attitudes, businessmen found it wise to avoid making enemies and to cultivate the authorities.[160]

Not until the First World War forced the pace of industrial growth, did Japanese capitalism begin to come into its own. Between 1913 and 1920, the output of finished steel jumped from 255 to 533 thousand tons. Electric power capacity also more than doubled during the same period, rising from 504 to 1214 thousand kilowatts.[161] Even after this spurt, however, capitalist industry had not advanced to the point reached in Germany, England, or the United States. For the years between the two World Wars it is possible to characterize the Japanese economy as mainly a small-factory system, indeed widely still a peasant and artisan system, dominated by a few large firms whose influence spread directly and indirectly into nearly every Japanese household.[162] The zai-

---

Brown, *Nationalism in Japan*, chap V. Foreign conquest was in the minds of important government leaders from the beginning. As noted above, the question was which should come first, reform or conquest. In 1871 Yamagata Aritomo, one of the founders of the modern army, told Saigo, the leader of the hothead *samurai* faction, that the time was not yet ripe. "Our army," he said, "is in the midst of reorganization at the present time; but in a year or so, foundations of the military system will be established, and there probably will not be any obstacles to prevent the sending of an army to the continent." See Ike, *Beginnings of Political Democracy*, 51.

[160] Scalapino, *Democracy*, 251, 253, 258, 262.

[161] Allen, *Short Economic History*, 107.

[162] Cf the comment by Ike, *Beginnings of Political Democracy*, 212.

batsu reached the zenith of their power in 1929, just before the depression. By advancing funds, through technical advice, and by their power over the market, they extended this influence even into minor agricultural products and small-scale enterprise generally.[163]

The main concrete issue dividing the industrialists and the agrarians during a large part of the modern era was the price of rice. The industrialists wanted cheap rice for their workers and put effective pressure on the government to prevent high supports for rice, which would have benefited mainly the landlords.[164] Though yields of rice per unit of cultivated area and total production continued to rise, after the turn of the century Japan was unable to produce enough to feed her own population and had to resort to imports. After 1925 imports amounted to between one-sixth and one-fifth of domestic production. Despite the imports, consumption per head dropped steadily.[165] The short-run successes of the Meiji era were by this time already beginning to display their dubious side.

Another divisive issue was taxation. Thus in 1923 the industrialists went so far as to propose the abolition of taxation on industry, a move that the agrarian interests resisted.[166] Again in 1932 there was a battle in the Diet "between the interests of rent and profit," over the extent of the farm relief program, a question rendered more acute by the depression then ravaging Japanese industry and agriculture. Business won. The effect was to intensify, at least temporarily, strains on the loose landlord-industrial coalition that controlled Japanese politics.[167]

These clashes help to bring out important structural differ-

[163] Allen, *Short Economic History*, 128.

[164] Dore, *Land Reform*, 99.

[165] Allen, *Short Economic History*, 201 (Table X). Allen's figures go only as far as 1937. According to Ohkawa and Rosovsky, "Role of Agriculture," 54 (Table 8) and 57 (Table 12), the same trends continued at least to 1942.

[166] Tanin and Yohan, *Militarism and Fascism*, 137. This is a Soviet work in translation, but relatively undogmatic and deserves serious consideration. Its main defect is unwarranted optimism about the "sharpening of the class struggle."

[167] Tanin and Yohan, *Militarism and Fascism*, 155–157.

ences between German and Japanese society during the more recent phases of modernization. Because Japan lacked any group comparable to the top Junker élite of late nineteenth-century Germany, there was no open deal comparable to the famous marriage of iron and rye, no agreement coupling naval expansion to suit the industrialists with tariffs on grain to suit the agrarians, which in 1901 represented the consummation of the marriage in Germany. Instead, as we have just seen, rice imports increased, though it is worth noticing that much of this rice came from areas under direct Japanese political control. A further consequence of the differences in social structure was that anticapitalist radicalism or pseudo-radicalism of the right, with strong roots among the smaller landlords in the villages, was a major component in the Japanese version of fascism while in Germany it was no more than a secondary current.

It remains necessary to see these conflicts between Japanese industrial and agrarian interests in their proper perspective. The forces that divided business from the landlord were less important than those that united them. As we shall see in the next section, when the chips were down, anticapitalist radicalism had to be sacrificed. Fundamentally both the Meiji land settlement and the program of industrialization brought agrarian and commercial interests together. Domestically they were united by the common threat that any successful popular movement posed to their respective economic and political interests. Externally they were held together by the threat of foreign partition, or a repetition of the fate of India and China, and by the lure of markets and glory. As business became more powerful, providing Japan with the means for an active foreign policy, the consequences of this combination became more visible and more dangerous.

It is legitimate to ask why business and the agrarians could agree only on a program of domestic repression and foreign expansion. Perhaps there was something else they *could* have done. There was, I believe, though it ran the risk of political suicide. To raise the standard of living of the peasants and workers and to create an internal market would have been a dangerous undertaking from the standpoint of the upper classes. It would have threatened the exploitative paternalism upon which their authority rested in the factory and which was one of the main mechanisms for profit-making. For the landlords, the consequences would have been more serious still. A prosperous peasantry in a genuine political democracy would have deprived them of their rents. That in turn would have meant the liquidation of their entire position.

To this explanation of the main features of the Japanese variant of totalitarianism some might be inclined to add the factor of continuity in the Japanese system of values, particularly the warrior tradition of the *samurai*. Continuity of a sort there certainly was. But one has to explain why the tradition continued. Human sentiments do not persist simply of their own momentum. They have to be drilled into each generation anew and kept alive through social structures that make them seem more or less sensible and appropriate. There was nothing in the warrior spirit as such that during the twentieth century propelled Japan forward on the path of conquest abroad and repression at home. The Tokugawa victory in 1600 doomed the feudal warrior. For nearly three hundred years the *Shōgun* managed with relatively little difficulty to hold in check the much-touted warrior spirit, blunting its edge through peace and luxury. When Japan began to play the imperialist game, at first tentatively and at least partly out of self-defense (as in the Sino-Japanese War of 1894 – 1895) and finally in earnest, the *samurai* tradition and the Imperial cult provided rationalizations and legitimations for the constellation of interests outlined above.

Repression at home and aggression abroad were then, in very general terms, the main consequences of the breakup of the agrarian system and the rise of industry in Japan. Without attempting a detailed political history, we may now look at the political outcome in somewhat more concrete detail.

4. *Political Consequences: The Nature of Japanese Fascism*

For our purposes the political history of modern Japan since the Restoration may be divided into three main phases. The first one, characterized by the failure of agrarian liberalism, comes to a close with the adoption of a formal constitution and some of the outward trappings of parliamentary democracy in 1889. The sec-

ond ends with the failure of democratic forces to break through
the barriers imposed by this system, a result that is clearly apparent
by the onset of the great depression in the early 1930s. The failure
of the 1930s inaugurates the third phase of a war economy and the
Japanese version of a right totalitarian regime. Obviously this division has its arbitrary features. If it helps to focus attention on important developments, it will serve the purpose.

The "liberal" movement arose, as the reader may recall, out of
the feudal and chauvinist reaction of *samurai* disappointed with the
outcome of the Meiji Restoration. Despite these auspices the movement has some claim to be called liberal, since it demanded wider
public participation in politics, from the standpoint of both discussion and voting, than the Meiji government was prepared to grant.

Economically the group that rallied to the cry "Liberty and
People's Rights" and that gave rise to the Liberal Party (*Jiyūtō*);
appears to have grown out of the protest of the smaller landlords
against the domination of the Meiji aristocratic and financial oligarchy. Norman attributes some of their liberal inclinations to the
fact that many landlords of the 1870s were small-scale commercial
capitalists on the side, brewers of *sake*, makers of bean paste, and
the like.[168] I am rather skeptical of this alleged connection between
brewing and democracy and believe that this is one of the rare
points at which Norman applies European parallels and Marxist
categories rather uncritically. The defeat of the Japanese democratic movement in the 1870s and 1880s was not one where a weak
commercial class throws itself into the arms of the feudal aristocracy for protection against the workers, trading, as Marx says, the
right to rule for the right to make money. Japan was not Germany,
at least not yet.

The Japanese problem, if we look at it from the viewpoint of
the Meiji rulers, was one of reconciling the upper classes in the
rural areas to the new order.[169] The Meiji government wanted to
create shipping, military supplies, and heavy industry, all of which
meant heavier taxes on the land. Thus the inaugural meeting of the
Jiyūtō in 1881 protested taxes listed under the name of increased

[168] *Japan's Emergence*, 169 – 170.
[169] Cf Ike, *Beginnings of Political Democracy*, 173.

naval expenditures.[170] As a group that felt that others, particularly government insiders, were reaping the main benefits of the Restoration, it tried to widen the basis of its support, reaching down even into the peasantry. But as soon as the landlords encountered radical peasant demands counter to the landed interest, the *Jiyūtō* split and collapsed. Somewhat leftish for its day, the *Jiyūtō* dissolved in 1884 rather than permit itself to become a really radical group — at that time quite impossible.

So ended Japan's first adventure with organized political liberalism. The movement sprang up among landlords who dropped it the moment they realized it was stirring up the peasantry. In no sense then was this an attempt, even an abortive one, by urban commercial classes to achieve "bourgeois democracy," as some writers have claimed.[171]

Nevertheless during the brief span of "liberal" agitation the Meiji government did not hesitate to turn to repressive measures. As early as 1880, at the first signs of emerging political parties, it decreed that "no political association . . . may advertise its lectures or debates, persuade people to enter its ranks by dispatching commissioners or issuing circulars, or combine and communicate with other similar societies."[172] However, the activities of the *Jiyūtō* shortly afterward show that the law was not strictly enforced. From the government's point of view, the peasant revolts of 1884 – 1885 were undoubtedly more important. Though some of these, as we saw, took on the character of a minor civil war, they were not coordinated with one another and soon failed. Relying on its new police force and conscript army, the government was able to suppress them moderately easily.[173]

In 1885, the year following the dissolution of the *Jiyūtō*, economic conditions began to improve. Time seemed to be on the side of the government. Yet when signs of a revival of political activity appeared, the government attempted once more to stamp out the

[170] Scalapino, *Democracy*, 101.
[171] For an account see Scalapino, *Democracy*, 96 – 107, and Ike, *Beginnings of Political Democracy*, 68 – 71, 88 – 89, 107 – 110.
[172] Quoted in Scalapino, *Democracy*, 65.
[173] See Ike, *Beginnings of Political Democracy*, chap XIV.

fire with its notorious Peace Preservation Law of December 25, 1887, drafted by the Chief of the Metropolitan Police Bureau and others under the direction of General Yamagata, the most powerful figure of the later Meiji era. The main provisions allowed the police to remove anyone who lived within a radius of about seven miles from the Imperial Palace if they judged him to be "scheming something detrimental to public tranquillity." This allowed General Yamagata to remove by force some five hundred persons including nearly all opposition leaders. Previously the police had received secret instructions to kill anyone who resisted. Nevertheless at least one major opposition figure, Gotō Shōjirō, continued to make speeches up and down the countryside, only to be effectively silenced by the offer of the Ministry of Communications a few days after the promulgation of the constitution.[174]

The main features of the government's strategy appear clearly from this sketch. It was a combination of straightforward police repression, economic policies designed to ameliorate some of the sources of discontent without endangering the position of the dominant group, and finally decapitation of the opposition by offering its leaders attractive posts in the Meiji bureaucracy. Except perhaps for certain stylistic features in the details of its execution or in the rhetoric of public statements, there is nothing in this policy that one can trace specifically to Japanese culture. Certainly the content of the policy is what one would expect from any intelligent and conservative set of rulers under roughly similar circumstances.

For the time being, the policy was successful. While it is unlikely that it could have succeeded against an energetic and united opposition determined to achieve modernization through democratic means — let us say roughly along the English pattern — such opposition could hardly emerge under the specific conditions of Japanese society at that time. The industrial working class was very rudimentary; the peasants, though a source of opposition, relatively weak and divided; the commercial classes, scarcely out from under the controls of the feudal aristocracy. The constitution, granted from above in 1889, reflected this balance of social forces

[174] Ike, *Beginnings of Political Democracy*, 181, 185 – 187.

and, by giving it the *cachet* of Imperial legitimacy, helped to stabilize and perpetuate it.

There is no need to continue the account of national politics in any detail down through the First World War. As is well known, the Diet's control of the purse strings was severely limited under the new constitution. While the army had unusual powers, its access to the throne was more a reflection of its power in Japanese society than the source of this power. Governments did not resign because they lost elections, whose outcome could generally be manipulated, but because they lost the confidence of an important section of the élite: aristocrats, bureaucrats, or militarists.[175] The resignation of Itō in 1901 marked the collapse of the civilian wing in the oligarchy. After his assassination in 1909, the soldier Yamagata dominated Japanese politics until he died in 1922.[176]

More significant for our purposes are certain intellectual currents that attracted the attention of the landlords after their limited enthusiasm for parliamentary government had waned. The movement known as *Nōhon-shugi* (literally, "agriculture-is-the-base-ism"), that flourished up until about 1914, was a curious mixture of Shinto nationalism, a belief in the unique mission of the Japanese, and what Westerners would recognize as physiocratic ideas. Prominent in this mixture was a "mystic faith in the spiritual values of rural life and . . . didactic emphasis on the beauties of the Japanese family system and paternalism, and on those virtues — of frugality, piety, hard work, resignation, and devotion to duty — which . . . made up the traditional teachings of the 'landlord paternalistic didactic.' "[177]

Patriotic exaltation of peasant virtues, especially those virtues that profit the agrarian upper classes, is a characteristic of agrarian societies suffering from the inroads of commerce. In Japan the continuation of agrarian problems into the era of industrialism made this reactionary patriotism more important than elsewhere. *Nōhon-shugi* was but one phase of a larger movement. Its antecedents can be found among leading thinkers of the Tokugawa; its

[175] Scalapino, *Democracy*, 206; Reischauer, *Japan*, 98.
[176] Reischauer, *Japan*, 121, 125.
[177] Dore, *Land Reform*, 56 – 57.

historical successors may be seen in the zealots of the Young Officers, the assassinations and attempted *coups d'état* that helped to
prepare the totalitarian regime of the 1930s.[178]

During the first decades of the Meiji era, *Nōhon-shugi*, despite its emphasis on the uniqueness of Japan, played some part in
the movement to introduce large-scale capitalist farming to Japan.
The attempt, as we have seen, came to nothing largely because it
was more profitable for Japanese landlords to rent their land out in
small plots than to farm it themselves.[179]

The movement's attitude toward the peasantry was more important, though it also failed to produce concrete results, because it
coincided with the general body of bureaucratic and even industrial opinion before World War I. Any reduction in the number of
small farmers — even those with a miserable half *chō* of land — was
something to be deplored. The "dean" of *Nōhon-shugi* scholars in
1914 spoke with emotion about the demoralization filtering through
the countryside as peasants took to buying lemonade, umbrellas,
clogs, and youths took to wearing Sherlock Holmes hats. Today we
may smile at this Japanese version of Colonel Blimp. But the government and the industrialists had good reasons to support it. Stable
peasant families, they reasoned, provided docile soldiers and a bulwark against subversion. Through their abundant numbers they
also kept wages down, enabling Japan to export and build an industrial base.[180]

Here once more one may see the material interests that tied
together the agrarians and the industrialists. For these interests
Nōhon-shugi, in its moderate versions perhaps scarcely distinct
from "normal" Japanese patriotism and emperor worship, provided
a useful legitimation and rationalization. In the light of current inclinations to take these ideas seriously, it is necessary to emphasize
again that they were rationalizations and nothing more.[181] Their

[178] Dore, *Land Reform*, 57.

[179] Dore, *Land Reform*, 58 – 59.

[180] Dore, *Land Reform*, 60 – 62.

[181] Cf Benedict, *Chrysanthemum and the Sword*. It is only honest to
confess that I took them seriously until I had studied Japanese history in
earnest.

éffect on policy was nil. When the time came to do something concrete for the peasants and tenants who were the subject of this sentimental moralizing, landlord interests in the Diet quickly put a stop to such efforts. While the Civil Code of 1898 gave some protection to tenants on issues important to them, its application was limited to one percent of the land under tenancy. As Dore concludes, "the vast majority of ordinary tenants were given no protection."[182]

Following the First World War, the balance of forces in Japanese society shifted to the disadvantage of the rural élite. The War served as a forcing period for Japanese industry, and the twenties marked the zenith both of Japanese democracy and of the influence of business on Japanese politics. General Yamagata died in 1922. For some years afterwards, power was visibly passing from the hands of the militarists to those of the commercial classes and the Diet.[183] Symptomatic of the change in the political climate is the fact that, after the Washington agreement on Naval Disarmament of 1922, some Japanese newspapers controlled by industrial interests went so far as to raise the cry "Keep the army out of politics."[184] Some students place the high point of parliamentary influence in the ratification of the London Naval Treaty of 1930.[185] The depression soon put an end to these hopes.

While the connection between the advance of business and parliamentary democracy, as well as that between the depression and the failure of efforts to attain constitutional democracy, are surely important ones, they do not reveal the heart of the situation. The depression merely gave the *coup de grâce* to a structure that suffered from grave weaknesses. Only a few of the favored got the benefits of Japanese capitalism, while its evil effects were visible to nearly everyone.[186] It did not, and under the circumstances almost

[182] *Land Reform*, 64:

[183] Allen, *Short Economic History*, 99.

[184] Tanin and Yohan, *Militarism and Fascism*, 176.

[185] See, for example, Colegrove, *Militarism in Japan*, 23 – 24.

[186] Western students of Japan are likely to balk at this thesis. Those with whom I have discussed the problem hold that the balance between antidemocratic and democratic potentialities was much more even than indicated here. This estimate, I think, gives too much weight to talk and political mechanics. Japan lacked the essential prerequisite for the democratic break-

certainly could not, distribute its material benefits in such a way as to build up a massive popular interest in the maintenance of capitalist democracy. Although the forms of its reliance on the state varied from one historical period to another, it never shook off this dependence on the state as a purchaser of its products and protector of its markets. Under capitalism, the absence of vigorous internal market sets up self-perpetuating forces as business finds that it can make profits in other ways. Finally, growing up in quite different circumstances, Japanese capitalism never became the carrier of democratic ideas to the extent that commercial and manufacturing interests did in nineteenth-century Europe.

During this relatively democratic phase the landlord interest, though showing some signs of decline, remained politically powerful and a factor with which commercial and industrial influences had to reckon. Up until the adoption of universal manhood suffrage in 1928, rural landowners controlled the majority of votes in both major parties in the Diet.[187] Agrarian interests in the twenties were also active behind a variety of protofascist and anticapitalist movements. To some extent government officials encouraged and took part in these movements, scarcely a favorable omen for the future. For the time being, however, agrarian patriotic extremism, as well as its urban counterpart, remained unable to attract significant mass support.[188]

Nevertheless, patriotic extremism was even during this period an important political force. The early years following World War I were a period of rural as well as urban radicalism that at times took violent forms. Patriotic organizations helped to break tenant and worker strikes, while hired bullies smashed labor unions and liberal newspapers.[189] The government too reacted with a campaign by the Ministry of Education against "dangerous thoughts," directed mainly against students. In April of 1925 the government

---

through: an industrial sector whose economic power was both fairly widely diffused among its members and sufficient to enable them to act with considerable independence vis-à-vis the government and other social formations. Nevertheless, the question would bear careful investigation.

[187] Scalapino, *Democracy*, 283; Dore, *Land Reform*, 86.
[188] Scalapino, *Democracy*, 353, 357, 360, 362.
[189] Reischauer, *Japan*, 138, 140.

passed a Peace Preservation Law (far more specific than that of 1887), punishing with imprisonment those who joined societies aimed at altering the system of government or repudiating private property. This law inaugurated in Japan the policy of mass incarcerations.[190]

An episode that took place in 1923 sheds a lurid light on the way patriotic extremism poisoned the political atmosphere of the day. The Tokyo earthquake in September of that year provided an excuse for the arrest of thousands of its inhabitants, mostly socialists. A captain of the gendarmerie strangled with his own hands a prominent labor leader, together with his wife and seven-year-old nephew. Though he was court-martialed and sentenced to ten years' imprisonment, several extremist newspapers called him a national hero.[191] A whole apparatus of terror, partly controlled by the government, partly unorganized and "spontaneous," was evidently necessary to keep in line large segments of a population that some writers describe as almost uniformly suffused with "feudal loyalty" to its superiors.

By the early thirties, Japanese parliamentary democracy, such as it was, was succumbing under the final blow of the Great Depression. It did not do so, however, in so dramatic a fashion as the Weimar Republic. In the political history of Japan it is much more difficult to draw a sharp distinction between a democratic and a totalitarian phase than it is in German history.[192] The occupation of Manchuria in 1931 is one boundary line often used by historians. It marks in foreign affairs a reversal of the Japanese government's position at the London Naval Conference of 1930. In domestic affairs the assassination of Premier Inukai and the attempt at a coup by the radical right on May 15, 1932, are events that authorities on Japan note as marking the end of the hegemony of the politicians.[193] The assassination of Inukai again reveals much about the character of contemporary Japanese politics and is worth outlining briefly.

[190] Reischauer, *Japan*, 143–144.

[191] Reischauer, *Japan*, 140–141.

[192] For Germany one can write *finis* to the tale of the Weimar Republic in 1932, the year of the last free election.

[193] Reischauer, *Japan*, 157; Scalapino, *Democracy*, 243.

In 1932 a small group of young peasants led by a Buddhist priest pledged themselves to assassinate the "ruling clique" responsible for Japan's agrarian misery. After drawing up a list from the world of business and politics, each member of the group chose his victim by lot. Former Finance Minister Inoue (February 9) and Baron Dan, chief director of Mitsui (March 5), were among the victims they killed before the plot was uncovered. Bands of young naval and army cadets were ready to continue the task and on May 15, 1932, struck at the *zaibatsu*, political parties, and men around the throne, "to save Japan from collapse," as they claimed. One unit shot Inukai, others attacked court officials, the Metropolitan Police, and the Bank of Japan.[194]

This episode inaugurated a period of semimilitary dictatorship rather than of outright fascism. Four years later in 1936, Japan had a moderately free election. The openly radical right obtained only 400,000 votes and 6 seats in the Diet, while a labor party (*Shakai Taishūtō*) doubled its previous vote and won 18 seats in the Diet. The party that unexpectedly obtained the largest number of votes (*Minseitō*: 4,456,250 votes and 205 seats) had used as one of its slogans "What shall it be, parliamentary government or Fascism?" To be sure, the results of the election were no popular endorsement of democracy: absenteeism was much higher than usual, especially in the cities, which suggests widespread disgust with politics and politicians. At the same time the election showed a lack of electoral support for patriotic radicalism.

To this check, a section of the army responded with another attempted coup, known in Japanese history as the February 26th [1936] Incident. Several high officials were killed. The rebels barricaded themselves in one section of the city for three days and issued pamphlets to explain their purposes: the destruction of the old ruling cliques and the salvation of Japan under a "new order." High army authorities were unwilling to restore order through the use of force. Finally the revolutionists surrendered upon the Emperor's personal command, the appointment of a negotiator they trusted, and the marshalling of formidable forces against them. Thus did

[194] Scalapino, *Democracy*, 369–370.

Japan recover — if one may use such an expression — from its most important domestic crisis since the Satsuma Rebellion.[195]

The February 26th [1936] episode was the prelude to further political maneuvers that need not detain us and to the imposition of a totalitarian façade, all of which took place between 1938 and 1940. According to one penetrating Japanese analysis, this attempted coup marked a defeat for "fascism from below," essentially the anticapitalist and popular Right, which was sacrificed to "fascism from above," or, we might say, to respectable fascism, the taking over by high government officials of those features they could use and the discarding of popular elements. Respectable fascism now made rapid strides.[196] National mobilization was decreed, radicals were arrested, political parties were dissolved and replaced by the Imperial Rule Assistance Association, a rather unsuccessful copy of a Western totalitarian party. Shortly afterward, Japan joined the anti-Comintern Triple Alliance and dissolved all trade unions, replacing them with an association for "service to the nation through industry."[197] Thus by the end of 1940 Japan displayed the principal external traits of European fascism.

As in Germany, the totalitarian façade concealed a tremendous amount of tugging and hauling among competing interest groups. In both countries the right-wing radicals never held real power, though in Japan no blood purge was necessary to keep them out. In Japan centralized control over the economy appears to have been rather more of a farce than in Germany.[198]

Japanese big business successfully resisted attempts to subordinate profits to patriotism. The whole period of military hegemony and fascism was very favorable to business. Industrial output rose from 6 billion yen in 1930 to 30 billion yen in 1941. The relative positions of light and heavy industry were reversed. In 1930 heavy industry accounted for only 38 percent of the total industrial out-

---

[195] Scalapino, *Democracy*, 381–383.
[196] See Maruyama, *Thought and Behavior*, 66–67.
[197] Reischauer, *Japan*, 186; Scalapino, *Democracy*, 388–389; Cohen, *Japan's Economy*, 30, note 62.
[198] For some details, see Cohen, *Japan's Economy*, 58–59.

put; by 1942 its share was 73 percent.[199] By nominally yielding to government control, the *zaibatsu* were able to obtain fairly complete domination of all industry.[200] The four great *zaibatsu* firms, Mitsui, Mitsubishi, Sumitomo, and Yasuda, came out of the Second World War with total assets of more than 3 billion yen, compared with only 875 millions in 1930.[201]

For the *zaibatsu*, anticapitalism actually amounted to little more than a minor nuisance, and one they were largely able to control after about 1936, a tiny price to pay for the policy of domestic repression and foreign expansion that filled their coffers. Big business needed fascism, patriotism, Emperor worship, and the military, just as the army and the patriots needed big industry to carry out their political program. This the agrarian radicals could not see, or at any rate refused to recognize. Particularly those tinged with the theories of *Nōhon-shugi* found themselves in a hopeless impasse. In these circles there was a marked anarchist streak and, among some, a romantic belief in acts of individual terrorism.[202] Their main theme was bitter hostility to the plutocracy and the traditional military élite whom they regarded as the plutocrats' servants. But they had nothing to put in their place except an idealized version of the Japanese peasant community. Since radical agrarian notions were in sharp conflict with the requirements of an expansionist policy executed by a modern industrial society, the more orthodox élites had little difficulty in elbowing them aside while appropriating some ideas to ensure popular support. Very much the same thing happened in Germany, though more suddenly and violently, with the destruction of the radical Nazis in the Blood Purge of 1934.

In Japan, the inherent limitations of agrarian rightist radicalism and frenetic Emperor worship appear even more clearly if we ex-

[199] Cohen, *Japan's Economy*, 1.

[200] Cohen, *Japan's Economy*, 59.

[201] Cohen, *Japan's Economy*, 101. For a more sympathetic treatment of the *zaibatsu*, see Lockwood, *Economic Development*, 563 – 571. Still it does not seem to me that Lockwood's evidence warrants the assertion (564), "In the end the *zaibatsu* were the victims of the system they helped to create."

[202] Storry, *The Double Patriots*, 96 – 100; Tsunoda et al, *Sources of Japanese Tradition*, 769 – 784 gives some samples of these writings.

amine the story briefly from the side of the army. Between 1920 and 1927, some thirty percent of those entering the cadet corps were sons of small landowners, rich farmers, and the urban petty bourgeoisie. At this time there were several cases of reservists taking the side of the peasants in their disputes with landowners.[203] Thus a new group with a new social basis and political outlook had by this time begun to replace the older, more aristocratic leadership of the army. By the 1930s General Araki was their chief spokesman, a major advocate of "independence" from the financial magnates and court cliques.[204] Consistent with this radical outlook, many of them became opposed to modernizing the army, to the new emphasis on economic planning, and to the adoption of a more advanced technology.[205] For a short time after 1932, Araki's talk about aid to agriculture caused a flurry among the industrialists. Even at this early date, however, faced with the difficulties of his position, he soon changed his tune and began to talk about the laziness of the Japanese peasant under the degrading influence of modern temptations.[206] During the war boom of the thirties, the profits made by the industrialists again disturbed the dissident army group with agrarian ties, leading to the resignation of the War Minister in 1940.[207] The army even went so far as to attempt to establish a self-sufficient base of operations in Manchuria, where it could be free, it hoped, from the influence of Japanese industrial combines. Manchuria remained predominantly agricultural until the Kwantung Army was forced to admit that it could not industrialize the area by itself and would have to utilize industrial aid even if reluctantly. The occupation of North China did not occur until the army had learned its lesson and until the need for industrial assistance in Manchuria had led to closer cooperation between military and business interests.[208]

The spectacle of the army, running away to escape the modern

[203] Tanin and Yohan, *Militarism and Fascism*, 180, 204.

[204] Tanin and Yohan, *Militarism and Fascism*, 182–183.

[205] Crowley, "Japanese Army Factionalism," 325. The February 26th episode marked a decisive defeat for the army radicals.

[206] Tanin and Yohan, *Militarism and Fascism*, 198–200.

[207] Cohen, *Japan's Economy*, 29.

[208] Cohen, *Japan's Economy*, 37, 42.

world, vividly demonstrates the futility of Japanese rightist agrarian doctrine and its ultimate dependence on big business. The abandonment of anticapitalism, in practice if not in slogans, was the price big business was able to exact from the agrarian and petty-bourgeois patriots in the *modus vivendi* of Japanese imperialism.

In the Japanese version of fascism, the army represented somewhat different social forces and played a different political role from the German army under Hitler. In Germany the army was a refuge for sections of the traditional élite unsympathetic to the Nazis. With the exception of the abortive conspiracy against Hitler in 1944, when the war was already lost, the army was mainly a passive technical instrument at Hitler's command. The generals may have feared and grumbled about the consequences, but they did what Hitler ordered them to do. In Japan the army was much more sensitive to pressures emanating from the countryside and small businessman in the towns who resented the *zaibatsu*. The difference can be traced in large measure to the difference between Japanese and German society. Japan was backward relative to Germany, and its agrarian sector was far more important. Hence the Japanese military leadership could not so easily dismiss these demands. For the same reason we find sections of the Japanese army intervening in the political arena and attempting *coups d'état* in a way that presents a distinct contrast to the behavior of the German army.

Japanese fascism differed from the German form and even Mussolini's Italy in several other respects. There was no sudden seizure of power, no outright break with previous constitutional democracy, no equivalent of a March on Rome, partly because there was no democratic era comparable to the Weimar Republic. Fascism emerged much more "naturally" in Japan; that is, it found congenial elements in Japanese institutions even more than it did in Germany. Japan had no plebeian *Führer* or *Duce*. Instead the Emperor served as a national symbol in much the same way. Nor did Japan have a really effective single mass party. The Imperial Rule Assistance Association was a rather second-rate imitation. Finally, the Japanese government did not engage in a massive policy of terror and extermination against a specific segment of the underlying population as did Hitler against the Jews. These differences, too, may be due to the relative backwardness of Japan. The problem of loyalty and obedience in Japan could be solved by an appeal to traditional symbols with a judicious application of terror, much of which could be left to "spontaneous" popular feeling. The secular and rationalist currents that in the early stages of industrialism eroded traditional European beliefs were a foreign import in the case of Japan and never took deep root. Much of their original force had been spent in their homeland by the time Japanese industrial growth gained momentum. Hence the Japanese were forced to rely more on traditional elements in their culture and social structure in facing both the economic problems of industrial growth and the political problems that accompanied this growth.

When all these differences have been recognized, the underlying similarities between German and Japanese fascism still remain as the fundamental features. Both Germany and Japan entered the industrial world at a late stage. In both countries, regimes emerged whose main policies were repression at home and expansion abroad. In both cases, the main social basis for this program was a coalition between the commercial-industrial élites (who started from a weak position) and the traditional ruling classes in the countryside, directed against the peasants and the industrial workers. Finally, in both cases, a form of rightist radicalism emerged out of the plight of the petty bourgeoisie and peasants under advancing capitalism. This right-wing radicalism provided some of the slogans for repressive regimes in both countries but was sacrificed in practice to the requirements of profit and "efficiency."

In Japan's authoritarian and fascist development, there remains one key problem for us to consider: what contribution, if any, did the peasants make? Were they, as some writers claim, an important reservoir of fanatic nationalism and patriotism?

In trying to answer these questions it might be helpful to review the major economic factors affecting the peasants of Japan during the years between the First and Second World Wars. Three points stand out in the standard accounts of Japanese agrarian life during this period. One is the failure of indigenous attempts to alter the tenancy system. The second is the increasing importance of silk in Japan's rural economy. The third is the impact of the Great Depression. All in all, the main trend in the post-Meiji period was to throw the Japanese peasant upon the mercy of the world market.

About the tenancy system, we can be brief since the major features have already been discussed. Immediately following the First World War a wave of landlord-tenant disputes spread over the countryside. In 1922 moderate socialists who had been active in the urban labor movement organized the first national tenants' union. The next five years were marked by numerous conflicts between landlords and tenants. By 1928, however, this movement had begun to lose momentum, though there was an even greater wave of disputes, if the statistics are to be trusted, in 1934 and 1935. Afterward it apparently petered out. As far as I have been able to discover, the reasons for failure have never received close examination, at least by Western scholars. Nevertheless, the main ones are moderately clear. Real class warfare never took hold in the Japanese village. Because of the structure inherited from the past, the landlord's influence spread into every nook and cranny of village life. Furthermore, for the individual tenant there always seemed to be the chance for a personal solution. Thus the struggle over tenancy did not seriously modify the system of authority in the countryside as it had emerged from the Meiji settlement.[209]

To the Japanese peasants, silk was important as a subsidiary source of income, and for some, even a major one. Silk growing produced badly needed cash and some of the security that can come from the diversification of products. In the 1930s there were about two million farmers, some forty percent of the total, who engaged in sericulture. The Japanese farmer sold the cocoons to a reeler, who was ordinarily financed by a commission merchant in Yokohama or Kobe. The reeler paid a high rate of interest and had to ship the raw silk to the commission merchant in return for the money advanced. The amount of the loan was such that the commission merchant virtually controlled the sale of raw silk. As for the peasant, he was as much at the mercy of the reeler as the reeler was at the mercy of the commission merchant. Growing cocoons

[209] Some details in Dore, *Land Reform*, 29; more in Totten, "Labor and Agrarian Disputes," 192–200, and Table 2 on 203.

was a family affair that allowed the head of the family to engage in other agricultural work. In this way sericulture did increase the income of the peasant families who engaged in it.[210] Nevertheless, under the prevailing organization of the market, the great firms in the cities could siphon off much of the benefit for themselves. Here was a situation made to order for the growth of peasant anticapitalism.

The depression struck a heavy blow at both rice and silk. The years 1927 – 1930 were years of large crops in rice. Prices collapsed.[211] Very likely the fall affected the landlords (and perhaps also the larger owner-cultivators) more than the tenants, since the tenants usually paid their rent in rice, while the landlords marketed 85 percent of their produce.[212] The fall in silk prices, which accompanied the collapse of American prosperity, hit the Japanese peasant more directly. In 1930 raw silk prices declined by half. Silk exports were only 53 percent by value of those in 1929. Many peasants were ruined. Some writers see a connection between these simultaneous blows at the rural economy, the overthrow of "liberal" government, and the transfer of power to those who favored military aggression. The key link in this chain of causation was supposedly the army, composed of peasant recruits and officered by *petit bourgeois* elements whose economic situation made them subject to hypernationalist appeals.[213]

This theory, I believe, oversimplifies the situation in such a way as to be seriously misleading. Among the peasantry there is little evidence of any enthusiastic support for hypernationalist movements.[214] The agrarian current of traditionalist patriotism, expressed in such movements as *Nōhon-shugi*, was mainly a town and

[210] Matsui, "Silk Industry," 52 – 57. See also Allen, *Short Economic History*, 64 – 65, 110.

[211] Allen, *Short Economic History*, 109.

[212] Ladejinsky, "Japanese Farm Tenancy," 431.

[213] Cf Allen, *Short Economic History*, 98 – 99, 111.

[214] One such movement was involved in the assassination of Premier Inukai in May 1932. But it was the premier himself who had the mass following in rural areas. See Borton, *Japan Since 1931*, 21 – 22, and Beardsley et al, *Village Japan*, 431 – 435.

landlord affair, directed *against* peasant interests and aiming to keep the peasant frugal and contented — in a word, in his place. At the most, agrarian superpatriotism probably had some appeal to the more prosperous owner-cultivators, who identified themselves with the landlords, for whose position as sellers of rice these notions provided a rationalization.

To be sure, there were certain aspects of the peasants' situation, particularly those derived from the silk trade, that could easily have made them susceptible to anticapitalist ideas. Anticapitalist sentiments among the peasants were very likely strong enough, when combined with other factors, to make the peasants follow the leadership of the rural élite. On the whole, the peasants' contribution to Japanese fascism — or nationalist extremism if one prefers such a term at this point — was mainly a passive one. The peasants did provide a large body of obedient recruits for the army and constituted in civil life a huge apolitical (i.e., conservative) and submissive mass that had a crucial effect on Japanese politics.

Now apolitical obedience to orders, regardless of what the orders are, is not simply a matter of psychology. The mentality that behaves in this way is the product of concrete historical circumstances, just as much as the self-reliant mentality still admired in the West. Furthermore, as the Japanese case demonstrates beyond any doubt, this passive attitude is not necessarily a product of advanced industrialism. Under specific circumstances it can occur in peasant societies as well.

In Japan these circumstances were embodied in the structure of the Japanese village, as inherited from late Tokugawa and early Meiji times and reinforced by more modern economic trends. The landlord remained the unchallenged leader of the peasant community. Through the structure of the village he was able to have his way locally. Likewise, the village gave him a political base from which to transmit his aims upward to the national scene, where they met the challenge and formed part of the overall compromise we have already discussed. Let us therefore look more closely at the reasons why the peasants remained so much under his influence.

The most prominent features of the Japanese village down to the time of the American land reform were its domination by the wealthy and the discouragement of open conflict.[215] The main basis of authority in the village was the ownership of landed property. The resulting relationships were supported by the state, on occasion with brute force. To some extent they were also softened and made more palatable by the patina of age, tradition, and custom. Resident landlords frequently managed village affairs, though larger ones might leave this chore to others, exercising their authority from behind the scenes. Tenants might on occasion have some minor share in village offices.[216] In a good many villages or larger areas there was a small circle of intermarrying landlord families, known vividly as the "kissing ring," that dominated local affairs.[217] Generally the smaller landlords supplied recruits for paid offices in the *mura*, as they could thus supplement the meager salary from their rents.[218]

Perhaps only in extreme cases could the landlord withdraw the tenant's sole source of livelihood at will or be likely to undertake so drastic an action.[219] But the landlord's power over the tenant's means of existence was constantly visible to the latter and to others in a hundred subtle ways. It was the ultimate sanction behind the elaborate code of deference that governed the peasant's relation to his superiors. The tenant carefully observed "the color of his land-

[215] A terminological difficulty arises here. The Japanese *buraku* has no appropriate counterpart in American experience. It is a community, usually of less than a hundred houses, all of whose members know one another personally. The borders of its land are only hazily defined, but its members have a strong sense of belonging to a clearly defined social unit. The *mura* is larger and its members do not know one another personally, though it is legally the smallest administrative unit in Japan. A *mura* ordinarily contains several *buraku*. R. P. Dore usually translates *buraku* by "hamlet," ordinarily saving "village" for the larger administrative unit. The problem does not arise for T.C. Smith, who deals in his *Agrarian Origins* exclusively with earlier times, and uses the term "village" to refer to a natural social unit. Therefore I have used the word village for *buraku*, except for a few occasions, indicated clearly by the context, where it refers to the *mura*. See Beardsley et al, *Village Japan*, 3 – 5, and glossary for further details.

[216] Dore, *Land Reform*, 325.

[217] Dore, *Land Reform*, 330.

[218] Dore, *Land Reform*, 337.

[219] Cf Dore, *Land Reform*, 373.

lord's face." R.P. Dore, the source of this observation, is one to minimize rather than to exaggerate the darker side of the landlord's authority. Yet even he concludes that the tenant's deference was due to the conscious calculation of advantage and of outright fear based on the brute fact of economic dependence.[220] Fear and dependence were thus the ultimate sources, at least in the countryside, of the elaborate Japanese code of deference that charms many American visitors by its novelty and contrast with their own experience. One may guess that such visitors are aware of the hostility behind much friendly breeziness in the United States but miss both the historical origins and present meaning of Japanese politeness. Where the relations of economic dependence have disappeared, as a consequence of the American land reform or for other reasons, the traditional structure of status and deference has crumbled away.[221] If anyone were inclined to doubt the economic basis of oligarchy in the village and of the Japanese code of politeness, the circumstances of their partial disappearance would seem to demonstrate the relationship conclusively.

The satellite system of large and small holdings continued into recent times because it could be adapted to a market economy through the device of tenancy and because no forces arose to challenge it. The solidarity and "harmony" of the Japanese village, its avoidance — perhaps we ought to say suppression — of open conflict are also a feudal legacy that has adapted itself more or less successfully to modern times. In the village before modern times, this solidarity arose out of the system of economic cooperation among the peasants as well as from the lord's policies of taxation and paternalistic supervision. In their modern forms both factors continued to operate between the two World Wars and continue to have many of the same effects even today. Without going into details, it is sufficient to remark that the continued spread of a money economy into the village has put some strain on older relationships, without so far modifying them very seriously.[222]

[220] *Land Reform,* 371 – 372.
[221] Dore, *Land Reform,* 367.
[222] For some details on the continuation of practices described earlier in this chapter, see Embree, *Suye Mura,* chap IV. Embree, however, is sin-

On the side of what may rather loosely be called politics there have also been several factors at work to continue the solidarity of the village. The "big" issues — those that divide rich and poor — were not decided at the local level in Tokugawa times, nor have they been decided there in modern ones.[223] "Little" issues that affect only the local community are handled in ways that seem familiar enough to anyone who has ever sat on an academic committee. One might give them the collective name of reaching agreement through boredom and exhaustion. Possibly we have here one of the universals or laws that some sociologists still seek so earnestly. Fundamentally the device consists of letting those who have opinions express them endlessly until the group as a whole is willing to undertake collective responsibility for a decision. In Japan, as perhaps elsewhere, the real discussions generally take place away from public eyes, which may increase both candor and the possibility of an acceptable compromise. The system puts a greater premium on the strength with which an individual holds opinions than on their rational grounds. At the same time it is democratic insofar as it allows for the thorough ventilation of opposing views. This clash can occur only when the contending parties are roughly equal outside the committee room. In modern Japanese villages where there were more than one leading family, there appear to have been vigorous discussions within this élite group, again — one must repeat — about strictly local issues. Although completely lacking any indigenous tradition about the virtues of democracy, Japan did develop some of its institutional features, it appears, quite out of her own soil.[224] More formally democratic countries are not in the best position to say that Japan developed democracy most effectively where it mattered least.

During the totalitarian phase of Japan's recent history, the vil-

---

gularly unenlightening on social classes and politics; further, on cultivation practices, in Beardsley et al, *Village Japan,* esp 151; Dore, *Land Reform,* 352 – 353.

[223] Dore, *Land Reform,* 338, 341.

[224] On village politics see Dore, *Land Reform,* chap XIII, and Beardsley et al, *Village Japan,* chaps 12, 13, esp pp. 354 – 385. Dore's account throws much light backward on political behavior before 1945.

lage was integrated into the national structure in a way that vividly recalls Tokugawa techniques for penetrating and controlling peasant society. Whether there was direct historical continuity is not clear from the sources.[225] Even if there was not, these arrangements show the way in which important aspects of Japanese feudalism were easily compatible with twentieth-century totalitarian institutions.

The reader may recall the Tokugawa organization of five-man groups among the peasantry for the purpose of mutual responsibility. These were widely reenforced by public notice boards in the village, exhorting the peasants to good behavior. After 1930, neighborhood groups were organized by the government, each with its own head. Dore observes that the system, together with the official administration above it, provided a method for the central government to reach every household through a descending face-to-face hierarchy of command. Orders came down from the Home Ministry to individual households by means of a circulating notice board. In the case of important matters, each householder had to append his seal to show that he had received the order. This device provided an effective way to organize the rural population for such purposes as rationing, the collection of controlled grain, war bond subscription, and general austerity measures. Though the American occupation authorities abolished the system of downward communication, the local organizations continued to exist because they had local functions to perform. Since they did remain, and provided a more efficient means of disseminating information than notice boards that the villagers might disregard, they soon resumed this function.[226]

*   *   *

As one looks back over the history of the Japanese village since the seventeenth century, the feature most likely to strike the historian is its continuity. The oligarchical structure, internal solidarity, and effective vertical ties with higher authority all survived with very little change the transition to modern production for the

[225] Embree, *Suye Mura,* 34 – 35 claims this continuity.
[226] Dore, *Land Reform,* 355.

market. At the same time, historical continuity itself provides no explanation; it is something that requires explanation, especially when so much else has changed. The essence of the explanation, I would urge, lies in the fact that the landlords maintained most of the old village structure because through it they could extract and sell enough of a surplus to stay on top of the heap. Those who did not make the grade provided recruits for agrarian pseudoradicalism. The substitution of tenancy relations for pseudokinship was the only institutional change needed. All this was possible only in a rice culture, where, as events were to show, traditional methods could greatly raise productivity. Unlike the English landlord of the eighteenth century, the Prussian Junker in the sixteenth, or Russian Communists in the twentieth, the Japanese ruling classes found that they could get their way without destroying the prevailing peasant society. If working through the traditional social structure had not brought results, I doubt that the Japanese landlord would have spared the village any more than did landlords elsewhere.

The adaptability of Japanese political and social institutions to capitalist principles enabled Japan to avoid the costs of a revolutionary entrance onto the stage of modern history. Partly because she escaped these early horrors, Japan succumbed in time to fascism and defeat. So did Germany for very broadly the same reason. The price for avoiding a revolutionary entrance has been a very high one. It has been high in India as well. There the play has not yet reached the culminating act; the plot and the characters are different. Still, lessons learned from all the cases studied so far may prove helpful in understanding what the play means.

CHAPTER SIX

Democracy in Asia:
India and the Price of Peaceful Change

1. Relevance of the Indian Experience

THAT INDIA BELONGS TO TWO WORLDS is a familiar platitude that happens to be true. Economically it remains in the preindustrial age. It has not had an industrial revolution in either of the two capitalist variants discussed so far, nor according to the communist one. There has been no bourgeois revolution, no conservative revolution from above, no peasant revolution. But as a political species it does belong to the modern world. At the time of Nehru's death in 1964 political democracy had existed for seventeen years. If imperfect, the democracy was no mere sham. There had been a working parliamentary system since Independence in 1947, an independent judiciary, and the standard liberal freedoms: free general elections in which the governing party had accepted defeat in an important part of the country, civilian control over the military, a head of state that made very limited use of formal extensive powers.[1] There is a paradox here, but only a superficial one. Political democracy may seem strange in both an Asian setting and one without an industrial revolution until one realizes that the appalling problems facing the Indian government are due to these very facts. Indeed that is the story I shall do my best to explain in this chapter: why the advent of the modern world has not led to political or economic upheavals in India and, more briefly, the legacy this process has left for present-day Indian society.

[1] Brecher, *Nehru*, 638.

Instructive in its own right, the story constitutes both a challenge to and a check upon the theories advanced in this book as well as others, especially those theories of democracy that were a response to the very different historical experience of Western Europe and the United States. Because obstacles to modernization have been especially powerful in India, we gain additional understanding of those factors that enabled other countries to overcome them. Once more, however, it is necessary to emphasize that in order to read the story at all correctly we have to realize that it is not a finished one. Only the future will reveal whether it is possible to modernize Indian society and retain or extend democratic freedoms.

By way of prologue, the reader may find it helpful to hear the story as I have gradually come to perceive it. By the time of Queen Elizabeth I, the Islamic conquerors of India ·had established over much of the subcontinent what an older and less inhibited generation of scholars would have called an oriental despotism. Today we must call it an agrarian bureaucracy or an Asian version of royal absolutism, rather more primitive than that in China, a political system unfavorable to political democracy and the growth of a trading class. Neither aristocratic nor bourgeois privileges and liberties were able to threaten Mogul rule. Nor were there among the peasants any forces at work that would have been likely to produce either an economic or a political break with the prevailing society. Cultivation was lackadaisical and inefficient over wide areas, partly due to Mogul tax farming, partly because of the peculiar structure of peasant society, organized through the caste system. In providing a framework for all social activity, quite literally from conception to the afterlife, at the local level of the village community, caste made the central government largely superfluous. Hence peasant opposition was less likely to take the form of massive peasant rebellions that it had taken in China. Innovation and opposition could be absorbed without change, by the formation of new castes and subcastes. In the absence of any strong impulse toward qualitative change, the Mogul system simply broke down, due to the dynamics of increasing exploitation produced by its system of tax farming. This collapse gave the Europeans the chance to establish a territorial foothold during the eighteenth century.

There were, then, powerful obstacles to modernization present in the character of Indian society prior to the British conquest. Others came to the surface as a result of this conquest. During the late eighteenth and the first part of the nineteenth centuries, the British introduced new systems of taxation and land tenure, as well as textiles that may have damaged artisan castes. The British further made visible the whole apparatus of Western scientific culture that was a threat to traditional priestly privilege. The response was the Mutiny of 1857, a reactionary convulsion and unsuccessful effort to expel the British. A deeper and more long-run effect of the introduction of law and order and taxes, and of an increasing population, was the rise of parasitic landlordism. Despite poor cultivation, the peasants did generate a substantial economic surplus. The British presence, the failure of the Mutiny, the character of Indian society ruled out the Japanese solution to backwardness: rule by a new section of the native élite which used this surplus as the basis for industrial growth. Instead, in India the foreign conqueror, the landlord, and the moneylender absorbed and dissipated this surplus. Hence economic stagnation continued throughout the British era and indeed into the present day.

On the other hand, the British presence prevented the formation of the characteristic reactionary coalition of landed élites with a weak bourgeoisie and thereby, along with British cultural influences, made an important contribution toward political democracy. British authority rested heavily on the landed upper classes. The native bourgeoisie, especially the manufacturers, on the other hand felt cramped by British policies, particularly on free trade, and sought to exploit a protected Indian market. As the nationalist movement grew and looked for a mass basis, Gandhi provided a link between powerful sections of the bourgeoisie and the peasantry through the doctrine of nonviolence, trusteeship, and the glorification of the Indian village community. For this and other reasons, the nationalist movement did not take a revolutionary form, though civil disobedience forced the withdrawal of a weakened British empire. The outcome of these forces was indeed political democracy, but a democracy that has not done a great deal toward modernizing India's social structure. Hence famine still lurks in the background.

Shorn of complexities and contradictions, shorn indeed to the point of grotesque baldness, this is the tale we are about to follow. Others who have studied India far more than I may be reluctant to recognize their subject in this preliminary sketch. It is my hope, and very likely my delusion, that the evidence which follows will make the resemblance more convincing.

2. Mogul India: Obstacles to Democracy

The last of the many conquerors that invaded India before the Western impact were the Moguls, a name applied to one large segment of the followers of the great Mongol leader, Genghis Khan. Early in the sixteenth century the first of their leaders invaded India. They reached the height of their power under Akbar (1556 – 1605), a contemporary of Queen Elizabeth I, though subsequent rulers did extend the territory under their control. By the end of the sixteenth century, an appropriate starting point for our account, this Islamic dynasty controlled the lion's share of India, approximately down the peninsula to a line running east and west somewhat north of Bombay. Hindu kingdoms to the south remained independent. As the Moguls adapted their rule to Hindu circumstances, there was little difference between them, beyond the fact that, at its best, the Mogul territory was better governed.[2]

According to a well-known description, the fundamental features of the traditional Indian polity were a sovereign who ruled, an army that supported the throne, and a peasantry that paid for both.[3] To this trio one must add, for an adequate comprehension of Indian society, the notion of caste. For the moment we may describe the caste system as the organization of the population into hereditary and endogamous groups in which the males perform the same type of social function, such as that of priest, warrior, artisan, cultivator, and the like. Religious notions of pollution sanction this division of society into theoretically watertight and hierarchically ordered compartments.[4] Caste served, and still serves, to organize

[2] Moreland, *India at Death of Akbar,* 6.
[3] Moreland, *Agrarian System,* xi.
[4] It seems somewhat strange that Moreland in his detailed descriptions of Mogul society has very little to say about the caste system, which was

the life of the village community, the basic cell of Indian society and the fundamental unit into which it tended to disintegrate wherever and whenever a strong ruler was lacking.

This institutional complex of village communities organized by caste, supporting by their taxes an army that was the main prop of the ruler, has proved to be a hardy one. It characterized the Indian polity throughout the British period. Even under Independence and Nehru, much of the Mogul system has remained intact.

Essentially the political and social system of the Mogul era was an agrarian bureaucracy imposed on top of a heterogeneous collection of native chieftains differing widely in resources and power. As the Mogul authority weakened in the eighteenth century, it reverted to looser forms. Under Akbar and succeeding strong rulers, there was no landed aristocracy of national scope independent of the crown, at least not in theory and to a considerable extent not in fact. Native chieftains did enjoy substantial independence, though the Mogul rulers were at least moderately successful in incorporating them into the Mogul bureaucratic system. The position of the native chieftain will require more detailed discussion shortly. In general, as Moreland says, "Independence was synonymous with rebellion, and a noble was either a servant or an enemy of the ruling power."[5] The weakness of a national aristocracy was an important feature of seventeenth-century India that, as in other countries,

---

flourishing at that time, as it had been for centuries. The reason may be that Moreland was compelled to construct his description from Mogul administrative documents and the accounts of contemporary travellers. Neither type of account focuses sharply on the village community where caste becomes a living reality as the basis for the division of labor. One could collect taxes, raise military recruits, or, if one were a foreigner, engage in trade, with minimal knowledge of the workings of caste. The *Ain i Akbari,* a general description of the Mogul realm compiled by Akbar's minister, Abul Fazl, mentions caste several times, but mainly as a curiosity. Habib, *Agrarian System* (1963), corrects and extends Moreland on a number of crucial points, particularly the role of the lower nobility and their connection with peasant rebellions. In others it confirms Moreland's analysis. It too touches rather lightly on caste, though somewhat more than Moreland.

[5] *India at Death of Akbar,* 63.

inhibited the growth of parliamentary democracy from native soil. Parliamentary institutions were to be a late and exotic import.

Land was held theoretically, and to a great extent in practice, at the pleasure of the ruler. It could not even be purchased except in small blocks for building houses.[6] The usual practice was to assign to an officer the revenue of a village, a group of villages, or some larger area, as the emolument for service in the Mogul Imperial Civil Service. Akbar disliked this arrangement, as it had the standard disadvantages of tax farming. The holder of an assigned area was under temptation to exploit the peasants and might also develop a territorial base for his own power. Therefore Akbar attempted to replace the system of assignments with regular cash payments. For reasons to be discussed later, the effort failed.[7]

Again, in theory, there was no such thing as the inheritance of office, and each generation had to make a fresh start. On the death of the officeholder, the wealth reverted to the treasury. The Hindu chiefs, local rulers whom the Moguls had conquered and left in authority in return for loyalty to the new regime, were an important exception. And a number of noble families did persist among the conquerors. Yet confiscation at death took place often enough to render the accumulation of wealth a hazard.[8]

In addition to these efforts to prevent the growth of property rights in office, the Indian political system displayed other bureaucratic traits. The tasks were graded and the conditions of service set down by the Emperor in great detail. After admission to the Imperial Service, a man received his appointment to a military rank. Then he was required to enroll a certain number of cavalry and infantry in accord with his designated rank.[9] On the other hand, the Mogul bureaucracy failed to develop some of the safeguards of bureaucratic authority common in modern societies. There were no

[6] Moreland, *India at Death of Akbar*, 256. Rights over the land were, however, purchasable according to Habib, *Agrarian System*, 154.

[7] Moreland, *India at Death of Akbar*, 67, and his *Agrarian System*, 9–10.

[8] Moreland, *India at Death of Akbar*, 71, 263; Moreland and Chatterjee, *Short History*, 211–212.

[9] Moreland, *India at Death of Akbar*, 65.

rules of promotion, no tests of fitness, no notion of competence in a specific function. Akbar apparently depended practically entirely on his intuitive judgment of character in advancing, degrading, or dismissing officers. The most·eminent literary man of the day performed excellent service in charge of military operations, and another met his death in command of. troops on the frontier after many years at court.[10] In comparison with the civil service of Manchu China, Akbar's system was relatively primitive. To be sure, the Chinese, too, explicitly rejected any notion of extreme specialization, and one might easily match from Chinese history the varied careers just mentioned. Yet the Chinese examination system was certainly much closer to the practice of contemporary bureaucracy than Akbar's haphazard methods of recruitment and promotion. An even more significant difference rests in China's substantial success in preventing the growth of property rights in bureaucratic office. At a later date, the Moguls were unsuccessful on this count, as we shall see in due course.

The risk of accumulating wealth and the barrier to its transmission by testament put a tremendous premium on display. Spending, not hoarding, was the dominant feature of the time. Such appears to be the origin of that magnificence rooted in squalor that still strikes visitors to India today and that made a vivid impression on European travellers in Mogul times. The emperor set the example of magnificence to be followed by his courtiers.[11] This court splendor was a device that helped to prevent an undesirable accumulation of resources in the hands of his associates, though, as we shall see, it also had unfortunate consequences from the ruler's standpoint. Courtiers spent more money on their stables than on any other branch of their household with the possible exception of jewelry. Sport and gambling flourished.[12] The abundance of human labor led to a profusion of retainers, a custom that has remained into modern times. Every ordinary elephant had four attendants, a number that was increased to seven in the case of animals chosen for the emperor's use. One of the later emperors assigned four

---

[10] Moreland, *India at Death of Akbar,* 69, 71.

[11] Moreland, *India at Death of Akbar,* 257.

[12] Moreland, *India at Death of Akbar,* 259.

human attendants to each of the dogs brought to him as presents from England.[13]

By skimming off most of the economic surplus generated by the underlying population and turning it into display, the Mogul rulers for a time avoided the dangers of an aristocratic. attack on their power. At the same time, such a use of the surplus seriously limited the possibilities of economic development or, more precisely, the kind of economic development that would have broken through the agrarian order and established a new kind of society.[14] The point deserves stressing since Marxists and Indian nationalists generally argue that Indian society was on the point of bursting through the fetters of an agrarian system when the advent of British imperialism crushed and distorted potential developments in this direction. This conclusion seems quite unwarranted on the basis of the evidence, which gives strong support to the opposite thesis: that neither capitalism nor parliamentary democracy could have emerged unaided from seventeenth-century Indian society.

Such a conclusion receives a reinforcement as we turn our attention to the towns and what germs there were of an Indian bourgeoisie. For germs of a sort there were, and even some traces of an outlook resembling that much disputed demiurge of social history, the Protestant ethic. Tavernier, a French traveller of the seventeenth century, speaks of the Banians, a caste of bankers and brokers, in these words:

> The members of this caste are so subtle and skillful in trade that
> . . . they could give lessons to the most cunning Jews. They accustom their children at an early age to shun slothfulness, and instead of letting them into the streets to lose time at play, as we generally allow ours, teach them arithmetic. . . . They are always with their fathers who instruct them in trade and do nothing without at the same time explaining it to them. . . . If anyone gets in a rage with them they listen with patience, not returning to see him for four or five days, when they anticipate his rage will be over.[15]

[13] Moreland, *India at Death of Akbar*, 88 – 89.
[14] As recognized clearly by Moreland, *India at Death of Akbar*, 73.
[15] *Travels in India*, II, 144.

But Indian society at that time was not one in which these virtues could find sufficient scope to overturn the prevailing system of production.

Cities there were, too. European travellers of the day refer to Agra, Lahore, Delhi, and Vijayanager as equal to the great European cities of the time, Rome, Paris, and Constantinople.[16] These cities did not, however, owe their existence primarily to trade and commerce. They were mainly political and, to some extent, religious centers. Traders and merchants were relatively insignificant. At Delhi, the French traveller Bernier remarks, "There is no middle estate. A man must be either of the highest rank or live miserably."[17] Merchants existed, of course, and even engaged in foreign commerce, though the Portuguese had by this time annexed most of the profits in this field.[18] Here is one fact that does support the thesis that European imperialism stifled native impulses toward modernization, though it seems to me very far from a decisive piece of evidence. There were also artisans who produced mainly luxuries for the wealthy.[19]

The main barriers to commerce were political and social. Some of these were perhaps no worse than in Europe of the same period, which also knew highway robberies, vexations, and expensive transit dues.[20] Others were worse. The Mogul legal system was behind that of Europe. The merchant who wished to enforce a contract or recover a debt could not put his case into the hands of a professional lawyer because the profession did not exist. He had to plead his case in person under a system of justice suffused with personal and arbitrary traits. Bribery was almost universal.[21]

More important still was the emperor's practice of claiming the earthly goods of wealthier merchants as well as of officials at the moment they died. Moreland quotes from a letter of Aurang-

[16] Moreland, *India at Death of Akbar*, 13.
[17] Quoted by Moreland, *India at Death of Akbar*, 26.
[18] Moreland, *India at Death of Akbar*, 239.
[19] Moreland, *India at Death of Akbar*, 160, 184, 187.
[20] Moreland, *India at Death of Akbar*, 41. See also Habib, *Agrarian System*, chap II.
[21] Moreland, *India at Death of Akbar*, 35 – 36.

zeb, the last of the Great Moguls (*d* 1707), a portion of which the
traveller Bernier preserved:

> We have been accustomed as soon as an Omrah (noble) or a
> rich merchant has ceased to breathe, nay sometimes before the vital
> spark has fled, to place seals on his coffers, to imprison and beat the
> servants or officers of his household, until they made a full dis-
> closure of the whole property, even of the most inconsiderable
> jewel. This practice is advantageous no doubt, but can we deny
> its injustice and cruelty?[22]

Probably this did not happen in every case. Yet, as Moreland dryly
observes, trade must have suffered by the risk of a sudden demand
for the whole visible capital at the moment when the death of its
owner had probably involved the business in temporary uncertainty.[23] One wonders, too, if the emperor always and conscien-
tiously refrained from hastening the natural processes of human
decay, whose eventual outcome would be for him such a happy
event. All these considerations must have circulated in the mercantile community and inhibited the growth of commerce.

In general, the attitude of the political authorities in India toward the merchant seems to have been closer to that of the spider
toward the fly than that of the cowherd toward his cow that was
widespread in Europe at the same time. Not even Akbar, the most
enlightened of the Moguls, had a Colbert. In the Hindu areas the
situation was probably somewhat worse. Local authorities, such as
the governor of a town, might at times take a different view,
though they too were under pressure to make and spend their
fortunes rapidly. All in all, I believe it is safe to conclude that the
establishment of peace and order (of a sort) did not create a situation in which the rise of mercantile influences could undermine the
agrarian order to the extent that it did in Japan. The Mogul system
was too predatory for that; not because its rulers and officers were
necessarily more vicious as human beings (though some of the later
rulers were drug sodden and bloodthirsty, perhaps out of boredom
and hopelessness), but because the system put the ruler and his

[22] Moreland, *From Akbar to Aurangzeb,* 277–278.
[23] *From Akbar to Aurangzeb,* 280.

servants in a situation where greedy behavior was often the only kind that made sense.

This predatory characteristic in time gravely weakened the Mogul system. During the eighteenth century the Mogul regime crumbled in the face of small European forces (engaged mainly in fighting one another) to the point where the Great Mogul became the recipient of a British stipend. An examination of the relationship between the Mogul bureaucracy and the peasantry reveals some of the reasons.

Prior to the Mogul conquest, the Hindu system was one in which the peasants paid a share of their produce to the king, who determined, within limits imposed by custom, law, and what the traffic would bear, the amount of his share as well as the methods of assessment and collection. The Moguls took over this arrangement from the Hindu kingdoms with very little change, partly because it was in any case congruent with their own traditions.[24] The Mogul administrative ideal, especially under Akbar, was one of direct relationship between the peasant and the state. Ideally both the assessment and the collection of the revenue were to be controlled from the center through officers who should account in detail for all receipts.[25] Except for brief periods and in relatively small areas, the Mogul rulers never achieved this ideal. To put it into effect would have required the creation of a large body of salaried officials under the direct control of the emperor. Such an arrangement seems to have been beyond the material and human resources of this agrarian society, much as it was beyond the achievement of the tsars.

Instead of paying cash directly out of the royal treasury to imperial officials, the most widespread arrangement was to assign the royal share of the produce in a specified area. The assignment carried with it the grant of executive authority sufficient to assess and collect the required amount. The area might be a whole province or no more than a single village, while the amount to be raised might represent the cost of maintaining troops or the performance of some other service. During the Mogul period most of the em-

[24] Moreland, *Agrarian System,* 5 – 6.
[25] Moreland, *India at Death of Akbar,* 33.

pire, sometimes as much as seven-eights of its area, was in the hands of such assignees.[26] In addition to collecting the revenue, this arrangement served as a method of recruiting troops for the army. A single set of officers performed these two fundamental tasks of the Mogul bureaucracy and was also responsible for keeping peace and order.[27]

There were numerous local variations on this basic pattern whose details we may safely ignore. As Moreland observes, Akbar's regime was eminently practical. "A chief or a raja who submitted and agreed to pay a reasonable revenue was commonly allowed to retain his position of authority: one who was recalcitrant or rebellious was killed, imprisoned, or driven away, and his lands taken under direct control." One aspect, nevertheless, deserves attention on account of its subsequent importance. Very widely, though not universally, the Mogul emperors found it necessary to rule and tax through native authorities. The general terms for these intermediaries was *zamindars*.

Both practice and the usage of the term fluctuated enough to create considerable confusion. Even if the line between them is occasionally shadowy, it is nevertheless possible to classify the *zamindars* into two broad types, depending on their degree of independence of the central authority. In many parts of the country, a series of conquests had led to a situation in which the members of a conquering caste had established their own rights to the collection of revenue from the peasants in a particular area. Fortresses belonging to the local aristocrats, who had their own bands of armed retainers, dotted much of the countryside. Though such *zamindars* had no recognized place in the Mogul scheme for collecting the revenue, they were normally called upon to pay revenue for territories over which they themselves claimed similar rights. Thus their rights of collecting taxes existed alongside those of the Mogul bureaucracy. In practice *zamindar* rights could be sold, subdivided, and transferred by inheritance, in much the same way as claims on the income of a modern corporation in the form of bonds and stocks. Naturally the Mogul authorities resisted this implicit chal-

[26] Moreland, *Agrarian System*, 9 – 10, 93.
[27] Moreland, *India at Death of Akbar*, 31.

lenge to their own authority and did their best to incorporate the *zamindars* into their own service. The Mogul doctrine was that the imperial government could resume or confer *zamindari* rights at its own pleasure. How far it was actually able to do so is not clear. Other *zamindars* amounted to nearly independent chieftains. As long as they paid taxes they were left alone. Though the richest and most populous areas (including those with the *zamindars* more or less successfully absorbed into the imperial service) were under direct imperial control, the territories of chiefs and princelings were far from negligible.[28]

Hence the empire was made up of local despotisms varying greatly in size and degree of independence, yet all owing revenue to the imperial coffers.[29] The smaller *zamindars* formed a series of local aristocracies. Divided from families near the crown by the fact that they were conquered subjects, too disunited and attached to their localities to play a role comparable to the English aristocracy as both challenge and substitute for royal absolutism these smaller *zamindars* nevertheless played a decisive political role.[30] As the imperial system decayed and became more oppressive, *zamindars* large and small became the rallying point for peasant rebellions. Native élites together with the peasants could not weld India into a viable political unit on their own. But they could punish the errors of foreigners and make their position untenable. This the peasants did under the Moguls and, with new allies, under the British; similar tendencies remain apparent even in the third quarter of the twentieth century.

The term *zamindar* has been at the center of a much larger question about whether Indian society had a system of private property in land. In time it has come to be realized that the question amounted to asking what were the relationships among men that governed the material objects all people used in order to provide themselves with food, shelter, and the accoutrements of civilization. In regard to land, the question is not difficult to answer, at least in its broad outlines. At that time land was abundant, often to be had

[28] Habib, *Agrarian System*, 154, 160, 165, 170, 174, 180, 183, 189.
[29] Habib, *Agrarian System*, 184.
[30] Cf Habib, *Agrarian System*, 165 – 167.

for the effort of working it. Hence, from the standpoint of the rulers, the problem was to make the peasants cultivate it. If a subject of the empire occupied land, he was required to pay a share of the gross produce to the ruler in return for protection. Mogul administrative theory and practice emphasized the duty of cultivation. Moreland mentions the case of a local governor who cut a village headman in two with his own hands for failing to sow his ground.[31] Even if the example is an extreme one, it reveals the fundamental problem. Private rights of ownership were definitely subordinate to and derived from the public duty of cultivation. This fact has affected social relationships on the land even under completely altered conditions down to the present day.

Mogul policy put a severe financial strain on the administrative system. While Jahangir (1605 – 1627), the successor to Akbar, endeavored to conciliate his Hindu subjects and did not try to extend the empire, Shah Jahan (1627 – 1658) engaged in a policy of magnificence, constructing numerous buildings, including the Taj Mahal and the Peacock Throne, whose construction took seven years and whose materials have been assessed at more than a million pounds sterling. He also began, though in a moderate way, to discriminate against Hindus.[32] Aurangzeb (1658 – 1707) simultaneously persecuted the Hindus on a wide scale and extended the empire by expensive and ultimately ruinous wars. These policies of magnificence and territorial expansion, probably connected through the fact that more land meant greater sources of revenue, brought to the surface inherent structural weaknesses.

If the emperor left an assignee in charge of a single area for a substantial period of time, he ran the risk of losing control over his subordinates as the latter developed an independent source of revenue and basis for his power. On the other hand, if the ruler changed the assignees frequently from one territory to another, the subordinates would be tempted to get as much out of the peasants as possible in the time available. Cultivation would then decline and, ultimately, the Imperial revenues. Eventually therefore the sinews

[31] *India at Death of Akbar*, 96 – 97; see also his *Agrarian System*, xi – xii.

[32] Moreland and Chatterjee, *Short History*, 241, 242.

of the central authority would slacken, and the emperor would lose the control that he had sought to maintain through frequent transfers. No matter which course the emperor followed, it appears that he was bound to lose out in the long run. The second of the two possibilities just sketched constitutes quite a close approximation to what actually happened.

As early as under Jahangir, we hear of agrarian instability due to frequent changes in assignments.[33] Bernier, who travelled in the middle of the seventeenth century, puts a much quoted remark into the mouth of the officials with which he was familiar:

> Why should the neglected state of this land create uneasiness in our minds? And why should we spend our money and time to render it fruitful? We may be deprived of it in a single moment, and our exertions would benefit neither ourselves nor our children. Let us draw from the soil all the money we can, though the peasant should starve or abscond, and we should leave it, when commanded to quit, a dreary wilderness.[34]

Though Bernier may have exaggerated, there is abundant evidence to show that he put his finger on the main defect in the Mogul polity.

Bernier's evidence, as well as that of other travellers, fits closely with what we know of the situation from Aurangzeb's orders. Together they portray a situation in which the peasants are heavily assessed and kept under strict discipline, while at the same time they are decreasing in numbers, partly through flight to areas outside the Mogul jurisdiction.[35] When the peasants fled, the assignee's income was necessarily reduced. An assignee with short and uncertain tenure would try to make good some part of his loss through increased pressure on those who remained at work. Hence the process tended to be cumulative. The Mogul system drove the peasants into the arms of more or less independent chieftains where conditions tended to be better. Bernier's statement that the peasants found less oppression in these areas finds confirmation in a number

[33] Moreland, *Agrarian System*, 130.

[34] Quoted by Moreland, *Agrarian System*, 205.

[35] Habib, *Agrarian System*, chap IX. See also Moreland, *Agrarian System*, 147; *From Akbar to Aurangzeb*, 202.

of independént sources. Smaller *zamindars*, engaged in an unequal contest with the Mogul bureaucracy, also found it to their advantage· to treat the peasants well. Thus the foci of independent authority that the Moguls had not been able to root out provided rallying points for peasant rebellions. Revolts were occurring fairly frequently even when the Mogul power was at its height.[36] As the Mogul bureaucracy became more oppressive and corrupt, the rebellions became more serious. Over wide areas the peasants refused to pay revenue, took to arms, and plundered. The chieftains who led the peasants showed no inclination to improve the condition of their subjects. One supposedly said of the common people "Money is inconvenient for them; give them victuals and an arse clout, it is enough."[37] Nevertheless, perhaps out of a combination of sheer desperation as well as patriarchal and caste loyalties, the peasants followed them willingly. Indeed, in their contradictory mixture of patriarchal loyalties, sectarian religious innovation, and outright protest against the injustices of the prevailing order as well as against acts of bloody vengeance and plunder, the peasant movements of the declining Mogul system display behavior similar to those of peasants in other societies under the same general conditions of very primitive commercial relationships which are making their intrusion into an oppressive agrarian order.[38]

By the middle of the eighteenth century the Mogul bureaucratic hegemony had decayed into a system of petty kingdoms frequently at war with one another. Such was the situation that the British encountered when they began to intervene in earnest in the Indian countryside.

As one looks back over the record, it is easy to conclude — perhaps a trifle too easy — that the dynamics of the Mogul system were unfavorable to the development of either political democracy or economic growth in anything resembling the Western pattern. There was no landed aristocracy that had succeeded in achieving independence and privilege against the monarch while retaining political unity. Instead their independence, if it can be called that, had

[36] Habib, *Agrarian System,* 335 – 336.
[37] Quoted by Habib, *Agrarian System,* 90 – 91; see also 350 – 351.
[38] See Habib, *Agrarian System,* 338 – 351.

brought anarchy in its train. What there was of a bourgeoisie likewise lacked an independent base. Both features are connected with a predatory bureaucracy, driven to become ever more grasping as its power weakened, and which by crushing the peasants and driving them into rebellion returned the subcontinent to what it had often been before, a series of fragmented units fighting with one another, ready prey for another foreign conqueror.

3. Village Society: Obstacles to Rebellion

The character of the upper classes and political institutions have suggested some reasons why there was not in India the kind of economic and political movement toward capitalism and political democracy that parts of Europe displayed from the sixteenth to the eighteenth centuries. A closer look at the place of the peasants in Indian society will help to account for two further features that have been of the utmost importance: widespread poor cultivation, which contrasts in the sharpest possible manner with the gardenlike peasant agriculture in China and Japan, and the apparent political docility of the Indian peasants. Though there were exceptions to this docility, best discussed in a separate section, peasant rebellions never assumed remotely the same significance in India that they did in China.

Crops and ways of growing them were very much the same in Akbar's time as they still are today over wide sections of India. Rice was prominent in Bengal. Northern India in general grew cereals, millets and pulses. The Deccan produced *jowar* (also spelled *jovār* and *juār*, a kind of millet or sorghum) and cotton, while rice and millets were again prominent in the South.[39] A good crop was and is dependent on the annual monsoon rains. An often repeated statement in standard works on India is that, over the greater part of the country, agriculture is a gamble in the rains. To some extent irrigation offset the gamble, even in pre-British days, though this was scarcely possible over the whole country. Failure of the monsoon has from time to time led to severe famines. They have oc-

[39] Moreland, *India at Death of Akbar*, 102, 104. More detailed survey in Habib, *Agrarian System,* chap I.

curred not only in earlier days but several times during the British era. The last severe one took place in 1945. It is often claimed that the unpredictability of natural forces has made the Indian peasant passive and apathetic and prevented the transition to intensive peasant cultivation. I doubt this very much. China has been as much subject to intermittent famine as India, yet her peasants are universally praised for their energy and careful cultivation from quite early times.

By contrast, Indian practices appear wasteful and inefficient, even if one makes considerable allowance for ethnocentric bias in the early British accounts. Technology too seems to have been stagnant. Agricultural implements and techniques did not change significantly between Akbar's time and the early twentieth century.[40] A light plow, drawn by bullocks, was and remains today the most important implement. The cow has thus been a source of power, of food (not of course meat), and fuel, as well as an object of religious veneration.[41] The advantages of transplanting rice were known, at least in some areas, in the early part of the nineteenth century and very likely earlier. But, in contrast with Japan, the organization of the work was so poor that the cultivators obtained only limited benefits. "About half of the whole [crop] is finally transplanted in the first month of the season," Buchanan reported in 1809 – 1810 for one district in the northeast corner of Bengal, "and is extremely productive; five-eighths of the rest are transplanted in the second month and give an indifferent crop; and three-eighths are transplanted in the third month, making so mis-

---

[40] Moreland, *India at Death of Akbar*, 105 – 106.

[41] O'Malley, *Popular Hinduism*, 15, quotes the work of a modern Indian writer on the attitude towards the cow: "The cow is of all animals the most sacred. . . . All its excreta are hallowed. . . . The water it ejects ought to be preserved as the best of holy waters — a sin-destroying liquid which sanctifies everything it touches, while nothing purifies like cow dung. Any spot which a cow has condescended to honor with the sacred deposit of her excrement is forever afterwards sacred ground." The use of cow dung for fuel cannot simply be due to the shortage of wood, since it is used where other fuel is abundant. See Buchanan, *Bhagalpur*, 445. Since it burns very slowly and evenly, requiring little attention, practical advantages may actually be important in accounting for its widespread use down to the present day.

erable a return that the practice would seem to be bad economy, but the people would otherwise be idle."[42]

Buchanan, one of the few sources to give details on agricultural practices at this time, also tells us that, instead of rotating crops, the cultivators in this district often mixed several crops on the same field. This was a crude form of insurance: though none of the crops grew well, seldom did all of them fail.[43] In another district on the banks of the Ganges it was common practice, again in sharp contrast with Japan, to sow large quantities of seed broadcast on dry earth without previous preparation of the soil, a practice he also noticed in the area just mentioned.[44] Throughout Buchanan's reports there runs the same theme of inefficient cultivation and low productivity that occurs in the earlier French accounts of the situation under the Moguls.

It is quite possible that the relative abundance of land may have been an important cause of both poor cultivation and the character of peasant opposition through much of Indian history prior to the British. Land in many places was plentiful and waiting for men with resources to cultivate it. Peasants, as we saw, often responded to an oppressive ruler simply by absconding en masse. In the words of a recent authority flight was "the first answer to famine or man's oppression."[45] Oppression and abundant land interacting with each other in this way account quite well for the wide areas of uncultivated and badly cultivated land that occur very frequently in the accounts of late Mogul and early British times.

[42] *Purnea*, 345. Buchanan was a doctor and a shrewd observer who did not accept uncritically whatever the Indians told him but tried to cross check the accounts wherever possible. He was also a man free of the grosser sorts of national prejudice. His detailed observations made in parts of both northern and southern India inspire considerable confidence. His full name was Francis Hamilton Buchanan; it appears that some of his work was published under the name of Francis Buchanan Hamilton.

[43] Buchanan, *Purnea*, 343.

[44] *Bhagalpur*, 410 – 412.

[45] Habib, *Agrarian System*, 117; see also Moreland, *Agrarian System*, xii, 161 – 163, 165, 169, 171. Flight to a forest area, however, involved huge difficulties of reclamation. See on this Baden-Powell, *Village Community*, 50 – 51.

Though very important, this explanation is nevertheless insufficient. Parts of India, such as the western Gangetic plain, may have been just as full of people in Akbar's time as in the earlier decades of the twentieth century. Furthermore, cultivation remained poor over wide areas of the country after land had become scarce. Such facts lead to the suspicion that social arrangements on the land also have an important part to play in the explanation.

One of these has already been mentioned, the Indian system of taxation. Like his counterpart in Japan, the Indian peasant was to the ruling classes mainly a producer of revenue. The Japanese tax, we saw, was a fixed assessment on the land, enabling energetic peasants to keep a surplus. Mogul and Indian taxation was mainly a fixed proportion of the crop. Thus in India the more the peasant grew, the more he had to turn over to the tax collector. Furthermore the Mogul system of tax farming contained a built-in temptation to squeeze the peasants heavily. Very likely this difference had a decisive influence on the character of the peasantry in the two countries. This situation, we know, had prevailed in India for a very long time. The headman, or in some areas a council of village notables, generally acted as collectors of the revenue, apportioning the amounts to be collected and the lands to be cultivated among the inhabitants. Though the headman or the council acted as a buffer between authority and the village in a way that resembles the system in Japan, there was in India much less tendency for the overlord to try to supervise what took place inside the village. Keeping peace and order was left almost entirely to village notables and the headman as long as the revenue was forthcoming.[46]

The organization of labor in the Indian peasant community also differed from that in Japan in a manner that helps to explain the relatively low level of cultivation. Here we encounter directly the caste system, which will shortly require fuller discussion. For the moment it is enough to recall that the Japanese system before it began to change in late Tokugawa times was based mainly on pseudo-kinship ties. The Indian one was based instead on the exchange of

[46] Spear, *Twilight of the Mughuls*, 123–124; Moreland, *Agrarian System*, 162, 203; Baden-Powell, *Village Community*, 13, 23–24; Habib, *Agrarian System*, 185.

labor and services for food between castes who had land and those who had little or none. Though closer to the modern system of hired labor, the Indian arrangement too was supported by custom and what we can loosely call traditional sentiments. It appears to have had some of the disadvantages of both customary systems based on emotional loyalties and modern ones without their respective advantages, and to have inhibited both changes in the division of labor and its intensive application to a specific task. On account of the flexibility of caste in actual practice, it would be unwise to press this point too far, though the tendency seems clear. Close supervision in the modern fashion was difficult. So was the cooperation found in many tightly knit traditional work groups. Most Indian laborers were at the very bottom of the caste system and in large measure excluded from the village community, as shown by the designation "untouchable." Strikes of the modern sort, the untouchables scarcely knew, partly because laborers were broken up into different castes, but "dilution of labor they understood," as a modern authority puts it.[47] This was one of the reasons for lackadaisical cultivation. Another was the fact that higher castes often preferred smaller returns, with less trouble and supervision, to standing over workers and trying to compel them to improve their ways.

A few words of caution are in order before going further into the question of caste and its political implications. At least in its full ramifications, the caste system is unique to Indian civilization. For this reason there is a strong temptation to use caste as an explanation for everything else that seems distinctive in Indian society. Obviously this will not do. For example, caste in older studies has been used to explain the apparent absence of religious warfare in India. Yet in modern times — not to mention Hindu resistance to Moslem proselytism in earlier days — religious warfare has taken on terrible proportions while caste has remained. Caste, and the theory of reincarnation, which forms an important part of caste doctrines, has also been used to explain the apparent political docility of the Indian peasants, the feebleness of the revolutionary upsurge in modern times. Yet we have seen that this upsurge was an important

[47] Spear, *Twilight of the Mughuls,* 120.

component in the forces that brought down the Mogul edifice. Nor is it altogether absent in later days. Still the overall evidence of submissiveness remains overwhelming. That caste has played a part in creating and supporting this behavior I see no sense in denying. Rather, the problem is to understand the mechanisms that produced passive acceptance.

The standard explanation runs about as follows. According to the theory of reincarnation, a person who obeyed the requirements of caste etiquette in this life would be born into a higher caste in the next. Submissiveness in this life was to be rewarded by a rise in the social scale in the next. This explanation requires us to believe that the ordinary Indian peasants accepted the rationalizations put forth by urban priestly classes. Perhaps the Brahmans did succeed in this way to some extent. But it can only be a small part of the story. As far as it is possible to recover the attitude of the peasants toward the Brahmans, it is fairly clear that the peasants did not passively and wholeheartedly accept the Brahman as a model of all that was good and desirable. Their attitude toward the monopolist of supernatural power seems to have been a mixture of admiration, fear, and hostility, much like that of many French peasants toward the Catholic priest. "There are three blood suckers in this world," runs a North Indian proverb, "the flea, the bug, and the Brahman."[48] Since the Brahman exacted payment for his services to the village, there were good reasons for this hostility. "The farmer does not reap his harvest without paying the Brahman to perform some ceremony; a tradesman cannot begin a business without a fee to a Brahman, a fisherman cannot build a new boat nor begin to fish . . . without a ceremony and a fee."[49] Secular sanctions were obviously part of the caste system. And in a general way we know that human attitudes and beliefs fail to persist unless the situations and sanctions that reproduce them continue to persist or, more crassly, unless people get something out of them. To these concrete supports we must obviously turn if we are to understand caste.

The first of these was and remains the ownership of land. The universal superiority of the Brahman is a priestly fiction that does

[48] O'Malley, *Popular Hinduism,* 190 – 191.
[49] Kaye, *Sepoy War,* I, 182 – 183.

not correspond to the workings of the caste system now and probably has not done so for ages. In modern villages the economically dominant group is also the dominant caste. In one village it may be the Brahmans, in another a peasant caste. Even where the Brahmans are on top, it is because of their economic function, not their priestly one.[50] Thus we see that caste has had and still has an economic base and a religious explanation and that the fit between the two has for long been far from perfect. The caste that holds the land in a particular locality — and caste is a reality only in its local manifestation — is the highest caste. To argue backward from a modern situation is, of course, not altogether safe. Before British influence made itself felt very widely and when land was in present-day terms abundant, the economic basis was perhaps less crassly obvious. Nevertheless it was there. The evidence is clear, even for earlier times, that the higher castes often held the best land and could command the labor of the lower castes.[51]

The main formal instrument for the enforcement of caste

[50] For the wide variety of occupations in which Brahmans were found in the late eighteenth and early nineteenth centuries, see the account by the Abbé Dubois, *Hindu Manners*, I, 295; for later times Senart, *Caste*, 35 – 36.

[51] See, for example, Buchanan, *Purnea*, 360, 429 – 430, 439. Bailey, *Caste and the Economic Frontier*, reports that in former times in this part of Orissa the warrior-joint families had outcaste client families that performed agricultural labor. The Abbé Dubois, *Hindu Manners*, I, 55, 57, 58, reports a form of serfdom verging on slavery among the outcastes, though he says that it had become relatively rare in his day.

Patel, *Agricultural Laborers in Modern India and Pakistan*, 9, claims that the traditional Indian community lacked any distinct class of agricultural laborers. His main evidence comes from Campbell, *Modern India*, 65 and a citation from Sir Thomas Munro taken from a modern Indian work. I believe that this claim represents an instance of the Indian nationalist tendency to idealize the pre-British period. Buchanan found agricultural laborers in many parts of southern India. See his *Journey from Madras*, I, 124, II, 217, 315, III, 398, 454 – 455. Slaves were common enough to have their absence specifically noticed in one part of his *Journey from Madras*, III, 398. Agricultural laborers as a distinct class turn up very frequently in his detailed reports on three northern districts. See *Purnea*, 119, 123, 162 – 164, 409, 429, 433, 443 – 446; *Bhagalpur*, 193, 423, 460, 468; *Shahabad*, 343, and others that I did not trouble to note. See also on this question Moreland, *India at Death of Akbar*, 90 – 91, 112 – 114; Habib, *Agrarian System*, 120.

regulations was and remains the caste councils, composed of a small group of leaders chosen from the members of each caste in all of the villages inhabiting a certain area. In some parts of India one finds a hierarchy of these councils. The council controls only the behavior of the members of its own caste. Presumably the geographical area for which each caste had a council was smaller in older times than at present, due to the greater difficulties in transportation. Nor is it always true that each caste had a council; on this score there was considerable local variation depending on local conditions. It is also important to notice that there was no such thing as a council for the caste as a whole throughout India.[52] Caste manifests itself strictly on the local level. Even in the village there is really no central organization with the task of seeing to it that the caste system as such remains in force, i.e., that members of the lower castes display the proper deference toward members of the higher ones. The lower castes disciplined themselves. Members of the lower castes had to learn to accept their place in the social order. On this score, the leaders of the lower castes evidently had an important task to perform. For doing so they received quite concrete rewards. Sometimes they received commissions on the wages of laborers from their castes as well as fines for any transgressions of caste regulations.[53]

The penalty for severe breaches of caste discipline was boycott, that is, denial of the facilities of the village community. In a society where the individual depended almost entirely on these facilities, the organized pattern of cooperation among his fellows, such a penalty was terrible indeed. In due course we shall see how the advent of the modern world has partly mitigated the impact of these sanctions.

What exactly did this system enforce? Quite obviously a local division of labor and a corresponding distribution of authority and power. But it evidently did a great deal more than this. In pre-British Indian society, and still today in much of the countryside,

---

[52] Caste councils are usually described in any detailed local account. See also Blunt, "Economic Aspect of the Caste System," in Mukerjee, *Economic Problems*, I, 69.

[53] Buchanan, *Bhagalpur*, 281–282.

the fact of being born in a particular caste determined for the individual the entire span of existence, quite literally from before conception until after death. It gave the range of choice for a marital partner in the case of parents, the type of upbringing the offspring would have and their choice of mate in marriage, the work he or she could legitimately undertake, the appropriate religious ceremonies, food, dress, rules of evacuation (which were very important), down to most details of daily living, all organized around a conception of disgust.[54]

Without this universal supervision and indoctrination it is difficult to imagine how and why the lower castes would accept caste in a way that would make it work without more centrally organized sanctions. It seems to me that its diffuseness and the fact that it extended beyond the areas Westerners consider to be economic and political, even in a broad and loose sense, constituted the essence of caste. Human beings in a wide variety of civilizations have an observable tendency to establish "artificial" distinctions, that is, those that are not derived from the necessities of a rational division of labor or a rational organization of authority, using rational here in the very restricted sense of providing effective social mechanism for performing an immediately given task in such a way as to enable the group to survive. Children elaborate artificial distinctions all the time in Western society. So do aristocrats when freed from the necessities of ruling. Indeed the need to perform a particular task may break down artificial distinctions: military etiquette in the field is generally much less elaborate than it is at headquarters. The reason for this tendency toward snobbishness — highly developed in some of the most "primitive" societies — is not easy to perceive.[55] Though I cannot prove it, I suspect that one of the few lasting and dependable sources of human satisfaction is making other people suffer and that this constitutes the ultimate cause.

Whatever the origins may be, the fact that in India caste served to organize so wide a range of human activities has had, I would urge, profound political consequences. As a system that arranges

[54] See Hutton, *Caste*, 79.
[55] See Lévi-Strauss, *Pensée sauvage*, 117 – 119.

life effectively in a specific locality, caste spells indifference to national politics. Government above the village was an excrescence generally imposed by an outsider, not a necessity; something to be borne with patience, not something to be changed when the world is obviously out of joint. Because it had really nothing to do in the village where caste took care of everything, government may have seemed especially predatory. The government was not necessary to keep order. Its role in the maintenance of irrigation systems, *pace* Marx, was quite minor.[56] Again these were often quite local affairs. The structural contrast with China is quite striking. There the imperial bureaucracy gave cohesion to the society and was what had to be changed when the villagers suffered prolonged disaster. Even so, to put the contrast that way remains on the surface. In China the local gentry needed the imperial bureaucracy as a mechanism for obtaining the economic surplus out of the peasantry that supported their position locally and nationally. At the local level such an arrangement was unnecessary in India. Caste regulations took its place. Where he existed, the *zamindar* had won an accepted place in the local scheme of things. He did not need the central government to help him extract his perquisites from the peasantry. Thus the character of the two systems meant that peasant opposition would take different forms in each. In China the main thrust was to replace a "bad" government by a "good" one of the same character; in India it was much more toward getting rid of government above the villages altogether. And in India for the most part we can scarcely speak of a strong thrust in any sense but, rather, a general direction to affairs imposed by the character of the society. By and large, government was more superfluous than actively resisted, though at times resistance occurred as well.

Because caste has embraced such a wide range of human behavior, there has also been a strong tendency in Indian society for opposition to the prevailing order to take the form of just another caste. It appears quite strikingly in the case of the criminal castes, notably the Thugs from whom the English word has come, which were so troublesome to the British in the first half of the nineteenth

[56] Habib, *Agrarian System*, 256.

century.[57] Similarly since caste was expressed very heavily in religious ritual, opposition to the oppressive features of caste was likely to be absorbed into the system in the form of an additional caste. Partly this was true because there was no religious hierarchy comparable to that of Roman Catholicism, indeed no very specific orthodoxy that could present a specific target. Thus caste was and indeed remains tremendously persistent and tremendously flexible, in its concrete manifestation, a huge mass of locally coordinated social cells that tolerate novelty by generating another cell. This was the fate that awaited foreign conquerors, as in the caste of Islam, and even of Europeans. These too became to all intents and purposes a separate caste, though their rating on the scale of disgust was opposite to that on the scale of political power. Somewhere I have read that good Hindus in early British times always used to take a thorough bath to wash away pollution after having dealings with an Englishman.

Opposition to the hierarchical system as such, however, was relatively rare even in a veiled form. Much more frequent in British times and very likely earlier has been the attempt by a caste as a whole to struggle up to a higher rung on the ladder of esteem and disgust by persuading its members to adopt the proper (i.e., Brahman) diet, occupation, and marital practices. To be able to burn widows was a decisive sign that a caste had arrived socially. By providing a form of collective upward mobility that required strict discipline and adherence to norms set by the upper castes, Indian society further limited the possibility of political opposition. Thus the system emphasized the individual's duty to caste, not individual rights against society. What rights there were against society tended to be group rights, those of the caste.[58] In the willing acceptance of personal degradation by its victims and the absence of a specific target for hostility, a specific locus of responsibility for misery, the

[57] They remained widespread down to quite recent times, and many, as far as my knowledge goes, still exist. For an interesting modern sketch see Blunt, *Caste System of Northern India*, 158.

[58] Cf Brown, "Traditions of Leadership," in Park and Tinker, eds, *Leadership and Political Institutions*, 7.

Indian caste system strikes a modern Westerner as a curiously intensified caricature of the world as Kafka saw it. To some extent these negative features may be the consequence of distortions introduced into Hindu society by the British occupation. Even if this is so, it is a distortion of features that were present before the British ever appeared, and their character is no small part of the cause of subsequent misery.

To sum up, at least provisionally and very tentatively, I would suggest that, as an organization of labor, caste in the countryside was a cause of poor cultivation, though certainly not the only one. Furthermore, as the organization of authority in the local community, caste seems much more clearly to have inhibited political unity. By its very flexibility Indian society seems to have rendered fundamental change very difficult. Still, it was not impossible. Indeed the new conquerors that replaced the Moguls were to plant seeds whose fruit neither they nor others could have guessed.

4. Changes Produced by the British up to 1857

One cannot discuss the impact of the British on Indian society as if it were the result of a uniform cause operating continuously over more than three centuries. British society and the character of the British who went to India changed enormously between Elizabethan times and the twentieth century. Some of the most significant alterations took place roughly during the century 1750 – 1850. In the middle of the eighteenth century the British were still organized for commerce and plunder in the Honorable East India Company and controlled no more than a small fraction of Indian territory. By the middle of the nineteenth century they had become in effect the rulers of India, organized in a bureaucracy proud of its tradition of justice and fair dealing. From the standpoint of modern sociological theories of bureaucracy, it is almost impossible to see how the change could have taken place since the historical raw materials were so unpromising: a company of merchants not too easily distinguished from pirates on the one hand, and a series of decaying Oriental despotisms on the other. One may legitimately press the sociological and historical paradox even further: from this equally unpromising amalgam there eventually emerged a state with valid claims to democracy!

On the British side of this strange mixture, the course of development was in very broad outline the following. In Elizabethan times, the British came to India for a combination of adventure, reasons of state, commerce, and plunder: motives and causes that were really indistinguishable during that burst of energy released all over Europe by the decay of the traditional Christian medieval civilization and the rise of a new and much more secular one. Though there were big fortunes to be made in India, it soon became apparent that a territorial base would be necessary. If one wanted to buy pepper or indigo, the only way to get it at a reasonable price was to leave a man on the spot to bargain for it at harvest time when prices dropped and to store it until a ship arrived. From depots and forts established for such reasons, the British began to range further back into the countryside, buying indigo, opium, jute, getting prices under their control in order to be able to trade. Since the behavior of native authorities seemed erratic and unpredictable, the tendency to seize more of the elements of real power was strong: likewise, of course, the tendency to oust other European rivals. Meanwhile, as we saw, the Mogul system was in full decay. After Clive's victory at Arcot in 1751, the Great Mogul was reduced to the character of a spectacle; Clive's victory at Plassey in 1757 ended the prospect of French hegemony. There was a defensive element, if not absentmindedness, in the British acquisition of empire: the Portuguese and the French were intriguing with native rulers to oust them. The British responded by counterattacks. In extending their territorial foothold, they seized the revenues of conquered sovereigns, thus forcing the Indians to pay in very substantial measure for their own conquest. As they acquired greater territorial responsibilities, they gradually transformed themselves from commercial plunderers to more pacific rulers seeking to establish peace and order with the very small forces at their disposal. Essentially the acquisition of territorial responsibility was the key to the whole process and to their transformation into a bureaucracy that, to be sure, owed something to English notions of justice but also showed striking resemblances to Akbar's political arrangements.[59] Down to the present day these resemblances have by no means disappeared.

Such then, if in sketchy outline, was the evolution of the British from piracy to bureaucracy. Three interrelated consequences for Indian society followed: the beginnings of an abortive commercialization of agriculture through the establishment of law and order, regular taxes, and property in the countryside; secondly, the partial destruction of rural handicrafts, and, finally, an unsuccessful attempt to throw off the British yoke in the Mutiny of 1857. In turn these three processes set the basic framework for what has taken place down to the present day.

Let us start with taxes, unravelling the connections from there. By the end of the eighteenth century, the older notions of making a fortune as quickly as possible and clearing out for home had largely died out among responsible British officials. In their efforts to establish a settled form of government there is no indication that they had the intention of bleeding the country as much as possible. Nevertheless, their primary interest was exactly what Akbar's had been, getting a source of revenue that would support their government, without creating dangerous unrest. A little later there were some who thought that India might become in a short time another England and a huge market for English goods. But among the English in India itself, this was a quite minor current. Commercial motives will not do as the main explanation for the British remaining in India once they had acquired a substantial foothold. The real one is probably much simpler. To pull out, which as far as I am aware was never seriously considered, would have been to acknowledge defeat without having been defeated. And, if they were to stay, they would have to find a workable basis for doing so, which meant collecting taxes.

The decisions about how taxes were to be assessed and col-

[59] For the whole process sketched above, see Woodruff, *Founders*, pt I, and chap 1 of pt II. Though the treatment is biographical, and even anecdotal, it is extremely good reading, and the main points gradually emerge. *Cambridge History of India*, V, 141 – 180 gives useful additional details at times, but is hard to follow. Spear, *Twilight of the Mughuls*, is a first-rate analysis, mainly of the late eighteenth-century situation near Delhi.

lected are known to students of Indian affairs as "settlements," a term that at first seems rather curious. Nevertheless, it is a very appropriate one since decisions about how to collect the revenue were indeed attempts to "settle" a complicated series of problems in such a way that the native inhabitants would go about their affairs peaceably. The actual settlements were the outcome of British policy and preconceptions as well as the structure of Indian society and immediate political situations in a particular area. All these factors varied substantially in both time and place.[60] Because some of the main differences became less and less important under the unifying impact of the British occupations as deeper economic and social trends worked themselves out during the rest of the nineteenth century and the first half of the twentieth, there is no need to examine them in detail. What is important for this inquiry is their place in the general course of Indian social developments. Very briefly, the settlements were the starting point of a whole process of rural change whereby the imposition of law and order and associated rights of property greatly intensified the problem of parasitic landlordism. More significant still they formed the basis of a political and economic system in which the foreigner, the landlord, and the moneylender took the economic surplus away from the peasantry, failed to invest it in industrial growth and thus ruled out the possibility of repeating Japan's way of entering the modern era. There were, of course, other obstacles too, and perhaps even other possible ways that India might have found to enter the modern era. But the agrarian system that emerged from this fusion of British administration and Indian rural society was enough to eliminate decisively the Japanese alternative.

[60] For a detailed analysis of the English preconceptions, see Stokes, *English Utilitarians,* pt II. When Baden-Powell, toward the end of the nineteenth century took up the task of presenting these systems of revenue collection with a minimum of background information in a form suitable for British administrators, he found three fat volumes barely adequate for the task. See his *Land Systems.* I have followed mainly this work in the sketch that follows. Stokes, *English Utilitarians,* 105, suggests that at times Baden-Powell overdoes the empirical aspects of British procedure; without knowing the subject in enough detail to pass firm judgment I find that Stokes's discussion overdoes the influence of English theories.

The first, and historically the most important of the settlements was the Permanent Settlement (also known as the *zamindari* settlement) put into effect in Bengal in 1793. On the British side it was an attempt to retain the income but to get out from under the difficulties of administering a complicated native system of taxation that they barely understood. Also it was a curious effort to introduce onto the Indian social scene the enterprising landlord who was then at the height of his importance as an influence for "progress" in the English countryside. The important feature on the Indian side was Mogul administrative practice utilizing *zamindars*, the native tax-collecting officials standing between the ruler and the peasant, as we have seen. When the Mogul system was working properly, a *zamindar* was not, formally at least, a property owner. As it declined he took over *de facto* possession in somewhat the same way as did a twentieth-century Chinese warlord. The British Governor-General, Lord Cornwallis, thought he saw in the *zamindar* a social specimen that conceivably might turn into an enterprising English landlord who would clear the country and establish prosperous cultivation if he were given the assurance that in the future he would not be taxed out of existence for his pains, as he certainly would have been under the Moguls. This was the source of the English insistence on making the settlement permanent. Under the new government the *zamindar* received a property right that promised to be stable. At the same time he remained a tax collector as he had been under the Moguls. By the terms of the Permanent Settlement, the British took nine-tenths of the revenue that the *zamindar* received from his peasant tenants, leaving to the *zamindars* the remaining tenth "for their trouble and responsibility."[61] Though the legal skeleton of the Permanent Settlement proved to deserve its name rather more than most human creations — it lasted until 1951 — its consequences were a sharp disappointment for the hopes of its founders. At first the British pitched the assessments too high and turned out those *zamindars* who failed to

[61] Baden-Powell, *Land Systems*, I, 401 – 402, 432 – 433; Griffiths, *British Impact on India*, 170 – 171; Gopal, *Permanent Settlement in Bengal*, 17 – 18. Habib, *Agrarian System*, points out strong precedents in local Mogul practice in Bengal.

bring in the revenues. As a result many *zamindars* lost their lands to be replaced by what we would now call collaborators. "Respectable natives" was the term that came into use among the British. By the middle of the nineteenth century, that is, shortly before the Sepoy Mutiny, about forty percent of the land in important parts of the permanently settled area had changed hands in this fashion.[62] Dispossessed *zamindars* were among the important causes of the Mutiny, while the newly established ones were a storm anchor for the British power. In turn the latter turned in large numbers into parasitic landlords as the rise in population drove up rents in the course of the nineteenth century, while their tax burden remained fixed.

It is important to recognize that in Bengal and the Permanent Settlement, British policy merely accelerated and intensified the trend toward parasitic landlordism. It did not create this new social specimen. A most instructive account of Bengal in the year 1794, shows very plainly that the main blights on Indian agrarian society (the same ones that receive heavy emphasis in twentieth-century descriptions) all antedate the British era.[63] These were indolent landlords, the multiple layering of tenant rights, and a class of propertyless laborers. A market economy had rendered these problems moderately acute in the heavily populated river valleys. In interior portions away from the market, they were much less severe. There the landlord had not yet emerged from the tax-gathering official. In Buchanan's three-volume account of a journey through Madras, I came upon no sign that the landlord had become parasitic in the eyes of the natives or the British. There was but a slight problem of debt. Though agricultural laborers and even slaves did exist in some areas, one could scarcely speak of an agricultural proletariat.[64]

Southern India is the part of the country in which the other main form of settlement came to prevail widely. This one is known

[62] Cohn, "Initial British Impact on India," 424–431.

[63] Sir Henry Thomas Colebrooke, *Remarks on the Husbandry and Internal Commerce of Bengal*, 30, 64, 92–93, 96–97.

[64] See Buchanan, *Journey from Madras*, on markets and commerce: I, 19, 39, 40, 265–266; II, 452, 459; on the overlord: I, 2–3, 124, 298; II, 67, 187–188, 213, 296, 477; III, 88 and index s.v. *ganda;* on peasants and land: I, 271; II, 309; III, 34, 385, 427–428. His account appeared in 1807.

as *ryotwari* (from *ryot*, also spelled in other ways, meaning cultivator) because the revenues were collected directly from the peasants instead of through intermediaries. In some areas this had been a Mogul practice as well. Unhappy experience with the Permanent Settlement, a considerable dose of paternalism, plus English economic notions about the desirability of a vigorous peasantry and the alleged parasitic character of their own landlords, expressed notably in Ricardo's theory of rent, helped to produce this result as well as to avoid making the rates permanent. More important, it seems to me, was the fact that in the Madras area, where the model was put into effect in 1812, there were no *zamindars* with whom to effect a settlement. This situation came about mainly because the local chieftains made the mistake in this area of opposing the British, who destroyed them while pensioning off a few.[65] From the standpoint of the present inquiry the main significance of the *ryotwari* settlement is negative: it did not prevent the emergence of parasitic landlordism which in due time became as much of a problem in many parts of southern India as it did in the North. As already indicated, although the differences among the various types of settlement bulk large in the contemporary literature and in more recent historical accounts, in the not so long run these differences tended to even out as the overall effect of security for property and a rising population made themselves felt.

Peace and property were then, broadly speaking, the first gift of British dominion that would set in motion slowly fermenting changes in the villages of the subcontinent. The second gift was the product of England's industrial revolution: textiles that from about 1814 to 1830 flooded much of the Indian countryside and destroyed a section of the native handicrafts. Those who bore the brunt of the suffering were the town weavers who produced goods of high quality or else villages, especially in Madras, that had come to specialize in textiles for the market. The ordinary village weaver who turned out coarse goods for local consumption was relatively unaffected. Indirect effects there were in forcing the town weavers back on the land and diminishing the opportunities for urban em-

[65] *Cambridge History of India*, V, 473, 463; Baden-Powell, *Land Systems*, III, 11, 19, 22.

ployment.[66] Though the impact on Indian society seems to have been most severe in the 1830s, the import of textiles continued through the nineteenth century. British officials in charge of Indian affairs defended Indian interests vigorously but unsuccessfully.[67] Ironically enough, the statements by English officials collected in the work of an Indian official and scholar, Romesh Dutt, appear to be the origin of the thesis, shared by Indian nationalists and Marxists, that India was a manufacturing nation whom the British reduced to an agricultural one for selfish imperialist reasons. In this bald form, the thesis is nonsense. Handicrafts were destroyed, not manufactures in the modern sense, and India at the time of booming handicrafts was still overwhelmingly an agricultural nation. Furthermore the destruction took place long before the development of modern monopoly capitalism. But it is not enough to dismiss the thesis in this offhand manner. The suffering was no less real even if mistaken theoretical inferences have been drawn from it. And it is also true, as we shall see in due course, that the British did to some extent oppose industrial development in India.

Between taxes and textiles enough of a shock was administered to Indian rural society — and most of the society was, of course, rural — to make the Mutiny seem to the modern historian quite comprehensible. The shocks did not end with those just sketched so briefly. Certain further ones along the same lines were among the important immediate causes of the outbreak. In the northern and western parts of India, a form of land settlement intermediate between the *zamindari* and *ryotwari* came into effect by 1833. Wherever possible, it favored corporate village groups rather than landlords, making these groups jointly responsible to the government for the revenue.[68] Similar events took place in the state of Oudh. There the British ousted the native landed élite, a variety of tax farmers who collected the revenue from the villages and lived

[66] Gadgil, *Industrial Evolution*, 37, 43, 45; Anstey, *Economic Development*, 146, 205, 208; Raju, *Economic Conditions in Madras*, 164, 175, 177, 181. See also Dutt, *India in the Victorian Age*, for much interesting concrete material now largely inaccessible, esp 101, 105 – 106, 108, 112.

[67] See the material in Dutt, cited above, and Woodruff, *Guardians*, 91.

[68] Baden-Powell, *Land Systems*, II, 21; see also Woodruff, *Founders*, 293 – 298, 301.

on the difference between what they collected and what they passed on to the native government. Oudh was also a rich center of recruitment for the soldiers of the Bengal army, who received a severe shock in learning that the British had annexed their country.[69] The final and immediate source of the outbreak was the famous greased-cartridge rumor that the new rifle required the soldier to bite cartridges deliberately polluted by grease from pigs and cows.

The liquidation of the landed élite in Oudh has, with other facts, inclined many writers to hold that the resentment of the landed élite was a main cause of the Mutiny and to contrast a reforming pro-peasant British policy prior to the Mutiny with a more conservative policy favorable to the landed élite after the Mutiny.[70] This seems to be another instance of a slightly exaggerated partial truth that obscures a more important and wider truth. There is rather more continuity to both the causes and the effects of British policy than such an interpretation reveals. A paternal attitude toward the peasantry, a romantic and self-serving notion that the strong and simple folk could and should be the source and justification of their power, constituted a powerful theme in British policy throughout the occupation, even if peasant benefits therefrom are dubious.

Although class relationships in the countryside were very important, they fail to make sense until they are set against a larger background. Agrarian conditions, especially in India, cannot be separated out from caste and religion as they all together formed a single institutional complex. The main cleavage in Indian society that the Mutiny revealed was one between a deeply offended orthodoxy supported through definite material interests and a luke-

[69] Chattopadhyaya, *Sepoy Mutiny*, 94–95. Metcalf, "Influence of the Mutiny," is a very illuminating article, though I feel that the author overemphasizes the contrast between British policies before and after the Mutiny.

[70] See Metcalf, "Influence of the Mutiny," for a good modern statement of the thesis; Kaye, *Sepoy War*, I, chap IV for a good older version of the view that resentment among the landed upper classes brought on the Mutiny.

warm attitude among those who either gained by British policy or were not too deeply disturbed by it. This cleavage cut across religious lines and to some extent material ones as well. Hindus and Moslems were on both sides in large numbers.[71] And in Oudh the peasants rose with their former masters to present a united opposition to British intrusion. Hence it seems fair to conclude that *whatever* the British did or tried to do — and as we have seen they did quite different things in different places and at different times — they were likely to stir up a hornet's nest. By and large as conquerors with only small forces at their command they tried to do no more than seemed absolutely necessary. The "reforms" of the era prior to the Mutiny were minimal.

At a deeper level of causation, the Mutiny shows how the intrusion of the West, with its stress on commerce and industry, its secular and scientific attitude towards the physical world, its emphasis on demonstrable competence in a job rather than on inherited status, posed a fundamental threat to Indian society. Together and separately, these features were incompatible with an agrarian civilization organized around caste and its religious sanctions. The English had proceeded rather gingerly. Those on the spot in India had little desire to make trouble for themselves by imposing their own social structure *en bloc*, introducing reforms only for the sake of commercial tranquillity, to provide material support for their own presence, or at a few points where Indian customs deeply offended British consciences.

One of the latter was *sati* (also spelled *suttee*), the term for the custom of burning or otherwise killing a widow as soon as her husband died. It revolted many British. In Bengal generally a widow "was usually tied to the corpse, often already putrid; men

---

[71] Chattopadhyaya, *Sepoy Mutiny*, 100 – 101. Some of the older British writers put the main blame for the Mutiny on the Moslems and have even held that it was a last-ditch attempt to restore the Mogul Empire, a view that attributes too much of a definite plan to what was a chaotic and in some areas a genuine, spontaneous uprising. However, the Mutiny was mainly confined to the Moslem area in northern India. See the interesting map, showing the main centers of the Mutiny in Chattopadhyaya, *Sepoy Mutiny*, facing 28, and his discussion on 150 – 153.

stood by with poles to push her back in case the bonds should burn through and the victim, scorched and maimed, should struggle free."[72] In the vast majority of cases, at least in the eighteenth and nineteenth centuries, the woman went to the flames in fear and horror. Many people know the remark of one famous British officer in the 1840s, in reply to Brahmans who argued that *sati* was a national custom: "My nation also has a custom. When men burn women alive, we hang them. . . . Let us all act according to national customs."[73] Such a custom might indeed test the beliefs of even the most firm present-day believer in the equal worth of all cultures. For a long time the British avoided taking more than sporadic action against *sati* for fear of arousing native hostility. Not until 1829 was it formally abolished in the main areas under British control.[74] That, however, was not the end of the story; nor is it altogether ended yet. I am told by those who know India that scattered instances of *sati* still take place.

Official British policies toward religion were enough to alarm the orthodox, both Hindu and Moslem, despite their contradictory character. (In this connection it is important to recall that even a small amount of empirical science was a threat to the priest who was source and sanction for native arts and charged fees for their use.) On the one hand, the British government spent large sums of money each year for the maintenance of mosques and temples. On the other hand, they permitted and in some local instances even encouraged Christian missionaries on a substantial scale. The missionaries claim to have had 22 societies and 313 stations, though only 443 missionaries as such, in the year 1852.[75] Vernacular schools started by missionaries to teach girls how to read and write aroused fears that such skills would facilitate female intrigues and that any

[72] Woodruff, *Founders*, 255.

[73] The remark is attributed to Sir Charles Napier, conqueror of Sind in 1843, in Woodruff, *Founders*, 327.

[74] Woodruff, *Founders*, 257. Evidently the tolerant Akbar had also disliked the custom and likewise refrained from interfering. Woodruff here quotes him as remarking, "It is a strange commentary on the magnanimity of men that they should seek their deliverance through the self-sacrifice of their wives."

[75] Chattopadhyaya, *Sepoy Mutiny*, 37.

woman who learned to read and write would become a widow.[76] Along with the response to the burning of widows, such evidence hints that one of the important causes of Indian hatred of the British was that the Europeans interfered in several ways with the sexual and personal prerogatives of the male, which are very highly stressed in Hindu civilization, a fact that does not exclude the dominance of elderly females in many domestic situations. Furthermore the exigencies of British day-to-day activities in the army, the jails, and the railroad, just coming into use before the Mutiny, aroused fears that the British intended to destroy the backbone of Hindu society, the caste system. Just how deep Hindu sensibilities were and are on this score is very difficult to judge. Some contemporary episodes where castes were mingled without causing trouble suggest the possibility that Westerners may have tended to overestimate the importance of these sentiments.[77] Nevertheless, it is clear that the British intrusion as a whole had generated enough inflammable material to produce a conflagration once the match had been set to it.

Partly because the Mutiny had the character of a series of spontaneous combustions, the British were able to survive the conflagration. In several areas, especially central India, the population seems to have been ready to revolt but was kept in check by native authorities. A combination of the old élite in the form of native princes and the new élites that had grown up under British protection appear to have been the chief social forces helping the British. Mainly in the northwestern provinces and in Oudh, peasant sentiment allied with that of the dominant classes to produce a massive revolt.[78] At bottom the Mutiny was an attempt to restore an idealized *status quo* that supposedly existed before the British conquest. In this sense it was an out-and-out reactionary upheaval. The fact that it attracted widespread support from the population seems to

[76] Chattopadhyaya, *Sepoy Mutiny*, 33–34.

[77] See Kaye, *Sepoy War*, I, 195–196 on the elimination of separate cooking facilities for different castes in the jails; also the assertion that in the armies of Madras and Bombay soldiers in the ranks were above caste prejudices in Chattopadhyaya, *Sepoy Mutiny*, 37. But note the revealing rebel proclamation quoted on p. 103 in the latter work.

[78] Chattopadhyaya, *Sepoy Mutiny*, 95–97, 159–160.

contradict such an assessment but, instead, under the conditions of the times, reenforces it.[79]

With the English present as conquerors and the main carriers of the new civilization, it is difficult to see how the Mutiny could have been anything else. Its failure ruled out for India any prospect of developing along Japanese lines. In any case such a prospect was so remote that it scarcely deserves serious consideration. This is not because the foreigner had such a strong foothold. That the English might have been driven out does not seem foolish. The crux of the matter is that, in the Indian situation, the foreign presence imposed a reactionary solution. India was too divided, too amorphous, and too big to be unified on its own under dissident aristocratic auspices, with some help from the peasants, as happened in Japan. Over long centuries a society had grown up that rendered central authority in substantial measure superfluous, perhaps inherently predatory and parasitic. In the Indian situation, around the middle of the nineteenth century, dissident aristocrats and peasants could work together only through passionate hatred of modernization. They could not, as in Japan, use modernization to drive the foreigner away. Ninety more years were to pass before the British were to be driven out. Though new factors entered the situation in the meantime, the reactionary component in the effort to drive them out remained very powerful, enough to handicap very seriously subsequent efforts at becoming an industrial society.

5. Pax Britannica *1857 – 1947: A Landlord's Paradise?*

After suppressing the Mutiny, the British were able to impose upon India nearly a century of law and order and a fair facsimile of political unity. Political disturbances there were, which increased in number and intensity after the First World War, and in the end complete unity was not achieved. Despite these qualifications the years 1857 – 1947 were within India years of peace that present the sharpest possible contrast with the history of the rest of the world.

Its price is another matter. A policy of law and order favors

[79] For a contrary interpretation which has the merit of bringing out popular components, see Chaudhuri, *Civil Rebellion in the Indian Mutinies* chap VI.

those who already have privileges, including some whose privileges are not very large. Such was the consequence of British policy in India, though it set in motion, however slowly, other and deeper forces. British rule rested mainly on the Indian upper classes in the countryside, native princes and larger landowners in many, but not all, parts of the country. At the courts of the more important princes was a British resident adviser who controlled "foreign" relations and interfered in domestic affairs as little as possible. In areas under their own control the British worked mainly with whatever forces were in the ascendant after the Mutiny.[80]

Some major political consequences of the tendency to rely on the upper strata in the countryside deserve to be noticed right away, though they will require more detailed explanation later. This tendency alienated the commercial and professional classes, the new Indian bourgeoisie, as it slowly put in an appearance during the course of the nineteenth century. By splitting the landed upper classes from the weak and rising urban leaders, the English presence prevented the formation of the characteristic reactionary coalition on the German or Japanese model. This may be judged a decisive contribution toward the eventual establishment of a parliamentary democracy on Indian soil, at least as important as the osmosis of English ideas through Indian professional classes. Without at least some favorable structural conditions, the ideas could scarcely have been more than literary playthings. Finally, the British presence drove the Indian bourgeoisie to an accommodation with the peasantry in order to obtain a massive base. How this somewhat curious feat was performed and some of its consequences, we shall see in the next section.

In addition to law and order, the British introduced into Indian society during the nineteenth century railroads and a substantial amount of irrigation. The most important prerequisites for commercial agriculture and industrial growth would seem to have been present. Yet what growth there was turned out to be abortive and sickly. Why? A decisive part of the answer, I think, is that *pax Britannica* simply enabled the landlord and now also the money-

[80] For some enlightening contrasts due to local conditions, see Metcalf, "Struggle over Land Tenure," 295 – 308.

lender to pocket the economic surplus generated in the countryside that in Japan paid for the painful first stages of industrialization. As foreign conquerors, the English were not in India to make an industrial revolution. They were not the ones to tax the countryside in either the Japanese or the Soviet fashion. Hence beneath the protective umbrella of Anglo-Saxon justice-under-law, parasitic landlordism became much worse than in Japan.

To lay all the blame on British shoulders is obviously absurd. There is much evidence, discussed in the preceding section, to demonstrate that this blight was inherent in India's own social structure and traditions. Two centuries of British occupation merely allowed it to spread and root more deeply throughout Indian society. More specifically, *pax Britannica* allowed the population to rise and rents to increase as competition for land drove them up. Though the new legal and political framework of property rights enforceable in British courts played a part in providing the landlord with new weapons, it is likely that the landlord depended less on these to increase his revenues and more on traditional sanctions through caste and the organization of the village, at least until fairly recent times.

As key links in a complicated chain of historical causation that explains India's prolonged backwardness, I would suggest that this particular method of extracting the economic surplus in the countryside and the consequent failure of the state to direct this surplus toward industrial growth are more important than some of the other commonly advanced explanations — such as the workings of the caste system, the inertia of associated cultural traditions, the shortage of entrepreneurial talent, and the like. Though such factors have played their part, there are grounds for regarding them as derivative from the method of extracting the surplus discussed above. Even in the rural areas where caste is much stronger, caste barriers have shown strong indications of crumbling where, due to local conditions, there has been some impulse toward a more thorough-going market economy. By and large, caste seems to be maintained by the top layer of the village élite for their own benefit and for the reasons just indicated. All this I shall try to show in due course.

This interpretation may seem moderately convincing when set

out in rather broad strokes. As one tries to grapple with the details
of contradictory and fragmentary evidence, either of two things
may happen. The certainty may evaporate into a chaos of ill-
assorted facts, or else the evidence may be selected to produce an
argument that runs too smoothly to be true. There is not much that
any author can do about this situation that would persuade a really
convinced skeptic. Nevertheless it may be appropriate to mention
that at one point in the study of this period of Indian history I sus-
pected that the parasitic landlord might well be a legendary social
species created by Indian nationalist and semi-Marxist writers. It
took a good deal of evidence to convince me that he was real, the
more important of which I shall now try to relate.

Some exceptions to the generalization that India has experienced no commercial transformation in agriculture may be discussed with profit at the start. Although India did not turn into a
plantation colony, producing raw materials for export to more economically advanced countries, there were during the nineteenth
century and earlier a few limited starts in this direction. Indians had
carried on the cultivation of cotton since quite ancient times. Jute
had been grown for local use and became a commercial crop during
the second quarter of the nineteenth century. Tea (mainly in
Assam), pepper, and indigo complete the list. Arrangements for
growing them ranged from something close to a straightforward
plantation to agrarian forms of a putting-out system by which advances were made to small individual cultivators.[81]

In terms of area and number of people involved, this semiplan-
tation economy remained small. Otherwise the establishment of political democracy might have faced altogether insuperable obstacles.
After our study of the American South, this point requires no further laboring. A combination of foreign competition with geographical and social factors accounts moderately well for the failure
of the plantation system to achieve a dominant position in India. In-

---

[81] On pepper see the interesting discussion in Buchanan, *Journey from
Madras*, II, 455, 465 – 466, 523; Gadgil, *Industrial Evolution*, 48 – 50 for
indigo and other aspects of the plantation system. Anstey, *Economic Development*, 115, remarks that straightforward plantations were generally in
European hands.

dian cotton was unable to compete with American; possibly the smothering of native textiles prior to our Civil War contributed to this result, though that is doubtful. The discovery of synthetic dyes ruined the indigo trade. Jute was grown only in one area, Bengal and Assam, though the possibility of growing it in other places cannot be excluded. The main limitation seems to be a sociological one. The agrarian variation of the putting-out system is not very efficient because it is difficult to control the practices of numerous small cultivators. On the other hand, a straightforward plantation system employing servile or semiservile labor is likely to need an efficient repressive apparatus. To create one on any large scale was beyond British or Indian resources, increasingly so as time went on.

As British authority became firmly established, land began to take on some of the characteristics of a manufactured commodity as it has elsewhere in the world under similar conditions. If it could not be reproduced for sale in the market like pots and pans, at least it could be bought and sold. It acquired a value measurable in money, and, with the increasing pressure of population under conditions where property was secure, this value rose rather steadily. The rise became quite apparent to competent observers soon after the Mutiny. There are some good indications that the process had begun considerably beforehand. The Famine Commission of 1880 asserted that there was evidence of an increase in the price of land all over India during the preceding twenty years.[82] Sir Malcolm Darling gives some striking figures that illustrate this point, mainly from the Punjab, though the process took place all over India. Worth about 10 rupees an acre in 1866, land sold at an average of 238 rupees an acre in 1921 – 1926. During the depression there was a check: the figure only reached 241 rupees by 1940. In 1862 – 1863 the government had congratulated itself that the sale price of

[82] Great Britain, *Report of Famine Commission 1880*, II, 125. Great Britain, *Report of Commission on Agriculture in India 1928*, 9, states that the rise was apparent as early as the famine of 1837 – 1838. Evidence from the census about population growth does not begin until the first census of 1871, although it is almost certain that the rise began earlier. A chart of the increases by decades shows substantial rises only in alternate ten-year periods up until 1921, after which the rate accelerates steadily and rapidly. See Davis, *Population of India and Pakistan*, 26, 28.

land stood as high as 7 years' purchase of the land revenue. In 1930 the corresponding figure was 261.[83]

The partial intrusion of the market and the rise in land values brought about changes in the role of the moneylender, an important figure in the rural scene with whom it now becomes necessary to make our acquaintance. He had been there for a long time and is no new creation of British authority. There are indications that, within the pre-British village, economic exchanges took place with little or no use of cash. The caste of craftsmen still today in many parts of the country receives payment for its services in the form of a specified share of the crops. Even in Akbar's day, on the other hand, and no doubt much further back, taxes were widely paid in cash. Here the moneylender entered the village economy. Frequently he belonged to a special caste, though this was not universally the case. Many of the peasant's complaints about having to sell his produce at low prices after the harvest only to buy some back later under pressure of need and at high prices were familiar in Mogul times.[84] He performed two useful functions in the traditional economy. First he served as a crude balance wheel to even out periods of scarcity and prosperity. Except in cases of severe famine, the peasant could go to the moneylender for a loan of grain when his own supplies ran short. Secondly, he was the customary source of cash when the peasant needed money for taxes.[85] Naturally he did not perform these tasks without profit to himself. On the other hand, the traditional village community seems to have imposed limits to extortion that became less effective under later conditions.[86] At the same time the traditional sanctions of a close-knit community helped to guarantee the debt and enable the moneylender to advance considerable sums with a minimum of formal security.[87] The situation as a whole seems to have been at least mod-

[83] Darling, *Punjab Peasant*, 208.

[84] Moreland, *India at Death of Akbar*, 111 – 112; *Agrarian System*, ii, 126; *From Akbar to Aurangzeb*, 304. Darling, *Punjab Peasant*, 168 – 169, cites numerous areas where the moneylender was an important figure in pre-British times.

[85] Darling, *Punjab Peasant*, 6 – 7.

[86] Darling, *Punjab Peasant*, xxiii, 170.

[87] Darling, *Punjab Peasant*, 6 – 7, 167.

erately acceptable to all concerned; Hindu law, it is worth noticing, lacks the Western antagonism to the collection of interest.

Before the British appeared on the scene, the moneylender generally sought the peasant's crop, not the land, which was abundant and of little value without someone to cultivate it. This situation continued until well into the second half of the nineteenth century, that is, until land values began to rise and British protection of property through the courts began to take hold widely, a tendency strengthened by the Mutiny and subsequent increased reliance on men of substance and standing in the countryside.[88] At this point the moneylender began to change his tactics and sought to gain possession of the land itself, still leaving the peasant on it to cultivate it for him and produce a steady income.[89]

This situation was at its height between 1860 and 1880. In 1879 in the Deccan Agricultural Relief Act came the first attempt to limit the rights of transfer and to protect the peasant. Similar legislation was passed during the rest of the nineteenth century in other parts of India. The chief provision has been a prohibition on the transfer of land to noncultivating castes, in other words moneylenders. The main effect was to contract the already limited supply of credit for the peasant and to encourage the growth of a class of wealthy peasants within the cultivating castes who could lend to their less fortunate neighbors.[90] Though there are no statistics to indicate what proportion of the land formally passed out of the cultivator's hand and into those of the moneylender or rich peasant, it is clear from the Famine Report of 1880 that the problem was already serious and had taken the form that it was to display for many years to come.[91] In most parts of the country the moneylender belongs to a noncultivating caste and, in the Punjab, to the Hindu rather than the Muslim section of the population. For a long time the typical figure has remained the village shopkeeper. Hence the

---

[88] Metcalf, "British and the Moneylender," 295 – 307.

[89] Darling, *Punjab Peasant*, 180; Gadgil, *Industrial Evolution*, 166.

[90] Anstey, *Economic Development*, 186 –187; Gadgil, *Industrial Evolution*, 30 – 31, 164; Darling, *Punjab Peasant*, 191, 197; India, *Report of Famine Inquiry Commission 1945*, 294.

[91] Great Britain, *Report of Famine Commission 1880*, II, 130.

legal transfer made no real difference to the system of cultivation as such. The former cultivator remained in possession of his plot, turning over his surplus in some areas by a high rental instead of interest on his debt.[92] This trend has continued well into recent times. Though no figures are available, competent observers hold that the tendency for land to pass out of the hands of the cultivators continued during the depression, to be checked, at least temporarily, only during the prosperity of the Second World War.[93]

One of the main effects therefore of limited modernization has been to direct the economic surplus extracted from agriculture into new hands. In the Punjab, interest on debt in the late 1920s amounted to 104 rupees a head annually for the agricultural population, compared with a land revenue rate of 4 rupees.[94] Not all of this debt was owed to the moneylender; a substantial amount was owed to the more prosperous peasants. Nor were the moneylenders rolling in luxury, even if one out of every four income-tax payers in the 1920s belonged to this group.[95] Rough though these figures are, they establish the point that the Indian peasant was generating a handsome surplus, and that this surplus was not going to the state. The Indian peasant was suffering many of the pains of primitive capitalist accumulation, while Indian society reaped none of the benefits.

The passing of the land into the hands of the moneylender brought no consolidation in the unit of cultivation. India experienced no substantial enclosure movement. Nor did it produce any improvement in the techniques of cultivation. Down to the present day, agricultural methods and tools have remained extremely backward. The *deshi* or native plow and other implements do not differ essentially from those of 1000 years ago, according to an Indian authority writing shortly after the Second World War.[96] The char-

[92] Cf Gadgil, *Industrial Evolution*, 166.

[93] India, *Report of Famine Inquiry Commission 1945*, 271.

[94] Darling, *Punjab Peasant*, 20; see also 218 – 222.

[95] Great Britain, *Report of Commission on Agriculture in India 1928*, 442.

[96] Thirumalai, *Postwar Agricultural Problems*, 178. This judgment may be somewhat severe. See Lewis, *Village Life*, for a list of technical innovations, some quite important, in a single village.

acteristic feature of Indian agriculture remains the consistently low yield per acre of most of the principal crops compared with that in other countries of the world. The most important are still rice and wheat, with rice much more significant than wheat. In 1945 these two grains accounted for nearly half the area devoted to food crops, while in terms of yield their proportion was very much higher.[97] In the absence of any substantial technical revolution, it is not surprising to learn that even in the twentieth century the bulk of the crops are still raised for subsistence, although most of the cultivators sell at least part of their produce.[98]

At this point it is well to desist from discussing India as a whole and examine at least very briefly the development and characteristics of landlordism in different parts of the country. We may begin with Bengal where, as we have seen, the main features of the problem antedated the full weight of the British impact. The information from this area shades and amplifies the image of the parasitic landlord by showing, first, that there were at times economic tasks that he performed and, secondly, that parasitism reached deep into the ranks of the peasantry itself.

The *zamindars* of Bengal did play a role, if scarcely an arduous one, in clearing the waste that formed so prominent a part of the rural landscape in that part of the country around 1800. This they accomplished mainly by putting a variety of pressures on the peasants. For example, by exemptions from the rent, they often induced relatively wild tribes to settle and clear the waste. As soon as the land had been reclaimed, the *zamindar* found legal ways to oust these tenants and replace them with more skillful tenants willing to pay handsome rents. Through this device and others, such as special levies on the tenants, the *zamindar* is said to have doubled his rates of rent between 1800 and 1850. After about 1850 the *zamindars* became more and more mere rent collectors and did little toward the extension of cultivation or the improvement of agriculture.[99]

By the time of the Mutiny the peasants' rights under the Permanent Settlement had deteriorated to the point where, in the judg-

[97] India, *Report of Famine Inquiry Commission 1945,* 288.
[98] Anstey, *Economic Development,* 154.
[99] India, *Census 1951,* VI, pt IA, 445 – 446.

ment of a modern student, they were substantially in the position of tenants-at-will. Shortly after the Mutiny the British undertook some steps to remedy the situation. They were able to do so because Bengal had escaped the worst effects of the Mutiny and there was therefore less necessity to conciliate the landlord class, already firmly entrenched.[100] By a series of tenancy acts beginning as early as 1859, the British tried to give the tenants some degree of security. Similar legislation was passed in other parts of India. The main provision was that twelve years of continuous cultivation formed the basis of occupancy rights and gave protection against eviction. Generally the landlords responded by evicting tenants before the twelve-year period was up. Furthermore, the new legislation made the rights of tenancy transferable like other property rights. Where this happened, competition for land intensified the practice of subletting. Numerous peasants turned into petty rent receivers as each peasant found it more profitable to make use of his right to sublet than to cultivate the soil.[101] As the difference became larger and larger between what the government took in taxes (limited by the Permanent Settlement) and what the pressure of competition for land would generate in the way of rent, the chain of tenancies and subtenancies grew longer and longer until it reached fantastic lengths in some parts of this area.

The older literature on the question of land tenures gives the impression that the burden of rent is heavier on the peasant where there is a large number of intermediaries between the landlord who pays the land revenue and the peasant who actually cultivates the land. Such is not the case. The large number of intermediaries arises merely from the wide difference between the rate of rent paid by the cultivator and the revenue or tax paid by the landlord.[102] In the 1940s the Land Revenue Commission of Bengal found that the rents paid in areas where the layering of tenancy rights was extreme

[100] Metcalf, "Struggle over Land Tenure," 299. For reasons indicated below, I think Metcalf's assessment of the favorable effects may be too optimistic.

[101] Mukerjee, *Economic Problems*, I, 221 – 223, 227 – 228, 230.

[102] India, *Report of Famine Inquiry Commission 1945*, 282.

were less than in many other parts of India. The Commissioners
even went so far as to conclude that "there would be justification
for enhancements rather than reductions of rent in Bengal."[103]
About the last point, opinions may differ. But one point emerges
clearly. The economic "surplus" was not, in many areas, entirely
skimmed off by the rich *rentier*. Instead the competition for land
led to its division among many mouths, the vast majority far from
wealthy. As the Indian census authorities are careful to point out,
the rural landlord in India is not merely the prosperous and relaxed
receiver of rents. He may be living at the margin of subsistence and
still making no economic contribution.[104] Among those living on
rents from land are likely to be a substantial proportion of widows
or infirm and decrepit landowners without grownup sons, incapable of cultivating the land themselves, who therefore lease it out
to others.[105] In some areas even the village servants, cobblers, barbers, washermen, carpenters, and others may be found among the
absentee landlords.[106] I know of no data that would permit an estimate of how many "poor landlords" there are in the various categories just described. Undoubtedly they vastly outnumber the
wealthy *rentier*. Nor are all landlords to be judged as wholly parasitic, that is, making no contribution to society either in an economic or in a wider sense, such as in the professions.

All these modifications of the thesis of parasitic landlordism
belong in any objective assessment of the problem. At the same
time, the detached social scientist must be very careful about decid-
ing what they really mean. There is a strong tendency to ward off
criticism of the *status quo* by pointing to exceptions and gaps in the
data until it may seem that the real problem does not exist or is
merely the product of a fevered imagination. In this instance, it is
about as clear as can be that parasitic landlordism was a real problem. The number of poor people who managed to squeeze in under
its umbrella to eke out a miserable existence does not constitute an

[103] India, *Report of Famine Inquiry Commission 1945*, 278.
[104] India, *Census 1951*, VI, pt IA, 355.
[105] India, *Census 1951*, IX, pt IA, 121–122.
[106] India, *Census 1951*, IX, pt IA, 119.

adequate defense of a social institution that was inherently wasteful and prevented economic advance. Nor does the fact that poor landlords greatly outnumbered wealthy ones, and that there is an absence of adequate statistics on the distribution of income within this sector, diminish the very strong probability that the lion's share of landlord income went to a small and wealthy sector.

Let us now have a look at developments in areas of southern India where under the *ryotwari* settlements the British collected taxes directly from the peasant villages instead of through intermediaries.

We may begin with a glimpse of the Madras Presidency in the last decade of the nineteenth century, an area that coincides roughly with that Buchanan travelled through ninety years before, looking through the eyes of an early Indian official in British service, the Inspector General of Registration, who in 1893 published a *Memorandum* on advances in Madras during the previous four decades.[107] The author was obviously a fair-minded scholarly official even if anxious to show as much progress as he could under the British, whose beneficiary he was. Yet the picture he paints is one of a small, enormously wealthy landed élite, squandering its resources in litigation and dissipation, resting on a mass of poor peasants. Of the 90 million acres in the Presidency 27½ millions, or between a third and a quarter, were held by 849 *zamindars*. Fifteen *zamindars* held nearly half a million acres each. Beneath them were some 4,600,000 peasant proprietors on *ryotwari* tenure.[108] The author calculates that about eight acres were necessary for a peasant family to procure subsistence without resorting to work for others.[109] Somewhat less than a fifth (17.5 percent) fell below this standard and had to eke out their living by working for others, while the average holding was only somewhat more than 3½ acres.[110] Again these figures, based on land-revenue returns, must be treated with caution. But I see no reason to reject the general picture that they present. As in Bengal, a number of the old landed families had lost their estates be-

[107] See Raghavaiyangar, *Madras.*
[108] Raghavaiyangar, *Madras,* 132, 134.
[109] Raghavaiyangar, *Madras,* 135 – 136.
[110] Raghavaiyangar, *Madras,* 137, 135.

tween 1830 and 1850, a period of low prices for grains, when they were unable to meet their taxes. Others evidently profited.[111] A comparison of Raghavaiyangar's 1893 *Memorandum* on Madras with Buchanan's sketches of the early nineteenth century leads to the conclusion that the main effects of British rule were a shortage of land among the peasants and the emergence of a small, enormously wealthy, and indolent class of landlords.

In Bombay at about the same time there were said to be no large landholders comparable to the *zamindars* in other parts of India. Most of the rural inhabitants were peasants paying land revenue directly to the government. On the other hand, the authors of the 1880 Famine Report took note of a tendency for many peasants to sublet their lands and live on the difference between the rents they received and the revenue they paid to the government.[112] This evidence indicates once more the familiar cluster of features: a rising population, an increasing demand for land, and the emergence of a class of petty landlord *rentiers* out of the peasantry. The problem of tenancy soon put in its appearance. Subtenants in *ryotwari* areas, such as Bombay and parts of Madras, lacked legal protection until toward the end of the British occupation. Efforts to protect traditional rights began in 1939.[113] By 1951 it had become official policy to minimize the existence of a landlord problem. Nevertheless the authors of the 1951 census reported, with some interesting details, the existence of a class of large landlords in the neighborhood of the city of Bombay. Almost one out of three among the agricultural rent receivers returned a secondary means of livelihood. Both facts indicate a close connection between landlordism and urban commercial interests, perhaps similar to that in the Chinese port cities.[114]

We may close this regional survey with a look at a section of the Punjab, a wheat-growing area now part of Pakistan. The Punjab is instructive because it is the home of a caste of peasants, the Jats,

---

[111] Raghavaiyangar, *Madras*, 133.

[112] Great Britain, *Report of Famine Commission 1880*, II, 123.

[113] Mukerjee, *Economic Problems*, I, 223; Gadgil, *Industrial Evolution*, ix.

[114] India, *Census 1951*, IV, pt I, 16, 60.

366   SOCIAL ORIGINS OF DICTATORSHIP AND DEMOCRACY

who are first-rate cultivators despite their martial background, (which appears to be a matter of the quite distant past). The Punjab is also a region where the British, at an early date, introduced irrigation on a large scale. Describing the situation in the 1920s Sir Malcolm Darling, an excellent and sympathetic observer, tells us that the landlords were concentrated along the valleys of the Indus. About 40 percent of the cultivated land was in their hands.[115] His remark agrees with the estimate cited by the Famine Commission of 1945 that 2.4 percent of the owners held 38 percent of the land.[116] In the main, these landlords are described as extravagant and without interest in improving their property, caring only for sport and their rents.[117] In the 1880s the British literally made the desert bloom through a large irrigation project and settled it with peasants of various-sized holdings, and a scattering of peasants with more land. The British hoped (shades of Cornwallis!) that the last group would become landed gentry, but these peasant owners turned into absentees, and that aspect of the experiment failed.[118] The picture was not, however, completely black. Darling at one point mentions progressive and commercially minded landlords from the towns. They did not come from the traditional landowning castes[119] that British policy generally tried to preserve. Together with what we know about the transfer of land out of the hands of the traditional native élite in other parts of India, this hint suggests that some form of capitalist revolution in agriculture was not completely out of the question in India. Rather than pursue the implications of this point now, it will be better to consider it later, along with efforts to set off a voluntary agricultural revolution undertaken during the Nehru era.

As this regional survey shows, one of the clearest consequences of the British occupation was to eliminate gradually the differences between the *ryotwari* and *zamindari* areas. Passionate debates over

[115] *Punjab Peasant*, 98.

[116] Great Britain, *Report of Famine Inquiry Commission 1945*, 442.

[117] *Punjab Peasant*, 99, 109 – 110, 257.

[118] Darling, *Punjab Peasant*, 48.

[119] *Punjab Peasant*, 157 – 158. See also the preface by E.D. Maclagan for the thinking behind British policy.

their relative merits largely ceased before the outbreak of the First World War as tenancy problems became more and more widespread. Even in the internal constitution of the village, according to one authority, there came to be few differences traceable to this distinction.[120] Nor is there any clear indication for the period between the wars that one of the two systems was more or less efficient than the other.[121]

By itself, the statistical evidence does not permit any judgment as to whether or not the number of tenants increased during the British era. The main difficulty arises from the fact that a peasant often owns one plot and rents one or more additional ones. Hence differences in the procedures used in collecting statistics at different points in time produce huge fluctuations in the results that completely misrepresent the real situation. There are some indications that up until 1931 the number of tenants was increasing. In the light of the indisputable increase in population and the competition for land, such an increase seems highly likely. The next census, in 1951, showed an astonishing reversal of this trend, which cannot be taken as serious evidence and is almost certainly due to a change in the definition of tenant and owner.[122] Nor is it certain beyond any shadow of doubt that the tenants' material situation deteriorated during the British era, as Indian nationalist writers are inclined to assert. Tenancy by itself is no proof, and, in any case, a similar relationship existed widely beforehand. Once again the most important fact is the increase in population. Combined with the absence of technical improvement in agriculture on any substantial scale, we may take this fact as strong evidence that deterioration did occur.

It is also impossible to get any accurate statistical measure of the extent to which the increase in the importance of the market, together with the new British legality, set in motion a process of concentrating landed property in fewer hands. Large holdings were

[120] Gadgil, *Industrial Evolution*, 63; Thirumalai, *Postwar Agricultural Problems*, 131; Great Britain, *Report of Famine Inquiry Commission 1945*, 258.

[121] India, *Report of Famine Inquiry Commission 1945*, 265.

[122] Good discussion in Thirumalai, *Postwar Agricultural Problems*, 133, where the relevant figures are given. See also Thorner and Thorner, *Land and Labour*, chap X, for a detailed analysis.

common in many parts of India before the British appeared. They were said to be relatively rare by the time the British departed.[123] The only statistical information on India as a whole comes from a study carried out in 1953 – 1954. Since the abolition of the *zamindari* system was taking place then (though as we shall see the abolition as such was far from complete) and since there would on this account have been a substantial premium on concealing the size of one's holdings from prying officials, the chances are that the study reports a substantially lower degree of concentration than prevailed at the end of the British period. Nevertheless, the main results are worth noticing. About one-fifth of India's rural households, some 14 to 15 millions, owned no land. Half of the rural households owned less than an acre. Their share of the land came to only 2 percent. At the upper end of the scale, we find that in all population zones the uppermost 10 percent of the rural households owned 48 percent or more of the total area. Big landowners, however, let us say those over 40 acres, held only about a fifth.[124] The image which emerges is that of a huge rural proletariat, about half the rural population; a small class of prosperous peasants, not much more than an eighth of the population; and a tiny élite.

Apparently the main change in rural social structure under the British impact was an increase in the size of the rural proletariat. For the most part, this stratum consists mainly of agricultural laborers, either landless or with a tiny plot sufficient to tie them effectively to the landlord. How big an increase there was in this group we cannot tell, because changes in the procedures of classification from one census to another make comparisons extremely risky. A scholar who has attempted to circumvent these difficulties concluded that the number of agricultural laborers increased from around 13 percent in 1891 to about 38 percent in 1931, levelling off subsequently since the decrease in the size of holdings that went with India's rising population meant that farms became easier to work with family labor.[125]

[123] India, *Report of Famine Inquiry Commission 1945*, 258.

[124] India, *National Sample Survey, Report. on Land Holdings*, iv, 16. See also Tables 4.3, 4.4, pp. 14, 15.

[125] Patel, *Agricultural Labourers*, 7 – 8, 14 –15. India, *Agricultural La-*

In India the landless or quasi-landless are not the product of any wholesale expropriation of the peasantry. That they are desperately poor is also beyond dispute. Among the outcastes who work as agricultural laborers in one district of Uttar Pradesh, it has long been an accepted custom to eat grain collected from the excreta of animals and cleaned. Apparently the practice is not regarded as repugnant, and about a fifth of the population in the district are said to resort to it.[126] No doubt this is an extreme example. Let it nevertheless stand as an instance of the degradation of civilized man under peaceful conditions. The average situation is bad enough.

Gross as these generalizations about the rural proletariat are, they are firm enough to stand the weight of the argument placed upon them here. The history of the bottom layers of the Indian countryside is obscure, with plenty of room, indeed a crying need, for further research. That the lower strata are not the straightforward creation of *pax Britannica* will bear repeating. One may even hesitate to claim that their relation to their employers changed fundamentally during the British period.[127]

The appalling misery of the bottom layers of Indian rural society (and that of the cities as well) brings the discussion back to a central question with which it began. Although the Indian peasants have undergone as much material suffering as the Chinese over the last two centuries, India has not yet experienced a peasant revolution. Some possible reasons are already evident from differences in their social structure prior to the Western intrusion, as well as from significant variations in the timing and character of that impact. Violence has been a part of the response, though, so far, only as a

bour Enquiry, I, 19, reports that about a third of the rural families were agricultural laborers, and of these half were landless. Thorner and Thorner, *Land and Labour*, chap XIII, subject the methods of collecting data to damning criticism by pointing out that the *Enquiry* concentrated on technical aspects of sampling to the almost complete neglect of social realities. Hence the categories and breakdowns are useless or, worse than useless, seriously misleading.

[126] Nair, *Blossoms in the Dust*, 83, citing data from the National Council of Applied Economic Research.

[127] For some valuable glimpses at an early date see Buchanan, *Purnea*, 443; *Bhagalpur*, 193, 460, 468.

very minor component. To explain why there has not been a great deal more, it will be necessary to discuss the character of the Indian nationalist movement and the violence that has sporadically erupted.

6. *The Bourgeois Link to the Peasantry through Nonviolence*

Early in this account there has been occasion to notice the obstacles Indian social structure placed in the way of commercial development before the coming of the Europeans: the insecurity of property, the barriers to its accumulation, the premium on luxurious display, and the caste system. The balance of forces was not entirely negative. Elsewhere luxury has often stimulated forms of commerce. Commerce was certainly present; even banking reached a high point of development.[128] Yet indigenous commerce was not destined to be the solvent that would destroy India's traditional agrarian society. To a very limited extent, the absence of commercial and industrial revolution may be attributed to the British occupation, its destruction of textile handicrafts and its reserved attitude toward commercial interests that might compete with its own. On the other hand, the British did not by any means completely succeed in preventing the emergence of a native modern business class. Nor does the record indicate that they tried very hard to prevent it.

Native industries, particularly cotton and jute, began to become important toward the end of the nineteenth century, when improvements in transportation made possible the import of machinery, as well as opening access to wider markets.[129] By the 1880s India had a distinct commercial and industrial class of the modern variety. She also had a vocal professional class. Lawyers were among the first and most important numbers of the modern bourgeoisie to put in an appearance on the Indian scene, because British legality and the British bureaucracy here provided one acceptable outlet for talent and ambition.[130] Quite possibly the law was also congenial to the Brahman tradition of authority and meta-

[128] See the short but penetrating essay by Lamb, "The Indian Merchant," in Singer, ed, *Traditional India*, 25 – 35.

[129] Anstey, *Economic Development*, 208.

[130] For further details see Misra, *Middle Classes*, chap XI.

physical speculation. Some forty-odd years later, official British visitors could speak with approval of the Indian merchant princes whose mansions stood on Malabar Hill in Bombay and tell us that most of the capital in the jute mills near Calcutta and the cotton factories of Bombay belonged to such as these.[131]

It was in these circles that doubts first arose about the benefits of the British connection. Commercial interests in England in the latter part of the nineteenth century feared the competition of their native counterpart in India. Free trade, Indian merchants felt, stifled the possibilities of growth. For a long time they sought protection, subsidy, and opportunities for the monopolistic exploitation of the Indian market.[132] Hence there came about a split between India's landed élite, who were the main beneficiaries of British rule after 1857, and the commercial classes who felt themselves cramped by the connection with England. This split remained down to Independence.

The split had very significant political consequences. Elsewhere we have observed that an alliance between influential segments of a landed élite and a rising but weak commercial class has been a crucial factor in producing a reactionary political phase in the course of economic development. The British presence in India prevented any such coalition and thereby contributed to the establishment of a parliamentary democracy.

But there is more to the story than that. The commercial classes were also linked through the nationalist movement to the peasantry. To understand this paradoxical connection between the most advanced sector of the population and the most backward, it is necessary to discuss briefly certain highlights in the history of the nationalist movement and examine Gandhi's writings and speeches with some care. That the connection was far from perfect and that some frictions existed will be apparent in due course.

The Indian National Congress and the first Indian Chamber of Commerce were formed in the same year, 1885. Up until the end of the First World War, the Congress was no more than a "timid

[131] Great Britain, *Report of Indian Statutory Commission*, I, 23.

[132] Gadgil, *Business Communities*, IX. The main economic facts may be found in Misra, *Middle Classes*, chap VIII.

annual gathering of English-speaking intelligentsia." Subsequently the connection with business interests remained one of the most important influences determining the Congress's stand, though there were brief periods when other forces managed to push them into the background.[133] Before the First World War, for example, B.G. Tilak became the leader of a violent nativist reaction seeking its inspiration from India's historic past. This turn toward violence was partly a response to widespread disappointment with the Congress's approach of polite and ineffective petitions. In 1906, under Tilak's influence, the Congress adopted the goal of *Swaraj*, then defined as the "system of government obtaining in the self-governing British colonies."[134] At a much later period another form of radicalism, this time with socialist overtones, was to influence the official stand of the Congress, as in the Karachi Resolution on Fundamental Rights of 1931, at which point the Congress agreed on a mildly socialist and democratic program.[135] In the absence of political responsibility these doctrinal gusts had limited significance, while business interests provided a steadying ballast. More important still, the presence of the British conqueror damped down internal clashes and imposed a degree of unity that extended from the Westernized and mildly radical intellectuals through the business community to the politically active section of the peasantry.

The Congress did not begin to reach the peasants until after the end of the First World War and the rise of Gandhi as the dominant figure in the nationalist movement, openly recognized at its session in Nagpur of 1920. At this point, the Indian National Congress ceased to be an upper-class club and started to become a mass organization. The following year the Congressmen turned to the peasantry, much as the Russian Narodniki had done in the 1870s.[136] From this time until his death, Gandhi remained the undisputed leader of that strange amalgam of Westernized intellectu-

[133] Gadgil, *Business Communities*, 30, 66; Brecher, *Nehru*, 52. Landed interests were also important at first in the Congress. See Misra, *Middle Classes*, 353.

[134] Majumdar et al, *Advanced History*, 895, 928, 981.

[135] Brecher, *Nehru*, 176 – 177.

[136] Brecher, *Nehru*, 72, 76.

als, merchants and industrialists, and of ordinary tillers of the soil that was the Indian nationalist movement. What enabled him to hold together such a disparate group of conflicting interests?

For intellectuals such as Nehru, Gandhi's program of non-violence seemed to offer a way out of the impasse created by two policies that had so far proved equally futile: the violence of a Tilak and the insipid constitutionalism of the Congress's earlier history.[187] Gandhi struck a responsive chord in Hindu culture, and struck it in such a way as to galvanize the country into opposition against the British without threatening vested interests in Indian society. Even the landed upper classes, though they feared him, were not the object of direct attack, as we shall see in a moment. It is unlikely that the absence of any elements of economic radicalism was the result of a deliberate Machiavellian choice by Gandhi. For our purposes his personal motives are unimportant. What is significant and revealing is Gandhi's program, set forth in his voluminous writings and speeches. In their main outlines his central ideas remained remarkably consistent from the beginning of his active leadership until the end of his life.

The goal of independence (*Swaraj*) and the method of non-violent noncooperation (*Satyagraha*), sometimes also referred to as passive resistance, the two main themes of his program, are quite familiar to educated Westerners. Rather less familiar is the social and economic content of Gandhi's program, symbolized by the famous spinning wheel and expressed by the term *Swadeshi*. In 1916 Gandhi defined the term in these words:

> *Swadeshi* is that spirit in us which restricts us to the use and service of our immediate surroundings to the exclusion of the more remote. Thus, as for religion, in order to satisfy the requirements of the definition, I must restrict myself to my ancestral religion. That is the use of my immediate religious surrounding. If I find it defective, I should serve it by purging it of its defects. In the domain of politics I should make use of the indigenous institutions and serve them by curing them of their proved defects. In that of economics I should use only things that are produced by my immediate

[187] Brecher, *Nehru*, 75.

neighbors and serve those industries by making them efficient and complete where they might be found wanting. . . .

If we follow the *Swadeshi* doctrine, it would be your duty and mine to find out neighbors who can supply our wants and to teach them to supply them where they do not know how to proceed, assuming that there are neighbors who are in want of healthy occupation. Then every village of India will almost be a self-supporting and self-contained unit, exchanging only such necessary commodities with other villages where they are not locally producible. This may all sound nonsensical. Well, India is a country of nonsense. It is nonsensical to parch one's throat with thirst when a kindly Mohammedan is ready to offer pure water to drink. And yet thousands of Hindus would rather die of thirst than drink water from a Mohammedan household.[138]

What Gandhi sought was a return to an idealized past: the Indian village community, purged of some of its more obviously degrading and repressive features, such as untouchability.[139]

Closely related to the conception of *Swadeshi* were Gandhi's ideas about property, expressed in the notion of trusteeship. Again it is advisable to let the Mahatma speak in his own words:

Supposing I have come by a fair amount of wealth either by way of legacy, or by means of trade and industry, I must know that all that wealth does not belong to me, what belongs to me is the right to an honorable livelihood, no better than that enjoyed by millions of others. The rest of my wealth belongs to the community and must be used for the welfare of the community. I enunciated this theory when the Socialist theory was placed before the country in respect to the possessions held by zamindars and ruling chiefs. They would do away with these privileged classes. I want them to outgrow their greed and sense of possession, and to come down in spite of their wealth to the level of those who earn their bread by labor. The laborer has to realize that the wealthy man is less owner of his wealth than the laborer is owner of *his* own, viz., the power to work.[140]

[138] *Speeches and Writings of Mahatma Gandhi*, 336 – 337, 341 – 342.
[139] Gandhi did not turn his main energies to the abolition of untouchability until 1933, a step welcomed by the British as they hoped it would divert attention from political issues. See Nanda, *Mahatma Gandhi*, 355.
[140] *Economic and Industrial Life*, I, 119.

The statement just quoted was made in a newspaper article in 1939. Five years earlier he had been asked why he tolerated private property since it appeared to be incompatible with nonviolence. His answer was that concessions had to be made to those who earn money but would not voluntarily use their earnings for the benefit of mankind. Pressed further with the question why did he not therefore advocate state ownership in the place of private property, he answered that, although it was better than private ownership, it was objectionable on the grounds of violence. "It is my firm conviction," he added, "that if the state suppressed capitalism by violence it will be caught in the evils of violence itself and fail to develop nonviolence at any time."[141]

Obviously this outlook contained nothing very terrifying to the holders of property, even to the landed aristocracy who were generally antagonistic to him. He maintained this point of view quite consistently, reproving the peasant movement for using violence, which he said in 1938 "would be something like fascism."[142] As far as I have been able to discover, the furthest step Gandhi took toward the view that the *zamindars* should be expropriated came in 1946, when he made the oblique threat that not every Congressman was an angel and hinted that an independent India might fall into unjust hands who would abolish the *zamindars*. Even on this occasion he was quick to add the hope that Congress would be just, as "Otherwise all the good it might have done would disappear in the twinkling of an eye."[143]

As implied by the notion of *Swadeshi*, the main thrust of Gandhi's program was the revival of traditional village India. It was with the peasants that Gandhi's heart really lay, and it was they who responded most enthusiastically to his movement. As he remarked in 1933:

I can only think in terms of the millions of villagers and can only make my happiness dependent upon that of the poorest amongst

[141] *Economic and Industrial Life*, I, 123.
[142] *Economic and Industrial Life*, III, 178, 180. See also his 1934 statement, III, 189.
[143] *Economic and Industrial Life*, III, 190 – 191.

them, and want to live only if they can live. My very simple mind cannot go beyond the little spindle of the little wheel which I can carry about with me from place to place and which I can manufacture without difficulty.[144]

To him the task of village uplift seemed a nonpolitical one upon which all groups could agree and cooperate.[145] Never did it occur to Gandhi that to maintain village India would be to condemn the mass of India's population to a life of squalor, ignorance, and disease. Industrialism, he felt, brought only materialism and violence. In his eyes the English were the victims of modern civilization, who deserved pity rather than hate.[146]

As is usually the case with backward-looking idealizations of peasant life, Gandhi's love of the village had antiurban and even anticapitalist overtones. There was a real basis for this outlook in Indian experience. The accounts of the destruction of the Indian village handicrafts, especially weaving, by British factory products made a deep impression on Gandhi. In 1922 he rejected with passion the familiar claim that the English had brought India the benefits of government by law. For him the law merely concealed a brutal exploitation. No juggling of figures, he asserted, could conceal "the evidence the skeletons in many villages present to the naked eye. I have no doubt whatsoever that both England and the town-dwellers of India will have to answer, if there is a God above, for this crime against humanity which is perhaps unequalled in history."[147] Many of his other speeches repeat the same theme. Village uplift he thought of mainly as "an honest attempt to return to the villagers what has been cruelly and thoughtlessly snatched away from them by the city dwellers."[148] Mechanization was good when there were not enough workers to carry on the task. In the contrary situation, it was evil. "Strange as it may appear, every mill generally is a menace to the villagers."[149]

[144] *Economic and Industrial Life*, II, 157.
[145] *Economic and Industrial Life*, II, 162.
[146] Nanda, *Mahatma Gandhi*, 188.
[147] *Speeches and Writings*, 699 – 700.
[148] *Economic and Industrial Life*, II, 159.
[149] *Economic and Industrial Life*, II, 160. See also II, 163.

Such ideas could scarcely have found favor with wealthy backers of the nationalist movement. Wealthy merchants too were scandalized by the admission of untouchables into Gandhi's *ashram*,[150] while his support of the workers in the Ahmedabad strike toward the end of World War I may have antagonized still others.[151] At first glance it seems contradictory that the wealthy urban classes should have been a source of support for the nationalist movement, while the landed aristocracy, on whose behalf he issued a number of soothing statements, were generally antagonistic.

Part of the contradiction disappears as we recall that the whole program of *Swadeshi* or local autonomy was in effect a doctrine of "buy Indian" and helped to cut down the competition of British goods. Furthermore, from the standpoint of the wealthy classes, there were useful aspects to Gandhi's doctrine of the dignity of labor. He opposed political strikes because they fell outside the framework of nonviolence and noncooperation. "It does not require much effort of the intellect," he said in 1921, "to perceive that it is a most dangerous thing to make political use of labor until laborers understand the political condition of the country and are prepared to work for the common good."[152] Even in the case of economic strikes, he urged "the necessity of thinking a hundred times before undertaking a strike." And as labor became better organized and better educated he hoped that the principle of arbitration would replace strikes.[153] These ideas found expression in the condemnation of socialist ideas, such as the confiscation of private property and class warfare, in a statement issued by the powerful Working Committee of the Congress in June 1934.[154]

Thus Gandhi's doctrines, despite some characteristic traces of peasant radicalism, brought water to the mills of the wealthy urban classes. His ideas competed effectively with Western radical notions (that were mainly limited to a few intellectuals) and in this way helped to bring the masses into the movement for independ-

[150] Nanda, *Mahatma Gandhi*, 135.
[151] Nanda, *Mahatma Gandhi*, 165.
[152] *Speeches and Writings,* 1049–1050.
[153] *Speeches and Writings,* 1048.
[154] Brecher, *Nehru*, 202.

ence, giving it power and effectiveness, while at the same time they helped to keep the movement safe for those with property.

Fundamentally Gandhi was the spokesman of the Indian peasant and village artisan. There is abundant evidence of the enthusiastic response they gave to his appeal. Large sections of this group, as we shall see in the next section, were suffering from the intrusions of capitalism, which were piled on top of ancient miseries. Thus the resentments that in Japan found part of their outlet in the Young Officers' Movement and superpatriotism, found in India under Gandhi quite another outlet in a different version of nationalism. Nevertheless, their similarities are at least as important as their differences. Both looked back to an idealized past for their model of the good society. Both were incapable of understanding the problems of the modern world. In the case of Gandhi this judgment may seem harsh. Many Western liberals, distressed by the horrors of modern industrial society, have found Gandhi a sympathetic figure, especially for his stress on nonviolence. To me this sympathy merely seems to be evidence for the *malaise* in modern liberalism and its incapacity to solve the problems that confront Western society. If one thing at least is certain, it is that modern technology is here to stay and will before long spread throughout the rest of the world. It is perhaps equally certain that whatever form the good society may take, if it ever comes, it will not be that of the self-contained Indian village served by the local artisan symbolized in Gandhi's spinning wheel.

7. A Note on the Extent and Character of Peasant Violence

The configuration of class relationships under the British occupation and the character of nationalist leaders imparted to their movement a quietist twist that helped to damp down what revolutionary tendencies there were among the peasants. Other factors were important too, especially the fact that the bottom layers of the peasantry were both fragmented along caste and linguistic lines and nevertheless tied by traditional rules and bits of property to the prevailing order. Still the glare of Gandhi's reputation together with the English desire to minimize the extent of disorder during their rule and in the course of transition to independence have partly concealed the amount of actual violence that did take place. Over the past two hundred years the Indian peasant has not behaved in quite so docile a fashion as once seemed the case. To examine the circumstances under which the peasants have turned to organized violence, though it is no easy task with the sources presently available, may shed some light on the factors that have in general prevented its occurrence.

There are some instructive gleanings to be had from the examination of peasant outbreaks between the establishment of British hegemony on the subcontinent after the battle of Plassey and the end of the Mutiny. An Indian scholar has recently performed the very useful task of pulling together an enormous mass of materials on civil disturbances in general during these hundred years. Among them one may find ten reasonably clear cases where large numbers of peasants have turned on their masters. At least five of these fall outside the boundaries of our problem insofar as they concern either Islamic movements among the peasantry or else aboriginal inhabitants.[155] The whole record of peasant uprisings is of course quite unimpressive in comparison with China. Nevertheless important points do emerge. The upheavals we will consider

---

[155] Chaudhuri, *Civil Disturbances*. Consult the index s.v. *peasantry* and *peasant movements*. Eight cases in Bengal are listed on 28, note 2. Of these notes 14, 15, 18, 22, 23 concern non-Hindu groups. There are two more episodes outside Bengal; see 141, 172 for some of the main events. My knowledge of India is not sufficiently detailed to enable me to judge exactly which cases do and do not reflect Hindu social conditions, since Islam is often a thin veneer on Hindu institutions. On the other hand, an Islamic nativist movement preaching the equality of all men (the Wahabis of case 14) does not seem relevant to the concerns of this discussion. A much briefer study from a socially radical, rather than a nationalist, standpoint is Natarajan, *Peasant Uprisings in India*. Natarajan has collected information about four major series of uprisings: 1) The Santal Rebellion of 1855 – 1856, by a non-Hindu aboriginal group; 2) the Indigo Cultivator's Strike of 1860, a special case involving a plantation economy; 3) Marathra Risings or the Deccan Riots of 1875, the only one that seems to have involved ordinary Hindu peasants; and 4) the Moplah Uprisings, spread out between 1836 to 1896, a series of outbreaks by Islamic cultivators against Hindu overlords. Useful though this little book is, it fails in its attempt to find a radical tradition of rebellion for the Indian peasants.

were on a substantial scale. All the instances involved the peasants' economic grievances quite prominently. One revolt took shape at the prospect of a survey; in others we hear of infuriated peasants hanging Brahman revenue officers from whom they had suffered extortions. In still other cases, Hindu peasants rose against Mohammedan tax collectors.[156] In the last instance, rebel bands of some hundreds of persons roamed about sacking the countryside and were joined by the inhabitants who for a time made common cause with them against the government, then far from firmly established. Another point worth stressing is that solidarity in rebellion could, at least temporarily, cross caste lines, including the sharp one separating peasants from the castes of artisans and village servants. In one instance milkmen, oilmen, and blacksmiths joined up; in another, barbers and house servants, including servants of the moneylender.[157] The fragmentation of the Indian village is evidently not in all circumstances a barrier to subversion. To sum up more generally what can be learned from this evidence, we may conclude that Indian peasants had very definite ideas about just and unjust rule, that economic grievances could drive even this supposedly docile population to rebellion on a local scale, finally that traditional leaders with close ties to the peasants played a part in such uprisings.

In the latter phases of *pax Britannica*, especially in the unsettled years following both the first and second World Wars, it is highly likely that there were generally similar outbreaks. However, the violence of this phase was not in the main revolutionary. What revolutionary component there may have been was masked by religious warfare about which it will be necessary to speak in a moment. Nevertheless, in one area, Hyderabad, smoldering discontent did flare into an open revolutionary upheaval for a brief time during the turmoils surrounding the British withdrawal. As an exception that throws much light on the general situation, the revolt in Hyderabad deserves more detailed discussion.

Before Independence, Hyderabad was one of the largest and most powerful of the princely states as well as one part of India

[156] Chaudhuri, *Civil Disturbances*, 172, 141, 65 – 66.
[157] Natarajan, *Peasant Uprisings in India*, 23, 26, 58.

where a political and social structure inherited from the days of Muslim rule had been preserved more·or less intact.[158] Around 80 percent of the underlying population was Hindu.[159] Perhaps somewhat backward in relation to the rest of India, there is still no evidence that the position of the peasants in Hyderabad was significantly worse than in many other parts of the country. Detailed descriptions report the usual fragmentation of land holdings, heavy pressure of population, perhaps only 1.15 acres a head in the food-growing areas in 1939 – 1940, tenancy problems, debt, and large numbers of quite miserable agricultural laborers, perhaps some 40 percent of the population.[160] Possibly the situation of some agricultural laborers, which verged on debt slavery, was worse than in other parts of India.[161] Still, generally similar conditions could be found in many areas where there were no revolts. Furthermore, the upheaval itself took place in a part of the country where tenancy problems were less acute.[162] And it spread into this area, Telingana, from neighboring Andhra where the Communists had established themselves among a relatively wealthy landowning caste.[163]

The Communists began their work among the Telingana peasants of Hyderabad in 1940. Their success was surprising. Village after village, especially in the areas along the Madras border, in 1943 – 1944 refused to obey landlords' orders, to supply forced labor, to pay rent and taxes.[164]

Confusion and the temporary breakdown of authority, as the Nizam of Hyderabad maneuvered in an effort to avoid absorption into the new Indian union, gave the Communists a further opportunity. They claimed at this time, late in 1947 or early in 1948, at least 2000 villages "liberated." Village soviets did spring up and take control of an extensive area. For a short time Communists

---

[158] Smith, "Hyderabad," 28 – 31, gives a good general description.
[159] Qureshi, *Hyderabad*, I, 30.
[160] Qureshi, *Hyderabad*, 39, 61, 67.
[161] Qureshi, *Hyderabad*, 72.
[162] Qureshi, *Hyderabad*, 133 – 134. The place was Telingana, also spelled Telengana, Tilangana.
[163] Smith, "Hyderabad," 32; Harrison, *India*, 162.
[164] Smith, "Hyderabad," 33.

broke landlord and police control, distributed land, cancelled debts, and liquidated their enemies in the classic manner. One scholarly observer has spoken of it as the "largest and for a brief moment perhaps the most effective peasant uprising in Asia outside of China."[165] The Nizam of Hyderabad tried to use the Communists, along with Muslim reactionary ruffians organized in fascist-type bands, to prevent the absorption of his territory. On September 13, 1948, the Indian army conquered the country in less than a week's time. But it took "some months" of intensive military and police operations, thousands of summary arrests, and the shooting of leaders out of hand to put down the Communist-led peasants in Telingana.[166]

The first lesson that the unsuccessful revolution in Hyderabad teaches is a negative one. Any notion to the effect that caste or other distinctive traits of Indian peasant society constitute an effective barrier to insurrection is obviously false. There *is* a revolutionary potential among the Indian peasants. In the second place, degrading material conditions in and by themselves are not the decisive factor in producing an outbreak, though they certainly contribute to the overall potential. There is no evidence to show that the material situation of the peasants was worse where the revolt broke out, and some substantial evidence to the contrary. It was the collapse of political authority from above that enabled the Communists to spread their authority temporarily, though not to establish themselves. Similar conditions in the past were the prerequisite of rural upheavals. In Hyderabad in 1947 and 1948, this collapse was exceptional and temporary. Should it recur elsewhere in the future, other pockets of Communist rule might easily spring up.

So far revolutionary extremism has gained no more than a precarious foothold and but a tiny influence in India.[167] Up until Nehru's death and beyond, the central government was strong enough to crush communism when it was revolutionary and to con-

[165] See Smith, "Hyderabad," 33 – 40.

[166] Smith, "Hyderabad," 45, 47.

[167] See Overstreet and Windmiller, *Communism in India,* for details. Unfortunately this large volume does very little to relate communism to Indian social trends.

tain it within legal bounds when it was reformist. Let us look back over the record to see why this has been so.

In pre-British times, I have suggested earlier, the institution of caste provided a way of organizing the local community in such a way as to make the central government something superfluous rather than something to be changed when things went wrong. Caste was also a way of organizing a highly fragmented society composed of many races, religions, and languages so that they could at least live together in the same territory. Though this fragmentation could at times be overcome in small ways and in specific localities, it must have been a barrier to widespread rebellion. Furthermore, the system of caste did enforce hierarchical submission. Make a man feel humble by a thousand daily acts and he will behave in a humble way. The traditional etiquette of caste was no mere excrescence; it had definite political consequences. Finally, as a safety valve, caste does provide a form of collective upward mobility through Sanskritization, but within the framework of the traditional system. On all points Indian society differed sharply from Imperial China.

These factors continued to operate in the countryside, even if with diminishing force, as limited modernization set in under the British. The way modernization took place also favored stability in many respects. The crisis of the Mutiny occurred before radical movements had learned how to turn reactionary longings into revolutions; whether they could have done so with this one is problematical. As the nationalist movement reached the peasants, it had strong pacifying tendencies for reasons that have already been discussed. Remarkably enough, the transfer of power to Indian hands was accomplished without a real crisis among the rulers; where a minor one did occur in Hyderabad, there was an abortive revolutionary outbreak.

One aspect deserves fuller exploration than I have been able to give it. Many of the hostilities generated by the intrusion of the modern world probably found their outlet in the horrors of communal warfare between Hindu and Moslem. As an indication of its importance, it is sufficient to recall the estimate of some 200,000 persons killed in the riots that accompanied Partition and Independence, while some 12,000,000 persons are said to have fled in opposite directions between the two states.[168] Hostility between the two religions has, of course, taken violent forms intermittently over a long period of Indian history. Mainly it seems to have been the result of efforts by Islamic rulers to convert Hindu subjects by force. Twentieth-century religious conflict and fanaticism are qualitatively different. They resemble more closely the well-known phenomenon of nativism. In many parts of the world, when an established culture was beginning to erode, threatening some of the population, people have responded by reaffirming the traditional way of life with increasing and frantic vigor. Often the reaffirmation has but tenuous connection with historical reality. Something of the sort apparently happened in India, a trend that would repay more detailed study than it has yet received. Communal sentiments played a part in India's faint version of a reactionary phase. Indeed, they have been by far its worst aspect. But they have been, at least for the Indian Republic and its leaders, strictly unofficial and anti-governmental trends. To their everlasting credit, both Gandhi and Nehru opposed communal violence with all the vigor they could command. Religious warfare may have been a substitute for revolution. It is also no more than an extreme manifestation of the fragmentation of Indian society that constitutes an obstacle to *all* effective political action, not merely revolutionary radicalism. The natural target for this radicalism might seem to be the outcastes and the rural proletariat. In addition to the tendency toward Sanskritization, radicalism encounters other obstacles here. Revolutionaries cannot appeal to the rural proletariat, even under peaceful guises, without antagonizing the mass of small and medium peasants. In any event, the real problem for a revolutionary movement is to detach whole villages and areas from the *status quo*, something very difficult to do on more than a limited local basis in India. The Communists in some areas could and did base part of their appeal on linguistic and regional loyalties. In other areas they have done this and tried to work through caste disputes as well.[169] The appeal to local and divisive sentiments may be at times good revolutionary

[168] Mellor, *India Since Partition*, 45.
[169] Harrison, *India*, 222–223, gives a good instance.

tactics. But when the time comes to fuse local discontents into a larger policy, these petty hostilities can do no more than neutralize each other in a cacophony of petty bickerings. Revolutions come with panhuman ideals, not trivial regional ones.

The problem of rapidly shifting tactics (for reasons that have nothing to do with conditions in India) and of identification with a foreign government, be it Russian or Chinese, are also severe obstacles faced by the only groups that at present have any claim to a revolutionary tradition. Most important of all, the Nehru regime had the top layer of the peasantry on its side. The forces of order hold strong cards, though they are all cards inherited from the past whose value will steadily depreciate unless India's political leaders can both initiate and control the deep-running currents that are already shaping the future of the Indian countryside. Though the outcome is inherently unpredictable, it may be possible to understand the problem itself through studying the reasons for what has been done and left undone.

8. *Independence and the Price of Peaceful Change*

By the time the British were driven out in 1947, a vicious circle had firmly established itself in Indian society. There was only a very small impetus toward industrialization because resources were not being tapped and collected for the construction of an industrial plant. Agriculture was stagnant and inefficient because the city was not reaching out into the countryside to stimulate productivity or transform rural society. For this same reason, the countryside was not generating resources that could be used for industrial growth. Instead, the landlord and the moneylender were skimming off what surplus there was, mainly for unproductive purposes.

To speak of a vicious circle may carry the implication that the situation was hopeless. This is not so. As historical experience in other recently industrialized countries shows, a policy exists which can break the circle. In their broad essentials, the problem and the answer are very simple. They amount to using a combination of economic incentives and political compulsion to induce the people on the land to improve productivity and at the same time taking a substantial part of the surplus so generated to construct an industrial society. Behind this problem there stands a political one, whether or not a class of people has arisen in the society with the capacity and ruthlessness to force through the changes. England had her squires and her early industrial capitalists, Russia her Communists, Japan her dissident aristocrats who could turn into bureaucrats. For reasons that have been discussed at some length by now, India was rather short on this score.

Before going any deeper, it is appropriate to warn once more against a certain kind of psychologism and acceptance of facts as they are — without really ascertaining *why* they are facts — in commenting on the absence of a stronger impulse toward change. For the moment we can limit matters to the countryside. Partly for lack of a better term, we have referred to the landlord as parasitic. This should not be taken to mean that everywhere he simply sat back in the shade to let the rents flow in, though this of course happened too, and perhaps even on a fairly wide scale. There were also many landlords who were active and energetic individuals. They showed as much entrepreneurial talent or desire for achievement as one could hope to find in the most model Protestant capitalist. But within the framework of Indian society such talents for innovation could only go into pulling the levers of the old repressive system. The landlord might find all kinds of ways to screw up his tenants' rents, alternating between British courts and the mechanisms provided by the political and social structure of the village.[170] It would be easy enough to pile up cases of innovation *within the system* to demonstrate that lack of this talent is not the problem. The people who have entrepreneurial ability are probably in a minority in any large group. The problem is one of releasing this talent and also of controlling it for larger social purposes. The creation of an appropriate situation to release it is in very broad terms a political problem.

If lack of innovating talent in the countryside is not an obstacle, neither is lack of resources. Potentially enough resources are there. To be convinced on this score, we may look at a single village through the eyes of an anthropologist:

[170] Some vivid examples are in Neale, *Economic Change*, 204–205.

The farmer of Gopalpur conducts his agricultural operations on a scale which only a very wealthy country could afford. Rather than use proper amounts of seed of good quality and known germinating ability, the farmer scatters vast wasteful quantities of unselected, untested seed. Failing to protect the young plants in the field, he perforce shares his seedlings with every bird, insect, and wild animal that comes around. He heaps his manure and compost carelessly outside his door, unprotected from sun and rain. Instead of carefully storing his harvested crop, he places it in his house in clay jars, or worse on a crudely made stone floor. What the rats don't eat is drilled and powdered by worms and weevils.[171]

Though not all villages are as badly off as this one — some are worse and a few are better — the situation is still characteristic all over India after seventeen years of Independence. There are more than 500,000 villages in India. Multiply the situation in this village by several hundred thousand and one can see the potential resources that exist merely by changing the way people conduct their agricultural practices.

They will not change simply because someone has told them to do so. That has been going on for some time. It is necessary to change the situation confronting the people on the land if they are going to alter their behavior. And if this has not yet happened, as by and large it has not, there are likely to be good political reasons. Here in this last portion of the discussion the task will be to find the reasons, to assess the obstacles of change, and what impulses might be present to overcome them. The task is not one of prediction, but merely one of analyzing a problem to suggest the range of possible solutions and their relative costs, including the cost of finding no solution.

It will be best to commence with another glance at the national political scene and the forces at work in Indian society as a whole, at the beginning of Independence in 1947. The British occupation had called into existence an opposition movement, the Congress Party, composed of intellectuals, such as Nehru, with a leaning toward socialism; solid businessmen to whom such notions were poison; journalists, politicians, and lawyers who gave articulate

[171] Beals, *Gopalpur*, 78.

expression to a wide variety of ideas — the whole resting on a peasant base newly awakened by Gandhi, who had in his makeup rather more of the traditional Indian holy man than of the modern politician. The industrial working class was still very small and as yet had not played any major political role. Common opposition to the British, whose regime provided everyone with a convenient explanation for everything that seemed wrong, had long muted conflict among the articulate leaders of these groups and accustomed them to work together. These conflicts came to the surface as soon as the common enemy disappeared. Yet, in the absence of any powerful radical movement among the industrial workers or the peasants, conservative elements so far have not had too much difficulty in keeping India moving along a moderate course that has not yet seriously threatened their interests.

The struggle over economic policy immediately after Independence sheds a revealing light on the reasons why the moderates have been so powerful. Backed by Sardar Vallabhbhai J. Patel, the business community launched into a successful attack on the system of price controls over food and other essentials. The government removed the controls only to face a first-class inflation. Prices rose some thirty percent in a few months. Then the government reimposed controls, after millions whose income was barely sufficient to purchase necessities under "normal" conditions had already suffered heavily. Now, Patel was one of the partners in the "duumvirate" — the other was Nehru — that ruled India from the Partition until Patel's death in 1950. As well as a spokesman for business, Patel was the leader to whom the landlords and orthodox Hindus looked for protection against threats of agrarian reforms and secularism. Gandhi by this time had come to intervene in politics only when he felt that serious moral principles were at stake. The debate over price control was one of these. Significantly, Gandhi's intervention tipped the scales effectively in favor of decontrol. Thus, on a crucial issue affecting the welfare of millions, and the first one to arise after Independence, the leader of the peasant masses threw his support to the conservatives.[172] In this episode we see the familiar link

[172] See Brecher, *Nehru*, 509–510, for the decontrol episode; 390, 395 for the duumvirate and character of Patel.

between the peasants and commercial interests that has for some time been one of the important facts of Indian politics.

Gandhi was assassinated in 1948. Sardar Patel died in 1950. Within a year Nehru, through a series of parliamentary and be-hind-the-scenes maneuvers had succeeded in making himself un-disputed leader of the Congress Party and the country. At long last, India was ready to move forward, or at least begin to cope seriously with her own problems. The Planning Commission had been estab-lished in March 1950 with Nehru as chairman. The First Five Year Plan began in 1951 and was followed directly by a Second and Third. However, not until 1955 did the government become com-mitted to a "socialist pattern of society."[173]

Though there has been considerable talk about socialism, enough to disturb the business community quite seriously, actually very little has been done. By 1961 the central government had be-gun to operate a number of firms in such diverse fields as atomic energy, electronics, locomotives, aircraft, electrical equipment, ma-chine tools, and antibiotics, while state governments owned or aided a number of others. But the share of private industry remained very large. According to the text of the Third Five-Year Plan, the government hoped to raise the contribution of the public sector in manufacturing from its level of under two percent in 1961 to nearly a fourth. However, the lion's share of investment funds was earmarked for transportation and communication, in other words for creating services needed by private industry.[174] There is noth-ing necessarily wrong in such a policy. But it does seem to be a serious mistake to refer to the Indian experiment as a form of social-ism. Progress there has been certainly in industry. I shall not try to assess it, beyond registering the very bare statistical assertions that the index of industrial production rose from 100 in 1956 to 158.2 in 1963, or by rather more than a half, and that per capita income has kept far enough ahead of population growth to register slow gains of about two percent a year from 1951 to 1961.[175] The warn-

[173] Brecher, *Nehru*, 432 – 436, 520, 528 – 530.
[174] India, Planning Commission, *Third Five Year Plan*, 14, 23.
[175] *Far Eastern Economic Review, 1964 Yearbook*, 174, 168. There was a slight drop in per capita income according to estimates for 1962 – 1963.

ing that such figures contain a good deal of guesswork will never-theless bear repeating. And the progress to date has taken place to a great extent under capitalist auspices.

In agriculture too the main lines of policy have been to seek for greater production within the framework of the prevailing system inherited from Akbar and the British. There were two major prongs in the policy of the Nehru period: an attack on the problems of landlordism and an effort, through the Community Development Program, to stimulate the peasants' output.

Shortly after the achievement of Indian independence, the government undertook a frontal attack on the long discussed prob-lem of *zamindars*. The *zamindar*, as we have seen, was not only a landlord but a collector of taxes who stood between the govern-ment and the actual cultivator. In the abolition of the *zamindar*, the objective was by no means a socialist form of agriculture but the encouragement of peasant agriculture by giving the actual tiller of the soil a permanent stake in the land he cultivates, and by prevent-ing rack-renting, the use of forced labor, and other abuses.[176] The actual legislation was left to the separate states of the new republic. The wide variety of local conditions provides one very good rea-son for so doing. On the other hand, leaving the question up to the states also increased the leverage of powerful local interest groups. These soon challenged the legality of the reform. When these de-lays became threatening, the central government altered the con-stitution to speed up the process.[177] By 1961 official sources could claim that intermediaries had been abolished throughout the coun-try, except for a few small pockets. Formerly intermediaries had rights over approximately 43 percent of the cultivated area of India, a share allegedly reduced to about 8.5 by 1961.[178] A closer look at the situation gives rise to the strong suspicion that the con-nection between these statistics and social realities in the country-side is largely fortuitous.

To speak of abolition *tout court* in the case of the *zamindars* would be highly misleading. In several states the governments set

176 Patel, *Indian Land Problem*, 402.
177 Patel, *Indian Land Problem*, 477.
178 See *Times of India Yearbook, 1960 – 1961*, 102.

no limit to the amount of land the *zamindars* might keep, as long as they used it for their residence and actually cultivated it. The purpose was the laudable one of avoiding the breakup of more efficient larger farms, though it is necessary to remember that in India a large farm is much more often a large holding rented out to many small tenants than it is an efficiently managed unit of cultivation. But the consequence in many areas was that *zamindars* campaigned to evict tenants, many of very long standing, in order to add to the area of their home farms. One cautious student referred to the result as an expropriation unheard of in the previous history of India.[179] Even the text of the Third Five Year Plan concedes that the impact of tenancy legislation in practice has been less than hoped for, because landlords have ejected tenants under the plea of voluntary surrenders. The record of the states in improving matters remained very spotty down to the end of 1963, more than a decade after the changes began.[180] Observations made on the spot and local studies indicate very little change. Daniel Thorner in 1960 concluded that "In essence the bigger people have held on to a lot of land, and they are getting others to cultivate it for them."[181]

Still the mighty in the countryside are a great deal less secure than they once were. The machinery of government no longer stands behind them as firmly as it did under British rule. About as close as one can come to the truth, I would venture, is to remark that the big people are not as big as they once were, and that the tenancy legislation of the Nehru period was a significant element in a general policy that had as its main consequence the promotion of petty landlords and rich peasants — the two often amount to the same thing — to become the dominant feature in the Indian rural landscape.[182] This impression is strengthened by a statistical study of the distribution of land ownership, carried out in 1953 – 1954,

[179] Patel, *Indian Land Problem*, 478 – 479.

[180] Planning Commission, *Third Five Year Plan*, 224 – 225. *Far Eastern Economic Review* (November·7, 1963) 294 cited continuing criticism of the states by the Planning Commission, for lack of progress in land reform.

[181] *Land and Labour*, 5. Note also on p. 4 his revealing first-hand observations on the original Community Development Project showplace at Etawah.

[182] Cf Neale, *Economic Change*, 257.

by which time the intermediaries were supposedly nearly eliminated. Such statistics are highly unreliable in India, for reasons that
have already been indicated. But the general conclusion, that about
half the total area was held by less than an eighth of the agricultural
population, is probably not too misleading.[183] Official agrarian policy has an equalitarian tinge that comes out more strongly in
speeches than in results. This has been equally true of the Community Development Program to which we may now turn.

The intellectual and institutional antecedents of the Community Development Program do not have the remotest connection
with Marxist socialism. One important ingredient is Gandhi's faith
in an idealized version of the Indian village as the most suitable
community for civilized man. A second element is American experience with our agricultural extension service. A third has been
the influence of British paternalism and, more specifically, movements for "village uplift." The last element seems to me the most
important. With the crucial exception of the scale on which it has
been tried, I can find nothing significant in the Community Development Program that has not been tried or recommended in such
accounts as F. L. Brayne's *The Remaking of Village India*[184] or the
writings of Sir Malcolm Darling.

This bizarre parentage has produced two main ideas that constitute the central doctrines of the Community Development Program. One is that India's peasants will want economic progress and
sustain it through their own efforts as soon as they have been shown
its advantages. The other theme is that the changes must and will
come about democratically, that is, in response to the "felt needs"
— a favorite phrase — of India's villagers, who will somehow be
able to participate in the planning of a better life for all. Much of
the preliminary discussion of the Program assumed that there was a
huge reservoir of popular energy and enthusiasm that could be
tapped on behalf of new and rather vaguely defined social ideals.

The atmosphere, as well as subsequent disappointments, recalls
the "movement to the people" of nineteenth-century Russian in-

[183] Figures given in Mitra, "Tax Burden," in Braibanti and Spengler,
eds, *Administration and Economic Development*, 299.
[184] 2d ed (Oxford, 1929).

tellectuals. The Indian Minister for Community Development and Cooperation once went so far as to deny that economic progress was the real objective:

> A project for community development does not aim at higher productivity in agriculture and industry, better roads and houses, more schools and clinics. None of thoses constitutes an end which the project pursues. For a community project, there is not a multiplicity of ends, but only one, and this single and indivisible goal is better living.[185]

Events were to show that the mass of the peasants were reluctant to adopt the new methods of cultivation brought in by outsiders and that democratic persuasion turned out to be a terribly slow and ineffective procedure when bureaucratic planners insisted on quick results. These difficulties form the core of the dilemma of democratic reform to which Nehru's government was deeply committed.

The Community Development Program began to function in 1952 and has thus been in effect for a dozen years at the time these lines are written. By the latter part of 1963, the press announced that development blocks (*i.e.*, areas of development projects) covered practically all of India.[186] Although the Congress party in early 1959 passed a resolution proclaiming a modified version of collectivism as a goal for the future, nothing was done to implement it.[187] In practice, the policy of the Community Development Program has been to proceed very gingerly with any changes affecting rural social structure. In the beginning, official instructions to program officials in contact with the villagers made no mention of caste, property relationships, or surplus manpower in

---

[185] Dey, "Community Projects in Action," in Park and Tinker, eds, *Leadership and Political Institutions*, 348. The essay as a whole is a good example of the official mystique about Community Development Programs.

[186] *Times of India*, November 27, 1963.

[187] According to the "Nagpur Resolution" as it has become known, "The future agrarian pattern should be that of co-operative joint farming, in which the land will be pooled for joint cultivation, the farmers continuing to retain their property rights and getting a share from the net produce in the proportion of the land." Landless laborers were also to get an unspecified share. See the text in *Congress Bulletin* (January – February 1959), 22 – 23.

the village — in other words, any of the real problems.[188] I have come upon no signs of change on this score. Most of the attempt at changes was directed toward reviving and reintroducing village democracy through the encouragement of village councils (*panchayats*). In some parts of the country the effect has been to weaken the authority of older landlords or even peasant élites. But the process has not gone very far. Fundamentally, the notion of village democracy is a piece of romantic Gandhian nostalgia that has no relevance to modern conditions. The premodern Indian village was probably as much of a petty tyranny as a petty republic; certainly the modern one is such. To democratize the villages without altering property relationships is simply absurd. (That the redistribution of land by itself is no answer is sufficiently obvious to require no comment.) Finally, the real sources of change, the factors that determine the fate of the peasantry, lie outside the boundaries of the village. Through the ballot box and through their pressure on state and national politics, the peasants can do something about those questions, but not within the framework of village politics. In any event, after the Program had begun to run into severe difficulties and some secondary criticism in one of its periodic evaluations, even some of the more Gandhian officials openly repudiated the conception of independent village republics and came out on behalf of stricter supervision from above.[189]

Without altering the content of the Program, closer supervision from above is unlikely to accomplish much. The content amounts in practice to bringing resources and techniques to the peasants' doorstep through bureaucratic procedures, while generally refraining from making or even trying to make any change in the social structure and general situation that prevents the peasants from adopting better methods. Here, in my judgment, lies the fundamental flaw in the whole policy. Neither the Community Development Program nor the land reform programs has taken any steps to tap the existing and potential surplus in agriculture to use

[188] See Dube, *India's Changing Villages*, 22.
[189] Tinker, "The Village in the Framework of Development," in Braibanti and Spengler, eds, *Administration and Economic Development*, 116–117. See also Retzlaff, *Case Study of Panchayats*, esp 43, 72, 110.

it for economic growth in a way that would ultimately benefit the peasants. Indeed one distinguished Indian economist has calculated that the government has spent a great deal more on agriculture than it has taken out![190]

To make this point is not to imply that the Nehru government should have put a Stalinist squeeze on the peasantry. It is not necessary to go nearly that far. There was plenty of room for greater accomplishments within a democratic framework. The point is rather that, by allowing old institutions to persist under a cloud of reformist rhetoric and bureaucratic make-work, the Nehru government 1) permitted the old forms of diverting the agricultural surplus to continue; 2) failed to introduce a market economy or a workable substitute to get food from the peasants to the cities; and 3) for these reasons failed to increase agricultural productivity or to tap the huge potential surplus that exists in the countryside. To be blunt, Nehru's agrarian program was an out-and-out failure. This harsh judgment requires an effort at proof and an explanation.

Seven years after the Community Development Program got under way, an official report could claim that more than three-quarters of India's food production never reached the market.[191] Eighty-five percent of the villager's credit still came from the moneylender and "other individuals," presumably the more prosperous peasants. As before, the grain that did reach the market was usually sold to local traders at depressed harvesttime prices. Cultivators still paid exorbitant rates for inadequate credit, much of which still went to finance customary forms of display such as dowries. Cooperatives still extended less than ten percent of the total agricultural credit used by cultivators.[192] Resentment against cooperatives as bureaucratic outside intruders, whose procedures in

[190] Mitra, "Tax Burden," 295.

[191] India, *Report of Food Crisis*, 98. Thorner, *Land and Labour*, chap VIII, dismisses the *Report* as a hurried political maneuver aimed at diverting the government from concentrating on industrial growth by creating a scare about agriculture. Though the *Report* does not in my judgment get at the root of the problem, its pessimistic observations have been partly justified by subsequent events; it also contains a number of valuable factual points.

[192] India, *Report of Food Crisis*, 6, 85, 71.

TABLE 2

INDIA'S REPORTED OUTPUT OF RICE*

Year	Yield (thousands of tons)	Year	Yield (thousands of tons)
1948 – 1949	22,597	1956 – 1957	28,282
1949 – 1950	23,170	1957 – 1958	24,821
1950 – 1951	20,251	1958 – 1959	29,721
1951 – 1952	20,964	1959 – 1960	30,831
1952 – 1953	22,537	1960 – 1961	33,700
1953 – 1954	27,769	1961 – 1962	33,600
1954 – 1955	24,821	1962 – 1963	32,500
1955 – 1956	27,122	(estimated)	or
			31,000

* Sources: For 1948 – 1957, see India, *Statistical Abstract; 1957 – 58,* 437; 1958 – 1961: *Times of India Yearbook, 1960 – 1961,* 113 and *1962 – 1963,* 282; 1961 – 1963: *Far Eastern Economic Review* (November 7, 1963), 294; the lower estimate for 1962 – 1963 comes from *Far Eastern Economic Review, 1964 Yearbook,* 174.

granting loans were slow and cumbersome compared to the money-lender, remained a common feature in village life.

The gravest weakness appears in the failure to achieve more than a very indifferent increase in the production of food. Before looking more closely at the reasons, it will be well to review some of the statistical evidence. Though figures on output and yield are far from dependable, the story that they tell is so plain that it would take an improbably large error to modify the general interpretation. Table 2 gives India's reported output of rice from 1948 to 1963. Because it has been by far the most important food crop, we may legitimately concentrate on rice alone. Nor is it necessary to carry the figures beyond 1963. By that time the existence of at least a potential crisis had begun to be common knowledge. Here our problem is to assess the reasons for failure, not to measure its extent in an ever-shifting present.

The Community Development Program was not expected to reach even a fourth of the population by 1956; by 1959 it had reached around 61 percent of the rural inhabitants; by 1963 supposedly nearly all were to have felt the impact.[193] According to this chronology, one should expect to see, if the program were effective in raising output, some slight effects by 1954 – 1955 and a more or less steady and accelerating rise thereafter. Though there is some rise in output, nothing of the sort appears. There is a drop of close to three million tons between 1953 – 1954 and 1954 – 1955, another drop of almost three and a half million tons between 1956 – 1957 and 1957 – 1958; after 1960 a steadily declining output, culminating in another sharp drop for 1962 – 1963. In October of that year the Calcutta mobs rioted for rice. Previous output had barely managed to keep ahead of population growth. The bad crop of 1962 – 1963 wiped out the margin, as per capita food consumption was reported to have dropped by two percent.[194]

Indian agriculture in a word remains today what it was in Akbar's and still was in Curzon's time: a gamble in the rains, where a bad crop means disaster for millions of people. In the second half of the twentieth century this is a social and political problem very much more than a geographical and material one. As the staff of the Community Development Program senses, the resources exist, even at a local level, to mitigate greatly the effects of climate. But this would mean some kind of a social as well as a technical revolution. Instead, what improvement there has been so far has come mainly from the spread of the old inefficient system into new and probably marginal areas of the country.

There is quite a bit of evidence that points in this direction. Some that is rather striking may be had in the statistics on yield per hectare. In any case, they provide a better notion of changes in productivity than do those on total output. Such figures also enable us to make a comparison between the situation under the British regime and the present one, even though the statistics should not be taken literally because there have been improvements in the

[193] Dube, *India's Changing Villages*, 12; *Times of India Yearbook, 1960 – 1961*, p. 264; *Times of India*, November 27, 1963.

[194] U.S. Department of Agriculture, *Foreign Agriculture* (February 10, 1964), 7.

TABLE 3

YIELD IN PADDY RICE FOR INDIA AND JAPAN*

Year	Yield in 100 kilograms per hectare India	Japan
1927 – 1928 } 1931 – 1932	14.4	35.4
1932 – 1933	14.1	34.7
1933 – 1934	13.8	41.8
1934 – 1935	13.9	30.6
1935 – 1936	12.3	33.6
1936 – 1937	14.5	39.3
1937 – 1938	13.9	38.6
1948 – 1949 } 1952 – 1953	11.1	40.0
1957 – 1958	11.8	44.3
1958 – 1959	14.0	46.2
1959 – 1960	14.1	47.5
1960 – 1961	15.3	48.6
1961 – 1962	15.1	47.0

* Sources: For 1927 – 1938, *Annuaire international de statistique agricole 1937 – 1938* (Rome, 1938), Table 77, p. 279; for 1948 – 1962, Food and Agriculture Organization of the United Nations, *Production Yearbook 1960*, XIV, 50, and ibid, 1962, XVI, 50.

way crop yields are estimated since the Second World War.[195] In Table 3 are presented data for certain years on the yield in wet or paddy rice for India and also for Japan. Those for India in the prewar period do not include Burma.

The figures scarcely require comment. Even under the new regime, India's productivity has fluctuated around the level of the late 1920s and early 1930s. Starting from a much higher base, Japan has forged steadily ahead in recent years. Her productivity is about three times that of India. Climate alone can scarcely account for such a big difference.

Though the grosser institutional factors that may explain India's low productivity lie outside the village and have already been

[195] For a fuller discussion of this point see "Food Statistics in India," *Studies in Agricultural Economics,* III, 8 – 11.

touched upon, it is helpful, indeed necessary for more adequate comprehension, to see their reflection at work within the peasant community. Furthermore, national averages conceal decisive facts. In some areas there has been distinct improvement. If we are to understand the obstacles, it is necessary to see why there has been improvement in some places and not in others. I shall try to bring these factors out, first by discussing one part of India where production has improved quite markedly and then by reviewing those aspects of the village community that still inhibit economic advance.

Madras constitutes one of the brighter spots on the map of India, where yields of rice are said to have risen by as much as 16 to 17 percent.[196] An effort to see what factors are involved produces an image that sharply contradicts official doctrines. In terms of land area, by far the most important crop is rice grown in paddies. About one-third of the area under cultivation in the State, 4.5 million acres out of a total of 14.27 million, is irrigated. Since only 344,000 acres have been brought under irrigation between 1952 and 1959,[197] improvements in irrigation cannot be the major reason for the rise in productivity. Rather, the answer appears to be that Madras has moved farther than other areas toward a capitalist form of agriculture.

The reasons for this change deserve at least passing mention because of their larger implications. At the end of the nineteenth century the tendency for land to pass out of the hands of the peasants became noticeable in Madras and aroused official concern, as it did in other parts of India. However, in Madras the professional moneylender was rare. Instead, money was lent by one cultivator to another. Furthermore, the line between the cultivator and the urban trading classes was not a sharp one. The latter kept their landed property and increased it by purchasing irrigated rice land. These tendencies appear to have been accelerated by legislation after Independence. The Fair Rent Act of 1956 forced the middling landlord who let out his land on a sharecropping basis to turn to direct exploitation of the land with hired labor, since wages were

[196] India, *Report of Food Crisis*, 180.
[197] *Madras in Maps and Pictures*, 41 – 42.

not raised at the same time.[198] The consequence has been that in the deltas, the best rice-growing areas, property has become highly concentrated. A minority in possession of the land faces a proletarian majority of laborers. Even though a well-to-do proprietor does not cultivate the land himself, he can, by careful supervision ·of hired labor, good use of fertilizer, and other measures, obtain yields of as high as 27 quintals a hectare (a quintal equals 100 kilograms), in comparison with the average of 17 for the area.[199]

Thus the rise in productivity, in this area at any rate, comes quite clearly from capitalism's entering wedge. It is not due to the government's policy of favoring the upper ranks of the peasantry. Among the agricultural workers and small peasants, the political consequences are also about what might be expected: increasing tension and disillusionment with the Congress Party and a rise in sympathy for the Communists.

A generous sampling of the literature on the villages (a first-rate cure, incidentally, for those who firmly believe in the infinite variety to be found in the Indian countryside) gives the same general impression of a limited capitalist intrusion, though generally less than in Madras.[200] Anthropologists have by now studied a substantial variety of villages in different parts of the country and at different stages in the process of modernization. Rather than try to set modernized villages against backward ones, something already

[198] Dupuis, *Madras*, 130 – 131, 144 – 145.

[199] Dupuis, *Madras*, 125, 132, 151 – 152.

[200] See e.g., Tinker, "The Village in the Framework of Economic Development," in Braibanti and Spengler, eds, *Administration and Economic Development*, 94 – 133, constitutes a good recent brief survey which draws on the evaluation reports of the Community Development Program, though it deals more with political than economic questions. Dumont, *Terres vivantes*, is very valuable but rather episodic. Epstein, *Economic Development and Social Change*, is perhaps the most useful of the individual case studies. Other valuable sources include Mayer et al, *Pilot Project India*, the first effort of the modern kind; the collection edited by Marriott, *Village India*, cited elsewhere; Mayer, *Caste and Kinship*; Lewis, *Village Life in Northern India*; Dube, *Indian Village* and *India's Changing Villages*, both done in the early stages but quite revealing of the main problems. Singer, ed, *Traditional India*, and Srinivas, *Caste in Modern India*, are more general but also bring out significant points.

done quite well for two nearby villages in one area,[201] I shall try to analyze each of the major obstacles and draw on specific instances where possible to demonstrate how they have been overcome and can be overcome.

The basic assumption of the Community Development Program, the reader may recall, has been that the Indian peasant would of his own free will, and because of his "felt needs," immediately adopt technical improvements the moment he was shown them. A good part of the trouble has been that a slow-moving and alien bureaucracy has been doing a great deal of the showing without knowing anything about local conditions. If the Program had directed its democratic inclinations more toward doing something about this aspect of the problem rather than *panchayat* reform, the results would probably have been better. As it is, the age-old split between the autonomous village and the government persists.

Of the government man sent into the village, one report says: "The hands of the Village-Level Worker are smooth and soft. His days are spent writing progress reports and keeping his office in order against the day when one of his superiors will pay a surprise visit." In this particular village the government worker had already urged the farmers to try some fertilizer. They applied it too liberally, and the crops withered and died. Next year, the same villagers, still friendly, accepted the advice to plant wheat in an empty irrigation reservoir. Rust attacked the crop. After that the men ruined an expensive German sprayer in an effort to kill the rust. Government officials ended up by regarding the peasants as hopelessly stupid and lazy. Peasants who could not afford to risk their crops stuck to traditional ways they knew would work after a fashion.[202] Such accounts could be duplicated endlessly. I will add only one more from the book by the prickly and commonsensical French agronomist, René Dumont, who left a United Nations evaluation team in disgust, because it started off as a feted showpiece tour, in order to tramp the dust and mud of Indian villages on his own. At one point he was shown with considerable pride a "cream puff" area of rice fields where the yields were at a record for India — but about forty

[201] Epstein, *Economic Development and Social Change*.
[202] Beals, *Gopalpur*, 79, 82.

percent below ordinary Japanese fields. Here the Indians had tried to introduce Japanese methods as they have done in many places. But the Japanese method cannot be taken over piecemeal. It requires not only transplanting, but careful regulation of the water supply and appropriate soil conditions. Local variations have to be taken into account and corresponding adaptations made to get proper results. Instead, what happened was that "everything was arranged on paper, nothing on the spot." Improvement plans, Dumont adds with italicized indignation, set up as advice for each development block, were just about the same for the entire country.[203]

Where the technology was appropriate to local conditions, on the other hand, and where it could be shown to work, peasants would often turn to it rapidly. In one village the peasants first drove their cattle away rather than allow them to be inoculated against the rinderpest, a fatal epidemic disease then raging in the area. Only forty-seven cattle were inoculated despite intensive efforts. When the inoculated cattle survived and the rinderpest killed some two hundred others, the peasants' attitude toward innovation in this area changed dramatically.[204]

In this instance innovation could gain an entry because the bureaucracy could and did offer a service that corresponded to "felt needs." Such is by no means always the case. "Felt needs" in any society are in large measure the product of the individual's specific social situation and upbringing. They are created, not simply the gift of nature. It is necessary to probe deeper and see what lies behind them to find what it is that is felt to be "normal." In the Indian village it amounts to the fact that "the felt needs" rest upon the petty tyranny of village oligarchs, fighting among themselves but maintaining their overall hegemony through caste and the traditional political structure of the village. There are strong vested interests at the back of grass-roots reluctance to adopt new ways. Essentially these are fears on the part of the dominant castes that they will lose their perquisites of labor and payments in kind. Dumont points out that, with very simple tools and equipment and by

[203] *Terres vivantes,* 144 – 145; see also 124 –127.
[204] Singh, "Impact of Community Development," in Park and Tinker, eds, *Leadership and Political Institutions,* 361 – 365.

drawing on labor that is available and unused most of the year, it would be possible to put in order the traditional system of irrigation by small reservoirs (tanks). Doing so would add enough good land with higher yields in his estimation to solve most of India's food problem. Why then does nothing happen? Because the proprietors who run the villages are afraid that the increased land made available from these tanks will cut into their rents and put the outcastes into a position to bargain about their labor.[205] All the endless talk about the persistence of Indian cultural traditions, the momentum of centuries behind the caste system, the apathy of the villagers constitutes, along with the new rhetoric of democracy, a huge billowing smokescreen before these interests.[206]

For the lower strata of the rural population, an overwhelming majority in India as a whole, the restriction of wants and ambitions, the acceptance of what seems to us an extraordinarily cramped horizon and the continuing wary skepticism about "outsiders" constitute realistic and sensible reactions to prevailing conditions. Where the cultivator is so poor that any minor disaster pushes him over the edge, he would be stupid to follow bureaucratic advice about new planting methods that fail because of inattention to important details and local conditions. Nor can he be expected to put out enormous efforts and display great enthusiasm where most of the benefits go to the local oligarchs. In such a situation his "felt need" is to lay low. Hence in a great many areas the Community Development Program came in like a whirlwind, aroused a bit of local enthusiasm — almost anyone likes to be the object of flattering attention — and moved on, retiring the area to the postintensive phase in official records. Afterward many villages slipped back into their old ways. When the authorities have had their pleasure, the world can go back to normal.

[205] *Terres vivantes,* 139; Beals; *Gopalpur,* 79, points out that the wealthy man stands to gain little from improvements in his clients' economic position. This situation differs sharply from that found in early Meiji Japan.

[206] For a good detailed study of caste as a means of domination see Gough, "Social Structure of a Tanjore Village," in Marriott, ed, *Village India,* 36 – 52. This function of caste appears more or less clearly in all the accounts, though Gough's seems to me the best and most concise.

None of these obstacles is insuperable, neither collectively nor individually, much as each one reenforces the others. The best evidence comes from the fact that the peasants do overcome them when the situation calls for it. Generally they adapt to the new situation those parts of the traditional social mechanism that will work.[207] But the peasants show little hesitation in discarding what is clearly unsuitable. One illuminating study contrasts the situation in a village where irrigation made possible the introduction of sugar cane on a wide scale with a nearby one to which the water could not be brought. In the irrigated areas the peasants showed no hesitation in going over to the cultivation of sugar cane, even though it involved a thorough reorganization of work patterns. Indeed the author suggests quite plausibly that a thorough reorganization may be easier than a partial one. Even in the face of caste prejudices against work in the fields, the farmers met out of their own households about half the total labor requirements for cane growing. All this could happen mainly because a local sugar cane factory was able to provide a steady market for the cane. In the same area, rice cultivation remained very inefficient. No one would go over to the Japanese methods. For rice, there was little or no market in the area. The introduction of sugar cane as a commercial crop, the transition to a cash economy, it is worth noting, produced relatively few differences in the general pattern of village life. The peasants remained peasants, though considerably more prosperous than before. Caste and the traditional system was by and large compatible with the transition, despite changes in work habits. In the nearby village that the water would not reach, the situation was quite different. There villagers had to scramble, by providing a variety of needed services, in order to take advantage of the general rise in the economic level that the surrounding area enjoyed. Hence the traditional order in

[207] Even caste may turn out to be reconcilable with democracy. See Rudolph and Rudolph, "Political Role of India's Caste Associations," 5 – 22, where the authors argue that caste associations may provide an adequate mechanism for bringing the illiterate peasantry into the democratic arena. For the negative side, the reactionary and utopian features of traditional Indian notions of consensus and the ways they limit the possibility of creative action on the part of the village in economic development, see the more pessimistic essay by Rudolph, "Consensus and Conflict," esp 396 – 397.

the dry village disintegrated much further. What emerges most clearly from the comparison is the range of adaptations that the original peasant society, generally the same over the entire area before the introduction of irrigation, could make under appropriate stimulus from the outside. Irrigation too would not have had these favorable results if a good market for the produce had not also arisen.[208] Elsewhere in India irrigation systems have rapidly deteriorated because the peasants had no use for them.

The introduction of a cash economy in the manner just discussed is instructive because it helps to dispose of preconceived notions about the difficulties involved. But it is not generally characteristic of what is taking place. A much more common situation is one where the more enterprising petty landlords and peasants show a strong inclination to go over to commercial activities, either selling their produce locally or taking up business sidelines where possible in the nearby town. This is partly an unintended consequence of the Community Development Program, whose major benefits have flowed to the wealthier peasants.[209] On this score, present-day India shows some strong resemblances to Soviet Russia during the days of the NEP. There is the same hustle and bustle as the energetic little fellows find all sorts of crevices in the system where they can establish themselves to make petty fortunes. This, too, is one more indication of the flexibility of the traditional order. Caste boycotts are much less effective than they used to be now that it is possible for even a peasant to buy services instead of being dependent on a closed system of economic changes. With the decline of the boycott, the whole caste system loses one of its most significant sanctions.

There are encouraging aspects to this chase after the fast rupee by petty landlords and the more well-to-do peasants. For one thing it demonstrates that, where there is a profitable alternative to work-

[208] Epstein, *Economic Development and Social Change;* on sugar cane, 30, 31, 34, 35, 53; on rice and contrasts, 63 – 65; on the "dry" village and general contrasts, see concluding chapter.

[209] Tinker, "Village, in the Framework of Development," in Braibanti and Spengler, eds, *Administration and Economic Development,* 130 – 131, points out this fact and some of its consequences quite explicitly.

ing the levers of the old society, there are many ambitious peasants who will grasp it. This may be the way in which India makes the transition to commercial agriculture, very roughly the French model of the late eighteenth and nineteenth centuries. Modern technology may also make it possible to eliminate the more back-breaking and stultifying aspects of intensive peasant agriculture. But there are political dangers. The rural proletariat in India is tied to the prevailing order through caste obligations and the tiny hand-kerchief plot. It seems likely that the direction of future changes will be toward further disintegration of traditional ties and toward wage labor, rather than in the direction of modified patriarchal ties as happened in Japan. Should prevailing trends continue, traditional bonds are liable to wear ever more thin. There is already a huge mi-gration to urban slums where communist agitation does find con-siderable response. If no place in society is found for the mass of floating labor released by this NEP-like transformation of the countryside, the political consequences might well be explosive.

What is the ultimate reason for this continuing stagnation and very halting progress, we may legitimately ask, as we leave the vil-lage behind and strive to gain a final perspective on the whole ques-tion. The proximate cause seems quite clearly to be the relative fail-ure of a market economy to penetrate very far into the countryside and put the peasants into a new situation to which they seem quite capable of responding with a sharp rise in output. The structure of village society is only a secondary obstacle, one that changes in re-sponse to external circumstances. To concentrate on local resist-ances, to send endless teams of anthropologists out to study the countryside, amounts to diverting attention from the main sources of difficulty, the makers of government policy in Delhi. More about that in a moment. Behind the weak push of the market lies the fail-ure to channel into industrial construction the resources that agri-culture does generate. One further step, taken with a glance at other countries, shows that the course of historical development in India was such that no class grew up with any very strong interest in rechanneling the agricultural surplus in such a way as to get the process of industrial growth started. The Nationalist movement owed its popular support to the peasantry and was, through Gandhi, suffused with its ideology.

This is about as far as a sociological analysis can penetrate. My own strong suspicion is that it already goes too far and that Nehru personally ought to bear a very large share of the blame. Too great a concentration on circumstances and objective difficulties leads to the mistake of forgetting that great political leaders are the ones who accomplish important institutional changes *despite* such obstacles. Nehru was a very powerful political leader. To deny that he had a great deal of room to maneuver seems absurd. Yet on the most decisive question of all, his policy was one of rhetoric and drift. The atmosphere of action became a substitute for action. On this score at least, Indian democracy is not alone.

In response to such an assessment, the Western liberal observer almost automatically responds that even if Indian agrarian policy, indeed her economic policy as a whole, has been rather long on talk and quite short on accomplishments, at least there has not been the brutality of communist modernization. Some sacrifice in speed, the argument runs, is necessary for the sake of democracy.

This comfortable generalization overlooks the dreadful costs in human suffering that a policy of *festina lente* imposes in the Indian situation. To measure these costs in cold statistics is impossible. But a few figures will give a rough notion of their magnitude. In 1924 and 1926 the All India Conference of Medical Research Workers estimated that India suffered from five to six million deaths a year from preventable diseases alone.[210] After the famine of 1943, the Bengal Famine Commission concluded that about a million and a half deaths occurred "as a direct result of the Famine and the epidemics which followed in its train."[211] Though wartime disruption contributed to the tragic results, fundamentally the famine was a product of the structure of Indian society.[212] The enormous death toll refers only to those who have fallen below the line that sepa-

---

[210] Quoted in Great Britain, *Report of Commission on Agriculture in India 1928*, 481.

[211] Quoted in India, *Census 1951*, VI, pt IA, 80.

[212] For a good account of the background from a British standpoint, see Woodruff, *Guardians*, 333 – 337.

rates success from failure in sheer biological survival. By themselves such figures say nothing about the disease, squalor, filth, and brutish ignorance perpetuated by religious beliefs among millions above the line. The upward thrust of population means also that the threat of death on a massive scale will hover in the background unless the rate of improvement rises sharply.

In addition it is necessary to point out that if democracy means the opportunity to play a meaningful part as a rational human being in determining one's own fate in life, democracy does not yet exist in the Indian countryside. The Indian peasant has not yet acquired the material and intellectual prerequisites for democratic society. The *panchayat* "revival," as I have indicated earlier, is mainly romantic rhetoric. Actually the Community Development Program has been imposed from above. Those who work in it have tended to shed much of their democratic idealism, to conclude that democratic processes are "too slow" and to orient their behavior toward "results" — often shallow statistical ones such as the number of compost pits dug — that will satisfy their superiors.

By itself, the fact that the Program has been imposed from above is not bad. It is the content of programs that matters. One can criticize bureaucratic leadership in the abstract only from a conception of democracy that excludes any interference whatever with the way human beings conduct their lives, no matter how ignorant or how cruel these people are as a consequence of their history. Anyone who holds this formalist conception of democracy would have to accept the fact that large sections of the Indian peasantry do not want economic development. They do not want it for reasons I have tried to explain. The only consistent program, from this standpoint, would be to dismantle any program and let the Indian peasants wallow in filth and disease until they starved. The results are scarcely likely to please any kind of democratic theorist.

More realistic policies might be grouped around the kinds of interference used and the costs of using one kind versus another. Whether any particular one will be adopted or none, with the Indian state breaking up along its present lines of cleavage, is another kind of question I do not propose to discuss.

If the prevailing policy in its essential outlines continues, as far as can be foreseen it would result in a very slow rate of improvement, mainly through the action of the upper stratum of the peasantry continuing to go over to peasant forms of commercial farming. The danger has already been pointed out: the steady swelling of an urban and rural proletariat on an ever larger scale. This policy could in time perhaps generate its own antithesis, though the difficulties of a radical takeover in India are enormous.

Much more desirable from a democratic standpoint would be for the government to harness and use these same tendencies for its own purposes. That would mean discarding the Gandhian doctrines (perhaps not so unlikely in the new administrative generation now coming to power), allowing the upper strata in the countryside free rein, but taxing their profits and organizing the market and credit mechanism in such a way as to drive out the moneylender. If the government in this way succeeded in tapping the present surplus generated in agriculture and encouraging the growth of a much bigger one, it could do a great deal more about industry on its own resources. As industry grew, it would sop up much of the surplus labor released in the countryside and spread the market ever more rapidly in a continually accelerating process. The efforts to bring technology and modern resources to the peasant's doorstep would then bear fruit.[213]

The third possibility would be to go over to much wider use of compulsion, more or less approaching the communist model. Even if it could be tried in India, it seems highly unlikely that it would work. Under Indian conditions for a long time to come, no political leadership — no matter how intelligent, dedicated, and ruthless — could, it seems to me, put through a revolutionary agrarian policy. The country is too diverse and too amorphous still, though that will gradually change. The administrative and political problem of forcing through a collectivization program against the barriers of

[213] The problem is recognized by some Indian students of agrarian questions. See, for example, Khan, "Resource Mobilization from Agriculture and Economic Development in Agriculture," 42 – 54, and Mitra, "Tax Burden," in Braibanti and Spengler, eds, *Administration and Economic Development*, 281 – 303, though the political aspects are muted in favor of economic technicalities.

caste and tradition in fourteen languages seems too formidable to require further discussion.

Only one line of policy then seems to offer real hope, which, to repeat, implies no prediction that it will be the one adopted. In any case, a strong element of coercion remains necessary if a change is to be made. Barring some technical miracle that will enable every Indian peasant to grow abundant food in a glass of water or a bowl of sand, labor will have to be applied much more effectively, technical advances introduced, and means found to get food to the dwellers in the cities. Either masked coercion on a massive scale, as in the capitalist model including even Japan, or more direct coercion approaching the socialist model will remain necessary. The tragic fact of the matter is that the poor bear the heaviest costs of modernization under both socialist and capitalist auspices. The only justification for imposing the costs is that they would become steadily worse off without it. As the situation stands, the dilemma is indeed a cruel one. It is possible to have the greatest sympathy for those responsible for facing it. To deny that it exists is, on the other hand, the acme of both intellectual and political irresponsibility.

PART THREE

*Theoretical Implications
and Projections*

CHAPTER SEVEN

The Democratic Route to Modern Society

FROM OUR PRESENT PERSPECTIVE we might now sketch with broad strokes the major features of each of the three routes to the modern world. The earliest one combined capitalism and parliamentary democracy after a series of revolutions: the Puritan Revolution, the French Revolution, and the American Civil War. With reservations discussed later in this chapter, I have called this the route of bourgeois revolution, a route that England, France, and the United States entered at succeeding points in time with profoundly different societies at the starting point. The second path was also a capitalist one, but, in the absence of a strong revolutionary surge, it passed through reactionary political forms to culminate in fascism. It is worth emphasizing that, through a revolution from above, industry did manage to grow and flourish in Germany and Japan. The third route is of course the communist one. In Russia and China, revolutions having their main but not exclusive origins among the peasants made possible the communist variant. Finally, by the middle of the 1960s, India had no more than haltingly entered upon the process of becoming a modern industrial society. That country had experienced neither a bourgeois revolution, nor a conservative revolution from above, nor so far a communist one. Whether India will be able to avoid the appalling costs of these three forms to discover some new variant, as it was trying to do under Nehru, or succumb in some way to the equally appalling costs of stagnation, remains the ghastly problem faced by Nehru's successors.

To a very limited extent these three types — bourgeois revolutions culminating in the Western form of democracy, conservative revolutions from above ending in fascism, and peasant revolutions leading to communism — may constitute alternative routes and choices. They are much more clearly successive historical stages. As such, they display a limited determinate relation to each other. The methods of modernization chosen in one country change the dimensions of the problem for the next countries who take the step, as Veblen recognized when he coined the now fashionable term, "the advantages of backwardness." Without the prior democratic modernization of England, the reactionary methods adopted in Germany and Japan would scarcely have been possible. Without both the capitalist and reactionary experiences, the communist method would have been something entirely different, if it had come into existence at all. It is easy enough to perceive, and even with some sympathy, that Indian diffidence is in good measure a negative critical reaction to all three forms of prior historical experience. Although there have been certain common problems in the construction of industrial societies, the task remains a continually changing one. The historical preconditions of each major political species differ sharply from the others.

Within each major type there are also striking differences, perhaps most striking in the democratic variant, as well as significant similarities. In this chapter we shall try to do justice to both, in analyzing certain agrarian social features that have contributed to the development of Western democracy. It is well to be explicit once more about what this rather sonorous phrase means, even if definitions of democracy have a way of leading away from real issues to trivial quibbling. The author sees the development of a democracy as a long and certainly incomplete struggle to do three closely related things: 1) to check arbitrary rulers, 2) to replace arbitrary rules with just and rational ones, and 3) to obtain a share for the underlying population in the making of rules. The beheading of kings has been the most dramatic and by no means the least important aspect of the first feature. Efforts to establish the rule of law, the power of the legislature, and later to use the state as an engine for social welfare are familiar and famous aspects of the other two.

Though a detailed consideration of the earlier phases of pre-modern societies lies outside the scope of this work, it is well to raise at least briefly the question of different starting points. Are there structural differences in agrarian societies that might in some cases favor subsequent development toward parliamentary democracy while other starting points would make this achievement difficult or rule it out altogether? Certainly the starting point does not completely determine the subsequent course of modernization. Fourteenth-century Prussian society exhibited many of the same features that were the ancestors of parliamentary democracy in Western Europe. The decisive changes that fundamentally altered the course of Prussian and eventually German society took place in the next two centuries. Yet even if the starting point is not decisive in itself, some may be much more favorable to democratic developments than others.

A good case can be made, I think, for the thesis that Western feudalism did contain certain institutions that distinguished it from other societies in such a way as to favor democratic possibilities. The German historian Otto Hintze in his discussion of the social orders of feudal society (*Stände*) has perhaps done the most toward rendering the thesis convincing, though it remains a topic of lively scholarly debate.[1] For our purposes, the most important aspect was the growth of the notion of the immunity of certain groups and persons from the power of the ruler, along with the conception of the right of resistance to unjust authority. Together with the conception of contract as a mutual engagement freely undertaken by free persons, derived from the feudal relation of vassalage, this complex of ideas and practices constitutes a crucial legacy from European medieval society to modern Western conceptions of a free society.

This complex arose only in Western Europe. Only there did that delicate balance occur between too much and too little royal

[1] See in Hintze, *Staat und Verfassung*, I, "Weltgeschichtliche Bedingungen der Repräsentativverfassung (1931)," 140–185; "Typologie der ständischen Verfassungen des Abendlandes (1930)," 120–139; and "Wesen und Verbreitung des Feudalismus (1929)," 84–119. For bringing some of the same ideas up to date see Coulborn, ed, *Feudalism* (1956).

power which gave an important impetus to parliamentary democracy. A wide variety of partial resemblances do occur elsewhere but seem to lack either a crucial ingredient or the crucial proportion among them found in Western Europe. Russian society did develop a system of estates, the *soslovii*. But Ivan the Terrible broke the back of the independent nobility. The attempt to recover their privileges came after the strong hand of Peter the Great had been removed and resulted in obtaining privileges without corresponding obligations or corporate representation in the process of governing. Bureaucratic China generated the conception of the Mandate of Heaven that gave some color of legitimacy to resistance to unjust oppression, but without a strong notion of corporate immunity, something the scholar officials created to a limited extent in practice and against the basic principle of the bureaucratic polity. Feudalism did arise in Japan, but with heavy stress on loyalty to superiors and a divine ruler. It lacked the conception of an engagement among theoretical equals. In the Indian caste system one can perceive strong tendencies toward the conception of immunity and corporate privilege, but again without the theory or practice of free contract.

The attempts to find a single comprehensive explanation of these differences, stimulated by a few offhand observations by Marx and culminating in Wittfogel's polemical conception of oriental despotism based on the control of water supplies, have not been very successful. This does not mean that they are misdirected. Water supply is probably much too narrow a notion. Traditional despotisms may arise where a central authority is able to perform a variety of tasks or supervise activities essential to the working of the whole society. In earlier times it was much less possible than it is now for a government to create situations that carry with them their own definition of what task is essential to society as a whole and make the underlying population accept it passively. Hence it is somewhat less risky to pursue this hypothesis about the locus of the performance of essential tasks for preindustrial societies than it would be for modern ones. On the other hand, there also seems to be a rather wider range of choice than was once supposed in the political level at which a society organizes the division of labor and the maintenance of social cohesion. The peasant village, the feudal fief, or even a crude territorial bureaucracy may constitute the decisive level under generally similar agrarian technologies.

With this brief assessment of variations in the starting point, we may turn to the process of modernization itself. One point stands out quite clearly. The persistence of royal absolutism or more generally of a preindustrial bureaucratic rule into modern times has created conditions unfavorable to democracy of the Western variety. The varied histories of China, Russia, and Germany converge on this point. It is a curious fact, for which I shall not try to offer an explanation, that powerful central governments that we can loosely call royal absolutisms or agrarian bureaucracies established themselves in the sixteenth and seventeenth centuries in all the major countries examined in connection with this study (except of course the United States), namely, England, France, the Prussian part of Germany, Russia, China, Japan, and India. Whatever the reason may be, the fact forms a convenient if partly arbitrary peg upon which to hang the beginnings of modernization. Though their persistence has had unfavorable consequences, strong monarchical institutions have performed an indispensable function at an early point in checking the turbulence of the nobility. Democracy could not grow and flourish under the shadow of prospective plunder and pillage by marauding barons.

In early modern times too, a decisive precondition for modern democracy has been the emergence of a rough balance between the crown and the nobility, in which the royal power predominated but left a substantial degree of independence to the nobility. The pluralist notion that an independent nobility is an essential ingredient in the growth of democracy has a firm basis in historical fact. Comparative support of this thesis is provided by the absence of such an ingredient in Akbar's India and Manchu China, or perhaps more accurately by the failure to work out an acceptable and legitimate status for the degree of independence that in fact existed. The ways in which this independence has been hammered out are equally important. In England the *locus classicus* for positive evidence, the Wars of the Roses decimated the landed aristocracy, making considerably easier the establishment of a form of royal absolutism rather milder than that in France. It is wise to recall that the achievement of such a balance, so dear to the liberal and pluralist tradition, has been the fruit of violent and occasionally revolutionary methods that contemporary liberals generally reject.

At this point one may ask what happens when and if the landed aristocracy tries to shake free from royal controls in the absence of a numerous and politically vigorous class of town dwellers. To put the question in less exact form, what may happen if the nobility seeks freedom in the absence of a bourgeois revolution? I think it is safe to say that the outcome is highly unfavorable to the Western version of democracy. In Russia during the eighteenth century the service nobility managed to have its obligations to the tsarist autocracy rescinded, while at the same time it retained and even increased its land holdings as well as its power over the serfs. The whole development was highly unfavorable to democracy. German history is in some respects even more revealing. There the nobility carried on its struggle against the Great Elector for the most part separately from the towns. Many of the aristocratic demands of the time resemble those made in England: for a voice in the government and especially in the government's ways of raising money. But the outcome was not parliamentary democracy. The weakness of the towns has been a constant feature in German history subsequent to their efflorescence in southern and western Germany in the late Middle Ages, after which they went into a decline.

Without going into the evidence further or discussing the Asian materials that point in the same direction, we may simply register strong agreement with the Marxist thesis that a vigorous and independent class of town dwellers has been an indispensable element in the growth of parliamentary democracy. No bourgeois, no democracy. The principal actor would not appear on the stage if we confined our attention strictly to the agrarian sector. Still the actors in the countryside have played a sufficiently important part to deserve careful inquiry. And if one wishes to write history with heroes and villains, a position the present writer repudiates, the totalitarian villain sometimes has lived in the country, and the democratic hero of the towns has had important allies there.

Such, for example, was the case in England. While absolutism was growing stronger in France, in a large section of Germany, and in Russia, it met its first major check on English soil, where to be sure the attempt to establish it was much feebler. In very large measure this was true because the English landed aristocracy at an early date began to acquire commercial traits. Among the most decisive determinants influencing the course of subsequent political evolution are whether or not a landed aristocracy has turned to commercial agriculture and, if so, the form that this commercialization has taken.

Let us try to perceive this transformation in its major contours and in comparative perspective. The European medieval system had been one in which the feudal lord had a certain portion of his land, the demesne, cultivated for him by the peasants in return for which the lord protected them and administered justice, very often, to be sure, with a heavy hand favoring his own material interests. The peasants used another section of the lord's land to grow food for their own support and on which to have their dwellings. A third part, generally consisting of woods, streams, and pasture, was known as the commons and served as a source of valuable fuel, game, and pastureland for both the lord and his peasants. Partly in order to assure the lord an adequate supply of labor, the peasants were tied in various ways to the soil. It is true that the market played an important part in the medieval agrarian economy, more important even at quite early times than was once realized. Yet, in contrast to later times the lord together with his peasants to a great extent constituted a self-sufficing community able to supply a large part of their needs from local resources and with local skills. With countless local variations, this system prevailed over large areas of Europe. It did not exist in China. Feudal Japan showed strong resemblances to this arrangement, and analogues can be found in parts of India.

The advance of commerce in the towns and the demands of absolutist rulers for taxes had among their many consequences the result that the overlord needed more and more cash. Three main responses occurred in different parts of Europe. The English landed aristocracy turned to a form of commercial farming that involved setting the peasants free to shift for themselves as best they could. The French landed élite generally left the peasants in *de facto* possession of the soil. In the areas where they turned toward commerce they did so by compelling the peasants to turn over a share of the produce which the nobles then marketed. In eastern Europe there occurred the third variant, the manorial reaction. East German Junkers reduced formerly free peasants to serfdom in order to grow and export grain, while in Russia a similar process took place due to political, much more than economic, causes. Only by the nineteenth century did grain exports become a major feature in the Russian economic and political landscape.

In England itself, the turn toward commercial farming by the landed aristocracy removed much of what remained of its dependence on the crown and generated a great deal of its hostility to fumbling Stuart attempts at absolutism. Likewise the form commercial farming took in England, in contrast to eastern Germany, created a considerable community of interest with the towns. Both factors were important causes of the Civil War and the ultimate victory of the parliamentary cause. Its effects continued to be important and to be reenforced by new causes in the eighteenth and nineteenth centuries.

The consequences appear even more clearly if we set the English experience alongside other varieties. Broadly speaking, there are two other possibilities. The commercial impulse may be quite weak among the landed upper classes. Where that happens, the result will be the survival of a huge peasant mass that is at best a tremendous problem for democracy and at worst the reservoir for a peasant revolution leading to a communist dictatorship. The other possibility is that the landed upper class will use a variety of political and social levers to hold down a labor force on the land and make its transition to commercial farming in this fashion. Combined with a substantial amount of industrial growth, the result is likely to be what we recognize as fascism.

In the next chapter we shall discuss the role played by the landed upper classes in the creation of fascist governments. Here we need only notice 1) that the form of commercial agriculture was just as important as commercialization itself and 2) that the failure of appropriate forms of commercial agriculture to take hold at an early point in time still left open another route to modern democratic institutions. Both features are apparent in French and American history. In parts of France, commercial agriculture left peasant society largely intact but took more out of the peasantry, thereby making a contribution to revolutionary forces. Over most of France the impulse among the nobility toward commercial agriculture was weak compared with England. But the Revolution crippled the aristocracy and opened the way toward parliamentary democracy. In the United States plantation slavery was an important aspect of capitalist growth. On the other hand, to put it mildly, this was an institution unfavorable to democracy. The Civil War overcame this obstacle, though only partially. Generally speaking, plantation slavery is only the most extreme form of repressive adaptations to capitalism. Three factors make it unfavorable to democracy. The landed upper class is likely to need a state with a powerful repressive apparatus and thus one that imposes a whole climate of political and social opinion unfavorable to human freedom. Further, it encourages the preponderance of the countryside over the towns, which are likely to become mere transshipment depots for export to distant markets. Finally, there are the brutalizing consequences of the élite's relationship to its work force, especially severe in those plantation economies where the laborers belong to a different race.

Since the transition to commercial agriculture is obviously a very important step, how is one to explain the ways in which it took place or failed to occur? A modern sociologist would be likely to seek an explanation in cultural terms. In countries where commercial agriculture failed to develop on a wide scale, he might stress the inhibiting character of aristocratic traditions, such as notions of honor and negative attitudes toward pecuniary gain and toward work. At the beginning stages of this research, my own inclination was to search for such explanations. As evidence accumulated, grounds appeared for taking a skeptical attitude toward this line of attack, though the general issues that are raised by its use will require discussion later.

To be convincing, a cultural explanation would have to demonstrate, for example, that among the English landed upper classes military traditions and notions of status and honor were substantially weaker than, let us say, in France. Although the English aristocracy was less of a closed group than its French counterpart and had no formal rule of derogation, it is doubtful that the cultural difference is sufficient to account for the difference in economic behavior. And what is one to make of the East German nobility who turned from colonization and conquest to the pursuit of exporting grain? An even more important consideration is the fact that among landed élites where the commercial impulse seems weak in comparison with England one often finds a substantial minority that has successfully made the attempt to engage in commerce where local conditions were favorable. Thus commercial agriculture for export did develop in parts of Russia.

Such observations lead to a renewed stress on the importance of differences in opportunities to adopt commercial agriculture, such as, above all, the existence of a market in nearby towns and the existence of adequate methods of transportation, mainly by water for bulky goods before the days of the railroad. Though variations in soil and climate are obviously important, the bourgeoisie once again lurks in the wings as the chief actor in the drama. Political considerations have also played a decisive role. Where it has been possible for the landlords to make use of the coercive apparatus of the state in order to sit back and collect rents, a phenomenon found widely in Asia and to some extent in prerevolutionary France and Russia, there is clearly no incentive to turn to less repressive adaptations.

Though the question of commercial agriculture among the peasants has less relevance for democracy, it will be well to say a word about it here. By and large, the elimination of the peasant question through the transformation of the peasantry into some other kind of social formation appears to augur best for democracy. Still, in the smaller client democracies of Scandinavia and Switzerland, the peasants have become part of democratic systems by taking up fairly specialized forms of commercial farming, mainly dairy products, for the town markets. Where peasants seem stubbornly to resist such changes, as for example in India, it is not difficult to construct an explanation around objective circumstances. A real market opportunity is often lacking. For peasants living close to the margin of physical existence, modernization is clearly too risky, especially if under the prevailing social institutions the profit is likely to go to someone else. Hence an abysmally low standard of living and set of expectations is the only adjustment that makes sense under such circumstances. Finally, where the circumstances are different, one can sometimes find dramatic changes in a short space of time.

So far the discussion has concentrated upon two major variables, the relationships of the landed upper classes with the monarchy and their response to the requirements of production for the market. There is a third major variable that has already crept into the discussion: the relationship of the landed upper classes with the town dwellers, mainly the upper stratum that we may loosely call the bourgeoisie. The coalitions and countercoalitions that have arisen among and across these two groups have constituted and in some parts of the world still constitute the basic framework and environment of political action, forming the series of opportunities, temptations, and impossibilities within which political leaders have had to act. In very broad terms, our problem becomes one therefore of trying to identify those situations in the relationship between the landed upper classes and the town dwellers that have contributed to the development of a relatively free society in modern times.

It is best to begin by recalling certain natural lines of cleavage between town and country and within these two sectors of the population. First, there is the familiar conflict of interest between the urban requirement of cheap food and high prices for the articles it produces and the rural desire for high food prices and cheap products from the artisan's shop and from the factory. This conflict may become increasingly important with the spread of a market economy. Class differences, such as those between landlord and peasant in the country, master and journeyman, factory owner and industrial worker in the city, cut across the rural-urban cleavage. Where the interests of the upper strata in town and country converge against the peasants and workers, the outcome is likely to be unfavorable to democracy. However, a great deal depends on the historical circumstances within which this alignment arises.

A very important instance of convergent interests between major segments of the landed aristocracy and the upper ranks of the town dwellers occurred in Tudor and Stuart England. There the convergence arose at an early stage in the course of modernization and under circumstances that led both groups to oppose the royal authority. These aspects are of crucial importance in explaining the democratic consequences. In contrast to the situation in France of the same period, where manufacturers were largely engaged in producing arms and luxury goods for the king and court aristocracy, the English bourgeoisie was vigorous and independent with far-flung interests in an export trade.

On the side of the landed nobility and the gentry, there was also a series of favorable factors. The wool trade had affected the countryside during the sixteenth century and before, leading to enclosures for sheep pasturing. The English sheep-raising upper class, a minority but an influential one, needed the towns which exported the wool, a situation quite different from that in eastern Germany where grain growing in Junker hands bypassed the declining towns.

The convergence between the landed and urban upper classes in England before the Civil War in such a way as to favor the cause of freedom was, among the major countries, a unique configuration. Perhaps the larger situation of which it was a part could occur only once in human history: the English bourgeoisie from the seventeenth through much of the nineteenth century had a maximum material stake in human freedom because it was the first bourgeoisie and had not yet brought its foreign and domestic rivals to their full powers. Nevertheless it may be useful to express certain inferences from the English experience in the form of tentative general hypotheses about the conditions under which collaboration between important sections of the upper classes in the towns and the countryside could be favorable to the growth of parliamentary democracy. As already indicated, it is important that the fusion take place in opposition to the royal bureaucracy. A second condition appears to be that the commercial and industrial leaders must be on their way to becoming the dominant element in society. Under these conditions the landed upper classes are able to develop bourgeois economic habits. This takes place not by mere copying, but as a response to general conditions and their own life circumstances. All these things can happen, it seems, only at an early stage in economic development. That they will be repeated anywhere in the twentieth century also seems highly unlikely.

Taking on a bourgeois hue makes it easier for the landed upper classes at a later stage to hold the posts of political command in what is basically a bourgeois society, as England was during the nineteenth century. Three further factors may be suggested as important here. One is the existence of a substantial degree of antagonism between commercial and industrial elements and the older landed classes. The second is that the landed classes maintain a fairly firm economic footing. Both factors prevent the formation of a solid front of upper-class opposition to demands for reform and encourage a certain amount of competition for popular support. Finally I would suggest that the landed élite must be able to transmit some of its aristocratic outlook to the commercial and industrial classes.

There is more to this transmission than the intermarriage in which an ancient estate may preserve itself by forming an alliance with new money. Many subtle changes in attitude are involved that are at present only very imperfectly understood. We only know the consequence: that bourgeois attitudes have to become stronger, rather than the other way around, as happened in Germany. The mechanisms by which this osmosis takes place are far from clear. No doubt the educational system plays an important part, though by itself it could scarcely be decisive. An exploration of biographical literature, very abundant for England, might yield a rich harvest here, despite the English tabu on frank discussions of social structure, a tabu that sometimes is just as strong as frank discussions of sex. Where the lines of social, economic, religious, and political cleavage do not coincide too closely, conflicts are less likely to be passionate and bitter to the point of excluding democratic reconciliation. The price of such a system is of course the perpetuation of a large amount of "tolerable" abuse — which is mainly tolerable for those who profit by the system.

A brief glance at the fate of the English peasantry suggests one more condition of democratic growth that may well be decisive in its own right. Though England's "final solution of the peasant question" through the enclosures may not have been as brutal or as thorough as some earlier writers have led us to think, there can be little doubt that the enclosures as part of the industrial revolution eliminated the peasant question from English politics. Hence there was no massive reservoir of peasants to serve the reactionary ends of the landed upper classes, as in Germany and Japan. Nor was there the mass basis for peasant revolutions as in Russia and China. For quite different reasons, the United States too escaped from the political plague of a peasant question. France did not escape, and the instability of French democracy during the nineteenth and twentieth centuries is partly due to this fact.

The admitted brutality of the enclosures confronts us with the limitations on the possibility of peaceful transitions to democracy and reminds us of the open and violent conflicts that have preceded its establishment. It is time to restore the dialectic, to remind ourselves of the role of revolutionary violence. A great deal of this violence, perhaps its most important features, had its origins in the agrarian problems that arose along the road that has led to Western democracy. The English Civil War checked royal absolutism and gave the commercially minded big landlords a free hand to play their part during the eighteenth and early nineteenth centuries in destroying peasant society. The French Revolution broke the power of a landed élite that was still mainly precommercial, though sections of it had begun to go over to new forms requiring repressive mechanisms to maintain its labor force. In this sense, as already noted, the French Revolution constituted an alternative way of creating institutions eventually favorable to democracy. Finally, the American Civil War likewise broke the power of a landed élite that was an obstacle in the way of democratic advance but, in this case, one that had grown up as part of capitalism.

Whether one believes that these three violent upheavals aided or hindered the development of liberal and bourgeois democracy, it remains necessary to recognize that they were an important part of the whole process. In itself this fact provides considerable justification for designating them as bourgeois or, if one prefers, liberal revolutions. Nevertheless there are real difficulties in grouping revolutions or, for that matter, any major historical phenomena. Before proceeding any further, it might be well to discuss this point.

Certain very general considerations make it necessary to adopt broad categories of this variety. It is or should be quite obvious that certain institutional arrangements such as feudalism, absolute monarchy, and capitalism rise, have their day, and pass away. The fact that any specific institutional complex develops first in one country and then in another, as did capitalism in Italy, Holland, England, France, and the United States, is no bar to a generally evolutionary conception of history. No single country goes through all the stages, but merely carries the development a certain distance within the framework of its own situation and institutions. Thus a revolution on behalf of private property in the means of production has a good chance of succeeding in some phases and not in others. It may be hopelessly premature and but a minor current in the fourteenth and sixteenth centuries and yet be hopelessly anachronistic in the second half of the twentieth. Over and beyond the concrete historical conditions at a given moment in a particular country, there are worldwide conditions, such as the state of the technical arts and the economic and political organization reached in other parts of the world, that influence heavily the prospects of revolution.

These considerations lead to the conclusion that it is necessary to group revolutions by the broad institutional results to which they contribute. Much of the confusion and unwillingness to use larger categories comes from the fact that those who provide the mass support for a revolution, those who lead it, and those who ultimately profit from it are very different sets of people. As long as this distinction remains clear in each case, it makes sense (and is even indispensable for the sake of drawing distinctions as well as perceiving similarities) to regard the English Civil War, the French Revolution and the American Civil War as stages in the development of *the* bourgeois-democratic revolution.

There are grounds for the reluctance to use this term, and it is worthwhile pointing out the way in which it can be misleading. To some writers the conception of a bourgeois revolution implies a steady increase in the economic power of the commercial and manufacturing classes in the towns up to a point where economic power comes into conflict with political power still in the hands of an old ruling class based mainly on the land. At this point there supposedly occurs a revolutionary explosion in which the commercial and manufacturing classes seize the reins of political power and introduce the main features of modern parliamentary democracy. Such a conception is not altogether false. Even for France, there are some good indications of an increase in the economic power of a section of the bourgeoisie hostile to the fetters imposed by the *ancien régime*. Nevertheless this meaning of bourgeois revolution is such a simplification as to be a caricature of what took place. To see that it is a caricature we need only recall 1) the importance of capitalism in the English countryside that enabled the English landed aristocracy to retain control of political machinery right through the nineteenth century; 2) the weakness of any purely bourgeois impulse in France, its close ties with the old order, its dependence on radical allies during the Revolution, the continuation of the peasant economy into modern times; 3) the fact that plantation slavery in the United States grew up as an integral part of industrial capitalism and presented an obstacle to democracy much more than to capitalism.

As pointed out a moment ago, the central difficulty is that such expressions as bourgeois revolution and peasant revolution lump together indiscriminately those who make the revolution and its beneficiaries. Likewise these terms confuse the legal and political results of revolutions with social groups active in them. Twentieth-century peasant revolutions have had their mass support among the peasants, who have then been the principal victims of modernization put through by communist governments. Nevertheless I shall remain candidly and explicitly inconsistent in the use of terms. In discussing peasant revolutions we shall be speaking about the main popular force behind them, well aware that in the twentieth century the result was communism. In discussing bourgeois revolutions the justification for the term rests on a series of legal and political consequences. Consistent terminology imposes the invention of new terms that, I fear, would only add to the confusion. The main problem, after all, is what happened and why, not the proper use of labels.

Now it seems just about as clear as such matters ever can be that the Puritan Revolution, the French Revolution, and the American Civil War were quite violent upheavals in a long process of political change leading up to what we recognize as modern Western democracy. This process had economic causes, though they were certainly not the only ones. The freedoms created through this process display a clear relationship to each other. Worked out in connection with the rise of modern capitalism, they display the traits of a specific historical epoch. Key elements in the liberal and bourgeois order of society are the right to vote, representation in a legislature that makes the laws and hence is more than a rubber stamp for the executive, an objective system of law that at least in theory confers no special privileges on account of birth or inherited status, security for the rights of property and the elimination of barriers inherited from the past on its use, religious toleration, freedom of speech, and the right to peaceful assembly. Even if practice falls short of profession, these are widely recognized marks of modern liberal society.

The taming of the agrarian sector has been a decisive feature of the whole historical process that produced such a society. It was just as important as the better-known disciplining of the working class and of course closely related to it. Indeed the English experience tempts one to say that getting rid of agriculture as a major social activity is one prerequisite for successful democracy. The political hegemony of the landed upper class had to be broken or transformed. The peasant had to be turned into a farmer producing for the market instead of for his own consumption and that of the overlord. In this process the landed upper classes either became an important part of the capitalist and democratic tide, as in England, or, if they came to oppose it, they were swept aside in the convulsions of revolution or civil war. In a word, the landed upper classes either helped to make the bourgeois revolution or were destroyed by it.

In closing this discussion it may be useful to set down the main conditions that have apparently been most important for the development of democracy and, as a rough test of these conclusions, set them alongside the Indian experience. If it turns out that the presence of some of these conditions has a demonstrable connection with the more successful aspects of parliamentary democracy in India or the historical origins of these aspects and, on the other hand, that the absence of other conditions displays a connection with the difficulties and obstacles to democracy in India, we may have greater confidence in these conclusions.

The first condition of democratic development that our analysis encountered was the *development of a balance to avoid too strong a crown or too independent a landed aristocracy*. In Mogul India at its zenith the power of the crown was overwhelming in relation to the upper classes. Lacking any secure property rights, the noble was, in Moreland's well-known phrase, either a servant or an enemy of the ruling power. The decay of the Mogul system freed the upper classes by tipping the balance in the opposite direction toward a polity of fighting local kinglets. Nevertheless the subsequent British effort in the eighteenth century to create on Indian soil a class of vigorous progressive squires similar to their domestic variety was a complete failure. Indian society has also failed to meet the second major prerequisite: *a turn toward an appropriate form of commercial agriculture* either on the part of the landed aristocracy or the peasantry. Instead, the protective umbrella of British law and order allowed population to increase and a class of parasitic landlords to skim off, together with the moneylenders, much of what the peasants did not eat themselves. In turn these conditions greatly inhibited capital accumulation and industrial growth. When Independence came, it arrived partly under the impetus of peasant yearning for a return to an idealized village past, which further limited and even dangerously delayed real modernization in the countryside. That these circumstances have been among the major obstacles to the establishment and working of a firmly based democracy needs no laboring here.

On the other hand, the departure of the British greatly weakened the political predominance of the landed élite. There are many who would claim that post-Independence reforms have even destroyed that power. To this limited extent, the development of democratic institutions has followed the Western pattern. Even more important, the British occupation, by resting its power on the landed élite and by favoring commercial interests in England, drove a substantial section of the urban commercial and trading classes into opposition, preventing the fateful coalition of a strong landed élite and weak bourgeoisie that, as we shall see in more detail in the next chapter, has been the social origin of rightist authoritarian regimes and movements in Europe and Asia. Thus two conditions have been met: *the weakening of the landed aristocracy and the prevention of an aristocratic-bourgeois coalition against the peasants and workers.*

India indeed constitutes an important instance where at least the formal structure of democracy and a significant portion of its substance, such as the existence of legal opposition and channels for protest and criticism, have arisen without a phase of revolutionary violence. (The Sepoy Mutiny was mainly a backward-looking affair.) Yet the absence of a fifth condition, *a revolutionary break with the past* and of any strong movement in this direction up to the present moment, are among the reasons for India's prolonged backwardness and the extraordinary difficulties that liberal democracy faces there. Some students of Indian affairs have expressed surprise that India's small Western-educated élite has remained faithful to the democratic ideal when they could so easily overthrow it. But why would they wish to overthrow it? Does not democracy provide a rationalization for refusing to overhaul on any massive scale a social structure that maintains their privileges? To be fair one must add that the task is a sufficiently formidable one to make any but the most doctrinaire radical quail at the thought of taking responsibility for it.

Though it would be tempting to discuss this point further,

Indian politics are relevant here only insofar as they serve to test a theory of democracy. The achievements and shortcomings of democracy in India, the obstacles and uncertainties it still faces, all find a reasonable explanation in terms of the five conditions derived here from the experience of other countries. That is not proof by any means. But I think it is fair to hold that these five conditions not only illuminate significant aspects of Indian history; they derive strong support from this history.

CHAPTER EIGHT

Revolution from Above and Fascism

THE SECOND MAIN ROUTE to the world of modern industry we have called the capitalist and reactionary one, exemplified most clearly by Germany and Japan. There capitalism took hold quite firmly in both agriculture and industry and turned them into industrial countries. But it did so without a popular revolutionary upheaval. What tendencies there were in this direction were weak, far weaker in Japan than in Germany, and in both were diverted and crushed. Though not the only cause, agrarian conditions and the specific types of capitalist transformation that took place in the countryside contributed very heavily to these defeats and the feebleness behind any impulse toward Western democratic forms.

There are certain forms of capitalist transformation in the countryside that may succeed economically, in the sense of yielding good profits, but which are for fairly obvious reasons unfavorable to the growth of free institutions of the nineteenth-century Western variety. Though these forms shade into each other, it is easy to distinguish two general types. A landed upper class may, as in Japan, maintain intact the preexisting peasant society, introducing just enough changes in rural society to ensure that the peasants generate a sufficient surplus that it can appropriate and market at a profit. Or a landed upper class may devise wholly new social arrangements along the lines of plantation slavery. Straightforward slavery in modern times is likely to be the creation of a class of colonizing intruders into tropical areas. In parts of eastern Europe, however, indigenous nobilities were able to reintroduce serfdom, which reattached the peasants to the soil in ways that produced somewhat similar results. This was a halfway form between the two others.

Both the system of maintaining peasant society intact but squeezing more out of it and the use of servile or semiservice labor on large units of cultivation require strong political methods to extract the surplus, keep the labor force in its place, and in general make the system work. Not all of these methods are of course political in the narrow sense. Particularly where the peasant society is preserved, there are all sorts of attempts to use traditional relationships and attitudes as the basis of the landlords' position. Since these political methods have important consequences, it will be helpful to give them a name. Economists distinguish between labor-intensive and capital-intensive types of agriculture, depending on whether the system uses large amounts of labor or capital. It may also be helpful to speak of labor-repressive systems, of which slavery is but an extreme type. The difficulty with such a notion is that one may legitimately ask precisely what type has not been labor-repressive. The distinction I am trying to suggest is one between the use of political mechanisms (using the term "political" broadly as just indicated) on the one hand and reliance on the labor market, on the other hand, to ensure an adequate labor force for working the soil and the creation of an agricultural surplus for consumption by other classes. Those at the bottom suffer severely in both cases.

To make the conception of a labor-repressive agricultural system useful, it would be well to stipulate that large numbers of people are kept at work in this fashion. It is also advisable to state explicitly what it does not include, for example, the American family farm of the midnineteenth century. There may have been exploitation of the labor of family members in this case, but it was done apparently mainly by the head of the household himself with minimal assistance from the outside. Again, a system of hired agricultural laborers where the workers had considerable real freedom to refuse jobs and move about, a condition rarely met in actual practice, would not fall under this rubric. Finally, precommercial and preindustrial agrarian systems are not necessarily labor repressive if there is a rough balance between the overlord's contribution to justice and security and the cultivator's contribution in the form of crops. Whether this balance can be pinned down in any objective sense is a moot point best discussed in the following chapter when the issue arises in connection with the causes of peasant revolutions. Here we need only remark that the establishment of labor-repressive agrarian systems in the course of modernization does not necessarily produce greater suffering among the peasants than other forms. Japanese peasants had an easier time of it than did English ones. Our problem here is in any case a different one: how and why labor-repressive agrarian systems provide an unfavorable soil for the growth of democracy and an important part of the institutional complex leading to fascism.

In discussing the rural origins of parliamentary democracy, we noticed that a limited degree of independence from the monarchy constituted one of the favorable conditions, though one that did not occur everywhere. While a system of labor-repressive agriculture may be started in opposition to the central authority, it is likely to fuse with the monarchy at a later point in search of political support. This situation can also lead to the preservation of a military ethic among the nobility in a manner unfavorable to the growth of democratic institutions. The evolution of the Prussian state constitutes the clearest example. Since we have referred to these developments at several points in this work, it will be appropriate to sketch them very briefly here.

In northeastern Germany the manorial reaction of the fifteenth and sixteenth centuries, about which we shall have still more to say in quite another context, broke off the development toward the liberation of the peasantry from feudal obligations and the closely connected development of town life that in England and France eventually culminated in Western democracy. A fundamental cause was the growth of grain exports, though it was not the sole one. The Prussian nobility expanded its holdings at the expense of the peasantry which, under the Teutonic Order, had been close to freedom, and reduced them to serfdom. As part of the same process, the nobility reduced the towns to dependence by short-circuiting them with their exports. Afterward, the Hohenzollern rulers managed to destroy the independence of the nobility and crush the Estates, playing nobles and townsmen off against one another, thereby .checking the aristocratic component in the move toward parliamentary government. The result in the seventeenth and eighteenth centuries was the "Sparta of the North," a militarized fusion of royal bureaucracy and landed aristocracy.[1]

From the side of the landed aristocracy came the conceptions of inherent superiority in the ruling class and a sensitivity to matters of status, prominent traits well into the twentieth century. Fed by new sources, these conceptions could later be vulgarized and made appealing to the German population as a whole in doctrines of racial superiority. The royal bureaucracy introduced, against considerable aristocratic resistance, the ideal of complete and unreflecting obedience to an institution over and above class and individual — prior to the nineteenth century it would be anachronistic to speak of the nation. Prussian discipline, obedience, and admiration for the hard qualities of the soldier come mainly from the Hohenzollern efforts to create a centralized monarchy.

All this does not of course mean that some inexorable fate drove Germany toward fascism from the sixteenth century onward, that the process never could have been reversed. Other factors had to intervene, some very important ones, as industrialization began to gather momentum during the nineteenth century. About these it will be necessary to speak in a moment. There are also significant variants and substitutions within the general pattern that has led to fascism, subalternatives one might say if one wished to be very precise and technical, within the major alternative of conservative modernization through revolution from above. In Japan the notion of total commitment to authority apparently came out of the feudal, rather than the monarchical, side of the equation.[2] Again in Italy, where fascism was invented, there was no powerful national monarchy. Mussolini had to go all the way back to ancient Rome for the corresponding symbolism.

At a later stage in the course of modernization, a new and crucial factor is likely to appear in the form of a rough working coalition between influential sectors of the landed upper classes and the emerging commercial and manufacturing interests. By and large,

[1] See Rosenberg, *Bureaucracy;* Carsten, *Origins of Prussia.*
[2] Sansom, *History of Japan,* I, 368.

this was a nineteenth-century political configuration, though it continued on into the twentieth. Marx and Engels in their discussion of the abortive 1848 revolution in Germany, wrong though they were on other major features, put their finger on this decisive ingredient: a commercial and industrial class which is too weak and dependent to take power and rule in its own right and which therefore throws itself into the arms of the landed aristocracy and the royal bureaucracy, exchanging the right to rule for the right to make money.[3] It is necessary to add that, even if the commercial and industrial element is weak, it must be strong enough (or soon become strong enough) to be a worthwhile political ally. Otherwise a peasant revolution leading to communism may intervene. This happened in both Russia and China after unsuccessful efforts to establish such a coalition. There also appears to be another ingredient that enters the situation somewhat later than the formation of this coalition: sooner or later systems of labor-repressive agriculture are liable to run into difficulties produced by competition from more technically advanced ones in other countries. The competition of American wheat exports created difficulties in many parts of Europe after the end of our Civil War. In the context of a reactionary coalition, such competition intensifies authoritarian and reactionary trends among a landed upper class that finds its economic basis sinking and therefore turns to political levers to preserve its rule.

Where the coalition succeeds in establishing itself, there has followed a prolonged period of conservative and even authoritarian government, which, however, falls far short of fascism. The historical boundaries of such systems are often somewhat blurred. At a rather generous estimate, one might hold that to this species belong the period from the Stein-Hardenberg reforms in Germany to the end of the First World War and, in Japan, from the fall of the Tokugawa Shogunate to 1918. These authoritarian governments acquired some democratic features: notably a parliament with limited powers. Their history may be punctuated with attempts to extend democracy which, toward the end, succeeded in

[3] See Marx, *Selected Works*, II, "Germany: Revolution and Counter-Revolution," written mainly by Engels.

establishing unstable democracies (the Weimar Republic, Japan in the twenties, Italy under Giolitti). Eventually the door to fascist regimes was opened by the failure of these democracies to cope with the severe problems of the day and reluctance or inability to bring about fundamental structural changes.[4] One factor, but only one, in the social anatomy of these governments has been the retention of a very substantial share in political power by the landed élite, due to the absence of a revolutionary breakthrough by the peasants in combination with urban strata.

Some of the semiparliamentary governments that arose on this basis carried out a more or less peaceful economic and political revolution from above that took them a long distance toward becoming modern industrial countries. Germany travelled the furthest in this direction, Japan only somewhat less so, Italy a great deal less, Spain very little. Now, in the course of modernization by a revolution from above, such a government has to carry out many of the same tasks performed elsewhere with the help of a revolution from below. The notion that a violent popular revolution is somehow necessary in order to sweep away "feudal" obstacles to industrialization is pure nonsense, as the course of German and Japanese history demonstrates. On the other hand, the political consequences from dismounting the old order from above are decidedly different. As they proceeded with conservative modernization, these semiparliamentary governments tried to preserve as much of the original social structure as they could, fitting large sections into the new building wherever possible. The results had some resemblance to present-day Victorian houses with modern electrical kitchens but insufficient bathrooms and leaky pipes hidden decorously behind newly plastered walls. Ultimately the makeshifts collapsed.

One very important series of measures was the rationalization of the political order. This meant the breakup of traditional and long established territorial divisions, such as the feudal *han* in Japan

[4] Poland, Hungary, Rumania, Spain, and even Greece went through approximately this sequence. On the basis of admittedly inadequate knowledge, I would hazard the suggestion that much of Latin America remains in the era of authoritarian semiparliamentary government.

or independent states and principalities in Germany and Italy. Except in Japan, the breakup was not complete. But in the course of time a central government did establish strong authority and a uniform administrative system, and a more or less uniform law code and system of courts appeared. Again, in varying degrees, the state managed to create a sufficiently powerful military machine to be able to make the wishes of its rulers felt in the arena of international politics. Economically the establishment of a strong central government and the elimination of internal barriers to trade meant an increase in the size of the effective economic unit. Without such an increase in size, the division of labor necessary for an industrial society could not exist, unless all countries were willing to trade peacefully with one another. As the first country to industrialize, England had been able to draw on most of the accessible world for material and markets, a situation that gradually deteriorated during the nineteenth century when others caught up and sought to use the state to guarantee their markets and sources of supply.

Still another aspect of the rationalization of the political order has to do with the making of citizens in a new type of society. Literacy and rudimentary technical skills are necessary for the masses. Setting up a national system of education is very likely to bring on a conflict with religious authorities. Loyalty to a new abstraction, the state, must also replace religious loyalties if they transcend national boundaries or compete with one another so vigorously as to destroy internal peace. Japan had less of a problem here than Germany, Italy, or Spain. Yet even in Japan, as the somewhat artificial revival of *Shintō* indicates, there were substantial difficulties. In overcoming such difficulties, the existence of a foreign enemy can be quite useful. Then patriotic and conservative appeals to the military traditions of the landed aristocracy can overcome localist tendencies among this important group and push into the background any too insistent demands of the lower strata for an unwarranted share in the benefits of the new order.[5] In carrying out the task of rationalizing and extending the political order, these

[5] Possibly one of the reasons the conservative Cavour had such difficulties with the relatively radical Garibaldi was the weakness of military traditions among the Italian landed aristocracy.

nineteenth-century governments were doing work that royal absolutism had already accomplished in other countries.

One striking fact about the course of conservative modernization is the appearance of a galaxy of distinguished political leaders: Cavour in Italy; in Germany, Stein, Hardenberg, and Bismarck, the most famous of them all; in Japan, the statesmen of the Meiji era. Though the reasons are obscure, it seems unlikely that the appearance of a similar leadership in similar circumstances could be pure coincidence. All were conservatives in the political spectrum of their time and country, devoted to the monarchy, willing and able to use it as an instrument of reform, modernization, and national unification. Though all were aristocrats, they were dissidents or outsiders of a sort in relation to the old order. To the extent that their aristocratic background contributed habits of command and a flair for politics, one may perhaps detect a contribution of the agrarian *ancien régimes* to the construction of a new society. But there were strong contrary pulls here too. To the extent that these men were aliens within the aristocracy, one may see the incapacity of this stratum to meet the challenge of the modern world merely with its own intellectual and political resources.

The most successful of the conservative regimes accomplished a great deal, not only in tearing down the old order but in establishing a new one. The state aided industrial construction in several important ways. It served as an engine of primary capitalist accumulation, gathering resources and directing them toward the building of an industrial plant. In the taming of the labor force it again played an important role, by no means entirely a repressive one. Armaments served as an important stimulus for industry. So did protectionist tariff policies. All of these measures at some point involved taking resources or people out of agriculture. Therefore they imposed from time to time a serious strain on the coalition between those sectors of the upper strata in business and in agriculture that was the main feature of the political system. Without the threat of foreign dangers, sometimes real, sometimes perhaps imaginary, sometimes as in the case of Bismarck deliberately manufactured for domestic purposes, the landed interests might well have balked, to the point of endangering the whole process. The foreign threat alone, however, need not bear the whole weight of explaining this behavior.[6] Material and other rewards — the "payoff" in the language of gangsters and game theory — were quite substantial for both partners as long as they succeeded in keeping the peasants and industrial labor in place. Where there was substantial economic progress, the industrial workers were able to make significant gains, as in Germany, where *Sozialpolitik* was invented. It was in those countries that remained more backward, Italy to some extent, probably Spain to a greater extent, that there was more of a tendency to cannibalize the indigenous population.

Certain conditions seem to have been necessary for the successes of conservative modernization. First, it takes very able leadership to drag along the less perceptive reactionary elements, concentrated among, though not necessarily confined to, the landed upper classes. In the beginning, Japan had to suppress a real rebellion, the Satsuma revolt, to control these elements. Reactionaries can always advance the plausible argument that modernizing leaders are making changes and concessions that will merely arouse the appetites of the lower classes and bring on a revolution.[7] Similarly, the leadership must have at hand or be able to construct a sufficiently powerful bureaucratic apparatus, including the agencies of repression, the military and the police (compare the German saying *Gegen Demokraten helfen nur Soldaten*), in order to free itself from the influence of both extreme reactionary and popular or radical pressures in the society. The government has to become separate from society, something that can happen rather more easily than simplified versions of Marxism would allow us to believe.

In the short run, a strong conservative government has distinct advantages. It can both encourage and control economic growth.

[6] For a brilliant analysis of the situation in Germany toward the end of the nineteenth century see Kehr, *Schlachtflottenbau*. Weber, "Entwickelungstendenzen in der Lage der Ostelbischen Landarbeiter," in *Gesammelte Aufsätze*, esp 471 – 476, brings out very clearly the position of the Junkers.

[7] Such arguments were also very prominent in England as part of the reaction to the French Revolution. Many have been collected in Turberville, *House of Lords*. Tory reform could work in nineteenth-century England, however, at least partly because it was a sham battle anyway: the bourgeoisie had won, and only the more obtuse could fail to see their power.

It can see to it that the lower classes who pay the costs under all forms of modernization do not make too much trouble. But Germany and, even more, Japan were trying to solve a problem that was inherently insoluble, to modernize without changing their social structures. The only way out of this dilemma was militarism, which united the upper classes. Militarism intensified a climate of international conflict, which in turn made industrial advance all the more imperative, even if in Germany a Bismarck could for a time hold the situation in check, partly because militarism had not yet become a mass phenomenon. To carry out thoroughgoing structural reforms, i.e., to make the transition to a paying commercial agriculture without the repression of those who worked the soil and to do the same in industry, in a word, to use modern technology rationally for human welfare was beyond the political vision of these governments.[8] Ultimately these systems crashed in an attempt at foreign expansion, but not until they had tried to make reaction popular in the form of fascism.

Before discussing this final phase, it may be instructive to glance at unsuccessful reactionary trends in other countries. As mentioned above, this reactionary syndrome can be found at some point in all the cases I have examined. To see why it has failed in other countries may sharpen awareness of the reasons behind its successes. A brief look at these trends in such widely differing countries as England, Russia, and India may serve to bring out important underlying similarities concealed beneath a variety of historical experiences.

Beginning in the latter years of the French Revolution and lasting until about 1822, English society passed through a reactionary phase that recalls both the cases just discussed and contem-

---

[8] On this score, Germany and Japan are not of course unique. Since the Second World War, Western democracy has begun to display more and more of the same traits for broadly similar reasons that, however, no longer have much to do with agrarian questions. Somewhere Marx remarks that the bourgeoisie in its declining phase reproduces all the evils and irrationalities against which it once fought. So indeed did socialism in the effort to establish itself, thus allowing twentieth-century democracy to fly its muddy and blood-spattered banner of freedom with something short of outright cynical hypocrisy.

porary problems of American democracy. During most of these
years England was fighting against a revolutionary regime and its
heirs, sometimes, it may have seemed, for national survival itself. As
in our own time, the advocates of domestic reform were identified
with a foreign enemy represented as the incarnation of all that was
evil. Again, as in our own time, the violence, repressions, and be-
trayals of the revolutionary movement in France sickened and dis-
couraged its English supporters, making easier and more plausible
the work of reactionaries eager to stamp out the sparks that floated
across the channel. Writing in the 1920s the great French historian
Elie Halévy, certainly not a man given to dramatic exaggeration,
asserted, "A reign of terror was established throughout England by
the nobility and middle class — a terror more formidable, though
more silent, than the noisy demonstrations [of the radicals]."[9] The
events of the four decades and more that have passed since Halévy
wrote these lines have dulled our senses and lowered our standards.
No one writing now would be likely to refer to this phase as a
reign of terror. The number of direct victims of repression was
small. In the "massacre" of Peterloo (1819) — a derisive reference
to Wellington's more famous victory of Waterloo — only eleven
persons were killed. Nevertheless the gathering movement to reform Parliament was placed outside the law, the press muzzled,
associations that smacked of radicalism forbidden, a rash of treason
trials initiated, spies and *agents provocateurs* let loose among the
people, the Habeas Corpus suspended *after* the war with Napoleon
had ended. Repression and suffering were real and widespread, only
partly mitigated by some continued articulate opposition: an aristocrat such as Charles James Fox (*d* 1806) who spoke up coura-
geously in Parliament, here and there a judge or a jury that refused
to convict on treason or other charges.[10]

[9] Halévy, *History of the English People*, II, 19.

[10] An excellent and detailed description of what life was like for the
lower classes in England during this period may be found in Thompson,
Making of Working Class. The main governmental measures and some of
their effects can be traced through Cole and Postgate, *British People*, 132 –
134, 148 – 149, 157 – 159, 190 – 193. For some valuable additional details see
Halévy, *History of the English People*, II, 23 – 25. Aristocratic opposition

Why was this reactionary upsurge no more than a passing phase in England? Why did not England continue along this road to become another Germany? Anglo-Saxon liberties, Magna Charta, Parliament and such rhetoric will not do for an answer. Parliament voted repressive measures by huge majorities.

An important part of the answer may be found in the fact that, a century before, certain extremist Englishmen had chopped off the head of their monarch to shatter the magic of royal absolutism in England. At a deeper level of causation, England's whole previous history, her reliance on a navy instead of an army, on unpaid justices of the peace instead of royal officials, had put in the hands of the central government a repressive apparatus weaker than that possessed by the strong continental monarchies. Thus the materials with which to construct a German system were missing or but feebly developed. Still, by now we have seen enough great social and political changes out of unpromising beginnings to suspect that the institutions could have been created if circumstances had been more favorable. But fortunately for human liberties they were not. The push toward industrialism had begun much earlier in England and was to render unnecessary for the English bourgeoisie any great dependence on the crown and the landed aristocracy. Finally, the landed upper classes themselves did not need to repress the peasants. Mainly they wanted to get them out of the way in order to go over to commercial farming; by and large, economic measures would be enough to provide the labor force they needed. Succeeding economically in this particular fashion, they had little need to resort to repressive political measures to continue their leadership. Therefore in England manufacturing and agrarian interests competed with one another for popular favor during the rest of the nineteenth century, gradually extending the suffrage while jealously opposing and knocking down each other's more selfish measures (Reform Bill of 1832, abolition of the Corn Laws in 1846, gentry support for factory legislation, etc).

In the English phase of reaction there were hints of fascist pos-

---

to repression may be found in Trevelyan, *History of England*, III, 89 – 92, and Turberville, *House of Lords*, 98 – 100.

sibilities, particularly in some of the antiradical riots. But these were no more than hints. The time was still too early. Fascist symptoms we can see very much more clearly in another part of the world at a later point in time — during a brief phase of extremism in Russia after 1905. This was extreme even by Russian standards of the day; one could make a strong case for the thesis that Russian reactionaries invented fascism. Thus this phase of Russian history is especially illuminating because it shows that the fascist syndrome 1) can appear in response to the strains of advancing industrialism independently of a specific social and cultural background; 2) that it may have many roots in agrarian life; 3) that it appears partly in response to a weak push toward parliamentary democracy; 4) but cannot flourish without industrialism or in an overwhelmingly agrarian background — points, to be sure, all suggested by the recent histories of China and Japan too, though it is illuminating to find stronger confirmation in Russian history.

Shortly before the Revolution of 1905 the tiny Russian commercial and industrial class showed some signs of discontent with the repressive tsarist autocracy and a willingness to flirt with liberal constitutional notions. Workers' strikes, however, and the promise contained in the Imperial Manifesto of October 17, 1905, to meet some of the demands of the strikers, brought the industrialists safely back within the tsarist camp.[11] Against this background appeared the Black Hundreds movement. Drawing partly on American experience, they made "lynch" into a Russian word and asked for the application of *zakon lyncha*, lynch law. They resorted to violence in storm-trooper style to suppress "treason" and "sedition." If Russia could destroy the "kikes" and foreigners, their propaganda asserted, everyone could live happily in a return to "true Russian" ways. This anti-Semitic nativism had considerable appeal to backward, precapitalist, petty bourgeois elements in the cities and among the smaller nobility. However, in still backward peasant Russia of the early twentieth century, this form of rightist extremism was unable to find a firm popular basis. Among the peasants it succeeded mainly in areas of mixed nationality, where the explana-

[11] Gitermann, *Geschichte Russlands*, III, 403, 409 – 410; Berlin, *Russkaya burzhuaziya*, 226 – 227, 236.

tion of all evil as being due to Jews and foreigners made some sense in terms of peasant experience.[12] As everyone knows, to the extent that they were politically active, the Russian peasants were revolutionary and eventually the major force in exploding the old regime.

In India, which is equally if not more backward, similar movements have likewise failed to obtain a firm basis among the masses. To be sure, Subhas Chandra Bose, who died in 1945, expressed dictatorial sentiments, worked for the Axis, and had a very large popular following. Though his fascist sympathies were consistent with other aspects of his public record and do not seem to be the outcome of momentary enthusiasm or opportunism, Subhas Chandra Bose has gone down in Indian tradition mainly as an extreme and perhaps misguided anti-British patriot.[13] There has also been a scattering of nativist Hindu political organizations, some of which developed the autocratic discipline of the European totalitarian party. They have reached the peak of their influence so far in the chaos and riots surrounding Partition, during which they helped to promote anti-Muslim riots and served as defense organs for Hindu communities against Muslim attacks, led, presumably, by similar organizations on the Muslim side. Their programs lack economic content and appear to be mainly a form of militant, xenophobic Hinduism, seeking to combat the stereotype that Hindus are pacific, divided by caste, and weak. So far their electoral appeal has been very small.[14]

One possible reason for the weakness of the Hindu variant of fascism to date may be the fragmentation of the Hindu world along caste, class, and ethnic lines. Thus a characteristically fascist appeal addressed to one segment would antagonize others, while a more general appeal, by taking on some color of universal panhumanism, begins to lose its fascist qualities. In this connection it is worth noticing that nearly all the extremist Hindu groups have opposed un-

[12] Levitskii, "Pravyya partii," *Obshchestvennoye dvizheniye v Rossii,* III, 347 – 472. See esp 432, 370 – 376, 401, 353 – 355.

[13] See Samra, "Subhas Chandra Bose," in Park and Tinker, eds, *Leadership and Political Institutions,* 66 – 86, esp 78 – 79.

[14] Lambert, "Hindu Communal Groups," in Park and Tinker, eds, *Leadership and Political Institutions,* 211 – 224.

touchability and other social disabilities of caste.[15] The main reason, however, is probably the simple fact that Gandhi had already pre-empted the antiforeign and anticapitalist sentiment of huge masses of the population: peasants and artisans in the cottage industries. Under the conditions created by the British occupation, he was able to tie these sentiments to the interests of a large section of the business class. On the other hand, the landed élite generally stood aloof. Thus reactionary trends have been strong in India and have helped to delay economic progress since Independence. But as a mass phenomenon the larger movements belong to an historical species distinct from fascism.

Though it might be equally profitable to undertake a parallel consideration of democratic failures that preceded fascism in Germany, Japan, and Italy, it is enough for present purposes to notice that fascism is inconceivable without democracy or what is sometimes more turgidly called the entrance of the masses onto the historical stage. Fascism was an attempt to make reaction and conservatism popular and plebeian, through which conservatism, of course, lost the substantial connection it did have with freedom, some aspects of which were discussed in the preceding chapter.

The conception of objective law vanished under fascism. Among its most significant features was a violent rejection of humanitarian ideals, including any notion of potential human equality. The fascist outlook stressed not only the inevitability of hierarchy, discipline, and obedience, but also posited that they were values in their own right. Romantic conceptions of comradeship qualify this outlook but slightly; it is comradeship in submission. Another feature was the stress on violence. This stress goes far beyond any cold, rational appreciation of the factual importance of violence in politics to a mystical worship of "hardness" for its own sake. Blood and death often acquire overtones of erotic attraction, though in its less exalted moments fascism was thoroughly "healthy" and "normal," promising return to a cosy bourgeois, and even prebourgeois peasant, womb.[16]

[15] Lambert, "Hindu Communal Groups," 219.
[16] To say that fascism was atavistic does not distinguish it sufficiently.

Plebeian anticapitalism thus appears as the feature that most clearly distinguishes twentieth-century fascism from its predecessors, the nineteenth-century conservative and semiparliamentary regimes. It is a product of both the intrusion of capitalism into the rural economy and of strains arising in the postcompetitive phase of capitalist industry. Hence fascism developed most fully in Germany where capitalist industrial growth had gone the furthest within the framework of a conservative revolution from above. It came to light as only a weak secondary trend in such backward areas as Russia, China, and India. Prior to World War II, it failed to take much root in England and the United States where capitalism worked reasonably well or where efforts to correct its shortcomings could be attempted within the democratic framework and succeed with the help of a prolonged war boom. Most of the anticapitalist opposition to big business had to be shelved in practice, though one should not make the opposite error of regarding fascist leaders as merely the agents of big business. The attraction of fascism for the lower middle class in the cities, threatened by capitalism, has often been pointed out; here we may confine ourselves to a brief review of the evidence on its varying relationships to the peasantry in different countries. In Germany the effort to establish a massive conservative base in the countryside long antedates the Nazis. As Professor Alexander Gerschenkron points out, the basic elements of Nazi doctrine appear quite distinctly in the Junkers' generally successful efforts, by means of the Agrarian League established in 1894, to win the support of the peasants in non-Junker areas of smaller farms. *Führer* worship, the idea of a corporative state, militarism, anti-Semitism, in a setting closely related to the Nazi distinction between "predatory" and "productive" capital, were devices used to appeal to anticapitalist sentiments among the peasantry.[17] There are a good many indications that in subsequent years down to the depression the substantial and prosperous peasants were slowly losing ground to dwarf peasants. The depression constituted a deep and general crisis, to which the main

---

So are revolutionary movements, as I have tried to show in some detail in the next chapter.

[17] *Bread and Democracy*, 53, 55.

rural response was National Socialism. Rural support for the Nazis came to an average of 37.4 percent, practically identical with that in the country as a whole in the last relatively free election of July 31, 1932.[18]

If one looks at a map of Germany showing the distribution of the Nazi vote in the rural areas and compares this map with others showing the distribution of land values, types of cultivation,[19] or of the areas of small, medium, and large farms,[20] the first impression will be that Nazism in the countryside shows no consistent relationship with any of these. However, as one studies the maps more closely, one can discern substantial evidence to the effect that the Nazis succeeded most in their appeal to the peasant whose holding was relatively small and unprofitable *for the particular area in which it existed.*[21]

To the small peasant, suffering under the advance of capitalism with its problems of prices and mortgages that seemed to be controlled by hostile city middlemen and bankers, Nazi propaganda

[18] For the rural vote see the map of Germany showing the distribution of Nazi voting for rural areas, July 1932, with *Stadtkreise* removed, in Loomis and Beegle, "Spread of German Nazism," 726. For the percentage of the Nazi vote in Germany as a whole, consult the election statistics from 1919 to 1933 assembled in Dittmann, *Das politische Deutschland.*

[19] Compare Loomis-Beegle map above with map inserts VIII, VIIIa, and I, in Sering, ed, *Deutsche Landwirtschaft.*

[20] Printed as appendices in *Statistik des Deutschen Reichs* and in less detail but on a single page as map insert IV in Sering, ed, *Deutsche Landwirtschaft.*

[21] Special studies too provide evidence for the view that the "little fellow" who was having a hard time of it under capitalist conditions was the one most receptive to the Nazi appeal. In Schleswig-Holstein the village communities where the Nazis won 80 to 100 percent of the vote were in what is known as the *Geest,* an area of small farms on poor soil, heavily dependent on sensitive markets for young cattle and hogs. On this, see Heberle, *Social Movements,* 226, 228. Parts of Hannover show the same combination. Near Nuremberg, too, the Nazi vote ranged from 71 to 83 percent in an area of relatively low land values, middle-sized family farms, and generally marginal agriculture dependent on the urban market. See Loomis· and Beegle, "Spread of German Nazism," 726, 727. Further evidence pointing in the same direction is summarized and cited in Bracher, et al, *Machtergreifung,* 389–390.

presented the romantic image of an idealized peasant, "the free man on free land." The peasant became the key figure in the ideology of the radical right as elaborated by the Nazis. The Nazis were fond of stressing the point that, for the peasant, land is more than a means with which to earn a living; it has all the sentimental overtones of *Heimat*, to which the peasant feels himself far more closely connected than the white collar worker with his office or the industrial worker with his shop. Physiocratic and liberal notions found themselves jumbled together in these doctrines of the radical right.[22] "A firm stock of small and middle peasants," said Hitler in *Mein Kampf*, "has still been at all times the best protection against social evils as we have them now." Such a peasantry constitutes the only way through which a nation can secure its daily bread. He goes on, "Industry and commerce retreat from their unhealthy leading position and fit into the general framework of a national economy based on need and equality. Both are then no longer the basis for feeding the nation, but only a help in this."[23]

For our purposes there is nothing to be gained by examining the fate of these notions after the Nazis came to power. While a few starts were made here and there, most of them were junked because they contradicted the requirements of a powerful war economy, necessarily based on industry. The notion of a retreat from industry was only the most obviously absurd feature.[24]

In Japan, as in Germany, pseudoradical anticapitalism gained a considerable foothold among the Japanese peasantry. There too the original impulse came from the landed upper classes. On the other hand, its more extreme forms, such as the assassins' bands among junior military officers, though they claimed to speak for the peasants, do not seem to have had a strong following among them. Extremism was in any case absorbed into the more general framework of "respectable" Japanese conservatism and military aggression, for which the peasantry provided a mass basis. Since the Japanese case

[22] Bracher et al, *Machtergreifung*, 390 – 391.

[23] *Mein Kampf*, 151 – 152. For the main factual aspects of Nazi policy see also Schweitzer, "Nazification," in *Third Reich*, 576 – 594.

[24] For the fate of the agrarian program, consult Wunderlich, *Farm Labor*, pt III, "The Period of National Socialism."

has been discussed in detail in an earlier chapter, there is no need to examine it further here.

Italian fascism displays the same pseudoradical and propeasant features found in Germany and Japan. In Italy, on the other hand, these notions were more of an opportunistic growth, a cynical decoration put on to take advantage of circumstances. Cynical opportunism was present in Germany and Japan too, of course, but seems to have been much more blatant in Italy.

Immediately after the 1914 war, there was a bitter struggle in the north Italian countryside between Socialist and Christian-Democratic trade unions on the one hand and the big landowners on the other. At this point, i.e., 1919 – 1920, Mussolini, according to Ignazio Silone, paid no attention to the countryside, did not believe in a fascist conquest of the land, and thought fascism would always be an urban movement.[25] But the struggle between the landowners and the unions, representing the interests of hired labor and tenants, gave fascism an unexpected opportunity to fish in troubled waters. Presenting themselves as the saviors of civilization against Bolshevism, *fasci* — bands of idealists, demobilized army officers, and just plain toughs — broke up rural union headquarters, often with the connivance of the police, and during 1921 destroyed the leftist movement in the countryside. Among those who streamed into fascist ranks were peasants who had climbed into the middle ranks of landowners, and even tenants who hated the monopolistic practices of the unions.[26] During the summer of this year Mussolini made his famous observation that "if Fascism does not wish to die or, worse still, to commit suicide, it must now provide itself with a doctrine. . . . I do wish that during the two months which are still to elapse before our National Assembly meets, the philosophy of Fascism could be created."[27]

Only later did Italian fascist leaders begin to declare that fascism was "ruralizing" Italy, championing the cause of the peasants, or that it was primarily a "rural phenomenon." These claims were

[25] Silone, *Fascismus*, 107.

[26] Schmidt, *Plough and Sword*, 34 – 38; Silone, *Fascismus*, 109; Salvemini, *Fascist Dictatorship*, 67, 73.

[27] Quoted by Schmidt, *Plough and Sword*, 39 – 40.

nonsense. The number of owner operators dropped by 500,000 between 1921 and 1931; that of cash-and-share tenants rose by about 400,000. Essentially fascism protected big agriculture and big industry at the expense of the agricultural laborer, small peasant, and consumer.[28]

As we look back at fascism and its antecedents, we can see that the glorification of the peasantry appears as a reactionary symptom in both Western and Asiatic civilization at a time when the peasant economy is facing severe difficulties. In part of the Epilogue I shall try to indicate some of the recurring forms this glorification has taken in its more virulent stages. To say that such ideas are merely foisted on the peasants by the upper classes is not true. Because the ideas find an echo in peasant experience, they may win wide acceptance, the wider, it seems, the more industrialized and modern the country is.

As evidence against the evaluation that such glorification constitutes a reactionary symptom, one might be tempted to cite Jefferson's praise of the small farmer and John Stuart Mill's defense of peasant farming. Both thinkers, however, in the characteristic fashion of early liberal capitalism, were defending not so much peasants as small independent property owners. There is in their thought none of the militant chauvinism and glorification of hierarchy and submission found in the later versions, though there are occasional overtones of a romantic attitude toward rural life. Even so, their attitude toward agrarian problems and rural society does indicate the limits that liberal thinkers had reached at their respective points in time. For such ideas to serve reactionary purposes in the twentieth century, they have had to take on a new coloring and appear in a new context; the defense of hard work and small property in the twentieth century has an entirely different political meaning from what it had in the middle of the nineteenth or the latter part of the eighteenth centuries.

[28] For figures and details see Schmidt, *Plough and Sword*, v, 132 – 134, 66 – 67, 71, 113.

CHAPTER NINE

The Peasants and Revolution

THE PROCESS OF MODERNIZATION begins with peasant revolutions that fail. It culminates during the twentieth century with peasant revolutions that succeed. No longer is it possible to take seriously the view that the peasant is an "object of history," a form of social life over which historical changes pass but which contributes nothing to the impetus of these changes. For those who savor historical irony it is indeed curious that the peasant in the modern era has been as much an agent of revolution as the machine, that he has come into his own as an effective historical actor along with the conquests of the machine. Nevertheless the revolutionary contribution has been very uneven: decisive in China and Russia, quite important in France, very minor in Japan, insignificant in India to date, trivial in Germany and England after initial explosions had been defeated. In this concluding chapter our task will be to relate these facts to each other systematically in the hope of discovering what kinds of social structures and historical situations produce peasant revolutions and which ones inhibit or prevent them.

The undertaking is not an easy one. The traditional general explanations run into important exceptions within the range of materials examined here. No theory emphasizing a single factor appears to be satisfactory. Since negative findings have their uses, I will begin with a brief summary of theories it has been necessary to discard.

The first one that a modern investigator might choose is a simple economic interpretation in terms of deterioration in the peasants' situation under the impact of commerce and industry.

Where such deterioration has occurred on a marked scale, it seems plausible to expect revolutionary outbreaks. Once again the case of India provides a useful check, especially when set alongside that of China. There is no indication that the deterioration in the economic position of the Indian peasantry has been worse than that of the Chinese during the nineteenth and twentieth centuries. Admittedly the evidence is far from perfect in both cases. Local and ineffective peasant upheavals there were in India. Still it is highly unlikely that whatever difference there may be is adequate to account for the contrast in the political behavior of Chinese and Indian peasants during the past century and a half. Since these differences also extend backward in time for centuries, it becomes obvious that no simple economic explanation will do.

One might object that this form of the economic explanation is too simple. Could it be that not merely a decline in the peasants' material situation but a massive threat to their entire mode of life, to the very foundations of peasant existence — property, family, and religion — brings about a revolutionary situation? Once more the evidence is clearly negative. It was not the English peasants turned adrift by enclosures who rose in massive revolt but the French ones who were merely threatened by them. Russian peasant society in 1917 was mainly intact. Again, as I shall have occasion to point out in more detail later in this chapter, it was not the peasants of eastern Germany rolled under by the manorial reaction and the reintroduction of serfdom who turned to bloody revolt in the sixteenth century but those of the south and west, who by and large retained and even extended their old way of life. Indeed the very opposite hypothesis comes closer to the truth, as we shall see in due course.

From the romantic and conservative tradition of the nineteenth century comes another familiar thesis that where the noble aristocrat lives in the countryside among his peasants there is less likelihood of acute peasant outbreaks than where he becomes a lover of luxury, living in the capital. Contrasts between the fate of the French and English aristocracy during the eighteenth and nineteenth centuries seem to be the origin of this notion. However, the Russian landlord of the nineteenth century often lived a large part of his life on his estate, a fact that did not deter peasants from burning manors and finally driving the *dvorianstvo* from the historical stage. Even for France itself, the thesis is doubtful. Modern research has shown that by no means all the nobility were hangers-on at the court; many lived morally exemplary lives in the countryside.

The notion that a large rural proletariat of landless labor is a potential source of insurrection and revolution may be somewhat closer to the truth. The huge size and appalling misery of India's rural proletariat might seem to refute the thesis. Many of these are, on the other hand, tied to the prevailing system through possession of a tiny plot of land and by the caste system. Where such bonds have been snapped or never existed at all, as in plantation economies operated with very cheap hired labor of a different race or by slaves, the possibilities of insurrection are much greater. Though slave owners in the American South seem to have had exaggerated fears, there has been reason enough elsewhere to fear insurrection: in ancient Rome, Haiti and other parts of the Caribbean during the eighteenth and nineteenth centuries, parts of Spain in modern times, and quite recently on the sugar plantations of Cuba. But, even if the hypothesis should turn out on more careful inquiry to be correct, it would not account for the historically significant cases. No rural proletariat of this type was important in the Russian Revolutions of 1905 or 1917.[1] Though the Chinese case is less well documented, and bands of wandering peasants driven from their land by a variety of causes have been important there, the revolutionary upsurges of 1927 and 1949 were certainly not those of a rural proletariat working huge landed estates. Nor was this the case in the revolutionary outbreaks of the nineteenth century. As a general explanation, this conception simply will not do.

Driven back from material explanations one might turn naturally to hypotheses about the role of religion. At first glance this seems a promising tack. Hinduism might go a long way toward explaining the passivity of the Indian peasantry. More generally an organic cosmology that conferred legitimacy on the role of the ruling classes, couched in some theory of the harmony of the universe that stressed resignation and the acceptance of individual fate, might conceivably serve as a strong bar to insurrection and rebel-

[1] Robinson, *Rural Russia*, 206, is explicit on this point.

lion if the peasants accepted its norms. Here at once a difficulty appears. Such religions are the product of urban and priestly classes. The extent of their acceptance among peasants is problematic. In general the existence of an undercurrent of belief distinct from that of the educated strata, often in direct opposition to it, characterizes peasant societies. Passed along by word of mouth from generation to generation, only fragments of this underground tradition are likely to find their way into the historical record, and then very likely in a distorted form.

Even in religion-soaked India there are numerous indications of widespread hostility to the Brahman. Possibly Indian and other peasants believe in the effectiveness of magic and ritual as such, while at the same time they resent the human agent who performs the rituals and the price that he exacts for their performance. Movements to do away with the priest, to attain direct access to the deity and the source of magic, have simmered underground in both Europe and Asia for long periods, to burst forth from time to time in heretical and rebellious movements. In this connection, too, we would want to know what circumstances make peasants receptive to these movements at some times and not at others. Nor are they a universal accompaniment of the more important peasant upheavals. There is little indication of any religious component in the peasant disturbances that preceded and accompanied the French Revolution. In the Russian Revolution it is highly unlikely that revolutionary notions from the towns, either religious or secular, were of any importance. G.T. Robinson in his study of Russian peasant life before 1917 points out that the religious and other intellectual currents impinging on the peasants from the outside were wholly on the side of conservatism and strongly discounts the role of revolutionary ideas from the towns.[2] Conceivably further research may reveal the role of underground traditions indigenous to the peasantry and couched in religious terms. Nevertheless, to be meaningful, such an explanation in the case of Russia, or of any society, requires information about the way in which ideas were related to concrete social circumstances. Religion by itself clearly provides no key.

[2] *Rural Russia,* 144.

The shortcoming of all these hypotheses is that they focus too much attention on the peasantry. A moment's reflection on the course of any specific preindustrial rebellion reveals that one cannot understand it without reference to the actions of the upper classes that in large measure provoked it. Another noticeable feature of rebellions in agrarian societies is their tendency to take on the character of the society against which they rebel. In modern times this tendency is obscured because successful rebellion has been the prelude to thorough and violent overhaul of the entire society. In earlier peasant rebellions, it is much more obvious. The insurgents battle for the restoration of the "old law," as in the *Bauernkrieg*, for the "real Tsar" or the "good Tsar" in Russian peasant upheavals. In traditional China the outcome has often been the replacement of a decaying dynasty by a new and vigorous one, that is, a restoration of essentially the same social structure. Before looking at the peasantry, it is necessary to look at the whole society.

With these considerations in mind we may raise the question whether certain types of agrarian and premodern societies are more subject to peasant insurrection and rebellion than others and what structural features may help to explain the differences. The contrast between India and China is sufficient to show that the differences exist and have prolonged political consequences. Likewise the existence of even one substantiated attempt at peasant revolt in India, that of Hyderabad in 1948, even leaving aside other smaller upheavals, strongly suggests that no social structure can be totally immune to revolutionary tendencies set up in the course of modernization. On the other hand, some societies are obviously much more vulnerable than others. For the moment we may set aside all problems that arise during the course of modernization and concentrate specifically on structural differences in premodern societies.[3]

[3] As the expressions "immune" and "vulnerable" show, English usage imposes a conservative bias on the analysis of revolutions: the implicit assumption is that a "healthy" society is immune to revolution. Hence it becomes necessary to make explicit the author's rejection of this assumption. The analysis of why revolutions do and do not occur carries no *logical* implication of approval or disapproval, even if no investigator is free of such preferences. Without trying to develop the argument here, I suspect that a

The contrast between India and China suggests an hypothesis perhaps more tenable than those just discussed. Indian society, as many scholars have remarked, resembles some huge yet very simple invertebrate organism. A central coordinating authority, a monarch, or to continue the biological analogy, a brain, was not necessary to its continued operation. Through much of Indian history down to modern times, there was no central authority imposing its will on the whole subcontinent. Indian society reminds one of the starfish whom fishermen used to shred angrily into bits, after which each fragment would grow into a new starfish. But the analogy is inexact. Indian society was even simpler and yet more differentiated. Climate, agricultural practices, taxation systems, religious beliefs, and many other social and culture features differed markedly from one part of the country to another. Caste, on the other hand, was common to them all and provided the framework around which all of life was everywhere organized. It made possible these differences and a society where a territorial segment could be cut off from the rest without damage, or at least without fatal damage, to itself or the rest of the society. Far more important, from the standpoint of our immediate problem, is the reverse of this feature. Any attempt at innovation, any local variation, simply became the basis of another caste. This has not been merely a matter of new religious beliefs. Since the distinction between sacred and profane is very dubious for Indian society, and since religiously tinged caste codes cover practically the whole range of human activities, any innovation or attempted innovation in premodern times was likely to become the basis for another caste. Thus opposition to society and preying on society became a part of society in the form of bandit castes or castes in the form of religious sects. In China, too, hereditary bandits were known.[4] In the Chinese context, their significance was quite different, aside from the fact that the absence of caste made recruitment easier. In China the landlord needed a strong central authority as part of the arrangement for extracting the surplus from the peasants. Until quite recent times, caste made this arrange-

strong case can be made for the thesis that sick societies are ones in which revolutions are impossible.

[4] Hsiao, *Rural China*, 462.

ment unnecessary in India. Chinese society for this reason required something resembling a brain, a more than rudimentary coordinating authority at the center. Bandits were a threat in China and could grow into peasant insurrections.

The general hypothesis that emerges from this brief recapitulation, hedged with that familiar ritual phrase *ceteris paribus* used by scholars to avoid thorny issues, might be put in the following way: A highly segmented society that depends on diffuse sanctions for its coherence and for extracting the surplus from the underlying peasantry is nearly immune to peasant rebellion because opposition is likely to take the form of creating another segment. On the other hand, an agrarian bureaucracy, or a society that depends on a central authority for extracting the surplus, is a type most vulnerable to such outbreaks. Feudal systems, where real power is diffused into several centers under the nominal authority of a weak monarch, belong somewhere in between. This hypothesis at least fits the main facts in this study. Peasant rebellion was a severe problem in traditional China and tsarist Russia; was somewhat less severe but frequently beneath the surface in medieval Europe; was quite noticeable in Japan from the fifteenth century onwards; and finds almost no mention in histories of India.[5]

Turning to the process of modernization itself, we notice once again that the success or failure of the upper class in taking up commercial agriculture has a tremendous influence on the political outcome. Where the landed upper class has turned to production for the market in a way that enables commercial influences to permeate rural life, peasant revolutions have been weak affairs. There are several very different ways in which this antirevolutionary transition has been able to take place. In early Meiji Japan, a landed upper class that was being rapidly renewed preserved much of the traditional peasant society as the mechanism for extracting a surplus. In other key cases, peasant society was destroyed, either by breaking

[5] Japanese revolts show some of the signs characteristic of the early phase of modernization in Europe, a fact compatible with Japan's more centralized feudalism, which resembled European efforts under absolute monarchies to preserve privilege and the *status quo*. See Sansom, *History of Japan*, II, 208–210.

the connection with the land as in England or by intensifying the connection as in the reintroduction of serfdom in Prussia. Conversely the evidence indicates that a revolutionary movement is much more likely to develop and become a serious threat where the landed aristocracy fails to develop a really powerful commercial impulse within its own ranks. Then it may leave beneath it a peasant society damaged but intact, with which it has few connecting links. Meanwhile it is likely to try to maintain its style of life in a changing world by extracting a larger surplus out of the peasantry. By and large this was the case in eighteenth-century France and in Russia and China during the nineteenth and twentieth centuries.[6]

The great German peasant war, the *Bauernkrieg* of 1524–1525, illustrates these relationships in a striking fashion, especially if one compares the areas in which it broke out violently with those parts of Germany where it was not more than a minor episode. Since it was the most important peasant revolution of early modern times in Europe, it will be well to discuss it briefly here. Once again its meaning becomes clearest through contrast with changes in English society. An influential sector of the landed upper classes in England wanted, not men, but land for sheep raising. The German Junkers, on the other hand, wanted men, more specifically men attached to the land, in order to grow the grain which they exported. Much of the subsequent history of the two countries goes back to this homely difference.

In Prussia the coming of grain exports brought about a sharp reversal of earlier trends that had been similar to those in Western Europe, where parliamentary democracy eventually triumphed. By the middle of the fourteenth century, Prussia still resembled West-

[6] India may seem an exception to this generalization about the survival of peasant society as a cause of modern revolution. It is partly explicable in terms of the impediments to rebellion and revolution inherent in India's premodern social structure, partly the way modernization has proceeded up to now. Most important of all, modernization has but barely begun in the Indian countryside. Such are the main grounds for holding that it is not really an exception. Perhaps it will become one. Historical generalizations are not immutable laws like those of physics: the course of history reflects mainly an effort to escape the bounds imposed by previous conditions expressed in such generalizations.

ern Europe, even if it had reached this stage by a different route. Then it was a land of prosperous and relatively free peasants. As in the rest of what later became northeastern Germany, the necessity to grant favorable conditions to immigrating German colonists had, along with the development of a strong central authority in the form of the Teutonic Order and a vigorous town life, been the main cause of this freedom. German peasants had the right to sell and bequeath their lands, as well as to market their produce in the nearby towns. Their dues to the overlord in both money and labor were small, the authority of the lord in village affairs was strictly limited, mainly to "higher justice," i.e., the more serious crimes. For the rest, villagers managed their own affairs.[7]

The villages throughout the colonized area were settled by the *locator*, often employed by the noble landholders, who procured the settlers, led them from their place of origin, allocated to them their holdings, measured the village fields, and in return became the hereditary mayor with larger holdings than the rest.[8] In a sense, therefore, the villages of northeastern Germany were artificial communities that received their rights in the form of charters (*Handfesten*) from above. Their situation on this score differed from that of southern German-speaking villages, which won their rights in the course of a prolonged struggle with the overlord. This difference may be partly responsible for the lack of resistance to later subjugation in the northeast, though other factors were probably more significant. Another difference from the south was the ethnically mixed character of the population, as Germans settled in Slavic territories. However, German villages were usually settled on unoccupied land, and the Slavic peasants soon gained the same favorable legal status as the Germans.[9]

Toward the end of the fourteenth century, certain changes began that later led to the enserfment of the peasants. The towns declined; the central authority weakened. But most important of all,

[7] Carsten, *Origins of Prussia*, pt I, esp 29 – 31, 41, 62, 64, 73 – 74, for details of the peasants' situation. Stein, *Agrarverfassung*, I, 431, 434, adds in a concise fashion some legal materials.

[8] Carsten, *Origins of Prussia*, 30 – 31.

[9] Carsten, *Origins of Prussia*, 32, 34 – 35, 37 – 39.

there appeared the beginnings of an export market for grain. To-·gether these forces altered the political balance in the countryside. Other parts of Germany and Europe were also hit by a debasement of the currency as part of a weakening of royal authority and by an agrarian crisis that led the nobility to press hard on the peasants, events that helped to produce the Peasants' War.[10] But only in the northeast did an important export trade in grain put in an appearance.

The consequences for the peasants were disastrous. The lords ceased to be interested in money dues from the peasants and turned instead to cultivating and increasing the demesne. For this the labor of the peasants was necessary. Labor services were extended; the peasants tied to the soil. Their rights to sell and bequeath their property were all but abolished, and they were no longer allowed to marry off the estate. Most of these changes took place during the sixteenth century, an era of booming grain prices. It is worth noticing that in this situation the scarcity of labor did not aid the peasants but led to severe discipline in order to prevent flight and that a numerous though rather poor nobility was able to establish a labor-repressive system without the assistance of a powerful central government. In fact the formal end of the Teutonic Order in 1525 was one of the more important political events that led to the results just mentioned.[11]

During the period of colonization, peasant villages had often been physically separate from the noble's estate and had been largely independent organisms. In the second half of the fifteenth century, this situation ceased,[12] as the lords penetrated the villages, economically by taking over peasant property, especially the larger holdings of the mayor, and politically by establishing a monopoly of justice.[13] Without this capture of the village community and the destruction of its autonomy, it is difficult to understand how a mass of scattered nobles could have imposed their will.

[10] Carsten, *Origins of Prussia*, 115.
[11] Carsten, *Origins of Prussia*, chap XI, esp 149 – 150, 154, 163 – 164.
[12] Aubin, *Geschichte des gutsherrlich-bäuerlichen Verhältnisses*, 155 – 156.
[13] Stein, *Agrarverfassung*, I, 437 – 439.

By the end of the seventeenth century, most of the nobles had become petty despots in the area of their estates, checked by no formal authority from above or below. The "capitalist" revolution of the sixteenth- and seventeenth-century Junker was almost entirely a social and political one. There is no indication in the literature of any important technical changes in agriculture that accompanied the Junker's rise to supremacy. The three-field system was still almost universal up until about the time of the Seven Years' War, and, by the eighteenth century, agricultural practices, especially on the big Junker estates, were far behind those in Germany's western provinces.[14]

The peasants did offer limited resistance. The only revolt of importance broke out in the vicinity of Königsberg in 1525, shortly after the abolition of the Teutonic Order. It is not surprising that the impetus came partly from the town itself and from those who had most to lose — the more prosperous free peasants. Its rapid suppression was due to weak support from the towns, where, in contrast to the *Bauernkrieg* area, guild life was relatively feeble.[15]

The situation that led to the *Bauernkrieg* of 1524 – 1525 was in its most important aspects almost the opposite of that in northeastern Germany and calls to mind some of the features that more than two centuries later produced the French Revolution. Since the *Bauernkrieg* and the numerous upheavals that led up to it were spread over a wide area, from what is now western Austria, through

[14] Stein, *Agrarverfassung*, I, 463 – 464.

[15] Carsten, "Bauernkrieg," 407. The weak resistance in Germany to the establishment of serfdom presents a sharp contrast with the peasant unrest and revolts that accompanied and followed its establishment during the same time period in Russia. The main reason for the difference is probably a fact to which attention has been drawn before: serfdom in Russia arose in response to a political situation. As part of the process by which absolutism established itself, Russian serfdom provided a method of working the lands granted to support the tsar's officials. Also serfdom in Russia seems to have damaged the peasant village far less than in Prussia. Though it lost much of its autonomy, the Russian village commune (*mir*, or more accurately *sel'skoe obshchestvo*) remained very much a going concern. For an excellent treatment of the changes during the sixteenth and seventeenth centuries in Russia, see Blum, *Lord and Peasant*, chaps 8 – 14; on peasant unrest, 258, 267 – 268; on the *mir*, 510 – 512.

nearly all of Switzerland, parts of southwestern Germany, and a large area of the upper Rhine Valley, there was naturally considerable variation in local conditions, a variation that has added to the difficulty in determining its causes and kept alive a vigorous controversy over them up to the present time.[16]

Nevertheless there is widespread agreement among a variety of scholars along the following lines. The territorial princes in this part of Germany were getting stronger, not weaker as in the northeast, and taking some of the early steps toward controlling their own nobility and setting up a modern uniform administration. This form of absolutism was, however, a petty, fragmented variety, as the Emperor had dissipated German energies in a vain struggle with the papacy. Town life flourished in this part of Germany; the late Middle Ages were the golden age of the German *Bürger*.

Thus the peasants could at times draw on the urban plebs for support. But to generalize about what social strata the peasants allied themselves with and which ones they opposed is very risky. At different times and places they were in opposition to nearly every conceivable group and in alliance with some other: in the Rhineland with the nobles against the monastic holdings,[17] against the nobility at others, with the nobility at still others, yet again in opposition to the bourgeoisie and the territorial prince.[18] All that one can say with confidence is that the conflict began chiefly with the moderate demands of well-to-do peasants and became more radical as it developed, turning later into the apocalyptic visions of Thomas Münzer. Partly this progressive radicalization was due to the refusal of early moderate demands,[19] partly to the tendency of peasants to turn to new religious notions emanating from the Reformation in justification of their economic, political, and social grievances.[20] The connection with the towns probably contributed to this radi-

[16] See the three maps at the end of Franz, *Bauernkrieg*.

[17] Waas, *Grosse Wendung*, 13 – 15, 19.

[18] Franz, *Bauernkrieg*, 84, 32, 26.

[19] The thesis of Waas, in *Grosse Wendung*.

[20] Nabholz, "Ursachen des Bauernkriegs," 144 – 167 brings out this connection very clearly for the Zürich area. Note especially 162 – 163, 165, 167.

calization, of which there were some foreshadowings at an early date.[21] It may also have derived from the complaints of lower strata among the peasantry, who were dividing into rich and poor much as in France of the late eighteenth century, though I have not found any explicit statement of this connection.

The nobility of the time were facing a double squeeze: from the efforts of the territorial princes to establish their authority and from the more general effects of the spread of a commercial economy. They needed money and tried in a variety of ways to get it, reviving where they could ancient rights, or — as it seemed to the peasants — trying to create new obligations. Indeed the first stirrings of peasant discontent took the form of efforts to retain or return to "das alte Recht."[22] What the nobles did *not* do, except here and there on a small scale, was to undertake farming for the market. Here lies the crucial difference between the area of the *Bauernkrieg* and Junker Germany.

As for the peasants themselves, the economic and social position of a large sector had been improving for some time. As one scholar observed more than twenty years ago, the evidence of prosperity among the peasants and *Bürger* in this part of Germany at the end of the Middle Ages has become so abundant that it is no longer possible to believe that general economic deterioration caused the revolt.[23] This fact is of course quite consistent with the view that hard pressed nobles tried to put the screw on the peasants in whatever way they could.[24] For centuries a see-saw struggle had been taking place between the peasant community and the overlord over their respective rights, a struggle that did not exclude shared interests on many issues. Periodically the outcome crystallized in a

[21] E.g., in the piper of Niklashausen. See Franz, *Bauernkrieg*, 45 – 52.

[22] Franz, *Bauernkrieg*, 1 – 40.

[23] Waas, *Grosse Wendung*, 40 – 42.

[24] Evidence on this score is presented by a Soviet scholar Smirin, *Ocherki istorii politicheskoi bor'by v Germanii*, chap II. Smirin does everything he can to prove the existence of a "seigneurial reaction" and at times strains the evidence to the point of being silly: as when he cites (p. 60) labor dues of three days a year as an indication of their importance. But he is probably correct in his assertion (p. 85) that the peasants were upset by the uncertainty and variation in their obligations.

written record known as a *Weistum*, the codification of customary law (*Rechtsgewohnheiten*) which was written down from answers to questioning under oath of the experienced older men of the community. The surviving records show a big increase in the number of *Weistümer* after 1300 with the largest number falling between 1500 and 1600, after which they fall off rapidly.[25] What these documents and other similar evidence reveal is a tightly knit village community, albeit one with increasing property differentials, existing in a slowly changing situation of antagonistic cooperation with the overlord.[26] Labor dues and the cultivation of the demesne appear to have been declining in importance and money dues increasing, the reverse of the situation in the northeast. A good many peasants had come close to attaining *de facto* property rights, having shaken off most of the stigmata of feudal tenure, though there were many pockets where the latter remained.[27]

In the early stages of the revolt, peasant demands often repeated themes taken from older *Weistümer*.[28] This fact is one more strong indication that the revolt began with the "legitimate" grievances of respected and substantial members of the village community.[29]

The *Bauernkrieg* was a failure and bloodily suppressed. Both its radical and conservative manifestations were driven underground. Partly because of the aristocratic victory, which as we have seen took place in the northeast for different reasons and against little resistance, the prospects for the emergence of liberal democracy in Germany were cut off for centuries. Not until the nineteenth century did Germany again take halting and, as it turned out, still unsuccessful steps in this direction.

[25] Wiessner, *Sachinhalt und Wirtschaftliche Bedeutung der Weistümer*, 26-29.

[26] Wiessner, "Geschichte des Dorfes," 43-44, 60, 63, 70-71. Though the account is limited to Austria, it is highly likely that the same type of differences was appearing elsewhere.

[27] For the Zürich area, Nabholz, "Ursachen des Bauernkriegs," 158-159; for Austria, Wiessner, "Geschichte des Dorfes," 49, 50, 67; for Germany, Waas, *Grosse Wendung*, 37-38.

[28] Waas, *Grosse Wendung*, 34-35.

[29] Cf Franz, *Bauernkrieg*, 1-40.

The respective victories·of the English squire and the German Junker constitute almost exactly opposite forms in which a landed upper class might make a successful transition to commercial agriculture. They also constitute exactly opposite ways of destroying the basis of political action by the peasantry. Even if defeated, this action was vigorous in the *Bauernkrieg* areas where the upper classes did not make an economic onslaught on peasant society but apparently tried to increase the amount of money it took from the peasants.

This excursion into a concrete case is sufficient, I hope, to indicate the main ways in which the response of the landed upper classes to the challenge of commercial agriculture creates situations that are favorable or unfavorable to revolts by the peasantry. The main areas where peasant revolutions have in modern times had the greatest importance, China and Russia, were alike in the fact that the landed upper classes by and large did not make a successful transition to the world of commerce and industry and did not destroy the prevailing social organization among the peasants.

Now we may leave the actions of the aristocracy aside to undertake a more analytic discussion of factors at work among the peasantry itself. Just what does modernization mean for the peasantry beyond the simple and brutal fact that sooner or later they are its victims? On general grounds, it seems obvious that the different types of social organization found in various peasant societies, together with the timing and character of the modernization process itself, can be expected to have considerable influence on whether or not the response will be a revolutionary or a passive one. But just what is the connection among these variables? Let us see first what general changes take place in this complex process.

In agriculture economic modernization means the extension of market relationships over a much wider area than before, and the replacement of subsistence farming more and more by production for the market.[30] Secondly, in politics successful modernization

[30] Markets were by no means absent in premodern peasant villages. And even the modern suburban businessman may take pride in a few tomatoes grown in his backyard. It would not be necessary to mention these points were it not for anticonceptual scholarship that delights in the

involves the establishment of peace and order over a wide area, the creation of a strong central government. There is no universal connection between the two processes: Rome and China both established powerful and far-flung governments for their time without generating any significant impetus toward a modern society. It is the combination of the two, nevertheless, that has yielded modernization in various parts of the world since the fifteenth century. The spread of the state's authority and the intrusion of the market, which may occur at quite different times, affect the bonds of the peasant to the overlord, the division of labor within the village, its system of authority, class groupings within the peasantry, tenure and property rights. At some point the influence of these external forces may produce changes in the technology and level of productivity in agriculture. To my limited knowledge, there is no instance of a major technical revolution in agriculture arising among the peasantry, though moderately important ones are reported for Japan, as we have seen, toward the end of the Tokugawa era. Technological changes so far have been far more important in the West; in the rice economies of Asia, added productivity has come mainly through intensified human labor.

In this complex of related changes three aspects are especially important politically: the character of the link between the peasant community and the overlord, property and class divisions within the peasantry, and the degree of solidarity or cohesiveness displayed by the peasant community. Because these three aspects are so closely related to each other, it is impossible to avoid some overlap and repetition in an effort to trace out characteristic patterns of modernization in each of them.

To return to the starting point of the process, one finds that there are certain very broad similarities among peasant communities or villages and their relationships to the outside world in many agrarian civilizations. It will be helpful to begin by sketching the general ground plan of these communities in very general terms, realizing that there are numerous politically significant departures

---

effort to trample down historical distinctions by pointing to such trivialities. Obviously what matters is the qualitative role played by the market in the countryside: its effect on social relationships.

from this plan. Indeed it is easier to perceive the meaning of these departures if we first grasp the general model. I shall limit the discussion to villages, conceived as compact settlements surrounded by cultivated fields. Though the system of scattered individual settlements also occurs quite widely, it was not the predominant form anywhere except perhaps in parts of the United States in colonial and frontier times. In itself this is one of the grounds for refusing the designation peasant to American farmers.

Either directly or indirectly the immediate overlord played a vital part in the life of the village. In feudal societies he was the seigneur; in bureaucratic China he was the landlord dependent on the Imperial bureaucracy; in parts of India the *zamindar*, a figure roughly halfway between the bureaucratic official and the feudal seigneur. The general task of the secular overlord was to provide security against the external enemies. Often, but not universally, he rendered justice and settled disputes among the inhabitants of the village. Alongside the secular overlord, there has often been the priest. His task has been to help give legitimacy to the prevailing social order and to provide a way of both explaining and coping with those misfortunes and disasters for which the individual peasant's traditional economic and social techniques were inadequate. In return for the performance of these functions, the overlord with the priest extracted an economic surplus from the peasants in the form of labor, agricultural products, or even money, though this was generally less important in precommercial times. How these obligations were distributed among the peasants varied considerably. The peasants' right to cultivate the soil and keep a portion of the products for their own use generally depended on fulfilling the above obligations.

There is considerable evidence to support the thesis that, where the links arising out of this relationship between overlord and peasant community are strong, the tendency toward peasant rebellion (and later revolution) is feeble. In both China and Russia, the links were tenuous and peasant upheavals endemic to these states, even though the structure of the peasant communities themselves were about as different as could be imagined. In Japan, where peasant revolution was kept under control, the linkage was very .

effective. There are some puzzles and contradictions in the evidence. In India, strictly political power did not reach into the village except in certain areas in pre-British times. But there was a strong linkage to authority through the priesthood.

Two conditions are probably essential for the link to be an effective agent of social stability. One is that there should not be severe competition for land or other resources between the peasants and the overlord. This is not simply a matter of how much land is available. Social institutions are just as important as the amount of land in determining whether or not peasants become land hungry. Thus, a second and closely related condition, I would suggest, is the following: political stability requires the inclusion of the overlord and/or the priest as members of the village community who perform services necessary for the agricultural cycle and the social cohesion of the village for which they receive roughly commensurate privileges and material rewards. This point requires more extensive discussion since it raises general issues that are a matter of lively dispute.

The difficulty arises from the notion of rewards and privileges commensurate with the services rendered by the upper class. In a feudal society just how many hens and eggs at stated times in the year, how many days of work on the lord's fields, would be a "fair" repayment for the lord's protection and justice? Is the matter not wholly arbitrary, one that can only be decided by a test of strength? More generally, is not the concept of "exploitation" a purely subjective one, no more than a political epithet, that cannot receive any objective pinning down or measurement? Very likely a majority of social scientists today would answer these questions with an affirmative. If one takes this position, the proposition just suggested becomes a trivial tautology. It means that peasants do not revolt as long as they accept the privileges of the aristocracy and their own obligations to them as legitimate. *Why* the peasants accept them remains as much of a problem as ever. Within the framework of this position, force and deception can be the only possible answers to this question because one set of rewards is just as arbitrary as any other. It seems to me that at this point the whole subjective interpretation of exploitation breaks down and becomes flagrantly self-contradictory. How can nine-tenths of the peasants' crop be no more and no less arbitrary an exaction than a third?

The opposite point of view, that exploitation is in principle an objective notion, I submit, makes better sense generally and at least provides the possibility of an explanation. The point at issue is whether or not one can make an objective assessment of the contributions of qualitatively different activities, such as fighting and tilling the soil, to the continued existence of a specific society. (Economists used to tell us that this was possible, at least through a competitive market, but would, I take it, be reluctant to go that far now.) It seems to me that this is possible for a detached observer and that he does so by asking the traditional questons 1) Is this activity necessary to the society? What would happen if it stopped or changed? 2) What resources are necessary in order to enable people to carry out this activity effectively? Though the answers to such questions must always have a substantial margin of uncertainty, they also have a common objective core.

Within limits broad enough for society to work, the objective character of exploitation seems so dreadfully obvious as to lead to the suspicion that the denial of objectivity is what requires explanation. It is not hard to tell when a peasant community gets real protection from its overlord and when the overlord is either unable to keep enemies out or is in league with them. An overlord who does not keep the peace, who takes away most of the peasants' food, seizes his women — as happened over wide areas of China in the nineteenth and twentieth centuries — is clearly exploitative. In between this situation and objective justice are all sorts of gradations where the ratio between services rendered and the surplus taken from the peasants is open to dispute. Such disputes may intrigue philosophers. They are not likely to rip society apart. The thesis put forward here merely holds that the contributions of those who fight, rule, and pray must be obvious to the peasant, and the peasants' return payments must not be grossly out of proportion to the services received. Folk conceptions of justice, to put the argument in still another way, do have a rational and realistic basis; and arrangements that depart from this basis are likely to need deception and force the more they do depart.

Certain forms of modernization are especially likely to upset any form of equilibrium that may establish itself in the relationship between the peasant community and the landed upper classes and to put new strains on the mechanisms linking them together. Where the royal authority has increased and intensified the burden on the peasantry in order to meet the costs of an expanding military establishment and administrative bureaucracy, as well as an expensive policy of courtly magnificence, the growth of royal absolutism may contribute heavily to peasant explosions.[31] The Bourbon kings and the Russian tsars each in their very different ways used this combination of devices to tame their respective nobilities at the cost of substantial suffering among the peasants. The reaction was intermittent eruptions, much more severe in Russia than in France. The Tudors and Stuarts in England faced an entirely different situation, and lost a royal head, partly because they attempted to protect the peasants against the "antisocial" behavior of a commercializing nobility. In Japan the Tokugawa *Shōgun* resolutely turned their backs on the outside world and therefore did not have to create as expensive a military and administrative establishment as did absolute monarchs in Europe. Peasant disturbances did not become important until the latter part of the era.

Generally the creation of centralized monarchy has meant that the peasants' immediate overlord lost his protective functions to the state. In both France and Russia this change took place in such a way as to leave still in large measure intact the rights of the lord to a series of obligations from the peasants. These lordly rights were backed up by the new power of the state because the royal authority could not afford to alienate the nobility altogether. In turn, gradual infiltration into the countryside of goods made in the towns that the lord needed or thought he needed, together with the requirements of conspicuous consumption at court, increased the lord's need to squeeze more out of the peasantry. The failure of commercial farming to take hold on any very wide scale made the situation worse, since it meant that there was scarcely any alternative to squeezing the peasant. As we have seen, what trends there

[31] For a detailed account of the relationship in seventeenth-century France, see Porchnev, *Soulèvements populaires.*

were toward commercial agriculture were labor-repressive. In France, Russia, and other parts of eastern Europe, the small lord became the most reactionary figure, perhaps because all alternatives were closed to him, such as the court, a good marriage, or an attempt at commercial farming. There is no need to labor the connection between these trends and peasant discontent, which have been pointed out by numerous historians.

Where the peasants have revolted, there are indications that new and capitalist methods of pumping the economic surplus out of the peasantry had been added while the traditional ones lingered on or were even intensified. This was true in eighteenth-century France, where the peasant movement that helped to bring down the *ancien régime* had strong anticapitalist as well as strong antifeudal features. In Russia the tsar's action in dismounting serfdom from above failed to satisfy the peasants. The redemption payments were too high and the grants of land too small, as the subsequent accumulation of arrears soon showed. In the absence of any thoroughgoing modernization of the countryside, the redemption payments merely became new ways of taking a surplus from the peasant while keeping him from getting the land that was "rightfully" his. Again, in China the peasant showed by his behavior that he resented the combination of the old tax-collecting official and commercial landlord embodied in the Kuomintang regime.

These facts do not imply that the total burden on the peasantry *necessarily* increased under these circumstances. Indeed it is an historical commonplace that improvement in the economic situation of the peasantry may be a prelude to revolt.[32] The fact seems

[32] Such improvement would seem to contradict the thesis that objective exploitation is a cause of revolt. This is not necessarily so. The relationship between the overlord and the peasant community can become more exploitative without the peasants becoming any poorer, indeed even if their material situation improves. This would happen wherever the lord's exactions increased and his contribution to the welfare of security of the village declined. A decline in the lord's contribution, along with general economic improvement and efforts by the lord to increase his "take," could be expected to generate tremendous resentment. To test this conception of objective exploitation carefully against several cases would be a very difficult but rewarding undertaking. I have not done this; the notion came to me in

moderately well established for the English countryside prior to the upheaval of 1381, for the *Bauernkrieg* in sixteenth-century Germany, and for the French peasantry prior to 1789. In other cases, the most important ones, Russia and China, the burden on the peasants very likely increased.

In any event, one of the greatest dangers for an *ancien régime* during the earlier phases of transition to the world of commerce and industry is to lose the support of the upper crust of the peasantry. One common explanation is a psychological one, to the effect that limited improvement in the economic position of this stratum leads to greater and greater demands and eventually to a revolutionary outbreak. This notion of a "revolution of rising expectations" may have some explanatory power. It will not do as a general explanation. For both Russia and China, even in the twentieth century, it strains the evidence beyond recognition. There are several different ways in which the richer peasants may turn upon the old order, depending on specific historical circumstances and the impact of these on different forms of peasant society.

The timing of changes in the life of the peasantry, including the number of people simultaneously affected, are crucial factors in their own right. I suspect that they are more important than the material changes in food, shelter, clothing, except for very sudden and big ones. Economic deterioration by slow degrees can become accepted by its victims as part of the normal situation. Especially where no alternative is clearly visible, more and more privation can gradually find acceptance in the peasants' standards of what is right and proper. What infuriates peasants (and not just peasants) is a new and sudden imposition or demand that strikes many people at once and that is a break with accepted rules and customs. Even the traditionally docile Indian peasants struck *en masse* and raised the specter of agrarian revolt over much of Bengal in the 1860s when English overlords tried to force them to grow indigo at starvation prices for the suddenly booming textile market.[33] Revolutionary

---

the course of a prolonged effort to make sense of the data, and I present it as a working hypothesis that finds some support in the evidence.

[33] An instructive account from a radical standpoint in Natarajan, *Peasant Uprisings,* chap IV.

measures against the priests in the Vendée had a very similar effect. To multiply instances is hardly necessary. The significant point is that under these conditions individual grievances in a flash become apparent as collective ones. If the impact is of the right kind (sudden, widespread, yet not so severe as to make collective resistance seem hopeless from the start), it can ignite the solidarity of rebellion or revolution in any kind of a peasant society. No type, as far as I can perceive, is immune. Nevertheless there are variations in the explosive potential that can be connected with types of peasant society.

In the course of this study we have noticed a substantial range of differences in the degree of cooperation and the associated division of labor in peasant communities. At one extreme one might place the peasants of the Vendée with their isolated farmsteads, rather atypical for peasants in civilized societies. At the other extreme might be the highly integrated Japanese village, an integration that has persisted through modern times. On general grounds, it seems obvious that the degree of solidarity displayed by peasants, since it is an expression of the entire network of social relationships within which the individual lives out his life, would have an important bearing on political tendencies. Nevertheless, because this factor is intertwined with so many others, the assessment of its importance presents difficulties. As I read the evidence, the absence of solidarity (or more precisely a state of weak solidarity, since some cooperation always exists) puts severe difficulties in the way of *any* political action. Hence its consequence is conservative, though the type of sudden shock just discussed can override this conservative tendency and arouse the peasants to violent action. Where solidarity is on the other hand strong, it is possible to distinguish between conservative forms and those favoring rebellion or revolution.

In a rebellious and revolutionary form of solidarity, institutional arrangements are such as to spread grievances through the peasant community and turn it into a solidarity group hostile to the overlord. There are strong indications that this was happening in the late nineteenth and early twentieth centuries in Russian villages. One of the main consequences of the periodic redivision of prop-

erty in the *mir*, or peasant commune, seems to have been to generalize land hunger, to align the richer peasants with the poorer
ones. Certainly this was the conclusion of Stolypin, who reversed
earlier official support for the *mir* and tried to establish a Russian
version of sturdy yeomanry to prop up the tottering throne of the
Romanoffs.[34] It is also worth recalling that the Chinese Communists,
before they took power, had to create this kind of solidarity out of
refractory social materials.

The opposite kind of solidarity, the conservative one, derives
its cohesion by tying those with actual and potential grievances
into the prevailing social structure. This takes place, as Japanese
and Indian materials show, through a division of labor that has behind it strong sanctions while at the same time it provides a recognized if humble niche for those with little property. Quite possibly
the key to the difference between radical and conservative forms
of solidarity rests on this point. Radical solidarity, as in the Russian
system, may represent an attempt to find an equitable distribution
of a scarce resource, namely land; conservative solidarity was
based on the division of labor. In general it seems easier to get people to cooperate on a common task than to cooperate peaceably in
the use of scarce resources.[35]

To put the same point in a slightly different fashion, property
arrangements vary a great deal in the way they tie the peasants to
the prevailing society and hence in their political effects. In order
to be a full member of the Chinese village and come under the conservative influences of the network of kinship and religious obligations, it was necessary to have a certain rough minimum of property.
The process of modernization apparently increased very considerably the number of those peasants below this minimum, something

[34] Robinson, *Rural Russia*, 153, points out that among the twenty
guberniias where landlords suffered heaviest losses during the peasant upheavals of 1905, sixteen showed a predominance of repartitional tenure
over hereditary holdings by individual peasant households. On the government's fear of solidarity among the peasants, see ibid, 264.

[35] For a humble illustration compare what happens when a large family
has to arrange a complicated picnic on a beach, where one child gathers
firewood, another builds the fire, etc, with what happens during the morning rush for the bathroom.

that may well have happened in premodern times as well, and hence the radical potential. Japanese and Indian villages, on the other hand, provided a legitimate if lowly status for those with little or no property both in premodern and later times.

The type of weak solidarity that inhibits political action of any variety is mainly a modern phenomenon. After the establishment of a capitalist legal framework and after commerce and industry have made a substantial impact, peasant society may reach a new form of conservative stability. This happened in much of France, parts of western Germany, and elsewhere in western Europe during the first half of the nineteenth century. Marx caught the essence of the situation when he compared French villages made up of small peasant holdings to sacks of potatoes.[36] The key feature is the absence of a network of cooperative relationships. This makes the modern peasant village the opposite of a medieval one. A recent study of a village of this type in southern Italy shows how the competition among the family units that make up the village inhibits any form of effective political action. The origin of "amoral familism" — a caricature of capitalism — is rooted in the specific history of this village, an extreme development that contrasts with more cooperative relationships in other parts of Italy.[37] More important and more general factors may be the disappearance of common rights and of the performance in common of certain tasks during the agricultural cycle; the overwhelming importance of the small plot worked by family labor; and the competitive relationships introduced by capitalism. At a more advanced stage of industrial development, this type of atomised small peasant village may, as we have seen in parts of Germany, become the seedbed of reactionary anticapitalist sentiment in the countryside.

To sum up, the most important causes of peasant revolutions have been the absence of a commercial revolution in agriculture led by the landed upper classes and the concomitant survival of peasant social institutions into the modern era when they are subject to new stresses and strains. Where the peasant community survives, as in

[36] See "Eighteenth Brumaire," 415.
[37] See Banfield, *Moral Basis of a Backward Society*, chap. 8, esp 147, 150 – 154.

Japan, it must remain closely linked to the dominant class in the countryside if revolution is to be avoided. Hence an important contributing cause of peasant revolution has been the weakness of the institutional links binding peasant society to the upper classes, together with the exploitative character of this relationship. Part of the general syndrome has been the regime's loss of the support of an upper class of wealthy peasants because these have begun to go over to more capitalist modes of cultivation and to establish their independence against an aristocracy seeking to maintain its position through the intensification of traditional obligations, as in eighteenth-century France. Where these conditions have been absent or reversed, peasant revolts have failed to break out or have been easily suppressed.

The great agrarian bureaucracies of royal absolutism, including China, have been especially liable to the combination of factors favoring peasant revolution. Their very strength enables them to inhibit the growth of an independent commercial and manufacturing class. At most, they are likely to encourage one that is fragmented and tied to royal apronstrings for the sake of magnificence and war as in seventeenth-century France. By taming the bourgeoisie, the crown reduces the impetus toward further modernization in the form of a bourgeois revolutionary breakthrough. This effect was very noticeable even in France. Russia and China, in escaping bourgeois revolution, became more vulnerable to peasant revolutions. Furthermore, an agrarian bureaucracy, through its heavy demands for taxes, risks driving the peasants into alliance with local élites in the towns, a particularly dangerous situation as it separates royal officialdom from the mass of the population.[38] Finally, to the extent that it takes over the protective and judicial functions of the locally residing overlord, royal absolutism weak-

[38] This is especially clear in the disturbances preceding and accompanying the *Fronde*. See Porchnev, *Soulèvements populaires*, 118–131, 392–466. The author has demonstrated beyond any possible doubt that the *Fronde* was much more than a piece of aristocratic mischief. For reasons that need no repetition here as they are part of the entire argument I have tried to present, I reject his effort and that of other Marxist writers to identify royal absolutism with feudalism.

ens the crucial link that binds the peasants to the upper classes. Or if it takes over these functions only partly and haphazardly it is likely to find itself in competition with local élites in extracting resources from the peasants. In such circumstances there is a temptation for the local notables to side with the peasants.

Variations in the types of solidary arrangements among the peasants, to continue with general factors, are important mainly insofar as they constitute focal points for the creation of a distinct peasant society in opposition to the dominant class and as the basis for popular conceptions of justice and injustice that clash with those of the rulers. Conservative or radical consequences depend on the specific forms of the institutions promoting peasant cohesion. Solidarity among the peasants could help the dominant classes or be a weapon against them, sometimes changing from one to the other. In some premodern societies one may also find, as seems to have been the case in China, a division of labor that creates much less cohesion. Hence, the revolutionary potential under the impact of modernization varies greatly from one agrarian society to another. On the other hand, the more extreme forms of atomization that severely inhibit any effective political action and that have powerful conservative results seem to occur at a somewhat later stage of capitalism. Such a culture of selfish poverty may be only a transitional stage in backwaters not yet reached by advanced industrialism.

The preceding factors may explain how a revolutionary potential arises among the peasantry. Whether or not this potential becomes politically effective depends on the possibility of a fusion between peasant grievances and those of other strata. By themselves the peasants have never been able to accomplish a revolution. On this point the Marxists are absolutely correct, wide of the mark though they are on other crucial aspects. The peasants have to have leaders from other classes. But leadership alone is not enough. Medieval and late medieval peasant revolts were led by aristocrats or townsmen and still were crushed. This point should serve as a salutary reminder to those modern determinists, by no means all Marxists, who feel that once the peasants have become stirred up, big changes are necessarily on the way. Actually peasant revolts have been repressed far more often than they have succeeded. For them to succeed requires a somewhat unusual combination of circumstances that has occurred only in modern times. Success itself has been of a strictly negative sort. The peasants have provided the dynamite to bring down the old building. To the subsequent work of reconstruction they have brought nothing; instead they have been — even in France — its first victims. The upper classes have to display a substantial degree of blindness, mainly the product of specific historical circumstances and to which there have always been some important individual exceptions, before a revolutionary breakthrough becomes feasible.

Naturally the peasant movement will not find its allies among the élite, though it may draw upon a section of it, especially a handful of discontented intellectuals in modern times, for its leaders. The intellectuals as such can do little politically unless they attach themselves to a massive form of discontent. The discontented intellectual with his soul searchings has attracted attention wholly out of proportion to his political importance, partly because these searchings leave behind them written records and also because those who write history are themselves intellectuals. It is a particularly misleading trick to deny that a revolution stems from peasant grievances because its leaders happen to be professional men or intellectuals.

The allies that peasant discontent can find depends upon the stage of economic development that a country has reached and more specific historical circumstances; these factors also determine the point at which the allies turn on the peasant movement to draw its teeth or suppress it. German peasants in the *Bauernkrieg* got some help from the towns as well as from dissident landed aristocrats but accomplished nothing; the collective power that the landed élite could bring to bear was still overwhelming. In France the peasant movement fused with bourgeois demands, mainly because the preceding feudal reaction had antagonized the well-to-do peasants. The connection seems to me to have been precarious and might have gone the other way, since many bourgeois had property in the countryside and were disturbed by peasant disorders. Another major revolutionary ally was the urban crowd in Paris, though the term ally should not be taken to mean that their policies were coordinated or that either stratum, for that matter, had a really coherent policy. The *sans-culottes* were mainly smaller artisans and journeymen, who have generally played a much more important revolutionary role than Marxist theory might lead us to believe.

In Russia of 1917 the commercial and industrial classes were not a suitable ally for the angry peasants. The Russian bourgeoisie was much smaller and weaker in the country as a whole than had been the case in France, despite a higher level of technology where trade and industry did exist. Though there had been flirtations with Western constitutional notions, the Russian bourgeoisie was tied by many strings to the tsarist government, which had encouraged, largely for military reasons, a certain amount of hothouse capitalist development. Perhaps most important of all, no significant segment of the Russian peasantry was interested in securing property rights against the remnants of feudalism, as had been the case in France. The demands of the Russian peasant were brutally simple: to get rid of the landlord, divide up the land, and of course stop the war. The Constitutional Democrats, the main party with a bourgeois flavor, had earlier considered giving in to peasant demands. But the peasants' frontal attack on property was too much for its stomach when the issue had to be faced squarely. On the other hand, there was nothing in the notion of dividing up the land to disturb the industrial workers, at least not for the moment. Stopping the war appealed to the peasants who were the main victims of the slaughter and had little interest in defending a government that refused concessions. Among the peasants, the Bolsheviks had no real following. But as the only party without ties to the existing order they could afford to give in temporarily to their demands for the sake of seizing power. This they did on taking over the government and again after the chaos of the Civil War. Subsequently of course the Bolsheviks found it necessary to turn on those who had brought them to power and to drive the peasants into collectives in order to make them the main basis and victims of the socialist version of primary capitalist accumulation.

In China we see still another combination of circumstances, about which less is known, partly because the events are still too recent to have been the subject of extensive historical investigation. It is difficult to point to any clear-cut stratum as an ally of the peasants, on whose backs the Communists finally rode to victory, even though, or perhaps partly because, disaffection with the Kuomintang had spread through all classes. As a contemporary scholar has convincingly demonstrated, the Communists made little headway as long as they clung to Marxist notions about the importance of the proletariat as the vanguard of the revolutionary and antiimperialist struggle.[39] In time they did get massive peasant support. Still, without urban leaders, it is unlikely that the peasants could have organized the Red Army and carried on the partisan warfare that distinguished this revolution from its predecessors and has set a model for subsequent attempts. The effect on their opponents has been curious; some of the Western enthusiasm for learning the "lessons" of guerilla warfare recalls nineteenth-century Japanese notions about democracy: the belief that it is a simple technique one can borrow that will bring in its train all the other advantages that the opponent enjoys.

In both Russia and China, the chances of halting the process of decay at some point short of peasant revolution were very slim, mainly due to the lack of any strong basis for either liberal or reactionary capitalism in the trading and manufacturing classes. Whether the same will be true of India is a question to which only the future will give a firm answer. To jump to conclusions about India on the basis of China is foolish, since their agrarian social structures are in major respects exactly opposite to one another. If the agrarian program of the present Indian government fails to solve India's food problem, and there is substantial evidence for a pessimistic evaluation, a political upheaval of some sort will become highly likely. But it will not necessarily take the form of a communist-led peasant revolution. A turn to the right or fragmentation along regional lines, or some combination of these two, seems much more probable in the light of India's social structure. The situation

[39] See Schwartz, *Chinese Communism.*

in India leads one to ask whether the great wave of peasant revolutions, so far one of the most distinctive features of the twentieth century, may not have already spent its force. Any attempt to consider the question seriously would require detailed study of Latin America and Africa, a huge task that must be left to others. Nevertheless one consideration is worth pointing out. By and large, during the process of modernization the circumstances of peasant life have seldom made peasants the allies of democratic capitalism, an historical formation that in any case is now past its zenith. *If* the revolutionary wave continues to sweep through the backward world in the years to come, that is scarcely the form it is likely to take.

Reactionary and Revolutionary Imagery

OUT OF THE WRENCHES AND FRACTURES that accompany the making of a new society — or of efforts to prevent its emergence — similar conceptions of what a society ought to be or ought not to be come to the surface in roughly comparable situations. To discuss adequately radical and conservative critiques of society in a comparative framework would obviously require another volume.[1] Here I shall merely comment briefly on a few themes taken from this wide range of ideas insofar as they are related to certain types of historical experience faced by the landed upper classes and the peasants. The ideas themselves are familiar enough to require no detailed exposition. As contributions to the general human conception of a free society, or as attacks upon such a conception, they belong together and display interesting relationships to each other. My observations on these ideas will be not only brief but provocative, in what I hope may be the good sense of the word, that of encouraging others to study these problems more closely. At the outset it will be helpful to make explicit the conception of the relationship between ideas and social movements which has been reached as a result of my investigations, even if it is unlikely that I have managed to adhere to it consistently throughout this study.

The issue has come up several times in considering the forces that aided or prevented the landed upper classes from taking up commercial agriculture. How much weight should one attribute to

[1] Eventually I hope to examine more carefully the situation under which a radical critique makes its appearance and those under which it fails to do so.

widely prevalent ideals, codes of behavior, or values in explaining the result? Though the evidence, I think, pointed in the direction of stressing as the crucial aspect of the explanation the situation that various groups faced, the attentive reader might suspect that ideas or cultural themes, to use still another term, have crept into the explanation somehow. His suspicions would be quite correct. I do not believe that they can be omitted and hold that there is a significant residue of truth in such explanations. My objection is to the way they are put into the explanation, which in my estimation creates a strong conservative bias under the color of scientific neutrality and objectivity. That this bias is no case of deliberate dishonesty goes without saying. Among serious thinkers deliberate deception is probably rather rare and in the long run much less significant than the direction imposed upon thought from its own structure and social milieu.

Common observation is enough to show that human beings individually and collectively do not react to an "objective" situation in the same way as one chemical reacts to another when they are put together in a test tube. This form of strict behaviorism is, I submit, just plain wrong. There is always an intervening variable, a filter, one might say, between people and an "objective" situation, made up from all sorts of wants, expectations, and other ideas derived from the past. This intervening variable, which it is convenient to call culture, screens out certain parts of the objective situation and emphasizes other parts. There are limits to the amount of variations in perception and human behavior that can come from this source. Still the residue of truth in the cultural explanation is that what looks like an opportunity or a temptation to one group of people will not necessarily seem so to another group with a different historical experience and living in a different form of society. The weakness of the cultural explanation is not in the statement of such facts, though there is room for a debate over their significance, but in the way they are put into the explanation. Materialist efforts to exorcise the ghost of idealism in cultural explanations are chanting at the wrong spook.

The real spook is a conception of social inertia, taken over probably from physics. There is a widespread assumption in modern social science that social continuity requires no explanation. Supposedly it is not problematical.[2] Change is what requires explanation. This assumption blinds the investigator to certain crucial aspects of social reality. Culture, or tradition — to use a less technical term — is not something that exists outside of or independently of individual human beings living together in society. Cultural values do not descend from heaven to influence the course of history. They are abstractions by an observer, based on the observation of certain similarities in the way groups of people behave, either in different situations or over time, or both. Even though one can often make accurate predictions about the way groups and individuals will behave over short periods of time on the basis of such abstractions, as such they do not explain the behavior. To explain behavior in terms of cultural values is to engage in circular reasoning. If we notice that a landed aristocracy resists commercial enterprise, we do not *explain* this fact by stating that the aristocracy has done so in the past or even that it is the carrier of certain traditions that make it hostile to such activities: the problem is to determine out of what past and present experiences such an outlook arises and maintains itself. If culture has an empirical meaning, it is as a tendency implanted in the human mind to behave in certain specific ways "acquired by man as a member of society," to quote the last phrase of Tylor's famous definition, which brought the term into scholarly and eventually popular usage.

The assumption of inertia, that cultural and social continuity do not require explanation, obliterates the fact that both have to be recreated anew in each generation, often with great pain and suffering. To maintain and transmit a value system, human beings are punched, bullied, sent to jail, thrown into concentration camps, cajoled, bribed, made into heroes, encouraged to read newspapers, stood up against a wall and shot, and sometimes even taught sociology. To speak of cultural inertia is to overlook the concrete interests and privileges that are served by indoctrination, education, and the entire complicated process of transmitting culture from one generation to the next. A member of the Chinese gentry in the nineteenth

[2] Parsons, *Social System*, 205, makes this view an explicit organizing assumption.

century, we may agree, usually judged economic opportunities in a way very different from that of a twentieth-century American businessman farmer. But he did so because he grew up in Chinese Imperial society whose class structure, system of rewards, privileges, and sanctions, penalized certain forms of economic gain that would have destroyed the hegemony and authority of the dominant groups. Finally, to take values as the starting point of sociological explanation makes it very difficult to understand the obvious fact that values change in response to circumstances. The perversion of democratic notions in the American South is an all too familiar example, incomprehensible without cotton and slavery. We cannot do without some conception of how people perceive the world and what they do or do not want to do about what they see. To detach this conception from the way people reach it, to take it out of its historical context and raise it to the status of an independent causal factor in its own right, means that the supposedly impartial investigator succumbs to the justifications that ruling groups generally offer for their most brutal conduct. That, I fear, is exactly what a great deal of academic social science does today.

Let us now return to more concrete problems. It is out of the question here to discuss fully the intellectual contributions to the conception of a free society that are traceable to the historical experience of the landed upper classes. It is sufficient to remind the reader that English parliamentary democracy was very largely the creation of this class, which remained in charge of its workings down to the eve of the First World War and has been very influential since then. Much of the modern conception of legitimate authority and of an open society derives from the struggles between this class, which was of course very far from united, and the royal authority. Instead I shall comment upon one theme, the ideal of the amateur, because the fate of this ideal illustrates how the ideals and rationalizations of what was once a dominant class can under certain circumstances become what Marxists call critical and progressive theories. This issue is worth raising because it has implications beyond the landed aristocracy. As will appear again from the discussion of the peasants, it may be dying classes that make decisive contributions to the vision of a free society.

Though the landed aristocracy has in many countries furnished a congenial social climate in which the ideal of the amateur has grown and flourished, this ideal has of course roots that ramify much further. In one form or another it is probably characteristic of most preindustrial civilizations. The main features in this cluster of ideas might be expressed in the following way. Because aristocratic status was supposed to indicate a qualitatively superior form of being, whose qualities were hereditary rather than the fruit of individually acquired merits, the aristocrat was not expected to put forth too prolonged or too earnest an effort in any single direction. He might excel, but not just in one activity as a consequence of prolonged training; that would be plebeian. The hereditary aspect, it is worth noticing, is not completely decisive. Thus the conception of the amateur and the gentleman were important in both classical Greece and Imperial China, societies that in theory minimized hereditary status above a certain level such as slaves. Nevertheless in such societies too only a limited number of persons were believed capable of achieving full aristocratic status. For them the "real" ruler-gentleman was a qualitatively distinct form of humanity. In these societies as well as others with a more explicit class or caste structure, the aristocrat was expected to do all things very well, but none of them, not even making love, *too* well. In Western society this conception largely disappeared with the triumph of industrial society. For example, in the United States the distinction between amateur and professional, with overtones of approval for the former, survives only in areas of life that the man in the street does not regard as completely serious. One can speak of an amateur athlete or an amateur actor, and in some circles even an amateur historian, but scarcely of an amateur businessman or an amateur lawyer except as a derogatory epithet.

As might be anticipated, the traditional conception of the amateur has survived most clearly in England, where the aristocracy, using the term broadly to include a large portion of the gentry, has maintained itself with least damage. Namier has observed, "More intellectual work is done by aristocrats in England than anywhere else, and in turn, scientists, doctors, historians and poets have been made peers . . . but no German *Gelehrter* was ever made a baron or a count." The critical stance of the aristocracy toward any notion that wealth is a desirable end in itself has helped the aristocracy to preserve the aesthetic dimension of life. Even today a few people still believe that art, literature, philosophy, and pure science are not merely decorative adjuncts to the serious business of making a living but the supreme end of human life. That such ideas can be taken seriously and have been taken seriously is in substantial measure due to the persistence of an independent aristocracy as a group that can lend the aura of its prestige and patronage to such notions, even if no aristocracy itself has adopted them as its real working code of behavior.

Similarly the critical stance toward the technician as the desiccated brain at the service of any master derives from the aristocratic conception of the amateur. Again Namier has noticed the importance of these ideas in twentieth-century England:

> We prefer to make it appear as if our ideas came to us casually — like the Empire — in a fit of absence of mind. . . . Specialisation necessarily entails distortion of mind and loss of balance, and the characteristically English attempt to appear unscientific springs from a desire to remain human. . . . What is not valued in England is abstract knowledge as a profession, because the tradition of English culture is that professions should be practical and culture should be the work of the leisured classes.[3]

At its best this ideal asserts that the educated man should attain a sufficiently accurate and informed understanding of broad issues and fundamental conceptions in the sciences and the arts to assess their social and political implications.

Even today this is no utopian ideal. The standard objection, that there is simply too much to know, dodges the main issue: what is worth knowing? The objection provides ideological cover for the technician and conceptual nihilist who fears that his own limited area of knowledge may not be able to compete with others in an open discussion of their relative significance. Thus the ancient struggle between aristocratic and plebeian, transposed into new forms, continues within academic walls.

[3] For both quotations see Namier, *England*, 14–15.

All these themes have strong negative aspects. The ideal of the amateur can and has served as an excuse for superficiality and incompetence. If the aristocracy has helped to preserve the independence of the aesthetic dimension, it has also exerted very strong pressures toward mere decoration and flattery. Sheer snobbishness, i.e., the drawing of social distinctions and the awarding of prestige without any rational basis, has played a tremendous part. Veblen's snide caricature in the *Theory of the Leisure Class* seizes essential aspects of the truth. Finally, it is necessary to recognize the very strong anti-intellectual streak in the Western European aristocracy, even in England. In many circles among the gentry and upward, any attempt at conversation beyond sports and gardens is likely to evoke pained surprise and the suspicion that the speaker has "Bolshie" sympathies. For every distinguished patron of the intellect, for every eccentric defender of unpopular causes, and certainly for every aristocrat who has used his independence as a stepping stone to real intellectual achievements, there are many empty and frivolous lives. For every Bertrand Russell, there are probably a score of Colonel Blimps. If the continued existence of an aristocracy has helped to preserve the life of the mind, it has in very great measure simultaneously contributed to the suffocation of the intellect. Though I know of no serious attempt to appraise the balance, it seems that only a tiny proportion of the economic and human resources appropriated by the aristocracy has found its way again into intellectual and artistic life. Hence this aristocratic contribution to the conception and realization of a free society has been purchased at terrific social cost.

If there is some justification for regarding the conception of the amateur as a positive contribution, there are clear grounds for a negative assessment of several other ideas. Those about to be discussed, however, arise in quite a different social context. Reactionary social theories are liable to flourish in a landed upper class that manages to hang onto political power successfully although it is losing out economically or perhaps is threatened by a new and strange source of economic power (a fear underlying some currents of thought in the American antebellum South). At several points in this book there has been occasion to notice that, where commercial relationships have begun to undermine a peasant economy, the conservative elements in society are likely to generate a rhetoric of extolling the peasant as the backbone of society. This phenomenon is not confined to modern times nor to Western civilization. The key elements in the rhetoric — advocacy of the sterner virtues, militarism, contempt for "decadent" foreigners, and anti-intellectualism — appear in the West at least as early as Cato the Elder (234–149 B.C.) who operated his own *latifundium* with slave labor. It is fitting, therefore, to label this complex of ideas with his name. A similar rhetoric, according to some authorities also in response to a threat to traditional peasant economy, had emerged in China with the Legalists, around the 4th century B.C. The function of Catonism is too obvious to require more than brief comment. It justifies a repressive social order that buttresses the position of those in power. It denies the existence of actual changes that have hurt the peasants. It denies the need for further social changes, especially revolutionary ones. Perhaps Catonism may also relieve the conscience of those most responsible for the damage — after all, military expansion destroyed the Roman peasantry.

Modern versions of Catonism arise too out of the adoption by the landed upper classes of repressive and exploitative methods in response to the increasing intrusion of market relationships into an agrarian economy. The main notions are prominent in nineteenth- and twentieth-century Junker circles, the *Nōhōn-shugi* movement in Japan, the Russian Black Hundreds after the turn of the century, the extreme conservatism in France that came to the surface as window dressing for Vichy.[4] Key elements occur among Southern apologists prior to the American Civil War. Catonism was an important component too in twentieth-century fascism in Europe and Asia, as well in Chiang Kai-shek's programmatic pronouncements for China. Naturally all these movements differ among themselves. Nevertheless it is not difficult to perceive a certain ground plan of related ideas and predispositions that all of them share.

A key element in this complex of symptoms is the appearance

[4] A penetrating brief discussion of French developments drawing attention to some of the larger issues may be found in "The Folklore of Royalism," *Times Literary Supplement,* September 7, 1962.

of a great deal of talk about the need for a thoroughgoing moral regeneration, talk that covers the absence of a realistic analysis of prevailing social conditions which would threaten the vested interests behind Catonism. Probably it is a good working rule to be suspicious about political and intellectual leaders who talk mainly about moral virtues; many poor devils are liable to be badly hurt. It is not quite correct to assert that the morality lacks content; Catonism seeks a specific kind of regeneration, though it is easier to specify what Catonism is against than what it is for. An aura of moral earnestness suffuses Catonist arguments. This morality is not instrumental; that is, policies are not advocated in order to make humanity happier (happiness and progress are contemptuously dismissed as decadent bourgeois illusions) and certainly not in order to make people richer. They are important because they are supposed to contribute to a way of life that has somehow proved its validity in the past. That Catonist views of the past are romantic distortions goes without saying.

This way of life is supposed to be an organic whole and, of course, being connected with the soil is essential to making it organic. Indeed "organic" and "whole" are favorite cloudy terms in Catonism. The organic life of the countryside is supposedly superior to the atomised and disintegrating world of modern science and modern urban civilization.[5] The peasant's alleged attachment to the soil becomes the subject of much praise and little action. Traditional religious piety with archaising overtones becomes fashionable. Actually, as in the case of Japanese *Shintō*, the tradition is to a substantial degree cooked to order, though not entirely. Obedience, hierarchy, often with overtones of race or at least biological metaphors about society, become the watchword. But the hierarchy is not supposed to take on the character of modern impersonal bureaucracy. Indeed there is much talk of comradeship, human warmth. *Gemeinschaft, Genossenschaft, Heimat*, words that carry emotional overtones far stronger than their English counterparts,

---

[5] Catonism draws heavily on the romantic protest against modern science and modern industrial civilization. Certainly not all of this protest is absurd. Many of the notions occur in Spengler. But Spengler's awareness that archaism never works is quite alien to Catonism.

community, association, home, are likely to steam the atmosphere and not merely in the German tongue.

Indeed the emphasis on human warmth seems to be as decisive an element as the notion of moral regeneration. The combination leads, in the context of the whole ideology, to contradictory attitudes toward sex. As part of the generally anti-intellectual and anti-industrial outlook of Catonism, modern urban civilization is seen as somehow devaluing sex, as making human relationships cold and impersonal. Hence the preoccupation with frigidity and impotence, the glorification of sex, as for example in *Lady Chatterley's Lover*. On the other hand, there is an air of guilty prurience about all this because sex has to be the basis of the home, the family, the state. The contradiction appears again between the orgies of the SS in Nazi Germany, the minor efforts to encourage illegitimate children by SS heroes, and the more general policy of trying to revive a "healthy" domestic environment of *Kinder, Kirche, Küche* for women. The political manifestations are of course "think with the blood," the rejection of rational analysis as something "cold" or "mechanical" that inhibits action. Action, on the other hand, is "hot," usually in the sense of combat. The effort to surround death and destruction with erotic overtones is also quite noticeable, especially in the Japanese version. Ultimately life is sacrificed for death, Mars absorbs Venus. *Dulce et decorum est. . . .*[6] For all the rhetoric of warmth Catonism expresses a deep fear of human affection as a form of softness.

There are other curious contradictions and ambivalences here as well. Catonism includes a horror of "unhealthy" preoccupation with death and decomposition, in the manner of a Baudelaire. This preoccupation Catonism identifies with the foreigner, with "decadent cosmopolitanism." Art must be "healthy," traditional, and above all easily comprehensible. Catonist artistic notions center around folk and provincial art, an effort on the part of educated urban classes to revive peasant costumes, dances, and celebrations. Once

[6] Medieval Christianity may also have put death ahead of life but scarcely with the same overt emphasis on violence and destruction. The elements of gentleness, pity, and mercy have not predominated in the practice of Christianity, but they do distinguish it from Catonism.

sharing power, it seems that the Catonist outlook on art merges with a general tendency noticeable in all regimes concerned with maintaining social cohesion, to promote traditional and academic art forms. There is, as has often been noted, a striking similarity between Nazi and Stalinist art. Both were equally strong in condemning *Kunstbolschewismus* and "rootless cosmopolitanism." Similar trends may be observed in Augustan Rome.[7]

In sketching what finds approval under Catonist notions, it has already been necessary to mention what Catonist theories oppose. Concretely they are hostile to traders, usurers, big money, cosmopolitanism, intellectuals. In America Catonism has taken the form of resentment against the city slicker and more generally any form of reasoning that goes beyond the most primitive folk wisdom. In Japan it manifested itself as violent antiplutocratic sentiment. The city appears as a cancerous sore full of invisible conspirators out to cheat and demoralize honest peasants. There is of course a realistic basis for these sentiments in the actual day-to-day experiences of peasants and small farmers who are at a serious disadvantage in a market economy.

As far as feelings (so far as we really know them) and the causes of hatred go, there is not a great deal to choose between the radical right and the radical left in the countryside. The main distinction depends on the amount of realistic analysis of the causes of suffering and on the images of a potential future. Catonism conceals the social causes and projects an image of continued submission. The radical tradition emphasizes the causes and projects an image of eventual liberation. The fact that the emotions and causes are similar does not mean that the emergence of one or the other as a politically significant force depends on skills in manipulating

[7] See the excellent discussion in Syme, *Roman Revolution*, chaps XXVIII – XXIX, esp 460 – 468 on Vergil and Horace. Note also the disgrace of Petronious, the attitudes of Roman historians toward the artistic interests of Nero and Caligula. The fact that Stalinist art displays traits I have labelled as Catonist or deriving from Catonism may seem to cast severe doubts on the whole interpretation suggested here. But is it ridiculous to suggest that socialism, especially under Stalin, borrowed and incorporated some of the most repressive features of its historical antagonists?

these discontents, as repeated failures to win over radicalized peasants to conservative causes (or vice versa) through the methods of psychological warfare clearly demonstrate. These psychological and organizational skills are important, but they work only when they are in line with the everyday experiences of the peasants whom such leaders attempt to set in motion.

Thus Catonism is not purely an upper-class mythology about the peasants, attributed to the peasants, but finds a response among the latter because it provides an explanation of sorts for their situation under the intrusion of the market. It is also quite clearly a body of notions that arises out of the life conditions of a landed aristocracy threatened by the same forces. If one glances at the major themes in the form of the aristocratic response that culminated in liberal democracy, one will notice that they also occur in Catonism — transposed to a different key. The criticism of mass democracy, the notions of legitimate authority and the importance of custom, opposition to the power of wealth and to mere technical expertise all constitute major themes in the Catonist cacophony. Again it is in the way they are combined, and even more important the ultimate purpose, that makes all the difference. In Catonism these notions serve the ends of strengthening repressive authority. In aristocratic liberalism they are brought together as intellectual weapons against irrational authority. Catonism, on the other hand, lacks any conception of pluralism or the desirability of checks on hierarchy and obedience.

As noted above, modern Catonism is mainly associated with the attempt to go over to labor-repressive forms of capitalist agriculture. It is also anti-industrial and antimodern through and through. Here may lie the basic limitations to the spread and success of Catonism. There is, I would suggest, this very significant residue of truth in Veblen's cautiously yet repeatedly expressed hope that the advance of the machine might somehow flush human irrationalities down the drain of history. The more extreme forms of labor-repressive or exploitative agriculture can be decisive adjuncts to capitalist development, as was the case in the connection between American slavery and both English and American industrial capi-

talism. But industrial capitalism has great difficulty establishing itself in the same area with a labor-repressive system.[8] As part of the
effort to hold down a subject population, the upper classes have to
generate an antirationalist, antiurban, antimaterialist, and, more
loosely, antibourgeois view of the world — one that excludes any
conception of progress. And it is very difficult to see how industrialism can take firm hold without a push from people who hold a
very materialist conception of progress that includes sooner or later
concrete improvement in the situation of the lower classes. In contrast with advancing industrialism, Catonism, it seems, finally com-
promises itself out of existence to fuse with more definitely urban
and capitalist forms of romantic nostalgia. These more intellectually respectable forms of the far right have become increasingly influential in the West during the past twenty years, especially in the
United States. Conceivably Catonism will some day appear to future historians, if any there are, as having contributed merely the
most explosive ingredients to this dangerous mixture.

In turning from ideas derived from the experience of the
landed upper classes to those of the peasants, the historian at once
runs into trouble because the materials are so sparse and their au-
thenticity often doubtful. To determine just what ideas have been
current among peasants is extraordinarily difficult because they
have left so few records of their own and have had a great many
ideas attributed to them by townsmen who had a political axe to
grind. Here there will be no attempt to undertake this task as a
whole, not even in the sketchiest fashion. Instead I shall explore
possible connections between familiar themes in the revolutionary
critique of modern society and the peasants' experience of their
own world as it came under attack in the modern era. Far more
than is generally realized, I suspect, the world of the village may
have been an important source of those half-conscious standards by

[8] Japan might be cited as an exception. Perhaps these obstacles to
industrialization are severe only in an agrarian economy closer to the plantation type. The Junker areas of Germany remained largely rural; so of
course did Russian society as a whole down to 1917. But in Japan too there
were difficulties, and much of the rural ideology had to be dumped over-
board in practice.

which men have judged and condemned modern industrial civilization, the background from which they have formed their conceptions of justice and injustice.

In an effort to distinguish genuine peasant conceptions from those ascribed to peasants by urban conservative and radical thinkers for their own political purposes, it will be useful to take one last fleeting glance at the conditions of peasant life prior to the modern impact. Certain recurring features stand out. As a form of insurance against natural hazards, and in some cases also in response to methods in the collection of taxes or dues to the overlord, peasants in many parts of the world have developed systems of tenure with a built-in tendency toward the equal distribution of resources. The system of holdings in strips, scattered over different parts of the territory belonging to the village, occurs widely in both Europe and Asia. In addition there is the custom of equal access for all to a segment of land held undivided, the commons. Though commons are more important in Europe where cattle took some of the burden off human shoulders, they have existed also in Asia; for example, in Japan as a source of supplementary resources such as fertilizer. Despite considerable variation, the main idea connected with these arrangements stands out very clearly: every member of the community should have access to enough resources to be able to perform obligations to the community carrying on a collective struggle for survival.[9] Everyone, including the lord and the priest, has a contribution to make. Romanticized by a variety of intellectuals, these notions have nevertheless a firm basis in the facts of peasant experience.

This experience, then, provides the soil out of which grow peasant mores and the moral standards by which they judge their own behavior and that of others. The essence of these standards is a crude notion of equality, stressing the justice and necessity of a minimum of land for the performance of essential social tasks. The standards usually have some sort of religious sanction, and it is

[9] In China the commons seem to have been absent, but the institution of the clan, where it existed, embodied to some extent the similar notion that a member should have access to resources in order to perform certain social functions.

likely to be in their stress on these points that the religion of the peasants differs from that of other social classes. In the course of modernization the peasants apply these standards, evaluating and to some extent explaining their own fate. Hence comes the frequent emphasis on the restoration of ancient rights. As Tawney well observes, the peasant radical would be astonished to hear that he is undermining the foundations of society; he is merely trying to get back what has long been rightfully his.[10]

As the world of commerce and industry began to undermine the structure of the village community, the European peasants reacted with a form of radicalism that stressed the themes of liberty, equality, and fraternity, but in a way distinct from the way that the townsmen, more specifically the more prosperous bourgeoisie, understood these themes. Throughout Europe and Asia, the current of rural response to modernization went its own course, sometimes joining that in the towns, sometimes flowing in the opposite direction. For the peasant, the first of the three was not liberty but equality. And peasant experience provided the background for a shattering critique of the bourgeois notion of equality, as I shall try to indicate more concretely in a moment. Briefly, the peasants asked, "What is the meaning of your fine political arrangements when the rich can still oppress the poor?" Liberty too meant getting rid of the overlord who no longer gave them protection but now used his ancient privileges to take away their land or make them work on his for nothing. Fraternity meant the village as a cooperative economic and territorial unit, little more. From the peasant, it seems, the idea may have passed to intellectuals who developed their theories about the depersonalization of modern life and the curse of bureaucratic bigness, looking backward through a romantic haze to what they thought they saw in the village community. All this would have seemed, I suspect, quite odd and incomprehensible to the peasant who had daily experience of the vicious quarrels over property and women common in his own village. For the peasant, fraternity was more a negative notion, a form of localism. The peasant had no abstract interest in feeding the towns. His organic conception of society stopped quite short of altruism. For

[10] *Agrarian Problem,* 333 – 334, 337 – 338.

him, "outsiders" were and are mainly a source of taxes and debt. Fellow villagers, on the other hand, even if they too were often creatures to be treated warily, were people with whom it was necessary to work at crucial stages in the agricultural cycle. Thus cooperation was the dominant theme within the group, hostility and distrust the dominant one toward outsiders, with many variations and shadings in concrete daily circumstances. Peasant localism, thus, is no innate trait (any more than attachment to the soil) but the product of concrete experiences and circumstances.

In the forms just sketched, these ideas also appealed to the smaller artisans and journeymen in the towns, oppressed by debt and the rise of larger traders. Since some of the smaller townsmen might be able to write, it was often they or a stray from the priesthood who put the grievances down in writing and so preserved them for historians to discuss. These circumstances make it doubly difficult to disentangle the purely peasant component. Yet if one looks at the extreme leftist manifestations of the English Civil War and the French Revolution, the Diggers and "Gracchus" Babeuf — the names in each case are revealing — as well as certain strands in pre-1917 Russian radicalism, it is not difficult to perceive their connection with peasant life and problems.

Some concrete details once more will help to give substance to these general observations. In the course of the English Civil War, on April 16, 1649, the Council of State received the disturbing news that a small but increasing band had set to work to dig up the land on St. George's Hill in Surrey and to sow it with parsnips, carrots, and beans and that they had some political design in hand. Before the Council could decide what to do about the situation, Digger leaders, including Gerrard Winstanley, appeared before them to justify their conduct and outline a program of agrarian communism. The most significant feature of the program, as it emerged from this and subsequent conflict with the authorities, was its criticism of the inadequacy of political democracy without social reform. "Wee know," said Winstanley, "that England cannott bee a free Commonwealth unless all the poore commoners have a free use and benefitt of the land; for if this freedome bee not granted, wee that are the poore commoners are in a worse case than we were in the King's days, for then wee had some estate about us, though wee were under oppression, but now our estates are spent to purchase freedome, and wee are under oppression still of Lords of Mannours' tyranny." Though a radical fringe, the Diggers were not an isolated movement; there were other similar ones, notably in areas where enclosures had proceeded rapidly. But they made little headway and the premature attack on property was soon crushed.[11]

The *cahiers* of the peasants in a section of northern France, studied by Georges Lefebvre, throw considerable light on their attitude in an area heavily exposed to the impact of modernization, though three-fourths of its population was still rural. While some historians regard the *cahiers* as a very dubious source of information about peasant problems, Lefebvre gives convincing reasons for accepting them with only occasional reservations. They are mainly concerned with quite concrete local abuses that we may neglect at this point. The general points of interest are negative ones: the peasants had little interest, as might be expected, in the question of the organization of power then agitating Paris. For the rest Lefebvre's own words are incisive: "Pour presque tous les paysans, être libre c'était être débarassé du seigneur; liberté, égalité, deux mots pour une seule chose qui était l'essence même de la Révolution."[12]

Lefebvre is also the author of two brief but instructive studies of a famous leader of the Revolution's extreme radical fringe, François-Emile (or "Gracchus") Babeuf.[13] Babeuf's ideas are a fusion of theories taken from books (especially from Rousseau and Mably) and also of his experiences in Picardy, where he was born and grew up in peasant surroundings. Among these experiences, the one that made the most powerful impact was his work as a petty feudal lawyer, *commissaire feudiste*, in the service of the aristocracy, examining the legal bases for seigneurial rights over the peasants in

[11] See James, *Social Problems*, 99–106; the quotation is on 102. For a full collection of texts and interpretation see Sabine, ed, *Works of Winstanley*, in which (269–277) "A Declaration from the Poor Oppressed People of England" is especially relevant to the points discussed above.

[12] Lefebvre, *Paysans du Nord*, 353; see also x, 344, 350–351.

[13] See Lefebvre, *Etudes*, 298–314.

this area where commercial influences were expanding rapidly.[14] From this combination of reading and experience emerged his firm conviction that the inequalities of wealth and property were the result of theft, violence, and cunning, covered with a cloak of hypocritical decency by the law. His remedy was to smash the prevailing system of property relationships and to introduce equality in distribution and the communal organization of production. As early as 1786, according to a recently discovered letter which he prudently refrained from sending to a certain liberal nobleman, Babeuf had thought of turning the large farms of the neighborhood into something very close to Soviet collective farms, though retaining the system of paying rent to a landlord.[15] To ensure that equality would remain in effect, as well as that production would remain guided by the requirements of use and a standard of decent comfort for all, he came to realize the need for strong centralized control.[16]

Like Winstanley before him, Babeuf regarded political equality as sheer deception if unsupported by economic rights. His criticism of the triumph of bourgeois democracy and the defeat of social democracy marked by the fall of Robespierre became vitriolic after initial hesitations. Just what there was to the Conspiracy of the Equals, for which Babeuf paid with his life in 1797, is a question for specialists. The main point for us is clear. The Babouvists looked forward to the day of real equality: "Never," they asserted, "has

[14] See the detailed description of social conditions in Picardy in Dalin, *Grakkh Babef*, chap 3; also 104 for a revealing quotation from Babeuf on what his experience as a *feudiste* meant to him.

[15] On Babeuf's letter of June 1, 1786, found in the archives of the Institute of Marxism-Leninism, see Dalin, *Grakkh Babef*, 95–109; on *fermes collectives*, see 99, where Dalin asserts that Babeuf advocated the notion of *fermes collectives* in a *mémoire* of 1785; I find no trace of the notion in a text of a *mémoire* of November 25, 1785 reproduced in Advielle, *Babeuf*, II, (pt 2), 1–14. Nor is the term mentioned in the index to Babeuf's correspondence with Dubois de Fosseux at the end of this volume.

[16] See Dommanget, *Babeuf*, esp 103–121, 250–264. On 268 Babeuf refers to the right of property as one of the most deplorable creations of human error. Other aspects of his thought relevant to this brief discussion are on 91, 96, 186, 209–211.

more vast a design been conceived and executed. At long intervals some men of genius, some sages have spoken of it in a low and trembling voice. None of them have had the courage to tell the whole truth. . . . The French Revolution is but the precursor of another revolution, far greater, far more solemn, which will be the last."[17]

Thus in the case of Babeuf, too, peasant experience contributed to a criticism of bourgeois society that became part of the current coin of later radical thought. The tradition of the armed insurrection, as well as the dictatorship of the proletariat, Lefebvre suggests, may all be part of the body of ideas that appear on the surface of the historical record with Babeuf, to return underground until later in the nineteenth century.

In the Russian village community of the eighteenth and nineteenth centuries, peasant notions of equality, as manifested in the periodic redistribution of the land, were at least as much of a response to the system of taxation as to physical conditions. Its central feature was the assumption that every family ought to have enough land to enable it to pay its share of dues and taxes that were assessed on the community as a unit. As is well known, the Russian Populists took their goals and many of their criticisms of modern industrial society from an idealized version of the village community. Despite the numerous differences within this group of nineteenth-century pre-Marxist radicals, there was general agreement on equality as their first principle and on the thesis that political forms of democracy were meaningless and useless to men who were starving.[18] Thus peasant practices are clearly the origin of this famous criticism in England, France, and Russia, though the role of the thinker in the towns becomes increasingly important in France and Russia.

To discern the other explicit political assumptions circulating among the Russian peasants is for obvious reasons more difficult than in western Europe. Despite the obstacles, serious investigation, of which there has been practically none on this particular topic,

---

[17] From the "Manifeste des Égaux" (1796) as translated in Postgate, *Revolution from 1789 to 1906*, 54, 55.

[18] Berlin, in the Introduction to Venturi, *Roots of Revolution*, vii, x, xvi, xxviii.

might conceivably turn up most illuminating material.[19] To judge from what Russian peasants actually did in the nineteenth century, especially at the time of emancipation, their first desire was to stop working the overlord's property for nothing. Since they felt that the tie between their own society and the overlord exploited them, they wanted to break the connection and run the village community themselves. This was their main conception of "true liberty."[20] The tsar they were quite willing to keep, thinking of him as an ally against the nobility, a mistaken notion that found many pathetic and dramatic expressions in the course of the nineteenth century but that, nevertheless, was not without some foundation in earlier historical experience. This notion of village autonomy remained an important peasant tradition, whose undercurrents have not yet, in all probability, died out. Perhaps its last open expression occurred in the slogan "Soviets without Communists" of the Kronstadt rebellion in 1921, whose suppression by the Bolsheviks revealed the "secret" of the Russian Revolution much as the repression of the Diggers had revealed the "secret" of the English Revolution.

In Asia peasant discontent has taken different forms up until the point where it has been captured by the communists. About intellectual content, there is very little information. We may close with a remark or two about similarities to and differences from European peasant movements. In India, peasant discontent has not yet taken on any significant revolutionary color and has therefore been mainly confined to Gandhi's version of the theme of fraternity, again a return to an idealized village community. China has witnessed an endless chain of religious rebellions, each against the backdrop of an extensive agricultural crisis. Very likely there is a good deal more to be discovered about Chinese peasant discontent than that it expressed itself in religious forms, as did that in Europe dur-

[19] Foreign and domestic observers continually put into the mouths of the peasants the notion that they belong to the landlord but that the land belongs to them. For some examples, see Venturi, *Roots of Revolution*, 68 – 69. To what extent does this statement represent actual peasant thinking and to what extent aristocratic distortions? The behavior of the peasants makes it very doubtful that they thought of themselves as belonging to the landlord.

[20] Venturi, *Roots of Revolution*, 211, 218.

ing the Middle Ages and in early modern times. Western sources, however, give little hint of any social criticism in China comparable to that in the West just discussed, except for the Taoist notion of a return to a primitive order of simplicity as a cure for the illnesses of a complex civilization.[21] Two reasons may be tentatively suggested. Confucian orthodoxy was in itself backward looking to a past golden age and may therefore have absorbed peasant tendencies to look to past models for criticizing present realities. Similarly the secular features in the Confucianism of the upper class may have encouraged peasant discontent to take mystical and religious forms, tendencies that are in any case very strong. More important than these considerations is another: Chinese peasants could scarcely be expected to develop an equalitarian critique of political democracy because in China there grew up no indigenous tradition of political democracy to criticize. Unrest and disorder among the Japanese peasants under the Tokugawa never seem to have found coherent political expression, or at least have left none in the historical record. In more modern times, peasant discontent has taken a conservative form. In the course of this discussion there have been several occasions to mention the backward-looking and reactionary aspects of peasant radicalism. Though these have been picked up and glorified by articulate reactionaries, they are by no means purely the creation of reactionaries. With this caveat as a reminder, we can forego fuller discussion.

Because peasant discontent has frequently expressed itself in reactionary forms, Marxist thinkers often regard peasant radicalism with a mixture of contempt and suspicion or, at best, with patronizing condescension. To smile at this blindness, to point out that Marxist successes have come out of peasant revolutions, have almost become favorite anti-Marxist pastimes, so much so as to conceal more significant issues. As one reviews the spread of modern revolution, from its starting points in the German *Bauernkrieg* and the Puritan Revolution in England, through its successful and abortive phases as it travels westward to the United States and eastward through France, Germany, Russia, and China, two points stand out.

[21] Yang, *Religion,* 114. See also ibid, chap IX, "Religion and Political Rebellion."

First, the utopian radical conceptions of one phase become the accepted institutions and philosophical platitudes of the next. Secondly, the chief social basis of radicalism has been the peasants and the smaller artisans in the towns. From these facts one may conclude that the wellsprings of human freedom lie not only where Marx saw them, in the aspirations of classes about to take power, but perhaps even more in the dying wail of a class over whom the wave of progress is about to roll. Industrialism, as it continues to spread, may in some distant future still these voices forever and make revolutionary radicalism as anachronistic as cuneiform writing.

For a Western scholar to say a good word on behalf of revolutionary radicalism is not easy because it runs counter to deeply grooved mental reflexes. The assumption that gradual and piecemeal reform has demonstrated its superiority over violent revolution as a way to advance human freedom is so pervasive that even to question such an assumption seems strange. In closing this book I should like to draw attention for the last time to what the evidence from the comparative history of modernization may tell us about this issue. As I have reluctantly come to read this evidence, the costs of moderation have been at least as atrocious as those of revolution, perhaps a great deal more.

Fairness demands recognition of the fact that the way nearly all history has been written imposes an overwhelming bias against revolutionary violence. Indeed the bias becomes horrifying as one comes to realize its depth. To equate the violence of those who resist oppression with the violence of the oppressors would be misleading enough. But there is a great deal more. From the days of Spartacus through Robespierre down to the present day, the use of force by the oppressed against their former masters has been the object of nearly universal condemnation. Meanwhile the day-to-day repression of "normal" society hovers dimly in the background of most history books. Even those radical historians who emphasize the injustices of prerevolutionary epochs generally concentrate on a short time span preceding the immediate outbreak. In that way, too, they may unwittingly distort the record.

That is one argument against the comforting myth of gradualism. There is an even more important one, the costs of going without a revolution. There have been the tragedies of the victims of fascism and its wars of aggression, the consequence of modernization without a real revolution. In the backward countries today, there continues the suffering of those who have not revolted. In India we have seen that this suffering has been in good measure the price of democratic slowness in the Asian context. To call the situation democratic stagnation may not stretch the truth unduly. There are also positive arguments on behalf of revolution. In the Western democratic countries revolutionary violence (and other forms as well) were part of the whole historical process that made possible subsequent peaceful change. In the communist countries too, revolutionary violence has been part of the break with a repressive past and of the effort to construct a less repressive future.

The gradualist argument seems shattered. But precisely at this point the revolutionary argument also collapses. It is clear beyond all shadow of doubt that the claims of existing socialist states to represent a higher form of freedom than Western democratic capitalism rest on promise, not on performance. There is no denying the patent fact that the Bolshevik Revolution did not bring liberation to the people of Russia. At most it·may have brought the possibility of liberation. Stalinist Russia was one of the bloodiest tyrannies the world has yet seen. Though much less is known about China, and the communist victory there probably meant some increase in personal security for the mass of the population after almost a century of widespread brigandage, foreign oppression, and revolution, it is safe enough to assert that in China too the claims of socialism rest on promise, not performance. Indeed communists cannot claim that the mass of the population has shouldered a lesser share of the burden of suffering under their form of industrialization than they did under the preceding forms of capitalism. On this score it is well to recollect that there is no evidence that the mass of the population anywhere has wanted an industrial society, and plenty of evidence that they did not. At bottom all forms of industrialization so far have been revolutions from above, the work of a ruthless minority.

To this indictment communists can reply that the repressive

features of their regimes have been in large measure a response to the imperative of creating their own industrial base in a tremendous hurry while surrounded by ravenous capitalist enemies. I do not think it is possible to make anything like that much of a case for what actually happened. The range and depth of Stalinist repression and terror were far too great to find explanation, let alone justification, through some conception of revolutionary necessity. In many ways the Stalinist terror probably did more to hinder than to aid revolutionary objectives, as in the decimation of the officer corps prior to the outbreak of the Second World War, very likely also in the way Stalinist rule produced a mixture of chaos and petrified rigidity all through the Soviet administrative structure, including the industrial sectors. Nor will it do to put all the blame on Stalin personally. The ugly side of the Stalinist era had institutional roots. Communism as a set of ideas and institutions cannot escape responsibility for Stalinism. In general one of the most revolting features of revolutionary dictatorships has been their use of terror against little people who were as much victims of the old order as were the revolutionaries themselves, often more so.

There is also the argument that we are too close to communist revolutions to judge them properly: the liberating effects of past revolutions took a long time to appear. Neither this argument nor the preceding one to the effect that the horrors of communism spring out of its defense against those of capitalism are arguments to be dismissed lightly. There are nevertheless grounds for holding that they display considerable naiveté toward the past and the future. They are naive about the past because every government blames its repressive features on its enemies: if the enemy would only go away, all subjects could live happily forever after. There is a sense in which all dominant élites, even when they fight one another, have a vested interest in their opponents' existence. They are naive about the future because they neglect the extent to which the deformations of a revolution create vested interests in domination. Altogether the communist defense requires an act of faith about the future that involves too great a surrender of critical rationality.

In the place of such a surrender, I would urge the view that both Western liberalism and communism (especially the Russian version) have begun to display many symptoms of historical obsolescence. As successful doctrines they have started to turn into ideologies that justify and conceal numerous forms of repression. That there are huge differences between the two goes without saying. Communist repression has been and remains so far mainly directed against its own population. The repression by liberal society, both under earlier imperialism and again now in the armed struggle against revolutionary movements in the backward areas, has been directed very heavily outward, against others. Nevertheless this common feature of repressive practice covered by talk of freedom may be the most significant one. To the extent that such is the case, the task of honest thinking is to detach itself from both sets of preconceptions, to uncover the causes of oppressive tendencies in both systems in the hope of overcoming them. Whether they can actually be overcome is dubious in the extreme. As long as powerful vested interests oppose changes that lead toward a less oppressive world, no commitment to a free society can dispense with some conception of revolutionary coercion. That, however, is an ultimate necessity, a last resort in political action, whose rational justification in time and place varies too much for any attempt at consideration here. Whether the ancient Western dream of a free and rational society will always remain a chimera, no one can know for sure. But if the men of the future are ever to break the chains of the present, they will have to understand the forces that forged them.

A Note on Statistics
and Conservative Historiography

ANYONE WHO GOES TO THE WRITINGS of other scholars in search of general instruction as well as information about specific problems is likely to notice sooner or later a conflict between generations at least as acute as that in Turgenev's famous novel. Conservative and radical interpretations of the same set of events succeed each other in fairly regular succession. Out of the conflict there does come an increase in historical understanding, as anyone can see for himself by looking first at, say, a Taine or a Michelet and then at almost any standard modern account of the French Revolution. Human nature being what it is, perhaps knowledge of human affairs can grow in no other way.

But there are a good many costs and losses in this procedure that get in the way of cumulative comprehension of the past. One loss comes from the tendency to accept uncritically the notion that the present generation has really settled certain questions more or less permanently. Whether this tendency in the long run prevails as much on the political left as on the right is not absolutely clear. I am somewhat more aware of it on the right than on the left for two reasons. One is partly accidental. This book happened to be written during a time when the political climate was conservative and the scholarly atmosphere contained strong revisionist currents against older works that might raise apprehension about our own society. By the time the book was finished there was already a noticeable reaction against this current. The other reason is simpler:

the bias of the doctrinaire left is often so crude as to be comic. Nobody has any trouble recognizing that.

For these reasons, the following remarks are addressed mainly to a certain form of conservative bias. Their purpose is to caution the curious layman and the fledgling scholar against extreme versions of conservative revisionism, views which hold in effect that hardheaded modern scientific and quantitative research has now "demolished" older interpretations and that adherence to any important aspect of them represents no more than an "affirmation of religious myth," a remark to be encountered more frequently in oral exchanges than in the cold print that compels most authors to veer back toward safe moderation. A close look at the statistical evidence upon which such criticism rests indicates, in some important instances to be discussed in a moment, that the statistics actually support the older views. After the technical discussion itself, I shall offer some reflections on the general tenor of these arguments. At the start, however, I would like to make explicit the spirit in which my observations are put forth. Without special competence in statistics, I still have no patience with the machine-breaking mentality that rejects figures out of hand. To name this deformation of the humanist mentality after the Luddites is actually unfair to them; they were rather more intelligent. Nor is this Appendix to be read as a hidden diatribe against all conservative revisionism. Anyone who knows a specific portion of the literature on which this book is based will recognize the similarity between some of my arguments and those of distinguished revisionist works. Finally, those scholars whose work is about to be discussed do not display that complacency found among those who make tentative conclusions part of the consensus of professional opinion — in the study of man the most treacherous of all opinions.

First I would like to take up an important study of the Long Parliament by Brunton and Pennington. It is a major work within the influential tradition of historical writing that is reluctant to recognize any broad social cleavage behind the English Civil War.[1]

[1] *Long Parliament.* Readers with a hazy knowledge of the events of the Civil War may wish to be reminded that the Long Parliament sat throughout the Civil War, from November 3, 1640, to March 16, 1660. Some weeks

At first glance, their research seems to bear out such a thesis and, more specifically, to refute Tawney's views.

At one point this statistical study claims that the only significant difference between Royalists and Parliamentarians in the Long Parliament concerned age: Royalists were generally younger. Greater and lesser gentry, conservative and improving landlords, metropolitan and provincial traders were found on both sides in proportions that were not widely distinctive.[2] Tawney generously observed, in his introduction to this study:

> As far . . . as the membership of the House of Commons, with which alone the present work deals, is concerned, the inference from the figures contained in it is plain. It is that the division between Royalists and Parliamentarians had little connection with diversities of economic interest and social class. Till equally comprehensive evidence to the contrary is adduced, that conclusion must stand.[3]

However, quite strong evidence about the importance of class and economic interest is available in the study itself, evidence that somehow escaped Tawney's notice. Good scholars that they were, the authors provided detailed figures that reveal the significance of these factors. They appear as soon as one looks at the geographical distribution of Parliamentary and Royalist strength among the members of the Long Parliament. Let us distinguish the areas where Parliamentarians were in a majority from those where they were in a minority. The relevant figures are in Table 4. They refer to the 552 "original" members who sat at some time between November 1640 and August 1642, that is, prior to the actual outbreak of hostilities.

Even if he knew nothing about the Civil War, any social historian who looked at these figures would be likely to guess that the

---

prior to the King's execution, which took place on January 30, 1649, the Long Parliament was purged by Colonel Pride and reduced to the Rump. Its membership fluctuated with other events both before and after the execution and during Cromwell's Protectorate (1653–1658), events that need not concern us here.

[2] Brunton and Pennington, *Long Parliament*, 19–20.

[3] Brunton and Pennington, *Long Parliament*, xix, see also xviii.

TABLE 4

MEMBERS OF THE LONG PARLIAMENT 1640 – 1642[*]

Areas of Parliamentary strength:

	East No.	East %	Midland No.	Midland %	Southeast No.	Southeast %
Royalist	14	20	32	37	28	27
Parliamentarians	55	80	51	59	70	68

Areas where Parliamentarians were in a minority:

	North No.	North %	West No.	West %	Southwest No.	Southwest %
Royalist	37	55	43	67	82	50
Parliamentarians	28	42	20	31	78	48

[*] Sources: Adapted from Brunton and Pennington, *Long Parliament*, 187, Table 1. See also p. 2 for definition of "original" members, and Appendix V for geographical divisions.

different geographical sections of England had, for historical reasons, developed quite distinct types of social structure that had somehow or other come into conflict with one another. (Only in the southwest is the division almost even.) These distinctions are of course well known to historians. Trevelyan discusses their meaning with great insight and in a fashion that makes very vivid the mixture of class interests, traditional ties of loyalty to superiors, religious principles, and sheer desire to remain neutral that were present among various strata in different parts of the country. The result is about what one would expect in a society where capitalist and more generally modern ways of thinking and acting were forcing their way up through an older social structure. This new world had its center in London, from which its influence radiated out most strongly to the south and east. The King's strength, on the other hand, lay in the more backward areas, especially in the north and west, with the exception of Puritan clothing districts and seaports.[4]

[4] Trevelyan, *History of England*, II, 185 – 187. See also the critique of Brunton and Pennington in Hill, *Puritanism*, 14 – 24; Hill draws attention to the geographical distinctions on p. 16.

To explain these regional differences with any thoroughness is beyond the scope of this note and my own limited knowledge; the almost even division in the southwest is, in all candor, puzzling to me. Nevertheless it is worthwhile mentioning several indications of a connection between the enclosing landlord and the Parliamentary cause that appear as a result of breaking down the figures in Brunton and Pennington by geographical regions. The Midlands and the east are the areas where, according to Tawney, the sixteenth-century enclosures had their most socially disruptive effects.[5] They are also areas of substantial Parliamentary majorities. About the south and east, major areas of Parliamentary strength, there is somewhat more information that enables us to grasp more clearly what was taking place. In Kent and Essex, to the south, there was little disruption during the sixteenth century since much of the area had been enclosed beforehand. Kent has been the subject of special inquiry and appears to be a classic area of neutralism, where the gentry rather reluctantly joined the Parliamentary cause and, after a period of turmoil, happily welcomed the Restoration, all out of a mixture of Anglicanism and due regard for established property rights.[6] Suffolk in the east, Cromwell's home territory, has also been the subject of special investigation and was a Parliamentary stronghold. The leadership of the Parliamentary forces is described in a recent monograph as "a kind of exclusive county club comprising most of the brains and much of the wealth of the shire." Like other eastern counties, its economy both rural and urban was exceptionally advanced. It was also one where the interpenetration of mercantile and agricultural enterprise had developed to an unusually high degree. Among landed families "few [were] without close commercial connections, and in the agricultural exploitation of their estates Suffolk landowners were as ardent as any."[7]

This description of a major Parliamentary stronghold matches almost perfectly what one would expect to find on the basis of Tawney's thesis. When one looks at the statistics in Brunton and

[5] Tawney, *Agrarian Problem*, 8.

[6] Tawney, *Agrarian Problem*, 8; Everitt, "County Committee of Kent," 9.

[7] Everitt, *Suffolk*, 16 – 17.

Pennington more closely and at the social variations behind these statistics, they turn out, I would suggest, to provide a rather strong argument for Tawney's views rather than demolishing them.

It is possible to reach the same judgment of statistical evidence that purports to contradict older writings which stressed the severity of the impact of the enclosure movement in the late eighteenth and early nineteenth centuries. In "The Size of Farms in the Eighteenth Century," Mingay discusses the question of the decline of small farming as a result of enclosures and other factors. With the essay as a whole, which concludes that there *was* a decline, I have no quarrel. Indeed it sheds valuable light on a number of questions, such as the legal and political rather than purely economic role of the "spirited landlord." The dubious part of his interpretation is a series of statistical observations with which the article opens. As I read Mingay's point here, nineteenth-century census statistics reveal a picture of English rural society inconsistent with any thesis to the effect that there had been a very serious deterioration in the position of the small farmer during the preceding century. "Anyone who is willing to believe that the small farms 'disappeared' in the eighteenth century must be prepared to explain how it was that they reappeared in such strength in the nineteenth century." The evidence from the census Mingay summarizes in a sentence (with a reference to Clapham, *Economic History*, II, 263 – 264): "In 1831 nearly half the farmers employed no labour other than that of their families, and in 1851 62 percent of the occupiers of 5 acres and over had less than 100 acres. The returns of 1885 show much the same picture. . . ."[8]

From these observations by Mingay it is easy to derive the impression that small farmers continued to flourish well into the nineteenth century and constituted a large proportion of the rural population, somewhere from "nearly half" to "62 percent." Part of the difficulty is a matter of terminology. Writing in an English scholarly periodical, Mingay was certainly under no obligation to point out that in English usage the word "farmer" generally refers to a tenant, who cultivates his holdings with or without the help of hired labor. More rarely does the term refer to someone

[8] Mingay, "Size of Farms," 470.

who owns and cultivates land. Hence the term "farmer" itself already excludes from consideration groups of people who played a decisive part in the life in the countryside, namely, landed proprietors at the top of the social scale and agricultural laborers at the bottom. Nevertheless it is insufficient to put Mingay's observations in perspective by recalling English usage. As best we can, we want to see what the situation was, and that means bringing into our picture of English society people other than small farmers. As soon as one does this, the impression given by Mingay's figures changes drastically. Small farmers and small farms may well have survived. But by the nineteenth century their social surroundings had become such that to speak of survival *tout court* is meaningless if not outright misleading. English rural society had become one largely made up of a small number of large landed proprietors and a huge number of near landless laborers, i.e., a land where small farming had become marginal.

Before going into the actual figures, an analogy may make plainer the character of my objection. Consider the number of dwellings of different kinds that might be found at different points in time on a tract of land the size of Manhattan Island, which begins the century as a cluster of farmhouses and ends it as a metropolis of glass and concrete. It is quite possible that the total number of small houses (even wooden ones) might increase as greedy speculators here and there demolished whole settlements of wooden shacks to erect skyscrapers. To stress the survival of the small houses in this instance would be quite misleading because it overlooks vastly more significant changes.

Now the figures. By 1831, the time of the first moderately dependable census, there were roughly 961,000 families engaged in agriculture in Great Britain. Of these[9]

    I. 144,600 were farming families of occupiers who hired labor.

    II. 130,500 were those of occupiers who hired no labor and might reasonably be considered small farmers.

    III. 686,000 were laboring families.

[9] Great Britain, Census of 1831, *Parliamentary Papers*, XXXVI, ix.

Mingay's remarks that in 1831 nearly half the farmers employed no labor other than that of their families apparently refers to the fact that Group II is almost as large as Group I and that both together make up the body of farmers. His observation is true. But Group II represents only about *one-seventh* of the total number of households engaged in agriculture. This fact, it seems to me, gives a much clearer idea of what the survival — if survival it was — of the small farmer actually amounted to.

The same critical observations apply to his comments on the information from the census of 1851. By that time, in England, Scotland, and Wales there were somewhat fewer than 2.4 million persons who retained an economic and social connection with the land. They were divided in roughly the following fashion:

A. About 35,000 were landed proprietors. Presumably this category included titled aristocrats and members of the still influential gentry.

B. About 306,000 were farmers (and graziers, the latter numbering only about 3000 persons). It appears that the farmers occupied the lion's share of the cultivated area, renting it from big landed proprietors and working it in the vast majority of cases with hired help or with their own families.

C. About 1,461,000 were men and women who did manual work on the land, mainly outdoor laborers.

The rest (not included in the table above) were in miscellaneous categories, including the wives, children, and other relatives of the farmers.[10] Drawing his figures from Clapham, Mingay in discussing the census of 1851 remarked, as we have noted above, that 62 percent of the occupiers of 5 acres and over had less than 100 acres. But Clapham's figures refer *only* to Group B in my table. He is not discussing the other two groups, A and C. Clapham states this point quite plainly.[11] However one might not realize what this limitation means without going back to the census figures themselves. Whether failure to go back to the original figures might be the source of the

---

[10] Great Britain, Census of 1851, *Parliamentary Papers*, LXXXVIII, xci and c. All figures rounded to nearest thousand.

[11] See Clapham, *Economic History*, II, 263 – 265.

misleading impression given by Mingay's brief observations, I of course do not know.

In closing it is necessary to repeat that these statistics amount to no more than rough estimates. The actual percentages are not to be taken literally. But the statistics themselves are perfectly consistent with the older thesis that the social changes of the eighteenth century eliminated the small farmer ?s a significant figure on the English social landscape.

The third and last study to be discussed is an older one, Greer's statistical interpretation of the impact of the Terror in the French Revolution. In its overt denial of the significance of class conflict, its thesis resembles closely the analysis of the Long Parliament by Brunton and Pennington. In his study of the social composition of the victims of the Terror, Greer found·that 84 percent of those executed belonged to the Third Estate. On this ground he concluded that "the split in French society was perpendicular, not horizontal. The Terror was an intra-class, not an inter-class war."[12] This conclusion has attracted considerable attention and, taken at face value, stands of course in glaring contradiction to any sociological interpretation. This is the kind of "evidence" that leads some scholars to regard a Mathiez and the like as antiquated. In the best tradition of scholarship, Greer gives enough data to dissolve the paradox and dismiss the conclusion.

Confining our attention to the lowest strata in the Third Estate, working class and peasants, together more than 79 percent of the victims, we may ask when and where they met their grisly fate. The answer is straightforward: the overwhelming majority died as victims of revolutionary repression exercised against the Vendée counterrevolution and that of Lyon. Though the statistical evidence points strongly toward this conclusion, there is not much sense in reproducing the figures because they are inherently, and through no fault of Greer, very incomplete. For instance they do

---

[12] *Incidence of the Terror*, 97–98. It will be recalled that those executed were only a minority of the victims and that there is no information about the rest. There is no need to raise the point whether such information might have called for modification of Greer's thesis, because the relevant issues can be discussed within the framework of established facts.

not include the victims of one of the most dramatic episodes of the Vendée counterrevolution, the drowning of some 2000 persons in the wintry waters of the Loire, nor the massive fusillade at Toulon that may have taken 800 lives.[13]

Thus the split in French society was between revolutionaries and counterrevolutionaries. Was it a perpendicular split? The counterrevolutionaries had, as Greer makes very clear, limited geographical bases whose social structure differed from that in other parts of France. It was not a war of peasant against peasant, bourgeois against bourgeois throughout France. To be sure, there were members of roughly the same social strata fighting on opposite sides. But they were fighting for opposed social objectives, the restoration of the old order or its abolition. Victory for one side or the other meant the victory or defeat of class privileges. On these grounds alone, it seems impossible to deny that the Terror was an instrument of class warfare, at least in its essential outlines.

There are also some general reasons for holding that in any violent conflict the social composition of the victims will not *by itself* reveal much about the social and political character of the struggle. Let us suppose that a revolution breaks out in some Latin American country where the government is under the control of wealthy landlords and a few rich businessmen. Let us suppose further that the army is made up mostly of peasant conscripts and that one section of the army breaks off and joins the rebels who are seeking to overthrow the government and establish a communist regime. After a few pitched battles, the statistician would no doubt find that the casualties on both sides were mainly peasants. To conclude that the main split in this case was a vertical one, to deny that class conflict was the key to the political struggles, would be patently absurd. If, on the other hand, the rebels put forth no social demands and merely sought to replace one set of landlords and business leaders with another, there would be grounds for the assertion that some sort of a perpendicular split existed. In a word, it is not only who fights but what the fight is about that matters. This aspect raises more general issues to which we may now turn.

[13] Greer, *Incidence of the Terror*, 35 – 37, 115; see also Table VIII, p. 165.

So far the discussion has proceeded within the framework of the statistical evidence alone. However, there are certain common themes in the statistical critique that raise questions transcending statistics. In order to bring out these points I will take the liberty of reformulating the general drift of the line of argument just discussed. Implicitly the burden of this argument seems to be the following: In what were supposedly the great revolutions *against oppressors* it is possible to show, by counting, that there was in reality little or no rising against oppression. No important differences distinguished the two sides in the Puritan and French Revolutions. Similarly, in what was supposed to be a revolutionary social transformation carried out *by an oppressive upper class*, the enclosure movement in England, it is possible to show by counting that in reality there was not much oppression. The victims grew and flourished. Hence the whole radical tradition is suffused with sentimental nonsense.

Quite possibly this formulation exceeds the intentions of the authors under discussion, though the implications do seem reasonably clear. Be that as it may, this type of argument does exist and requires discussion. In part this thesis demands an answer in its own terms. I have already tried to show that the statistics do not yield such a result. Now I should like to raise a new issue by suggesting that, although statistics can shed considerable light on this thesis and similar ones, there may also be a point at which quantitative evidence becomes inapplicable, where counting becomes the wrong procedure to use. In the analysis of qualitative changes from one type of social organization to another, let us say from feudalism to industrial capitalism, there may be an upper limit to the profitable use of statistical procedures.

The remark is attributed to Lord Kelvin that everything that exists exists in quantity. But this aphorism does not mean that everything that exists can be measured on the same scale or that all differences can be reduced to quantitative differences. To my limited knowledge, statisticians do not make such a claim; certainly it is not the general claim of mathematics. Up to a point, changes in social structure do indeed find their reflection in changes in statistical measurements. For example, changes over time in the number of people in different occupations tell us a great deal about changes in social structure. But where the time period is long or the changes in the structure of society very marked, difficulties arise with the yardstick.[14] The same proportion between rural and urban population may have very different meanings in two different societies if one is like the antebellum South and the other a precommercial society. Again, up to a point statistical investigation can take care of these difficulties by carefully defining its categories. Nevertheless there may be an upper limit to such readjustments that involves a matter of principle. Counting necessarily involves ignoring all differences except the one being measured. It requires reducing evidence to similar units. Human beings have to be sorted into statistical piles by age, sex, marital status, and a host of other criteria. The necessities of counting, I suggest, make it necessary to ignore structural distinctions sooner or later. The more definitions the investigator makes in order to catch up with structural changes, the smaller and less useful and· trustworthy become the statistical piles with which he works. At bottom, the sizes of the different piles are consequences of structural changes. They are not the changes themselves.

These changes are qualitative alterations in the relations men have with one another. They concern such differences as those between owning property and producing goods with a few simple tools and one's own hands, and owning no property, working for someone else, and producing goods with complicated machines. To speak in very neutral and abstract terms .for a moment, they are changes in the form of social patterns. The distinctions in these forms and patterns do not seem to me reducible to any quantitative differences; they are incommensurable.[15] Yet it is precisely such

[14] For the sake of simplicity I leave out of account the problem of obtaining reliable statistical data. This problem is a very severe one. In my estimation no one should try to draw on statistical information without pondering carefully Morgenstern, *Accuracy of Economic Observations*, which brings out these difficulties in societies with advanced methods of collecting statistics, and the Thorners' *Land and Labour in India* (esp chap XIII), which brings them out for a backward country.

[15] Note in this connection Whitehead, *Modes of Thought*, 195: "Thus beyond all questions of quantity, there lie questions of pattern, which are

differences that matter most to human beings. They are the ones where change has produced the most violent conflict, the source of the great historical issues.

Even if statistical methods may have inherent limitations, could it still be possible to describe and explain these qualitative changes in an objective fashion? In principle, I think, it is possible, although shortcomings in the evidence and human failures in the historian mean that objectivity remains no more than an ever receding ideal. Objectivity implies belief in truth with a small t, the conception that social events happen the way they do for ascertainable reasons. Since this conception can lead to assessments very different from prevailing conservative views and also different from some versions of the radical tradition, I will try to spell out its implications very briefly.

There is a respectable intellectual tradition which denies that objectivity is possible at all, even in principle. This denial seems to rest on a confusion between the causes of historical events and their consequences or meaning. The causes of the American Civil War had run their course by the time the first shot was fired at Fort Sumter. No historian's opinion about these causes can have the remotest effect on what they actually were. The consequences are another matter. They are with us today and may be with us as long as human history continues. This second aspect of the thesis about the permanent ambiguity of history seems to me perfectly valid. Statements by historians about the causes of the Civil War have polemical results *now*, no matter what their authors intend. It is in this sense that impartiality is an impossibility and an illusion. Whether he knows it or not, to continue the argument, the historian has to adopt some principle in selecting and ordering his facts. The same is true for the sociologist studying contemporary affairs. By virtue of what they include and exclude, highlight or deemphasize, these principles have political and moral consequences.

---

essential for the understanding of nature. Apart from a presupposed pattern, quantity determines nothing." Whitehead's reservations about the procedures of the natural sciences and mathematics are to be taken very seriously because, unlike many other critics, he knew thoroughly what he was talking about.

Hence they are unavoidably moral principles. It is impossible to opt out of the struggle. The very act of trying to opt out, of trying to take a nonpartisan position, means taking up a form of apolitical pseudo-objectivity that in effect supports the *status quo*.

The thesis that neutrality is impossible is a powerful one, convincing at any rate to me. But I do not think that it leads to a denial that objective social and historical analysis is possible. Different perspectives on the same set of events should lead to complementary and congruent interpretations, not to contradictory ones. Furthermore the denial that objective truth is possible in principle flings open the door to the worst forms of intellectual dishonesty. A crude version goes something like this: since neutrality is impossible I will take my stand with the underdog and write history to serve the underdog, helping in this way to reach a "higher Truth." In plain language that is just cheating. No matter what his unavoidable moral premises and predilections, any student of human affairs is bound sooner or later to come across evidence that is profoundly disturbing. Then he has the task of coming to terms with it honestly.

Gradations of Truth with a capital T, rightly in my estimation, arouse angry suspicion. But this does not mean that objectivity and truth with a small t lead to comfortable complacency. Objectivity is not the same thing as conventional judiciousness. A celebration of the virtues of our own society which leaves out its ugly and cruel features, which fails to face the question of a connection between its attractive and its cruel ones, remains an apologia even if it is spoken in the most measured academic tones. There is a strong tendency to assume that mild-mannered statements in favor of the *status quo* are "objective" and that anything else is a form of "rhetoric."

This type of bias, this misinterpretation of objectivity, is the one most common in the West today. It confuses objectivity with triviality and meaninglessness. For reasons already mentioned, any simple straightforward truth about political institutions or events is bound to have polemical consequences. It will damage some group interests. In any society the dominant groups are the ones with the most to hide about the way society works. Very often therefore truthful analyses are bound to have a critical ring, to seem like exposures rather than objective statements, as the term is conventionally used. (This will be true in communist countries too if they ever get to the point of allowing moderately candid accounts of their own past to see the light.) For all students of human society, sympathy with the victims of historical processes and skepticism about the victors' claims provide essential safeguards against being taken in by the dominant mythology. A scholar who tries to be objective needs these feelings as part of his ordinary working equipment.

Bibliography

THERE ARE THREE KINDS OF WORKS listed below. The first contains works on Germany and Russia which are the basis of my interpretation of the social history of these countries, as indicated in the Introduction. The second and main body of references consists of works cited in each of the chapters in the order in which each country is discussed. Finally, the usual stragglers that do not fit elsewhere are lumped together in a catch-all category. This is then in no sense a complete or selected bibliography. It merely identifies the main sources of the evidence I have considered.

I.

Germany

Aubin, Gustav, *Zur Geschichte des gutsherrlich-bäuerlichen Verhältnisses in Ostpreussen von der Gründung des Ordensstaates bis zur Steinschen Reform*. Leipzig, 1911.

Bracher, Karl Dietrich, Sauer, Wolfgang, and Schulz, Gerhard, *Die nationalsozialistische Machtergreifung*. Köln and Opladen, 1960.

Carsten, F. L., *The Origins of Prussia*. London, 1954, reprinted 1958.

——— "Der Bauernkrieg in Ostpreussen 1525," *International Review for Social History*, III (1938), 398–409.

Dittmann, Wilhelm, *Das politische Deutschland vor Hitler*. Zürich, 1945.

Franz, Günther, *Der deutsche Bauernkrieg*. Darmstadt, 1956.

Gerschenkron, Alexander, *Bread and Democracy in Germany*. Berkeley, 1943.

Hamerow, Theodore S., *Restoration, Revolution, Reaction: Economics and Politics in Germany, 1815–1871*. Princeton, 1958.

Heberle, Rudolf, *Social Movements: An Introduction to Political Sociology*. New York, 1951.

Hitler, Adolf, *Mein Kampf.* 141st ed., München, 1935.

Kehr, Eckart, *Schlachtflottenbau und Parteipolitik 1894–1901.* Berlin, 1930.

Krieger, Leonard, *The German Idea of Freedom.* Boston, 1957.

Loomis, Charles P., and Beegle, J. Allen, "The Spread of German Nazism in Rural Areas," *American Sociological Review,* XI (December, 1946), 724–734.

Nabholz, Hans, "Zur Frage nach den Ursachen des Bauernkriegs 1525," reprinted in *Ausgewählte Aufsätze zur Wirtschaftsgeschichte* (Zürich, 1954). First published in 1928.

Preradovich, Nikolaus von, *Die Führungsschichten in Österreich und Preussen (1804–1918).* Wiesbaden, 1955.

Rosenberg, Hans, *Bureaucracy, Aristocracy and Autocracy: The Prussian Experience 1660–1815.* Cambridge, Massachusetts, 1958.

Schorske, Carl E., *German Social Democracy 1905–1917.* Cambridge, Massachusetts, 1955.

Schweitzer, Arthur, "The Nazification of the Lower Middle Class and Peasants," in *The Third Reich,* a collection of essays published by the International Council for Philosophy and Humanistic Studies (London, 1955), 576–594.

Sering, Max, editor, *Die deutsche Landwirtschaft unter volks-und weltwirtschaftlichen Gesichtspunkten dargestellt . . . ,* published as Sonderheft 50, Neue Folge, *Berichte uber Landwirtschaft* (Berlin, 1932).

Smirin, M. M., *Ocherki istorii politicheskoi bor'by v Germanii pered reformatsiei.* 2nd ed., Moscow, 1952.

Stein, Robert, *Die Umwandlung der Agrarverfassung Ostpreussens durch die Reform des neunzehnten Jahrhunderts.* Vol. I, Jena, 1918.

Waas, Adolf, *Die grosse Wendung im deutschen Bauernkrieg.* München, 1939.

Weber, Max, "Entwickelungstendénzen in der Lage der Ostelbischen Landarbeiter," in *Gesammelte Aufsätze zur Sozial- und Wirtschaftsgeschichte* (Tübingen, 1924), 470–507.

Wiessner, Hermann, *Beiträge zur Geschichte des Dorfes und der Dorfgemeinde in Österreich.* Klagenfurt, 1946.

—— *Sachinhalt und Wirtschaftliche Bedeutung der Weistümer im Deutschen Kulturgebiet.* Baden, 1934.

Wundèrlich, Frieda, *Farm Labor in Germany 1810–1945.* Princeton, 1961.

Russia

Berlin, P. A., *Russkaya burzhuaziya v staroye i novoye vremya*. Moscow, 1922.

Blum, Jerome, *Lord and Peasant in Russia: From the Ninth to the Nineteenth Century*. Princeton, 1961.

Gitermann, Valentin, *Geschichte Russlands*. 3 vols. Zürich, 1944 – 1949.

Kliuchevskii, V., *Kurs russkoi istorii*. 5 vols. Moscow, 1937.

Levitskii, V., "Pravyya partii," in *Obshchestvennoye dvizheniye v Rossii v nachale XX-go veka*, III (St. Petersburg, 1914), 347 – 472.

Maynard, Sir John, *Russia in Flux: Before October*. London, 1946.

Miliukov, P., *Ocherki po istorii russkoi kultury*. St. Petersburg, 1909.

Robinson, Geroid T., *Rural Russia Under the Old Regime: A History of the Landlord Peasant World and a Prologue to the Peasant Revolution of 1917*. New York, 1932.

Venturi, Franco, *Roots of Revolution: A History of the Populist and Socialist Movements in Nineteenth Century Russia*. Translated by Francis Haskell. London, 1960.

II.

England

Ashton, T. S., *An Economic History of England: The Eighteenth Century*. London, 1955.

Aston, Trevor, editor, *Crisis in Europe 1560 – 1660: Essays from* PAST AND PRESENT. London, 1965.

Aydelotte, W. O., "The Business Interests of the Gentry in the Parliament of 1841 – 47," an appendix in Clark, *The Making of Victorian England*, 290 – 305.

Bowden, Peter J., *The Wool Trade in Tudor and Stuart England*. London, 1962.

Briggs, Asa, *The Age of Improvement*. London, 1959.

——— editor, *Chartist Studies*. London, 1962.

Brunton, D., and Pennington, D. H., *Members of the Long Parliament*. London, 1954.

Cam, Helen M., "The Decline and Fall of English Feudalism," *History*, New Series, Vol. XXV, No. 99 (December, 1940), 216 – 233.

Campbell, Mildred, *The English Yeoman under Elizabeth and the Early Stuarts*. 2nd ed., London, 1960.

Carus-Wilson, E. M., editor, *Essays in Economic History*. Vol. I: London, 1954. Vol. II: London, 1962.

Cecil, Lord David, *Melbourne*. Reprinted, New York, 1954.

Census of Great Britain in 1851: An Analytical Index. London, 1854.

Chambers, J. D., "Enclosure and Labour Supply in the Industrial Revolution," *Economic History Review*, 2nd Series, Vol. V, No. 3 (1953), 319 – 343.

Clapham, J. H., *An Economic History of Modern Britain*. 3 vols. Reprinted, Cambridge, 1950 – 1952.

Clark, G. Kitson, *The Making of Victorian England*. London, 1962.

Cole, G. D. H., and Postgate, Raymond, *The British People, 1746 – 1946*. New York, 1947.

Cooper, J. P.,. "The Counting of Manors," *Economic History Review*, 2nd Series, Vol. VIII, No. 3 (April, 1956), 377 – 389.

Davies, E., "The Small Landowner, 1780 – 1832, in the Light of the Land Tax Assessments," reprinted in Carus-Wilson, editor, *Essays in Economic History*, 270 – 294.

Deane, Phyllis, and Cole, W. A., *British Economic Growth 1688 – 1959: Trends and Structure*. Cambridge, 1962.

Everitt, Alan Milner, "The County Committee of Kent in the Civil War," *Occasional Papers*, No. 9 (1957), published by the University College of Leicester, Department of English Local History.

————— editor, *Suffolk and the Great Rebellion 1640 – 1660*. Ipswich, 1961.

Firth, C. H., *Cromwell's Army*. 3rd ed., London, 1921; reprinted 1962.

Gallagher, John, and Robinson, Ronald, "The Imperialism of Free Trade," *Economic History Review*, 2nd Series, VI, No. 1 (August, 1953), 1 – 15.

Gonner, E. C. K., *Common Land and Enclosure*. London, 1912.

Goodwin, A., editor, *The European Nobility in the Eighteenth Century*. London, 1953.

Great Britain, Census of 1831, *Parliamentary Papers*, Session: 29 January – 29 August 1833, Vol. XXXVI, Accounts and Papers, Vol. 12.

————— Census of 1851, *Parliamentary Papers*, Session: 4 November 1852 – 20 August 1853, Accounts and Papers, Vol. 32, Part I.

– 20 August 1853, Accounts and Papers, Vol, 32, Part I.

Habakkuk, H. J., "English Landownership, 1680 – 1740," *Economic History Review*, Vol. X, No. 1 (February, 1940), 2 – 17.

Halévy, Elie, *A History of the English People in the Nineteenth Cen-*

tury. Translated by E. I. Watkin. 6 vols. 2nd revised edition, London, 1949 – 52.

Hammond, J. L. and Barbara, *The Village Labourer 1760 – 1832*. London, 1911.

Hardacre, Paul H., *The Royalists during the Puritan Revolution*. The Hague, 1956.

Hexter, J. H., *Reappraisals in History*. Evanston, 1961.

Hill, Christopher, *Puritanism and Revolution*. London, 1958.

Hoskins, W. G., *The Midland Peasant: The Economic and Social History of a Leicestershire Village*. London, 1957.

James, Margaret, *Social Problems and Policy during the Puritan Revolution 1640 – 1660*. London, 1930.

Johnson, Arthur H., *The Disappearance of the Small Landowner*. Oxford, 1909; reprinted 1963.

Kerridge, Eric, "The Returns of the Inquisition of Depopulation," *English Historical Review*, Vol. LXX, No. 275 (April, 1955), 212 – 228.

Langer, William, "Europe's Initial Population Explosion," *American Historical Review*, Vol. LXIX (1963), 1 – 17.

Levy, Hermann, *Large and Small Holdings*. Translated with additions by the author. Cambridge, 1911.

Lipson, E., *The Economic History of England*. Vol. I: *The Middle Ages;* reprinted London, 1956, from the 7th ed., 1937. Vols. II and III: *The Age of Mercantilism;* reprinted London, 1956, from the 3rd ed., 1943.

Manning, Brian, "The Nobles, the People, and the Constitution," in Aston, editor, *Crisis in Europe 1560 – 1660*, 247 – 269.

Mather, F. C., "The Government and the Chartists," in Briggs, editor, *Chartist Studies*, 385 – 394.

Mingay, G. E., *English Landed Society in the Eighteenth Century*. London, 1963.

———— "The Land Tax Assessments and the Small Landowner," *Economic History Review*, 2nd Series, Vol. XVII, No. 2 (December, 1964), 381 – 388.

———— "The Size of Farms in the Eighteenth Century," *Economic History Review*, 2nd Series, Vol. XIV, No. 3 (April, 1962), 469 – 488.

Namier, Sir Lewis, *England in the Age of the American Revolution*. 2nd ed., London, 1961.

Nef, John U., *Industry and Government in France and England 1540 – 1640*. Reprinted from 1940 edition, Ithaca, 1957.

Plumb, J. H., *England in the Eighteenth Century*. Penguin Books, 1950.

Power, Eileen, *The Wool Trade in English Medieval History*. Oxford, 1941.

Sabine, George H., editor, *The Works of Gerrard Winstanley*. Ithaca, 1941.

Semenov, V. F., *Ogorazhivaniya i krest'yanskiye dvizheniya v Anglii XVI veka*. Moscow, 1949.

Stone, Lawrence, *The Crisis of the Aristocracy 1558 – 1641*. Oxford, 1965.

Tate, W. E., "Members of Parliament and the Proceedings upon Enclosure Bills," *Economic History Review*, Vol. XII (1942), 68 – 75.

Tawney, R. H., *The Agrarian Problem in the Sixteenth Century*. London, 1912.

―――― "The Rise of the Gentry 1558 – 1640," reprinted in Carus-Wilson, editor, *Essays in Economic History*, 173 – 214.

Thirsk, Joan, "The Restoration Land Settlement," *Journal of Modern History*, Vol. XXVI, No. 4 (December, 1954), 315 – 328.

―――― *Tudor Enclosures*. London, 1959.

Thompson, E. P., *The Making of the English Working Class*. London, 1963.

Thompson, F. M. L., *English Landed Society in the Nineteenth Century*. London, 1963.

Trevelyan, G. M., *History of England*. 3 vols. Reprinted from 2nd revised edition, New York, 1953 – 56.

Trevor-Roper, H. R., "The Gentry 1540 – 1640," *Economic History Review Supplement*, No. 1 (1953).

Turberville, A. S., *The House of Lords in the Age of Reform 1784 – 1837*. London, 1958.

Woodward, E. L., *The Age of Reform 1815 – 1870*. Oxford, 1949.

Yule, George, *The Independents in the English Civil War*. Cambridge, 1958.

Zagorin, Perez, "The English Revolution 1640 – 1660," *Journal of World History*, Vol. II, No. 3 (1955), 668 – 681.

―――― "The Social Interpretation of the English Revolution," *Journal of Economic History*, Vol. XIX (1959), 376 – 401.

France

Advielle, Victor, *Histoire de Gracchus Babeuf et du Babouvisme*. 2 vols. Paris, 1884.

Augé-Laribé, Michel, *La Politique agricole de la France de 1880 à 1949*. Paris, 1950.

Barber, Elinor G., *The Bourgeoisie in Eighteenth Century France*. Princeton, 1955.

Bloch, Marc, *Les Caractères originaux de l'histoire rurale française*. 2 vols. 2nd ed., Paris, 1955 – 1956.

——— "La lutte pour l'individualisme agraire dans la France du XVIIIe siècle," *Annales d'histoire économique et sociale*, Vol. II, No. 7 (15 July 1930), 329 – 381, and No. 8 (15 October 1930), 511 – 556.

——— "Sur le passé de la noblesse française; quelques jalons de recherche," *Annales d'histoire économique et sociale*, VIII (July, 1936), 366 – 378.

Bois, Paul, *Paysans de l'Ouest*. Le Mans, 1960.

Bourgin, Georges, editor, *Le Partage des biens communeaux*. Paris, 1908.

Carré, Henri, *La Noblesse de France et l'opinion publique au XVIIIe siècle*. Paris, 1920.

Cobb, Richard, *Les Armées révolutionnaires*. 2 vols. Paris, 1961 – 1963.

Cobban, Alfred, "The *Parlements* of France in the Eighteenth Century," *History*, New Series, Vol. 35 (February – June, 1950), 64 – 80.

——— *The Social Interpretation of the French Revolution*. Cambridge, 1964.

Dalin, V. M., *Grakkh Babef*. Moscow, 1963.

Dommanget, Maurice, *Pages choisies de Babeuf*. Paris, 1935.

Duby, Georges, *L'Economie rurale et la vie des campagnes dans l'occident médiéval*. 2 vols. Paris, 1962.

"The Folklore of Royalism," *Times Literary Supplement* (London), September 7, 1962.

Ford, Franklin L., *Robe and Sword: The Regrouping of the French Aristocracy After Louis XIV*. Cambridge, Massachusetts, 1953.

Forster, Robert, *The Nobility of Toulouse in the Eighteenth Century*. Baltimore, 1960.

——— "The Noble Wine Producers of the Bordelais in the Eighteenth Century," *Economic History Review*, 2nd Series, XIV, No. 1 (August, 1961), 18 – 33.

——— "The Provincial Noble: A Reappraisal," *American Historical Review*, Vol. LXVIII, No. 3 (April, 1963), 681 – 691.

Göhring, Martin, *Die Ämterkäuflichkeit im Ancien Régime*. Berlin, 1938.

———— *Die Frage der Feudalität in Frankreich Ende des Ancien Régime und in der französischen Revolution (bis 17 Juli 1793).* Berlin, 1934.

Goubert, Pierre, *Beauvais et le Beauvaisis de 1600 à 1730.* Paris, 1960.

Greer, Donald, *The Incidence of the Terror during the French Revolution.* Cambridge, Massachusetts, 1935.

Guérin, Daniel, *La Lutte de classes sous la première république.* 2 vols. Paris, 1946.

Hunter, Neil, *Peasantry and Crisis in France.* London, 1938.

Jaurès, Jean, *Histoire socialiste de la Révolution française,* édition revue par A. Mathiez. Vol. VI: *La Gironde* (Paris, 1923).

Labrousse, C. E., *La Crise de l'économie française à la fin de l'ancien régime et au début de la Révolution.* 2 vols. Vol. I (Paris, 1944).

———— *Esquisse du mouvement des prix et des revenus en France au XVIIIe siècle.* Paris, 1932.

Lavisse, Ernest, editor, *Histoire de France illustrée depuis les origines jusqu'à la Révolution.* Vol. VII (Paris, 1911).

Lefebvre, Georges, *Etudes sur la Révolution française.* Paris, 1954.

———— *La Grande Peur de 1789.* Paris, 1932.

———— *Les Paysans du Nord pendant la Révolution française.* Bari, 1959.

———— *Questions agraires au temps de la Terreur.* 2nd revised edition, La Roche-sur-Yon, 1954.

———— *La Révolution française.* Paris, 1957.

Lhomme, Jean, *La Grande bourgeoisie en pouvoir 1830 – 1880.* Paris, 1960.

Mathiez, A., *La Révolution française.* 3 vols. 12th ed., Paris, 1954 – 1955.

———— *La Vie chère et le mouvement social sous la Terreur.* Paris, 1927.

Nef, John U., *Industry and Government in France and England 1540 – 1640.* Ithaca, 1957, reprint of 1940 edition.

Porchnev, Boris, *Les Soulèvements populaires en France de 1623 à 1648.* Paris, 1963.

Postgate, R. W., editor, *Revolution from 1789 to 1906.* New York, 1962.

Rudé, George, *The Crowd in the French Revolution.* Oxford, 1959.

Sagnac, Philippe, *La Formation de la société française moderne.* 2 vols. Paris, 1945.

Saint Jacob, P. de, *Les Paysans de la Bourgogne du Nord au dernier siècle de l'ancien régime.* Paris, 1960.

Sée, Henri, *Evolution commerciale et industrielle de la France sous l'ancien régime.* Paris, 1925.

———— *Histoire économique de la France.* 2 vols. Paris, 1939.

Soboul, Albert, *Les Sans-culottes parisiens en l'an II.* 2nd edition, Paris, 1962.

Soreau, Edmond, "La Révolution française et le prolétariat rural," *Annales historiques de la Révolution française,* Vol. IX, No. 50 (March – April, 1932), 116 – 127.

Tilly, Charles, *The Vendée.* Cambridge, Massachusetts, 1964.

Usher, Abbot Payson, *The History of the Grain Trade in France 1400 – 1710.* Cambridge, Massachusetts, 1913.

Wright, Gordon, "Agrarian Syndicalism in Postwar France," *American Political Science Review,* Vol. XLVII, No. 2 (June, 1953), 402 – 416.

———— "Catholics and Peasantry in France," *Political Science Quarterly,* Vol. LXVIII, No. 4 (December, 1953), 526 – 551.

———— *Rural Revolution in France.* Stanford, 1964.

United States

Andreano, Ralph, editor, *The Economic Impact of the American Civil War.* Cambridge, Massachusetts, 1962.

Aptheker, Herbert, *American Negro Slave Revolts.* New York, 1943.

Beale, Howard K., *The Critical Year: A Study of Andrew Johnson and the Reconstruction.* Republished New York, 1958; first published, 1930.

———— "What Historians Have Said About the Causes of the Civil War," in *Theory and Practice in Historical Study,* A Report of the Committee on Historiography, Social Science Research Council (New York, 1946), 53 – 102.

Beard, Charles A. and Mary R., *The Rise of American Civilization.* 2 vols. in one; revised edition, New York, 1940.

Bennett, H. S., *Life on the English Manor: A Study of Peasant Conditions, 1150 – 1400.* Cambridge, 1956; first published, 1937.

Cochran, Thomas C., "Did the Civil War Retard Industrialization?" reprinted in Andreano, editor, *Economic Impact of the American Civil War,* 148 – 160.

Conrad, Alfred H., and Meyer, John R., "The Economics of Slavery in the Ante Bellum South," *Journal of Political Economy,* Vol. LXVI, No. 2 (April, 1958), 95 – 130.

Craven, Avery O., *The Coming of the Civil War.* 2nd ed., Chicago, 1957.

———— *The Growth of Southern Nationalism.* Baton Rouge, 1953.

Current, Richard Nelson, *Old Thad Stevens: A Story of Ambition.* Madison, 1942.

Davis, Lance E. *et al., American Economic History.* Homewood, 1961.

Elkins, Stanley M., *Slavery: A Problem in American Institutional and Intellectual Life.* Chicago, 1959; reprinted New York, 1963.

Foner, Philip S., *Business and Slavery: The New York Merchants and the Irrepressible Conflict.* Chapel Hill, 1941.

Gates, Paul W., *The Farmer's Age: Agriculture 1815 – 1860.* New York, 1962.

Gray, Lewis C., *History of Agriculture in Southern United States to 1860.* New York, 1941.

Hacker, Louis M., *The Triumph of American Capitalism.* New York, 1940.

Nevins, Allan, *The Emergence of Lincoln.* Vol. I: *Douglas, Buchanan and Party Chaos 1857 – 1859.* Vol. II: *Prologue to Civil War 1859 – 1861.* New York, 1950.

―― *Ordeal of the Union.* Vol. I, New York, 1947.

Nichols, Roy F., *The Disruption of American Democracy.* New York, 1948.

North, Douglass C., *The Economic Growth of the United States 1790 – 1860.* Englewood Cliffs, 1961.

Owsley, Frank L., *Plain Folk of the Old South.* Baton Rouge, 1949.

Phillips, Ulrich B., *Life and Labor in the Old South.* Boston, 1929.

Randall, J. G., and Donald, David, *The Civil War and Reconstruction.* 2nd ed., Boston, 1961.

Rayback, Joseph G., "The American Workingman and the Antislavery Crusade," *Journal of Economic History,* Vol. III, No. 2 (November, 1943), 152 – 163.

Schlesinger, Arthur M., Jr., *The Age of Jackson.* Boston, 1945.

Shannon, Fred A., *American Farmers Movements.* Princeton, 1957.

Sharkey, Robert P., *Money, Class, and Party: An Economic Study of Civil War and Reconstruction.* Baltimore, 1959.

Shortreed, Margaret, "The Antislavery Radicals: From Crusade to Revolution 1840 – 1868," *Past and Present,* No. 16 (November, 1959), 65 – 87.

Stampp, Kenneth M., *The Causes of the Civil War.* Englewood Cliffs, 1959.

―― *The Era of Reconstruction 1865 – 1877.* New York, 1965.

―― *The Peculiar Institution.* New York, 1956.

[Stevens, Thaddeus], *Reconstruction, Speech of Hon. Thaddeus*

*Stevens of Pennsylvania, delivered in the House of Representatives
. . . December 18, 1865.* Washington, 1865.

Woodward, C. Vann, *Reunion and Reaction.* Revised ed., New York,
1956.

Zahler, Helene S., *Eastern Workingmen and National Land Policy,
1829 - 1862.* New York, 1941.

China

Agrarian China: Selected Source Materials from Chinese Authors. London, 1939.

Allen, G. C., and Donnithorne, A. G., *Western Enterprise in Far Eastern Commercial Development.* London, 1954.

Balázs, Etienne, "Les aspects significatifs de la société chinoise," *Etudes Asiatiques,* Vol. VI (1952), 77 - 87.

———— *Chinese Civilization and Bureaucracy: Variations on a Theme.*
Selections from his writings, translated by H. M. Wright, edited
by Arthur F. Wright. New Haven, 1964.

Beal, Edwin George, Jr., *The Origin of Likin* (1853 - 1864). Cambridge, Massachusetts, 1958.

Berkov, Robert, *Strong Man of China: The Story of Chiang Kai-shek.*
Cambridge, Massachusetts, 1938.

Bland, J. O. P., and Backhouse, E., *China Under the Empress Dowager.*
London, 1911.

Brandt, Conrad, *Stalin's Failure in China 1924 - 1927.* Cambridge, Massachusetts, 1958.

————, Schwartz, Benjamin, Fairbank, John K., *A Documentary History of Chinese Communism.* Cambridge, Massachusetts, 1952.

Buck, John Lossing, *Land Utilization in China.* Chicago, 1937.

Cameron, Meribeth E., *The Reform Movement in China 1898 - 1912.*
Stanford, 1931.

Chang, Chung-li, *The Chinese Gentry.* Seattle, 1955.

———— *The Income of the Chinese Gentry.* Seattle, 1962.

Ch'en, Jerome, *Mao and the Chinese Revolution.* London, 1965.

Chiang Kai-shek, *China's Destiny.* Authorized translation by Wang
Chung-hui. New York, 1947.

Chiang, Siang-tseh, *The Nien Rebellion.* Seattle, 1954.

China - United States Agricultural Mission. *Report* (U.S. Office of
Foreign Agricultural Relations, Report No. 2). Washington, 1947.

Ch'ü, T'ung-tsu, *Local Government in China under the Ch'ing*. Cambridge, Massachusetts, 1962.

Crook, David and Isabel, *Revolution in a Chinese Village: Ten Mile Inn*. London, 1959.

DeGroot, J. J. M., *Sectarianism and Religious Persecutions in China*. 2 vóls. Amsterdam, 1903 – 1904.

Eberhard, Wolfram, *Chinas Geschichte*. Bern, 1948.

———— *Conquerors and Rulers: Social Forces in Medieval China*. Leiden, 1952.

Fei, Hsiao-tung, *Peasant Life in China: A Field Study of Country Life in the Yangtze Valley*. New York, 1946.

———— and Chang; Chih-i, *Earthbound China: A Study of Rural Economy in Yunnan*. London, 1948.

Feuerwerker, Albert, *China's Early Industrialization: Sheng Hsuan-huai (1844 – 1916) and Mandarin Enterprise*. Cambridge, Massachusetts, 1958.

———— "China's History in Marxian Dress," *American Historical Review*, Vol. XLVI, No. 2 (January, 1961), 323 – 353.

Fitzgerald, C. P., *Revolution in China*. London, 1952.

Franke, Wolfgang, *The Reform and Abolition of the Traditional Chinese Examination System*. Cambridge, Massachusetts, 1960.

Freedman, Maurice, Book review of Chung-li Chang, *The Chinese Gentry*, *Pacific Affairs*, Vol. XXIX, No. 1 (March, 1956), 78 – 80.

Fried, Morton H., *The Fabric of Chinese Society: A Study of the Social Life of a Chinese County Seat*. New York, 1953.

Gamble, Sidney D., *Ting Hsien: A North China Rural Community*. New York, 1954.

Hinton, Harold C., *The Grain Tribute System of China 1845 – 1911*. Cambridge, Massachusetts, 1956.

Ho, Ping-ti, *The Ladder of Success in Imperial China*. New York, 1962.

———— *Studies on the Population of China 1368 – 1953*. Cambridge, Massachusetts, 1959.

Holcombe, Arthur N., *The Chinese Revolution*. Cambridge, Massachusetts, 1930.

Hsiao, Kung-chuan, *Rural China: Imperial Control in the Nineteenth Century*. Seattle, 1960.

Isaacs, Harold R., *Tragedy of the Chinese Revolution*. Revised ed., Stanford, 1951.

Jamieson, George, *et al.*, "Tenure of Land in China and Condition of the Rural Population," *Journal of the Royal Asiatic Society of*

Great Britain and Ireland, North China Branch (Shanghai), n.s., XXIII (1888) (published Shanghai, 1889), 59 – 174.

Johnson, Chalmers A., *Peasant Nationalism and Communist Power: The Emergence of Revolutionary Power 1937 – 1945*. Stanford, 1962.

Khokhlov, A. N., "Agrarnye otnosheniya v Kitai vo vtoroi polovine XVIII – nachale XIX v.," *Kratkie soobshcheniya narodov Azii*, No. 53 (1962), 95 – 115.

Lamb, Jefferson D. H., *Development of the Agrarian Movement and Agrarian Legislation in China 1912 – 1930*. Peiping, 1931.

Lang, Olga, *Chinese Family and Society*. New Haven, 1946.

Lattimore, Owen, "The Industrial Impact on China, 1800 – 1950," in *First International Conference of Economic History, Stockholm, August, 1960* (Paris, 1960), 103 – 113.

Lee, Mabel Ping-hua, *The Economic History of China*. New York, 1921.

Levy, Marion J., Jr., and Shih, Kuo-shen, *The Rise of the Modern Chinese Business Class*. Mimeographed, New York, 1949.

Linebarger, Paul M., *The China of Chiang K'ai-shek*. Boston, 1941.

Liu, F. F., *A Military History of Modern China 1924 – 1949*. Princeton, 1956.

Liu, Hui-chen Wang, *Traditional Chinese Clan Rules*. Locust Valley, 1959.

Maspero, Henri and Escarra, Jean, *Les Institutions de la Chine*. Paris, 1952.

Morse, H. B., *Trade and Administration of the Chinese Empire*. London, 1908.

North, Robert C., *Moscow and the Chinese Communists*. Stanford, 1953.

Schwartz, Benjamin I., *Chinese Communism and the Rise of Mao*. Cambridge, Massachusetts, 1951.

Shen, N. C., "The Local Government of China," *Chinese Social and Political Science Review*, Vol. XX, No. 2 (July, 1936), 163 – 201.

Tawney, R. H., *Land and Labour in China*. London, 1932. Reprinted, New York, 1964.

Weber, Max, "Konfuzianismus und Taoismus," *Gesammelte Aufsätze zur Religionssoziologie*, Vol. I (4th ed., Tübingen, 1947), 276 – 536.

Wittfogel, Karl A., *Oriental Despotism: A Comparative Study of Total Power*. New Haven, 1957.

Wright, Mary Clabaugh, *The Last Stand of Chinese Conservatism*. Stanford, 1957.

Yang, C. K., *The Chinese Family in the Communist Revolution*. Cambridge, Massachusetts, 1959.

———— *A Chinese Village in Early Communist Transition*. Cambridge, Massachusetts, 1959.

———— *Religion in Chinese Society: A Study of Contemporary Social Functions of Religion and Some of Their Historical Factors*. Berkeley, 1961.

Yang, Martin C., *A Chinese Village: Taitou, Shantung Province*. New York, 1945.

Japan

Allen, G. C., *A Short Economic History of Modern Japan: 1867.–1937*. London, 1946. 2nd ed., London, 1962.

Asakawa, K., "Notes on Village Government in Japan, Part I," *Journal of the American Oriental Society*, Vol. XXX (1910), 259–300, and "Notes on Village Government in Japan, Part II," in Vol. XXX (1911), 151–216.

Beardsley, Richard K., *et al.*, *Village Japan*. Chicago, 1959.

Beasley, W. G., "Feudal Revenue in Japan at the Time of the Meiji Restoration," *Journal of Asian Studies*, Vol. XIX, No. 3 (May, 1960), 255–271.

Bellah, Robert N., *Tokugawa Religion: The Values of Pre-Industrial Japan*. Glencoe, 1957.

Benedict, Ruth, *The Chrysanthemum and the Sword*. New York, 1946.

Borton, Hugh, *Japan Since 1931: Its Political and Social Developments*. New York, 1940.

———— *Peasant Uprisings in Japan of the Tokugawa Period*. [New York], 1937.

Brown, Delmar M., *Nationalism in Japan*. Berkeley, 1955.

Cohen, Jerome B., *Japan's Economy in War and Reconstruction*. Minneapolis, 1949.

Colegrove, Kenneth W., *Militarism in Japan*. Boston, 1936.

Courant, Maurice, "Les clans japonais sous les Tokougawa," *Conférences faites au Musée Guimet*, 15, Part 1 (Paris, 1903–1905).

Craig, Albert M., "The Restoration Movement in Chōshū," *Journal of Asian Studies*, Vol. XVIII, No. 2 (February, 1959), 187–197.

———— *Chōshū in the Meiji Restoration*. Cambridge, Massachusetts, 1961.

Crowley, James B., "Japanese Army Factionalism in the Early 1930's," *Journal of Asian Studies*, Vol. XXI, No. 3 (May, 1962), 309 – 326.

Dore, R. P., "Agricultural Improvement in Japan: 1870 – 1900," *Economic Development and Cultural Change*, Vol. IX, No. 1, Part II (October, 1960), 69 – 91.

———— *Land Reform in Japan*. Oxford, 1959.

———— "The Meiji Landlord: Good or Bad?", *Journal of Asian Studies*, Vol. XVIII, No. 3 (May, 1959), 343 – 355.

———— and Sheldon, C. D., letters in *Journal of Asian Studies*, Vol. XVIII, No. 4 (August, 1959), 507 – 508 and Vol. XIX, No. 2 (February, 1960), 238 – 239.

Embree, John F., *Suye Mura: A Japanese Village*. Chicago, 1939.

Fukuda, Tokuzo, *Die Gesellschaftliche und Wirtschaftliche Entwickelung in Japan*. Stuttgart, 1900.

Hall, John W., "Feudalism in Japan — A Reassessment," *Comparative Studies in Society and History*, Vol. V, No. 1 (October, 1962), 15 – 51.

Harootunian, Harry D., "The Economic Rehabilitation of the Samurai in the Early Meiji Period," *Journal of Asian Studies*, Vol. XIX, No. 4 (August, 1960), 433 – 444.

Honjo, E., *Social and Economic History of Japan*. Kyoto, 1935.

Ike, Nobutaka, *The Beginnings of Political Democracy in Japan*. Baltimore, 1950.

Ladejinsky, W., "Farm Tenancy and Japanese Agriculture," *Foreign Agriculture* (issued by Bureau of Agricultural Economics, U.S. Department of Agriculture), Vol. I, No. 9 (September, 1937), 425 – 446.

La Mazelière, Antoine Rous de, *Le Japon, histoire et civilisation*. . . . 8 vols. Paris, 1907 – 1923.

Lockwood, William W., *The Economic Development of Japan*. Princeton, 1954.

Maruyama, Masao, *Thought and Behavior in Modern Japanese Politics*. Oxford, 1963.

Matsui, Shichiro, "Silk Industry," *Encyclopaedia of the Social Sciences* (New York, 1937), Vol. XIV, 52 – 57.

Morris, Morris D., "The Problem of the Peasant Agriculturist in Meiji Japan, 1873 – 1885," *Far Eastern Quarterly*, Vol. XV, No. 3 (May, 1956), 357 – 370.

Murdoch, James, *A History of Japan*. 3 vols. London, 1925 – 1926.

Nasu, Shiroshi, *Aspects of Japanese Agriculture*. New York, 1941.

Norman, E. Herbert, "Andō Shōeki and the Anatomy of Japanese Feudalism," *Transactions of the Asiatic Society of Japan*, 3rd Series, Vol. II (December, 1949).

———— *Japan's Emergence as a Modern State: Political and Economic Problems of the Meiji Period.* New York, 1940.

———— *Soldier and Peasant in Japan: The Origins of Conscription.* New York, 1943.

Ohkawa, Kazushi and Rosovsky, Henry, "The Role of Agriculture in Modern Japanese Economic Development," *Economic Development and Cultural Change*, Vol. IX, No. 1, Part II (October, 1960); 43 – 67.

Ramming, Martin, "Die Wirtschaftliche Lage der Samurai am Ende der Tokugawa-periode," *Mitteilungen der Deutschen Gesellschaft für Natur und Völkerkunde Ostasiens*, Band XXII, Teil A (Tokyo, 1928), 1 – 47.

Reischauer, Edwin O., "Japanese Feudalism," in Coulburn, Rushton, editor, *Feudalism in History* (Princeton, 1956).

Reischauer, Robert K., *Japan: Government-Politics.* New York, 1939.

Sansom, Sir George, *A History of Japan.* 3 vols. Vol. I: *To 1334* (Stanford, 1958). Vol. II: *1334 – 1615* (Stanford, 1961). Vol. III: *1615 – 1867* (Stanford, 1963).

———— *Japan: A Short Cultural History.* New York, 1943.

———— *The Western World and Japan.* New York, 1950.

Scalapino, Robert A., *Democracy and the Party Movement in Prewar Japan.* Berkeley, 1953.

Scott, J. W. Robertson, *The Foundations of Japan.* New York, 1922.

Sheldon, Charles David, *The Rise of the Merchant Class in Tokugawa Japan 1600 – 1868.* Locust Valley, 1958.

Smith, Thomas C., *Agrarian Origins of Modern Japan.* Stanford, 1959.

———— "The Land Tax in the Tokugawa Period," *Journal of Asian Studies*, Vol. VIII, No. 1 (November, 1958), 3 – 19.

———— "Landlords' Sons in the Business Elite," *Economic Development and Cultural Change*, Vol. IX, No. 1, Part II (October, 1960), 93 – 107.

———— *Political Change and Industrial Development in Japan: Government Enterprise, 1868 – 1880.* Stanford, 1955.

Storry, Richard, *The Double Patriots: A Study of Japanese Nationalism.* Boston, 1957.

Taeuber, Irene B., *The Population of Japan.* Princeton, 1958.

Takekoshi, Y., "Land Tenure, China and Japan," *Encyclopaedia of the Social Sciences* (New York, 1937), IX, 112 – 118.

Takizawa, Matsuyo, *The Penetration of Money Economy in Japan and Its Effects upon Social and Political Institutions*. New York, 1927.

Tanin, O., and Yohan, E., *Militarism and Fascism in Japan*. New York, 1934.

Totten, George O., "Labor and Agrarian Disputes in Japan Following World War I," *Economic Development and Cultural Change*, Vol. IX, No. 1, Part II (October, 1960), 192 – 200.

Tsunoda, Ryusaku, *et al.*, compilers, *Sources of Japanese Tradition*. New York, 1958.

India

Anstey, Vera, *The Economic Development of India*. 4th edition, London, 1952. First published 1929.

Baden-Powell, B. H., *The Indian Village Community*. London, 1896.

———— *Land Systems of British India*. 3 vols. Oxford, 1892.

Bailey, F. G., *Caste and the Economic Frontier*. Manchester, 1959.

Beals, Alan R., *Gopalpur: A South Indian Village*. New York, 1963.

Blunt, E. A. H., *Caste System of Northern India*. London, 1931.

———— "Economic Aspect of the Caste System," in Mukerjee, *Economic Problems*, 63 – 81.

Braibanti, Ralph, and Spengler, Joseph J., editors, *Administration and Economic Development in India*. Durham, 1963.

Brayne, F. L., *The Remaking of Village India*. 2nd ed., Oxford, 1929.

Brecher, Michael, *Nehru: A Political Biography*. Oxford, 1959.

Brown, D. Mackenzie, "Traditions of Leadership," in Park and Tinker, editors, *Leadership and Political Institutions in India*, 1 – 17.

Buchanan, Francis, *An Account of the District of Bhagalpur in 1810 – 1811*. Patna, 1939.

———— *An Account of the District of Purnea in 1809 – 1810*. Patna, 1928.

———— *An Account of the District of Shahabad in 1809 – 10*. Patna, 1934.

———— *A Journey from Madras through the Countries of Mysore, Canara, and Malabar*. . . . 3 vols. London, 1807.

Cambridge History of India. 6 vols. Cambridge, 1922 – 1937.

Campbell, Sir George, *Modern India*. London, 1852.

Chattopadhyaya, Haraprasad, *The Sepoy Mutiny 1857: A Social Study and Analysis.* Calcutta, 1957.

Chaudhuri, S. B., *Civil Disturbances During the British Rule in India 1765 – 1857.* Calcutta, 1955.

———— *Civil Rebellion in the Indian Mutinies 1857 – 1859.* Calcutta, 1957.

Cohn, Bernard S., "The Initial British Impact on India," *Journal of Asian Studies,* Vol. XIV, No. 4 (August 1960), 424 – 431.

Colebrooke, Sir Henry Thomas, *Remarks on the Husbandry and Internal Commerce of Bengal.* Calcutta, 1804.

Darling, Sir Malcolm, *The Punjab Peasant in Prosperity and Debt.* 4th ed., Oxford, 1947.

Davis, Kingsley, *The Population of India and Pakistan.* Princeton, 1951.

Dey, Sushil K., "Community Projects in Action in India," in Park and Tinker, editors, *Leadership and Political Institutions in India,* 347 – 357.

Dube, S. C., *India's Changing Villages,* Ithaca, 1958.

———— *Indian Village.* London, 1955.

Dubois, (Abbé) Jean Antoine, *Hindu Manners, Customs and Ceremonies.* Translated and edited by Henry K. Beauchamp. 2 vols. Oxford, 1897.

Dumont, René, *Terres vivantes: Voyages d'un agronome autour du monde.* Paris, 1961.

Dupuis, Jacques, *Madras et le Nord du Coromandel.* Paris, 1960.

Dutt, Romesh, *The Economic History of India in the Victorian Age.* 7th ed., London, 1950. First published 1903.

———— *The Economic History of India Under Early British Rule.* 7th ed., London, 1950. First published 1901.

Epstein, T. Scarlett, *Economic Development and Social Change in South India.* Manchester, 1962.

Far Eastern Economic Review (Hongkong). Issues of 1963 and 1960 – 1964 *Yearbooks.*

Ford Foundation, *Report.* See India: Agricultural Production Team.

Gadgil, D. R., *The Industrial Evolution of India in Recent Times.* 4th ed., Oxford, 1942. First published in 1924.

———— *Notes on the Rise of the Business Communities in India,* a Preliminary Memorandum Not for Publication, by Members of the Staff of the Gokhale Institute of Politics and Economics, Poona, with Introduction by D. R. Gadgil. New York, 1951.

Gandhi, M. K., *Economic and Industrial Life and Relations*, compiled and edited by V. B. Kher. 3 vols. Ahmedabed, 1957.

—— *Speeches and Writings of Mahatma Gandhi.* 4th ed., Madras, 1933.

Gopal, S., *The Permanent Settlement in Bengal and Its Results.* London, 1949.

Gough, Kathleen, "The Social Structure of a Tanjore Village," in Marriott, editor, *Village India*, 36 – 52.

Great Britain: Indian Famine Commission, *Report of the Indian Famine Commission. . . . Presented to Parliament.* Parts I and II. London, 1880.

——: Indian Statutory Commission, *Report of the Indian Statutory Commission. . . . Presented by the Secretary of State for the Home Department to Parliament. . . . May 1930.* 17 vols. London, 1930.

——: Royal Commission on Agriculture in India, *Report. . . . Presented to Parliament June, 1928.* Abridged, London, 1928.

Griffiths, Sir Percival, *The British Impact on India.* London, 1952.

Habib, Irfan, *The Agrarian System of Mogul India 1556 – 1707.* London, 1963.

Harrison, Selig, *India: The Most Dangerous Decade.* Princeton, 1960.

Hutton, J. H., *Caste in India.* Cambridge, 1936.

India: Agricultural Production Team, *Report of India's Food Crisis and Steps to Meet It.* Sponsored by the Ford Foundation. Issued by the Ministry of Food and Agriculture and Ministry of Community Development and Cooperation, April, 1959.

——: Cabinet Secretariat, Central Statistical Organisation, *Statistical Abstract, India 1957 – 58.* New Series, No. 8, New Delhi, 1959.

——: Cabinet Secretariat, Indian Statistical Institute, *The National Sample Survey. Eighth Round: July 1954 – March 1955. No. 10: First Report on Land Holdings, Rural Sector.* Delhi, 1958.

—— *Census 1951.* Several volumes, published in the different states, 1953. Vol. VI (West Bengal, Sikkim, and Chandernagore), Part IA – Report. Delhi, 1953.

——: Directorate of Economics and Statistics, *Studies in Agricultural Economics*, III, Third Issue (Delhi, 1960), containing "Food Statistics in India."

—— Famine Inquiry Commission, *Final Report.* Delhi, 1945.

————: Ministry of Labour, *Agricultural Labour Enquiry*, Vol. I: *All India*. New Delhi, 1954.

————: Planning Commission, *Third Five Year Plan*. Delhi, 1961.

Indian National Congress, All-India Congress Committee. *Congress Bulletin*, January – February, 1959.

Kaye, John William, *A History of the Sepoy War in India 1857 – 1858*. 3 vols. London, 1864 – 76.

Khan, N. A., "Resource Mobilization from Agriculture and Economic Development in India," *Economic Development and Cultural Change*, XII, No. 1 (October, 1963), 42 – 54.

Lamb, Helen, "The Indian Merchant," in Singer, editor, *Traditional India*, 25 – 35.

Lambert, Richard D., "Hindu Communal Groups," in Park and Tinker, editors, *Leadership and Political Institutions in India*, 211 – 224.

Lewis, Oscar, *Village Life in Northern India*. Urbana, 1958.

Madras in Maps and Pictures. Issued by the Director of Information and Publicity. Madras, 1959.

Majumdar, R. C., Raychaudhuri, H. C., and Datta, K., *An Advanced History of India*. London, 1950.

Marriott, McKim, editor, *Village India: Studies in the Little Community* American Anthropological Association, Memoir No. 83, June, 1955.

Mayer, Adrian C., *Caste and Kinship in Central India*. London, 1960.

Mayer, Albert, *et al.*, *Pilot Project, India: The Story of Rural Development at Etawah, Uttar Pradesh*. Berkeley, 1958.

Mellor, Andrew, *India Since Partition*. London, 1951.

Metcalf, Thomas R., "Struggle over Land Tenure in India 1860 – 1868," *Journal of Asian Studies*, Vol. XXI, No. 3 (May, 1962), 295 – 308.

————, "The British and the Moneylender in Nineteenth-Century India," *Journal of Modern History*, Vol. 34, No. 4 (December, 1962), 295 – 307.

———— "The Influence of the Mutiny of 1857 on Land Policy in India," *The Historical Journal*, Vol. 4, No. 2 (1961), 152 – 163.

Misra, B. B., *The Indian Middle Classes*. Oxford, 1961.

Mitra, Ashok, "Tax Burden for Indian Agriculture," in Braibanti and Spengler, editors, *Administration and Economic Development in India*, 281 – 303.

Moreland, W. H., *The Agrarian System of Moslem India*. Cambridge, 1929.

———— *From Akbar to Aurangzeb: A Study in Indian Economic History*. London, 1923.

———— *India at the Death of Akbar*. London, 1920.

———— and Chatterjee, A. C., *A Short History of India*. 4th ed., London, 1957.

Mukerjee, Radhakamal, editor, *Economic Problems of Modern India*. Vol. I: London, 1939.

Nair, Kusum, *Blossoms in the Dust*. Oxford, 1961.

Nanda, B. R., *Mahatma Gandhi: A Biography*. Boston, 1958.

Natarajan, L., *Peasant Uprisings in India 1850 – 1900*. Bombay, 1953.

Neale, Walter C., *Economic Change in Rural India: Land Tenure and Reform in Uttar Pradesh 1850 – 1955*. New Haven, 1962.

O'Malley, L. S. S., *Popular Hinduism*. Cambridge, 1935.

Overstreet, Gene D., and Windmiller, Marshall, *Communism in India*. Berkeley, 1959.

Park, Richard L., and Tinker, Irene, editors, *Leadership and Political Institutions in India*. Princeton, 1959.

Patel, Govindlal D., *The Indian Land Problem and Legislation*. Bombay, 1954.

Patel, Surendra J., *Agricultural Labourers in Modern India and Pakistan*. Bombay, 1952.

Qureshi, Anwar Iqbal, *The Economic Development of Hyderabad*. Bombay, 1949.

Raghavaiyangar, S. Srinivasa, *Memorandum on the Progress of the Madras Presidency during the Last Forty Years of British Administration*. Madras, 1893.

Raju, A. Sarada, *Economic Conditions in the Madras Presidency 1800 – 1850*. Madras, 1941.

Retzlaff, Ralph H., *A Case Study of Panchayats in a North Indian Village*. Berkeley, 1959.

Rudolph, Lloyd I. and Susanne H., "The Political Role of India's Caste Associations," *Pacific Affairs*, XXXIII, No. 1 (March, 1960), 5 – 22.

Rudolph, Susanne H., "Consensus and Conflict in Indian Politics," *World Politics*, XIII, No. 3 (April, 1961), 385 – 399.

Samra, Chattar Singh, "Subhas Chandra Bose," in Park and Tinker, editors, *Leadership and Political Institutions in India*, 66 – 86.

Senart, Emile, *Caste in India*. Translated by E. D. Ross. London, 1930.

Singer, Milton, editor, *Traditional India: Structure and Change*. (American Folklore Society, "Bibliographical and Special Series," Vol. X.) Philadelphia, 1959.

Singh, Baij Nath, "The Impact of Community Development on Rural Leadership," in Park and Tinker, editors, *Leadership and Political Institutions in India*, 361 – 365.

Smith, Wilfred Cantwell, "Hyderabad: Muslim Tragedy," *Middle East Journal*, IV, No. 1 (January, 1950), 27 – 51.

Spear, T: G., *Twilight of the Mughuls*. Cambridge, 1951.

Srinivas, M. N., *Caste in Modern India*. London, 1962.

Stokes, Eric, *The English Utilitarians and India*. Oxford, 1959.

Tavernier, Jean-Baptiste, *Travels in India*. Transl. by V. Ball. 2nd ed., edited by William Crooke, Oxford, 1925.

Thirumalai, S., *Postwar Agricultural Problems and Policies in India*. New York, 1954.

Thorner, Daniel and Alice, *Land and Labour in India*. London, 1962.

Times of India: Directory and Year Book, 1960 – 61. Bombay, Delhi, Calcutta, and London, 1961.

Tinker, Hugh, "The Village in the Framework of Development," in Braibanti and Spengler, editors, *Administration and Economic Development in India*, 94 – 133.

Woodruff, Philip., *The Men Who Ruled India*. Vol. I: *The Founders*. Vol. II: *The Guardians*. London, 1953.

III.

General and Miscellaneous

Annuaire internationale de statistique agricole, 1937 – 38. Issued by the International Institute of Agriculture. Rome, 1938.

Banfield, Edward C., *The Moral Basis of a Backward Society*. Glencoe, 1958.

Coulborn, Rushton, editor, *Feudalism in History*. Princeton, 1956.

Foreign Agriculture, weekly publication of the U.S. Department of Agriculture, Washington, D.C.

Hintze, Otto, *Staat und Verfassung: Gesammelte Abhandlungen zur allgemeinen Verfassungsgeschichte*. Edited by Gerhard Oestreich. 2nd ed., Göttingen, 1962.

Homans, George C., *The Human Group*. New York, 1950.

Klein, Julius, *The Mesta: A Study in Spanish Economic History 1273 – 1836*. Cambridge, Massachusetts, 1920.

Lévi-Strauss, Claude, *La Pensée sauvage*. Paris, 1962.

Marx, Karl, *Selected Works*. Translation edited by C. P. Dutt. 2 vols New York, n.d.

Morgenstern, Oskar, *On the Accuracy of Economic Observations*. 2nd revised edition, Princeton, 1963.

Parsons, Talcott, *The Social System*. Glencoe, 1951.

Pirenne, Henri, *Histoire économique de l'occident médiéval*. [Brussels], 1951.

Postgate, R. W., editor, *Revolution from 1789 to 1906: Documents selected and edited with Notes and Introductions*. London, 1920, reprinted New York, 1962.

Salvemini, Gaetano, *The Fascist Dictatorship in Italy*. London, 1928.

Schmidt, Carl P., *The Plough and the Sword: Labor, Land, and Property in Fascist Italy*. New York, 1938.

Schweinetz, Karl de, Jr., *Industrialization and Democracy: Economic Necessities and Political Possibilities*. New York, 1964.

Silone, Ignazio, *Der Fascismus*. Zürich, 1934.

Syme, Sir Ronald, *The Roman Revolution*. Oxford, 1956.

United Nations: Food and Agriculture Organization, *Production Yearbook*, XIV (1960) and XVI (1962).

Whitehead, Alfred N., *Modes of Thought*. New York, 1938; reprinted 1958.

Index